Interact with your text

→ each book in the **complete** series offers free
learning solutions online

www.oxfordtextbooks.co.uk/orc/complete/

complete: law solution

 online resource centre
www.oxfordtextbooks.co.uk/orc/clements_complete4e/

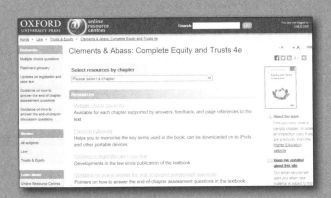

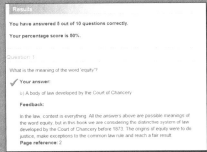

Visit the website for access to addition resources:

→ Interactive multiple choice questions with answers and feedback

→ Flashcard glossary

→ Guidance to end-of-chapter questions

→ Updates on legislation and case law

complete

Equity and Trusts

Text, Cases, and Materials

Fourth Edition

Richard Clements

Ademola Abass

OXFORD

UNIVERSITY PRESS

OXFORD
UNIVERSITY PRESS

Great Clarendon Street, Oxford, OX2 6DP,
United Kingdom

Oxford University Press is a department of the University of Oxford.
It furthers the University's objective of excellence in research, scholarship,
and education by publishing worldwide. Oxford is a registered trade mark of
Oxford University Press in the UK and in certain other countries

Published in the United States of America by Oxford University Press
198 Madison Avenue, New York, NY 10016, United States of America

British Library Cataloguing in Publication Data
Data available

Library of Congress Control Number: 2015936004

ISBN 978–0–19–872624–1

Printed in Great Britain by
Bell & Bain Ltd., Glasgow

To Eche and Kobi Abass

Guide to Using the Book

Complete Equity and Trusts: Text, Cases, and Materials is complemented by a number of features which are designed to enrich your learning and provide additional support as you progress through your equity and trusts module. This guided tour highlights the various features to help you to get the most out of your textbook.

● *Tinsley v Milligan* (1993) 3 All ER 65

Two single women lived together and ran a profitable lodging in the sole name of the plaintiff. They defrauded the Departme false benefit claims. The defendant later repented and info Following a quarrel between the two, the plaintiff moved out occupation. The plaintiff later served a notice to quit on the possession and ownership of the property. The defendant

Cases and materials

Cases play a pivotal role in shaping equity and trust law, so it is important to read first-hand reports in order to fully understand the subject. This book includes extracts from a wide range of cases, legislation, and academic material which complement and illustrate the author commentary.

Learning objectives

This chapter will help you to:

• realize that many different types of property can be held o
• understand the many purposes for which trusts can be use
• realize that trusts can be defined in different ways

Learning objectives

Each chapter begins with a bulleted outline of the main concepts you will encounter. These provide a helpful signpost to what you can expect to learn from the chapter.

thinking points

Trusts can be traced back at least as far as the 13th ce evolving to meet new challenges and provide a solutio statutory framework for regulating trusts has not char remains, although the investment power of trustees h (see Chapter 11). Many issues remain to be updated, a seldom interest Parliament. *See Sir William Goodhart* Trust Law International *38*.

Thinking points

Why was a particular decision reached in a certain case? Is the law on this point logical and coherent? Thinking points draw out these issues and help you to stop and reflect on these questions.

KEY POINT The trust fund may 'belong' to the benefic trustees to enforce the trust, e.g. to sue people who ow

Key points

Key points provide a commentary on cases and emphasize the essential points of law.

The trustee has the full legal pro not...All that the latter can do is trust and to compel the trustee t than any legal right, but it is not i 'belong' to the beneficiary or mak it leaves the hand of the party wh

Eo instanti— Latin—loosely translated it means 'there instantly'.

Definition boxes

Key terms are highlighted when they first appear and are concisely explained in definition boxes. These terms are collected in a glossary which can be found at the back of the book. Test your knowledge of terms and definitions using the flashcard glossary available on the Online Resource Centre.
www.oxfordtextbooks.co.uk/orc/clements_complete4e/

Diagram 3.1
A classification of
the different types
of property

| Real Property or Realty | Personal Prope |
| Land - ground, buildings or parts of buildings, water. Easements, servitudes and other rights over land. Land is immovable property which can be recovered by a real action. | Any property v Movable prope action for dama Includes Chatt leasehold prop Land. And Chattels movable, tang property |

Diagrams

Diagrams provide a visual representation of concepts, processes, and cases. Use these in conjunction with the text to clarify your understanding of even the most complex concepts.

Conclusion

The purpose of this chapter was to introduce the reader considered later in the book. Many different kinds of prope can be used to achieve many different purposes. There a so much so that it is difficult to find an overall unifying *Landesbank Girozentrale v Islington London Borough Cou*

Chapter conclusions

The central points and concepts covered in each chapter are distilled into conclusions at the ends of chapters. These reinforce your understanding and can be used for quick revision.

Key cases

- *Westdeutsche Landesbank Girozentrale v Isli* AC 669 **(at 3.5)**

- *Barclays Bank v Quistclose* [1970] AC 567 **(at 3**

Key case list

These clearly distinguish between the key 'law-making' precedent setting authorities and those authorities given by way of example of the operation of an established doctrine or rule. Section references guide you to where each case appears within the book.

Self-test questions

Self-test questions at the end of chapters help you recap on the topic covered and encourage you to test your understanding of the law.

Questions

Self-test questions

1 What are trusts used for?

2 What sort of property can be held on trust?

Discussion questions

1 Consider the many different types of trust. Can you see

2 A key feature of the trust is the 'split' between the legal e Consider the difference between rights in equity and rig

3 How do Quistclose-type trusts fit into the classification c

Discussion questions

Discussion questions at the end of each chapter help you to develop analytical and problem-solving skills. The Online Resource Centre contains guidance on how to approach these questions.

Assessment question

From reading this chapter, you should now have some understa What is the meaning of the following words in trust law?

Settlor	Will
Testator	Deed
Trust	Covenants

Assessment questions

Assessment questions provide examples of the types of problem and essay questions you will encounter in the exams. The Online Resource Centre contains guidance on how to approach these questions.

Further readin

N Hopkins 'The Pallant v Morgan "equity" again' [20 Constructive trusts seem capable of future development, bu defined limits.

Further reading

Selected further reading is included at the end of each chapter to provide a springboard for further study.

Guide to the Online Resource Centre

The Online Resource Centre that accompanies this book provides students and lecturers with ready-to-use learning resources. They are free of charge, and are designed to complement the book and maximize the teaching and learning experience.

www.oxfordtextbooks.co.uk/orc/clements_complete4e/

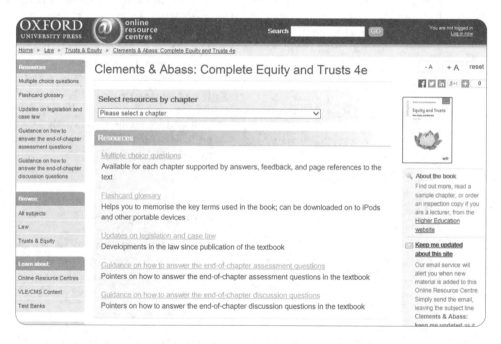

For students

These resources are available to all, enabling students to get the most from their textbook; no registration or password is required.

Updates

The authors will update this section of the site to account for recent cases and developments in equity and trusts that have occurred since publication of the book.

Guidelines to answering the end-of-chapter discussion questions

Here is where you can find guidance on how best to approach the discussion questions posed at the end of chapters in the book.

Guidelines to answering the end-of-chapter assessment questions

Here is where you can find guidance on how best to approach the exam-style questions posed at the end of chapters in the book.

Flashcard glossary of key terms

Test your knowledge and understanding of the specialized terminology used in equity and trusts. This is a useful way of ensuring that you are using terms correctly in your assignments and exams.

Preface

The main objective was to write a book suitable for undergraduate study. This volume is not intended as a rival to the many excellent, detailed, academic accounts of the law of equity and trusts. The aim was to produce a book that was accessible to those new to the subject and to write it in a clear and readable style. It is hoped that the layout and the pedagogical features, such as key points and thinking points, will help the student to gain some understanding of this difficult, contradictory, and complex subject. For ease of explanation it did not prove possible to go into every academic controversy, in a subject where there are many such disputes. The thinking points and the further reading at the end of each chapter should give a starting point to the keen student who wishes to investigate further the controversial areas. Some difficult choices had to be made on which cases to include and which to leave out. There was not room for them all and we apologize to lecturers and tutors if we have omitted some of their favourites. Our thanks go to colleagues with whom we have taught, whose ideas we may have borrowed and to students, whose questions and, sometimes errors, enabled us to devise what we hope are helpful key points. Similarly, the reviewers of the draft chapters were very helpful in fashioning the final version. We are now on our fourth edition and we hope that we have improved on the previous editions and made it a better book. Finally, we have tried to make the book as up to date and accurate as we could, but we would accept that errors will have crept in. Those mistakes are the sole responsibility of the authors.

Richard Clements

Ademola Abass

March 2015

New to this Edition

- *Prest v Petrodel Resources Ltd* [2013] and *Patel v Mirza* [2014] on resulting trusts.
- *Day v Harris, Robert Arnold, Katherine Arnold* [2013] in relation to the transfer of gifts and intention.
- *Southwell v Blackburn* [2014] on proprietary estoppel.
- *In Re Lucian Freud (Deceased)* [2014] on secret trusts.
- *Vallee v Birchwood* [2013] on contemplation of death.
- *R (Hodkin) v Registrar General of Births Deaths and Marriages* [2013] on charitable trusts.
- *Jeffery v Gretton* [2011] on powers of investment for trustees,
- *Shergill v Khaira* [2014] on the appointment of trustees.
- *AIB Group (UK) plc v Mark Redler & Co Solicitors* [2014] on breach of trust.
- *FHR European Ventures v Cedar Capital Partners* [2014] on tracing.

Acknowledgements

Grateful acknowledgement is made to all the authors and publishers of copyright material which appears in this book, and in particular to the following for permission to reprint material from the sources indicated.

Crown copyright material reproduced with the permission of the Controller, HMSO (under the terms of the Click Use licence).

Incorporated Council of Law Reporting for extracts from the *Law Reports: Appeal Cases* (AC), *Chancery Division* (Ch), *Family Law Reports* (Fam), *Queen's Bench* (QB), and *Weekly Law Reports* (WLR).

Oxford University Press for extracts from Gary Watt: *Trusts and Equity* (OUP, 2014) and Philip H. Pettit: *Equity and the Law of Trusts* (OUP, 2012). By permission of Oxford University Press.

Reed Elsevier (UK) Ltd trading as LexisNexis for extracts from *All England Law Reports* (ALL ER).

Taylor & Francis Books UK for *Equity and Trusts* (8th edition), Alastair Hudson, (Routledge, 2015), reproduced by permission of Taylor & Francis Books UK.

Contents

....

Chapter 4 Trusts and powers and the three certainties

Contents

xvii

Contents

xx

Table of Cases

Table of Statutes

Table of Statutory Instruments

Table of International Treaties and Conventions

The birth of equity and trusts

Learning objectives

This chapter will help you to:

- understand the origin and meaning of equity
- consider whether equity and common law were 'fused' or simply 'amalgamated' by the Judicature Acts 1873–5
- assess the effects of the Judicature Acts of 1873–5
- consider whether equity is of any relevance to modern society
- understand the origin of trusts and their functions.

Introduction

This chapter discusses the origin of equity and trusts as distinctive aspects of the English legal system and the subsequent merger of equity with the common law. In order for students to appreciate how equity functions in the modern society, first they need to understand the origin of equity, its individual operation before being merged with the common law, as well as the development of trusts which, as will be seen later, took shape in the court of equity. The chapter will also consider the effects of the merging of equity and common law—a topic that continues to generate debates among academics and judges—and considers whether equity has any relevance to modern society. It is hoped that this chapter will lay a solid foundation for discussion in the second chapter of the maxims of equity, the main tools through which equity expresses its characters, and the specific topics of subsequent chapters.

1.1 What is equity?

If you put the question 'what is equity?' to anyone, they are likely to respond that: equity is to do what is fair; it means to do justice; it is to do what is right. The list could continue. If the question is posed after the year 1875—which was the year when the rules of equity became fully developed—the addressee could easily say, as Maitland once said, that 'it is that body of rules which is administered only by those courts which are known as Courts of Equity' (Maitland *Equity* (Cambridge: Cambridge University Press, 1947) at 1). But it would be incorrect to define equity as such today because there are no courts that can now be called courts of equity.

One may also define equity in the years post 1875 as 'that body of rules administered by the English courts of Justice which, were it not for the operation of the Judicature Act, would be administered only by those courts known as Courts of Equity' (Maitland at 1). As with the previous definition, this latest one is misleading because, despite acknowledging that equity forms a part of the substantive English law, it describes this part and distinguishes it from other aspects of the law by reference to courts that are no longer in existence.

Equitable—certain rights are regarded as equitable. The basis is historical. They were once rights recognized by the court of Chancery.

We may even add another drawback to such a handicapped definition of equity as just given. In stating that **equitable** rules, or the rules of equity, are administered by English courts of justice after 1875, we raise certain ambiguities as to what part of equity is *now* administered with common law. As will be seen later, while the Judicature Acts undoubtedly brought equity and common law together within one judicial system, the question remains as to what the exact effects of these Acts are. Did the Acts 'fuse' the rules of equity and common law—which undoubtedly used to be administered separately by different courts before 1875—or did they simply 'unify' or 'amalgamate' the previous different administrations of equity and common law and entrust this upon the shoulder of a single court? While this issue will be fully considered later, it is necessary first to consider how other writers have attempted to define equity, marking out essential features of such definitions in italics.

Phillip H Pettit *Equity and the Law of Trusts* (12th edn, Oxford: Oxford University Press, 2012) at 2:

> If law be regarded in general terms as the rules enforced in the courts for the promotion of justice, equity may be described as that part of the law which, immediately *prior* to the coming into force of the Supreme Court of Judicature Acts 1873 and 1875 on 1 November 1875, was enforced *exclusively* in the Court of Chancery and not at all in the courts of common law—Common Pleas, Exchequer, and King's Bench. [Emphasis added.]

Alastair Hudson *Equity and Trusts* (8th edn, Abingdon: Routledge, 2015) at 4:

> Equity is the means by which a system of law balances out the need for certainty in rule-making with the need to achieve fair results in individual circumstances.

Robert Pearce and Warren Barr *Pearce & Stevens' Trusts and Equitable Obligations* (Oxford: Oxford University Press, 2015) at 4:

> Legally, the term 'equity' describes a particular body of law, consisting of *rights* and *remedies*, which evolved historically through the Courts of Chancery. [Emphasis added.]

Aristotle *The Nichomachean Ethics* (1955) 198 para 1137a17 x (quoted by Alastair Hudson at 8):

> For equity, though superior to justice, is still *just* ... justice and equity coincide, and although they are good, *equity* is superior. What causes the difficulty is the fact that equity is just, but not what is legally just: it is the rectification of legal justice ... the explanation of this is that all law is universal, and there are some things about which it is not possible to pronounce rightly in general terms; therefore in cases where it is necessary to make a general pronouncement, but impossible to do so rightly, the law takes account of the majority of cases, though not unaware that in this way errors are made ... so when the law states a general rule, and a case arises under this that is exceptional, then it is right, where the legislator owing to the generality of his language has erred in not covering that case, to correct the omission by a ruling such as the legislator himself would have given if he had been present there, and as he would have enacted if he had been aware of the circumstances.

Gary Watt *Trusts and Equity* (6th edn, Oxford: Oxford University Press, 2014):

> Equity is a body of principles, doctrines, and rules, developed originally by the old Court of Chancery in constructive competition with the rules, doctrines, and principles of common law courts, but now applied, since the Judicature Acts 1873–5, by the unified Supreme Court of England and Wales.

Michael Haley and Dr Lara McMurtry *Equity & Trusts* (4th edn, London: Sweet & Maxwell, 2014) at 1:

> The term 'equity' is, in a general sense, associated with notions of fairness, morality and justice. It is an ethical jurisdiction, originally of canon law descent. On a more legalistic level, however, 'equity' is the branch of law that was administered in the Court of Chancery prior to the Judicature Acts 1873 and 1875.

- Before 1875, equity was administered separately from common law.

- Equity balances the rules of law with judicial discretion based on individual factual circumstances.

- Equity consists of rights and remedies.

- Equity is rectificatory.

- Equity was, to some extent, administered jointly with common law after 1875.

 ## 1.2 Origin of equity

The origin of equity can be traced back to the existence, in the 13th-century reign in England of Edward I, of three distinct courts: the King's Bench, the Common Bench or Court of Common Pleas, and the Exchequer. These courts operated independently, entitling plaintiffs to a choice from the three. However, predominantly they all administered traditional and statute law, collectively known to the Edwardian lawyer as common law, a collection of legal principles and rules dating back to 1189.

However, of these three courts the Exchequer performed more than just judicial functions and, according to Maitland, it served as a 'government office', a modern-day treasury. This court is headed not by a judge, but by a chancellor, a person equivalent to the Chancellor of the Exchequer in modern-day Britain.

As a government official, the chancellor oversees many departmental works such as issuing of writs for the commencement of actions in the courts of law. Even to this day, it is not possible to commence a legal action without issuing a writ of summons or other kinds of writs—depending on the nature of the action—to the defendant. When issued by the chancellor, these writs are sealed with the king's seal. Evidently, the chancellor occupies a very important position. He sits in a court, although he is not a judge, issues writs to other courts (and this places him above the judges), and what is more, he is the only one who can encrypt the writs with the king's seal, a symbol of monarchical authority.

Although the chancellor issues writs already known to the English legal system, he however could issue writs to cover cases not covered by the existing writs. Yet, not being a learned man himself, he often found such writs quashed by the courts, especially as he often would not have had the benefit of the defendant's claim.

The fact that innovative writs issued by the chancellor are subject to being quashed by common law courts must sometimes distress him. However, like a good card player, the chancellor holds another ace: although the courts of common law dispense justice, there is also room for the king himself to do justice, even if only occasionally. If the courts do not satisfy the claimants, they simply go to the king. But towards the end of the 13th century, these extrajudicial petitions were so many as to involve the chancellor—as the king's prime minister—in the direct administration of these types of cases. And, it must be emphasized, he is involved in the king's council as well. It should be noted that it is in the administration of justice through or under the auspices of the king that the chancellor began to develop his judicial powers.

In the *Earl of Oxford* case (1615) 1 Rep Ch 1 at 6, Lord Ellesmere summarized the rationale for the chancery thus:

> [M]en's actions are so diverse and infinite that it is impossible to make any general rule which may aptly meet with every particular and not fail in some circumstances. The office of the Chancellor is to correct men's consciences for frauds, breaches of trusts, wrongs and oppressions of what nature so ever they be, and to soften and mollify the extremity of law.

Lord Ellesmere's justification of equity, as a response to the inadequacy of the common law, was theatrically espoused in the MGM classic, *The Magnificent Seven* (John Sturges (dir), Metro Golden Mayer, 1960, quoted by Gary Watt at 15), where two characters, Chris and Vin, played by Yul Bryner and Steve McQueen, converse thus:

Chris: 'We took a contract.'

Vin: 'It's not the kind any court would enforce.'

Chris: 'That's just the kind you gotta get.'

The chancellor's judicial powers are divided into two: the common law sides and an equity side. How do these work?

1.2.1 The common law side of the chancellor

How is it that the chancellor can administer common law? After all, we have said he is not a judge.

As the chancellor began to operate justice through the king, a division between two forms of justice ensued as already noted. In the first category, several people petitioned to and against the king. It must be pointed out that some of the kings at this time were great wrongdoers. They were notorious for seizing people's lands without apparent justification and they did this because they knew their subjects could not seek writs against them in any court, let alone before the kings themselves. So what the chancellor did was to devise a means by which, if a case involved the king, and a plaintiff from whom land is seized petitions the king, the chancellor sends the case down to the King's Bench for trial, and should there arise a need for the plaintiff to prove facts of ownership of the land, a jury is assembled to deal with the case. It must be borne in mind, however, that this particular form of action deals essentially with legal issues as between two parties, one of which is appearing before the king because he is not satisfied by the court, or as between one party who petitions against the king for the latter's own wrongdoing. It was not until the 1854 Common Law Procedure Act that common law courts were granted limited powers to award injunctions, while the 1858 Chancery Amendment Act (popularly called Lord Cairns's Act) would empower the Chancery to award damages. It was the Common Law Procedure Act that also abolished the writ system.

1.2.2 The equitable side of the chancellor: 'For the love of God and in the way of Charity'

In that great age of poverty, ignorance, bribery, and corruption, not many litigants could afford to seek remedies in courts of law. They are sometimes old, and pitched against the rich and famous, the powerful, and the celebrities of the day. So, such plaintiffs would rather send their petitions to the king, through his chancellor to do what is right, as the saying goes, *for the love of God and in the way of Charity*. Due to the number of these piteous petitions, petitioners began to send them directly to the chancellor himself.

The original response of the chancellor—again, now wanting to circumvent the courts of the land, the common law courts—was to issue special writs to such claimants to go to the courts. These writs, need it be mentioned, would mirror the particular circumstances of the litigants. But as is well known, by this time in the 14th century, the common law courts were so conservative that any such writs, which deviated from the laws and practices of the day, were regularly quashed. So one might be poor and his poverty written on the writs or old and the age inscribed therein, but this did not sway the common law court. The dictum of common law, it must always be remembered, is let justice be done even if heavens must fall! The common law at this time, one could say, was a slave to formality.

However, the chancellor had an alternative. Instead of sending a piteous plaintiff to the regular courts—where his writ might be quashed—he could, after listening to the plaintiff's complaint, order the defendant to appear before him. He does this by issuing a *subpoena*, which orders the defendant to appear before him or forfeit a sum of money. Now, while subpoenas are issued just as ordinary writs to make a person appear before the chancellor, they are in fact distinguishable from writs. Whilst writs merely inform a defendant as to what action is against him in the court, a subpoena forces him to appear and respond to a plaintiff's claim, and this he must do *upon oath*, unlike with writs.

Indeed, the whole process of subpoena, the oath, makes the procedure before the chancellor more like the ecclesiastical procedure rather than mirroring the day's English judicial process although, as some have observed, if the chancellor were to be asked about his intentions, he would likely deny that he deliberately set out to adopt a different judicial process from the ordinary courts of the land. This might be true if it is remembered that the complaints that come before the chancellor are normal issues tried by the courts.

1.2.3 So the next question is how does the chancellor begin to go it alone despite his lack of intention to do so?

The extraordinary justice dispensed by the chancellor began to attract bitter and rabid criticism from lawyers. Parliament was angry. The courts were irritated. The chancellor was giving justice to the poor and the indolent, as common law courts would regard these people, and at the same time the king was dispensing controversial justice to criminals. This double 'assault', shall we say, on the common law courts and the law of the land (Parliament) would soon result in the common law courts forbidding the chancellor to deal with common law cases! Luckily, by the time the chancellor was rebuffed by the common law courts, he had already begun to enforce breaches of trusts, a system which he carried over from the ecclesiastical church, which would normally punish breaches of such trusts by spiritual censures such as excommunication. We shall say more about the development of 'trust' later in this chapter.

The common law courts, with their difficult and conservative procedures could still not deal with 'fraud, accident, and breach of confidence'. The chancellor stepped in even deeper, strengthening his hold on power with no one being able to set any limit to his ever-growing powers. So, by the end of the 15th century, the chancellor would demonstrate clearly that when it comes to inventing rules to cover cases that would not normally be covered by common law courts the *sky is the limit*.

1.2.4 From love of God and charity to the rules of equity and good conscience: 16th century

Not much is today known about how chancellors developed their practice in the course of the 14th and 15th centuries. But we do know—thanks to reports in chancery dating back to

1557—that by the 16th century, his rules were known as 'rules of equity and good conscience'. The second part of the 16th century witnessed a more settled chancellor's rules of engagement. No more the ecclesiast. The chancellor had consolidated his jurisdiction by issuing what are called 'common injunctions'. The chancellor issued common injunctions to restrain the parties from continuing their action in common law courts or, where these have been concluded, from enforcing the judgment obtained. Underlining these common injunctions is the need for the chancellor to be able to enforce his new powers of trusts against the rich and powerful who could buy the court, but not the equity. Hence, if despite breaching trusts, a defendant obtains judgment, the chancellor does not controvert the judgment; he does not annul it; he does not question the legal validity of the judgment. All he does is to appeal to the party's conscience against enforcing the judgment against the party appearing before him. Of course, this is a threat more like: If you enforce your judgment, you shall go to jail.

The tension between the chancery and the common law courts was animated by Lord Ellesmere, the Lord Chancellor, and Chief Justice Coke, the head of the common law courts, both of whom wanted the question of validity or invalidity of common injunctions to be decided once and for all. In the *Earl of Oxford* case, the common law court had awarded judgment against a defendant to an action. The defendant petitioned the chancery on the basis that the judgment was obtained by fraud, an occurrence not uncommon in those days. The essence of the petition was to prevent an enforcement of the judgment against the defendant. Chief Justice Coke immediately indicted the defendant, but Lord Ellesmere issued an injunction to restrain the plaintiff from enforcing the judgment. Common law and the chancery clashed. Upon recourse to the monarch, it was all too easy for King James—forever wanting to overshadow his courts—and upon the advice of Francis Bacon, the Attorney General, and other eminent lawyers of the day, to decree in favour of the chancery.

From this period of victory over common law courts, the court of equity became an extremely busy court, with Bacon claiming that as many as 16,000 causes were pending before it at a time. It began to fall into arrears. Many called for its abolition. But it survived with restoration. The King's Seal, as was recorded, was always guided by eminent lawyers. By the 19th century equity made it to the textbooks, the first—and by then regarded as the greatest—of which is *Blackstone's Commentaries*.

Thus equity was born. But its growth began to pose threats to the indolence of the common law system. Surely, if tension between two distinct but often dovetailed and intermingling things is not properly managed, an explosion is inevitable. The *Earl of Oxford* case was the theatre of the conflict between equity and the common law. All that follows from this moment was a triumphant operation of equity until 1873 when the first of the Acts that would further establish its rules—and subject its development to a much stricter regulation—emerged.

thinking points

- *Do you think the decision in the* Earl of Oxford *case was fair to common law?*
- *What is the rationale for the chancellor, a non-lawyer, meddling in its administration of justice?*
- *Do you agree with Aristotle's explanation that the legislator would have given the same judgment as equity did were he present in the court, and would have made a similar equitable enactment were he aware of the circumstances? The fact that King James was very interested in preserving the dignity of the Court of Chancery, over which the king and his Lord Chancellor had a great influence, contributed to the decision in the* Earl of Oxford *case. Many scholars believe that in order for law to be responsive to the people, it is important that it remains dynamic at all times and its excessive rigidity is mitigated by the more liberal approach of equity. Aristotle's explanation shows clearly why equity has to complement law. Whether or not one agrees with his explanation depends largely on how individuals see the role of equity vis-à-vis law, especially in the post Judicature Act environment. See Anthony Mason 'The Place of Equity and Equitable Remedies in the Contemporary Common Law' (1994) 110 LQR 238).*

What became of the chancery jurisdiction after *Earl of Oxford* but before the Judicature Act?

Before we come to the Judicature Acts, let us consider briefly what became of the chancery jurisdiction after the *Earl of Oxford* case. After all, before that case, in the famous dictum of Selden (see the 'Table Talks of John Selden' (1927)), equity was:

> ...a roguish thing. For [common law] we have a measure...equity is according to the conscience of him that is Chancellor, and as that is longer or narrower so is equity. 'Tis all one as if they should make the standard for the measure a Chancellor's foot.'

This dictum is nowadays best expressed as: 'equity is as wide as the chancellor's foot', which, in plain language, means: equity had no systematic rules; equity does not follow or recognize precedents; equity was unpredictable just as the strides of individual chancellors; or, for equity, one could say, anything goes!

However, after the *Earl of Oxford* case, but before the Judicature Acts, equitable rules were thought to have become more systematized, rigid, and, in fact, cases of equity began to be reported. Phillip Pettit captioned well this new status of equity:

> This state of affairs [the loose nature of equity] began to be less true in the later seventeenth century, as the principles of equity began to become more fixed. Cases in the Chancery began to be reported around the middle of the century and were increasingly cited, relied on and followed in subsequent cases. The Chancellors began to say that although they had a discretion, it should be exercised not according to conscience, but in accordance with precedent. Lawyers rather than ecclesiastics became appointed Chancellors, the last of the non-legal Chancellors being Lord Shaftesbury, who held office during 1672–73. With his successor, Lord Nottingham (1673–82), often called the 'father of modern equity', the development of a settled system of equity really began, to be continued under succeeding Chancellors—notably Lord Hardwicke (1736–56)—and completed in the early nineteenth century by Lord Eldon (1801–06 and 1807–27). The result of their work was to transform equity into a system of law almost as fixed and rigid as the rules of the common law.

In *Gee v Pritchard* (1818) 2 Swans 402 at 414, Lord Eldon strongly rebuffed thoughts that equitable rules have remained loose, whimsical, and as varied as the chancellor's foot:

> Nothing would inflict on me greater pain, in quitting this place, than the recollection that I had done anything to justify the reproach that the equity of this court varies like the Chancellor's foot...

In *Re Telescriptor Syndicate Ltd*, Buckley J declared that '[t]his Court is not a Court of Conscience' and in *Re National Funds Assurance Co* (1878) 10 ChD 118, Jessel MR also stated that the Chancery Division of the High Court (one of the new divisions that the Judicature Acts divided the new High Court into) 'is not, as I have often said, a Court of Conscience, but a Court of Law'.

The maturation of the rules of equity, from a bundle of inconsistent, flexible, and unregulated rules, into a full, systematic body of rules, was recognized by the House of Lords in *Co-operative Insurance Society Ltd v Argyll Stores (Holdings) Ltd* [1997] 3 All ER 297 thus:

> Of course the grant or refusal of specific performance remains a matter for the judge's discretion. There are no binding rules, but this does not mean that there cannot be settled principles, founded on practical considerations…which do not have to be re-examined in every case, but which the courts will apply in all but exceptional circumstances.

But it should not be assumed that victory for equity led to a clear-cut relationship between it and the common law. Far from it. Equity had become a victim of its own success. On the one hand, equity rules became more systematized. On the other hand, equity's relationship with the common law became even less clear. There was an endless chain of actions and reactions as regards cases between these courts. The nature of this relationship was brilliantly captured by Charles Dickens's *Bleak House* (first instalment published in 1850) that:

> Equity sends questions to Law, Law sends questions back to Equity; Law finds it can't do this, Equity finds it can't do that; neither can so much as say it can't do anything, without this solicitor instructing and this counsel appearing…

The need to strike a balance between the failures of common law and the intervention of equity had long been foreshadowed by one of the earliest scholars of equity, Richard Francis. In his preface to his 1727 *Maxims of Equity*, Francis stated:

> [t]hat the court of law rigidly adheres to its own established rules, be the injustice arising from thence, ever so apparent; whereas the court of equity will not adhere to its own most established rules, if the least injustice arises from thence . . .

KEY POINTS

- Equity developed through activities of the chancellor.
- Equity was supplementary to common law and afforded remedies where common law was inadequate or rigid.
- The *Earl of Oxford* case gave prevalence to equity over common law.
- The chancellor never disregarded common law judgments, he only appealed to the conscience of common law victors.

 ## 1.4 The reform of the Court of Equity

Due to the situation we have described, steps were taken by the 18th century to reform the chancery. Gary Watt (at 7–8) summarized the process thus:

> The appointment, in 1729, of the Master of the Rolls (the chief Chancery Master) to sit as a second judge in certain cases had done little to reduce the burden on the Chancellor, because any decision of the Master of the Rolls could still be appealed to the Chancellor. It was not until 1833 that the Master of the Rolls could still be appealed to the Chancellor. It was not until 1833 that the Master of the Rolls could still be appealed to rent jurisdiction. In 1813, a Vice-Chancellor was appointed to assist the Chancellor and the Master of the Rolls. Yet when, in 1816, Sir Launcelot Shadwell VC was asked by a Commission of Inquiry whether the three judges could cope, he is said to have replied: '*No; not three angels.*'

> The Chancery judges were, indeed, overworked and increasingly unable to cope with the demands made upon them. In 1616, the supremacy of equity had been established as a means of escaping the common law jurisdiction, but by the nineteenth century, because

9

of the backlog of administration in the Court of Chancery, escape was often sought in the other direction. Even as late as 1852, it appears that claimants were attempting to avoid the queue to the Chancellor's door by asserting concurrent common law rights arising out of facts that ought to have been the exclusive concern of the Court of Chancery. Thus in *Edwards v. Lowndes*, Lord Campbell CJ had to remind litigants that a trustee is accountable to the beneficiaries of his trust in equity, but not at common law: 'no action at law for money had and received can be maintained against him, though he has money in his hands which under the terms of the trust he ought to pay over to the cestui que trust.'

The Court of Chancery Act 1850 and the Court of Chancery Procedure Act 1852 were early attempts to wrestle with the procedural problems in the Court of Chancery. However, the major step towards expediting the procedure of chancery did not come until Lord Chancellor Selborne introduced the Judicature Act 1873 into Parliament. Ironically, it was due to administrative delays that the statute did not come into force until 1875, when it was re-enacted with amendments. We now refer collectively to the Judicature Acts 1873–5. By these enactments the Supreme Court of Judicature was established with concurrent jurisdiction to administer the rules of equity and law within uniform procedural code.

1.5 The Supreme Court of Judicature Acts 1873–5: Fusion of rules or amalgamation of administrations?

The Judicature Acts 1873–5 established a Supreme Court in replacement of the previously existing Courts of Chancery, King's Bench, Common Pleas, Exchequer, Admiralty, Probate, and the London Court of Bankruptcy. The Judicature Acts divided the Supreme Court into the High Court and the Court of Appeal. The High Court, which was to sit as the court of first instance, was divided into the Chancery Division, King's Bench Division, Common Pleas Division, Exchequer Division, and the Probate, Divorce, and Admiralty Division. Each of these divisions is headed by a judge who, by virtue of art. 24 of the 1873 Act, must recognize and give effect to both legal and equitable rights, claims, defences, and remedies.

However, since 1875, the exact effect of the Judicature Acts has been very controversial. The single most important question about the Acts that continues to divide writers and judges is: What did the Judicature Acts do? Did they fuse the rules of equity and common law so that they now become one, or did they simply amalgamate the rules of equity and common law so that the rules still retain their individual identity but are administered by a single court?

Opinions are sharply divided on this matter. Some writers and judges believe that the rules of equity and common law are now fused and it is no longer sensible to talk about the two distinct rules of equity and common law. Others think that the effect of the Judicature Acts is purely procedural so that only the administrations, and not the rules, are fused. This latter view is partly based on the provision of s. 49 of the Supreme Court Act 1981 which provides that:

> (1) Subject to the provisions of this or any other Act, every court exercising jurisdiction in England or Wales in any civil cause or matter shall continue to administer law and equity on the basis that, wherever there is any conflict or variance between the rules of equity and the rules of the common law with reference to the same matter, the rules of equity shall prevail.

It is proposed to consider the contending positions on the effect of the Judicature Acts.

1.5.1 A fusion of administration, not rules

In 1954 Ashburner (*Principles of Equity*, 2nd edn at 18) famously set the orthodox view about the effect of Judicature Acts thus:

> …the two streams of jurisdiction, though they run in the same channel run side by side and do not mingle their waters.

According to eminent English Legal historian Professor JH Barker (*Sources of English Legal History: Private Law to 1750* (London: Butterworths, 1986)) at 132–3, cited by Watt at 12–13:

> If, for reasons of history, equity had become the law peculiar to Court of Chancery, nevertheless in broad theory equity was an approach to justice which gave more weight than did the law to particular circumstances and hard cases.

Gary Watt also observes that there remains a functional distinction between equity and common law and that 'it is because equity is functionally distinct from the common law that both approaches of law survived the Judicature Acts, which brought about the physical and jurisdictional unification of the old Court of Chancery with the courts of common law'. He describes the functional distinction in the following terms (at 14):

> The function of common law is to establish rules to govern the generality of cases; the effect of those rules is to recognize that certain persons will acquire certain legal rights and powers in certain circumstances. Legal rules allow the holders of legal rights and powers to exercise them in confidence that they are entitled to do so. But '*in some cases it is necessary to leave the words of the Law, and follow that* [which] *Reason and Justice requireth, and to that intent Equity ordained; that is to say, to temper and mitigate the rigor of the Law.*' The function of equity is to restrain or restrict the exercise of legal rights and powers in particular cases, whenever it would be unconscionable for them to be exercised to the full. It is also said that equity 'supplements' the shortcoming of the common law, but if that is correct it is nevertheless the case that equity only supplements the common law when, by doing so, it can prevent unconscionable reliance on the shortcomings of the common law … It may be true, as Millett LJ suggested in *Jones & Sons (a firm) v. Jones* that the common law itself had sometimes had regard for considerations of conscience, but if the common law has ever prevented a person from placing unconscionable reliance upon a legal rule or right or power, it was then performing an equitable function.

Some judicial authorities have lent much support to the view that despite the Judicature Acts, the rules of equity and common law retained their separate identities and that the effect of the Acts was simply procedural, that is, to fuse the administration of the two and not the rules.

In *Salt v Cooper* (1880) 16 ChD 544 at 549, Jessel MR pronounced that:

> …the main object of the Act was to assimilate the transaction of Equity business and Common Law business by different Courts of Judicature. It has been sometimes inaccurately called 'the fusion of Law and Equity'; but it was not any fusion, or anything of the kind; it was the vesting in one tribunal of the administration of Law and Equity in every cause, action or dispute which should come before that tribunal.

In *MCC Proceeds Inc v Lehman Bros International (Europe)* [1998] 4 All ER 675 (CA) at 691 Mummery LJ stated that the Judicature Acts:

> [w]ere intended to achieve procedural improvements in the administration of law and equity in all law courts, not to transform equitable interests into legal titles or to sweep away altogether the rules of the common law, such as the rule that a plaintiff in an action for conversion must have possession or a right to immediate possession of the good.

Writing extrajudicially (see Anthony Mason 'The Place of Equity and Equitable Remedies in the Contemporary Common Law' (1994) 110 *LQR* 238 at 239) on the issue of whether equity always follows the law, the Australian Chief Justice, Sir Anthony Mason, states that:

> [b]y providing for the *administration* of the two systems of law by one supreme court and by prescribing the paramountcy of equity, the Judicature Acts freed equity from its position on the coat-tails of the common law and positioned it for advances beyond its old frontiers.

1.5.2 A fusion of rules, not just administration

On the other divide to these views are those who believe that the Judicature Acts did not merely fuse the administration of equity and the common law, but that the Acts also fused the substantive rules of those jurisdictions. Not only have judges supported this view in judicial pronouncements, but they have also written in favour of it.

In *Errington v Errington and Woods* [1952] 1 KB 290 at 298, Lord Denning stated that 'law and equity have been fused for nearly eighty years now'. In *Boyer v Warbey* [1953] 1 QB 234, his Lordship would further clarify what he actually meant by 'fuse' when, while pronouncing on the common law principle of privity of estate and equitable leases, he stated:

> I know that before the Judicature Act 1873 it was said that the doctrine of covenants running with the land only applied to covenants under seal and not to agreements under hand...But since the fusion of law and equity the position is different. The distinction between agreements under hand and covenants under seal has largely been obliterated.

Whereas, in the terse and brisk statement in *Errington* it may be difficult to decipher what Lord Denning meant by 'fusion', his pronouncement in *Boyer* can hardly be understood to mean any more than that the 'fusion' is of rules of common law and equity. For, in referring to the 'fusion of law and equity', in the context of leases, there is little doubt that he meant the fusion of the substantive rules governing obligations that run with covenants in land and not *how* matters arise from claims originating from the application of the rules.

A little over two decades later in *United Scientific Holdings Ltd v Burnley Borough Council* [1977] 2 All ER 62 at 68, Lord Diplock would forcefully make the case for the fusion of the rules of equity and law. His Lordship began by offering what he understood the context of Ashburner's metaphor of 'two streams running side by side' to mean:

> ...by 1977 this metaphor has in my view become both mischievous and deceptive. The innate conservatism of English lawyers made them slow to recognise that by the Supreme Court of Judicature Act 1873 the two systems of substantive and adjectival law formerly administered by the Courts of Law and Courts of Chancery...were fused. As at the confluence of the Rhône and Saone, it may be possible for a short distance to discern the source from which each part of the combined stream came, but there comes a point at which this ceases to be possible. If Professor Ashburner's fluvial metaphor is to be retained at all, the waters of the confluent streams of law and equity have surely mingled now...
>
> My Lords, if by 'rules of equity' is meant that body of substantive and adjectival law, that prior to 1875, was administered by the Court of Chancery but not by courts of common law, to speak of the rules of equity as being part of the law of England in 1977 is about as meaningful as to speak similarly of the Statutes of Uses or of Quia Emptores. Historically all three in their time have played an important part in the development of the corpus juris into what it is today; but to perpetuate a dichotomy between rules of equity and rules of common law which it was a major purpose of the Supreme Court of Judicature Act 1873 to do away with, is, in my view, conducive to erroneous conclusions as to the ways in which the law of England has developed in the last 100 years.

Interest—the period for which a person is entitled to hold property. Since the Law of Property Act 1925, all interests in land that are not regarded as Legal Estates are recognized only in Equity, as equitable interests, e.g. a life interest.

Land—the statutory definition of land can be found in s. 205(1)(ix) of the Law of Property Act 1925 and includes not only land, but buildings, parts of buildings, rights over mines and minerals, and other rights, privileges, or benefits in, over, or derived from land.

More recently, judicial opinions in English courts have tended to favour the 'fusion of rules' approach. In *Tinsley v Milligan* [1993] 3 All ER 65, Lord Browne-Wilkinson had to decide whether a plaintiff who had acted illegally could assert a claim to an equitable **interest** in **land** through resulting trust. As will be seen in Chapter 2 'Maxims of Equity', one of the strongest maxims of equity is that he who comes to equity must come with clean hands, meaning a claimant who wants to seek an equitable remedy must not have done anything to tarnish his or her conduct. In the instant case, the claimant had tarnished her conduct by acting illegally (see Chapter 2 for a fuller analysis). At common law, the approach is that anyone who wishes to assert ownership of property the acquisition of which was tainted by illegal conduct can do so insofar as the claimant does not rely on the illegal conduct. Rejecting such distinction of the approaches of the two systems, Lord Browne-Wilkinson states that:

> ...to draw a distinction between property rights enforceable at law and those which require the intervention of equity would be surprising. More than 100 years has elapsed since the fusion of the administration of law and equity. The reality of the matter is that, in 1993, English law has one single law of property made up of legal and equitable interests. Although for historical reasons legal estates and equitable estates have differing incidents, the person owning either type of estate has a right of property, a right in rem not merely a right in personam. If the law is that a party is entitled to enforce a proprietary right acquired under an illegal transaction, in my judgment the same rule ought to apply to any property right so acquired, whether such right is legal or equitable.

In *Lord Napier and Ettrick v Hunter* [1993] 1 All ER 385 at 401, Lord Goff stated:

> No doubt our task nowadays is to see the two strands of authority, at law and in equity, moulded into a coherent whole; but for my part I cannot see why this amalgamation should lead to the rejection of equitable proprietary right...

13

thinking points

- Do you think it makes any sense to deny a party a remedy in one court only to entitle him or her to one in another court? In other words, why should the common law court blind its eye to an illegal conduct in respect of a proprietary interest just because the party does not rely on the illegal conduct in making its claims? What is the rationale for the chancellor, a non-lawyer, meddling in its administration of justice?
- Law does not operate on the basis of emotions or assumptions about what parties intend to do or achieve in any situation, as against what they actually do. This is why the common law is often regarded as unduly rigid. The problem, however, is that once the law begins to get involved in trying to discover the intention of parties, it may accidentally open Pandora's Box. Once a case does not fall within the legal perimeters of the law, it is the business of equity to attempt to make sense of the issues involved. The common law courts have traditionally not functioned in this respect and it may be precarious if they are encouraged to undertake such tasks that only equity courts perform. However, the merging of common law and equity has considerably narrowed the gap between these two aspects. See Anthony Mason 'The Place of Equity and Equitable Remedies in the Contemporary Common Law' (1994) 110 LQR 238.

1.5.3 The Commonwealth approach to the Judicature Act

Judicial approach in most Commonwealth jurisdictions concerning the effect of the Judicature Acts has leaned more heavily towards asserting that the Judicature Acts fused equity and common law rules and not just their administration. But it must be noted that, although they are of persuasive effect, decisions from Commonwealth jurisdictions do not prevail over decisions of English courts.

In *Aquaculture Corpn New Zealand v Green Mussel Co Ltd*, the New Zealand Appeal Court had to deal with issues concerning whether damages, which had traditionally been a common law remedy, should be made available for breach of trust which, clearly, is an equitable duty. The court (Cook P) pronounced that:

> [f]or all purposes now material, equity and common law are mingled or merged. The practicality of the matter is that in the circumstances of the dealings between parties the law imposes a duty of confidence. For its breach a full range of remedies should be available as appropriate, no matter whether they originate in common law, equity or statute.

In *Mouat v Clark Boyce* [1992] 3 NZLR 299, a New Zealand court held that breach of an equitable duty can lead to an award of exemplary damages or damages for mental distress. Traditionally, this remedy was only available in common law courts. (See also Pearce and Stevens at 14.)

. . . .

Fiduciary—a person in a position of trust or confidence, who may act on behalf of their principal. The position of the fiduciary is similar to that of the trustee and the position of the principal is similar to that of the beneficiary.

. . . .

Canadian courts have generally echoed the principle laid down by Lord Diplock in the *United Scientific Holdings* case. In *Le Mesurier v Andrus* (1986) 54 OR (2d) 1 and in *Canson Enterprises Ltd v Broughton & Co* (1991) 85 DLR (4th) 129, the common law principle of remoteness of damage was held applicable to an equitable claim for damages for breach of **fiduciary** duty (see also Pearce and Stevens at 15). The main difference between the approach of Canada and the rest of the Commonwealth (especially New Zealand) was that whereas Canada followed the general trend of regarding the fusion as one of the rules of law and equity, it recognizes that in some cases, however, there may yet be a need to retain a distinction. As La Forest J put it:

> There might be room for concern if one were indiscriminately attempting to meld the whole of the two systems. Equitable concepts like trusts, equitable estates and consequent equitable remedies must continue to exist apart, if not in isolation, from common law rules.

Academic analysis of the effects of the Judicature Acts has tended to focus more on the actual construction of the relevant provisions of the Judicature Acts as well as the preservation of the rationale for the existence of the different proprietary rights which, in proponents' views, justify the continued distinction between equity and common law rules which the likes of Lord Goff want abolished. We consider the two issues now.

As Phillip Pettit notes (at 10–11):

> It is respectfully submitted that these propositions [that the rules of equity and common law are fused] cannot be accepted. Baker has pointed out that no one thinks that the rules of equity have remained unchanged since 1875—they have developed in the same way as the rules of common law. As to the comparison with Quia Emptores [which Lord Diplock made in justification of the 'fusion of rules' proposition], Baker observes that this is still in force today and is said to be 'one of the pillars of the law of real property'. Most importantly, it is a complete misapprehension to think that it was a purpose

of the Judicature Acts to do away with the dichotomy between rules of equity and rules of common law. Introducing the second reading, the Attorney General said in terms that 'The Bill was not one of the fusion of law and equity' and he went on to explain what the purpose of the Bill was:

The defect of our legal system was, not that Law and Equity existed, but that if a man went for relief to a Court of law, and an equitable claim or an equitable defence arose, he must go to some other Court and begin afresh. Law and Equity therefore would remain if the Bill passed, but they would be administered concurrently, and no one would be sent to get in one Court the relief which another Court has refused to give...Great authorities had no doubt declared that law and equity might be fused by enactment; but in his opinion, to do so would be to decline to grapple with the real difficulty of the case. If an Act were passed doing no more than fuse law and Equity, it would take 20 years of decisions and hecatombs of suitors to make out what Parliament meant and had not taken the trouble to define. It was more philosophical to admit the innate distinction between Law and Equity, which you could not get rid of by Act of Parliament, and to say not that the distinction should not exist, but that the Courts should administer relief according to legal principles when these applied, or else according to equitable principles. That was what the Bill proposed, with the addition that, whenever the principles of Law and Equity conflicted, equitable principles should prevail.

The author of *Hanbury and Martin Modern Equity* (19th edn, London: Sweet & Maxwell, 2012 at 23, citing P Baker in (1977) 93 *LQR* 529 at 532) attempted to create a balance between these contending views on the effect of the Judicature Acts on equity and common law. First, they argue that a separation exists between the two despite the Judicature Acts. Accordingly, they reason that, if by fusion of equity and common law it is meant there is now no distinction or difference between legal rights and remedies and equitable rights and remedies, this cannot be supported:

It is still clear that legal ownership is different from equitable ownership; all the provisions of legislation of 1925, dealing with unregistered land, are based on that assumption. Again, the law of trusts assumes a distinction between legal and equitable rights. The equitable nature of the duties of a mortgage has been emphasised, although Sir Richard Scott V.C. has said: 'I do not, for my part, think that it matters one jot whether the duty is expressed as a common law duty or as a duty in equity. The result is the same.'

However, they also reject the other extreme view that both equity and common law are so separately administered after 1875 as to banish any relationship between them. Thus:

Nor is it true, at the other extreme, to say that rights exercisable in the High Court today are the same as those existing in 1875; nor that the application of equitable doctrines in the court has not had the effect of refining and developing common law rules. Both legal and equitable rules have developed since 1873; and the development of legal rules has sometimes been influenced by established equitable doctrine, with the effect that a situation which would at one time have been treated differently at law and equity is now treated in the same manner. If that is what is meant by fusion, there is evidence of it...It is a healthy and welcome development; and there are other situations which might be candidates for future inclusion.

After reviewing the current position in Canada, Professor Jeff Berryman noted:

My point here is not to discuss the current metes and bounds of the fusion debate other than to say that in Commonwealth jurisdictions there is still recognized a separate place for equity and recognition that within that sphere there are methodological differences in how equity applies the doctrines to any particular factual pleading. ('The Role of Equity's Maxims in Canada', <http://ssrn.com/abstract=1817858>, at p. 17).

> **thinking points**
>
> To what extent do you think that what we have discussed represents a better approach to reconcile the divergent views on the effect of the Judicature Acts? The approach adopted by countries like Canada and New Zealand towards the effect of the Judicature Acts is to emphasize the fusion of the rules of equity and common law rather than merely their administrations. This runs contrary to what most British lawyers and judges hold, but was prompted by Canada's far more liberal approach towards granting equitable remedies. For instance, Canada believes strongly in the 'conscionability principle', which tends to look at the circumstances of a case to see whether it is or is not conscionable to do justice in the circumstances even if the formal legal rules do not necessarily favour such a solution. Thus, holding that the rules of common law and equity have been fused affords such jurisdictions as Canada a greater latitude to discharge equitable justice more readily. See Elisabeth Peden 'When Common Law Trumps Equity: The Rise of Good Faith and Reasonableness and the Demise of Unconscionability' (2005) 21 Journal of Contract Law 226.

1.6 The modern relevance of equity

1.6.1 Equity after the Judicature Acts: Has it gone past childbearing?

Whether one believes that the Judicature Acts fused the rules of common law and equity or fused only the administrations, there is a general consensus that the rules of equity became more formal and rigid after the Acts. This new perception of equity has led to concern about whether, in the modern society, equity is still capable of inventing new principles; after all, equity derives its pedigree from its ability to respond, and provide alternatives, to the rigidity of the common law. So, the relevant question to ask is whether equity has now passed the age of childbearing.

Commenting on this issue, Pettit writes (at 6) that:

> [a]lthough there is no fiction in equity as there has been said to be at common law that the rules have existed from time immemorial, and although 'it is perfectly well known that they have been established from time to time—altered, improved and refined from time to time. In many cases we know the names of the Chancellors who invented them', yet, it is in principle doubtful whether a new right can now be created.

In 1952 ((1952) 5 *CLP* 8) Lord Denning wrote that 'the Courts of Chancery are no longer courts of equity...they are as fixed and immutable as the courts of law ever were'. In 1953 ((1953) 6 *CLP* 11 at 12) Lord Evershed stated that the Judicature Acts halted or, at least, severely restricted the inventive faculties of future chancery judges. In *Re Diplock* [1948] 2 All ER 204 at 218, the English Court of Appeal held that if a claim in equity exists:

> [i]t must be shown to have an ancestry founded in history and in the practice and precedents of the courts administering equity jurisdiction. It is not sufficient that because we may think that the 'justice' of the present case requires it, we should invent such a jurisdiction for the first time.

In their work *Equity, Doctrines and Remedies* (2nd edn, Sydney: Butterworths, 1984 at 68–9), Meagher, Gummow, and Lehane write that equity's naked power of improvization had long been spent. In *Western Fish Products Ltd v Penwith District Council* [1981] 2 All ER 204 (CA) at

218, Megaw LJ stated that 'the creation of new rights and remedies is a matter for Parliament, not judges'.

Statutory development in the law of equity and trusts has also been perceived as affecting the extent to which equity can generate new principles in the contemporary society. Pettit observes that as far as equitable interest in land is concerned:

> Section 4(1) of the Law of Property Act 1925 provides that, after 1925, such an interest is only capable of being validly created in any case in which an equivalent equitable interest in property real or personal could have been created before 1926. In principle, it is very doubtful, therefore, whether new equitable interests can any longer be created, except through the extension and development of existing equitable interests by exactly the same process as extension and development may take place at law.

In *Allen v Synder* [1977] 2 NSWLR 685 at 689, an Australian judge, Glass JA, commenting on the issue of creating new rules, stated that:

> [i]t is inevitable that judge made law will alter to meet the changing conditions of society. That is the way it has always evolved. But it is essential that new rules should be related to funda-mental doctrines. If the foundations of accepted doctrine be submerged under new principles, without regard to the interaction between the two, there will be high uncertainty as to the state of the law, both old and new.

Clearly, Judge Glass does not specifically rule out the possibility of equity (or judges) develop-ing new principles in the present society, contrary to what his statement has been taken to mean by some writers (Pettit at 6). All the judge did was to premise the basis for judge-made rules on fundamental doctrines so as to avoid a situation whereby a doctrine is submerged by a new principle.

However, Bagnall J, as with several other judges, was of the opinion that equity is now meas-ured and can no longer behave purely on the basis of the chancellor's discretion, but that does not mean that the adaptability of equity is now dead. As his Lordship stated, measuring the chancellor's feet does not mean that 'equity is past child-bearing; simply that its progeny must be legitimate—by precedent out of principle' (*Cowcher v Cowcher*, cited earlier, at 948).

This moderate view is shared by Bagnall J who, in *Cowcher v Cowcher* [1972] 1 All ER 943 at 948, proclaimed:

> I am convinced that in determining rights, particularly property rights, the only justice that can be attained by mortals, who are fallible and are not omniscient, is justice according to law; the justice which flows from the application of sure and settled principles to proved or admitted facts. So in the field of equity the Chancellor's foot has been measured or is capable of measurement. This does not mean that equity is past child bearing; simply that its progeny must be legitimate—by precedent out of principle. It is well that this should be so; otherwise no lawyer could safely advise on his client's title and every quarrel would lead to a law suit.

As will be seen in the next chapter, rather than its ability to invent new principles, the modern relevance of equity has emerged more in the form of the application of its many principles—generally embodied by maxims—to various kinds of transactions. Maybe equity is still as fertile as ever; but instead of producing new offspring itself, unwittingly making its breed susceptible to birds of prey, it has ingenuously and generously decided to donate its eggs to surrogates. If that be the case, then equity would, undoubtedly indirectly, father many more children than it ever did in the obscurity of its evolution; and who can question the paternity of equity's children in those circumstances except, of course, the uninitiated and unperceptive?

1.7 Trusts

In narrating the history of equity, we indicated briefly that the chancellor began to exercise certain powers over trusts. Thus, since it was through the activities of the chancellor that equity evolved, it is correct to describe trusts as a creation of equity. According to Maitland at 23:

> Of all the exploits of Equity the largest and the most important is the invention and development of the Trust...it is the most distinctive achievement of English Lawyers...It is an 'institute' of great elasticity; as elastic, as general as contract.

But this effusion does not tell us what trust is. Does the term mean to 'trust' people as in people trusting each other to act in a particular given way within certain contexts? Or is 'trust' the kind of trust that a master has in his or her servant to carry out his or her instructions in accordance to his or her wishes?

'Trust', as a concept, does not mean to 'trust' someone as in daily use. In fact, 'trust' can be set up and commissioned to an untrusted character and it would still be called trust! It is the operation of the law that makes a trust a trust, not the content or the character of who administers it. Trust is an interesting but complex concept. It is an institution that defies easy definition. It is a concept but at the same time a process. Trust is an enigma; no wonder authors do not generally define it. Instead, they speak of trust in various terms:

> It is a unique way of owning property under which assets are held by a trustee for the benefit of another person, or for certain purposes, in accordance with special equitable obligations (Watt at 36).

Martin at 47 describes trust as 'a relationship recognized by equity which arises where property is vested in (a person or) persons called the trustees, which those trustees are obliged to hold for the benefit of other persons called *cestuis que trust* or beneficiaries'. JG Ridall describes trusts as 'an arrangement recognised by law under which one person holds property for the benefit of another' (*The Law of Trusts* (London: Butterworths, 2002) at 1). For Alastair Hudson, 'a trust is created where the absolute owner of property (the **settlor**) passes the legal title in that property to a person (the trustees) to hold that property on **trust** for the benefit of another person (the **beneficiary**) in accordance with the terms set out by the settlor'.

However, some of these descriptions are somewhat misleading. For, while a trust is indeed applied to ownership of property, the property is not necessarily owned by someone for the benefit of *another* person. The person holding the property in trust could him or herself be a beneficiary. Additionally, although usually it is the owner of the property who dictates the terms upon which his or her property is to be held by another in trust, there are occasions when the law does intervene to set such terms.

We have seen various terms and descriptions, but these do not explain how the concept of trust emerged. A good historical account of the evolution of trust is found in Phillip Pettit's book. According to this author:

> Even before the Conquest [of 1066] cases have been found of land being conveyed to one man to be held by him on behalf of or 'to the use of' another, but for a considerable time this seems to have been done for a limited time and a limited purpose, such as for the grantor's family while he went away on a crusade. From the early thirteenth century the practice grew up of conveying land in a general way for more permanent purposes. For various reasons a landowner might convey land by ordinary common law conveyance to

persons called 'feoffees to uses' directing them to hold the land for the benefit of persons, the cestuis que use, who might indeed be or include the feoffor himself. After early doubts the common law refused to take any account of uses, i.e. the direction given to the feoffees to uses, who, though they were bound in honour, could not be sued either by the feoffor or the cestuis que use.

It was clearly highly unsatisfactory that feoffees to uses should be able to disregard the dictates of good faith, honour, and justice with impunity, and from the end of the fourteenth or the early fifteenth century, the Chancellor began to intervene and compel the feoffees to uses to carry out the directions given to them as to how they should deal with the land. The Chancellor never, however, denied that the feoffees to uses were the legal owners of the land; he merely ordered the feoffees to uses to carry out the directions given to them, and failure to carry out the order would be a contempt of court which would render the feoffees liable to imprisonment until they were prepared to comply.

The device of the use was adopted for various purposes. It enabled a landowner, for example, to evade some of the feudal dues that fell on the person seized of land, to dispose of his land by his will, to evade mortmain statutes, and more effectively to settle his land. The use developed considerably during the fifteenth and early sixteenth centuries, so much so that it was said, in 1500, that the greater part of the land in England was held in use [YB Mich 15 Hen VII 13 pl (Frowike CJ)] and the rights of the cestuis que use were so extensive that it became recognised that there was duality of ownership. One person, the feoffee to uses, was the legal owner according to the common law—a title not disputed by the Chancellor. But the feoffee to uses had only the bare legal title; beneficial ownership was in the equitable owner, the cestuis que use. A stop was put to the development of uses in 1535, however, when, largely because the King was losing so many feudal dues by the device of the use, the Statute of Uses was passed to put an end to uses, or at least severely to limit them. In cases in which the Act applied the use was 'executed'—that is, on the one hand, the feoffees to uses were deprived of their seisin of the land (indeed, they commonly dropped out of the picture altogether) and, on the other hand, the equitable estates of the cestuis que use were turned into equivalent legal estates carrying seisin. Although the Act executed the vast majority of uses there were cases to which it did not apply—those in which, for instance, the feoffees to uses had active duties to perform—and thus the use never became completely obsolete.

One special case which should be mentioned was the use upon a use, as where land is limited to A and his heirs to the use of B and his heirs to the use of C and his heirs. It was decided before 1535 that C took nothing in such a case: A had the legal fee simple, B the equitable fee simple, but the limitation to C was repugnant to B's interest and accordingly void. After the Statute of Uses the second use was still held to be void, though the first use was executed so as to give B the legal fee simple and leave A, like C, with nothing at all. Eventually, however, by steps which are not very clear, the Chancellor, at about the middle of the seventeenth century or perhaps earlier, began to enforce this second use and it had become a well-established practice by the end of the century. As a matter of terminology, the second use thus enforced became called a 'trust', and, as a matter of drafting, the basic formula was 'unto and to the use of B and his heirs in trust for C and his heirs'. B took the legal fee simple at common law, but the use in his favour prevented the second use from being executed by the Statue of Uses, leaving it to be enforced in equity as a trust. The result was to restore duality of ownership, B being the legal and C the equitable owner. The use was, in effect, resuscitated under the name of 'trust'.

From the above exposé, it is clear there are generally three parties to a standard trust transaction: the 'feoffor'—who is today called the settlor, the 'feoffee to uses'—the modern-day **trustee**, and the 'cestuis que trusts', called nowadays the beneficiaries. Now, let us discard the ancient terms and speak with a modern tongue. A trust takes place when A (the settlor) puts property, real or personal, into the care of B, the trustee to hold in trust for the benefit or use of C, the beneficiary. But note that a settlor is one whose trust is executed during his lifetime, but where the instrument is executed (i.e. when it comes into effect) after his death, then the settlor is referred to as the '**testator**' or, if a woman, the '**testatrix**' (see Diagram 1.1).

thinking points

- *Is it possible for a trustee to be a beneficiary or must a trustee at all times hold the property for persons other than him or herself?*
- *What are the reasons for the abolition of uses in 1535?*
- *Contrary to the impressions often given by definitions, a trustee can also double as a beneficiary, although, in most cases, trustees are separate from beneficiaries. However, it must always be borne in mind that a sole trustee cannot be a beneficiary since a trust is an arrangement between a trustee and a beneficiary. See P Baker 'The Future of Equity' (1971) 93 LQR 529.*

Settlor—one who intends to part with his or her property and leave it for the benefit of others by an instrument executed when he—the settlor—is still alive.

Testator/testatrix—one who intends to part with his or her property and leave it for the benefit of others by an instrument executed when he—the settlor—is dead.

Trustee—the middle person, the bridge between a settlor and the person whom the property is to benefit. It is the trustee that the property is 'vested' in, in trust for another.

Beneficiary—the ultimate person who would enjoy the property. Beneficiaries could include a trustee.

Trust—an arrangement created for the purpose of transferring property to the beneficiary via the trustee. It usually states the conditions of the trust with regard to the time of its maturity, termination, variation, and so on. A trust arrangement can either be made in writing through a legal instrument or orally.

Diagram 1.1

Diagram of settlor/trustee/ beneficiary

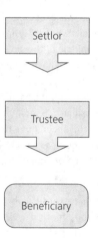

1.8 Types of trusts

There are various forms of trusts, depending on how and for what purpose they are created (as will be seen in subsequent chapters). Trusts can be express, implied, resulting, or constructive. Under these general forms are subsumed several sub-categories such as bare trusts; fixed trusts; executed and executory trusts; discretionary trusts; public, secret, and statutory trusts; and employee, pensions, and protective trusts. All these are sub-categories of express trusts (see Haley and McMurtry at 16–21). See Chapter 3 'The different types of trust' for a discussion of types of trusts.

1.9 Nature of trusts

The fact that a trust involves transactions concerning several persons having different but distinguishable rights and obligations under the arrangement has led to some confusion as to the exact nature of trusts. Some have conceived of trusts as a contractual arrangement or something that fits perfectly into a contractarian idea, while others have construed it as an agency between principal and agent. The following section briefly considers some of the most common concepts with which trust has been compared.

1.9.1 Trust and contract

According to Langbein, a trust is 'functionally indistinguishable from the modern third-party beneficiary contract' ('Contractarian Basis of the Law of Trusts' (1995) 105 *Yale LJ* 625 at 627). This implies that trusts are, to a large extent, synonymous with contracts. Several writers have challenged this view. The learned authors of Hanbury and Martin (at 27, 16th edn, London: Sweet & Maxwell, 2001), emphasizing the basic features of contract, in contradistinction from trusts, have noted that:

> … [t]here is a historical distinction that contract was developed by the common law courts while trusts was a creature of equity. In general the purposes are different: a contract usually represents a bargain between the contracting parties giving each some advantage, while the beneficiary under a trust is commonly a volunteer, and the trustee himself usually obtains no benefit at all. It is of the essence of a contract that the agreement is supported by **consideration**, but in the case of trust there is no need for consideration to have been given in order to be enforceable. This distinction is blurred by the fact that a contract by deed is enforceable at law without value having been given.

· ·

Consideration—each party to a contract must promise something of value. The consideration need not be adequate, i.e. of equal value to the promise made by the other party, but it must be of some financial value.

· ·

Alastair Hudson (at 70) observes that:

> [a] contract is a bilateral agreement (resulting from an offer, an acceptance of that offer, and consideration passing between the parties). An express trust arises from the unilateral act of settlor in declaring a trust. There is no contract between settlor and trustee in ordinary circumstances. It will be the case that if a professional trustee is appointed (perhaps a bank or a solicitor), then the trustee will require payment from the settlor to act as

trustee. In such circumstances there will be a trust and also a contract between settlor and trustee. However, the contract does not form part of the trust—rather, it is collateral to it.

As laid down in *Saunders v Vautier* (1841) 4 Beav 115, 'beneficiaries who are absolutely entitled to the trust property, and acting *sui generis*, are empowered to direct the trustees to deliver the trust property to them' (Hudson at 39).

In an even more elaborate exposé, Gary Watt (at 19–20) successfully lays out some crucial distinctions between trusts and contracts:

> There are a number of reasons why it does not make sense to regard the arrangement entered into between settlor and trustee as being contractual in nature. For one thing, whereas a contracting party always has the right to enforce his contractual rights against the other party, the power of enforcing trusts lies with the beneficiaries of the trust, so the settlor of a trust has no power to enforce it against the trustees unless he happens to nominate himself to be a beneficiary or becomes a beneficiary under a resulting trust. Otherwise, the settlor of a trust drops out of the picture just as the donor of an absolute gift drops out of the picture when he has made his gift. Of course, many settlement trusts do not come into effect until the death of the testator, so the testator patently 'drops out' of the picture in those cases.
>
> The most significant distinction between a trust and a contract, even a contract entered into for the benefit of a third party, is the nature of the beneficiary's rights. In some ways, the beneficiary's rights resemble contractual rights, in that they are enforceable against the trustee personally, but the beneficiary's right is not merely a personal right against the trustee; it is also a proprietary right in the asset itself. This is the feature that most clearly distinguishes the English trust from concepts that perform similar functions in other jurisdictions. The significance of the proprietary status of the beneficiary's right under the trust is essentially twofold. First, the beneficiary's right under the trust can be enforced not only against the trustee, but also against the trustee's successors in title. This is useful where the trustee has wrongfully transferred trust property into the hands of a third party and is particularly useful if a trustee dies or becomes insolvent. At no time does the beneficiary's proprietary right become part of the trustee's personal estate, so, when a trustee dies, the beneficiary's proprietary right in the trust assets is binding on the trustee's personal representatives and, when a trustee becomes insolvent, the beneficiary's right is binding on the 'trustees in bankruptcy', or, if the trustee was corporate (as many trustees are), on its successor in insolvency. Second, the proprietary status of the beneficiary's right under the trust means that the beneficiary is free to alienate the property wholly (say by selling it or giving it away, for example) or partially (by leasing it or subjecting it to a charge such as a mortgage, for example). It is even possible for a beneficiary to declare a trust of her equitable interest, thereby creating a sub-trust, although that possibility is somewhat controversial.

The crucial issue is often whether in given circumstances a trustee can be regarded as having been contracted by a settlor to hold property for the beneficiary in the same sense as obtains under the common law concept of contract. The situation is not normally easy to ascertain. Thus, problems have commonly arisen whether a settlor can order specific performance of a contract and whether the trustee can generally be treated as a contractual party.

. . . .

● *Re Schebsman* [1944] Ch 83 (CA)

The debtor was employed by a Swiss company and its subsidiary, an English company. On 31 March 1940 his employment ended and, on 20 September 1940, he entered into an agreement with the companies, by clause 2 of which: 'In consideration of the agreement which has already been made between the parties hereto the English company also agree to pay by way of compensation for loss of the debtor's employment a sum of 5,500l. to be paid to the persons at the dates in the amounts and subject to the conditions more particularly specified in the schedule hereto'. The schedule began with a list of six sums totalling 5,500l. to be paid to the debtor, the first for the year ending 31 March 1941, and the others for the years ending on the five succeeding anniversaries of that date. By paras (a) to (f) of the schedule, if the debtor died before the completion of the payments to him, provision was made for payments to his widow of sums varying in amount according to the date of the debtor's death, such sums amounting, with those which would already have been paid to the debtor, in some cases to less, in some cases to more, than 5,500l., while the period of payment, in certain events, was to continue to 31 March 1950…On 5 March 1942, the debtor was adjudicated bankrupt. On 12 May 1942 he died. By this motion the official receiver, as his trustee in bankruptcy, asked for a declaration that all sums payable under the agreement to the widow and, possibly, to the daughter, after the receiving order, formed part of the **estate** of the debtor, on the grounds inter alia that, although the sums were, by the agreement, to be paid to the widow or the daughter, the debtor always had the right to intercept them, which right was at the date of the motion in the trustee.

Uthwatt J held that the contract did not create a trust in favour of the widow or daughter and that Schebsman had not been contracted as trustee. Nevertheless, the court was content to allow the wife and the daughter to take priority over the trustee in bankruptcy since the latter's right could not have been greater than those of Schebsman were he alive. While there is no doubt that by fresh agreement with his ex-employer Schebsman could have deprived his wife and daughter of their benefits had he so chosen, he could not have done so unilaterally without breaching the contract.

On the issue of whether a trust constitutes a contract, Lord Greene MR states that:

> [a]n examination of the decided cases does, it is true, show that the courts have on occasions adopted what may be called a liberal view on questions of this character, but in the present case I cannot find in the contract anything to justify the conclusion that a trust was intended. It is not legitimate to import into the contract the idea of a trust when the parties have given no indication that such was their intention. To interpret this contract as creating a trust would, in my judgment, be to disregard the dividing line between the case of a trust and the simple case of a contract made between two persons for the benefit of a third. That dividing line exists, although it may not always be easy to determine where it is to be drawn. In the present case I find no difficulty.

On the same question about the status of the agreement, du Parcq LJ notes thus:

> It now remains to consider the question whether, and if so to what extent, the principles of equity affect the position of the parties. It was argued by Mr Denning that one effect of the agreement of 20 September 1940, was that a trust was thereby created, and that the debtor constituted himself trustee for Mrs Schebsman of the benefit of the covenant under which payments were to be made to her. Uthwatt J rejected this contention, and the argument has not satisfied me that he was wrong. It is true that, by the use possibly of unguarded language, a person may create a trust, as Monsieur Jourdain talked prose, without knowing it, but unless an intention to create a trust is clearly to be collected from the language used and the circumstances of the case, I think that the court ought not to be astute to discover indications of such an intention. I have little doubt that in the present case both parties (and certainly the debtor) intended to keep alive their common law right to vary consensually the terms of the obligation undertaken by the company, and if circumstances had changed in the debtor's life-time injustice might have been done by holding that a trust had been created and that those terms were accordingly unalterable.

KEY POINT In coming to his decision, Uthwatt J, in the court of first instance, applied and relied on the rationale in *Re Stapleton-Bretherton* [1938] Ch 799. This was approved by the Court of Appeal in the instant case.

1.9.2 Trust and agency

Another concept with which common comparison with trust is often made is agency. Writing in 1898, Spencer Brodhurst argued that an agent is a trustee for his principal of property belonging to the principal committed to his care, either generally or specifically in situations where a particular confidential relationship exists (see also Keeton and Sheridan *Law of Trusts* (12th edn, Chichester: Barry Rose Publishing, 1993) at 246; Pettit at 27; FE Dowrick (1954) 17 *MLR* 24; JD Stephens (1975) *CLP* 39).

As Pettit noted (at 27–8), 'there is no doubt that a principal can commonly exercise the same remedies against his agent as a cestuis que trust can against his trustee', but Professor Powell has pointed out that this

> does not necessarily mean that an agent is a trustee or that a trustee is an agent. It simply means that agents and trustees have something in common—and that 'something in common' is that they both hold a fiduciary position which imposes on them certain obligations. Thus both agents and trustees are under a duty not to delegate responsibilities, not to let their interests conflict with their duties, not to make any unauthorised profits and to keep proper account. There are however considerable differences. Thus the relationship of principal and agent is created by their agreement, but this is not so in case of trustees and beneficiary. The trustee does not represent the beneficiaries, though he performs his duties for their benefits, as the agent represents his principal. Further the trustee does not bring his beneficiaries into any contractual relationship with third parties, while it is the normal function of an agent to do so. Again the concept of a trust necessarily involves the concept of trust property over which the trustee has at least nominal control, but an agent need never have any control over any property belonging to his principal. An agent is subject to control of his principal, but a trustee is not subject to the control by the beneficiaries except in the sense that the beneficiaries can take steps to compel him to carry out the terms of the trust.

The view that trust and agency are similar was explained, about one hundred years ago, by McCardie J who, in *Armstrong v Jackson* [1917] 2 KB 822 at 826, said that:

> [t]he position of principal and agents gives rise to particular and onerous duties on the part of the agent, and the high standard of conduct required from him springs from the fiduciary relationship between his employer and himself. His position is confidential. It readily lends itself to abuse...The rules of English law as they now exist spring from the strictness originally required by the Courts of Equity in cases where the fiduciary relationship exists.

thinking points

- *Do you think it is always easy to tell, from the given facts of a case, whether an arrangement is a trust or an agency? What are those clues that you must look for to aid your analysis and decisions one way or the other?*
- *It is indeed easy to confuse an agency relationship with a trust arrangement, especially when we consider the general features of each in isolation. This is why some writers have argued that the two are identical. However, there are remarkable similarities between the two and the best way to tell them apart is by looking at how each of the arrangements is created, the nature of the responsibility of agents and trustees, and what specific objectives they each strive to achieve. See FE Dowrick (1954) 17 MLR 24.*

Alastair Hudson adds a different distinction to the two concepts. The author notes at 72 that:

> [t]he trust bears some superficial similarities to ... agency arrangement. At first blush a trustee may appear to operate as a form of agent, dealing with the legal title in property according to the terms of the trust. However, there is not necessarily a contract between settlor and trustee, nor between trustee and beneficiary. Furthermore, in an agency arrangement, a principal would not ordinarily acquire equitable interests in property acquired by the agent in the way that a beneficiary under a trust acquires equitable interests once the declaration of trust takes effect. It may, however, be possible for the principal to assert that the contract of agency would transfer equitable rights by means of specific performance.

As will be seen in later chapters, it is possible to set up a trust which operates without the knowledge of a beneficiary of either existence of the trust or of themselves as the beneficiary, until such time, or such conditions, nominated by the testator, for its disclosure arrives. This is often the case with secret trusts, which were originally used to protect children born out of wedlock who, without the creation of secret trusts in their favour, would be left without the benefit from their parents' estates. Secret trusts are the most discrete kind of trusts and are generally set up without conformity with the rules governing the creation of trusts in order to protect the identity of the beneficiaries. It is thus difficult to conceive of the relationship between a trustee and a beneficiary under this category as agency. Whereas an agent can occasionally exceed the scope of his or her authority and, provided there is subsequent ratification of the otherwise ultra vires acts he or she performs by the principal, such acts are deemed valid. But there still needs to be the knowledge that a relationship exists between the principal and agent before the latter can so act. Where there is no such relationship at all, as where there is no knowledge by one of the other's existence (as in secret trusts), a relationship cannot be uncontroversially presumed to exist. One cannot owe a duty to a principal who one does not know exists.

The other common law concepts with which trust has been compared, but which are not discussed in this book, are power, bailment, conditions and charges, and debt. (For these, see especially, Martin and Hanbury at 47–67; Paul Todd and Gary Watt *Cases and Materials on Equity and Trusts* (4th edn, Oxford: Oxford University Press, 2003) at 18–36; Pettit at 25–40; Haley and McMurtry at 21–4; and Hudson at 36–41.)

1.10 The recognition of trusts

The next issue to consider briefly is how the concept of trusts has been perceived within and outside the UK. Hanbury and Martin at 45ff write that:

> ... [t]he trust is an English concept which has spread to common law, but not civil law, jurisdiction. The 1984 Hague Convention on the Law applicable to Trusts and their Recognition establishes common principles between states on the law governing trusts and provides guidelines for their recognition. The United Kingdom, by means of the Recognition of Trusts Act 1987, has ratified the Convention.

> The ratification does not have the effect of changing the substantive law of trusts of the United Kingdom, nor of importing trusts into civil law jurisdictions. The Convention seeks to establish uniform conflict of law principles and to assist civil law states to deal with trusts issues arising within their jurisdiction. Recognition implies, for example, that the trust property is a separate fund and is not part of the trustee's estate. A trust is to be governed by the settlor, expressly or by implication. In the absence of any such choice, the trust is to be governed by the law with which it is most closely connected. The applicable law governs the validity and construction of the trust, and its effects and administration.

Conclusion

As we have seen, one of the advantages of equity over common law is its flexibility and ability readily to meet the challenges of changing circumstances of modern society. But then, the rapidity and intensity of today's commercial interactions and human relations means that people and businesses are much less attentive to legal rules governing their relations with others in general. In such an atmosphere, genuine mistakes—with devastating legal consequences—are made.

Spouses provide cash support for their spouses to help them to purchase property or other chattels, without ever signing any paper to evidence their intention to possess any interest in the property. The dubious spouse returns later to claim that, in the absence of any formal agreement, the cash advance was a gift. Company directors use knowledge derived from their position to profit themselves at the expense of their companies; a rich neighbour perennially annoys his poorer counterpart by throwing mindless night parties and buys the 'right' to do so at law by paying small compensations every now and then to the displeasured neighbour; a debtor, unwilling to settle his debt to a claimant certain to get justice against him, decides to remove or dissipate his money within the jurisdiction or elsewhere so as to frustrate the judgment. A trustee thinks because he has charge of certain trust funds he can deal with them as he likes, regardless of his status under the trusts and the rules of engagement. A dubious businessman believes by simply designating that all his money should go to a charity set up to benefit members of his family, he cheats the law.

The scenarios to which equity and trusts respond vary significantly. As will be seen in the following chapters, equity tries to keep pace with modern developments. As already seen, equity does not allow formality to defeat intentions; but such intentions must be genuine, and the mistake must have been honest. Equity will not aid the indolent. A nonchalant spouse, who, despite being aware of legal rules decides nonetheless to throw away caution, will have no respite in the court of equity. Nor will someone who has not done what is right, or who is not prepared to do so, receive any sympathy in the court of equity. Equity does not intend to destroy the common law but to fulfil it. Like the common law, equity believes in rules and principles, but in attempting to achieve that a practical and useful balance needs to be struck. It is a balance between extreme formality and sensibility. Nor is there any point for a person to seek legal and equitable justice from different courts. Why should a single court not be able to apply the rules of law and the principles of equity to the same case? Is it not much easier, time saving, and more practical to do so than to toss claimants from one court to another as though they are involved in a game of ping-pong? This is what the Judicature Act of 1875 started and which has now been furthered by more recent legislation.

Questions

Self-test questions

1 What is equity?

2 What are trusts?

3   Do you think the Judicature Acts fused the rules or administration of equity and common law?

4   What is the difference, if any, between the English and the Commonwealth approaches to the Judicature Acts? Do you think one is to be preferred, assuming that there is a difference?

5   Is it the same meaning to say someone is a trustee and that Mr A trusts Mr B?

6   What is the rationale behind the emergence of trusts?

7   Is there a difference between equity and trusts?

8   Do you think there is any justification in the merging of equity and trusts?

9   What is the relevance of equity in today's world?

Discussion questions

1   The Judicature Acts do nothing that fuses the administration of equity and common law. Both still retain their distinctive rules and although they now run side by side, they do not mingle. Discuss.

2   The fact that equity was besieged by serious problems before the Judicature Acts is a clear indication that they should never have been introduced into the English legal system in the first place. It is nothing but an avoidable waste of time. Do you agree?

3   There is no distinction between trusts and contract. It is the chancellor's lust for power, and nothing more, that led to the development of trusts as a distinct category. To what extent do you think this statement represents the rationale and use of trusts?

4   Is it true that once a person has been named as a trustee, he can deal with the property as he likes?

5   Equity is so flexible it can apply to anything; it is so powerful it can revoke or nullify a judgment given by a common law court. Is this true?

Assessment questions

It does not matter what the effects of the Judicature Acts are. What is indisputable today is that equity has passed the age of childbearing. In light of this chapter, would you agree with this assertion?

How do you deal with issues or questions concerning the effects of the Judicature Acts?

 # Key cases

- *Earl of Oxford* (1615) 1 Rep Ch 1 **(at 1.2, 1.2.4, and 1.3)**

- *Gee v Pritchard* (1818) 2 Swans 402 **(at 1.3)**

- *MCC Proceeds Inc v Lehman Bros International (Europe)* [1998] 4 All ER 675 (CA) **(at 1.5.1)**

- *Errington v Errington and Woods* [1952] 1 KB 290 **(at 1.5.2)**

- *Western Fish Products Ltd v Penwith District Council* [1981] 2 All ER 204 **(at 1.6.1)**

- *Cowcher v Cowcher* [1972] 1 All ER 943 **(at 1.6.1)**

- *Saunders v Vautier* (1841) 4 Beav 115 **(at 1.9.1)**

# Further reading

FW Maitland *Equity* (Cambridge: Cambridge University Press, 1947)
For a detailed history of the origin of equity.

P Baker 'The Future of Equity' (1971) 93 *LQR* 529
For the relevance of equity in the modern day.

A Mason 'The Place of Equity and Equitable Remedies in the Contemporary Common Law'
(1994) 110 *LQR* 238
Placing equity and its remedy in the contemporary world.

FE Dowrick 'The Relationship of Principals and Agents' (1954) 17 *MLR* 24
For the relationship between agency and trust.

Maxims of equity

Learning objectives

This chapter will help you to:

- understand the meaning of maxims of equity
- understand the functions of maxims and their practical significance in the development of equity
- appreciate the relevance of equitable maxims in the modern world
- understand which maxims apply to different situations.

Introduction

What do we mean by maxims of equity and what functions do they perform? How can one tell what maxim applies to which situation? Are maxims relevant to today's world? These are some of the questions one frequently hears equity students ask. These are indeed important questions because equitable maxims, although they may not be as complicated as their Latin expressions often make them out to be, do not lend themselves to easy understanding. As will be seen later, there are instances in which genuine difficulty can arise in identifying which of the several equitable maxims apply to a given situation and courts too do face such problems. This chapter explores the most commonly applied maxims of equity. It is often said that maxims are best appreciated in the context of substantive topics of equity. It is our view that students first need to understand the meaning, content, characteristics, and functions of maxims as a distinct equitable theme before attempting to understand them in the context of other topics.

 ## 2.1 Defining equitable maxims

Broadly speaking, a maxim is defined as 'general truth or rule of conduct expressed in a sentence' (*Oxford Compact English Dictionary* (1996) at 616). It originated from the medieval Latin *maxima* (*propositio*). Thus, to speak of a maxim of equity is to mean a 'general truth' or a 'rule of conduct' about the operation of equity. An example would be if two thieves set out to rob a bank and agree, in advance, to share the proceeds on a 50–50 basis. Suppose after the robbery the stronger thief, let us say an ex-boxer, threatens to punch the lights out of the weaker one unless he accepts a 30 per cent share compared with his own 70. The weaker thief threatens to go to the court to challenge the stronger one. Under the law of contract, such an agreement will not be enforceable because, as we say, 'out of an illegal contract no action can lie' (*ex turpi causa, non oritur actio*). This is a maxim (i.e. it is a statement of general truth), but it is not a maxim of equity because it operates in the sphere of law. Whether a contract is legal or illegal, or whether one can bring an action or not before a court to enforce agreements reached under the contract is determined by the *rules of law,* not by the *maxims of equity.* As we will see later, it is not the function of equity to replace the law, but to prevent an unfair operation of the law. Were we to allow the weaker thief to bring an action to enforce an illegal contract, we would thus be permitting equity to replace the rules and principles of law. We shall also explain later how to distinguish between legal principles and equitable maxims so that the two are not confused in their application to facts.

KEY POINT Common law has principles, just like equity. A good example of a common law principle is 'out of an illegal contract, no claim can arise'.

We now turn to a few passages from some texts to see what writers make of the idea of maxims of equity.

Sarah Wilson *Textbook on Trusts* (7th edn, Oxford: Oxford University Press, 2005) at 9:

> As equity became more formalized a framework emerged within which its development could become shaped. These principles became embodied in the form of equitable maxims. The maxims are not rules to be construed like statutes, but rather a general basis around which much of the law of equity has formed. They frequently appear as part of the reasoning of judgments.

Alastair Hudson *Equity and Trusts* (4th edn, London: Cavendish Publishing, 2005) at 24:

> Equity is based on a series of fundamental principles . . . As drafted, they are a collection of vague ethical statements, some more lyrical than others . . . At first blush, it is obvious that they are too vague to be meaningful in the abstract. They do not assert any particular view of the world other than that people should behave reasonably towards one another—hardly an alarming proposition in itself. They are . . . capable of many interpretations and . . . they constitute moral prescriptions for the values according to which people should behave. But they are not to be dismissed as merely lyrical pronouncements, because they are still applied by the courts.

Robert Pearce and Warren Barr *Pearce & Stevens' Trusts and Equitable Obligations* (6th edn, Oxford: Oxford University Press, 2015) at 28:

> . . . the key principles underlying the operation of the whole of the equitable jurisdiction, which the maxims of equity are an attempt to formulate in short, pithy phrases. They are not binding rules, nor do they provide guidance for every situation in which equity operates. Nevertheless, they provide useful illustration of some of the principal recurrent themes which can be identified within the corpus of the rules of equity.

2.2 The application of the maxims of equity

There are several maxims of equity. The most common are as follows:

1. He who comes to equity must come with clean hands
2. Equity follows the law
3. Equity does not suffer a wrong without a remedy
4. Equity does not aid the volunteer
5. When equities are equal the first in time prevails/where there is equal equity the first in time prevails
6. Equity looks at the substance, not the form
7. He who comes to equity must do equity
8. Equity acts in personam, not in rem
9. Equity regards as done that which ought to be done
10. Delay defeats equity
11. Equity will not permit the law to be used as an engine of fraud.

2.2.1 He who comes to equity must come with clean hands

This maxim epitomizes the very essence of equity. Equity means fairness. Thus, a person who wishes to bring a case in a court of equity to challenge what could otherwise be a valid legal principle or judgment will have to show that he has acted reasonably and fairly, that is, that his hands are clean. To have clean hands means to have done nothing or taken any action that could degrade or tarnish an applicant's claim in the court. Thus, a claimant whose conduct has been unfair in the past cannot invoke this maxim.

● ***Cross v Cross*** (1983) 4 FLR 235 (Wood J):

> He who comes to equity must come with clean hands and any conduct of the plaintiff, which would make a grant of specific performance inequitable, can prove a bar.

This maxim is mainly concerned with the specific, not the general conduct of a claimant, and the court may consider the past conduct of the claimant. But even when the court looks into the past conduct of the claimant, it only does so in respect of conduct that may affect the specific issue at hand. The court cannot prevent a person from invoking this maxim simply because he is of a generally bad character.

● ***Dering v Earl of Winchelsea*** (1787) 1 Cox 318

In this case, three people—Sir Edward Dering, the Earl of Winchelsea, and another person—acted as sureties for the earl's brother, Thomas, for the due performance of the office of Collector of Customs. Following Thomas's default, the Crown obtained a judgment from Sir Edward to make good losses incurred by his brother. In turn, Sir Edward approached the other two sureties for contributions. The earl objected, claiming that Sir Edward could not claim the share because of his own misconduct.

Eyre LCB, the deciding judge, reviewed Sir Edward's misconduct, as alleged by the earl. The judge found that indeed Sir Edward was guilty of general misconduct such as encouraging his brother Thomas to gamble with government money, and that this conduct placed Sir Edward in a bad point of view. But on the relevance of such general conduct to the case at hand, the judge stated that:

> ...a man must come into a Court of Equity with clean hands; but when this is said, it does not mean a general depravity; it must have an immediate and necessary relation to the equity sued for, it must be a depravity in a legal as well as a moral sense.

Thus, the court distinguished between Sir Edward's general moral laxity, which undoubtedly marks him out as a person of low character, and his specific conduct with respect to his brother's behaviour occasioning the loss of money. The court found that the fact that Sir Edward suffered general moral laxity did not prevent the recovery of sureties from the other parties, as Sir Edward's general conduct did not affect the specific conduct of his brother leading to the loss of funds.

● ***Argyll v Argyll*** (1967) Ch 32

The court held here that the fact that a wife's adulterous conduct contributed to the breakdown of the marriage and divorce proceeding does not prevent her from getting an injunction restraining the husband from publishing confidential materials about their marriage.

● *Tinsley v Milligan* [1993] 3 All ER 65

Two single women lived together and ran a profitable lodging business, and bought a house in the sole name of the plaintiff. They defrauded the Department of Social Security by making false benefit claims. The defendant later repented and informed the DSS of their fraud. Following a quarrel between the two, the plaintiff moved out, leaving the defendant in sole occupation. The plaintiff later served a notice to quit on the defendant and also claimed for possession and ownership of the property. The defendant counterclaimed that the house was held by the plaintiff on trust for both parties in equal shares. The judge dismissed the plaintiff's claim and allowed the counterclaim. On appeal by the plaintiff, the Court of Appeal (by a majority) dismissed the appeal on the ground that in the circumstances the public conscience would not be affronted if the defendant's counterclaim were to succeed.

On further appeal by the plaintiff to the House of Lords:

HELD: Dismissing the appeal (Lord Keith of Kinkel and Lord Goff of Chieveley dissenting), that a claimant to an interest in property, whether based on a legal or equitable title, was entitled to recover if he was not forced to plead or rely on an illegality, even though it transpired that the title on which he relied was acquired in the course of carrying through an illegal transaction; that, in the circumstances, by showing that she had contributed to the purchase price of the property and that there was a common understanding between the parties that they owned the property equally the defendant had established a resulting trust; that there was no necessity to prove the reason for the conveyance into the sole name of the plaintiff, which was irrelevant to the defendant's claim, and that since there was no evidence to rebut the presumption of a resulting trust the defendant was entitled to succeed on her counterclaim.

Although the House of Lords affirmed the decision of the Court of Appeal—that the defendant was entitled to beneficial ownership of the property in question—their Lordships rejected the flexible approach adopted by the Court of Appeal concerning the relevance of the illegality in actions for equitable relief. The Lords (with Lord Goff dissenting) held that such illegality should not matter where a party could assert an equitable title without relying on the illegality of his conduct as stated in *Bowmaker v Barnet Instruments* [1944] 2 All ER 579. In *Bowmaker*, the court laid down the rule that:

> No claim founded on an illegal contract will be enforced by the court, but as a general rule a man's right to possession of his own chattels will be enforced against one who, without any claim of right, is detaining them, or has converted them to his own use, even though it may appear from the pleadings, or in the course of the trial, that the chattels in question came into the defendant's possession by reason of an illegal contract between himself and the plaintiff, *provided that the plaintiff does not seek, and is not forced, either to found his claim on the illegal contract, or to plead its illegality in order to support his claim. An exception to this general rule arises in cases in which the goods claimed are of such a kind that it is unlawful to deal in them at all.* [Emphasis added.]

Also, in *Holman v Johnson* (1775) 1 Cowp 341 at 343, Lord Mansfield ruled that:

> ...the objection, that a contract is immoral or illegal as between plaintiff and defendant, sounds at all times very ill in the mouth of the defendant...No court will lend its aid to a man who founds his cause of action upon an immoral or an illegal act.

However, the courts recognized that the rule in *Bowmaker* does not apply where the claimant intends to use the equitable relief sought to achieve an illegal purpose as in *Taylor v Chester* (1869) LR 4 QB 309. Nevertheless, in *Tinsley v Milligan*, Lord Goff preferred the strict rule established in *Muckleston v Brown and Another* 6 Ves 52 when dealing with the effect of illegality on an equitable relief. In *Muckleston*, Lord Eldon LC stated that:

> … [t]he plaintiff stating that he had been guilty of a fraud upon the law, to evade, to disappoint, the provision of the legislature to which he is bound to submit, and coming to equity to be relieved against his own act, and the defence being dishonest, between the two species of dishonesty the court would not act, but would say: 'Let the estate lie where it falls'.

For further views of judges on this maxim, see generally the Lord Chief Baron Sir William Alexander in *Groves v Groves* 3 Y & J 163 at 174 and by Salmon LJ (with whom Cross LJ agreed) in *Tinker v Tinker* [1970] P 136 at 143; *Curtis v Perry* 6 Ves 739 at 746 (Lord Eldon LC); *Childers v Childers* (1857) 3 K & J 310 at 315 (Page Wood VC); and *Cantor v Cox* 239 EG 121 at 122 (Plowman VC).

KEY POINT Note that the court is not really concerned with determining who, as between the claimant and the defendant, has cleaner hands; the business of the court is with the hands of the person who seeks the protection of the court, the claimant.

● *Lee v Haley* (1869) 5 LR Ch App 155

The plaintiff had carried on business for some years at 22 Pall Mall, under the name 'The Guinea Coal Company'. In March 1869, the defendant, who had been the plaintiff's manager, set up a rival business under the name of 'The Pall Mall Guinea Coal Company' and at the end of August removed it to 46 Pall Mall. Upon finding out that many customers had been misled into believing that the defendants were the same as the plaintiff, the latter brought an action for a restraining injunction against the defendant. Among other defences, the defendant alleged that the plaintiff had knowingly and habitually sold short weight, and that the plaintiff had no exclusive right to the name 'Guinea Coal Company', which was used by various other establishments about London. Vice Chancellor Malins granted an injunction restraining the defendant from using the name 'The Pall Mall Guinea Coal Company' in Pall Mall. On appeal motion by the defendant:

HELD: Dismissing the appeal Sir GM Giffard LJ:

> … if the Plaintiffs had been systematically and knowingly carrying on a fraudulent trade, and delivering short weight, it is beyond all question that this Court would not interfere to protect them in carrying on such trade; but there is no evidence that proves anything of the sort.

For in that case, they would have been found to have unclean hands (while seeking equitable relief of injunction), not because they dealt in coal, but because they would have tainted their case by the deceit and fraud.

● *Ingram v Kasey's Associates* 340 SC 98, 531 SE 2d 287 (2000)

The plaintiff leased a property with an option to purchase. He told the lessor he did not intend to exercise the option. The lessor leased out the property to another party with the same option, and spent money to improve the property. The plaintiff then informed the lessor that he in fact intended to exercise his option to purchase. The Southern Carolina Supreme Court held, stating that Ingram's hands were unclean, that his initial representation to the lessor constituted a bar to his action.

thinking points

If equity insists on an applicant for an equitable relief to come to it with clean hands, what does this mean? Does 'clean hands' relate to acts already done by the applicant or that which he/she must do? To what extent must the applicant's hands be clean? Does it mean that he/she should have been fair in all manner of dealing with the defendant or only in relation to the specific conduct affecting the application? The main purpose of equity is to ensure that justice is done at all times and that the party who seeks equitable relief has himself/herself done nothing to prejudice his/her claim. This is a fair and straightforward principle, otherwise a situation in which the pot is calling the kettle black! But then, it does not mean that applicants for equitable relief must at all times be pure, or that any untoward act done against the person against whom they claim invariably adversely affects their claims. What is required is that nothing they have done before the claim compromises their claim, and whatever past acts will be deemed to affect their claims must solely relate to the particular claim in question. See Roger Young and Stephen Spitz 'SUEM—Spitz's Ultimate Equitable Maxim: In Equity, Good Guys Should Win and Bad Guys Should Lose' (2003–4) 55 South Carolina L Rev 175.

2.3 Equity follows the law

This maxim is crucial to the relationship between equity and common law in general. As noted in Chapter 1 'The birth of equity and trusts', equity developed in response to the inadequacies and inflexibility of the common law, not because the principles of common law are not sound or that common law judgments are not based on sound legal reasoning. Equity was developed simply to give a human face to the sometimes draconian application of common law. Hence equity follows the law. For instance, equity cannot take a less flexible attitude to illegality than common law, otherwise, as Lord Goff stated in *Tinsley v Milligan*, that 'would constitute a remarkable reversal of the traditional functions of law and equity'.

Richard Edwards and Nigel Stockwell *Trusts and Equity* (11th edn, London: Pearson, 2013) at 45:

> This is an attempt to indicate the relationship between common law and equity, which is a complex one. The traditional role of equity, as stated in 'Doctor and Student' 1523 by Christopher St German, was to 'temper and mitigate the rigour of law', which implies that equity would intervene and overrule the common law if justice required it. It was stressed, even at that time, however, that it did not attempt to overrule common law judgments, but rather to act in personam on the parties to prevent injustice...This maxim indicates that, where possible, equity will ensure that its own rules are in line with the common law ones.

2.3.1 Application of the maxim

This maxim applies to different situations but more frequently to property transactions. The following are some of the well-known examples of instances in which the maxim has been applied.

. . . .

● *Tulk v Moxhay* (1848) 2 Ph 774

One of the main uses of the maxim 'equity follows the law' is when equity is used to enforce restrictive covenants attached to a property. (As to restrictive covenants, see *Halsbury's Laws*

The rule is that a covenant between vendor and purchaser on the sale of land, that the purchaser and his assigns shall use or abstain from using the land in a particular way, will be enforced in equity against all subsequent purchasers with notice, independently of the question whether it be one which runs with the land so as to be binding upon subsequent purchasers at law.

The basis of this rule is that 'a negative covenant was enforceable in equity on the ground that it deprived the owner of a right over property and his successor in title was to be prevented from exercising a right which he had never acquired'.

The facts of the case were these. In 1808 the plaintiff sold some of its land in Leicester Square, London to one Elms. The deed of conveyance contained a covenant by Elms, for himself, his heirs, and assigns, to maintain and keep the property and the features attaching to it such as the iron railing as a square garden and pleasure ground, in an open state, uncovered with any buildings, in neat and ornamental order. The piece of land passed into the hands of the defendant, whose purchase deed contained no similar covenant with his seller, but he admitted that he had purchased with notice of the covenant in the deed of 1808. The defendant decided to alter the character of the square garden and proposed to build on it. The plaintiff, who remained owner of several houses in the square, applied for a restraining order which was granted. The defendant appealed to discharge the order.

HELD: If an equity is attached to property by the owner, no one purchasing with notice of that equity can stand in a different situation from that of the party from whom he purchased.

Thus the rule in *Tulk v Moxhay* allows negative covenants, that is, covenants not to do an act, to be enforced against any subsequent owner of the concerned property. The next question is, can equity enforce a positive covenant, that is, the covenant to do something? The court took a negative view in the following case.

. . . .

● *Indigo Realty Co v Charleston* 281 SC 234, 314 SE 2d 601 (1984)

Following a threat of condemnation, certain private property owners in South Carolina reluctantly agreed to sell property to the City of Charleston. Six months later, the City decided that it no longer needed the property and put them up for sale. The original owners' attempt to repurchase the property was rejected by the City, which asserted its right to sell to whom it pleased. The lower court decided that the former owners had a right to buy. On appeal, the South Carolina Supreme Court reversed the judgment on the basis that there was no legal obligation to resell property to the previous owners. Although the Supreme Court itself recognized, in its dictum, that this decision might appear unfair, it stated that the lower court's use of equity to resolve the problem 'undermines the legal rule and exceeds the court's of equity powers' (at 236). While the Supreme Court did not explicitly invoke the maxim, there is no doubt that it was guided by it in coming to the conclusion.

. . . .

● *Rhone v Stephens* [1994] 2 All ER 65

The owner of a cottage sold it by a conveyance in which he covenanted 'for himself and his successors in title . . . to maintain to the reasonable satisfaction of the purchasers and their successors in title such part of the roof of [the house] as lies above the property conveyed in wind and watertight condition'. The condition of the cottage deteriorated. The plaintiffs brought an action to enforce the covenant against the defendant, the successor in title to the original owner of the house. The judge held that the plaintiffs were entitled to enforce the covenant. Upon appeal, it was held that 'the burden of *positive* covenants did not run with freehold land' and that the principle that a party deriving benefit from a transaction entered into by his predecessor had to accept any burden therein was not applicable, since the benefits to the defendant's property from the disputed roof, in the form of eavesdrop and support, were minimal.

thinking points
- *Equity follows the law; it does not abolish the law.*
- *Equity mitigates the rigour of the law.*
- *Equity enforces a restrictive covenant—Tulk v Moxhay.*
- *Equity will not enforce a positive covenant.*

2.4 Equity acts in personam, not in rem

One of the most important principles of equity is that it does not act directly against an object being the subject of a lawsuit; rather, it acts on a person's conscience. This means that a court of equity, unlike common law, is not concerned about the physical presence of an asset or anything which is the subject of its order. Rather, the purpose of equitable courts is to bind the conscience of the person so that wherever the object of an order might be on earth, a court of equity is able to make an order regarding it. This maxim is very useful, for instance, with regard to trusts. As will have been noted from the history of equity and trusts in Chapter 1, a beneficiary of a trust has a property right in an asset (hence he can recover property or an asset from a trustee or any third party who wrongfully comes into contact with that thing). However, the beneficiary is also able to proceed against the trustee as a person in personam, for instance, to ensure that the property is well cared for until the beneficiary takes possession of it (see also Gary Watt *Todd and Watt's Cases and Materials on Equity and Trusts* (7th edn, Oxford: Oxford University Press, 2009) at 10).

This maxim is a useful strategy generally adopted by the court of equity to avoid being perceived as confronting common law. In Chapter 1 we noted that the early relationship of equity and the common law was not an easy one, leading, as the history discloses, to a confrontation between Lord Coke and Lord Ellesmere, and the ultimate fusion of equity and common jurisdiction in 1873–5 by the Judicature Act. Thus, instead of equity challenging a property being subject to a common law court's judgment, a judgment which, it must always be borne in mind, may in fact be based on very sound legal reasoning, equity is able to appeal directly to the conscience of the person who has obtained judgment with the singular aim of using moral, not legal, reasoning to sway him/her from pursuing the judgment.

Although this maxim applies to a wide variety of situations, it is today commonly used in situations where property is situated abroad or in respect of freezing injunctions (originally called Mareva injunctions, see Chapter 19 'Equitable remedies' on equitable remedy). This is the type of injunction used by a claimant in one jurisdiction to prevent a defendant in that jurisdiction from dealing with his assets in another jurisdiction. So, if an Englishman brings an action against a Frenchman in London for a debt, and the Englishman hopes to settle the judgment debt only by assets owned by the Frenchman in Paris, the English court is able to grant the Englishman a Mareva injunction, preventing the Frenchman from dissipating or quickly wasting his assets in France in order to frustrate the judgment.

2.4.1 Grounds for applying this maxim

- The person to be bound must be *within* the court's jurisdiction.
- The maxim cannot be relied on to grant an order in personam when such will violate legal rules of another country.
- The maxim will not normally be relied upon to grant an order which will not be enforceable overseas since equity does not act in vain.

For the English court to be able to bind the conscience of a person to an equitable order, that is, to be able to act in personam, it is essential that that person must be present within the court's jurisdiction, and the order in personam must be capable of enforcement overseas. Otherwise the order will be contrary to the principle asserted in 1861 by Lord Campbell LC, where he stated in *Norris v Chambers* at 583 that:

> An English court ought not to pronounce a degree, even if in personam, which can have no specific operation without the intervention of a foreign Court, and which in the country where the lands to be charged by it would probably be treated as *brutum fulmen* (an empty threat).

KEY POINTS

- Lord Campbell did not lay down a general law that the English courts *cannot*, but that they *ought not to* act in personam without the cooperation of the foreign court where the assets to which a person's consent is to be bound lie outside England and without taking into consideration the laws of that country. Otherwise the order by the English court would be regarded as an empty threat.

- The real force of Lord Campbell's dictum is that a court of equity cannot be seen to be trampling legal rules of another jurisdiction and also should not make an order that will be in vain, another equitable maxim we will come to later. Let us consider a few cases that illuminate the application of this maxim.

● ***Richard West and Partners (Inverness) Ltd v Dick*** [1969] 2 Ch 424

The plaintiffs sold certain property in Scotland to the defendant who lived in England. The defendant paid a deposit and instructed the plaintiffs' solicitors to act for him too. The defendant however decided to withdraw from buying the property upon realizing that it would cost a lot more than he expected for obtaining building plans and requested the return of his deposit. The plaintiffs refused that request and sought a decree of specific performance of the contract. On an application by the plaintiffs under RSC Ord 86 r 1 for summary judgment, Megarry J held that he had jurisdiction to grant a decree of specific performance of a contract relating to foreign land and that there was no issue or question which ought to be tried. He accordingly granted the plaintiffs a decree of specific performance.

After a careful consideration of the facts and the legal principle involved, Megarry J held that:

> ...at all events, without cogent evidence to establish it (and there is none) I refuse to assume that the Scottish courts will stand aghast at the spectacle of a purchaser living within the English jurisdiction being ordered by an English court to carry out his agreement to purchase land in Scotland.

The Court of Appeal held:

> …that, equity acting in personam, the English courts had jurisdiction to grant a decree of specific performance of a contract for the sale or purchase of foreign land, provided that the defendant was domiciled within the jurisdiction and that since the defendant in the present case was so domiciled the court had jurisdiction (at 436C–E).

Harman LJ stated:

> There remains the point on which Megarry J, learned man that he is, exhibited a very interesting and powerful judgment n(3) whereby he expressed the view that there is no objection to a grant of specific performance of a contract for foreign land by an English court. As far as I am concerned I am content to adopt the elaborate reasoning by which he reached that conclusion. I have always thought, and I still think, that the Court of Chancery, acting as it does in personam, is well able to grant specific performance of a contract to buy or sell foreign land, provided the defendant is domiciled within its jurisdiction. I say nothing about a case where the defendant is domiciled outside; but the purchaser here lives at Enfield: the vendors (if that be relevant; I do not think it is) have their registered office in England: and I see nothing difficult about a vendors' decree of specific performance in the circumstances. There might be difficulties raised by matters of Scottish title; but here the title was accepted. The decree (I suppose: I have not looked at it) contains the usual recital that the purchaser has accepted the vendors' title to the property, about which I gather there is no doubt.

KEY POINTS

- The fact that a court may not be able to supervise or enforce a decree it makes in personam, in respect of an asset abroad, is not a sufficient reason to bar an order. This fact came out in the judgment of Lord Hardwicke LC, who decreed an order of specific performance in respect of an agreement relating to the boundaries between Pennsylvania and Maryland, despite the inability of the court to enforce the order in rem.

- The defendant against whom the order is granted must be resident in England.

- Where there is a problem with the title to the property under the foreign law, this may present a difficulty.

● ***Penn v Lord Baltimore*** (1750) 1 Ves Sen 444

Lord Hardwicke LC:

> As to the court's not enforcing the execution of their judgment, if they could not at all, I agree that it would be in vain to make a decree, and that the court cannot enforce their own decree in rem in the present case, but that is not an objection against making a decree in the cause, for the strict primary decree in this court as a court of equity is in personam, long before it was settled whether this court could issue to put into possession in a suit of lands in England, which was first begun and settled in the time of James I, but ever since done by injunction or writ of assistant to the sheriff, but the court cannot to this day as to lands in Ireland or the plantations. In Lord King's time [1725–33] in *Richardson v Hamilton (Attorney General of Pennsylvania)*, which was a suit of land and a house in the town of Philadelphia, the court made a decree, though it could not be enforced in rem. In the case of *Lord Anglesey* of land lying in Ireland, I decreed for distinguishing and settling the parts of the estate, though

impossible to enforce that decree in rem, but, the party being in England, I could enforce it by process of contempt in personam and sequestration, which is the proper jurisdiction of this court. In the present case, if the parties want more to be done, they must resort to another jurisdiction and it looks by the order in 1735, as if that was in view, liberty being thereby given to resort to that board.

For further cases and an endorsement of the above line of reasoning, see *Ewing v Orr-Ewing* (1883) 9 App Cas 34; *Webb v Webb* [1991] 1 WLR 1410.

thinking points

Under what circumstances may an English court refuse to grant an injunction or specific performance in respect of property outside England? A court will not grant equitable relief where such cannot be enforced against the defendant since equity does not act in vain. This principle underlines why English courts will not decree equitable relief in respect of property outside their jurisdiction and under foreign laws. The courts cannot supervise such orders. That does not mean, however, that a court cannot grant an equitable relief in respect of a property outside its jurisdiction where the defendant is within the court's jurisdiction. After all, equity acts in personam so that the defendant's conscience may yet be bound in respect of a property outside the court's jurisdiction. See RH Graveson 'Admiralty Jurisdiction in Respect of Foreign Immovables: Notes on "The Tolten"' (1947) 10(3) MLR 306.

2.5 Equity regards as done that which ought to be done

One significant advantage of equity is that it is able to presume the completion of a deal which requires, to all intents and purposes, only a minor formality to perfect it. This maxim commonly applies to orders of specific performance such as the sale of land. A typical scenario is where A has sold a piece of land to B, under an enforceable contract. A therefore holds the land on constructive trust for the benefit of B, so that A cannot deny the contract on the basis that there remains some formality to observe, provided that the contract between the parties is specifically enforceable at law.

● **Walsh v Lonsdale** (1882) 21 ChD 9

An agreement for the lease of a cotton-weaving mill provided for a term of seven years, at a rent of 30s per annum for each loom worked, if the lessor provided steam power; the lessee not to work less than 300 looms in the first year, and not less than 540 in any subsequent year. It also contained provisions by reference to another lease whereby it was provided that one year's rent (in that case a fixed rent) should always be payable in advance on demand. The lessee having been, on 1 July 1879, let into possession, paid rent quarterly up to January 1881. On 13 March 1882 the lessor served the lessee with notice of a demand for a year's rent in advance, reckoned at 30s a loom upon all the looms he was then working, being 560 in number.

The main question for determination here is whether, in the absence of specifically writing some of the terms of the agreement in the contract, the defendant could rely on the construction of those terms written down in order to recover possession as the plaintiff prayed the court.

HELD: Jessel MR:

> ...He (the plaintiff) holds, therefore, under the same terms in equity as if a lease had been granted, it being a case in which both parties admit that relief is capable of being given by specific performance.

· ·

● **Re Flint (A Bankrupt)** [1993] Ch 319

On 18 July 1990 Mr Registrar Shaw, sitting at Crewe County Court, made an ancillary relief order in divorce proceedings requiring the husband, Ronald Flint, to transfer to the wife, Brenda Flint, within 28 days all his estate and interest in 7 Galway Grove, Shavington, near Crewe, the former matrimonial home. On 24 July 1990 the husband was adjudicated bankrupt in the Shrewsbury County Court. On 16 December 1991 Judge Roberts, sitting at Shrewsbury County Court, made a declaration that the order of 18 July was void under s. 284(1) of the Insolvency Act 1986, as having been a disposition of property by a person against whom a bankruptcy petition had been presented, and refused to ratify the disposition.

By a notice of appeal dated 13 January 1992 the wife appealed against the order of 16 December and sought an order that the disposition of 18 July was valid on the grounds (1) that the judge erred in law in holding that the order of 18 July was a disposition by a person adjudged bankrupt and void under s. 284 of the Act of 1986; (2) that the judge ought to have held that the order was a disposition of the property by the court and not by the husband, so that s. 284 did not apply; and, in the alternative, (3) that if s. 284 did apply, the judge failed to exercise his discretion whether or not to ratify the disposition properly or at all.

On the effect of the order made by the court, it was held that the transfer took effect in equity as an immediate consequence of the making of the order, and the terms of the order when complied with by the husband did no more than confirm that which had already happened in equity. Accordingly, the transfer to the wife was not a disposition by the husband but a disposition by the court and by operation of equity so that s. 284 of the Insolvency Act 1986 did not apply to it.

The ratio in *Re Flint* was followed in *Mountney v Treharne* [2003] Ch 135, the facts of which are similar to those of *Re Flint*. On the question of the effect of an order made by the court in a divorce proceeding, but which order has not been executed, the court held that:

> ...a property adjustment order was capable of conferring an equitable interest in the property, notwithstanding that the transfer had not been executed, in the same way that an order which directed a party to provide security and which contemplated the completion of the security by the execution of the appropriate deed created an immediate equitable charge, provided that the property subject to the charge could be sufficiently identified.

See also *AG for Hong Kong v Reid* [1994] 1 AC 324, [1994] 1 All ER 1, [1993] 3 WLR 1143 (PC); *Beer v Higham (A Bankrupt)* [1997] BPIR 349; *Bendall v McWhirter* [1952] 2 QB 466, [1952] 1 All ER 1307 (CA); *Burton v Burton* [1986] 2 FLR 419; *Re Condon, ex p James* (1874) LR 9 Ch App 609, [1874–80] All ER Rep 388 (CA); *F v F (Divorce: Insolvency)* [1994] 2 FCR 689, [1994] 1 FLR 359.

2.6 Those who come to equity must do equity

Halsbury's Laws of England (4th edn, vol 16, 1976) stated at 874 para 1303:

> The rule means that a man who comes to seek the aid of a court of equity to enforce a claim must be prepared to submit in such proceedings to any directions which the known principles of a court of equity may make it proper to give; he must do justice as to the matters in respect of which the assistance of equity is asked.

In *Story's Commentaries on Equity Jurisprudence*:

> ...The interference of a court of equity is a matter of mere discretion...and in all cases of this sort...the court will, in granting relief, impose such terms upon the party as it deems the real justice of the case to require...The maxim here is—emphatically applied—he who seeks equity must do equity.

This maxim relates to the future conduct (as against the past conduct) of someone who wishes to seek an equitable relief from the court. It requires such person to show that he/she is prepared to do equity so as to mitigate hardship to be caused to the defendant. This maxim, as with 'he who comes to equity must come with clean hands' and 'delay defeats equity', shows the discretionary nature of equitable reliefs in general and that the court is not unlimited in its discretion (see Lord Romilly MR in *Hartwood v Cope* (1858) 25 Beav 140).

For the maxim therefore to apply, a claimant must be ready to do equity, otherwise the court will refuse the order.

. . . .

● ***Chappell v Times Newspapers*** (1975) 2 All ER 233

In September 1974 a dispute occurred between the Newspapers Publishers Association (NPA) and the National Graphical Association (NGA) over the latter's refusal to be paid equally with other unions' members in the industry on the ground that the NGA members had traditionally earned more. In order to force the NPA to yield to their demands, the NGA went on strike, badly affecting the industry. After a series of strikes and more threatened, the NPA informed the NGA that, unless the NGA called off their disruptive action, the publishers would treat all members of the NGA as having terminated their contracts of employment. The plaintiffs, who were members of the NGA, brought an action against those of the publishers who were their employers seeking injunctions to restrain them from terminating the plaintiffs' contracts. Up to the time of the hearing of that application none of the plaintiffs had been involved in any industrial action organized by the NGA. At the hearing, however, they refused to give an undertaking not to engage in disruptive activities. The judge refused to grant an interlocutory injunction and the plaintiffs appealed, contending that, since they had not taken part in any disruptive action and were not members of any of the groups which had stopped production of the newspapers affected, they had not repudiated their contracts of employment and, therefore, the publishers had no right to dismiss them or threaten them with dismissal.

HELD:

> ...in seeking an equitable remedy the plaintiffs had to be prepared to do equity, and by refusing to give an undertaking not to disrupt newspaper production they were in effect

telling the employers that they must keep to their part of the contract even though the plaintiffs were not themselves ready or willing to keep to theirs. Accordingly, even though the plaintiffs might not have been in breach of their individual contracts of employment, they were not entitled to the equitable relief claimed in the interlocutory application and the appeal would fail.

Thus, those who seek equity may be required by the court to compensate the defendant.

....

● **Re Berkeley Applegate (Investment Consultants) Ltd (In Liquidation) Harris v Conway and Others** [1989] Ch 32

The business of the company, now in voluntary liquidation, was to place funds on behalf of individual investors on the security of first mortgages of freehold property, which were taken in the company's name. All investors were provided with an investment scheme which stated, inter alia, that no costs whatsoever would be incurred by them. Apart from the free assets of the company, moneys held in clients' accounts awaiting investment and the benefit of mortgages were held on trust by the company for the investors. At the time of winding up, the company had cash of €400,000 and debts of €5.6 million with €1.1 billion nominal value. The expenses and remuneration of the liquidator were very considerable and likely greatly to exceed the company's free assets. On the liquidator's application for the determination of the question whether any part of his expenses and remuneration could be paid out of the trust assets either directly or by way of payment to the company:

HELD:

> ...Although the liquidator was not in the position of a trustee and the legal title to the mortgages and the clients' accounts remained vested in the company, the court had jurisdiction to enforce the investors' equitable interests in that property and, in doing so, it had a discretion to require an allowance to be made for costs incurred and skill and labour expended in the administration of the property; that, since the work done by the liquidator had been of substantial benefit to both the trust property and the investors and was work that would have had to be done either by the investors themselves or by a receiver appointed by the court whose fees would have had to be borne by the trust property, the court would exercise its inherent jurisdiction to ensure that a proper allowance was made to the liquidator; and that, notwithstanding that the investors were relieved from liability for further payments under the investment scheme, the liquidator was to be compensated out of the trust funds to the extent that the company's assets were insufficient to compensate him adequately for his costs, skill and labour.

The court gave the rationale for awarding remuneration in this type of case when it proclaimed that:

> ...the jurisdiction to allow the liquidator remuneration can be based on the general jurisdiction of the court over trusts and trustees and on settled equitable principles. The principles are (a) that 'he who seeks equity must do equity' and (b) that the court exercises its jurisdiction over trusts so as to promote their administration.

It must be noted that the allowance of fair compensation to the liquidator, which is a proper application of the rule that he who seeks equity must do equity, 'decides nothing in itself; for you must first inquire what are the equities which the defendant must do, and what the plaintiff ought to have'.

● **Neesom v Clarkson** (1845) 4 Hare 97 at 101 (Wigram VC):

> ...where a litigant requires the assistance of a court of equity to enforce his claim, he can be made to submit to conditions. See *In re Northern Milling* Co [1908] 1 IR 473; *Falcke v Scottish Imperial Insurance Co* [1886] 34 ChD 234, 251 (Bowen LJ). So an allowance was made to the defendant in *Phipps v Boardman* [1964] 1 WLR 993, and consignees have been remunerated for the expense of managing estates: *Morrison v Morrison* [1854] 2 Sm & G 564 and *Scott v Nesbitt* [1808] 14 Ves Jun 438.

For further application of this principle see *Re Anglo-Austrian Printing and Publishing Union* [1895] 2 Ch 891.

KEY POINT Unlike the maxim 'he who comes to equity must come with clean hands', 'he who comes to equity must do equity' relates to the future conduct of the applicant.

2.7 Delay defeats equity

Equity does not abolish law. Thus, it is important that the operation of equitable maxims is guided by the temporal limitations laid down for the enforceability of legal rules. Therefore, anyone seeking equitable relief must act timeously, as time is very often the essence of an equitable claim.

An award of an equitable principle may be affected by the Limitation Act 1980 (an Act to consolidate the Limitation Acts 1939 to 1980, 13 November 1980) and where a particular matter is not limited by the Act, such might still be limited by the doctrine of laches.

Limitation Act 1980, s. 21

....

(3)...an action by a beneficiary to recover trust property or in respect of any breach of trust, not being an action for which a limitation is prescribed by other provisions of this Act, shall not be brought after the expiration of six years from the date on which the right of action accrued.

However, by virtue of s. 26 of the Limitation Act 1980, nothing shall affect any equitable jurisdiction to refuse relief on the grounds of acquiescence or otherwise.

In more recent times, some jurisdictions, such as Australia, have taken steps to formally apply Limitation statutes to equitable reliefs. In 2005 the Western Australian state legislature passed the Limitation Act 2005. The Act, which applies to all legal and equitable claims, entered into force on 15 November 2005. (For a discussion of this Act, see Natalie Skead 'Limitation Act 2005 (WA) and the Equitable Actions: A Fatal Blow to Judicial Discretion and Flexibility— How Other Australia Jurisdictions Might Learn from Western Australian's Mistakes' (2009) 11 *University of Notre Dame Australia L Rev* 8.

Delay is crucial when there has been acquiescence by a party to particular conduct. Hence, it is possible for the court of equity to infer from a person's delay that he/she has consented to the particular act or conduct. However, despite the fact that delay and acquiescence seem inseparable, the court may not always infer acquiescence from delay. Whether delay has occasioned acquiescence in any particular case is to be decided in light of the particular circumstances of the case. This is where equity deploys its discretionary power effectively.

The case of *Allcard v Skinner* [1886–90] All ER Rep 90 illustrates how courts determine not only when it is appropriate to apply the maxim delay defeats equity, but also when such delay warrants acquiescence so as to prevent a claimant from seeking an equitable relief.

● *Allcard v Skinner* [1886–90] All ER Rep 90

In 1867 the plaintiff, an unmarried woman aged 27, sought as a confessor N, a clergyman who was the spiritual director of a Church of England sisterhood. In 1868, on his introduction, she became an associate of the sisterhood, and as such, without becoming a member of the body or residing with the sisters, she joined in their charitable work. In January 1870 she became a postulant, that is, a member of the lowest order of the sisterhood. In April 1870 she became a novice. In 1871 she was admitted as a full member of the sisterhood, embracing for life vows which enjoined (i) poverty, that is, denuding herself of all her present and future property, either in favour of the sisterhood or otherwise; (ii) obedience; and (iii) chastity. She also agreed to the rules of the sisterhood, one of which forbade a member of the sisterhood to communicate with any person outside the sisterhood except by leave of the mother superior. While a sister, and without independent advice, she made gifts of money and stock to the mother superior on behalf of the sisterhood. In 1879 she left the sisterhood and joined the Roman Catholic Church. In 1884, hearing that another woman, on leaving the sisterhood, had obtained the return of the money which she had given to the sisterhood, the plaintiff claimed the return of the stock which she had given. In 1885 the present proceedings were begun against the mother superior for declarations that the plaintiff had been induced by undue influence to make over the property to the mother superior who held it as trustee for her.

On the question whether her delay had occasioned acquiescence, the court held that the equitable title of the mother superior to the property given by the plaintiff was imperfect by reason of her influence over the plaintiff, which inevitably resulted from her position, and so the gifts made by the plaintiff were voidable. Explaining the ratio of this case, Cotton LJ stated that:

> ...mere delay in enforcing a right is not in itself a defence. It is very different from raising no objection to an act while it is being done, which may be treated as assent to the act, and, therefore, as being acquiescence so as to be an equitable defence...I do not think that the delay in itself is an absolute bar, though it is a fact to be considered in determining the inference of fact, which appears to me to be the one that we must draw on one side or the other.

On the specific relevance of the plaintiff's delay to her ability to recover the gift she gave to the sisterhood, Cotton LJ proceeded thus:

> Has she lost this right by delay? The case is not like that of a contract voidable for fraud. There the party defrauded must elect, and within a reasonable time, for, until he does so, he retains the right or the benefits, however inadequate, secured to him by the contract. It is to such a case that the judgment in *Clough v London and North Western Rail Co* applies, and not to a case of voluntary gift like the present, where the person seeking to set aside the transfer never received any benefit whatever from the transaction.

It thus appears from this dictum that delay operates in cases of fraud where the plaintiff who seeks an equitable relief has benefited from the delay by receiving certain benefit which accrues by the fact of his delay. In such cases, acquiescence kicks in to deny him an equitable relief. However, Bowen LJ chose a different line of reasoning from Cotton LJ. He stated:

> ...then comes the question of the time which has elapsed since. What effect has time upon a right to the protection of this rule? The rule is an equity arising out of public policy. I do not

think that the delay in itself is an absolute bar, though it is a fact to be considered in determining the inference of fact which appears to me to be the one that we must draw on one side or the other. I have described, to the best of my imperfect powers, what to my mind the principle of the rule is. It is a principle arising out of public policy, and one which imposes a fetter upon the conscience of the recipient of the gift. When is that barrier removed from the conscience of the recipient of the gift? It seems to me that the common sense answer ought to be—and I think the right answer is—as soon as the **donor** escapes from the religious influence which hampered her at the time, as soon as she becomes free and determined to leave the gift where it is. If she has so acted—if her delay has been so long as reasonably to induce the recipient to think, and to act upon the belief that the gift is to lie where it has been laid—then, by **estoppel**, it appears to me that the donor of the gift would be prevented from revoking it.

Donor—person who makes a gift

Estoppel—the principle that a person cannot deny what they have represented to another

In support of Bowen's reasoning, Lindley LJ also believed that delay is not enough to infer acquiescence and must be coupled with other facts and considerations such as he found to be present in the instant case. According to the Lord Justice:

The case by no means rests on mere lapse of time. There is far more than inactivity and delay on the part of the plaintiff. There is conduct amounting to confirmation of her gift.

Also, in *Duke of Leeds v Earl of Amherst* 2 Ph 117 at 123 (1846) Lord Cottenham ruled that:

...the term 'acquiescence'...does not accurately express any known legal defence; but if used at all, it must have attached to it a very different signification according to whether the acquiescence alleged occurs while the act acquiesced in is in progress or only after it has been completed. If a person having a right, and seeing another person about to commit, or in the course of committing, an act infringing upon that right, stands by in such a manner as really to induce the person committing the act, who might otherwise have abstained from it, to believe that he assents to its being committed, he cannot afterwards be heard to complain of the act... acquiescence in that sense may be defined as acquiescence under such circumstances as that assent may be reasonably inferred from it, and is no more than an instance of the law of estoppel by words or conduct. But when once the act is completed without any knowledge or assent upon the part of the person whose right is infringed, the matter is to be determined on very different legal considerations.

See also *Lindsey Petroleum v Hurd* (1874) LR 5 PC 221.

2.8 Equity will not permit a statute to be used as an instrument of fraud

As stated earlier on, equity does not abrogate legal rules. Where legal rules govern a particular transaction, equity will not deviate from such rules since equity follows the law. A major exception to the rule that equity will not deviate from legal prescriptions is where a party seeks to rely on legal rules in order to perpetuate fraud.

Intestate—when a person dies without making a will

A common application of this maxim is to secret trusts. A secret trust 'arises when an intending settlor makes a gift of property in his will or leaves an existing will unrevoked or dies **intestate** on the strength of undertaking by the person entitled under his will or intestacy to hold whatever property he receives on trust for the third party' (Parker and Mellows *The Modern Law of*

Trusts (7th edn, London: Sweet & Maxwell, 1998) at 62). However, secret trusts directly contravene s. 9 of the Wills Act 1837, which states that no will is valid unless it satisfies four conditions. But then, the whole essence of secret trusts is to preclude the identity of the beneficiary of a secret trust from the testamentary disposition or any formally attested document. Thus, to insist that secret trusts do not comply with the Wills Act 1837 is to deny the efficacy of the trust.

In *McCormick v Grogan* (1869) LR 4 HL 82 at 89, Lord Hatherley LC said of the concept of secret trusts:

> It is in itself a doctrine which involves a wide departure from the policy which induced the Legislature to pass the Statute of Frauds, and it is only in clear cases of fraud that this doctrine has been applied—cases in which the Court has been persuaded that there has been a fraudulent inducement held out on the part of the apparent beneficiary in order to lead the testator to confide to him the duty which he so undertook to perform.

The maxim is also applied to prevent fraud from being perpetuated in cases where there has been no compliance with the Law of Property Act 1925, s. 53(1)(b) which provides, inter alia, that a transfer of interest in property must be made in writing.

· ·

● ***Bannister v Bannister*** [1948] 2 All ER 153

On the plaintiff's oral undertaking that the defendant would be allowed to live in a cottage rent free for as long as she desired, the defendant agreed to sell to her that and an adjacent cottage. The plaintiff's undertaking was not included in the formal conveyance. Subsequently, with the defendant's consent, the plaintiff occupied the whole of the first-named cottage with the exception of one room, which the defendant continued to occupy. In an action for the recovery of possession of that room the plaintiff claimed that the defendant had been occupying it as a tenant at will and that her tenancy at will had been duly determined by notice to quit. The defendant counterclaimed for a declaration that the plaintiff held the cottage in trust for her for her life.

HELD: The oral undertaking given by the plaintiff created a life interest in the cottage in favour of the defendant, determinable on the defendant ceasing to live in it.

2.9

Where equities are equal, the law prevails. Where there are equal equities, the first in time prevails

Occasions may arise where equities compete. This situation could occur where one equitable transaction, such as a **mortgage**, is created after another. In such a case, if the two interests created are equitable interests, then it is said that equities are equal. However, if one of the interests is an equitable one and the other is a legal interest, then it is said that there is equal equity as between the two. Where this happens, that is, where equity is equal, the logical cause of action should normally be for the court of equity to decide which of the equities is created first. However, such mathematical precision cannot be applied where the latter equity is created through a 'bona fide purchaser of the legal **estate** without notice' of the previously existing equitable interest. Of course, if the court would consider the order of creating the competing interests, there is no doubt that the person with the equitable interest (having being created first) takes free of all others. However, as will be seen in later chapters, a bona fide purchaser of legal estate without notice is the king of all equities, as he takes free of all others, irrespective of whether these are created before or after his legal interest accrues. All the bona fide purchaser needs to show is that he is bona fide, that is, he has no notice of the previously existing equitable interest.

. . . .

Estate—the period for which a person is entitled to hold property. Estate usually refers to land. Under s. 1 of the Law of Property Act 1925 only two legal estates are recognized in law: the fee simple and the term of years.

Mortgage—a loan secured on property, e.g. a mortgage. If the loan is not repaid, the loaner may claim the property.

. . . .

Lord James states, of the position of the bona fide purchaser without notice, as follows:

> [A]ccording to my view of the established law of this Court, such a purchaser's plea of a purchase for valuable consideration without notice is an absolute, unqualified, unanswerable defence, and an unanswerable plea to the jurisdiction of this Court. Such a purchaser, when he has once put in that plea, may be interrogated and tested to any extent as to the valuable consideration which he has given in order to shew the bona fides or mala fides of his purchase, and also the presence or the absence of notice; but when once he has gone through that ordeal, and has satisfied the terms of the plea of purchase for valuable consideration without notice, then, according to my judgment, this Court has no jurisdiction whatever to do anything more than to let him depart in possession of that legal estate, that legal right, that legal advantage which he has obtained, whatever it may be. In such a case a purchaser is entitled to hold that which, without breach of duty, he has had conveyed to him.

Where there is a claim between two equitable interests, the court will apply the order of creation as between the two equitable interests; none can be said to take priority in terms of significance being that in neither is a legal interest purchased without notice of a pre-existing one present. However, the court may postpone consideration of the order of creation if there is an act that militates against the first to be created of these two so that that equity is lost to the one created later.

. . . .

● ***Leather v Simpson*** [1871] LR 11 Eq 398

The defendant had discounted for the drawer certain bills of exchange, to which bills of lading were attached. The plaintiff, the drawee of the bills of exchange, paid them to the defendant on the faith of the bills of lading. The bills of lading turned out to be forged. The plaintiffs then sought to recover the money as money paid by mistake, but failed.

Malins, VC, stated that:

> [t]he equities between these parties are equal; the parties are equally innocent in the transaction; they have all been imposed upon; but there is this difference, that one of them, by the course of the transaction, has been in possession of the money, and I am at a loss to see any ground upon which I can be justified in making a decree that that money should be returned.

Clearly in this case, the court had prioritized one equity over the other, despite the equities being equal, on the ground that one of the parties (whose equity was created later) had received the money and there was no good reason to deny him.

In *Shropshire Union Railways v R* (1875) LR 7 HL 496, Lord Cain stated at 506 that:

> [a] pre-existing and undoubted equitable title may be defeated by a supervening legal title obtained by transfer; and I agree with what has been contended, that it may also be defeated by conduct, by representations, by misstatements, of a character which would operate and enure to take away the pre-existing equitable title. But I conceive it to be clear and undoubted law, and law the enforcement of which is required for the safety of mankind, that, in order to take away any pre-existing admitted equitable title that which is relied upon must be shown and proved by those upon whom the burden lies, and that it must amount to something tangible and distinct, which can have the grave and strong effect to accomplish which it is produced.

· ·

● *Abigail v Lapin* [1934] AC 491

Registered proprietors of two parcels of land under the provisions of the Real Property Act 1900 of New South Wales, on 5 December 1923 transferred those properties to OH, the wife of BH, by transfers in the form prescribed by the Act. The transfers, although absolute in form, were given only as security for payment of costs owing to BH and of an amount owing to a bank. The mortgage to the bank was paid off, and the transfers were registered on 18 December 1923, whereupon OH became the registered proprietor in fee simple of the land. On 14 March 1924 OH mortgaged the land to another bank and these mortgages were duly registered. On 2 September 1925 the mortgages were discharged out of moneys lent by a mortgagee which were secured by a statutory mortgage of the same date granted by OH as 'being the registered proprietor of an estate in fee simple' in the specified properties. On 4 September 1925 the mortgagee lodged a caveat under the Act in respect of these two properties. On 24 February 1926 the mortgagee lodged the mortgage for registration, but it was referred back, and before it was finally relodged the original registered proprietors lodged caveats. The mortgagee had no notice of the outstanding equity of the original registered proprietors, but had not searched the register.

HELD: The original proprietors' equity ought to be postponed to that of the ultimate mortgagee because the original proprietors were bound by the natural consequences of their acts in arming OH with the power to go into the world as the absolute owner of the lands and thus execute transfers or mortgages of the lands to another person: *Butler v Fairclough* (1917) 23 CLR 78, approved; *Rice v Rice* (1854) 2 Drew 73, approved in part and applied; *Dixon v Muckleston* (1872) 8 Ch App 155, applied; *Shropshire Union Railways and Canal Co v R* (1875) LR 7 HL 496, distinguished.

The Privy Council stated (at 502) that:

> [i]n dealing with such equitable rights the courts in general act upon the principles which are applicable to equitable interests in land which is not subject to the Acts. In the case of a contest between two equitable claimants the first in time, all other things being equal, is entitled to priority. But all other things must be equal, and the claimant who is first in time may lose his priority by any act or omission which had or might have had the effect of inducing a claimant later in time to act to his prejudice. Thus, if an equitable mortgagee of lands allows the mortgagor to retain possession of the title deeds, a person dealing with the mortgagor on the faith of that possession is entitled to priority in the absence of special circumstances to account for it.

For a general discussion of these maxims and the circumstances under which courts may vary their application, see JB Ames, 'The Doctrine of *Price v Neal*' (1891) 4(7) *Harvard L Rev* 297.

(2.10) Equity looks to the substance and not the form

The main purpose of equity is to operate on the conscience of parties to a suit. In doing so, equity must not treat formal legal requirements governing transactions between parties with levity or with discourtesy, or overlook such requirements non-compliance with which is not fatal to a transaction or defeat the real essence thereof. Certainly, it would be incorrect to say that equity, which follows the law, seeks to cast to the outer darkness legal requirements imposed for the purpose of certainty and validity of transactions. Rather, what equity seeks to do is to remove the veil of formality which, if allowed irredeemably to determine the validity of a transaction, might result in gross unfairness.

Alistair Hudson in *Equity & Trusts* (8th edn) states (at 32):

> It is a common principle of English Law that the courts will seek to look through any arti-fice and give effect to the substance of any transaction rather than merely to its surface appearance. In this sense, equity will consider the parties' intentions and not simply the form which any documents may have taken. Equity will not ignore formalities altogether—for example, in relations to the law of express trusts, equity is particularly astute to observe formalities—but it will not observe unnecessary formalities.

In *Walsh v Lonsdale*, the court of equity was able to enforce a contract despite the absence of a deed since there was consideration furnished by the plaintiff (see 2.5 'Equity regards as done that which ought to be done', for facts). Also in *Parkin v Thorold* (1852) 16 Beav 59, Lord Romilly MR laid down the guiding principle of this maxim thus:

> The court of equity makes a distinction in all cases between that which is matter of sub-stance and that which is matter of form; and it finds that by insisting on the form, the sub-stance will be defeated, it holds it inequitable to allow a person to insist on such form, and thereby defeat substance.

● *Midland Bank plc v Wyatt* [1995] 1 FLR 696, [1995] Fam 299

In December 1981 the defendant and his wife purchased a property which was registered in their joint names. They executed a legal charge with the plaintiff bank to secure a mortgage advance. The defendant decided to set up his own textile company and accordingly, as he alleged, in order to protect his family from long-term commercial risk, and acting on advice from his solicitor, he entered into a trust arrangement with his wife, giving the equity in their home to the wife and their two daughters. The trust deed was dated 17 June 1987 and was signed by the defendant and his wife, although the wife was not aware of its import or effect. Thereafter, the defendant negotiated further loans with the bank to finance his business on the security of his interest in the property. He separated from his wife in 1989 and in 1991 the business went into receivership. Neither the bank nor the husband's business partners nor the solicitors acting for the wife in the separation arrangements were made aware of the declaration of trust, and all dealings were entered into on the basis that the husband and wife were the beneficial owners of the property. Following judgment for the plaintiff against the defendant for £63,134.50 plus costs, the bank obtained a charging order nisi on the defendant's interest in the property. The defendant, in reliance on the declaration of trust, resisted the making absolute of the charging order. The bank contended that if the declaration of trust was executed on the date named, it was either void as being a sham transaction or voidable by reason of s. 423 of the Insolvency Act 1986 as a transaction to defraud creditors.

HELD: The court would proceed on the basis that it had to be fully satisfied as to the true nature and object of the transaction in question, bearing in mind that it was not necessary to establish a fraudulent motive in order to prove that there had been a sham, and that for a sham to be established there was no requirement that the wife, as well as the defendant, should have intended that the declaration of trust should have no effect: *Snook v London and West Riding Investments Ltd*, distinguished.

DEM Young QC said:

> As such I consider the declaration of trust was not what it purported to be but pretence or, as it is sometimes referred to, a 'sham'. The fact that Mr Wyatt executed the deed with the benefit of legal advice from Mr Ellis does not in my view affect the status of the transaction. It follows that even if the deed was entered into without any dishonest or fraudulent motive but was entered into on the basis of mistaken advice, in my judgment such a transaction will still be void and therefore an unenforceable transaction if it was not intended to be acted upon but was entered into for some different or ulterior motive.

KEY POINTS

- Note that in applying this maxim, it is important to create a balance between the injustice that arises by a rigid insistence on formal requirements and the justice that will be done by tempering formality with essence.

- Equity does not discard formality altogether. It only precludes formality where insisting on it will lead to injustice.

Equity will not assist a volunteer

Who is a volunteer? A volunteer at law is not the same thing as someone who volunteers to do an act with no expectation of financial or other rewards. A volunteer at law is one who enters into a contract or other form of transaction without furnishing consideration, that is, to give anything towards the contract to make it legally binding. However, although as a general rule equity does not aid a volunteer, there is a category of true volunteers whom equity will aid. These are trustees.

In *Milroy v Lord* (1862) 4 De GF & J 264, Knight-Bruce LJ stated that:

> …in order to render a voluntary settlement valid and effectual the settlor must have done everything which, according to the nature of the property, was necessary to transfer the property and render the settlement binding upon himself; that might be done by an actual transfer either to the persons intended to be benefited or to a trustee for them, or by a declaration that the settlor himself held on trust for them.

2.12 Equity imputes an intention to fulfil an obligation

Where a person is already under an obligation to perform an act and does something which is not necessarily required to fulfil that obligation, equity may treat the act as a fulfilment of the obligation (see *Sowden v Sowden* (1785) 1 Bro CC 582). For instance, suppose that A rented an apartment from B at a rent of £100 per month. A is in arrears for ten months. A died before he could repay the debt but instructed, in his will, that the sum of £100 should be paid to B without expressly mentioning the arrears. In these circumstances, equity will assume that the £100 is in partial fulfilment of the rent owed to B.

2.13 Equity will not suffer a wrong without a remedy

The maxim—equity will not suffer a wrong without a remedy—prevents the defeat of justice by technicalities in the common law. Thus, this maxim acts in opposition to the maxim equity follows the law, and seems to be saying that 'equity follows the law but not blindly or slavishly'. In *Sears, Roebuck & Co v Camp* 124 NJ Eq 403 at 411–12 (E & A 1938), Heher J aptly set out the broad extent of equity's power to remedy a wrong:

> Equitable remedies are distinguished for their flexibility, their unlimited variety, their adaptability to circumstances, and the natural rules which govern their use. There is in fact no limit to their variety and application; the court of equity has the power of devising its remedy and shaping it so as to fit the changing circumstances of every case and the complex relations of all the parties.

This maxim is a correlation of the common law principle—*ubi jus ubi remedium* (where there is a right there is a remedy). However, the courts are sometimes notorious for sacrificing justice on the platter of technicalities contained in common law principles. Thus, a person with a meritorious case may lose judgment to a less meritorious party—or be robbed of the full effect of justice—because of technical difficulties that arise during the trial or attend to the facts and/or substance of the case.

As was stated in *Westinghouse Electric Corp v United Electrical, Radio and Machine Workers of America Local No 410* 139 NJ Eq 97 at 108 (E & A 1946): 'A wrong suffered without a remedy is a blot upon the sound administration of justice'. In *Graf v Hope Building Corp* 254 NY 1 at 9 (1930), Cardozo CJ declared: 'Let the hardship be strong enough and equity will find a way, though many a formula of inaction may seem to her the path.'

This maxim is extremely useful especially in situations where the application of a statute of limitation will occasion injustice to a party. As Nicholls LJ stated in *Billson and Others v Residential Tenancies Ltd* [1992] 1 AC 494 as to the exercise of relief in equity outside the limitation period:

> This is not to say that courts of equity should now grant relief without any regard to statutory provisions. Equity follows the law, but not slavishly nor always.

In the United States, the maxim has been applied to a wide variety of cases: master/servant relationships, constitutional matters, and landlord and tenants. See *Texas and New Orleans Railroad Co v Brotherhood of Railway & Steamship Clerks* 281 US 548, 50 S Ct 427, 74 L Ed 1034 (1930); *Phelps Dodge Corp v National Labor Relations Board* 313 US 177 at 187, 61 S Ct 845 at 855, L Ed 1271 at 1279 (1941); *Ross v Butler* 19 NJ Eq 294 [97 Am Dec 654] (1868).

In fact, this maxim has found a very radical and extensive use by the US courts and, certainly, the scope covered by the operation of the maxim in the US is today much wider than in most jurisdictions. (For a good discussion of the maxim, see *Donna M Shimp v New Jersey Bell Telephone Company* Docket No C-3904-75, available at <http://www.members.tripod.com/medicolegal/shimporder.htm>.)

2.14 Distinguishing between common law principles and equity maxims

Apart from confusion arising from which maxim to apply to what situation, one common problem that students often confront is how to tell the principles of common law from the maxims of equity. Broadly formulated, the puzzle is: How does one tell what 'general truth' operates in equity and not in law? Put differently, how does one tell a maxim of equity from general principles of law? To recognize a maxim of equity, it is necessary to look for clues. The following clues may be sought, although they are by no means fool-proof or exhaustive!

- The court of equity is always eager to help a distressed party. The Lord Chancellor, who was in charge of administering equity in the early days, was always delighted to assist those who appeared before him to seek protection from the injustice that might arise from the operation of common law. Search for sentences such as 'equity will not suffer a wrong without a remedy'. Mark out a party to a suit who is not happy either because a strict application of legal rules threatens to truncate his right or prevent him from obtaining justice. If such situations are disclosed by the facts of a case, an equitable maxim may be relevant.

- Equitable maxims usually contain the word 'equity' or 'equitable', although not always, as part of the sentence or as our definition of maxims goes, as part of the 'general truth'. Search for sentences that do not just contain equity, but contain facts which disclose some kind of unfairness.

- Equitable maxims are always about correcting or giving effect to intention over form. Thus, if the facts of a case refer to a transaction in which one of the parties has not fulfilled his formal obligations—such as executing a deed, etc.—and the other party seeks to rely on this fact to obtain judgment, an equitable maxim may apply.

The Canadian Supreme Court recently pronounced on the relevance of equitable maxims. In *Pro Swing Inc v Elta Golf Inc* (2006) 2 SCR 612, Deschamps J stated that:

> [a]t common law, the typical remedy is an award for damages. However a wide range of equitable remedies are available and they take various forms. Their commonality is that they are able to be awarded at the judge's discretion. Judges do not apply strict rules, but follow general guidelines illustrated by . . . maxims . . . the application of equitable principles is largely dependent on the social fabric.

Conclusion

Equitable maxims constitute the very foundation upon which equity is constructed. They give meaning, content, and context to the notion of fairness which is the rationale for the existence of equity. To understand the fate of equity without its maxims is to appreciate the life of a fish out of water.

As shown earlier, equitable maxims are many and vary in their application. They are also subject to different interpretations by different courts. But this is not a rarity given that equitable reliefs are, to a reasonable extent, a matter for courts' discretion. Nevertheless, equitable maxims are as relevant to today's world as they were during the time of the Court of Chancery. They are adaptable and adjust readily to emerging challenges of modern times. As will be seen in subsequent chapters, several judges have helped in shaping maxims and in making them the very useful tools that they are today.

Questions

Self-test questions

1 What is a maxim of equity and what function does it perform?

2 Distinguish between the following maxims: 'He who comes to equity must come with clean hands' and 'He who comes to equity must do equity.'

3 When it comes to ascertaining the intention of parties, equity is as rigid as the common law. Is this true?

4 What maxim(s) of equity applies(y) to the situation and why do you think the maxim you chose is the appropriate one and not another?

5 If the business of equity is to follow the law, then is equitable jurisdiction of courts in modern society not an unnecessary duplication of the judicial system?

6 The maxims of equity are nothing more than an irritation in the skin of common law. Discuss.

7 On what basis would equity act against a person's conscience?

8 To what extent can it be said that equity does not abolish the law?

Discussion questions

1 It is not always easy to distinguish between one maxim and another in some cases. With the aid of decided cases, select two such maxims and discuss the similarities and differences between them.

2 Is a court sitting in England able to grant injunctive relief against a defendant at all times, provided the defendant lives within the English jurisdiction?

3 Delay will always defeat equity no matter what happens. Discuss this assertion and indicate if there are any limitations to this maxim.

4 No one who has witnessed the rigidity of the common law rules should have sympathy for it whenever equitable maxims are used to exclude the application of common rules in certain cases. In your understanding of the relationship between equity and common law, do you think this is a correct view?

Assessment question

A newly married couple goes out for an evening meal at La Tasca. Then after much champagne to celebrate the husband's promotion at work, he announces to his wife that he wishes to take out a mortgage to buy a house with the aid of a loan obtained from a bank or another lender so that they can have a place of their own. She, being tipsy at that moment of the announcement, says to him 'Honey, that's great!' The husband responds that he still needs £1,000 to complete the deposit for the mortgage, and she, having no money, gleefully takes off her necklace and hands it to him, saying 'Here! I have no money, but that is worth £1,200.' After the purchase of the house and moving in, problems start. One day, after an argument he says to her: 'Get out of my house, I don't want to see you ever again!', whereupon she retorts: 'Fine, but what of my share in the house?' The husband looks truly puzzled, saying 'What *share*? It is *my* house. I alone paid for it. Surely, we have no agreement that you'll have any share in the house. Or did we? We did not write anything down to that effect. Happily we are both lawyers and you know what s. 53 of the Law of Property Act 1925 says about registering an interest in property.'

Advise.

Key cases

- *Dering v Earl of Winchelsea* (1787) 1 Cox 318 **(at 2.2.1)**

- *Tinsley v Milligan* (1993) 3 All ER 65 **(at 2.2.1 and 2.3)**

- *Tulk v Moxhay* (1848) 2 Ph 774 **(at 2.3.1)**

- *Penn v Lord Baltimore* (1750) 1 Ves Sen 444 (Lord Hardwicke LC) **(at 2.4.1)**

- *Walsh v Lonsdale* (1882) 21 ChD 9 **(at 2.5 and 2.10)**

Further reading

C McLachlan 'The Jurisdictional Limits of Disclosure Orders in Transnational Fraud Litigation' (1998) 47(1) *International and Comparative Law Quarterly* 3
On understanding how jurisdictional limits work.

S Wilson *Todd & Wilson's Textbook on Trusts* (7th edn, Oxford: Oxford University Press, 2005), 9ff
On the nature of equitable maxim.

R Young and S Spitz 'SUEM—Spitz's Ultimate Equitable Maxim: In Equity, Good Guys Should Win and Bad Guys Should Lose' (2003–4) 55 *South Carolina L Rev* 175
The nature of equitable maxims.

A Hudson *Equity & Trusts* (4th edn, London: Cavendish Publishing, 2005), 25ff
A comprehensive discussion of the nature of equity and trusts.

L Collins 'The Territorial Reach of Mareva' (1989) 105 *LQR* 262
The use of freezing orders.

D McClean *International Judicial Assistance* (Oxford: Clarendon Press, 1992)
On the nature of equitable maxim.

RH Graveson 'Admiralty Jurisdiction in Respect of Foreign Immovables: Notes on "The Tolten"' (1947) 10(3) *MLR* 306
The reach of jurisdiction.

C McLachlan 'Transnational Interlocutory Measures for the Preservation of Assets' in Lye Hin Heng (ed) *Current Legal Issues in the Internationalization of Business Enterprises* (Singapore: Butterworths, 1996)
The extra-territorial nature of freezing orders.

G Watt 'Laches, Cause of Action Estoppel and Election in Breach of Trusts' in P Birks and A Pretto (eds) *Breach of Trust* (Oxford: Hart Publishing, 2002)
The operation of estoppel as an equitable principle.

N Skead 'Limitation Act 2005 (WA) and the Equitable Actions: A Fatal Blow to Judicial Discretion and Flexibility—How Other Australian Jurisdictions Might Learn from Western Australia's Mistakes' (2009) 11 *University of Notre Dame Australia L Rev* 8
On the operation of Limitation Acts on equitable reliefs.

The different types of trust

Learning objectives

This chapter will help you to:

- realize that many different types of property can be held on trust
- understand the many purposes for which trusts can be used
- realize that trusts can be defined in different ways
- appreciate the many different types of trust
- understand the nature of an equitable interest
- contrast the legal position of trustees and personal representatives.

Introduction

We have already seen in Chapter 1 'The birth of equity and trusts' how the trust concept came into existence and how the trust differs from other legal concepts. Here we look at the different types of trust and how they are used. Trusts are used for many different purposes and can do things that no other arrangement of property can. We will also investigate the nature of a trust: what does it mean when we say that someone has an equitable interest? By the end of the chapter, you should at least have some idea about what a trust is and why many people continue to use them.

3.1 What is a trust?

The trust was created in England, by English law courts. Since then it has been exported all over the world, chiefly the common law world. Those countries that were once ruled by Britain were also given its legal system. So countries from the USA, to Canada, to Nigeria, to India and Malaysia all use the trust. Trusts can seem very strange and technical, particularly when they are used for purposes such as tax avoidance, but the basic idea of a trust is very simple.

A trust involves the notion of holding property on behalf of someone else. The property can be any sort of property, not just land, as was the case historically.

The trust property could be money or it could be chattels (goods). Many trusts consist of intangible property, where a document represents a valuable right. Shares are a good example of this. A share certificate is a worthless piece of paper, but it represents rights to part of a company and the profit that it produces.

Legal—certain rights are regarded as legal. The basis is historical. They were once rights recognized by the Common Law courts.

KEY POINTS

- The trustees hold the **legal** estate in the property.

- The beneficiaries hold the equitable interest in the property.

This means that the trustees look after the property on behalf of the beneficiaries. In most trusts the trustees invest the trust property (the capital) and pay the profit (the income) produced by the investments to the beneficiaries. When the trust ends, the capital is distributed to the beneficiaries. Who the trustees are, what the property held on trust is, the identity of the beneficiaries, and what they should be paid are all laid down in the trust. Commonly, this is put in writing in a document known as the 'trust instrument'.

The real 'owners' of the trust are the beneficiaries. Hence it is the equitable interest that is taxed by the tax authorities in most countries, not the legal estate.

What is property?

In trust law it is necessary to keep an open mind about what could be 'property' and therefore held on trust. It could be some sort of contractual right or even a **licence** to produce something. Although most trusts are put in writing, a trust could be created in an informal manner. It is not even necessary to use the word 'trust' as long as the intention is clear. Three fairly recent cases are a good example of rather odd types of 'property' being held on trust.

. . . .

Licence—permission to do some act which otherwise could not lawfully be done. A licence often refers to land and is permission to do what would otherwise be a trespass. A licence does not grant an estate or interest in the land.

. . . .

. . . .

● ***Don King v Warren*** [1998] 2 All ER 630 (HC)

This case concerned agreements between the US boxing promoter Don King, and Frank Warren, a British boxing promoter. They formed a partnership jointly to promote European boxers, the most famous of whom was Naseem Hamed. There was a problem. Each boxer's contract with his promoter did not allow the contract to be assigned (transferred) to anyone else. To try to avoid this, the partnership agreement had, in clause 7.2, the following words:

> Don King Productions or Sports Network Ltd...shall hold all promotional and management agreements relating to the business of the Partnership...to the benefit of the partnership absolutely...

Did this mean that the employment contract of the boxer was held on trust for the partnership?

HELD: Lightman J agreed that it was at 630:

> For this purpose it makes no difference that the subject matter is a chose in action. 'The scope of the trusts recognised in equity is unlimited. There can be a trust of a chattel or of a chose in action, or of a right or obligation under an ordinary legal contract, just as much as a trust of land': see *Lord Strathcona Steamship Co Ltd v Dominion Coal Co Ltd* [1926] AC 108 at 124.
>
> As a matter of general principle it is, I think, quite clear that a trust may exist of a contract, and this may extend, not merely to the benefit of the rights conferred, but also the benefit of being a contracting party.

NB: This case later went to the Court of Appeal [1999] 2 All ER 218, but the issue there was the duty of the trustees. It was accepted that a trust existed.

. . . .

● ***Swift v Dairywise*** [2000] 1 All ER 320

The issue here was whether a 'milk quota' could be held on trust. The European Union restricts the amount of milk that farmers may produce. To gain exemption from this, farmers must have a 'milk quota', in effect permission to produce a stated amount of milk from their land. Farmers buy and sell these quotas, often independently from the sale of their land, and, as in this case, use them as security for loans. But could a milk quota be held on trust? (See Diagram 3.1.)

Diagram 3.1

A classification of the different types of property

> **Real Property or Realty**
>
> Land–ground, buildings or parts of buildings, water. Easements, servitudes and other rights over land. Land is immovable property which can be recovered by a real action.

> **Personal Property or Personalty**
>
> Any property which is not land. Movable property. A personal action for damages is possible. Includes **Chattels Real** which is leasehold property, now regarded as Land. And **Chattels Personal** which are movable, tangible articles of property.

> *Chose in Possession*
> A movable chattel in the custody or control of the owner e.g. car, jewellery, painting, etc.

> *Chose in Action*
> Right of proceeding in a court of law to recover a sum of money. An intangible right, e.g. contractual right, share in a company, patent, trademark, insurance policy, bill of exchange, etc.

HELD: Jacob J at 326 and 327:

Value—something of financial worth. 'Value' is sometimes used as another word for consideration.

> Quota has commercial **value** and legal effect. Merely because there are limitations on how it may be held or conveyed is not a reason for equity not to impose a trust where conscience so requires.
>
> Licences can be 'property' as shown by a previous case *Re Celtic Extraction Ltd (in liquidation)* [1999] 4 All ER 684 at 694:
>
> (1) There must be a statutory framework conferring an entitlement on one who satisfies certain conditions even though there is some element of discretion exercisable within that framework...
>
> (2) The exemption must be transferable...
>
> (3) The exemption or licence will have value.

The High Court returned to the issues raised in *Swift v Dairywise* [2000] 1 All ER 320, in *Armstrong DLW GmbH v Winnington Networks Ltd* [2012] 3 All ER 425, which concerned carbon emission allowances and whether they could be held on a constructive trust. For this to be possible, the carbon emission allowances, known as European Union Allowances (EUAs), had to be a form of property recognized by the law. The European Union issues what are in effect licences to emit carbon as part of their strategy to reduce the burning of fossil fuels and slow global warming. These licences have no physical existence and are held on an electronic register, the Emission Trading Schemes Registry, but they are bought and sold, and traded between companies. The court looked at several definitions of 'property' and decided that the EUAs qualified, although they did not fit neatly into the traditional categories.

● *Armstrong DLW GmbH v Winnington Networks Ltd* [2012] 3 All ER 425

Stephen Morris QC explored the nature of property.

At para 44:

> Tangible properties, otherwise referred to as 'choses in possession', are corporeal things, which are tangible, moveable and visible and of which possession can be taken. They are capable of transfer by delivery.

If EUAs were property they would have to be choses in action, otherwise known as intangible property.

At para 45: *Halsbury's Laws of England* (5th edn, vol 13, London: Butterworths, 2005) para 1:

> The expression chose in action or thing in action in the literal sense means a thing recoverable by action, as contrasted with a chose in possession, which is a thing of which a person may have physical possession. The meaning has expanded over time, and is now used to describe all personal rights of property which can only be claimed or enforced by action, and not by taking physical possession.

At para 58:

> ...an EUA is certainly 'property' and intangible property...First, there is, here, a statutory framework which confers an entitlement on the holder of an EUA to exemption from a fine. Secondly, the EUA is an exemption which is transferable, and expressly so, under the statutory framework. Thirdly, the EUA is an exemption which has value...

At para 61:

> In my judgment, strictly an EUA is not a chose in action in the narrow sense, as it cannot be claimed or enforced by action. However to the extent that the concept encompasses wider matters of property, then it could be so described.

3.3 What trusts are used for

Most members of the general public have little knowledge of what a trust is, but unbeknown to them many of them are, if not beneficiaries, trustees as well. There are many examples of the use of the trust in everyday life and you might note how varied and flexible trusts can be.

Historically trusts were used to keep property in the family. Usually it was land, but it could be valuable heirlooms such as paintings, furniture, silverware, jewellery, or any other chattels. Even today such dynastic trusts are not unknown.

● *Hambro v Duke of Marlborough* [1994] Ch 158

This case drew attention to a trust created by an Act of Parliament of 1706, which ensured that Blenheim Palace and its estates would pass down the male line of the Churchill family forever. This was given as a reward to the military hero, the first Duke of Marlborough. The court altered the trusts to prevent the current heir, the Marquis of Blandford, from inheriting the life interest, which would have given him the power to sell or mortgage the estate. This was done because he suffered from depression and a drug problem. Instead, the court set up a 'protective trust', which protects the life tenant from his creditors if he or she gets into debt. When that event occurs, the life interest 'determines' or ends and a discretionary trust comes into effect for him, his spouse, and their children. It is most unusual for courts to alter a trust (called 'variation of trust') for an adult beneficiary who has not given his consent, but the unusual circumstances persuaded the court to do it in this particular case.

(See Chapter 12 'Maintenance and advancement and protective trusts' and 14.2.4 'Settled Land Act 1925'.)

Millions of people in the UK pay part of their salary towards a pension fund or have already retired and are receiving their pensions. Many pension funds are trusts run by trustees; and the employees and pensioners, the members of the scheme, are beneficiaries. As in most trusts, the trustees are obliged to invest the trust capital, here the contributions made by the employees and their employers. This should make a profit with which to pay the pensions. A few years ago, in a lively stock market, pension funds amassed more profit than they needed to pay the pensions and this 'surplus' was sometimes used by employers for other business purposes. This is unlawful, because the trust fund belongs to the beneficiaries. A notorious example was the late businessman Robert Maxwell, the owner of the 'Mirror' group of newspapers. Following this, the Goode Report in 1993 led to greater protections for pension funds in the Pensions Act 1995. Now the problem is reversed. In a quieter stock market, many pension funds report that they have not made enough money from their investments to pay the pensions. Both surpluses and shortfalls produce legal problems. Trusts create enforceable equitable rights for beneficiaries, which cannot just be ignored.

Many investors unknowingly participate in trusts. A common form of investment is known as a unit trust. Banks, building societies, and other financial organizations receive an investor's money and invest it in shares, government stocks, etc. on the investor's behalf. They hold the investor's money on trust.

Many couples, both married and unmarried, buy houses together. They would often be surprised to be told that, because of their shared ownership, the land is held on trust. Under the Trusts of Land and Appointment of Trustees Act 1996 this is known as a trust of land. They might be even more surprised to discover that this made them both trustees of the trust. Usually, they would be its only beneficiaries as well. There is no legal problem for the same person to be both a beneficiary and a trustee. (See Chapter 18 'Trusts of the family home'.)

Children or minors cannot hold property in their own names until they reach the age of majority, which is nowadays 18, but was 21 before the Family Law Reform Act 1969 reduced it. Property for children is commonly held on trust. Indeed, in a short-lived experiment, under the Child Trust Funds Act 2004, every child in the country born after 31 August 2002 had a trust fund set up on his or her behalf, started off with government money. The government has now discontinued this practice and no new child trust funds were set up after January 2011. The idea for the Child Trust Funds already in existence is that the children's families will add to this money, so that when the children grow up they will have money to start on their careers, go to university, etc. Trusts are also established for those who are thought not competent to manage their own affairs, for reasons such as mental disability.

Trusts are commonly employed in all sorts of business situations, as we saw in *Don King* [1998] 2 All ER 630 and *Dairywise Farms* [2000] 1 All ER 320 at 3.2. They are also often used as a device to save taxation. A simple example would be for a wealthy businessperson to set up trusts for the benefit of his or her children and grandchildren. A wealthy person pays a great deal of tax. Children rarely have earnings, so they do not. Similarly, even moderately wealthy people sometimes transfer their houses to their children before they die, to save the children paying inheritance tax. Trusts can also be used to hide the real owners of property, by the simple device of trustees holding it on trust for them. The register of shareholders of any public company is open to public inspection. Trustees (here called 'nominees') are registered as the shareholders, so that the name of the real owner, the beneficiary, does not appear on the register.

Some organizations have little option but to hold their property on trust. Trade unions have to do this, as, unlike companies, they have no separate legal personality. Many clubs and societies also have to hold their property on trust. They are not incorporated as companies, so there is no 'company' to own the property. It would be highly inconvenient if all the members held the property together, so trustees are appointed to hold the property on behalf of the members. (See 9.1 'Unincorporated associations have no legal personality' and 9.2 'Possible legal structures for unincorporated associations'.)

Lastly, billions of pounds are held by charities. These are often trusts and the trustees have to fulfil the charity's purpose, such as helping the sick or helping the poor. (See Chapter 10 'Charitable trusts'.)

The courts can also decide that a trust existed, even though the parties did not create it intentionally and probably did not realize that there was a trust, until the court told them so. These trusts, known as constructive and resulting trusts, are based on the presumed intention of the parties. If the parties had thought about it they would have established a trust. (See Chapter 8 'Resulting trusts' and Chapter 16 'Constructive trusts'.)

Such trusts can be very useful to the courts, providing a just and 'equitable' solution, where the common law would suggest a different answer. Here are two examples.

. . . .

● *Prest v Petrodel Resources Ltd* [2013] 3 WLR 1

Mr and Mrs Prest were divorcing and Mrs Prest was seeking a financial settlement. She alleged that her husband had used offshore companies (PRL) to hold legal title to seven London houses, which, in reality, belonged beneficially to him. The houses had been transferred by Mr Prest to these companies for nominal sums, such as £1. Mr Prest failed to comply with court orders to disclose his financial position.

HELD: Equity presumes that if person A transfers property to B, and does not receive anything in return, A does not intend just to give their property away. Unless there is evidence to the contrary, B holds the property on resulting trust for A. This could be applied to Mr Prest: his companies held the houses on resulting trust for him and his wife could claim them.

Lord Sumption at page 28:

> Since no explanation has been forthcoming for the gratuitous transfer of these properties to PRL, there is nothing to rebut the ordinary presumption of equity that PRL was not intended to acquire a beneficial interest in them. (See 3.7.2 'Presumed resulting trust'.)

A bizarre example of the constructive trust is revealed in the next case. (See 3.8 'Constructive trusts'.)

. . . .

● *Re West Norwood Cemetery* The Times 24 February 2005

Sylvia and Dennis Swaden were buried in plot 177 of the West Norwood Cemetery in 1992 and 2003, respectively. One of the couple's seven children, Paul, objected to his father's burial there. Paul was the registered owner of the burial plot, but his father Dennis and five of the other children had contributed to part of the cost of the burial.

HELD: The family members had a common intention of who should be buried in the plot and by their expenditure had acted to their detriment.

> ...a constructive trust was established and Paul had no right to refuse his consent to Dennis's interment thereby defeating the common purpose of the trust.

thinking points

Trusts can be traced back at least as far as the 13th century, but as we have seen they are still capable of evolving to meet new challenges and provide a solution to new problems. Strangely, though, the basic statutory framework for regulating trusts has not changed much since 1925. The Trustee Act 1925 still remains, although the investment power of trustees has now been modernized by the Trustee Act 2000 (see Chapter 11 'The duties of trustees: with special reference to investment'). Many issues remain to be updated, as trusts may be regarded as 'lawyers' law' and seldom interest Parliament. See Sir William Goodhart 'Trust Law for the Twenty-First Century' (1996) 10(2) Trust Law International *38.*

3.4 What is an equitable interest?

3.4.1 Property rights

Historically, only the trustees had rights in rem, meaning rights against the thing itself. They could claim the actual land itself and not just financial compensation. The beneficiaries only had a right in personam: they could sue the trustees and force them to take action on their behalf and gain financial compensation if they would not. Whether rights are in rem or in personam is a somewhat academic question nowadays and a better question is to whom does the property really belong, the trustees or the beneficiaries? Equitable interests are generally regarded as a property right (**proprietary**) and were defined in the case below.

Proprietary—an interest or estate that gives the right to actual property, usually land.

● *National Provincial Bank v Ainsworth* [1965] AC 1175 at 1248 (Lord Wilberforce):

> ...it must be definable, identifiable by third parties, capable in its nature of assumption by third parties, and have some degree of permanence and stability.

3.4.2 Rights in equity

So equitable interests can be bought, sold, mortgaged, and left by will. They are only unenforceable against a 'bona fide purchaser for valuable consideration without notice', who is sometimes called 'equity's darling'. If someone buys the trust property from the trustees and does not know about the equitable interests, that person takes free of them and is not bound by them (see 17.4.1 'Bona fide purchaser for value without notice'). The beneficiaries would be left to sue the trustees. So equitable interests may be property rights, but they are not quite as good as legal rights.

● *Baker v Archer-Shee* [1927] AC 844

Lady Archer-Shee was a US citizen but resident in England. She was the beneficiary of a trust established in New York, where the trustees received dividends from the trustee investments, paid local taxes, deducted their fees and expenses, etc., and kept the balance for her on account in New York. Did she 'own' these dividends, which would mean that she was liable for tax in the UK?

HELD: The answer was 'Yes'.

Lord Carson said at 870 that she 'was sole beneficial owner of the interest and dividends of all the securities, stocks and shares forming part of the trust fund'.

Yet according to Viscount Sumner at 850:

> The trustee has the full legal property in the whole of the trust fund and the beneficiary has not...All that the latter can do is to claim the assistance of a court of equity to enforce the trust and to compel the trustee to discharge it. This right is quite as good and often is better than any legal right, but it is not in any case one, which for all purposes makes the trust fund 'belong' to the beneficiary or makes the income of it accrue to him *eo instanti* and directly as it leaves the hand of the party who pays it.

Eo instanti—Latin—loosely translated it means 'there instantly'.

The point Viscount Sumner is trying to make is that money owing to the trust goes to the trustees first. Then the trustees pay it out to the beneficiaries, according to the terms of the trust.

KEY POINT The trust fund may 'belong' to the beneficiary, but the beneficiary relies on the trustees to enforce the trust, e.g. to sue people who owe the trust money.

3.5 Trusts today—a definition

An overall definition of the trust is difficult. Coke and Maitland give historical explanations:

> A confidence reposed in some other, not issuing out of the land, but as a thing annexed in privity to the estate of the land, and to the person touching the land, for which the cestui que trust has no remedy but by subpoena in the Chancery. (Coke, Co Litt 272b)

When a person has rights which he is bound to exercise upon behalf of another or for the accomplishment of some particular purpose, he is said to have those rights in trust for that other or for that purpose and he is called a trustee. (Maitland, *Lectures on Equity* (2nd edn, 1936) 44)

An international treaty was agreed to aid the international recognition of trusts, which as we have explained in this book, are a distinctively English concept.

Hague Convention on the Law Applicable to Trusts and on their Recognition (1985) Article 2

For the purposes of this Convention, the term 'trust' refers to the legal relationships created—inter vivos or on death—by a person, the settlor, when assets have been placed under the control of a trustee for the benefit of a beneficiary or for a specified purpose.

A trust has the following characteristics:

(a) the assets constitute a separate fund and are not part of the trustee's own estate;

(b) title to the trust assets stands in the name of the trustee or in the name of another person on behalf of the trustee;

(c) the trustee has the power and the duty, in respect of which he is accountable, to manage, employ, or dispose of the assets in accordance with the terms of the trust and the special duties imposed upon him by law.

The reservation by the settlor of certain rights and powers, and the fact that the trustee may himself have rights as a beneficiary, are not necessarily inconsistent with the existence of a trust.

The problem with this definition is that it is fairly easy to frame a general definition of what a trust is, but hard to come up with a definition that can cover every type of trust. That is why the definition mentions trusts for 'a specified purpose', because charitable trusts do not have any beneficiaries with equitable interests who can enforce the trust. (See 3.6.2 'Public trusts'.)

The House of Lords has also attempted to describe the main elements of a trust.

• **Westdeutsche Landesbank Girozentrale v Islington London Borough Council** [1996] AC 669 at 705 (Lord Browne-Wilkinson):

The relevant principles of trust law

(i) Equity operates on the conscience of the owner of the legal interest. In the case of a trust, the conscience of the legal owner requires him to carry out the purposes for which the property was vested in him (express or implied trust) or which the law imposes on him by reason of his unconscionable conduct (constructive trust).

(ii) Since the equitable jurisdiction to enforce trusts depends upon the conscience of the holder of the legal interest being affected, he cannot be a trustee of the property if and so long as he is ignorant of the facts alleged to affect his conscience, i.e. until he is aware that he is intended to hold the property for the benefit of others in the case of an express or implied trust, or, in the case of a constructive trust, of the factors which are alleged to affect his conscience.

(iii) In order to establish a trust there must be identifiable trust property. The only apparent exception to this rule is a constructive trust imposed on a person who dishonestly assists in a breach of trust who may come under fiduciary duties even if he does not receive identifiable trust property.

(iv) Once a trust is established, as from the date of its establishment the beneficiary has, in equity, a proprietary interest in the trust property, which proprietary interest will be enforceable in equity against any subsequent holder of the property (whether the original property or substituted property into which it can be traced) other than a purchaser for value of the legal interest without notice.

These propositions are fundamental to the law of trusts and we would have thought uncontroversial.

3.6   Classification of trusts

Trusts can be classified in various ways.

3.6.1 Private trusts

The beneficiaries are people.

3.6.2 Public trusts

These are trusts for purposes, not people, but only charitable purposes are allowed. As we shall see in Chapter 10, the legal definition of charity can create anomalies. For example, a trust to relieve the poverty of 'the working classes' is not charitable (*Re Sanders* [1954] Ch 265), but a trust to provide a hostel for 'working men' is (*Re Niyazi* [1978] 1 WLR 910). (See 10.4.1 'The definition of poverty'.)

However, there is an exceptional category of purpose trusts that are allowed, but are not charitable. These are trusts to maintain a grave, trusts to look after a pet, trusts to say masses for the deceased, and trusts to promote fox-hunting (see *Re Astor* [1952] Ch 534 in 9.4.1 'The beneficiary principle').

3.6.3 Express trusts

The trust is intentionally created. The 'certainty' and 'formality' rules must be obeyed. All trusts must be 'certain'. This is a long-standing rule and there are three certainties that all trusts must satisfy (*Knight v Knight* (1840) 3 Beav 148 at 173):

- Certainty of intention: it must be clear from the wording used that a trust was intended. The word 'trust' does not have to be used, but the intention must be clear. It is not intended that the trustee can keep the property for himself/herself, but it is held on behalf of another.
- Certainty of subject matter: the words used must clearly indicate the property subject to the trust.
- Certainty of objects: the trust must have beneficiaries and the wording must clearly indicate who they are.

See 4.6 'The three certainties'.

Ever since the 17th century and the Statute of Frauds 1677, there have been 'formality' requirements for trusts. The formality rules require that certain transactions must be put in writing and, although the Statute of Frauds has long since been repealed, most of its requirements survive, for example in the Law of Property Act 1925. Most transfers or **assignments** of property have to be made in writing, the main exception being chattels or goods which can simply be handed over, e.g. if I want to give you my valuable gold ring, I simply hand it over.

Assignment—transferring a right or interest in property to another.

KEY POINT
Transactions involving *land* require writing. (See Chapter 5 'The formality requirements and incompletely constituted trusts'.)

If I want to give you my house, I need a written document according to s. 2 of the Law of Property (Miscellaneous Provisions) Act 1989. I also need a deed (a formal signed legal document) to transfer the legal estate to you according to s. 52 of the Law of Property Act 1925.

Declarations of trust can be made orally, e.g. I just say 'I hold these shares on trust for you.' However, if it is land, then the declaration of trust can be made orally, but there must be some written proof: s. 53(1)(b) of the Law of Property Act 1925. So it is easier to make declarations of trust of land in writing and that is what most people do. In fact most people deliberately creating a trust involving *any valuable property* would put it in writing, so that there could be no dispute later. However, it is only required by law if land is involved.

Many trusts are set up in wills. Wills must comply with the Wills Act 1837, which means that the will must be in writing, signed by the testator, and the signature witnessed by two or more people. (See 7.1.1 'General characteristics of wills'.)

3.6.4 Fixed trusts

This is a type of trust with which you might already be familiar from your legal studies. The trust instrument (the document that sets out the trust) will lay down the share or interest that each beneficiary is to take. In other words the beneficiaries are clearly identified, as is their equitable interest, e.g. to A for life, remainder in fee simple to my children B and C in equal shares.

3.6.5 Discretionary trusts

The trustees choose amongst a specified group or class of beneficiaries (objects). An example would be 'my trustees shall hold my shares in the Loch Ness Whale Farm plc on trust for my children. The trustees shall apply the income from these shares for the benefit of all or any of my children in such amounts and at such times as they think fit.'

No beneficiaries (often called 'objects' here) have any equitable interest (see 3.5 'Trusts today—a definition'), or right to the property unless the trustees choose him or her.

The trustees have a choice or discretion as to whom they give the property. This gives maximum flexibility to help the poorer children, to protect those who have fallen into debt, or even to pay out to the children who will pay the least tax. Discretionary trusts are quite commonly used and an unusual example of their use can be seen in *Annabel's (Berkeley Square) Ltd v Revenue and Customs Commissioners* [2009] 4 All ER 55.

. . . .

● ***Annabel's (Berkeley Square) Ltd v Revenue and Customs Commissioners***
   [2009] 4 All ER 55

The employers were private members' clubs and restaurants, and customers gave them tips for the staff when they paid their bills by credit card, debit card, and cheque. These tips were passed on to a member of staff called the troncmaster, who would distribute the tips to the staff, according to their length of service. The employers were accused of not paying their staff the minimum wage and argued that these tips were part of the staff's wages.

HELD: Court of Appeal. The tip money never belonged to the employer and so could not be part of the staff wage. Instead, the troncmaster was holding this money on a discretionary trust for the staff.

Rimer LJ at 66:

> The correct analysis is that the money paid to the troncmaster became held by him upon trust for the employees, a trust requiring him to distribute it between them in accordance with the tronc scheme. Accordingly, the legal and beneficial interest in the money left the employer when it was paid to the troncmaster, who thereupon held it for the employees beneficially. So long as the money remained in the hands of the troncmaster, no payment was made to the employees. Until then they had at most a collective beneficial interest in the money entitling them to have the trust executed.

This case accurately describes how the legal and beneficial interests are held in discretionary trusts. (See Chapter 4 'Trusts and powers and the three certainties' for more detail.)

3.6.6 Secret trusts

These are imposed upon the beneficiary under a will, when the beneficiary has promised the testator to give the property to a person or purpose not mentioned in the will. An example would be where A leaves his house to B in the written document of his will. In fact B has promised A that he, B, will give the house to C, but there is no mention of this in the will. Wills become documents that are publicly available once a person has died, so if the testator or testatrix does not want other people to know who the real beneficiary is, the secret trust is a useful device. The courts will make B keep his promise, by imposing a trust in favour of C upon the house that B has inherited.

There is disagreement upon what type of trust a secret trust is.

It could be an express trust, because A has deliberately created it. On the other hand, it could be a constructive trust because B is being forced by the courts to keep his promise; as to allow him to keep the property for himself would be 'unconscionable'. (See 7.2 'Secret trusts'.)

3.6.7 Bare trusts

The trustees hold for the beneficiaries, but there are no duties for the trustees to perform.

These are sometimes called simple or even naked trusts. A holds on trust for B and there is nothing more to it. A, the trustee, does not have to invest, think of other beneficiaries, or do anything except look after the property. The bare trust is often used to hide the real owner of shares. (See 3.3 'What trusts are used for' for 'nominees'.)

A good example of a bare trust is the old case of *Saunders v Vautier*.

. . . .

● ***Saunders v Vautier*** [1841] 4 Beav 115

Trustees held £2,000 of East India stock on trust for Vautier. They were to accumulate the dividends paid on the stock until Vautier attained the age of 25, and then transfer the capital and accumulated dividends to Vautier. When Vautier reached the age of majority, which was then 21, he wanted the whole fund transferred to him and did not want to wait until he was 25.

HELD: Vautier could have the whole fund now as he had 'an absolute indefeasible interest in the legacy'.

This rule in *Saunders v Vautier*, allowing beneficiaries to end the trust and tell the trustees to hand over the property, only applies if all the beneficiaries agree and if they are all of full age and sound mind. Most trusts have many beneficiaries, so it is not often a usable rule, unless we are dealing with a bare trust, which often has only one beneficiary. (See Chapter 14 'Variation of trust'.)

3.6.8 Blind trusts

This is not a technical term but it is used to describe a situation where a number of donors or settlors pay into the trust. Their donations are held on trust for the beneficiary or beneficiaries, who do not know who has donated the money. Politicians use this device when supporters donate money to help them in their work. Under the blind trust the politician is the beneficiary, so the politician does not know who has donated money to him or her and so cannot be accused of favouring them.

3.6.9 STAR trusts

Many countries want to attract foreign investment and part of this can involve encouraging trusts and their trustees to be located in that country. This is done by having very 'relaxed' rules for trusts that often allow a lot of secrecy. The Cayman Islands enacted the Special Trusts (Alternative Regime) Law in 1997. These are discretionary trusts (see 3.6.5 'Discretionary trusts'), but they do not follow the English rules about certainty of objects (see 3.6.3 'Express trusts'). The trustees can choose amongst wide categories of beneficiaries and even purposes. Tax authorities cannot easily discover to whom trust funds are being paid and even the family of the settlor may be unable to discover whether they are a beneficiary, which might save the settlor from unwelcome pleas for money! 'Protectors' are appointed to enforce the beneficiaries' interests and, commonly, settlors provide a 'letter of wishes' to give the trustees guidance on what he or she wants them to do. By not putting these 'wishes' into the trust document itself it again makes it harder for anyone to find out where the money is actually going. Other 'offshore' tax havens, such as Bermuda, the Isle of Man, and the Channel Islands have followed suit with legislation allowing similar types of trusts.

3.7 Resulting trusts

(Resulting trusts are covered in more detail in Chapter 8 'Resulting trusts'.)

These occur when person A is held to be holding property on trust for person B. The trust has not been deliberately created and so is not an express trust. The trust arises by operation of law or, in other words, a court decision. These trusts arise in a number of different situations. Megarry J identified two main categories of resulting trust in *Re Vandervell's Trusts (No 2)* [1974] 1 All ER 47, which were the automatic resulting trust and the presumed resulting trust.

....

● *Re Vandervell's Trusts (No 2)* [1974] Ch 269

Megarry J at 289:

KEY POINT
This is the presumed resulting trust.

> The distinction between the two categories of resulting trusts is important because they operate in different ways. Putting it shortly, in the first category, subject to any provisions in the instrument, the matter is one of intention, with the rebuttable presumption of a resulting trust applying if the intention is not made manifest.

KEY POINT
This is the automatic resulting trust.

> For the second category, there is no mention of any expression of intention in any instrument, or of any presumption of a resulting trust: the resulting trust takes effect by operation of law, and so appears to be automatic. What a man fails effectually to dispose of remains automatically **vested** in him, and no question of any mere presumption can arise. The two categories are thus of presumed resulting trusts and automatic resulting trusts.

....

Vest—the beneficiary becomes fully entitled, e.g. if the trust said 'to A for life, remainder to the children of A upon marriage'. A child of A does not become fully entitled until he/she marries and A dies. When the child marries, his/her equitable interest vests in interest. When A dies, the interest vests in possession.

....

3.7.1 Automatic resulting trust

A trust fails for some reason and the property returns to the settlor. Megarry J did not think that this depended on any intention on the part of the original settlor. In *Vandervell* [1974] Ch 269 itself, Mr Vandervell was trying to rid himself of his shares to minimize his tax burden.

Yet the court decided that he had not done so, so the shares 'resulted' back to him. A good example of this type of resulting trust is *Re Gillingham Bus Disaster*.

. . . .

● ***Re Gillingham Bus Disaster*** [1958] Ch 300

In 1951 24 Royal Marine cadets were killed, and others injured, when, while marching through the streets of Gillingham in Kent, they were hit by a runaway bus. What we would nowadays call a 'disaster fund' was set up and money was donated by the public to help to pay for funerals, help the disabled, 'and then to such worthy cause or causes . . .'. As the bus company and the driver had to pay damages and 'worthy causes' was too vague to be charitable, there was a surplus in the fund.

HELD: Harman J at 310:

> The general principle must be that where money is held upon trust and the trusts declared do not exhaust the fund it will revert to the donor or settlor under what is called a resulting trust. The reasoning behind this is that the settlor or donor did not part with his money absolutely out and out but only sub modo —under a condition or restriction to the intent that his wishes as declared by the declaration of trust should be carried into effect. When therefore this has been done any surplus still belongs to him. This doctrine does not, in my judgment, rest on any evidence of the state of mind of the settlor, for in the vast majority of cases no doubt he does not expect to see his money back; he has created a trust which so far as he can see will absorb the whole of it.

The court made this decision despite the practical difficulty of returning the property to the original donors to the charity. Many of them gave to street collections or sent their contribution in anonymously. In fact most of the money could not be returned and in 1993 the remainder was used to build a memorial to those who died.

More recently the House of Lords put forward the view that *both* types of resulting trust ultimately depend upon the intention of the donor or settlor: if they had thought that the trust property could not be used for the trust, they would want it back.

In *Westdeutsche Landesbank Girozentrale v Islington London Borough Council* [1996] AC 669, Lord Browne-Wilkinson said at 708:

> Both types of resulting trust are traditionally regarded as examples of trusts giving effect to the common intention of the parties. A resulting trust is not imposed by law against the intentions of the trustee (as is a constructive trust) but gives effect to his presumed intention.

(Once again—see Chapter 8 'Resulting trusts'.)

3.7.2 Presumed resulting trust

This depends upon the presumed intention of the settlor (original owner or holder of the property). In other words what they would have intended if they had thought about it. There are two types of resulting trust in this category.

The purchase money resulting trust

If A pays for property and puts it legally into the name of B, it is presumed, as A paid for it, that A intended to keep it. B holds the property on resulting trust for A.

If A and B both contribute to the purchase of property it is presumed that they hold it in proportion to the amount that they contributed. The way this is accomplished is to recognize their shares in equity. So if A pays £50,000 towards the purchase of a house and B pays £100,000 and it is legally in their joint names, they hold it on resulting trust, one-third for A and two-thirds for B.

The classic statement can be found in the next case.

....

● **Dyer v Dyer** [1788] 2 Cox Eq Cases 92

Eyre CB at 93:

> The clear result of all the cases, without a single exception, is that the trust of a legal estate, whether freehold, copyhold, leasehold; whether taken in the names of the purchasers and others jointly, or in the name of others without that of the purchaser; whether in one name or several; whether jointly or successive, results to the man who advances the purchase money.

Presumption of resulting trust

If A legally transfers property to B and receives nothing in return, unless there is evidence that A actually intended a gift, it is presumed that B, who holds the property legally, holds it on resulting trust for A, who has the equitable interest. (See *Prest v Petrodel Ltd* [2013] 3 WLR 1 at 3.3.)

This seems contrary to common sense, but is based on the deep-seated idea in the law that someone must give consideration, something of value, in return to gain any right to property. This is sometimes stated in the equitable maxim 'Equity will not assist a volunteer'. A volunteer is someone who has not given consideration. (See 2.11 'Equity will not assist a volunteer'.)

Remember, however, that if there is evidence that a gift was intended, there will be no resulting trust and the property will belong to B.

3.8 Constructive trusts

(See Chapter 16 'Constructive trusts' for more detail.)

These are imposed by the court in a variety of situations, usually when someone has wrongfully acquired the property of another, e.g. by breaking a promise or knowingly taking someone else's property. As *Westdeutsche Landesbank* says at 3.7.1, something affects the 'trustee's' conscience. Often the parties involved will not have intended any sort of trust, but 'Equity says that in certain circumstances the legal owner of property must hold it on trust for others'. (Hanbury and Martin *Modern Equity* (19th edn, London: Sweet & Maxwell, 2012 at 74.)

These circumstances can vary so much that it is difficult to frame an overall definition, so it is probably easier just to learn to recognize the different situations in which constructive trusts can be imposed.

3.8.1 Constructive trusts and 'good conscience'

It is hard to pin down exactly what a constructive trust is, so in some cases the courts concentrate on obtaining a result that they consider 'just' and 'fair'. A number of cases heard by Lord Denning in the 1970s are good examples of this:

● **Hussey v Palmer** [1972] 3 All ER 744

Mrs Hussey lived with her daughter and son-in-law in their house. She paid £607 for an extension to be built. They quarrelled and Mrs Hussey left the house, but she claimed for the return of her money.

HELD: Lord Denning found for her, but made a sweeping statement at 747:

> Although the plaintiff alleged that there was a resulting trust, I should have thought that the trust in this case if there was one, was more in the nature of a constructive trust, but that is more a matter of words than anything else. The two run together. By whatever name it is described, *it is a trust imposed by law whenever justice and good conscience require it...*
>
> It is an equitable remedy by which the court can enable an aggrieved party to obtain restitution...
>
> Thus we have repeatedly held that when one person contributes towards the purchase price of a house, the owner holds it on constructive trust for him, proportionate to his contribution, even though there is no agreement between them, and no declaration of trust to be found, and no evidence of any intention to create a trust.

Controversially, Lord Denning MR makes no distinction between resulting trusts and constructive trusts. To him, constructive trusts just depend on the property holder's 'bad conscience'; has he/she done something wrong? Although this approach goes far back to the origins of equity, in that all that the court does is to do justice as the judge sees it, the problem is that it leads to uncertainty and unpredictability. What seems just to one person may not seem just to another.

Westdeutsche Landesbank [1996] AC 669 was an attempt by the House of Lords to restate an orthodox position that there are clearly defined categories of trust. Despite this there is still the occasional case where courts use a constructive trust in an innovative way to obtain a just result. (See 3.5 'Trusts today—a definition'.)

● **Banner Homes v Luff** [2000] 2 All ER 117

Banner Homes and Luff Developments had orally agreed to acquire a site at White Waltham for development as a joint venture. Luff eventually took up the opportunity alone, even though Banner still thought that they had a joint agreement.

HELD: The court agreed that there was no contract between them, but still thought that Banner had a claim. A constructive trust was imposed upon Luff to hold half of the proceeds for each of them. It was thought 'unconscionable' and 'inequitable' to allow Luff to take this advantage. This was an 'inominate equity of an entirely different nature' meaning that it resembled other uses of constructive trust, but was not exactly like them.

The case of *Banner Homes v Luff* [2000] 2 All ER 117 was considered in the House of Lords case, *Yeoman's Row Management Ltd v Cobbe* [2008] 4 All ER 713. The House confirmed that this type of constructive trust, based on the older case of *Pallant v Morgan* [1952] Ch 43, did exist, but did not apply on the facts of the case. 'Unconscionable behaviour' was not enough, by itself, to found a constructive trust.

● **Yeoman's Row Management Ltd v Cobbe** [2008] 4 All ER 713

Mrs Lisle-Mainwaring owned a block of flats through her company, Yeoman's Row, and negotiated with Cobbe, an experienced property developer. Cobbe would obtain planning permission for the flats, at his own expense, and then buy the flats from her for £12 million. He would redevelop the site and build houses. If the houses sold for more than £24 million he would give Mrs Lisle-Mainwaring 50 per cent of the proceeds above that figure. Cobbe obtained planning permission, but then Mrs Lisle-Mainwaring wanted to renegotiate the terms of the agreement and obtain a much bigger share of the profits. Cobbe insisted that they keep to the terms of the original agreement.

HELD: Cobbe sued for breach of contract, but as the agreement was oral and involved land, there was no contract under s. 2(1) of the Law of Property (Miscellaneous Provisions) Act 1989. So he claimed that there was a constructive trust.

His claim was rejected. The type of constructive trust found in *Banner Homes v Luff* [2000] 2 All ER 117 only applies when the parties engage in a 'joint venture' to acquire an identified piece of land. Mrs Lisle-Mainwaring already owned the block of flats and their alleged agreement was too vague and uncertain. They were really still in the negotiation stage. The fact that Mrs Lisle-Mainwaring behaved 'unconscionably' did not make it a constructive trust.

(Mr Cobbe also argued **proprietary estoppel**, but failed on those grounds as well, for very similar reasons. See Chapter 6 'Proprietary estoppel'.)

KEY POINT
The House of Lords did not overrule the constructive trust cases based solely on 'good conscience', but did not wish to encourage further development of this idea.

....

Proprietary estoppel—if party A represents to party B that party B has a right to some property held by party A, then if party B relies on this representation and acts to their detriment, party A cannot deny the right of party B.

....

In *Crossco No 4 Unlimited v Jolan Ltd (Note)* [2012] 2 All ER 754, the Court of Appeal followed the approach of the House of Lords in *Yeoman's Row Management v Cobbe* [2008] 4 All ER 713. They conceded that the constructive trust used in *Banner Homes v Luff* [2000] 2 All ER 117 existed, but declined to apply it to the facts of the case.

....

● ***Crossco No 4 Unlimited v Jolan Ltd (Note)*** [2012] 2 All ER 754

There was an alleged oral agreement not to end a written lease, but a constructive trust was not established, as there was no proof that the oral agreement ever existed.

thinking points

The type of constructive trust found in Yeoman's Row v Cobbe, *descends from the older case of* Pallant v Morgan *[1953] Ch 43. The majority of judges in* Crossco No 4 Unlimited v Jolan Ltd *thought that this type of trust was a kind of common intention constructive trust, more often used in disputes about the family home. (See Chapter 18 'Trusts of the family home'.) Etherton LJ delivered a strong dissent in* Crossco No 4, *to the effect that it would be better if the 'equity in Pallant v Morgan' was confined to its own very distinct facts. The indiscriminate use of common intention constructive trusts could lead to uncertainty in business and commercial dealings. See Nicholas Hopkins 'The* Pallant v Morgan *"equity"—again' [2012]* Conveyancer *327–33.*

Implied trusts

These are mentioned in the Law of Property Act 1925, s. 53(2).

> **Law of Property Act 1925**
>
> . . . .
>
> 53 Instruments required to be in writing
>
> (1) Subject to the provisions hereinafter contained with respect to the creation of interests in land by parol—
>
> ...
>
> (b) a declaration of trust respecting any land or any interest therein must be manifested and proved by some writing signed by some person who is able to declare such trust or by his will.
>
> (c) a disposition of an equitable interest or trust subsisting at the time of the disposition, must be in writing signed by the person disposing of the same, or by his agent thereunto lawfully authorised in writing or by will.
>
> (2) This section does not affect the creation or operation of resulting, implied or constructive trusts.

It is, however, uncertain to which type of trust the section is referring. The section also refers to constructive and resulting trusts, so it is likely that something similar is meant. Neither constructive nor resulting trusts are created deliberately and intentionally by the parties involved, so they could both be said to be 'implied'. Usually the parties involved do not realize that it is a trust, until the court tells them so! As we have seen, in cases such as *Hussey v Palmer* [1972] 3 All ER 744, the courts do not always distinguish carefully between constructive and resulting trusts. The full section requires that trusts of land should only be declared in writing (s. 53(1)(b)), and that disposing of or transferring the equitable interest in a trust of any type of property can also only be done in writing. Section 53(2) exempts resulting, constructive, and implied trusts from this requirement, because if the parties do not even realize that they have created a trust, they can hardly be expected to put it into writing.

Quistclose-type trusts

3.10.1 Distinctive characteristics of 'Quistclose' trusts

It is possible to create a trust without an express declaration of trust. Payments for a particular purpose may create a trust. If the purpose of the trust fails, a resulting trust returns the property to the settlor.

A small group of cases has attracted some attention because the cases illustrate a number of key points about trust law.

1. It is easy to declare a trust. Unless land is involved, no particular formalities are required. All that is required is that a clear intention is shown.
2. If the purpose of a trust fails, a resulting trust comes into operation. The current owner of the property holds it upon trust for the original owner.
3. A trust can protect property from creditors. The trustees must protect the property for the beneficiaries.

3.10.2 An express trust followed by a resulting trust

● **Barclays Bank v Quistclose** [1970] AC 567

Rolls-Razor owed money to its bankers Barclays. It was also unable to pay its shareholders. So Rolls borrowed money from Quistclose to pay dividends to the shareholders. This money was placed in a separate account at Barclays. Rolls-Razor went into liquidation and the question was: who was entitled to the money in the separate account? Normally in a liquidation all the creditors receive a proportion of whatever property is left.

HELD: The money was for a special purpose and was therefore held on trust. That purpose had failed so it went back to Quistclose on a resulting trust. They gained 'priority' over the claims of Barclays, as Barclays' claim was only a contractual one. (A debt is a contract.)

Lord Wilberforce at 580:

> That arrangements of this character for the payment of a person's creditors by a third person give rise to a relationship of a fiduciary character or trust, in favour, as a primary trust, of the creditors, and secondarily, if the primary trust fails, of the third person, has been recognised in a series of cases over some 150 years.... when the money is advanced, the lender acquires an equitable right to see that it is applied for the primary designated purpose ...

● **Re Kayford Ltd (In Liquidation)** [1975] 1 WLR 279

Kayford was a mail order firm that was in financial difficulties. Its customers paid in advance for the goods that they ordered, so Kayford placed the money sent in by its customers in a separate bank account designated 'Customers' Trust Deposit Account'. Kayford went into liquidation.

HELD: This account was clearly a trust, as K had taken 'suitable steps' to establish it. The purpose had failed and so it was held on resulting trust for the customers. The customers took in advance of the other creditors because their property was protected within the trust.

● **Re EVTR** [1987] BCLC 646

Barber won £240,000 on the Premium Bonds and wanted to use it to enable his employers, EVTR, to buy new equipment. He deposited £60,000 of it with his solicitors and authorized them to release it 'for the sole purpose of buying new equipment', but the money was not held in any special fund. The money was handed over to EVTR and the equipment was ordered, but had not yet arrived when EVTR went into receivership. Barber wanted to protect the money that he had given to EVTR from the **receiver**.

Receiver—a person appointed to collect debts that are owed.

HELD: This was enough to create a trust. So when EVTR went into liquidation, the purpose of buying the new equipment had failed and the money was held on resulting trust for Barber.

● **Carreras Rothman v Freeman Matthews Treasure** [1985] Ch 207

Rothmans had a contract with Freeman, an advertising agency, and paid it for its services. It also paid a monthly sum into a specially designated account at Freeman's bank. The purpose of this account was so that Freeman could in turn pay the artists, photographers, etc. that it employed to produce the advertising. It was done this way because Freeman was in financial difficulties and could not pay the people that it hired. Unfortunately, Freeman still went into liquidation.

Could Rothmans get its money back?

HELD: No. Although the money in the account was held on trust, the purpose of that trust had *not* failed. The original beneficiaries, the artists, photographers, etc. could still be paid for their services with this money. Therefore, there was no need for the resulting trust back to Rothmans.

3.10.3 Other views on how these trusts work

'Quistclose' trusts have been much debated, as they are certainly an unusual type of trust and the courts have not explained exactly how they work. Dr Chambers argues in his book *Resulting Trusts* (Oxford: Oxford University Press, 1997), that these are not really trusts at all, but simply a contract. The lender gives the money to the borrower as a loan and that is just a contract, not a trust. The money belongs to the borrower; he has the entire beneficial interest, which leaves the lender with no type of property right to the money. The rights that the lender has are based on contract and the lender has a contractual right to ensure that the loan is used for the stated purpose. If the purpose fails, then a resulting trust springs into life as a kind of remedy. This has a type of logic to it, but the courts have insisted that these cases involve a trust from the outset. The problems are who is the trustee, who is the beneficiary, and what is the trust property? This is examined by Lord Millett in the following case.

. . . .

● *Twinsectra Ltd v Yardley* [2002] AC 164

Twinsectra had lent £1,000,000 to Mr Yardley for the purpose of buying land. He spent £357,720.11 on other purposes and that is why Twinsectra sued. The £1 million had been advanced to Yardley's solicitor, Sims, who signed an undertaking that provided, among other things, that '[t]he loan monies will be utilised *solely* for the acquisition of property on behalf of our client *and for no other purpose'*. The question was whether this formed a trust.

HELD: Lord Millett considered the nature of the 'Quistclose' trust at 185:

> It does not matter whether the parties involved understand what a trust is, it is what they actually do that counts. A settlor must, of course, possess the necessary intention to create a trust, but his subjective intentions are irrelevant. If he enters into arrangements which have the effect of creating a trust, it is not necessary that they should appreciate that they do so; it is sufficient that he intends to enter into them.

Then Lord Millett states that there are problems with the traditional analysis in the original *Quistclose* case at 187:

> These passages suggest that there are two successive trusts, a primary trust for payment to identifiable beneficiaries, such as creditors or shareholders, and a secondary trust in favour of the lender arising on the failure of the primary trust. But there are formidable difficulties in this analysis, which has little academic support. What if the primary trust is not for identifiable persons, but as in the present case to carry out an abstract purpose? Where in such a case is the beneficial interest pending the application of the money for the stated purpose or the failure of the purpose? There are four possibilities: (i) in the lender; (ii) in the borrower; (iii) in the contemplated beneficiary; or (iv) in suspense.

Lord Millett favours the first possibility, but first he has to dispose of the other three. He said at 187–8:

> *[ii] The borrower.* It is plain that the beneficial interest is not vested unconditionally in the borrower so as to leave the money at his free disposal. That would defeat the whole purpose of the arrangements, which is to prevent the money from passing to the borrower's trustee in bankruptcy in the event of his insolvency.

It would be a bit odd if Sims were holding on trust for Yardley, because then, as the only beneficiary, Yardley could do as he liked with the money.

(iii) It was usually thought that the trust was for some of the creditors, such as the shareholders in Quistclose or the customers in Kayford. This is awkward, as the category of shareholders or customers fluctuates, causing problems with the certainty of objects rule, with which all trusts must comply.

At 189:

> The most serious objection to this approach is exemplified by the facts of the present case. In several of the cases the primary trust was for an abstract purpose with no one but the lender to enforce performance or restrain misapplication of the money.

Re EVTR is an example of this, where the trust was for the purpose of buying new equipment. Trusts must have human beneficiaries, purpose trusts are not allowed (see 3.6.3 'Express trusts').

(iv) This is Dr Chambers' idea that it is a contract followed by a resulting trust. The problem with this is that *Quistclose* insists that it is a trust from the start and that the lender can enforce it if the money is not spent for the stated purpose. The obvious solution for Lord Millett is to say that the lender must be the beneficiary, right from the start. His conclusion is that it is a resulting trust (at 193):

> A trust must have certainty of objects. But the only trust is the resulting trust for the lender. The borrower is authorised (or directed) to apply the money for a stated purpose, but this is a mere power and does not constitute a purpose trust.

And at 192–3:

> The lender pays the money to the borrower by way of loan, but he does not part with the entire beneficial interest in the money, and in so far as he does it is held on a resulting trust for the lender from the outset.

When the purpose fails, the money is returnable to the lender, not under some new trust in his favour which only comes into being on the failure of the purpose, but because the resulting trust in his favour is no longer subject to any power on the part of the borrower to make use of the money.

None of the other judges attempted to explain the Quistclose-type trust, so it remains to be seen whether Lord Millett's analysis is adopted.

Subsequent cases, such as *Wise v Jimenez* [2013] Al ER (D) 123, merely cite the two competing theories from *Quistclose* and *Twinsectra*, but do not give any indication which is correct.

KEY POINTS 'Quistclose' trusts are:

- an express trust for one particular group of creditors. When the purpose fails there is a resulting trust back for the person who loaned the money; or

- a contractual loan. When the purpose fails there is a resulting trust back for the person who loaned the money; or

- a resulting trust for the person who loans the money right from the start. The borrower, who is the trustee, has the power to use the money for a specified purpose.

thinking points

Was the original decision in Barclays Bank v Quistclose *[1970] AC 567 correct? That case decided that there was a particular form of trust, henceforward known as the Quistclose trust, which consisted of an express trust, followed by a resulting trust if the purpose of the express trust failed. Various other solutions have been suggested, such as one based on contract, advocated by Chambers and, in 2002, the House of Lords had the opportunity to consider the matter again in* Twinsectra v Yardley. *Lord Millett took the opportunity to draw on his own writings, at (1985) 101 LGR 269 'The Quistclose Trust: Who Can Enforce It?' and concluded that the Quistclose trust was really just a resulting trust and maybe not a distinctive type of trust. Lord Millett's thinking on resulting trusts can also be seen in* Air Jamaica v Charlton *[1999] 1 WLR 1399 at 8.3. See TM Yeo and H Tijo 'The Quistclose Trust' (2003) 119 LQR 8.*

(3.11) Wills and intestacies

Executors are named in a will. If there is no will, known as an intestacy, the court must appoint administrators who would usually be close relatives of the deceased. Both executors and administrators are known as personal representatives. Personal representatives, of either kind, have very similar duties to trustees and are often regarded in the same way legally. Indeed the definition of a trustee in s. 68 of the Trustee Act 1925 includes personal representatives.

It is not unusual when making a will, if the testator is trying to establish a trust after his death, to nominate the same people as executors and trustees.

3.11.1 The differences between trustees and personal representatives

There are, however, differences between trustees and personal representatives. The period within which they can be sued for their actions, known as the limitation period, is different. Under the Limitation Act 1980, it is six years for a trustee (s. 21) and 12 years for a personal representative (s. 22). (See 15.7 'Limitation' for limitation periods.) Trustees can retire from their position under s. 39 of the Trustee Act 1925, but personal representatives cannot.

The task of trustees is to run the trust, which may last for many years, but personal representatives must gather in the deceased's property, possibly sell it, and distribute it to the beneficiaries according to the terms of the will or if it is an intestacy to the 'statutory next of kin'. Then the function of the personal representative ends. Although personal representatives are referred to as trustees, the estate of the deceased as a 'trust', and the recipients of the property as beneficiaries, this arrangement is not actually a trust in the sense that we usually use the word. This is explained in the following case.

Real property—rights over land, especially freehold rights over land.

Personal property—all property that is not land. This includes moveable and intangible property.

● *Commissioner of Stamp Duties (Queensland) v Livingston* [1965] AC 694

Mr Livingston died while living in New South Wales leaving his **real and personal property** to his widow, Mrs Coulson, who also lived in New South Wales. Before the administration of his estate had been completed, his widow also died. Mr Livingston's property was in New South Wales and Queensland and the Queensland authorities claimed that Mrs Coulson was liable to pay tax on inheriting the property in Queensland. The law there required the payment of succession duty upon 'every devolution by law of any beneficial interest in property...upon the death of any person...'. The argument was that she had inherited an equitable interest in her husband's property in the period between his death and her own.

HELD: This was not the case.

Viscount Radcliffe at 707–8:

> *Virtute officii*—Latin—literally, by virtue of their office, meaning that the executor does not hold the property for their personal use, but for the benefit of the beneficiaries.

...whatever property came to the executor *virtute officii* came to him in full ownership, without distinction between legal and equitable interests.

The whole property was his. He held it for the purpose of carrying out the functions and duties of administration, not for his own benefit; and those duties would be enforced upon him by the Court of Chancery, if application had to be made for that purpose by a creditor or beneficiary interested in the estate. Certainly, therefore, he was in a fiduciary position with regard to the assets that came to him in the right of his office, and for certain purposes and in some aspects he was treated by the court as a trustee. 'An executor,' said Kay J in *Re Marsden* (1884) 26 ChD 783 at 789, 'is personally liable in equity for all breaches of the ordinary trusts which in Courts of Equity are considered to arise for his office.' He is a trustee 'in this sense'.

It may not be possible to state exhaustively what those trusts are at any one moment. Essentially, they are trusts to preserve the assets, to deal properly with them, and to apply them in a due course of administration for the benefit of those interested according to that course, creditors, the death duty authorities, legatees of various sorts, and the residuary beneficiaries. They might just as well have been termed 'duties in respect of the assets' as trusts. What equity did not do was to recognize or create for residuary legatees a beneficial interest in the assets in the executor's hands during the course of administration. Conceivably, this could have been done, in the sense that the assets, whatever they might be from time to time, could have been treated as a present, though fluctuating, trust fund held for the benefit of all those interested in the estate according to the measure of their respective interests. But it never was done. It would have been a clumsy and unsatisfactory device from a practical point of view; and, indeed, it would have been in plain conflict with the basic conception of equity that to impose the fetters of a trust upon property, with the resulting creation of equitable interests in that property, there had to be specific subjects identifiable as the trust fund. An unadministered estate was incapable of satisfying this requirement. The assets as a whole were in the hands of the executor, his property; and until administration was complete no one was in a position to say what items of property would need to be realized for the purposes of that administration or of what the residue, when ascertained, would consist or what its value would be. Even in modern economies, when the ready marketability of many forms of property can almost be assumed, valuation and realization are very far from being interchangeable terms.

And at 717:

> ...their Lordships regard it as clearly established that Mrs Coulson was not entitled to any beneficial interest in any property in Queensland at the date of her death. What she was entitled to in respect of her rights under her deceased husband's will was a chose in action, capable of being invoked for any purpose connected with the proper administration of his estate; and the local situation of this asset, as much under Queensland law as any other law, was in New South Wales, where the testator had been domiciled and his executors resided and which constituted the proper forum of administration of his estate.

KEY POINTS Wills and trusts

- Unlike trustees, personal representatives hold both the legal estate and the equitable interest in the deceased's properties. This is so that they can more easily sell it.

- Unlike under a normal trust, the beneficiaries do not have an equitable interest, merely a right, a chose in action, to see that the estate is properly administered.

Conclusion

The purpose of this chapter was to introduce the reader to many of the issues that will be considered later in the book. Many different kinds of property can be held on trust and trusts can be used to achieve many different purposes. There are many different kinds of trust, so much so that it is difficult to find an overall unifying concept, although *Westdeutsche Landesbank Girozentrale v Islington London Borough Council* [1996] AC 669 tried. Lastly, wills can be important in the study of equity and trusts (see for example Chapter 7 'The disposal of property on death') and it is important to understand the differences between trustees and personal representatives.

Questions

Self-test questions

1   What are trusts used for?

2   What sort of property can be held on trust?

3   What common features can be found in the different types of trust?

4   Why have Quistclose trusts caused so much difficulty?

5   How do beneficiaries under a trust and under a will differ?

Discussion questions

1   Consider the many different types of trust. Can you see any common features in them?

2   A key feature of the trust is the 'split' between the legal estate and the equitable interests. Consider the difference between rights in equity and rights in law.

3   How do Quistclose-type trusts fit into the classification of trusts?

Assessment question

From reading this chapter, you should now have some understanding of the words below. What is the meaning of the following words in trust law?

Settlor	Will
Testator	Deed
Trust	Covenants
Settlement	Conveyance
Trustee	Trust instrument
Beneficiary	Value
Legal	Consideration
Equitable	Volunteer
Estate	Chose in action
Interest	Negotiable instrument
Real property	Assignment
Personal property	Charge
Proprietary	Personal representative
Licence	Executor
Estoppel	Administrator
Fiduciary	Intestacy

Check the suggested answer in the Glossary at the end of the book.

Key cases

- *Westdeutsche Landesbank Girozentrale v Islington London Borough Council* [1996] AC 669 **(at 3.5 and 3.7.1)**

- *Barclays Bank v Quistclose* [1970] AC 567 **(at 3.10.2)**

- *Twinsectra v Yardley* [2002] 2 AC 164 **(at 3.10.3)**

Further reading

N Hopkins 'The Pallant v Morgan "equity" again' [2012] *Conveyancer* 327–33.
Constructive trusts seem capable of future development, but the courts are keen to keep such trusts within defined limits.

Sir W Goodhart 'Trust Law for the 21st Century' (1996) 10(2) *Trust Law International* 38.
How trust law might develop in the future.

TM Yeo and H Tijo 'The Quistclose Trust' (2003) 119 *LQR* 8.
A review of the Quistclose case law.

4

Trusts and powers and the three certainties

Learning objectives

This chapter will help you to:

- distinguish between a bare power of appointment and a fiduciary power of appointment
- distinguish between a discretionary trust and a fixed trust
- understand that a trust must satisfy the three certainties: Certainty of Intention, Certainty of Subject Matter, Certainty of Objects
- distinguish gifts subject to a condition from fiduciary powers and discretionary trusts.

Introduction

We are dealing here with private property which belongs to settlors and testators. It is up to them how they dispose of it to their families, friends, or other beneficiaries. The law does not stand in their way if they wish to set up complex arrangements, which may seem puzzling and pointless to the layperson! Settlors and testators are often aiming for maximum flexibility and often they are trying to minimize their tax liability.

The courts are concerned with what they call 'certainty'. This means that the wording of the trust must be clear enough for the courts to enforce the trust if necessary. It must be clear from the words used by the testator or settlor that a trust was actually intended. If it is a trust, we must then decide what sort of trust it is. Is it a fixed or discretionary trust? Does the trust contain a power of appointment and, if so, is it a bare power or a fiduciary power? Has the settlor or testator clearly indicated what property is to be subjected to the trust? Lastly, and most importantly, is it possible for the courts and trustees to work out who the beneficiaries are?

4.1 The different types of trust and powers

An express, private trust begins with property that belongs to a settlor or testator. It is their property, so the law allows them plenty of freedom to dispose of it in the way that they wish. Establishing a trust is one way of doing this and in furtherance of the same policy, the courts have allowed several different types of trust to develop. We will start off by trying to make some basic distinctions.

4.1.1 Powers of appointment

An authorization given by the donor to the donee (appointor) to appoint (transfer) property in which he may or may not have an interest to another person or persons (objects or appointees). As part of a wider trust, it is common to stipulate that someone, usually a beneficiary or a trustee, has the power to decide who is to receive the property.

Example: to my trustees Tim and Tom to hold for A for life, remainder to such of my nephews and nieces as A may decide, but in default of appointment, to my sister absolutely.

In this example, A has the power to decide who receives the property after him. A would stipulate in his **will** which nephews or nieces receive the property after he dies. It is as well to stipulate what happens if A fails to choose. This is known as a gift over in default of appointment. Here the property would go to the sister. The whole point of a power of appointment is that A is free to choose or not choose the next beneficiaries. A power is based on *discretion*.

> **Will**—the document that states to whom the property of the deceased should be distributed. A will must be signed by the testator or testatrix and the signature must be witnessed by two people.

4.1.2 Fixed trust

Example: to my trustees Tim and Tom to hold for A for life, remainder to all my nephews and nieces in equal shares.

Here, the trustees must carry out the instructions in the trust to allow A to enjoy the property for his life, and when he dies the property is divided equally between the nephews and nieces. The fixed trust is based on *duty*, not discretion.

4.1.3 Discretionary trust

The settlor or testator might want to be sure that his wishes are carried out, but might also want to ensure that there was some flexibility built in. This can be done by combining the features of a fixed trust with a power of appointment. This is known as a discretionary trust.

Example: to my trustees Tim and Tom to hold for A for life, remainder on trust for such of my nephews and nieces in such shares as my trustees shall in their absolute discretion decide.

Because it is a trust, the trustees must choose one or more of the nephews and nieces to whom to give the property. Who they choose is up to the trustees. There is a mixture of duty *and discretion*.

Settlors and testators are more or less free to combine elements of trusts and powers as they choose. This makes it very difficult to categorize accurately all the different types of trusts and powers that might exist. We will identify four basic types.

Perhaps it is easier to think of a 'sliding scale' from power to fixed trust, where the duties of the trustees or appointor become more onerous and the ability of the beneficiaries to enforce strengthens.

Mere (bare) power— **Fiduciary** power—Non-exhaustive discretionary trust—Exhaustive discretionary trust—Fixed trust.

> **Fiduciary**—a person in a position of trust or confidence, who may act on behalf of their principal. The position of the fiduciary is similar to that of the trustee and the position of the principal is similar to that of the beneficiary.

4.2 Power (mere or bare or personal)

4.2.1 The duties of the appointor

The person who is given the power of appointment is known as the appointor. The appointor is not a trustee and is often a fellow beneficiary. It is A in the examples in 4.1.1. The appointor has no duties to carry out and has unfettered discretion. A can choose someone or not choose someone and does not even have to consider making a choice.

The position of an appointor holding a mere power is contrasted with that of a trustee holding a fiduciary power in:

● **Re Gulbenkian** [1970] AC 508

Lord Reid at 518:

> It may be that when a mere power is given to an individual he is under no duty to exercise it or even to consider whether he should exercise it. But when a power is given to trustees as such, it appears to me that the situation must be different. A settlor or testator who entrusts a power to his trustees must be relying on them in their fiduciary capacity so they cannot simply push aside the power and refuse to consider whether it ought in their judgment to be exercised.

(See 4.3 'Fidiciary power' for fiduciary power.)

4.2.2 The rights of the beneficiaries

The people that the appointor may choose can be referred to as the appointees, beneficiaries, or 'objects' of the power. They are the nephews or nieces in our examples at 4.1.1.

Spes—Latin—hope.

Their legal position is weak, in that they only have a **spes** that they will be chosen.

The appointees are not regarded as having any equitable interest, so they have no right to go to court in order to challenge the decisions of the appointor, which are completely in his or her discretion.

Those entitled in default of appointment have an equitable or legal right to the property. So they do have the right to challenge the decisions of the appointor in court. The usual basis would be that a non-object (someone who is not qualified) has been chosen.

● **Re Dick** [1953] Ch 343

The will of William Dick left property to his youngest daughter, Mrs Sherman, with a power to appoint to her brothers and sisters and their issue. If she did not appoint, the property was to go to her brothers and sisters anyway. Mrs Sherman instead wanted to provide for the family, the Claytons, who looked after her. To do this she appointed by will her sister, but coupled this with a request that her sister should provide an annuity for the family. Her sister was able to challenge this appointment, as she was also one of the beneficiaries entitled in default of appointment.

HELD: This was not permitted, as the property was being diverted away from the objects. This is known as a fraud on a power.

Fiduciary power

4.3.1 The difference between a mere power and a fiduciary power

The difference between a mere power and a fiduciary power is that the fiduciary power is held by *trustees*. The trust, which contains the fiduciary power, will make clear that the trustees hold the power in their trustee capacity and not as beneficiaries, which the trustees might also be, and not as private individuals. If the power was held as a beneficiary or private individual, then it would be a mere power.

4.3.2 The duties of the trustees in a fiduciary power

Trustees have fiduciary duties and therefore they must properly consider their choice.

There are three main aspects of this, according to the following case.

● **Re Hay's Settlement Trusts** [1982] 1 WLR 202

The court was considering a power held by the trustees for such persons or purposes as the trustees shall by deed...executed within 21 years from the date hereof appoint. The trustees could not appoint to the settlor, husband, or past or present trustees.

HELD: Megarry VC at 209:

> In the case of a trust, of course, the trustee is bound to execute it, and if he does not, the court will see to its execution. A mere power is very different.

[Here Megarry VC means a *fiduciary* power. He is contrasting a fiduciary power with a trust, so he is stressing that it is only a power, not a trust.]

> Normally the trustee is not bound to exercise it, and the court will not compel him to do so. That, however, does not mean that he can simply fold his hands and ignore it, for normally he must from time to time consider whether or not to exercise the power, and the court may direct him to do this.
>
> When he does exercise the power, he must, of course (as in the case of all trusts and powers) confine himself to what is authorized, and not go beyond it. But that is not the only restriction. Whereas a person who is not in a fiduciary position is free to exercise the power in any way that he wishes, unhampered by any fiduciary duties, a trustee to whom, as such, a power is given is bound by the duties of his office in exercising that power to do so in a responsible manner according to its purpose. It is not enough for him to refrain from acting capriciously; he must do more. He must 'make such a survey of the range of objects or possible beneficiaries...' as will enable him to carry out his fiduciary duty. He must find out 'the permissible area of selection and then consider responsibly, in individual cases, whether a contemplated beneficiary was within the power and whether, in relation to other possible claimants, a particular grant was appropriate': *In re Baden (No 1)* [1971] AC 424, 449, 457 (Lord Wilberforce).

And at 210:

> If I am right in these views, the duties of a trustee which are specific to a mere power seem to be threefold. Apart from the obvious duty of obeying the trust instrument, and in particular of

making no appointment that is not authorised by it, the trustee must, first, consider periodically whether or not he should exercise the power; secondly, consider the range of objects of the power; and thirdly, consider the appropriateness of individual appointments.

NB: In a fiduciary power, there is nothing to stop the trustees carefully considering and deciding to choose no one. That is why most fiduciary powers contain a 'gift over in default of appointment', i.e. if the trustees do not choose, the property goes to my sister, in our example.

thinking points

Re Hay *[1982] 1 WLR 202* is a useful case on how fiduciary powers and discretionary trusts actually work, but it is not beyond criticism. It usefully summarizes the fiduciary duties of trustees in a discretionary trust and a fiduciary power, but does not satisfactorily distinguish between the two. The trustees of a discretionary trust would have more onerous duties, but exactly what extra things would they have to do? The fiduciary power in Re Hay to appoint to any person or purposes is very wide, but held by Megarry to be precisely defined and therefore passed the certainty of objects test (see 4.9 'Certainty of objects'). But would it be too wide if this were a discretionary trust, where the trustees ultimately have to make a choice of whom to appoint? See A Grubb 'Powers, Trusts and Classes of Objects—Re Hay's Settlements' [1982] Conv 432.

KEY POINT Trustees who hold a fiduciary power cannot just ignore it. Periodically, they must think about whether they want to choose anyone to appoint. They must look at the range of choice open to them, e.g. in *Re Hay* [1982] 1 WLR 202 they could choose practically anyone, but their choice might be more limited, e.g. to the children of the settlor. Then they would have to set up some sort of procedure for choosing amongst the beneficiaries. Do they want to look at personal circumstances, do they want beneficiaries to apply to them, etc.…? The trustees must make their choices in a proper manner, but the point of it being a power is that they may decide to choose no one.

4.3.3 The rights of beneficiaries in a fiduciary power

Objects do not have equitable interests, they only have a *spes* (hope that they are chosen). They can, however, challenge the trustees' decisions, or lack of decisions, if the trustees fail to consider properly or bona fide (in good faith). An example of this can be found in the next case.

● *Turner v Turner* [1984] Ch 100

The settlor, John Turner, appointed his father, sister-in-law, and brother as trustees. None of them knew anything about trusts and the settlor made the decisions. The trustees had power to appoint two members of the Turner family and made three appointments.

HELD: Mervyn Davies J at 110:

Accordingly the trustees exercising a power come under a duty to consider. It is plain on the evidence that here the trustees did not in any way 'consider' in the course of signing the three deeds in question. They did not know they had any discretion during the settlor's lifetime, they did not read or understand the effect of the documents they were signing and what they were doing was not preceded by any discussion. They merely signed when requested. The trustees therefore made appointments in breach of their duty, in that it was their duty to 'consider' before appointing and this they did not do…

The appointments were therefore void.

The consequences of this were that the trustees had to take their decisions again, but this time they were to consider properly. It is possible for the courts to go further than this.

● *Mettoy Pension Trustees v Evans* [1991] 2 All ER 513

The court could instruct the trustees on how to distribute the property; they could appoint new trustees or the court could ask representative beneficiaries to draw up a scheme of distribution.

KEY POINT The rights of the beneficiaries are limited. Although they can force the trustees to consider properly, they cannot compel the trustees to choose them. The beneficiaries do not have any right to the property. The equitable interests belong to those who are entitled in default of appointment.

4.4 Trust power (trust in default of appointment)

This is based on the unusual case of *Burrough v Philcox*.

● *Burrough v Philcox* [1840] 5 My & Cr 72

The testator John Walton gave life interests to his two children and remainders to their issue, but if his children died without leaving any lawful issue, then the survivor of the children should have power to dispose, by will, amongst the nephews and nieces, or their children, either all to one of them or to as many of them as Walton's surviving child should think proper. Walton's children had no children and the survivor died without making any appointment to the nephews and nieces. Walton's will failed to state what was to happen in this situation, i.e. there was no gift over in default of appointment.

HELD: Lord Cottenham at 89:

The question is, whether these nephews and nieces and their children, take any interest in the property, independently of the power; that is, whether the power given to the survivor of the son and daughter is a mere power, and the interests of the nephews and nieces and their children were, therefore, to depend upon the exercise of it, or whether there was a gift to them, subject only to the power of selection given to the survivor of the son and daughter.

> ...when there appears a general intention in favour of a class to be selected by another person, and the particular intention fails, from that selection not being made, the Court will carry into effect the general intention in favour of the class.

> ...and, in such a case, the Court will not permit the objects of the power to suffer by the negligence or conduct of the donee, but fastens upon the property a trust for their benefit.

This seems to comprise a mere or bare power possessed by whichever child survived, which was not exercised (i.e. no choice of object was made). The court decided that, as there was a clear intention to benefit a class, there was then a fixed trust in favour of the objects. This is why the trust in *Burrough v Philcox* (1840) 5 My & Cr 72 is sometimes referred to as a 'trust power'. It can be confusing, as discretionary trusts, our next category, are also sometimes called 'trust powers'. The language used by Lord Cottenham can also seem to describe a discretionary trust. It is probably better to regard this as a unique and different category of trust. The courts have not seemed keen to follow *Burrough v Philcox* as illustrated by *Re Weekes' Settlement* (1897) 1 Ch 289.

4.5 Discretionary trust (sometimes called a trust power or power in the form of a trust)

These are extremely similar to fiduciary powers.

4.5.1 The duties of trustees in a discretionary trust

The trustees have a duty to consider their choice, as with fiduciary powers in 4.3 'Fiduciary power'. It is thought that the trustees must choose more carefully in a discretionary trust than in a fiduciary power.

● *McPhail v Doulton* [1971] AC 424

Lord Wilberforce at 457:

> As to the trustees' duty of enquiry or ascertainment...in each case the trustees ought to make such a survey of the range of objects or possible beneficiaries as will enable them to carry out their fiduciary duty. A wider and more comprehensive range of enquiry is called for in the case of trust powers [discretionary trusts] than in the case of powers.

One difference between a fiduciary power and a discretionary trust is that the discretionary trust is a *trust* and the trustees must distribute the trust property, i.e. they must come to a decision. This is summarized in *Re Hay's Settlement Trusts*.

● **Re Hay's Settlement Trusts** [1982] 1 WLR 202

Sir Robert Megarry VC at 213–14:

> I consider that the duties of trustees under a discretionary trust are more stringent than those of trustees under a power of appointment [see, for example, *In re Baden (No.1)* [also called *McPhail v Doulton* [1971] AC 424]], and as at present advised I think that I would, if necessary, hold that an intermediate trust such as that in the present case is void as being administratively unworkable. In my view there is a difference between a power and a trust in this respect. The essence of that difference, I think, is that beneficiaries under a trust have rights of enforcement which mere objects of a power lack.

4.5.2 The rights of beneficiaries under a discretionary trust

The objects only have a *spes* (hope) that they are chosen, but they can challenge the trustees' decisions, or lack of decisions, if they can prove that the trustees did not consider properly or did not decide bona fide (in good faith). This was explained in the following case.

● **Gartside v IRC** [1968] AC 553

Lord Reid at 605:

> There are in some of the cases indications of a view that, while each of the objects of a discretionary trust has an interest in the trust fund, this does not extend to the whole or any part of the interest accruing from the fund. But on the other hand, all the objects together have a single class or group interest which does extend to the whole interest of the fund.

At 606:

> No object of a discretionary trust has, as such, any legal right to or in the capital. His sole interest, if it be an 'interest' within the scope of these provisions, is with regard to the income: he can require the trustees to exercise, in bona fide, their discretion as to how it shall be distributed, and he can take and enjoy whatever part of the income the trustees choose to give him.

The *trust* property 'belongs' to the beneficiaries and they could combine together to claim this property and end the trust. This is known as the rule in *Saunders v Vautier* (1841) 4 Beav 115. (See 14.1 'Adult beneficiaries'.) In discretionary trusts it is usually impossible to list all the beneficiaries (see 4.9 'Certainty of objects'), so this is usually only a theoretical possibility.

A rare example of *all* the beneficiaries of a discretionary trust being able to combine together to end the trust can be found in *Re Smith* [1928] Ch 915. There were only four beneficiaries.

● **Re Smith** [1928] Ch 915

The trustees held a fund on trust 'to pay or apply the whole or any part of the annual income...thereof or if they shall think fit from time to time any part of the capital thereof unto and for the maintenance and personal support and benefit of...Lilian Aspinall'. After her death the remaining income and capital were to be held on trust for her sons who attained 21 and her daughters who attained 21 and married. Mrs Aspinall had three children, all of whom were 21 and one of whom had died. She was past the age of childbearing.

HELD: Romer J at 917:

> Mrs Aspinall, the two surviving children and the representatives of the deceased child are between them entitled to the whole fund. In those circumstances it appears to me, notwithstanding the discretion which is reposed in the trustees, under which discretion they could select one or more of the people I have mentioned as recipients of the income, and might apply part of the capital for the benefit of Mrs Aspinall and so take it away from the children, that the four of them, if they were all living, could come to the Court and say to the trustees: 'Hand over the fund to us'.

The trustees do not have to explain to the beneficiaries how they have exercised their discretion, as can be seen in the following case.

● *Re Beloved Wilkes Charity* [1851] 3 Mac & G 440

Lord Truro LC at 447:

> The question, therefore, is, whether it was the duty of the trustees to enter into particulars, or whether the law is not, that trustees who are appointed to execute a trust according to discretion, that discretion to be influenced by a variety of circumstances . . . are not bound to go into a detail of the grounds upon which they come to their conclusion, their duty being satisfied by shewing that they have considered the circumstances of the case, and have come to their conclusion accordingly.

KEY POINT Under a discretionary trust, the trustees must consider more carefully than in a fiduciary power, because, ultimately, they must choose some beneficiaries to whom to distribute the property. Individual beneficiaries still have no right to the trust property, but collectively the trust property belongs to all of the beneficiaries.

4.5.3 Exhaustive and non-exhaustive discretionary trusts

It is possible further to subdivide discretionary trusts into two types: exhaustive where the trustees are instructed to distribute all the money, and non-exhaustive where the trustees are told that they can keep some of the money back. The difference would be in the wording of the trust instrument. A non-exhaustive discretionary trust would include words such as 'surplus' and 'accumulate'.

(a) Exhaustive:

● *Re Locker's Settlement Trusts* [1978] 1 All ER 216

The terms of this trust were that ' . . . the trustees shall . . . pay, divide or apply the income of the trust fund to or between or for the maintenance, support, education or benefit of all or any one or more to the exclusion of the other or others of the beneficiaries as the trustees shall in their absolute discretion determine'. Their discretion was described as 'absolute and uncontrolled'. The trustees did not make a distribution between 1965 and 1968, and asked the court's advice on whether they should do so.

HELD: Goulding J: Contrasted this trust with a fiduciary power and a non-exhaustive discretionary trust and told the trustees it was their duty to distribute for those years.

At 1325:

> It is common ground that it was the duty of the trustees to distribute the trust income within a reasonable time after it came into their hands.

And at 1326:

> In the case of an obligatory power (in other words a compelling trust to distribute), the failure to execute the trust promptly is an unfulfilled duty still in existence.

This decision can be contrasted with the fiduciary power case *Turner v Turner* in 4.3.3. There the trustees were told to consider again, because unlike a discretionary trust, in a fiduciary power the trustees do not have to choose anyone and the property does not belong to the beneficiaries.

(b) Non-exhaustive. There must be an express power to accumulate.

. . . .
● *Gartside v IRC* [1968] AC 553

A discretionary trust for the maintenance or benefit of all or any of his son, his son's wife, or children, accumulate the surplus income as an addition to capital with power at any time to resort to the accumulations and to apply them as current income.

The difference between an exhaustive and non-exhaustive discretionary trust can be very subtle.

. . . .
● *Sainsbury v IRC* [1970] Ch 712

The trustees held the property on trust to apply the income at the trustees' absolute discretion for Elsie Sainsbury during her life and to accumulate the surplus income for 21 years after the testator's death. The trust then went on to say that this surplus should be applied for the benefit of her husband and issue and the testator's other children and issue. This was an exhaustive discretionary trust.

HELD: Ungoed-Thomas J at 723:

> *Gartside* was non-exhaustive in that it did not require the whole of the income to be distributed between the objects: whereas in our case that trusts are exhaustive in the sense that the trustees are required to distribute the whole of the income and have merely discretion as to whether any and what part of the whole which must be distributed is to be distributed to or for the benefit of any individual object.

KEY POINT Non-exhaustive discretionary trusts and fiduciary powers look very similar. The difference would be that in a fiduciary power the trustees do not have to choose any beneficiaries and could distribute no money at all. In a non-exhaustive discretionary trust they would have to make some choices and distribute some of the money, they just do not need to distribute it all. It all depends upon what the wording of the trust tells them to do and, as we can see in *Sainsbury v IRC* [1970] Ch 712, how that wording is interpreted.

4.6 The three certainties

It is a basic principle of trust law that, for a trust or fiduciary power to be valid, it must satisfy the three certainties. This was laid down by Lord Eldon in the early 19th century and has been accepted ever since.

....

● ***Wright v Atkyns*** [1823] Turn & R 143

Lord Eldon at 157:

> In order to determine whether the trust is a trust this court will interfere with, it is a matter of observation, first that the words must be imperative, secondly, that the subject must be certain and, thirdly, that the object must be as certain as the subject.

4.7 Certainty of intention

Equity looks to the intent rather than the form. Has the settlor/testator used sufficiently imperative words to impose an equitably binding obligation? There is a difference between a request which forms an unenforceable *moral* obligation and an instruction which forms a binding *equitable* obligation. Only the equitable obligation will be enforced by the courts.

4.7.1 Older cases involving precatory words

In early trust cases the courts took a very generous attitude and often accepted that a trust had been created even if words like 'confidence', 'wish', 'belief', 'desire', or 'hope' were used rather than 'trust'. After 1858, the Court of Chancery took over cases involving wills from the ecclesiastical courts and took a stricter approach. **Precatory words** were not regarded as creating a binding trust.

....

Precatory words—
requesting words.

....

Just asking someone to do something with the property is not enough to establish a trust; the words used must tell them what they must do with the property.

....

● ***Lambe v Eames*** [1871] 6 Ch App 597

The will of the testator left his estate to his widow 'to be at her disposal in any way she may think fit, for the benefit of herself and her family'. His widow tried to dispose of some of the property outside the family.

HELD: The words used meant that this was just a gift, with a request as to how she used the property. It was not a trust, so the property was hers to do with as she liked.

● **Re Adams & the Kensington Vestry** (1884) LR 27 ChD 394

The will of the testator left all his property to his wife, Harriet Smith, 'in full confidence that she will do what is right as to the disposal thereof between my children, either in her lifetime or by will after her decease...'.

HELD: Cotton LJ at 409:

> The motive of the gift is, in my opinion, not a trust imposed upon her by the gift in the will. He leaves the property to her; he knows that she will do what is right, and carry out the moral obligation which he thought lay on him, and on her if she survived him, to provide for the children.

There are no special words that create a trust. The court must look at all the words used and 'spell out' the intention of the testator. This can be seen in the next case.

● **Comisky v Bowring-Hanbury** [1905] AC 84

The will of the testator left all his property to his wife

> in full confidence that she will make use of it as I should have made myself and that at her death she will devise it to such one or more of my nieces as she may think fit and in default of any disposition by her thereof by her will...I hereby direct that all my estate and property acquired by her under this my will shall at her death be equally divided among the surviving said nieces.

HELD: This was a trust. Although the wording seems vague at first with the phrase 'in full confidence' used again, the greater detail on how the property is to be divided indicates a trust.

4.7.2 More modern declarations of trust

In some of the more modern cases, the courts seem to have taken a more relaxed attitude to the words necessary to create a trust. These cases involve oral declarations of trust, though, where perhaps precise language is not to be expected. The principle remains the same: to discover the true intention of the settlor. It is not necessary to use the word 'trust'. What the settlor did with the property can support what he said.

● **Paul v Constance** [1977] 1 WLR 527

Mr Constance was separated from his wife and living with Ms Paul. He received £950 in damages from an accident at work and he and Paul decided to put it into a deposit account at the bank. Because they were embarrassed at opening an account in joint names, the account was in Mr Constance's name only. Mr Constance died and his wife claimed the money in the account. Ms Paul claimed that Mr Constance held the money on trust for her.

HELD: Scarman LJ at 532:

> When one bears in mind the unsophisticated character of the deceased and his relationship with the plaintiff during the last years of his life, Mr Wilson submits that the words that he did use on more than one occasion, 'this money is as much yours as mine', convey clearly a

present declaration that the existing fund was as much the plaintiff's as his own. The judge accepted that conclusion. I think that he was well justified in doing so and, indeed, I think that he was right to do so.

● *Hunter v Moss* [1994] 3 All ER 452

Mr Moss employed Mr Hunter to work for his company. The company had 1,000 shares and Mr Moss had 950 of them. He said that he wanted to give Hunter 5 per cent of the shares in the company, but because of tax problems he needed to work out a way of doing this. Mr Moss paid Mr Hunter the dividends on the shares. Later the parties quarrelled and Mr Moss refused to transfer the shares.

HELD: Dillon LJ at 455–6:

> Mr Hunter says that, during that conversation, Mr Moss asked him if he would mind if he, Mr Moss, held on to Mr Hunter's shares for him until a solution was found and that, in the meantime, he would ensure that Mr Hunter received all the dividends that he was entitled to. Mr Hunter is unsure whether Mr Moss said in terms that he would, in the meantime, hold the shares 'in trust' for him, but he says that that is the sense of what Mr Moss said to him.

Then the Lord Justice quoted from the trial judge.

> I find that, as from that conversation in early September 1986, Mr Moss held 5% of MEL's issued shares (i.e. 50 shares) on trust for Mr Hunter. Even if he did not in terms use the words 'in trust', the sense of what he then said was that he would thenceforth hold the shares on such a trust.

● *Gold v Hill* [1999] 1 FLR 54

Mr Gilbert was married to Antoinette Gilbert and made a will naming his solicitor, Mr Hill, as the executor, leaving his estate to Antoinette or if she died to his two daughters by his previous wife, Jennifer. There were four other children by a wife before Jennifer, but these were not mentioned in the will.

Mr Gilbert left Antoinette and began living with Carol, who changed her name to Gilbert. Carol had two children by her previous marriage. Mr Gilbert never divorced his wife, Antoinette.

KEY POINT
There is no 'test' to decide whether the settlor or testator really intended a trust. All that a court can do is to try to interpret the words used.

Mr Gilbert was a deep sea diver and took out a life insurance policy through his company. He completed the company's 'enrolment card' nominating the beneficiary as Max Gold, who was Carol's solicitor, and described him as 'executor'. At dinner in the Beverley Arms hotel he told Mr Gold:

> If anything happens to me you will have to sort things out—you know what to do—look after Carol and the kids. Don't let that bitch get anything.

The law report describes Mr Gilbert as a 'flamboyant character'.

Mr Gilbert died of a heart attack and the two solicitors, Gold and Hill, wanted to know whether the $350,000 insurance payout went to Antoinette or Carol.

HELD: Carnwath LJ at 64:

> Applying that approach, it seems to me that the most likely interpretation of Mr Gilbert's intentions, as expressed in the 'enrolment card' and elaborated by his conversation with Mr Gold, was, as pleaded in the amended statement of claim, namely that he should hold them as trustee for her to apply those moneys for the use and benefit of her children.

Mr Gilbert had declared a trust for 'Carol and the kids'.

4.8 Certainty of subject matter

It is necessary for the settlor or testator clearly to define the trust property and to identify clearly the separate equitable interests of the beneficiaries. One of the problems in determining certainty of subject matter is that the courts have never stated a test, or defined exactly what they are looking for. The underlying principle seems to be that, if there was a problem and the court had to enforce the trust, would they be able to sufficiently identify the trust property to (say) order A to hand it over to B?

4.8.1 Clearly describing the trust property

● *Palmer v Simmonds* [1854] 2 Drew 221

The problem here was that the testatrix had left 'the bulk of my said residuary estate' to Thomas Harrison to hold on trust for various people.

The meaning of residue was clear, but what did 'the bulk' of the residue mean?

HELD: Kindersley VC at 227:

His Honour consulted a dictionary and then said:

> Its popular meaning we all know. When a person is said to have given the bulk of his property, what is meant is not the whole but the greater part ... When, therefore, the testatrix uses that term, can I say she has used a term expressing a definite, clear, certain part of her estate, or the whole of her estate? I am bound to say that she has not designated the subject ...

The problem is that 'bulk' could mean anything between 51 per cent and 99 per cent of the property, so the trust was not established.

It also has to be clear which property goes to which beneficiary.

● *Boyce v Boyce* [1849] 16 Sim 476

A fixed trust was set up by will, which consisted of two houses for two beneficiaries, Maria and Charlotte. Maria was to choose which house she wanted and Charlotte was to have the other. Unfortunately, Maria died before the testator and did not make her selection.

HELD: The trust failed because the beneficial shares were uncertain. It was impossible to know which house Charlotte should have.

This can be contrasted with the following case.

● *Re Golay's Will Trusts* [1965] 1 WLR 969

The will directed the executors 'to let Tossy...Mrs F Bridgewater...to enjoy one of my flats during her lifetime and to receive a reasonable income from my other properties'.

HELD: There was no problem with the flat because, unlike *Boyce v Boyce* (1849) 16 Sim 476, there was still someone able to choose which flat; the executors.

The phrase 'reasonable income' did not cause the trust to fail for uncertainty.

Ungoed-Thomas J at 972:

> The court is constantly involved in making such objective assessments of what is reasonable and it is not to be deterred from doing so because subjective influences can never be wholly excluded.

The court could look at Tossy's current income and standard of life and come up with a figure.

4.8.2 The type of property involved

Certainty of subject matter can depend upon the type of property:

● *Re London Wine* [1986] PCC 121

Customers bought wine, but they did not take it home. Instead, it was stored for them in a number of warehouses. London Wine got into financial difficulty and receivers were appointed. Some customers claimed that their wine was protected because it was held on trust for them. Their lawyers argued that there was no need for a 'direct and express declaration' of trust, because a trust could be created by the actions of the parties involved.

HELD: Oliver J:

> It is with regret that I feel compelled to reject these submissions, for I feel great sympathy with those who paid for their wine and received an assurance that they had title to it. But I find it impossible to spell either out of the acknowledgements signed by the company or out of the circumstances any such trust as is now sought to be set up. It seems to me that in order to create a trust it must be possible to ascertain not only what the interest of the beneficiary is to be but to what property it is to attach.

The objection is that the customer cannot identify specific bottles of wine that belong to them. There might be 1,000 cases of a particular wine in the warehouse and the customer might have paid for 100 cases, but the customer cannot identify which particular cases belong to him. Sometimes customers would be given their certificates of title to the wine before it was even delivered to the warehouse. The trust property must be 'specific or ascertained' for a trust.

A later case came to different conclusions.

● *Hunter v Moss* [1994] 3 All ER 215 (also to be found in 7.7.2)

Moss told Hunter that he would hold 5 per cent of the shares in his company for Hunter. There were 1,000 shares in the company, all the same type of shares, and Moss had previously told

Hunter that he would give him 50 shares. So there was no doubt about the number of shares to be held on trust.

HELD: Dillon LJ at 231 referring to *Re London Wine* [1986] PCC 121:

> It seems to me that that case is a long way from the present. It is concerned with the appropriation of chattels and when the property in chattels passes. We are concerned with a declaration of trust, accepting that the legal title remained in Mr Moss and was not intended, at the time the trust was declared, to pass immediately to Mr Hunter. Mr Moss was to retain the shares as trustee for Mr Hunter.

At 232:

> Just as a person can give, by will, a specified number of his shares of a certain class in a certain company, so equally, in my judgment, he can declare himself trustee of 50 of his ordinary shares in MEL or whatever the company may be and that is effective to give a beneficial proprietary interest to the beneficiary under the trust.

The court could see no problem with this, as all the shares were the same and it did not matter which 50 it was. Presumably, though, 100 cases of Chateau Rotgut 1994 are no different from another 100 cases. *Hunter v Moss* [1994] 3 All ER 215, is a case that has been criticized, but was followed in one of several cases that have resulted from the collapse of Lehman Brothers, the global investment bank.

● ***Re Lehman Brothers International (Europe) (In Administration). Also known as Pearson v Lehman Brothers Finance S.A.*** [2011] EWCA Civ 1544

Lehman brothers took investments from numerous parties in the form of bonds and stocks. These individual deposits were bought and sold and exchanged for other shares and often mixed together with other deposits. Did these deposits have sufficient certainty of subject matter to be held on trust?

HELD: Lloyd LJ at para 70:

> Its duties as such trustee were more limited than those of an ordinary trustee, because it did not have to keep the holding segregated, and could not only mix it with other assets, with different beneficial ownership, but could deal with it, on a short term basis, for its own benefit or that of others than LBF. However, its trusteeship was constituted at once, and difficulties in accounting as a result of what happened later do not subvert the proposition that the securities were held on trust from the time of their first acquisition.

Another case, involving the same company, but decided by the Supreme Court, took a similar line.

● ***Lehman Bros International (Europe) (a company) (in admin), Re*** [2012] 3 All ER 1

Lord Clarke at 59:

> There is no doubt that money in a mixed fund may be held on trust, and that a trust of money can be created without an obligation to keep it in a separate account: *Re Kayford Ltd* [1975] 1 All ER 604 at 607, per Megarry J.

These might seem convenient decisions, giving claimants an extra remedy against Lehmans, but seem to break two basic principles of trust law. It is odd to allow a trustee to use trust property for their own benefit, and as far as certainty of objects goes, it seems to contradict the basic principle, that the courts should be able to identify exactly what property they are granting enforcement against.

KEY POINTS

- Some see the difference in the cases in the type of property involved. Bottles of wine are chattels and therefore have a tangible existence. They can be separated and set aside from other bottles. Shares, though, are intangible property. They are just certificates which grant valuable rights. It is not possible to actually pick up a share and put it in another place.

- Another difference is that there was an actual declaration of trust in *Hunter v Moss* [1994] 3 All ER 215. In *Re London Wine* [1986] PCC 121 it was merely a somewhat theoretical argument that there could be a trust.

thinking points

Is there really any difference between a trust of 100 bottles of wine and a trust of 100 shares? David Hayton was not convinced by the distinction between tangible and intangible property and did not think that the court in Hunter v Moss *considered the matter sufficiently.* Hunter v Moss *does not seem to follow previous cases such as* Re London Wine *and* MacJordan Construction Ltd v Brookmount Erostin Ltd *[1992] BCLC 350. See D Hayton 'Uncertainty of Subject-Matter of Trusts' (1994) 110 LQR 335.*

(4.9) Certainty of objects

The basic principle, like much else in trusts law, comes from Lord Eldon in the early 19th century.

● *Morice v Bishop of Durham* [1805] 9 Ves Jun 401

The will of Ann Cracherode left all her real and personal estate to the Bishop of Durham 'to such objects of benevolence and liberality as the Bishop of Durham in his own discretion shall most approve of . . .'.

HELD: Lord Eldon at 405:

> If there be a clear trust, but for uncertain objects, the property, that is the subject of the trust, is undisposed of, and the benefit of such trust must result to those, to whom the law gives the ownership in default of disposition by the former owner. But this doctrine does not hold good with regard to trusts for charity. Every other trust must have a definite object. There must be somebody, in whose favour the court can decree performance.

The will did not fall into any of the Four Heads of Charity (see Chapter 10 'Charitable trusts'), so it failed the certainty test and the property returned on resulting trust to the estate of Cracherode.

Therefore, all trusts, except charities, must have identifiable human beneficiaries.

The court needs to know who the beneficiaries are, because they need to know who has the right to sue the trustees. Ultimately, trust property belongs to the beneficiaries, so the court also needs to know who all the beneficiaries are, in case the property has to be divided between the beneficiaries.

The trustees need to know who the beneficiaries are, so that they can correctly distribute the property to them.

4.9.1 Certainty of objects in fixed trusts

The traditional rule and the rule for *fixed trusts* (see 4.1.2 'Fixed trusts') is that the number and identity of the beneficiaries must be known. It must be possible to make a *list* of all the beneficiaries: in other words, identify all of them. (This is known as the Rule of Exhaustive Enumeration.) The court would read the words used in the trust and decide whether this was possible. If it was not, the trust fails and the property results back to the settlor or testator.

● ***OT Computers Ltd v First National Tricity Finance Ltd*** [2003] EWHC 1010

OT traded as Tiny Computers and was making large losses. So it instructed its bank to open two separate trust accounts: one for customers' deposits and one to pay 'urgent suppliers'. The company went into receivership, so if these were valid trusts the money there would be protected from other creditors and held on trust for the customers and urgent suppliers, respectively.

HELD: There was no difficulty about the customers' trust. The beneficiaries could be clearly identified. What is more, the company had actually created a list of customers.

The urgent suppliers trust was not valid because the word 'urgent' was too vague. The company had made a partial list of suppliers, but even if it had been a full list it would have made no difference, as 'urgent' was too vague to define any class of beneficiaries.

● ***Gold v Hill*** [1999] 1 FLR 54

This was a trust for 'Carol and the kids'. Mr Gilbert had six children from previous marriages. (This case also appears in 4.7.2, on the issue of whether it was a trust at all.)

HELD: Carnwath J at 64:

As to certainty, Mr Chapman submits that a trust for 'Carol and the kids' is insufficiently precise, first as to which of Mr Gilbert's children by his various relationships were intended to be included, and secondly as to the nature of the interest as between Carol and the children respectively. I can see no serious doubt that the 'kids' referred to were Carol's children. The children by Mr Gilbert's previous marriages were grown up and would hardly have been referred to as 'kids'. In any event, Mr Gilbert had been recently living with and maintaining Carol's children, and the remark was made at a dinner in Carol's presence.

As to the precise terms of the trust, there is potential ambiguity in the words used, but the general intention is clear, that it is to provide help for Carol to look after herself and her children.

[It could be interpreted in several ways: to Carol, to the three of them jointly, to Carol on trust, etc.]

> It would be unfortunate if the difficulty of distinguishing precisely between these possibilities, which are probably of little practical difference, should have the effect of defeating the gift altogether and producing a result directly contrary to Mr Gilbert's intention.

The judge then quoted Lord Upjohn in *Re Gulbenkian's Settlements* [1970] AC 508 at 522 (see 4.9.7 'Applying the certainty of objects test to a discretionary trust') that the task of the courts was to use their common sense to try to make sense of what a settlor or testator really meant and not just strike it down for lack of certainty.

So, the courts must be satisfied that the beneficiaries are identifiable, but must try to interpret the terms of a trust in a reasonable and realistic way.

4.9.2 Certainty of objects in fiduciary powers

The exhaustive enumeration or list rule would make most fiduciary powers invalid, because the class of objects is usually a large and fluctuating group of individuals. It would be very difficult or impossible to draw up a complete list of all the beneficiaries. Even if such a list were made, the beneficiaries might change within a few days. For example, it might be possible to list all the employees of a company, but employees leave and employees join, so soon the list would be wrong.

The issue came before the courts in the early 1950s. Settlors and testators were increasingly using fiduciary powers with large classes of beneficiaries, both to provide maximum flexibility and to reduce tax liability. The courts do not wish to strike down the wishes of the settlor or testator, unless they absolutely have to do so. In the following case, the courts worked out a way of allowing such wide fiduciary powers.

. . . .

● **Re Gestetner** [1953] Ch 672

The trustees had a power to make gifts to any of the following class:

(a) four named individuals;

(b) any person living or thereafter to be born who was a descendant of the settlor's father David Gestetner or of his uncle Jacob Gestetner;

(c) spouse, widow, or widower of aforesaid;

(d) five named charities;

(e) former employee, widow, or widower of former employee of settlor and his wife;

(f) employee or director, former employee or director, wife or husband or widow or widower of former director or employee of Gestetner Ltd. Or of any company which had one or more directors who were also directors of Gestetner Ltd.

HELD: Harman J at 683:

> It is impossible to know at any one moment the names of all the members of the specified class.

At 684:

> ...powers which do not impose a trust upon the conscience of the donee, then I do not think that it can be the law that it is necessary to know of all the objects in order to appoint to one of them.

KEY POINT
The list principle, or rule of exhaustive enumeration, requires a high degree of precision in the definition of who the beneficiaries are.

At 688:

> ...but there is not...any duty, as I see it, on the trustees to distribute the whole of either income or capital among the members of the specified class; and if the whole of those members could join together, they could still, as I understand it, not divide the fund between them...there is no obligation on the trustees to do more than consider—from time to time—I suppose—the merits of such persons of the specified class as are known to them and, if they think fit, to give them something.
>
> In fact, there is no difficulty, as has been admitted, in ascertaining whether any given postulant is a member of the specified class.

And at 689:

> There is no uncertainty in so far as it is quite certain whether particular individuals are objects of the power. What is not certain is how many objects there are.

A new test for certainty of objects was being proposed which was: 'In fact there is no difficulty, as has been admitted, in ascertaining whether any given postulant is a member of the specified class.'

The idea is that the court reads the definition of the category or class of beneficiary and decides whether the class of objects is defined with sufficient precision. We imagine that any possible person in the world comes forward to claim under the fiduciary power. Looking at the words used to describe the category of objects in the fiduciary power, we should be able to decide whether they qualify or, in other words, meet the definition. It would be possible to tell whether someone is an employee, director, or widow, for example.

The theory behind this is that a fiduciary power is not a trust, so there is no possibility of all the beneficiaries grouping together to claim the trust property under the rule in *Saunders v Vautier* (see 4.5.2 'The rights of beneficiaries under a discretionary trust'). Therefore, a complete list of beneficiaries is unnecessary. All the trustees need to know is whether someone is qualified or not, so all that is required is a definition of the class of beneficiaries that is clear enough for them to be able to determine that.

4.9.3 What does the new test mean?

Unfortunately the test has proved hard to understand and apply. Some cases have allowed a looser test. In these cases the class of objects is not defined so tightly that it is possible to say of any person that might apply whether they qualify or not. The courts accept a definition of the class, where some people certainly qualify, although there would be other, doubtful cases. The classic examples are powers where a named person can give or appoint property to 'friends' of the testator or settlor.

. . . .

● *Re Coates* [1955] Ch 495

The will included the term: 'If my wife feels that I have forgotten any friend I direct my executors to pay to such friend or friends as are nominated by my wife a sum not exceeding £25 per friend with a maximum aggregate payment of £250, so that such friends may buy a small memento of our friendship'.

HELD: From the summary of the judgment:

(1) It was not essential to the validity of the power of selection conferred on the wife that the whole class of beneficiaries could be ascertained **a priori**.

(2) That having regard to the language and context of the will the wife, or the court with the assistance of her evidence, would have no difficulty in determining whether any **propositus** was or was not a proper object of the power, so that the power did not fail for uncertainty.

. . . .

A priori—Latin—from the start.

Propositus—Latin—anyone who could come forward to claim. Plural 'propositi'.

. . . .

Roxburgh J at 498–9:

> This question of uncertainty is a vexed question. Of course, language draws a series of mental pictures in the mind of the person hearing the words spoken. Those pictures are sometimes fairly well defined, and sometimes blurred in outline, but they are never very precise. Language is a medium which disdains mathematical rules. I, for my part, accept as my guide the words of Lord Tomlin *In re Ogden* [1933] Ch 678 at 682:
>
> > The question is one of degree in each case, whether, having regard to the language of the will, and the circumstances of the case, there is such uncertainty as to justify the court coming to the conclusion that the gift is bad.

Coates was considered in *Re Gibbard*.

. . . .

● **Re Gibbard** [1966] 1 All ER 273

Part of the will of Mark Gibbard allowed the survivor of two named persons to leave money by will to '…any of our old friends…'. They were to consult with his solicitor, Jervis, before choosing and were not to give any money to 'idlers'!

HELD: Plowman J interpreted the certainty test to mean that it would be satisfied if at least one person would definitely qualify as a 'friend'. It was clear that at least some people could be identified as 'friends', although there might be many doubtful cases.

At 49:

> Applying that test to the present case, is it impossible for any conceivable person who comes along and says 'I am an old friend of the testator' to show that he is within that description? It does not seem to me that it is…suppose that the testator had been at preparatory school with X and had gone on from prep. school to public school with X, and then to University with X; each had become god-father to one of the other's children, perhaps lived in the same neighbourhood, perhaps belonged to the same club, perhaps played golf together, perhaps dined in each other's house and had been doing that for 50 years. Could X, coming along and stating that that was the relationship between the testator and himself, fail to satisfy the description 'any of my old friends'?

thinking points

- *Those of you who read 4.2 carefully might note that these two cases actually involve mere or bare powers of appointment, rather than fiduciary powers, because the person holding the power is not a trustee. The courts are not making any distinction in the certainty test required.*
- *Do you think that the word 'friend' is a word with a clear-cut meaning? Could you say for certain whether someone was your friend or not? Or does it depend upon what we mean by friend?*

4.9.4 Restating the certainty of objects test

The issue returned to the House of Lords in the case of *Re Gulbenkian*.

· ·

● *Re Gulbenkian* [1970] AC 508

The House disapproved of the two 'friends' cases *Re Coates* [1955] Ch 495 and *Re Gibbard* [1966] 1 All ER 273 which we have just considered and reasserted the *Re Gestetner* [1953] Ch 672 test.

Part of the trust was a fiduciary power which stated that the trustees:

> shall at their absolute discretion pay all or any part of the income of the property hereby settled and the investments for the time being representing the same (hereinafter called the trust fund) to or apply the same for the maintenance and personal support or benefit of all or any one or more ... of the following persons ...

> any person or persons in whose house or apartments or in whose company or under whose care and control or by or with whom the said Nubar Sarkis Gulbenkian may from time to time be residing.

Nubar was a wealthy person who could not be trusted with money, so the trustees were being given power to pay for everything that he needed.

HELD: Lord Upjohn at 521:

> ... a mere or bare power of appointment

[he actually means fiduciary power, but he says mere power to contrast it with a discretionary trust]

> among a class is valid if you can with certainty say whether any given individual is or is not a member of the class; you do not have to be able to ascertain every member of the class.

At 524 he disapproved of 'my old friend' type cases unless there is evidence that the testator further identified them. One could say that one particular person qualified, but that was not enough.

> But I should add this: if the class is sufficiently defined by the donor the fact that it may be difficult to ascertain the whereabouts or continued existence of some of its members at the relevant time matters not.

KEY POINT The certainty of objects test for a fiduciary power of appointment among a class is that it is valid if you can with certainty say whether any given individual is or is not a member of the class; you do not have to be able to ascertain every member of the class. The last part decisively rejects the older certainty test: that it must be possible to list every object of the fiduciary power.

A way around this strict test is to set up a class that is so wide that everyone in the world qualifies. That way no one can be outside the class.

As part of the trust, the trustees had power to appoint to various members of Edward Manisty's immediate family. The trustees also had the power to add to the list of beneficiaries any person or persons, corporation or corporations, or charity or charities that they thought fit. There was an excluded class of persons, which they could not add, including the settlors and their wives.

The trustees wanted to know whether this power was too wide to be valid.

HELD: Templeman J at 23:

This passed the certainty test.

> In my judgment, however, the mere width of a power cannot make it impossible for trustees to perform their duty nor prevent the court from determining whether the trustees are in breach.

In reality, the trustees would only add other members of the Manisty family as beneficiaries.

Widely drafted powers are also acceptable in wills.

● *Re Beatty* [1990] 3 All ER 844

The testatrix bequeathed her personal estate and a legacy of £1.5 million to her trustees to 'allocate...to or among such person or persons...as they think fit'.

4.9.5 Certainty of objects in discretionary trusts

The traditional approach

Discretionary trusts look very like fiduciary powers in that the trustees have to choose amongst a large and fluctuating class of beneficiaries. Originally, however, the fixed trust certainty rule of exhaustive enumeration was applied here. (See 4.9.1 'Certainty of objects in fixed trusts'.)

● *IRC v Broadway Cottages Trust* [1955] Ch 20

Alan Timpson gave money to his trustees, of which he was one, for the trustees on trust to apply income for the benefit of all or any of a class of beneficiaries...in such shares, proportions, and manner as the trustees in their absolute discretion thought fit.

(a) All persons past and present employed by the settlor, wife of settlor, father of settlor, mother of settlor, William Timpson Ltd or successor and other Limited Companies of which the settlor is a director.

(b) Wives or widows of the above.

(c) All issue, however remote, of the settlor and wife's fathers.

(d) Named persons and their spouses and issue.

(e) Godchildren of the settlor and wife.

(f) Broadway Cottages and Sunnylands Trust charities.

Settlement—this is another word for trust. It often refers to a trust established in order to provide for a family. A settlement is usually made in a deed.

> ...the beneficiaries for the purposes of the **settlement**, comprise an aggregate of objects which is incapable of ascertainment, in the sense that it would be impossible at any given time to achieve a complete and exhaustive enumeration of all the persons then qualified for inclusion in the class of beneficiaries...
>
> ...the trust...must be void for uncertainty, inasmuch as there can be no division in equal shares amongst a class of persons unless all the members of the class are known.

The court still felt itself bound by *Morice v Bishop of Durham* (see 4.9 'Certainty of objects') and felt that they must know the identity of all the beneficiaries, in case they had to equally divide the trust property. This did not apply to fiduciary powers, because ultimately the property belongs to the beneficiaries entitled in default of appointment.

4.9.6 The modern certainty of objects test for discretionary trusts

Finally, the House of Lords decided to regularize the position. In many cases it was argued that the instrument was really a fiduciary power to take advantage of the more generous certainty test. In *McPhail v Doulton* [1971] AC 424, the High Court and Court of Appeal thought that they were looking at a fiduciary power. The House of Lords decided it was a discretionary trust, but it did not matter much what it was, for the certainty test should be the same.

● ***McPhail v Doulton*** [1971] AC 424

In 1941 Bertram Baden set up trusts for the employees of Matthew Hall and Co Ltd and their relatives and dependants. Clause 9(a) caused the court problems and it read:

> The trustees shall apply the net income of the fund in making at their absolute discretion grants to or for the benefit of any of the officers and employees or ex-officers and ex-employees of the company or to any relatives or dependants of any such persons in such amounts, at such times and in such conditions (if any) as they think fit.

The trustees did not have to exhaust the income of any one year in making these distributions.

HELD: Lord Wilberforce: He decided that what the court was considering was a discretionary trust.

Extracts from 448–57:

> Naturally read, the intention of the deed seems to me clear: clause 9(a), whose language is mandatory ('shall'), creates together with a power of selection, a trust for distribution of the income, the strictness of which is qualified by clause 9(b), which allows the income of any one year to be held up and (under clause 6(a)) either placed, for the time, with a bank, or if thought fit, invested.

The use of the mandatory word 'shall' was the crucial test.

His Lordship went on to say that there was no great difference between fiduciary powers and discretionary trusts.

> Before dealing with these two questions some general observations, or reflections, may be permissible. It is striking how narrow and in a sense artificial is the distinction, in cases such as the present, between trusts or as the particular type of trust is called, trust powers, and powers.

[Discretionary trusts as opposed to fiduciary powers.]

> A layman and, I suspect, also a logician would find it hard to understand what difference there is.
>
> It does not seem satisfactory that the entire validity of a disposition should depend on such delicate shading. And if one considers how in practice reasonable and competent trustees would act, and ought to act, in the two cases, surely a matter very relevant to the question of validity, the distinction appears even less significant.
>
> Any trustee would surely make it his duty to know what is the permissible area of selection and then consider responsibly, in individual cases, whether a contemplated beneficiary was within the power and whether, in relation to other possible claimants, a particular grant was appropriate.
>
> Correspondingly a trustee with a duty to distribute, particularly among a potentially very large class, would surely never require the preparation of a complete list of names, which anyhow would tell him little that he needs to know.
>
> Assuming, as I am prepared to do for present purposes, that the test of validity is whether the trust can be executed by the court, it does not follow that execution is impossible unless there can be equal division.
>
> I would venture to amplify this by saying that the court, if called upon to execute the trust power, will do so in the manner best calculated to give effect to the settlor's or testator's intentions. It may do so by appointing new trustees, or by authorising or directing representative persons of the classes of beneficiaries to prepare a scheme of distribution, or even, should the proper basis for distribution appear by itself directing the trustees so to distribute.

So the 'list' certainty test did not need to be used for discretionary trusts, because there would never be a need to divide the trust property equally.

> So I think that we are free to review the *IRC v Broadway Cottages Trust* [1955] Ch 20 case. The conclusion which I would reach, implicit in the previous discussion, is that the wide distinction between the validity test for powers and that for trust powers is unfortunate and wrong, that the rule recently fastened upon the courts by *IRC v Broadway Cottages Trust* ought to be discarded, and the test for the validity of trust powers ought to be similar to that accepted by this House in *Re Gulbenkian* [1970] AC 508 for powers, namely, that the trust is valid if it can be said with certainty that any given individual is or is not a member of the class.

[Powers mean fiduciary powers and trust powers mean discretionary trusts.]

The certainty test is now the same for fiduciary powers and discretionary trusts.

> I desire to emphasise the distinction . . . between linguistic and semantic uncertainty which, if unresolved by the court, renders the gift void, and the difficulty of ascertaining the existence or whereabouts of members of the class, a matter with which the court can appropriately deal on an application for directions.

The certainty of objects test requires the words used to define the class clearly or the trust is void. This is not the same as whether the beneficiaries can actually be located, once the trustees have decided to exercise their discretion in their favour.

thinking points

McPhail v Doulton [1971] AC 424 was thought at the time to be an important change in the law. To understand the background to the case see Y Grbich 'Baden: Awakening the Conceptually Moribund Trust' (1974) 37 MLR 643. The article makes the dramatic claim that '[t]his crucial decision has given legitimacy to a much wider and more flexible concept of trust'. By not insisting on the listing of every beneficiary in order to pass the certainty of objects test, McPhail v Doulton recognizes that it is not essential in a trust for each beneficiary to have an identifiable piece of trust property or, as he puts it, 'each beneficiary has a finite right to a finite portion of the trust fund'. Instead, under a discretionary trust, each beneficiary has a right for their claims to be properly considered, which enables them to enforce the trust.

KEY POINT The certainty of objects test for discretionary trusts states that the trust is valid if it can be said with certainty that any given individual is or is not a member of the class.

4.9.7 Applying the certainty of objects test to a discretionary trust

The case was then sent to the High Court, in order to apply the new certainty test to the facts, where it was heard by Brightman J. It was appealed to the Court of Appeal in the following case.

. . . .

● ***Re Baden (No 2)*** [1973] Ch 9

The judges had difficulty applying the test. The House of Lords above had given a strong hint that they thought the discretionary trust was valid. The words 'dependant' and 'relative' caused problems. Do they have a clear and agreed meaning?

It had been argued that this discretionary trust failed the certainty of objects test, if it was impossible to prove that a potential applicant was *not* in the class, e.g. if it was impossible to prove that a potential applicant was *not* a relative.

HELD: This argument was rejected and all three judges thought that the discretionary trust was valid, but for different reasons!

Sachs LJ at 20:

> Once the class of persons to be benefited is conceptually certain it then becomes a question of fact to be determined on evidence whether any postulant has on inquiry been proved to be within it: if he is not so proved, then he is not in it. That position remains the same whether the class to be benefited happens to be small (such as 'first cousins') or large (such as 'members' of the X Trade Union' or 'those who have served in the Royal Navy'). The suggestion that such trusts could be invalid because it might be impossible to prove of a given individual that he was not in the relevant class is wholly fallacious . . .

At 21–2:

> As regards 'relatives' Brightman J, after stating, at 625, at 995, 'It is not in dispute that a person is a relative of an . . . employee . . . , if both trace legal descent from a common ancestor'; a little later said: 'In practice, the use of the expression 'relatives' cannot cause the slightest difficulty.

Megaw LJ at 24:

> In my judgment, much too great emphasis is placed in the executor's argument on the words 'or is not'. To my mind, the test is satisfied if, as regards at least a substantial number of

objects, it can be said with certainty that they fall within the trust; even though, as regards a substantial number of other persons, if they ever for some fanciful reason fell to be considered, the answer would have to be, not that 'they are outside the trust', but 'it is not proven whether they are in or out.' What is a 'substantial number' may well be a question of common sense and of degree in relation to the particular trust: particularly where, as here, it would be fantasy, to use a mild word, to suggest that any practical difficulty would arise in the fair, proper and sensible administration of this trust in respect of relatives and dependants.

Stamp LJ at 28:

Validity or invalidity is to depend upon whether you can say of any individual—and the accent must be on that word 'any' for it is not simply the individual whose claim you are considering who is spoken of—[that he] 'is or is not a member of the class', for only thus can you make a survey of the range of objects or possible beneficiaries.

If the matter rested there, it would in my judgment follow that, treating the word 'relatives' as meaning descendants from a common ancestor, a trust for distribution such as here in question would not be valid.

At 29:

…a discretionary trust for 'relations' was a valid trust to be executed by the court by distribution to the next of kin. The class of beneficiaries thus becomes a clearly defined class and there is no difficulty in determining whether a given individual is within it or without it.

Sachs LJ accepts that the test is about conceptual certainty: can the class of beneficiaries be defined with sufficient precision so that there can be no doubt who qualifies?

Stamp LJ agrees. Where they differ is in their definition of the problem word 'relative'. Sachs LJ has a wide definition of descent from a common ancestor, but Stamp LJ uses a phrase 'next of kin', that is often used in wills and trusts and has the advantage of a statutorily defined meaning, i.e. near, blood relative. Despite this difference, both judges think that one can tell whether someone is a relative or not.

Megaw LJ is not sure. He thinks that usually one can tell whether someone is a relative or not, but that there would be some, doubtful, borderline cases.

---

thinking points

How easy is it to apply this certainty test? See CT Emery 'The Most Hallowed Principle—Certainty of Beneficiaries in Trusts and Powers of Appointment' (1982) 98 LQR 551. Emery helps us to think more clearly about the certainty of objects rule by looking at how it works in fixed trusts, conditions precedent, fiduciary powers, the discretionary trust in Burrough v Philcox, and the discretionary trust in McPhail v Doulton. He explains that there are four different certainty 'problems' and confusion has been caused by failing to distinguish between them. They are conceptual certainty, where the language must be precise enough to define the class; evidential certainty, where the issue is the evidence needed to identify specific members of the class; ascertainability, which is discovering the whereabouts or continued existence of members of the class; and administrative workability, which is whether it is practicable for the trustees to discharge their duties. The main certainty problem in fiduciary powers and discretionary trusts is the first one, conceptual certainty.

The problem with the certainty of objects test is that it is really about the meaning of words and whether a testator or settlor could ever use words, where there would be absolutely no doubt about what they meant. This is considered in the case below.

● *Re Hay's Settlement Trusts* [1982] 1 WLR 202

Megarry VC at 209:

> It is now well settled that no mere power

[he means fiduciary power, but this also applies to discretionary trusts]

> is invalidated by it being impossible to ascertain every object of the power; provided the language is clear enough to make it possible to say whether any given individual is an object of the power, it need not be possible to compile a complete list of every object.

And at 211:

> Certainly it is not void for linguistic or semantic uncertainty; there is no room for doubt in the definition of those who are or are not objects of the power.

KEY POINT The three judges in *Re Baden (No 2)* [1973] Ch 9 thought that 'relative' was clear enough for the trust to operate without difficulty. They differed, however, in what 'relative' actually meant. That is the problem with this test: different people, even judges, define words in different ways and therefore come to different conclusions upon whether the words used clearly define a class.

The House of Lords had cited a number of old cases where discretionary trusts for relations had been allowed and none of the judges really wanted to obstruct Baden's wishes. One could argue that interpreted literally, 'relatives' is too vague; after all some would argue that the whole human race is related to one another, albeit distantly. But, the courts generally go for a 'realistic' interpretation of problem words in trusts and powers.

● *Re Gulbenkian's Settlements* [1970] AC 508

Lord Upjohn at 522:

> ...very frequently, whether it be in wills, settlements or commercial agreements,...the draftsman has used words wrongly, his sentences border on the illiterate and his grammar may be appalling. It is then the duty of the court by the exercise of its judicial knowledge and experience in the relevant matter, innate common sense and desire to make sense of the settlor's or party's expressed intentions, however obscure and ambiguous the language that may have been used, to give a reasonable meaning to that language if it can do so without doing violence to it. The fact that the court has to see whether the clause is 'certain' for a particular purpose does not disentitle the court from doing otherwise than, in the first place, trying to make sense of it.

4.10 Administrative unworkability

4.10.1 Discretionary trusts

As suggested in *McPhail v Doulton* [1971] AC 424, even if a discretionary trust passes the certainty of objects test, it can still be struck down for *administrative unworkability*, i.e. there are simply too many beneficiaries in the class. The trustees would not be able to do their job of carefully selecting.

● *McPhail v Doulton* [1971] AC 424

Lord Wilberforce at 457:

> There may be a third case where the meaning of the words used is clear but the definition of beneficiaries is so hopelessly wide as not to form 'anything like a class' so that the trust is administratively unworkable or in Lord Eldon's words one that cannot be executed: *Morice v Bishop of Durham* (1805) 10 Ves 522 at 527. I hesitate to give examples for they may prejudice future cases, but perhaps 'all the residents of Greater London' will serve. I do not think that a discretionary trust for 'relatives' even of a living person falls within this category.

Finally, a real case, where there was a huge class of beneficiaries, appeared before the courts.

● *R v District Auditor, ex p West Yorkshire MCC* [1986] RVR 24

In order to try to avoid central government controls over local government spending, West Yorkshire Metropolitan County Council established a trust for the trustees 'to apply and expend the Trust Fund for the benefit of any or all or some of the inhabitants of the County of West Yorkshire'.

HELD: Lloyd LJ at 26:

> The class might be on the large side, containing as it does some two and a half million potential beneficiaries. But the definition, it was said, is straightforward and clear cut. There is no uncertainty as to the concept. If anyone were to come forward and claim to be a beneficiary, it could be said of him at once whether he was within the class or not.
>
> I cannot accept counsel for the county council's argument. I am prepared to assume in favour of the council, without deciding, that the class is defined with sufficient clarity. I do not decide the point because it might, as it seems to me, be open to argument what is meant by 'an inhabitant' of the county of West Yorkshire. But I put that difficulty on one side. For there is to my mind a more fundamental difficulty. A trust with as many as two and a half million potential beneficiaries is, in my judgment, quite simply unworkable.

One might note the caution of the judge, who did not wish to apply the certainty of objects test, as there was an easier way to decide the case. There were too many beneficiaries for the trustees to make a meaningful choice between them, so this discretionary trust failed for administrative unworkability.

4.10.2 Fiduciary powers

A similar approach can be taken for fiduciary powers, which can pass the certainty of objects test, but be struck down for 'capriciousness'. As the trustees do not have to make any choice at all, a fiduciary power could not be called 'administratively unworkable', but if the trustees have to choose amongst a huge class, with no real connection between the members of the class, they might find their task of proper consideration impossible.

• **Re Manisty** [1973] 2 All ER 1203

Templeman J at 27:

> A power to benefit 'residents of Greater London' is capricious because the terms of the power negative any sensible intention on the part of the settlor.

And at 29:

> The settlor neither gives the trustees an unlimited power which they can exercise sensibly, nor a power limited to what may be described a 'sensible' class, but a power limited to a class, membership of which is accidental and irrelevant to any settled purpose or to any method of limiting or selecting beneficiaries.

4.11 Certainty of objects in conditional gifts

4.11.1 At least one person meets the condition

Some of the apparent contradictions in the case law concerning certainty of objects in trusts and powers may be caused by confusion with the less stringent test for *individual gifts* with a condition attached. Discretionary trusts and fiduciary powers concern choosing amongst a *class*, which might be large. The whole class has to be defined. In individual gift cases the courts only have to be satisfied that someone can claim the gift. Certainty is satisfied if at least one person could meet the condition and claim the gift.

• **Re Allen** [1953] Ch 810

Life interests went to the eldest of the sons of his nephew F 'who shall be a member of the Church of England and an adherent to the doctrine of that Church'.

HELD: Evershed MR at 817:

> All that the claiming **devisee** has to do is at the relevant date to establish if he can, that he satisfies the condition or qualification whatever be the appropriate test.

Devisee—person to whom real property (land) is left in a will.

A condition for a 'tall man' would also satisfy the certainty test, for although there would be doubt about many applicants, a man of six feet six inches would definitely meet the condition. So the condition was certain enough if at least one person could meet it.

Re Allen [1953] Ch 810 was cited in the 'old friends' case *Re Gibbard* [1967] 1 WLR 42, indicating the confusion between cases involving fiduciary powers and individual gifts. (See 4.9.3 'What does the new test mean?'.)

4.11.2 'The independent expert'

Sometimes the uncertainty about the meaning of a condition is resolved where a person, who is named in the will or trust, can decide what the condition means.

. . . .

● *Re Tuck* [1978] Ch 49

The condition here was that the beneficiary could receive income if he should be of the Jewish faith and be married to and live with an 'approved wife'. There was then a lengthy definition of what it meant for the wife to be Jewish. The Chief Rabbi of that particular Jewish community was given the power to decide whether someone was an 'approved wife'.

HELD: Lord Denning thought that this was a good and useful device.

Such a device also found favour in *Re Gibbard* [1967] 1 WLR 42, where a named solicitor was to be consulted before appointments were made. Whether this is still legitimate, in a fiduciary power, is open to doubt, as the stricter certainty test in *Re Gulbenkian's Settlements* [1970] AC 508 disapproved of cases such as *Re Gibbard*, without specifically condemning the use of an 'independent expert'. (See 4.9.4 'Restating the certainty of objects test'.)

The effects of absence of the three certainties

. . . .

Donee—person to whom a gift is made.

. . . .

1. If there is no intention to create a trust, the only interpretation must be that an outright *gift* was intended. The **donee** can keep the property for themselves, as they are not a trustee.

2. If it is not clear what the trust property is intended to be, there can be no trust. The likely result is the complete failure of the attempted disposition. If the beneficial interests are not indicated, the property is still held on trust, but as it is not clear for whom, the trustees hold the trust property on resulting trust for the settlor or testator. (See 8.2 'The automatic resulting trust'.)

3. If there is no certainty of objects, then, as above, the trustees hold the property on resulting trust for the testator or settlor.

Conclusion

One of the great difficulties in this area is trying to work out what exactly the settlor or testator has established. The differences between a fiduciary power and the various kinds of discretionary trust are small. Although they are theoretically different, for most practical purposes the duties of the trustees are the same. If imperative words, like 'shall' or 'must', are used, it is a discretionary trust. If permissive words, like 'may', are used and there is a gift over in default of appointment, then it is a fiduciary power.

Words are also a problem for the three certainties. There is no requirement to use the word 'trust'; just imperative words that have the same meaning. Similarly, there is no particular test for certainty of subject matter, only that the words used must clearly indicate the property subjected to a trust. With certainty of objects there are the two tests of exhaustive enumeration and whether 'any given individual is or is not a member of the class', but they are just another way of saying that the class of beneficiaries must be clearly defined. For a fixed trust, exhaustive enumeration is suitable, as the trustees need to know who all the beneficiaries are. In a discretionary trust and fiduciary power, the trustees merely need to know whether a possible beneficiary qualifies for the class or not.

Questions

Self-test questions

1   What is the difference between a fixed trust and a discretionary trust?

2   What is the difference between a mere power and a fiduciary power?

3   What is the difference between a fiduciary power and a discretionary trust?

4   How does the court decide that a trust was intended?

5   How does the court decide that there is certainty of subject matter?

6   What are the tests for certainty of objects?

7   How was the class test applied in *Re Baden (No 2)*?

8   How would large numbers of beneficiaries make a trust or power unworkable?

Discussion questions

1   Are the differences between a trust and a power theoretical or real?

2   Do the cases on certainty of objects indicate a consistent approach by the courts?

3   Is the *McPhail v Doulton* test for certainty of objects workable?

4   How do beneficiaries enforce the duties of the trustees in a fiduciary power or discretionary trust?

Assessment question

Bob was a builder. He therefore amassed a lot of money. Before his death he made a will. In his will he makes the following disposition (amongst others):

On trust to Farmer Pickles in the hope that he will distribute a large slice of my considerable fortune to any or all of my customers who were satisfied with my work during my lifetime.

The will further provides that if there is any doubt about the above, 'Farmer Pickles is to refer to Wendy—my loyal assistant and worker for many years.' The residue of the estate is left to Bob's sister, Ethel.

Advise Farmer Pickles as to whether the disposition is valid as a trust or power and whether Mrs Broadbent (a former customer of Bob's), Farmer Pickles, or Ethel can claim any of the money.

Key cases

- *Re Gulbenkian's Settlement Trusts (No 1)* [1970] AC 508 **(at 4.2.1, 4.9.4, and 4.9.7)**

- *Re Hay's Settlement Trusts* [1982] 1 WLR 202 **(at 4.3.2, 4.5.1, and 4.9.7)**

- *McPhail v Doulton* [1971] AC 424 **(at 4.5.1, 4.9.6, and 4.10.1)**

- *Hunter v Moss* [1994] 3 All ER 215 **(at 4.7.2 and 4.8.2)**

- *IRC v Broadway Cottages Trust* [1955] Ch 20 **(at 4.9.5)**

- *Re Baden's Deed Trusts (No 2)* [1973] Ch 9 **(at 4.9.7)**

Further reading

CT Emery 'The Most Hallowed Principle—Certainty of Beneficiaries in Trusts and Powers of Appointment' (1982) 98 *LQR* 551
Emery suggests that some of the confusion is caused by there being four different kinds of uncertainty. Only the two in italics cause the trust to fail.

(a) *Conceptual uncertainty*

(b) Evidential uncertainty

(c) Ascertainability

(d) *Administrative workability*.

D Hayton 'Uncertainty of Subject-Matter of Trusts' (1994) 110 *LQR* 335
This article ponders on whether there really is a distinction between *London Wine* and *Hunter v Moss*.

Y Grbich 'Baden: Awakening the Conceptually Moribund Trust' (1974) 37 *MLR* 643

An article about the most important cases in this area, the *McPhail v Doulton* litigation, and what seemed, at the time, a dramatic change in the law.

A Grubb 'Powers, Trusts and Classes of Objects—*Re Hay's Settlements*' [1982] Conv 432

An article about a case that explains the duties of trustees and how this relates to the certainty of objects test.

5

The formality requirements and incompletely constituted trusts

Learning objectives

This chapter will help you to:

- distinguish between the different formality requirements for different types of property
- recognize that transactions in land require writing
- distinguish between a declaration of trust and a transfer of property
- understand that the disposition of an equitable interest must be in writing
- understand that contracts to transfer property to trustees can only be enforced by the parties to the contract, not the beneficiaries (incompletely constituted trusts)
- understand that marriage settlements are an exception in that beneficiaries within the marriage consideration may enforce a contract to transfer property to the trustees.

Introduction

What we mean by formality requirements is that certain transactions must be made in writing. Most of these originated in the Statute of Frauds 1677, when it was felt that certain transactions were so prone to fraud that written evidence of them was necessary. Many of these provisions survive to the present day, mostly in the Law of Property Act 1925. Nowadays, some of the distinctions may not strike us as terribly logical, for instance it is usually possible to declare a trust of any type of property, except of land, orally, even though it might be a multi-million pound transaction. Nevertheless, it is important to be clear about these rules. As we shall see, public ignorance of them can cause many legal problems.

 ## 5.1 Analyse the transaction

To work out the answer to a problem question in this area it is important to be *analytical*.

5.1.1 What sort of property is it?

First, see what sort of property is involved, because the formalities are different for different types of property (see Diagram 5.1).

It can be seen from the diagram that a basic distinction is made between land, real property, and all other types of property, known as personal property.

Personal property is divided into articles that have a physical existence, chattels, and rights to something valuable, which are known as choses in action.

5.1.2 What are the parties trying to do?

Once you have clearly identified the type of property, *then* see what sort of transaction is being attempted. There are two ways of establishing a trust:

1. Transfer of the property to the trustees and declaration of trust by the **settlor**.
2. There is another possibility; the settlor could just make a declaration of trust. Then the settlor would be the trustee.
3. *But* do not forget that the 'settlor' might not want to establish a trust and might just intend an outright gift. Then only a transfer is needed and there are no trustees. The transfer would be directly to the person to whom the settlor wants to give. The donor gives to the donee.

A transfer can also be called an assignment.

Diagram 5.1

Types of property

> **Real Property or Realty**
>
> Land—ground, buildings or parts of buildings, water. Easements, servitudes, and other rights over land.
> Land is immovable property which can be recovered by a real action.

> **Personal Property or Personalty**
>
> Any property which is not land. Movable property. A personal action for damages is possible.
> Includes **Chattels Real** which is leasehold property, now regarded as Land.
> And **Chattels Personal** which are movable, tangible articles of property.

> *Chose in Possession*
> A movable chattel in the custody or control of the owner e.g. car, jewellery, painting, etc.

> *Chose in Action*
> Right of proceeding in a court of law to recover a sum of money. An intangible right, e.g. contractual right, share in a company, patent, trademark, insurance policy, bill of exchange, etc.

Settlor—the person who establishes the trust. Trusts are sometimes called 'settlements'. Alternatively a trust could be established in a will. This is a written document signed by the testator and witnessed—Wills Act 1837, s. 9. The will effects both the transfer and the declaration. (See 7.1 'Wills'.)

There are different writing requirements for different types of property

5.2.1 Land

Transfer

The legal estate can only be transferred by deed.

The Law of Property Act 1925

Section 52(1) states that all conveyances of land or of any interest therein are void for the purpose of conveying or creating a legal estate unless made by deed.

KEY POINTS

- A deed is a formal legal document. It is not just any piece of writing, but has to meet the following requirements:

- Traditionally, at common law it had to be written on parchment or paper. Each party to it had to execute it by doing three things:

  1. he/she had to sign it and the signature had to be witnessed;

  2. he/she had to seal it;

  3. he/she had to 'deliver' it. Delivery is words or conduct expressly or impliedly acknowledging that he/she intends to be bound by whatever they have promised to do in the deed.

- The Law of Property (Miscellaneous Provisions) Act 1989, s. 1 has modernized the law for deeds delivered after 31 July 1990.

- The paper or parchment rule has been abolished.

- Deeds no longer have to be sealed.

- The document must clearly state that it is intended to be a deed.

Even today, when documents are commonly word processed and sent electronically, rather than on paper, the courts will insist that the formalities for a deed are observed and, for example, that the *final* document is signed. 'The requirement that a party sign an actual existing authoritative version of the contractual document gives some, albeit not total, protection against fraud or mistake' (Underhill J at para 39, *Mercury Tax Group Ltd, Masters v Her Majesty's Commissioners of Revenue and Customs* [2008] EWHC 2721 (Admin)).

Transfer, disposal, or assignment of land also requires an additional piece of writing to the deed. This would usually be a contract and would be drawn up before the deed.

Law of Property (Miscellaneous Provisions) Act 1989, s. 2

(1) A contract for the sale or other disposition of an interest in land can only be made in writing . . .

Many people will be familiar with this two-stage process when buying a house. First there has to be 'exchange of contracts', followed by 'completion' when the deed is drawn up. A deed, in this situation, can also be called a conveyance.

Exception

An oral agreement to settle a boundary dispute does not require writing.

● *Joyce v Rigolli* [2004] EWCA Civ 79, (2004) 68 Conv 224

Mrs Joyce had sold part of 6 Chanton Drive to Mr Rigolli. Mr Rigolli's plot became 7 Chanton Drive, but unfortunately the transfer did not clearly identify the boundary line between the two plots. Later, Mr Joyce, on behalf of his wife, agreed a boundary line with Mr Rigolli. Could an *oral* agreement relating to land be binding?

HELD: This issue had been dealt with in an earlier case, *Neilson v Poole* [1969] 20 P & CR 909, as Arden LJ explained:

> In *Neilson v Poole*, Megarry J analysed boundary agreements into two different types: those that constitute an exchange of land and those by which the parties merely intend to 'demarcate' an unclear boundary referred to in title documents. He held it to be presumed that when parties informally agree a boundary, they are making an agreement of the latter class. The latter class of agreements have as their purpose the identification of a boundary, not the conveyance of land (para 26).

On the facts of this case, Mr Rigolli had thought that he was transferring a small piece of land to Mrs Joyce.

Arden LJ chose to go further than Megarry J and accept that minor boundary disputes of either of Megarry J's two types could be settled orally.

> As Megarry J put it, a boundary agreement is 'an act of peace quieting strife and averting litigation'. If s. 2(1) applies where trivial transfers of land are consciously involved, the expense to the parties will also be disproportionate to the value of the land involved. Accordingly, in my judgment, it can in this case properly be concluded that s. 2 does not apply to trivial dispositions of land consciously made pursuant to an informal boundary agreement of the 'demarcating' kind (para 34).

thinking points

'Boundary disputes are a particularly painful form of litigation. Feelings can run high and disproportionate amounts of money are spent.' The problem is made worse by 'sloppy' conveyancing where the boundaries of the land are insufficiently defined and the attached plan is inaccurate. Joyce v Rigolli went further than Neilson v Poole *in that it was clearly not a case of demarcating an existing boundary, but involved the transfer of a small piece of land. An alternative basis for the decision was that the oral agreement could be enforced on the basis of a proprietary estoppel. (See Chapter 6 'Proprietary estoppel'.) See MP Thompson 'Oral Boundary Agreements' (2004) 68* Conv *224.*

Declaration

This too must be made in writing, or at least there must be written evidence of it.

KEY POINT

Only trusts of *land* require the declaration to be made in *writing*. It can be *oral* for all other types of property.

Law of Property Act 1925, s. 53

. . . .

(1) (b) ...a declaration of trust respecting any land or any interest therein must be manifested and proved by some writing signed by some person who is able to declare such trust...

5.2.2 Chattels, goods

These can also be called *choses in possession*.

Transfer

There must be an intention to give and manual delivery or a deed.

This seems very straightforward in that the donor or settlor simply has to hand the item over to the donee. Complications arise because the donor or settlor also has to have the intention to part with the goods, not just, say, to entrust them to the safe-keeping of the other party. That is why a deed can be useful to make clear that the handover, 'manual delivery', is intended as a gift/transfer.

● *Day v Harris, Robert Arnold, Katherine Arnold* [2013] EWCA 191

Sir Malcolm Arnold was a famous composer and in his will he left most of his property to his carer, Day. The will specifically mentioned his manuscripts and the scores to his musical compositions. Sir Malcolm died in 2006. When he was moving house in 1976, he had sent various boxes of household contents to his daughter Katherine. In the boxes were many of his musical scores. At the same time, he sent a postcard to his son, Robert, on which he had written:

> "All the books, pictures, sculptures, etc. are for you and Katherine to share and keep or sell if you like! Dad."

The issue in the case was whether Sir Malcolm had intended to make a gift of his musical scores to his children or whether he just wanted them to look after them.

HELD: There had been delivery of the scores and Sir Malcolm's intention to make a gift of the scores to his children was clear. Katherine had been unsure whether the scores were hers or not, but only Sir Malcolm's intention was relevant. A gift had been made, so the scores did not pass via his will to Day.

Transfer can be a little confusing in some of the cases. In *Day v Harris* [2013] EWCA 191, the attempted transfer was just intended to be a gift. In other cases, the transfer can be part of setting up a trust, as the trust property needs to be properly transferred to the trustees. If a trust is intended, there also has to be a declaration.

DECLARATION. Oral

However valuable the property is, a trust can still be declared orally.

● *Rowe v Prance* [1999] 2 FLR 787

Mr Prance and Mrs Rowe had been lovers from about May 1982, although Mr Prance was married and remained married. Mr Prance said that he would divorce his wife, sell his house, and they would move in together. He never did this, but eventually he did sell his house and used part of the proceeds to buy a boat with the plan that they would both sail around the world. The boat was registered in Mr Prance's sole name and he lied to Mrs Rowe, by telling her that was because only he had an Ocean Master's Certificate. Mrs Rowe moved on to the boat and Mr Prance reassured her that the boat was her security and that she had an interest in it. Mr Prance referred to it as 'our boat'. They separated and Mrs Rowe claimed her share of the boat.

HELD: It was argued that Mrs Rowe had an equitable interest in the boat under the type of constructive trust discussed in the leading 'family home' case *Lloyds Bank v Rosset* [1991]

1 AC 107. This was not necessary though because, unusually, the 'family home' here was not land. There could be an express trust.

Nicholas Warren QC at 794H:

> It is pointed out that there is no need for writing in the case of an item of personal property such as a boat to create an express trust. There is therefore no need to rely on the case law concerning the circumstances where, absent writing, it is necessary to rely on a constructive trust to establish the beneficial interest.

(The judge is referring to 'Trusts of the family home', see Chapter 18, which usually involve land.)

Mrs Rowe was awarded half the value of the boat, because Mr Prance's use of the words 'our boat' was an express declaration of trust and 'equality is equity'.

5.2.3 Choses in action

This is property that is not tangible, i.e. a physical item that can be held in the hand, but is instead a valuable right, perhaps represented by a piece of paper, e.g. a share certificate.

Transfer

Some form of writing is required. The exact detail varies according to the type of property, but the basic structure is that the person transferring or giving has to put it in writing and notify the person against whom the property is claimed.

> **Law of Property Act 1925, s. 136**
> . . . .
> . . . by writing under the hand of the assignor . . . and . . . express notice in writing to the debtor . . .

So if we take as our example a bank account, the customer writes that he is transferring his account, say, to his friend and notifies the bank, the 'debtor' in writing.

Stocks and shares

A certificate is issued, stating how many stocks or shares the person owns. These certificates usually have a 'transfer form' attached to them. The owner writes the name of the new owner on the transfer form and sends the certificate to the company. The company registers the name of the new owner. Both writing on the transfer form *and* registration by the company are essential to transfer legal ownership of the shares: s. 1 of the Stock Transfer Act 1963 and s. 544 and Part 21 of the Companies Act 2006.

Nowadays the procedure would often be electronic, but the basis is still the same. Other types of intangible property also require writing in order to be transferred, e.g. bills of exchange—writing (endorsement), s. 31 of the Bills of Exchange Act 1882 and copyright—writing, s. 90(3) of the Copyright, Designs and Patents Act 1988.

DECLARATION. Oral

As with chattels, this could involve valuable property.

● **Paul v Constance** [1977] 1 All ER 195

Mr Constance was separated from his wife and living with Mrs Paul. Mr Constance received £950 as damages for an injury at work and they both decided to put it into a deposit account at Lloyds Bank. They were embarrassed about using joint names so the account was only in the name of Mr Constance. Mr Constance died, still married, and his wife, Mrs Constance, claimed the money in the account.

HELD: In order to transfer half the bank account to Mrs Paul, Mr Constance would need to have put it in writing and notified the bank in writing (see earlier). If he was declaring a trust over the shares, he could do this orally.

Scarman LJ at 198:

> In this court the issue becomes: was there sufficient evidence to justify the judge in reaching that conclusion of fact? In submitting that there was, Mr Wilson draws attention first and foremost to the words used. When one bears in mind the unsophisticated character of the deceased and his relationship with the plaintiff during the last few years of his life, Mr Wilson submits that the words that he did use on more than one occasion, 'This money is as much yours as mine', convey clearly a present declaration that the existing fund was as much the plaintiff's as his own. The judge accepted that conclusion. I think that he was well justified in doing so, and, indeed, I think that he was right to do so.
>
> It might, however, be thought that this was a borderline case, since it is not easy to pinpoint a specific moment of declaration, and one must exclude from one's mind any case built upon the existence of an implied or constructive trust, for this case was put forward at the trial and is now argued by the plaintiff as one of express declaration of trust. It was so pleaded and it is only as such that it may be considered in this court. The question, therefore, is whether, in all the circumstances, the use of those words on numerous occasions as between the deceased and the plaintiff constituted an express declaration of trust. The judge found that they did. For myself, I think that he was right so to find. I therefore would dismiss the appeal.

Another useful case, *Hunter v Moss* [1994] 3 All ER 215, illustrates the same point as *Paul v Constance*. A trust of a chose in action, this time shares, can be declared orally and no particular wording needs to be used.

● **Hunter v Moss** [1994] 3 All ER 215

Mr Hunter agreed to work for Bennett & Fountain Group plc and, as part of his remuneration, the majority shareholder, Mr Moss, agreed to give him a 5 per cent shareholding in the company. As the company had 1,000 shares, this amounted to 50 shares, but because of concerns about tax liability Mr Moss came up with the following scheme.

Dillon LJ at 218:

> Mr Hunter says that, during the conversation, Mr Moss asked him if he would mind if he, Mr Moss, held on to Mr Hunter's shares for him until a solution was found and that, in the meantime, he would ensure that Mr Hunter received all the dividends that he was entitled to.

The dividends were paid to Mr Hunter in 1989, but after that Moss and Hunter quarrelled and Mr Hunter claimed to be entitled to the shares.

HELD: This was a declaration of trust, which could be made orally.

KEY POINT

There is no need to use the word 'trust' in order to declare a trust. The intention of the settlor, here Mr Constance, is the important thing.

Dillon LJ at 219:

> I find that, as from that conversation in early September 1986, Mr Moss held 5 per cent of MEL's issued shares (i.e. 50 shares) on trust for Mr Hunter. Even if he did not in terms use the words 'in trust', the sense of what he then said was that he would thenceforth hold the shares on such a trust.

Paul and *Hunter* might seem to be fair decisions, but did the parties really intend to declare trusts? These cases could be accused of blurring the distinction between a gift and a declaration of trust.

KEY POINTS

- Analysing the transaction can be difficult.

- The rules are different for different types of property.

- You need to identify what the parties intended.

- 'Unsophisticated' parties may not understand what they intended.

- Carefully distinguish between a declaration of trust and a transfer, they are not the same.

 5.3

Dispositions of equitable interests must be in writing

> **Law of Property Act 1925, s. 53**
>
> . . . .
>
> (1) (c) ...a disposition of an equitable interest or trust subsisting at the time of the disposition must be in writing signed by the person disposing of the same or by his agent...

Diagram 5.2

Disposition of an equitable interest

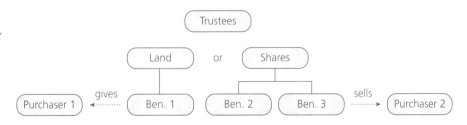

There are two sets of rights in any item of property: the legal estate and the equitable interests (see Diagram 5.2). If there is a trust, the trustees hold the legal estate for the beneficiaries, who hold the equitable interests. Section 53(1)(c) tells us that the disposition of an equitable interest must be in writing. Therefore, any transfer (assignment) of an equitable interest must be written.

There have been a number of ingenious attempts to avoid the writing requirement in this subsection because, at one time, a written document transferring an equitable interest was taxed. It was liable to stamp duty, a percentage of the value of the equitable interest transferred.

5.3.1 In some cases the court held that writing was required

. . . .

● *Grey v IRC* [1960] AC 1

Mr Hunter wanted to transfer shares to his grandchildren, but he did not want to pay stamp duty. So what he tried to do was to say that he was declaring a trust, which as the property involved was shares, could be done orally.

First he established six settlements of nominal sums in favour of his grandchildren. Then he transferred 18,000 shares to the same trustees, but they were to hold them on trust for him.

On 18 February 1955 Mr Hunter *orally* directed the trustees to hold the shares on trust for his grandchildren. On 25 March Mr Hunter and the trustees executed a deed declaring this new trust, which repeated what had been said on 18 February 1955 and declared that the shares had been held on trust since 18 February. (What they were doing was providing a permanent record of what had been done, but insisting that the effective declaration of trust had been oral.)

HELD: The words of 18 February could not transfer the equitable interest, because s. 53(1)(c) required this to be done in writing. Therefore, the deed of 25 March transferred the equitable interest and stamp duty had to be paid (see Diagram 5.3).

Diagram 5.3

Grey v IRC

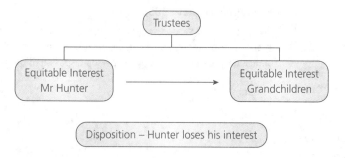

Lord Radcliffe at 15:

> My Lords, if there is nothing more in this appeal than the short question whether the oral direction that Mr Hunter gave to his trustees on 18 February 1955, amounted in any ordinary sense of the words to a 'disposition of an equitable interest or trust subsisting at the time of the disposition', I do not feel any doubt as to my answer. I think that it did. Whether we describe what happened in technical or in more general terms, the full equitable interest in the eighteen thousand shares concerned, which at that time was his, was (subject to any statutory invalidity) diverted by his direction from his ownership into the beneficial ownership of the various equitable owners, present and future, entitled under his six existing settlements.

KEY POINT In other words Mr Hunter starts by 'owning' or holding the equitable interest in the shares. What he does transfers the equitable interest to his grandchildren. This means that he has 'disposed' of his equitable interest and this requires writing.

Lord Radcliffe at 16:

> Moreover, there is warrant for saying that a direction to his trustee by the equitable owner of trust property prescribing new trusts of that property was a declaration of trust. But it does not necessarily follow from that that such a direction, if the effect of it was to determine completely or **pro tanto** the subsisting equitable interest of the maker of the direction, was not also a grant or assignment . . . and therefore required writing for its validity. Something had to happen to that equitable interest in order to displace it in favour of the new interests created by the direction: and it would be at any rate logical to treat the direction as being an assignment of the subsisting interest to the new beneficiary or beneficiaries or, in other cases, a release or surrender of it to the trustees.

Pro tanto
Latin—literally
'for so much'. It
means the same as
'completely' here.

KEY POINT Lord Radcliffe looked at the history of the law in this area and concluded that even though Mr Hunter claimed it was only a declaration of trust, which could be oral, that did not stop it *also* being a disposition which had to be in writing.

An even more ingenious attempt to find a way around the writing requirement in s. 53(1)(c) can be found in *Oughtred v IRC* [1960] AC 206.

● ***Oughtred v IRC*** [1960] AC 206

The parties tried intentionally to establish a constructive trust which requires no writing and use the exception in s. 53 of the Law of Property Act 1925.

Law of Property Act 1925, s. 53

....

(2) This section does not affect the creation or operation of resulting, implied or constructive trusts.

Shares in a private company were held on trust for Mrs Oughtred for life, with the remainder for her son Peter. If the trust took its course and Peter inherited when his mother died, then estate duty (now called inheritance tax) would have to be paid. So to prevent this Mrs Oughtred and Peter orally agreed that he would transfer his remainder to his mother. This would make her the absolute owner, the only beneficiary under the trust. In return, Mrs Oughtred orally agreed to transfer some other shares, which she owned outside the trust, to Peter. They made these agreements orally to try to avoid paying stamp duty.

Subsequently, documents were drawn up, a deed stating that the trust shares were now held in trust for Mrs Oughtred alone and another document transferring the other shares to Peter. The trustees then transferred the trust shares to Mrs Oughtred and she transferred the other shares to Peter.

The Inland Revenue (now HM Revenue & Customs) claimed that the deed was a disposition of Peter's equitable interest to his mother and stamp duty had to be paid.

The Oughtreds claimed that their oral agreement was a contract that could be enforced, if necessary, by specific performance. The courts had long held that in that situation, the vendor, Peter, held the property on constructive trust for the purchaser, his mother. Under that reasoning his mother already held the equitable interest, s. 53(2) applied, and no further writing was required.

This was a very clever argument and caused the House of Lords some difficulty.

HELD: The Lords found for the Inland Revenue by a 3:2 majority. The majority thought that the oral agreement did not transfer *all* the equitable interest.

Lord Jenkins at 240:

> This interest under the contract is no doubt a proprietary interest of a sort, which arises, so to speak, in anticipation of the execution of the transfer for which the purchaser is entitled to call. But its existence has never (so far as I know) been held to prevent a subsequent transfer, in performance of the contract, of the property contracted to be sold from constituting for stamp duty purposes a transfer on sale of the property in question.
>
> In truth, the title secured by a purchaser by means of an actual transfer is different in kind from, and may well be superior to, the special form of proprietary interest which equity confers on a purchaser in anticipation of such transfer.

KEY POINT Lord Jenkins accepts that the contract creates an equitable interest for Mrs Oughtred. But it is not the full equitable interest, which can only be disposed of in writing.

The minority accepted the arguments of the Oughtreds: the contract created a constructive trust which moved the equitable interest to Mrs Oughtred.

The argument that contractual agreements can move the equitable interest, without the need for additional writing, has been accepted in other cases.

● *Neville v Wilson* [1996] 3 WLR 460

Trustees held 120 shares in Universal Engineering Co Ltd on trust for JE Neville Ltd, a family company. In 1969 the shareholders of Neville Ltd entered into an agreement with one another for the informal liquidation of their company. As part of this, they decided to divide the equitable interest in the Universal shares among themselves, in proportion to their existing shareholding. These were oral agreements, for consideration, disposing of an equitable interest.

HELD: This case did not involve tax questions, but instead the ownership of shares in a company.

The Court of Appeal was satisfied here that an oral contract to dispose of an equitable interest could create a constructive trust and use s. 53(2) to avoid the writing requirement.

The court felt able to distinguish *Oughtred* [1960] AC 206 on the grounds that the judges in the majority did not specifically decide the constructive trust point.

Perhaps the true policy reason behind *Oughtred* was that the Oughtreds had discovered a simple loophole in the tax laws that the courts agreed should be closed.

Oughtred was followed in the next case.

● *Parinv v IRC* [1998] STC 305

Parinv (Hatfield) had purchased land at Bishops Square, Hatfield for £37,223,000 and the Inland Revenue claimed stamp duty, at 1 per cent, of £372,230. Parinv claimed that the vendor had first declared a trust in their favour, which had the effect of transferring the equitable interest to them. So the later transfer of the land to them had no real effect as they already had the equitable interest. Stamp duty should be a nominal 50p.

HELD: Lord Millett found for the Inland Revenue.

> A transfer to a purchaser of the legal estate in property contracted to be sold was a conveyance on sale notwithstanding that the beneficial interest in the property had already passed to the transferee under a preceding contract for sale and the whole of the purchase consideration had been paid before the transfer.
>
> An alternative argument raised by the purchaser was that … it was the declaration of trust which was the instrument which constituted the conveyance on sale and that as the property could not be conveyed twice over, the transfer was not a conveyance on sale.
>
> Its alternative argument had been knocked on the head almost 40 years ago in *Oughtred v IRC* [1960] AC 206.

thinking points

One of the problems in this area is that although s. 53(1)(c) is a re-enactment of s. 9 of the Statute of Frauds 1677, there was very little authority on this point. For a long time it was thought that s. 9 only applied to equitable interests in real property, but these cases confirm that it also applies to personal property, such as shares. Many of the cases on s. 53(1)(c) have distinctive facts and it might be difficult to derive general principles from the judgments. For instance, were the minority in Oughtred *correct and is it simply policy considerations that influenced the majority? See B Green 'Grey, Oughtred and Vandervell: A Contextual Reappraisal' (1984) 47 MLR 385.*

Declaration of a sub-trust

Section 53(1)(c) of the Law of Property Act 1925 states that a disposition of an equitable interest must be in writing. Yet a declaration of trust of any property, except land, can be made orally. In some situations it is hard to tell whether a declaration of trust has been made or whether there has been a disposition of an equitable interest. It was thought that a declaration of a sub-trust, sometimes called an intermediate trust, did not count as a disposition and therefore did not require writing (see Diagram 5.4). This view can be found in the American Restatement 'Trusts' and was approved by Lord Evershed in *Grey v Inland Revenue Commissioners* [1958] Ch 690 at 715. This was, however, merely an obiter dictum and was not mentioned when the case went to the House of Lords [1960] AC 1, but it was approved in a subsequent case, *Drakeford v Cotton* [2012] 3 All ER 1138.

However, when the issue arose in *Nelson v Greening and Sykes (Builders) Ltd* [2007] EWCA Civ 1358, the Court of Appeal declined to follow Lord Evershed's view, which was not binding upon them.

Diagram 5.4

A sub-trust

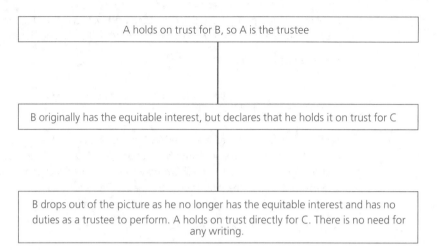

A holds on trust for B, so A is the trustee

B originally has the equitable interest, but declares that he holds it on trust for C

B drops out of the picture as he no longer has the equitable interest and has no duties as a trustee to perform. A holds on trust directly for C. There is no need for any writing.

● **Nelson v Greening and Sykes (Builders) Ltd** [2007] EWCA Civ 1358

Nelson had exchanged contracts with Greening to buy a plot of land and Nelson had paid the required price. Nelson refused to complete, so Greening sued him. Greening sought an order for costs against Nelson. Nelson argued that, because of the contract, Greening held the land on constructive trust for him. In fact, the purchase price had been provided by Ms Hanley, so Nelson also argued that he, in turn, held on a resulting trust for Ms Hanley. He was B in Diagram 5.4 and dropped out of the picture entirely, so Greening could not sue him for costs.

HELD: Collins LJ at para 57:

> These authorities do not bind this court to hold that as a matter of law an intermediate trustee ceases to be a trustee. I accept the submission for G & S that saying (as Lord Evershed MR said) that the practical effect would seem to amount to or be capable of amounting to the 'getting rid' of the trust of the equitable interest then subsisting, is not the same as saying that as a matter of law it does get rid of the intermediate trust. What he was saying was that in the case of a trust and sub-trust of personal property the trustees may decide that as a matter of practicality it is more convenient to deal directly with the beneficiary of the sub-trust.

KEY POINT

According to the Court of Appeal, the declaration of a sub-trust requires writing, because it is the disposition of an equitable interest.

In any case, the authorities did not apply to this kind of constructive trust. Mr Nelson still held on trust for Ms Hanley and could still be sued for costs. Nelson would have had to transfer his equitable interest to Hanley in writing.

The s. 53(1)(c) writing requirement can cause unexpected problems. It is common in company pension schemes for the member to be able to nominate a person to receive a death benefit if he/she dies in service.

● **Re Danish Bacon** [1971] 1 WLR 248

Megarry J thought that this nomination might be a disposition of an equitable interest, but on the facts there had been sufficient writing anyway.

● *Baird v Baird* [1990] 2 AC 548

HELD: Lord Oliver at 561 confirmed this, but said that, under some pension schemes, if the member had 'a full power of disposition during his lifetime over the amount standing to his credit under the scheme', then the nomination would be a will. The formalities there are different: a will requires a signature and two witnesses.

(See 7.1 'Wills'.)

5.3.2 In two celebrated cases the court held that writing was not required

Section 53(1)(c) only applies if the equitable interest is being transferred separately from the legal estate.

● *Vandervell v IRC* [1967] 2 AC 291

Mr Vandervell was subject to extremely high rates of tax, so he wanted to reduce his tax liability. He decided to give money to a charity, the Royal College of Surgeons, so that it could endow a Chair of Pharmacology. The National Provincial Bank held shares in Vandervell Products Ltd on trust for Mr Vandervell, who was the only beneficiary.

As he held the entire equitable interest in the shares he was perfectly entitled to instruct his trustees to transfer the shares to the Royal College of Surgeons.

His trustees transferred the legal estate in the shares to the Royal College.

HELD: Section 53(1)(c) did not apply, because the equitable interest was being transferred together with the legal estate. The section only applies when the equitable interest is being transferred separately.

Lord Upjohn at 311:

> Those words [s. 53(1)(c)] were applied in Grey and Oughtred to cases where the legal estate remained outstanding in a trustee and the beneficial owner was dealing and dealing only with the equitable estate. That is understandable; the object of the section, as was the object of the old Statute of Frauds, is to prevent hidden oral transactions in equitable interests in fraud of those truly entitled, and making it difficult, if not impossible, for the trustees to ascertain who are in truth his beneficiaries. But where the beneficial owner owns the whole beneficial estate and is in a position to give directions to his bare trustee with regard to the legal as well as the equitable estate there can be no possible ground for invoking the section where the beneficial owner wants to deal with the legal estate as well as the equitable estate.
>
> But if the intention of the beneficial owner in directing the trustee to transfer the legal estate to X is that X should be the beneficial owner I can see no reason for any further document or further words in the document assigning the legal estate also expressly transferring the beneficial interest; the greater includes the less.

KEY POINT
When the equitable interest is transferred, *together* with the legal estate, no separate writing is required.

(See Diagram 5.5.)

Unfortunately Mr Vandervell lost on another ground. He wanted to have the ability to recover the shares from the Royal College of Surgeons, so the college had agreed to an option to allow

133

Diagram 5.5
Vandervell v IRC
Part 1

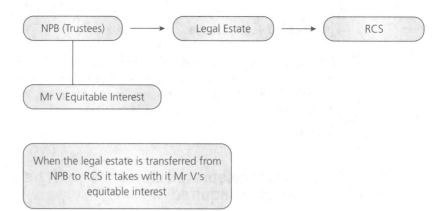

the repurchase of the shares for £5,000. This agreement was with the Vandervell Trustees Ltd, who were trustees of a number of Vandervell family trusts. An option is just a contractual right to acquire property on payment of consideration. A contractual right is also a form of property. The majority in the House of Lords decided that the trustees could not have the option for themselves, but must be holding on trust. Mr Vandervell had neglected to declare the trusts on which the option was held, so the option was held back for him on resulting trust. Therefore, the IRC could successfully argue that he still had some form of beneficial interest in the shares and was still liable for tax on it.

(See 8.2.1 'Resulting trusts'.)

Lord Wilberforce at 329:

> The conclusion on the facts found, is simply that the option was vested in the trustee company as a trustee on trusts, not defined at the time, possibly to be defined later. But the equitable, or beneficial interest, cannot remain in the air: the consequence in law must be that it remains in the settlor.

Lords Reid and Donovan disagreed on this point.

Mr Vandervell then tried to rid himself of these shares to reduce his tax bill, which led to another court case with the Inland Revenue. This time he was more successful, as the court agreed that a new trust had been created. Therefore, it was a declaration of trust and, as the trust property was shares, no writing was required. (See 8.2.3 'Surplus after completion of purpose'.)

● *Re Vandervell (No 2)* [1974] Ch 269

Mr Vandervell, as the only beneficiary of the resulting trust of the option, instructed his trustees, Vandervell Trustees Ltd, to exercise the option. They did this and bought back the shares from the Royal College of Surgeons. The Vandervell trustees used £5,000 from a trust that they held for Mr Vandervell's children to pay for the shares. With Mr Vandervell's consent, the trustees made it clear that these shares were now held on trust for the children and informed the Inland Revenue of this. The High Court had decided that Mr Vandervell had done nothing to rid himself of the shares, so they were still held by the trustees for him (see Diagram 5.6).

Mr Vandervell's argument, in the Court of Appeal, was that he had declared a new trust over the shares and that this did not need writing.

KEY POINT
If the settlor does not specify the beneficiaries, the trustees hold the property back on resulting trust for the settlor.

Diagram 5.6

Vandervell v IRC
Part 2

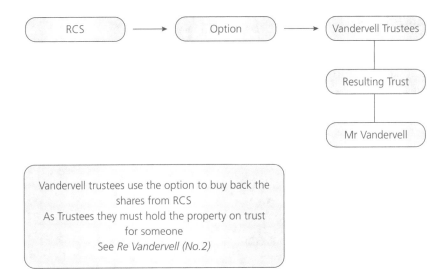

HELD: Fortunately for Mr Vandervell, Lord Denning gave the leading judgment in the Court of Appeal. By this stage, Mr Vandervell was dead and the Inland Revenue had withdrawn from the case. The dispute was about whether the shares belonged to his children or to his estate, which would go to their stepmother.

Lord Denning concluded that Mr Vandervell had done enough to declare a trust.

At 319:

> In October and November 1961, the trustee company exercised the option...Thereupon the trustee company became the legal owner of the shares. This was a different kind of property altogether. Whereas previously the trustee company had only a chose in action of one kind—an option—it now had a chose in action of a different kind—the actual shares.

At 320:

> Such being the intention, clear and manifest, at the time when the shares were conveyed to the trustee company, it is sufficient to create a trust.
>
> A resulting trust for the settlor is born and dies without any writing at all. It comes into existence whenever there is a gap in the beneficial ownership. It ceases to exist whenever that gap is filled by someone becoming beneficially entitled. As soon as the gap is filled by the creation or declaration of a valid trust, the resulting trust comes to an end. In this case, before the option was exercised, there was a gap in the beneficial ownership. So there was a resulting trust for Mr Vandervell. But as soon as the option was exercised and the shares registered in the trustees' name, there was created a valid trust of the shares in favour of the children's settlement. Not being a trust of land, it could be created without any writing. A trust of personalty can be created without writing.

And at 322:

> Equity was introduced to mitigate the rigour of the law. But in the present case it has been prayed in aid to do injustice on a large scale—to defeat the intentions of a dead man—to deprive his children of the benefits he provided for them—and to expose his estate to the payment of tax of over £600,000. I am glad to find that we can overcome this most unjust result.

A new trust was created, therefore it was a declaration of trust and no writing was required (see Diagrams 5.7 and 5.8).

Diagram 5.7

Superficially Vandervell No. 2 looks just like Grey v IRC

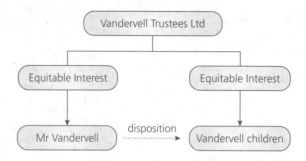

Diagram 5.8

Re Vandervell No. 2—a declaration of trust, not a disposition of an equitable interest

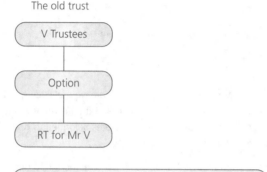

KEY POINTS

- The problem with this decision is that it seems to contradict *Grey v IRC* [1960] AC 1.

- In both cases we start with trustees holding shares on trust for Mr Hunter and Mr Vandervell respectively, the only beneficiary. They tell their trustees to hold the shares for their children instead. In *Grey* writing is required, but in *Vandervell* it is not.

- There seem to be two main differences:

  1. In *Vandervell* the first trust is a resulting trust, which, according to Lord Denning, just ceases to exist when it is no longer needed;

  2. In *Vandervell* the two trusts involve different property: first the option to buy the shares and then the shares themselves. It is easier to see the share trust as the declaration of a completely new trust.

- Against that, if we read the facts of *Vandervell* closely, there is little evidence that Vandervell ever declared a trust! Nonetheless, Lord Denning's decision has been followed in *Drakeford v Cotton* [2012] 3 All ER 1138.

thinking points

There is a distinction between declaring a fresh trust and disposing of an equitable interest under a trust that already exists. For the former, s. 53(1)(b) applies, but for the latter it is s. 53(1)(c). Graham Battersby explores the various cases on s. 53(1)(c) and tries to see whether this distinction is made consistently. His conclusion is that '[i]t is submitted that the complexity of the present position reflects no credit on the law, and that the time has come for long cool look—would the Law Commission or the Law Reform Committee be interested?' See G Battersby 'Formalities for the Disposition of an Equitable Interest under a Trust' [1979] Conv 17.

5.4 When the writing requirements can be waived

An equitable maxim states that 'Equity will not permit a statute to be used as an instrument of fraud'. Equity has the power, if it desires, to disregard statutory requirements if this is necessary to prevent injustice. This will only be done in exceptional circumstances.

(See 2.8 'Equity will not permit a statute to be used as an instrument of fraud'.)

5.4.1 Oral declarations of trust over land

There are many examples where the courts have allowed this, despite the clear wording of s. 53(1)(b) of the Law of Property Act 1925 that this must be evidenced in writing.

● *Rochefoucauld v Boustead* [1897] 1 Ch 196

The Comtesse de la Rochefoucauld needed money to pay to her ex-husband, but as her estates were already heavily mortgaged it was difficult for her to raise money. She came to an agreement with Boustead and Duff that they should buy her estates so that she could pay off her debts. Instead they mortgaged the estates and went bankrupt. Rochefoucauld claimed that the agreement was that Boustead and Duff would hold the estates on trust for her, even though this had never been put in writing.

HELD: Lindley LJ at 206:

> …and that it is a fraud on the part of a person to whom land is conveyed as a trustee, and who knows it was so conveyed, to deny the trust and claim the land himself. Consequently, notwithstanding the statute, it is competent for a person claiming land conveyed to another to prove by parol [oral] evidence that it was so conveyed upon trust for the claimant, and that the grantee, knowing the facts, is denying the trust and relying upon the form of conveyance and the statute, in order to keep the land himself.

In more modern times it is more likely that the courts would regard such trusts as constructive trusts. This is covered by s. 53(2) of the Law of Property Act 1925.

> **Law of Property Act 1925, s. 53**
> ....
> (2) This section does not affect the creation or operation of resulting, implied or constructive trusts.

● *Bannister v Bannister* [1948] 2 All ER 133

The defendant owned two adjoining cottages and agreed to sell them to her brother-in-law for £250, when the real value was nearer £400. In return for this the defendant wanted to rent one of the cottages, but the brother-in-law said; 'I do not want to take any rent, but will let you stay as long as you like rent-free'. The written conveyance did not mention that she could stay in one of the cottages and, a few years later, her brother-in-law sought possession.

HELD: The brother-in-law held the cottages on constructive trust and the defendant had a life interest in the cottage in which she lived. The oral agreement could be enforced, even though the words 'trust' had never been used.

'Fraud' did not have to mean that the defendant had misled the plaintiff in order to obtain the conveyance, but only that he was insisting on enforcing the written conveyance, when he had orally agreed that the plaintiff had an interest in the property. He could not hide behind the writing requirements of the Law of Property Act 1925, but had to respect the 'real bargain'.

5.4.2 Oral contracts for the sale of land

The Law of Property (Miscellaneous Provisions) Act 1989 tightened up the law on the need for writing in contracts for the sale of land. Section 2 says that the contract must be written and not just evidenced in writing (see 5.2.1 'Land'). The doctrine of part performance of a contract was also abolished. Despite this, if justice requires it, a constructive trust can still be used to enforce an oral agreement relating to land.

● *Yaxley v Gotts* [2000] Ch 162

Alan Gotts bought a house. Previously, his father, Brownie Gotts, had orally agreed with Keith Yaxley, a builder, that Yaxley could have the ground-floor flat in return for work on the other flats in the building and for managing these flats. Neither the contract nor the conveyance gave any interest in the property to Yaxley. A few years later Alan Gotts excluded Yaxley from the house.

HELD: Even though the oral agreement was void and unenforceable under the Law of Property (Miscellaneous Provisions) Act 1989, s. 2(5) did not affect 'the creation or operation of resulting, implied or constructive trusts'. Yaxley could claim the ground-floor flat under a proprietary estoppel or constructive trust. (See Chapter 16 'Constructive trusts' and Chapter 6 'Proprietary estoppel'.)

KEY POINT
'Fraud' means failing to abide by what was really agreed. If there is a fraud, the courts may disregard the writing requirements.

Incompletely constituted trusts

5.5

5.5.1 The proper legal procedure must be followed

There are two main problems in this area of the law.

1. If the donor/settlor wants to give property to someone (donee) there are three distinct ways in which he/she can do this.

    If the donor/settlor gets the legal procedures wrong, equity will *not* usually intervene and say legal formalities do not matter if we know what the parties were really trying to do. This is unusual in equity where the usual policy is to give effect to what the parties really intended even if they get the legal formalities wrong. (See 5.4, 'When the writing requirements can be waived', for example.)

2. A settlor promises to transfer property to the trustees of a trust. The settlor does not keep his/her promise. In most cases, equity will *not* force the settlor to keep his/her promise. This is dealt with in more detail at 5.8 'Incompletely constituted trusts: covenants to settle property'.

    This might seem odd. Equity usually makes parties *keep* their promises. (See, for example, Chapter 7 'The disposal of property on death' and Chapter 18 'Trusts of the family home'.)

Both situations 1 and 2 are covered by the maxim 'There is no equity to perfect an imperfect gift'.

5.5.2 The three methods to make a gift

Just to remind you, there are three main methods by which the donor/settlor may make his 'gift'.

1. Transfer directly to the donee. There is no trust; this is just an outright gift.
2. Transfer to the trustees and declaration of trust.
3. Declaration of trust. The settlor becomes the trustee.

Method 3 is the easiest because, unless land is involved, a declaration of trust can be oral. Transfer of property, as in 1 and 2, usually involves some form of writing and, in the case of land, a deed.

If the settlor attempts method 1 or 2, but does not transfer the property properly, usually because there is no writing, equity will *not* say 'Oh well, let's just call it a declaration of trust and then everything will be alright.' That is the meaning of the equitable maxim in 5.5.1 'The proper legal procedure must be followed'.

The settlor/donor must observe the correct formalities for the method of benefiting the donee/beneficiary that he/she has chosen. He/she must choose one of the three methods. They cannot be mixed.

The main authority for these rules is *Milroy v Lord* (1862) 4 De GF & J 264, which laid down a strict rule.

. . . .

● ***Milroy v Lord*** (1862) 4 De GF & J 264

The settlor, Thomas Medley, executed a deed which tried to transfer 50 shares in the Bank of Louisiana to Samuel Lord to hold on trust for Milroy. Later the settlor handed the share certificates to Lord. To transfer shares, the change in ownership must be registered by the company, but this was never done either by Medley or Lord, even though Lord had a power of attorney to act for Medley.

HELD: The shares were not held on trust for Milroy as they had never been properly transferred to the trustee. [Method 2 had been attempted, but had not been successful.]

Lord Turner LJ in the Court of Appeal at 274–5:

> I take the law of this Court to be well settled, that, in order to render a voluntary settlement valid and effectual, the settlor must have done everything which, according to the nature of the property comprised in the settlement, was necessary to be done in order to transfer the property and render the settlement binding upon him. He may of course do this by actually transferring the property to the person for whom he intends to provide, and the provision will then be effectual, and it will be equally effectual if he transfers the property to a trustee for the purposes of the settlement, or declares that he himself holds it in trust for those purposes; and if the property be personal, the trust may, as I apprehend, be declared either in writing or by parol [oral]; but in order to render the settlement binding, one or other of these modes must, as I understand the law of this Court, be resorted to, for there is no equity in this Court to perfect an imperfect gift. The cases I think go further to this extent, that if the settlement is intended to be effectuated by one of the modes to which I have referred, the Court will not give effect to it by applying another of those modes. If it is intended to take effect by transfer, the Court will not hold the intended transfer to operate as a declaration of trust, for then every imperfect instrument would be made effectual by being converted into a perfect trust. These are the principles by which, as I conceive, this case must be tried.
>
> Applying, then, these principles to the case, there is not here any transfer either of the one class of shares or of the other to the objects of the settlement, and the question therefore must be, whether a valid and effectual trust in favour of those objects was created in the defendant Samuel Lord or in the settlor himself as to all or any of these shares. Now it is plain that it was not the purpose of this settlement, or the intention of the settlor, to constitute himself a trustee of the bank shares. The intention was that the trust should be vested in the defendant Samuel Lord, and I think therefore that we should not be justified in holding that by the settlement, or by any parol declaration made by the settlor, he himself became a trustee of these shares for the purposes of the settlement. By doing so we should be converting the settlement or the parol declaration to a purpose wholly different from that which was intended to be effected by it, and, as I have said, creating a perfect trust out of an imperfect transaction...

Medley had not properly transferred the shares to the trustee Lord. As he had chosen method 2 he needed *both* a proper transfer *and* a declaration of trust. A declaration of trust by itself could not set up a trust for Milroy, as Medley had not chosen method 3.

5.5.3 An ineffective transfer will not be treated as an effective declaration

Older cases adhered closely to *Milroy v Lord*. The Court of Chancery wanted to apply the strict legal rules of property transfer, in order to provide certainty in business dealings. This is an example of the equitable maxim, 'Equity follows the law' (see 2.3 'Equity follows the law'). Two examples are given here.

● *Jones v Lock* (1865) LR 1 Ch App 25

Robert Jones was an ironmonger in Pembroke with a second wife and a nine-month-old son. He returned from a business trip to Birmingham and the child's nurse said, 'You have come back from Birmingham and have not brought baby anything.' Robert Jones had brought back a cheque for £900, payable to himself and he produced it saying: 'Look you here, I give this to baby; it is for himself, and I am going to put it away from him, and will give him a great deal more along with it.' He then handed the cheque to his baby son, but his wife was worried that the baby might tear it, so Robert added: 'Never mind if he does, it is his own, and he may do what he likes with it.' Then he did take the cheque back and locked it in the safe. Nothing further was done with the cheque and six days later Robert Jones was dead. His will left his property to the children of his first marriage.

HELD: Robert Jones had clearly intended a gift to his son, but had not used the correct procedure to transfer it to him. He should have 'endorsed' the cheque for his son. (Written on it transferring it to his son. This cannot be done with crossed cheques, which are more common nowadays.)

Lord Cranworth LC at 28–9:

> Therefore the question in each case is one of fact; has there been a gift or not, or has there been a declaration of trust or not? I should have every inclination to sustain this gift, but unfortunately I am unable to do so; the case turns on the very short question whether Jones intended to make a declaration that he held the property in trust for the child; and I cannot come to any other conclusion than he did not. I think it would be of very dangerous example if loose conversations of this sort, in important transactions of this kind, should have the effect of declarations of trust.

Robert Jones intended a gift, which requires writing. He could have declared a trust orally, but he did not intend a trust.

The same principle applies, whatever the type of property.

. . . .

● ***Richards v Delbridge*** (1874) LR 18 Eq 11

John Delbridge leased premises where he carried on the business of a bone manure merchant. His grandson, Edward Benetto Richards, who was under age, helped him. Shortly before his death, Delbridge wrote on the lease deed itself: 'This deed and all thereto belonging, I give to Edward Benetto Richards from this time forth, with all the stock in trade'. He then gave the document to the mother of Richards and died. The lease was not mentioned in his will.

HELD: Sir George Jessel MR:

The clear intention of Delbridge was to make a gift. To do this he would need to execute a fresh deed, as he was attempting to transfer a legal estate in land.

Writing would have been enough to declare a trust, but this was not his intention.

At 14:

> It is true he need not use the words 'I declare myself a trustee' but he must do something which is equivalent to it and use expressions which have that meaning. For a man to make himself a trustee there must be an expression of intention to become a trustee.

5.6 Moderating the rule

The rule laid down by *Milroy v Lord* (1862) 4 De GF & J 264 can seem harsh, particularly if the failure to transfer the property has been caused by a minor procedural error or by someone else's fault. In some cases, the courts have been prepared to depart from these strict rules.

● **Re Rose** [1952] Ch 499

This case might be explainable by its unusual facts, where the exact date of the transfer was very important. As in *Milroy,* the problem was the registration of shares.

Rose filled in two share transfer forms correctly on 30 March 1943. One was in favour of his wife absolutely and one was to his wife and one other person to hold as trustees. The company, whose shares they were, delayed in registering the transfer until 30 June 1943. Rose died on 16 February 1947. If he had transferred his shares before 10 April 1943, then estate duty (now inheritance tax) would not have to be paid on them.

HELD: Evershed MR at 507:

> Now I agree that on the face of the document it was obviously intended (if you take the words used) to operate and operate immediately as a transfer—'I do hereby transfer to the transferee' these shares 'to hold unto the said transferee, subject to the several conditions on which I held the same at the time of the execution hereof'. It plainly was intended to operate immediately as a transfer of rights.

He then considers *Milroy v Lord* at 510:

> Those last few sentences form the gist of the Crown's argument and on it is founded the broad, general proposition that if a document is expressed as, and on the face of it intended to operate as, a transfer, it cannot in any respect take effect by way of a trust—so far as I understand the argument to go. In my judgment, that statement is too broad and involves too great a simplification of the problem; and is not warranted by authority.

He follows an earlier case, also called by coincidence, *Re Rose* [1949] Ch 78 and quotes from p. 89 of that case at 511–12:

> I was referred on that to the well known case of *Milroy v Lord*, and also to the recent case of *Re Fry* [1946] Ch 312. Those cases, as I understand them, turn on the fact that the deceased donor had not done all in his power, according to the nature of the property given, to vest the legal interest in the property in the donee. In such circumstances it is, of course, well settled that there is no equity to complete the imperfect gift. If any act remained to be done by the donor to complete the gift at the date of the donor's death the court will not compel his personal representatives to do that act and the gift remains incomplete and fails. In *Milroy v Lord* the imperfection was due to the fact that the wrong form of transfer was used for the purpose of transferring certain bank shares. The document was not the appropriate document to pass any interest in the property at all.
>
> Then he refers to *In Re Fry*, which is another illustration. 'In this case, as I understand it, the testator had done everything in his power to divest himself of the shares in question to Mr Hook. He had executed a transfer. It is not suggested that the transfer was not in accordance with the company's regulations. He had handed that transfer together with the certificate to Mr Hook. There was nothing else the testator could do.'

Evershed MR resumed:

> I venture respectfully to adopt the whole of the passage I have read which, in my judgment, is a correct statement of the law. If that be so, then it seems to me that it cannot be asserted on the authority of *Milroy v Lord*, and I venture to think it also cannot be asserted as a matter of logic and good sense or principle, that because, by the regulations of the company, there had to be a gap before Mrs Rose could, as between herself

and the company, claim the rights which the shares gave her vis-à-vis the company, the deceased was not in the meantime a trustee for her of all his rights and benefits under the shares.

KEY POINTS

- *Milroy v Lord* held that to transfer property the transferor has to do *everything necessary* for that type of property.

- *Re Rose* held that if the transferor had done *everything in his power* to transfer that type of property, the property transfer would be effective in equity.

Some more recent cases have followed the *Re Rose* interpretation.

● ***Mascall v Mascall*** (1985) 49 P & CR 119

Mascall wanted to give his house to his son and in 1976 had said 'If you want, it is yours'. With his father's approval, the son then treated the house as his own, carrying out work on it and paying bills, etc. . . . In 1991, because of worries about capital gains tax, the father agreed to sell the house for £9,000 to his son. The father filled out a Land Registry form of transfer, which was signed and witnessed, and handed the land certificate to his son. Both were sent to the Stamp Office, but the Inland Revenue were concerned whether the son was really going to pay him for the house, so there was a delay. Then the Mascalls quarrelled, with the effect that the sale was never registered by the Land Registry. Some years later the son sought to prove that the house was his.

HELD: Lawton LJ considered *Milroy v Lord* and commented that it was once thought that that case meant that 'everything had to be done before a gift was perfected'.

At 124:

> He thought that it meant that the donor had to do everything in his power to effect the transfer of the legal interest. The donor had done this here as he had the intention, had filled in all the necessary forms and handed them over to his son, the donee. The son had merely to have the transfer stamped and to ask the Land Registry to register his title.

Browne-Wilkinson LJ at 126:

> The basic principle underlying all the cases is that equity will not come to the aid of a volunteer. Therefore, if a donee needs to get an order to complete his title, he would not get it. If on the other hand the donee has under his control everything necessary to constitute his title completely without any further assistance from the donor, the donee needs no assistance from equity and the gift is complete. It is on this principle, which is laid down in *Re Rose* that in equity it is held that a gift is complete as soon as the settlor or donor has done everything that the donor has to do, that is to say, as soon as the donee has within his control all those things necessary to enable him, the donee, to complete his title.

KEY POINT
So the test changes again. Now the donee has to have in his control everything necessary to complete the title.

In the 21st century the courts have had the opportunity to reconsider *Milroy v Lord* (1862) 4 De GF & J 264 yet again.

The Privy Council looked at the issue of imperfect gifts in *T Choithram International v Pagarini* [2001] 1 WLR 1, a case with unusual facts.

● *T Choithram International v Pagarini* [2001] 1 WLR 1

Thakurdas Choithram Pagarini was a very wealthy man, who ran a worldwide chain of supermarkets. He was seriously ill and nearing death and decided to set up a charitable foundation, by drawing up a trust deed and making himself one of the seven trustees. He put £1,000 into the trust and always said that he intended to transfer more of his wealth to the trustees, but died before he could go through the necessary legal formalities. Different witnesses gave different accounts of what he said, but it was something like 'I now give all my wealth to the trust'.

HELD: Lord Browne-Wilkinson: The Court of Appeal had decided that Thakurdas Choithram Pagarini had not succeeded in transferring his wealth to his charity. This was neither an outright gift nor was it a declaration of trust.

Lord Browne-Wilkinson disagreed and considered that Thakurdas Choithram Pagarini's words could be interpreted as a declaration of trust.

At 11:

> The facts of the case are novel and raise a new point.

And at 12:

> Therefore the words 'I give to the foundation' can only mean 'I give to the trustees of the foundation trust deed to be held by them on the trusts of the foundation trust deed'. Although the words are apparently words of outright gift they are essentially words of gift on trust.
>
> There can in principle be no distinction between the case where the donor declares himself to be sole trustee for a donee or a purpose and the case where he declares himself to be one of the trustees for that donee or purpose. In both cases his conscience is affected and it would be unconscionable and contrary to the principles of equity to allow such a donor to resile from his gift.

What is 'novel' about the *T Choithram International v Pagarini* case is that Thakurdas Choithram Pagarini did not need to transfer the legal estate to anyone else, because he already held it. So it was not a situation where equity was obliged to follow the common law rules, it just depended upon rules of equity. In equity it would be 'unconscionable' to prevent the dead man's gift from taking effect. That said, this case sits uneasily with the basic principle laid down by *Milroy v Lord* (1862) 4 De GF & J 264, that equity will not perfect an imperfect gift, but the theme of not allowing something that was 'unconscionable' was followed subsequently in *Pennington v Waine* [2002] 1 WLR 2075.

● *Pennington v Waine* [2002] 1 WLR 2075

Ada Crampton wanted to make a gift of 400 shares in Crampton Brothers to her nephew Harold Crampton, to qualify him to become a company director. Ada prepared and signed a share transfer form and gave it to Pennington, an auditor to the company. This was the wrong person, as the company secretary usually registers changes in the names of shareholders.

The form was kept on file and nothing was done to register the shares to Harold. When Ada died, he claimed the shares.

HELD: The facts are quite similar to *Milroy v Lord*, although the share transfer forms are at least sent to the company here. Ada, though, was only attempting to make an outright gift to Harold, not set up a trust for him.

Once again the court was willing to make an exception to *Milroy v Lord*. Ada's intention was clear. It would be unconscionable not to let Harold have the shares, even though he had not been given control of the necessary documents.

Ada could be regarded as having declared a trust over the shares in favour of Harold.

Arden LJ at 2087:

> Thus explained, the principle that equity will not assist a volunteer at first sight looks like a hard-edged rule of law not permitting much argument or exception. Historically the emergence of the principle may have been due to the need for equity to follow the law rather than an intuitive development of equity. The principle against imperfectly constituted gifts led to harsh and seemingly paradoxical results. Before long, equity had tempered the wind to the shorn lamb (i.e. the donee). It did so on more than one occasion and in more than one way . . .

At 2090–2:

> What then are the relevant facts here? Ada made the gift of her own free will: there is no finding that she was not competent to do this. She not only told Harold about the gift and signed a form of transfer which she delivered to Mr Pennington for him to secure registration: her agent also told Harold that he need take no action. In addition Harold agreed to become a director of the company without limit of time, which he could not do without shares being transferred to him.
>
> However, that conclusion as to the ratio in *Rose v Inland Revenue Comrs* does not mean that this appeal must be decided in the appellant's favour. Even if I am correct in my view that the Court of Appeal took the view in *Rose v Inland Revenue Comrs* that delivery of the share transfers was there required, it does not follow that delivery cannot in some circumstances be dispensed with. Here, there was a clear finding that Ada intended to make an immediate gift. Harold was informed of it. Moreover, I have already expressed the view that a stage was reached when it would have been unconscionable for Ada to recall the gift. It follows that it would also have been unconscionable for her personal representatives to refuse to hand over the share transfer to Harold after her death. In those circumstances, in my judgment, delivery of the share transfer before her death was unnecessary so far as perfection of the gift was concerned.

The maxim 'Equity will not assist a volunteer' here means that the court would not normally allow Harold to take the gift, as an incorrect procedure has been used. However, Ada's intention was so clear that it would just be unfair and 'unconscionable' not to enforce the gift.

KEY POINTS

- *Milroy v Lord* still stands and it would be wise to stick to formal procedures to transfer property.

- The courts will accept exceptions, enforceable in equity, if it would be unconscionable not to do so.

thinking points

A recent case, Curtis v Pulbrook *[2011] EWHC 167 (Ch), tried to summarize the exceptions to the* Milroy v Lord *principle and decided that there were three types. The first was that the donor had done everything in their power to make the transfer as shown in* Re Rose. *The second was that there was detrimental reliance by the donee, so it would be unconscionable for the donor to recall the gift.* Pennington v Waine *was an example of this estoppel-type doctrine. The third type was where what looked like a gift could be interpreted as a declaration of trust:* Choithram v Pagarini. *Although the arguments of Briggs J in* Curtis *seem convincing and would help to restrict exceptions being made to the* Milroy v Lord *principle, the judgments in* Pennington *do not seem to be based on an estoppel principle. See Peter Luxton 'In search of perfection: the Re Rose rationale' [2012]* Conveyancer *70.*

5.7 Consequences of a completely constituted trust

Once property has been correctly transferred to the trustees, the settlor cannot change his/her mind and require the property to be returned.

(Some settlors get round this by putting a specific clause in the trust enabling them to do just that. This is known as a revocation clause.)

· ·

Marriage settlement—a trust is established, on marriage, to provide for the husband and wife and the children that they hope to have. Commonly, the husband and wife would covenant, in a deed with the trustees, that they would transfer any property that they acquired in the future to the trust. The spouses and the children of the marriage may enforce the promise in the covenant despite the fact that the children do not provide any consideration, i.e. they do not promise anything in return.

· ·

· ·

● *Paul v Paul* (1882) 20 ChD 742

This was a **marriage settlement**, which is a trust established when a couple marry to provide for the married couple and the children that they hope to have. Such trusts usually have a 'default' clause stating that the property is held for the next of kin if there happen to be no children. The Pauls set up just such a trust, but had no children, and had in fact separated, so they wanted to recover the property that the wife had transferred to the trustees.

HELD: Jessel MR at 744:

> In this case a trust was declared by the settlement for the next of kin of the lady, and the fund has been transferred to the trustees. The fact of their being volunteers does not enable the trustees to part with it without the consent of their cestuis que trust. That has been the rule ever since the Court of Chancery existed. The appeal must be dismissed.

A volunteer is someone who has not provided consideration. (See 2.11 'Equity will not assist a volunteer' and 5.8.3 'Equity will not aid a volunteer'.)

5.8 Incompletely constituted trusts: covenants to settle property

To call these trusts 'incompletely constituted' is misleading, because usually some property has been transferred to the trustees, so the trust has been constituted. The problem is that someone, who is usually not only a settlor, but a beneficiary as well, has promised to transfer property to the trustees, but does not do so. When can this promise be enforced?

5.8.1 Marriage settlements

The problem usually arises in marriage settlements. Both families establish a trust for the couple that takes effect upon their marriage. Typically the terms of the trust would be 'to the husband and wife for life, then to the issue of the marriage, remainder to the next of kin'. The settlement is established by deed and the settlors, trustees, and husband and wife are all parties to the deed. Each spouse promises to transfer any property that might be acquired in the future to the trustees. (This is known as an 'after-acquired property clause'.) Typically it would be property inherited from their parents. At one time marriage settlements were the normal way in which married couples held their property. It had advantages, particularly before the Married Women's Property Act 1884, when married women could not own their own property. The trustees could protect the wife and children from the husband spending all the family money.

. . . .

● **Re Densham** [1975] 1 WLR 1519

Here the house was legally in the name of the husband, but the wife had made a contribution to the purchase price through their joint savings. This gave her an equitable interest in the house under the principles in *Gissing v Gissing* [1971] AC 886. (See Chapter 18 'Trusts of the family home'.)

The court attempted to define the essential elements of a marriage settlement.

HELD: Goff J at 734:

(1) it must be made on the occasion of marriage;

(2) it must be conditional only to take effect on the marriage taking place;

(3) it must be made by a person for the purpose of or with a view to encouraging or facilitating the marriage.

This was not a marriage settlement, because it only satisfied condition 1. It was not a trust deliberately created by the marrying couple and their families to provide for the couple and their future children.

Another example would be *Re Kay* [1939] Ch 329 (see 5.8.3 'Equity will not aid a volunteer'), where the trust was established in 1907, but Mary Kay married in 1913, so it could not satisfy conditions 1 and 2 in *Re Densham* [1975] 1 WLR 1519 and could not be a marriage settlement.

5.8.2 Equitable or marriage consideration

In equity, those within the marriage settlement are regarded as giving consideration and can enforce the promise to transfer after-acquired property, i.e. husband, wife, and their issue. The next of kin, who are often residuary beneficiaries in this sort of trust, are not regarded as being within the marriage consideration.

Children of previous marriages are *not* included in the 'marriage consideration'.

....

● *AG v Jacobs-Smith* [1895] 2 QB 341

Mrs Smith, a widow with children, married Jacobs-Smith. The children of her first marriage could not enforce the marriage settlement.

HELD: Lindley LJ at 348:

> ...the consideration of marriage extends only to the husband and wife and the children of that marriage, and that all other persons whether they are children of a former marriage or children of a subsequent marriage, or whether they are brothers, or whether they are illegitimate children, or whether they are strangers altogether, are volunteers in some sense.

The only exception would be where the trust was set out in such a way that it could not be enforced for the children of the marriage settlement without enforcing it for previous children.

Lopes LJ at 351–2:

> He accounts for it by saying that in that case the limitations in favour of the children of the first marriage and the children of the second marriage were so complicated and mixed up, and that they were so much dealt with together as a class, that it was impossible to give effect to the limitations in favour of the one without giving effect to the limitations in favour of the other.

If there is a marriage settlement, then the husband, wife, and children can come to court and enforce the other spouse's promise to transfer property to the trustees.

....

● *Pullan v Coe* [1913] 1 Ch 9

Here the couple married in 1859 and a marriage settlement was established for them. There was a provision that the wife should settle after-acquired property above the value of £100. In 1875 she received £285 from her mother, which she put into her husband's bank account. In 1909 the husband died and the trustees, acting on behalf of the wife and children, claimed the return of this money.

HELD: Swinfen Eady J at 14–15:

> In my opinion as soon as the £285 was paid to the wife it became in equity bound by and subject to the trusts of the settlement.
>
> Again the trustees are entitled to come into a Court of Equity to enforce a contract to create a trust, contained in a marriage settlement, for the benefit of the wife and the issue of the marriage, all of whom are within the marriage consideration.

All that equity has done is to say that the husband, wife, and children, in a marriage settlement, are also parties to the contract. The policy reason behind this is to keep property within the immediate family of husband, wife, and their children.

5.8.3 Equity will not aid a volunteer

If there is not a marriage settlement, or if there is, but it is the next of kin who are trying to enforce the promise to transfer property to the trustees, the courts will not enforce these promises.

Looked at in simple contractual terms, these claimants are not parties to the contract.

● ***Re D'Angibau*** (1880) 15 Ch 228 (CA)

Cotton LJ at 242:

> But as a rule the Court will not enforce a contract as distinguished from a trust at the instance of persons not parties to the contract. The Court would probably enforce a contract in a marriage settlement at the instance of the children of the marriage, but this is an exception from the general rule in favour of those who are specially the objects of the settlement.

KEY POINT Volunteers are not parties to the contract. They have given no consideration. They are beneficiaries of the trust, but this is not enough to allow them to enforce the covenant.

There is a line of authority to support this rule, that the courts will only enforce promises to transfer property to the trustees on behalf of those within the marriage consideration (see Diagram 5.9).

● ***Re Plumptre*** [1910] 1 Ch 609

There was a marriage settlement in 1878. Money came from Mrs Plumptre's mother to Mr Plumptre, who used it to purchase stock in Mrs Plumptre's name in 1884. She did not keep to the covenant in the trust and, on her death in 1909, this after-acquired property had still not been transferred to the trust. The Plumptres had had no children, so the next of kin, who were the only other beneficiaries, wanted the trustees to take legal action to enforce the wife's promise. The trustees sought the advice of the court.

Diagram 5.9

The covenant in a marriage settlement

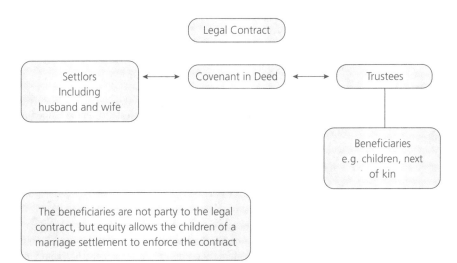

Settlors Including husband and wife ←→ Covenant in Deed ←→ Trustees

Beneficiaries e.g. children, next of kin

The beneficiaries are not party to the legal contract, but equity allows the children of a marriage settlement to enforce the contract

HELD: The trustees could not sue at common law for an ordinary breach of contract (the trust deed formed a legally binding contract), because the breach of contract was in 1884 and action was now barred by the Statute of Limitations. (There is a six-year time limit.)

Eve J at 618:

> The collaterals [next of kin] are not parties to the contract; they are not within the marriage consideration and cannot be considered otherwise than as volunteers...

And at 619:

> I therefore answer the second question by saying that the applicants [the trustees] are not bound to take any steps.

● ***Re Pryce*** [1917] 1 Ch 234

This case had very similar facts except that this time it was the husband who did not keep his promise. Again there were no children, so the next of kin were the beneficiaries.

HELD: Eve J at 241–2:

> In these circumstances, seeing that the next of kin could neither maintain an action to enforce the covenant nor for damages for breach of it, and that the settlement is not a declaration of trust constituting the relationship of trustee and cestui que trust between the defendant and the next of kin, in which case effect could be given to the trusts even in favour of volunteers, but is a mere voluntary contract to create a trust, ought the Court now for the sole benefit of these volunteers to direct the trustees to take proceedings to enforce the defendant's covenant? I think it ought not; to do so would be to give the next of kin by indirect means relief that they cannot obtain by any direct procedure...

As the next of kin are not parties to the contract they cannot sue to enforce it. To let the trustees, who are parties to the contract, sue on their behalf seems illogical to the judge, as that would let the next of kin obtain indirectly what they cannot obtain directly, by suing themselves.

Of course, if it is not a marriage settlement there can be no question of enforcing covenants to transfer property.

● ***Re Kay*** [1939] Ch 32

Mary Winifred Kay, who was then unmarried, made a settlement with her trustees on 24 December 1907 in a deed establishing a trust for herself, any future husband, and then the children she might have.

As part of the trust, Mary promised (covenanted) to transfer any property that she inherited from her father and mother and their relatives to the trustees to hold on these trusts. Mary married in 1913 and had three children. Her mother died in 1937 and Mary inherited property from her.

At 331:

> The settlor [Mary] informed the trustees that she did not consider she should have to bring the above mentioned items of property into settlement, and contended that, the settlement

being purely voluntary, the trustees ought not to take any steps against her to compel performance by her of or sue for damages for her failure to implement the provisions of the after-acquired property clause contained in the settlement.

The trustees sought advice in a summons for direction.

HELD: Simonds J at 338–40:

> But, be it observed, though beneficiaries, her children are, for the purpose of this settlement, to be regarded as volunteers, there being no marriage consideration, which would have entitled them to sue, though they are parties to this application. The trustees ask whether, in the event which has happened of the settlor having become entitled to certain property, they should take proceedings against her to compel performance of the covenant or to recover damages on her failure to implement it.
>
> She [Mary Kay] has said that the question before me is not primarily whether, if she were sued, such an action would succeed (as to which she might have a defence, I know not what), but whether, in the circumstances as they are stated to the Court, the trustees ought to be directed to take proceedings against her.
>
> As to that, the argument before me has been, on behalf of the children of the marriage, beneficiaries under the settlement, that, although it is conceded that the trustees could not successfully take proceedings for specific performance of the agreements contained in the settlement, yet they could successfully, and ought to be directed to, take proceedings at law to recover damages for the non-observance of the agreements contained in the settlement, first, the covenant for further assurance of the appointed share of the first-mentioned 20,000 and, secondly, the covenant with regard to after-acquired property. In the circumstances I must say that I felt considerable sympathy for the argument which was put before me by Mr Winterbotham on behalf of the children, that there was, at any rate, on the evidence before the Court to-day, no reason why the trustees should not be directed to take proceedings to recover what damages might be recoverable at law for breach of the agreements entered into by the settlor in her settlement. But on a consideration of *In Re Pryce* [1917] 1 Ch 234 it seemed to me that so far as this Court was concerned the matter was concluded and that I ought not to give any directions to the trustees to take the suggested proceedings.

And at 342:

> In those circumstances it appears to me that I must follow the learned Judge's decision and I must direct the trustees not to take any steps either to compel performance of the covenant or to recover damages through her failure to implement it.

It may be noted that, although the court confirmed the rule that these promises to transfer would only be enforced if they appeared in a marriage settlement, the judge felt some doubt about the justice of this rule. However, in more modern times the rule was confirmed and explained.

. . . .

● ***Re Cook's Settlement Trusts*** [1965] Ch 902

This clearly was not a marriage settlement. The Cook family had built up a considerable collection of works of art, mainly old master paintings. These were held on trust for Sir Herbert Cook for life, and then the remainder absolutely for his son Sir Francis Cook. Sir Herbert wanted to give most of his collection to the nation, so he and his son agreed to end this trust and create a new one. A new trust was created for Sir Francis, his wife, then his children and next of kin. The trust property consisted of money, land, and some of the paintings from

the collection in addition to paintings that had belonged to Sir Herbert outside the trust. As part of the agreement, Sir Francis covenanted that if he sold a painting he would pay the proceeds to the trustees to be held on the trust. There was a legally binding contract here, with consideration, between Sir Francis, his father, and the trustees.

Sir Francis, who married several times, gave one of the paintings, a Rembrandt picture of 'Titus', away to a wife to provide for her. She was now proposing to sell it.

The trustees sought the advice of the court upon whether they should sue Sir Francis to make him keep his covenant, on behalf of the ultimate beneficiaries, his children.

HELD: The trustees were not required to enforce the promise of Sir Francis, because the children were not party to the contract and this was not a marriage settlement. There was a brief justification of this rule.

Buckley J at 914:

> In contrast to all these cases, this covenant upon its true construction is, in my opinion, an executory contract to settle a particular fund or particular funds of money which at the date of the contract did not exist and which might never come into existence.

thinking points

Do Plumptre, Pryce, Kay, and Cook *actually tell the trustees that they cannot enforce the covenant? Professor Elliott disagreed and thought that although the beneficiaries could not compel the trustees to enforce the covenant, if the trustees wanted, they could sue for breach of contract, at common law, and recover substantial damages, which they would hold for the beneficiaries.* Re Pryce and Re Kay *had misunderstood the original authority of* Re D'Angibau. *JA Hornby went further and argued that the trustees must hold the benefit of the covenant on trust for all the beneficiaries. Authority for this could be found in* Fletcher v Fletcher *and* Davenport v Bishopp *(1843) 2 Y & CCC 451, where, in* Bishopp, *the trustees had successfully sought specific performance of the covenant to transfer after-acquired property, on behalf of volunteer beneficiaries. Hornby argued that as the trustees held the promise to transfer on trust, they were bound to enforce it for all beneficiaries, whether they were volunteers or not. See JA Hornby 'Covenants in Favour of Volunteers' (1962) 78 LQR 228, replying to DW Elliott 'The Power of Trustees to Enforce Covenants in Favour of Volunteers' (1960) 76 LQR 100.*

5.8.4 Exceptions to this rule

In equity there are many cases and at least some have come to a different conclusion on whether these covenants to transfer property can be enforced. *Re Cook* [1965] Ch 902 (at 5.8.3) distinguishes them by saying that there is a crucial difference between:

1. Promises to transfer property that a person hopes to acquire in the future (executory contracts). These are not enforceable unless it is a marriage settlement and it is being enforced on behalf of someone within the marriage consideration.

2. Promises to transfer property that the person already possesses. These are enforceable.

● *Re Cavendish-Brown's ST* [1916] WN 341

Catherine Penelope Cavendish-Brown covenanted to transfer property to the trustees. At the date of her death, she had not transferred real estate in Canada to the trustees. The administrators wanted to know whether the value of the real estate should be paid to the trustees by way of damages for breach of covenant.

Cases such as *Re Plumptre* [1910] 1 Ch 609 and *Fletcher v Fletcher* (1844) 4 Hare 67, among others, were cited.

HELD:

> Younger J without delivering a final judgment, held, on the authority of the above cases, that the trustees were entitled to recover from the plaintiffs substantial damages for breach of the covenant to assure, and that the measure of such damages was the value of the property which would have come to the hands of the trustees if the covenant had been performed.

It is hard to explain this decision, but perhaps the judge thought that Catherine had only promised to transfer property that she already had, rather than property that she only hoped to inherit in future.

It is hard to say more about the judge's reasons, because the extract above is the complete judgment! One of the precedents cited was *Fletcher v Fletcher* (1844) 4 Hare 67, which allowed the enforcement of the covenant.

· ·

● ***Fletcher v Fletcher*** [1844] 4 Hare 67

Four or five years before his death, Ellis Fletcher drew up a deed stating that within one year from his death his executors should pay £60,000 to five named trustees to hold for his two illegitimate sons, John and Jacob, if they survived him. No one, not even the trustees, knew about this deed until it was discovered some years after the death of Ellis. Jacob, the surviving son, brought the case to court. The surviving trustees declined to enforce the covenant of Ellis 'unless the Court should be of opinion that they were bound to act'.

HELD: The court considered two lines of authority, one that saw no reason why such covenants should not be enforced and the other that took the conventional approach that Jacob was not a party to the contract between his father and the trustees, so it could not be enforced.

It was decided that Jacob could enforce the covenant.

Sir James Wigram VC at 567:

> According to the authorities I cannot, I admit, do anything to perfect the liability of the author of the trust, if it is not already perfect. This covenant, however, is already perfect. The covenantor is liable at law, and the Court is not called upon to do any act to perfect it. One question made in argument has been whether there can be a trust of a covenant the benefit of which shall belong to a third party; but I cannot think there is any difficulty in that...
>
> The proposition therefore, that in no case can there be a trust of a covenant is clearly too large, and the real question is whether the relation of a trustee and cestui que trust is established in the present case.

There are several possible explanations of this case.

1. This case involved a promise relating to property that Ellis Fletcher already possessed. Jacob, the beneficiary, sued. It was not a case of the trustees seeking advice.

2. Read literally, the words of Wigram VC seem to suggest that the trustees held Ellis Fletcher's promise on trust. This meant that the trust was constituted, in that the trustees held some

property for Jacob, so there was no difficulty in Jacob enforcing the trust, as a beneficiary, rather than having to sue on the covenant. There is no difficulty with a contractual promise being held on trust, because it is a form of property (see 3.2 'What is property?'). If this was so, it would provide a way of enforcing these covenants to transfer property in all cases. The counter-argument is that there is no evidence that Ellis ever declared that the covenant was itself held on trust.

3. It is possible to interpret the judgment in a simpler way: it merely sees no reason why a covenant which is so clearly for Jacob's benefit should not be enforced by the trustees. This was at an early date when the rule that these covenants could not be enforced except by those within the marriage consideration had yet to become a firm rule. Why should not trustees enforce a covenant when it is clearly for the benefit of a beneficiary?

5.8.5 Contracts for third parties

The law may have turned full circle! The Contracts (Rights of Third Parties) Act 1999 allows third parties to enforce a contract that has clearly been made for their benefit.

Contracts (Rights of Third Parties) Act 1999, s. 1

. . . .

(1) Subject to the provisions of this Act, a person who is not a party to a contract (a 'third party') may in his own right enforce a term of the contract if—

(a) the contract expressly provides that he may, or

(b) subject to sub-section (2), the term purports to confer a benefit on him . . .

(3) The third party must be expressly identified in the contract by name, as a member of a class or as answering a particular description, but need not be in existence when the contract is entered into.

The wording of subsections (1)(b) and (3) seems to apply to the beneficiaries of a trust, but it is uncertain whether that was the intention of the Act. The Act only applies to covenants entered into after 11 May 2000, so we await cases. If the courts find in favour of beneficiaries, then this area of law will disappear and become merely of historical interest.

 # Conclusion

The transfer of property is not a straightforward business. Different types of property require different writing requirements. It also depends upon what the parties are trying to do with the property. They may be trying to establish a trust by transferring property to the trustees and declaring a trust. Alternatively they might simply be declaring themselves a trustee or they may be making an outright gift, with no trust intended. Disposing of an equitable interest also requires writing, unless the equitable interest is being transferred together with the legal estate: *Vandervell v IRC* [1967] 2 AC 291. A declaration of a new trust also does not require writing according to *Re Vandervell (No 2)* [1974] Ch 269, whereas declaring a trust of an existing equitable interest does: *Grey v IRC* [1960] AC 1.

Milroy v Lord (1862) 4 De GF & J 264 states that the writing requirement for the type of property and transaction chosen must be rigorously followed. Nowadays the court might be persuaded to make an exception, when *not* to do so would be unconscionable: *Pennington v Waine* [2002] 1 WLR 2075.

Lastly, a contract to transfer property to a trust raises different problems. The contract can only be enforced by the parties to it, unless it is a marriage settlement, when the husband, wife, and children of the marriage can also enforce the contract.

Questions

Self-test questions

1 What is a deed and what is its legal significance?

2 In terms of formalities, what is different about land?

3 When does the disposition of an equitable interest occur?

4 When will the courts ignore a writing requirement?

5 What is the importance of the decision in *Milroy v Lord*?

6 When can the beneficiaries enforce a covenant to transfer property to the trust?

Discussion questions

1 Are the writing requirements inconsistent and out of date?

2 Is there really a significant difference between the disposition of an equitable interest and a declaration of trust?

3 Is there any consistency in the exceptions to *Milroy v Lord*?

4 If the beneficiaries in a marriage settlement can enforce a covenant to transfer property to the trustees, why cannot all beneficiaries do this?

Assessment question

Sam and Janet marry and establish a trust with the following terms: 'To Sam and Janet for life, remainder to the children of their marriage, if there is a failure of issue, remainder to the next of kin.' Sam and Janet are parties, with the trustees, Tabitha and Tatiana, to the trust deed. Janet covenants that she will transfer any after-acquired property to the trust. Sam does not covenant, because he comes from a poor family and does not expect to inherit anything.

When her mother dies, Janet inherits a house, Paisleyacre, and shares in Everlast plc. Janet does not transfer Paisleyacre to the trust, but instead puts it into the joint names of herself and her husband, Sam. She promises to transfer the shares to the trustees, but merely fills in the transfer section on the share certificate and hands the certificate to the trustees.

Janet and Sam do not have any children of their own, but adopt a child, Pablo. There is only one next of kin, Janet's brother Sebastian.

Sam and Janet both die. The trustees wonder whether they should enforce Janet's covenant and try to obtain Paisleyacre and the shares in Everlast plc for the trust. The beneficiaries, Pablo and Sebastian, are keen that they should do so.

Advise the trustees, Tabitha and Tatiana.

Key cases

- *Paul v Constance* [1977] 1 All ER 195 **(at 5.2.3)**
- *Vandervell (No 2)* [1974] Ch 269 **(at 5.3.2)**
- *Grey v IRC* [1960] AC 1 **(at 5.3.1)**
- *Yaxley v Gotts* [2000] Ch 162 **(at 5.4.2)**
- *Milroy v Lord* (1862) 4 De GF & J 264 **(at 5.5.2 and 5.6)**
- *Pennington v Waine* [2002] 1 WLR 2075 **(at 5.6)**
- *Re Pryce* [1917] 1 Ch 234 **(at 5.8.3)**

Further reading

MP Thompson 'Oral Boundary Agreements' [2004] 68 *Conv* 224
The case of *Joyce v Rigolli* [2004] EWCA Civ 79. An exception to the normal writing requirements.

B Green 'Grey, Oughtred and Vandervell: A Contextual Reappraisal' (1984) 47 *MLR* 385
An attempt to explain these rather difficult cases.

G Battersby 'Formalities for the Disposition of an Equitable Interest under a Trust' [1979] *Conv* 17
Another attempt to explain the difficult cases on s. 53(1)(c) of the Law of Property Act 1925.

P Luxton 'In search of perfection: the Re Rose rationale' [2012] *Conveyancer* 70.
Can a unifying principle, consistent with the general principles of trust law, be found in cases such as *Pennington v Waine* and *T Choithram International v Pagarini*?

JA Hornby 'Covenants in Favour of Volunteers' (1962) 78 *LQR* 228 and
DW Elliott 'The Power of Trustees to Enforce Covenants in Favour of Volunteers' (1960) 76 *LQR* 100
Most academic opinion seeks to argue that the main cases on incompletely constituted trusts are wrong, but for different reasons.

6

Proprietary estoppel

Learning objectives

This chapter will help you to:

- understand the principle of estoppel
- identify the key elements of proprietary estoppel
- recognize the importance of the principle of unconscionability
- identify the need for a clear representation or acquiescence
- understand that the claimant must act as they did because they believed that they had a right to the property
- identify the different types of detriment
- understand that an equitable remedy is flexible
- understand the similarities and differences between a proprietary estoppel and a constructive trust.

Introduction

Equitable estoppel appears to be an ancient doctrine and remedy of equity, which was revived after the Second World War. Lord Denning played a leading role in this, as part of his campaign to revive the equitable jurisdiction of the courts: a judge should not be bound by the strict legal rules if this would lead to an unjust result. Estoppel basically means that a person must keep their promise, if another relies upon the promise and acts to their detriment. It has provided a very useful means for dealing with difficult situations when the law would seem to lead to an undesirable result. Its disadvantage is that it has proved very difficult to pin down precisely what is needed to prove the existence of an estoppel. It relies on general concepts such as 'detriment' and 'unconscionability', but how exactly do we define these? As we shall see, even the highest courts can disagree on the relative importance of the different elements that make up an estoppel.

 ## 6.1 The different types of estoppel

Several different kinds of estoppel can be found in both common law and equity. The basic principle is quite simple: A makes a promise to B and, in certain circumstances, A will be prevented from going back on that promise. Hudson has a useful overall definition:

> Estoppel achieves justice by preventing a person from going back on her word. The difference between an ordinary promise and a promise giving rise to an estoppel is that it is a requirement of the latter that the claimant must have suffered some detriment in reliance on that promise (Alasdair Hudson *Equity and Trusts* (8th edn, London: Routledge-Cavendish, 2015) at 684).

6.1.1 Promissory estoppel

One of the best-known types of estoppel is promissory estoppel in contract, famously associated with Lord Denning.

● **Central London Property Trust Ltd v High Trees House** [1947] KB 130

Flats were let on a 99-year lease at £2,500 a year, but during the Second World War the landlord had agreed to reduce the rent to £1,250 because of the difficulty of finding tenants. Could the landlord go back on this promise, which was not legally binding, because of the lack of any consideration in return?

HELD: Lord Denning considered that, in the right circumstances, such promises could be binding, although not on these facts, as the war was now over (at 134–5):

> The courts have not gone so far as to give a cause of action in damages for the breach of such a promise, but they have refused to allow the party making it to act inconsistently with it. It is in that sense, and that sense only, that such a promise gives rise to an estoppel. The decisions

are a natural result of the fusion of law and equity: for the cases of *Hughes v Metropolitan Rly Co* (1877) 2 App Cas 439, *Birmingham and District Land Co v London & North Western Railway Company* (1888) 40 ChD 268 and *Salisbury (Marquess) v Gilmore* [1942] 2 KB 38, afford a sufficient basis for saying that a party would not be allowed in equity to go back on such a promise.

It might be noted that this promissory estoppel can only be used as a *defence* to an action; the contract cannot be enforced. As we shall see later in the chapter, proprietary estoppel is different, as it forms the basis of a claim.

6.1.2 Is there one principle of equitable estoppel?

Some are of the view that there is only one principle of equitable estoppel and that it is not helpful to separate it into promissory estoppel, proprietary estoppel, etc. This can be seen in the quotations from Hudson and Lord Denning at 6.1 'The different types of estoppel'. This view was propounded in the House of Lords case *Yeoman's Row Management Ltd v Cobbe* [2008] 1 WLR 1752.

. . . .

● *Yeoman's Row Management Ltd v Cobbe* [2008] 1 WLR 1752

Lord Scott at 1761:

> An 'estoppel' bars the object of it from asserting some fact or facts, or, sometimes, something that is a mixture of fact and law, that stands in the way of some right claimed by the person entitled to the benefit of the estoppel. The estoppel becomes a 'proprietary' estoppel—a sub-species of a 'promissory' estoppel—if the right claimed is a proprietary right, usually a right to or over land but, in principle, equally available in relation to chattels or choses in action.

Other judges are more sceptical as to whether these fine distinctions make any real difference as to how a case is actually going to be decided.

. . . .

● *Crabb v Arun District Council* [1976] Ch 179

Lord Scarman at 193:

> In pursuit of that inquiry I do not find helpful the distinction between promissory and proprietary estoppels. This distinction may indeed be valuable to those who have to teach or expound the law; but I do not think that, in solving the particular problem raised by a particular case, putting the law into categories is of the slightest assistance.

However, for the purposes of this book, we are going to concentrate on how estoppel affects rights over land, so we will call it proprietary estoppel.

6.2 Defining proprietary estoppel

Equity developed a doctrine of proprietary estoppel, which enabled the plaintiff to claim an interest in land (hence the name 'proprietary'), because they had been promised it, had believed the promise, and acted upon it. Proprietary estoppel is the basis of the claim, not just a defence to an action, so in that respect it differs from promissory estoppel. The claim could be established without the need for writing, deeds, or other formalities. The doctrine is ancient and there have been many judicial attempts to define its precise elements.

6.2.1 Building on someone else's land

The general situation required is laid out in:

. . . .

● ***Ramsden v Dyson*** (1866) LR 1 HL 129

Lord Kingsdown at 170:

> If a man under a verbal agreement with a landlord for a certain interest in land, or, what amounts to the same thing, under an expectation, created or encouraged by the landlord, that he shall have a certain interest, takes possession of such land, with the consent of the land-lord, and upon the face of such promise or expectation, with the knowledge of the landlord, and without objection by him, laid out money on the land, a Court of Equity will compel the landlord to give effect to such promise or expectation.

Lord Cranworth at 140:

> . . . if a stranger begins to build on any land supposing it to be his own, and I, perceiving his mistake, abstain from setting him right, and leave him to persevere in his error, a Court of Equity will not allow me afterwards to assert my title to the land on which he had expended money on the supposition that the land was his own.

6.2.2 'The five probanda'

There have been attempts to strictly define what is required.

The requirements for proprietary estoppel were set out in *Willmott v Barber* (1880) 15 ChD 96. All of five things had to be proved in order to establish a proprietary estoppel. These are sometimes known as 'the five **probanda**'.

. . . .
Probanda
Latin—things requiring to be proved.
. . . .

. . . .

● ***Willmott v Barber*** (1880) 15 ChD 96

Fry J at 105–6:

> A man is not to be deprived of his legal rights unless he has acted in such a way as would make it fraudulent for him to set up those rights. What, then, are the elements or requisites necessary to constitute fraud of that description?
>
> [1] In the first place the plaintiff must have made a mistake as to his legal rights.
>
> [2] Secondly, the plaintiff must have expended some money or must have done some act (not necessarily upon the defendant's land) on the faith of his mistaken belief.
>
> [3] Thirdly, the defendant the possessor of the legal right, must know of the existence of his own right which is inconsistent with the right claimed by the plaintiff. If he does not know of it he is in the same position as the plaintiff, and the doctrine of acquiescence is founded upon conduct with a knowledge of your legal rights.

[4] Fourthly, the defendant, the possessor of the legal right, must know of the plaintiff's mistaken belief of his rights. If he does not, there is nothing which calls upon him to assert his own rights.

[5] Lastly, the defendant, the possessor of the legal right, must have encouraged the plaintiff in his expenditure of money or in the other acts which he has done, either directly or by abstaining from asserting his legal right.

Where all these elements exist, there is fraud of such a nature as will entitle the court to restrain the possessor of the legal right from exercising it, but, in my judgment, nothing short of this will do.

6.2.3 Unconscionability

Later cases have not had such a rigid insistence that all five elements must be present. One element was missing in the following case, but an estoppel was still made out.

· ·

● *Taylor Fashions v Liverpool Victoria* [1982] QB 133

Taylor Fashions had a lease on a shop, but unknown to them, because their option to renew the lease had not been registered, they had no right to extend the lease. They had asked their landlords' permission to carry out extensive improvements on the shop, assuming that they would be using the shop for some time. The landlords, Liverpool Victoria, had granted permission. Liverpool did not know either that there was no right to renew the lease. Counsel for Victoria had argued that the fourth of the 'probanda' in *Willmott v Barber* (1880) 15 ChD 96 was not present, as Liverpool Victoria did not know that Taylor's belief as to renewal of the lease was 'mistaken', as they also thought that the lease could be renewed.

HELD: It was not essential for all five probanda to be established.

Oliver J at 151–2:

> Furthermore the more recent cases indicate, in my judgment, that the application of the *Ramsden v. Dyson*, L.R. 1 H.L. 129 principle—whether you call it proprietary estoppel, estoppel by acquiescence or estoppel by encouragement is really immaterial—requires a very much broader approach which is directed rather at ascertaining whether, in particular individual circumstances, it would be unconscionable for a party to be permitted to deny that which, knowingly, or unknowingly, he has allowed or encouraged another to assume to his detriment than to inquiring whether the circumstances can be fitted within the confines of some preconceived formula serving as a universal yardstick for every form of unconscionable behaviour.

In a number of subsequent cases, 'unconscionability' became the key concept. This can be seen in cases like *Re Basham* [1986] 1 WLR 1498 (at 6.3.1 'A presentation of future rights') and *Gillett v Holt* [2000] 2 All ER 289.

· ·

● *Gillett v Holt* [2000] 2 All ER 289

Robert Walker LJ at 301:

> Moreover the fundamental principles that equity is concerned to prevent unconscionable conduct permeates all the elements of the doctrine. In the end the court must look at the matter in the round.

6.2.4 By itself, unconscionability is not enough

The House of Lords reacted against the 'unconscionable' approach in *Yeoman's Row Management Ltd v Cobbe* [2008] 1 WLR 1752 and said that there could be no estoppel unless a promise or representation was made or encouragement given that the claimant was to receive an interest in land.

● *Yeoman's Row Management Ltd v Cobbe* [2008] 1 WLR 1752

Mrs Lisle-Mainwaring owned a block of flats through her company, Yeoman's Row, and negotiated with Cobbe, an experienced property developer. Cobbe would obtain planning permission for the flats, at his own expense, and then buy the flats from her for £12 million. He would redevelop the site and build houses. If the houses sold for more than £24 million he would give Mrs Lisle-Mainwaring 50 per cent of the proceeds above that figure. Cobbe obtained planning permission, but then Mrs Lisle-Mainwaring wanted to renegotiate the terms of the agreement and obtain a much bigger share of the profits. Cobbe wanted her to keep to the terms of the original agreement.

HELD: Cobbe sued for breach of contract, but as the agreement was oral and involved land, there was no contract under s. 2(1) of the Law of Property (Miscellaneous Provisions) Act 1989. So he claimed that there was a proprietary estoppel.

For there to be an estoppel Cobbe would have to be under an expectation, created or encouraged by Mrs Lisle-Mainwaring, that he was to have a certain interest in land and Cobbe would have to rely on that representation and act to his detriment.

Cobbe had no expectation, because it was always clear that they were still negotiating the terms of the contract and the terms that they had agreed were not intended to be binding. Cobbe's 'expectation' was that he would be allocated a particular share of the profits, not that he was to receive an interest in land. Therefore, Cobbe had no claim based on estoppel.

The House considered that business people, who could take legal advice, should be expected to make proper contracts, if they wanted an 'agreement' to be binding. The same level of formality should not be expected in domestic or family situations.

Lord Walker at 1782:

'Unconscionability' could not be the crucial element. The other elements of representation, reliance, and detriment had to be present.

> In the commercial context, the claimant is typically a business person with access to legal advice and what he or she is expecting to get is a *contract*. In the domestic or family situation context, the typical claimant is not a business person and is not receiving legal advice. What he or she wants and expects to get is an *interest* in immovable property, often for long-term occupation as a home. The focus is not on intangible legal rights but on the tangible property which he or she expects to get. The typical domestic claimant does not stop to reflect (until disappointed expectations lead to litigation) whether some further legal transaction (such as a grant by deed, or the making of a will or codicil) is necessary to complete the promised title.

Lord Walker at 1775:

> [Proprietary estoppel is] not a sort of joker or wild card to be used whenever the Court disapproves of the conduct of a litigant who seems to have the law on his side. Flexible though it is, the doctrine must be formulated and applied in a disciplined and principled way. Certainty is important in property transactions.

KEY POINT

Representation, reliance, and detriment are more important elements of estoppel than unconscionability.

'Unconscionability' was a check at the end to ensure that the three vital elements of a proprietary estoppel were present.

Lord Walker at 1788:

> As such it [unconscionability] does in my opinion play a very important part in the doctrine of equitable estoppel, in unifying and confirming, as it were the other elements. If the other elements appear to be present but the result does not shock the conscience of the court, the analysis needs to be looked at again.

thinking points

There seems to be some sort of representation in Cobbe, *even though it is not very explicit. It is clear that Cobbe acted to his detriment, as he spent a lot of money. Surely what happened to him was unconscionable? The court also seem to insist that the Law of Property (Miscellaneous Provisions) Act 1989 and its writing requirements are an impediment to successfully claiming an estoppel. If we apply* Cobbe *to many of the subsequent cases in this chapter, a fair number of them would no longer seem to be a valid estoppel. Can this decision be correct? See Macfarlane and Robertson 'The Death of Proprietary Estoppel' [2008] LMCLQ 449.*

6.2.5 Is there a distinction between business and domestic cases?

Some thought that *Yeoman's Row Management Ltd v Cobbe* [2008] 1 WLR 1752 was so strict that it spelled the end of proprietary estoppel, but in the following year the House of Lords was able to look at a new case on estoppel, with very different facts.

● *Thorner v Major and others* [2009] 1 WLR 776

Peter Thorner owned Steart Farm, near Cheddar in Somerset. His younger cousin, David Thorner, helped him to run the farm and worked without pay for 29 years. Peter indicated by various remarks to David that David would inherit the farm when he died, an example being giving David details of life assurance policies and saying 'That's for my death duties.' Peter, however, never made any definite statement to David that he would inherit the farm. Unknown to David, Peter had made a will to this effect in 1997, but he revoked it and died intestate in 2005. Other relatives claimed the farm under the intestacy rules, as Peter had no wife or children.

HELD: The House was able to distinguish this case from *Yeoman's Row Management Ltd v Cobbe* [2008] 1 WLR 1752.

Lord Neuberger at 803–4:

> However, there was total uncertainty as to the nature or terms of any benefit (property interest, contractual right, or money), and, if a property interest, as to the nature of that interest (freehold, leasehold, or charge), to be accorded to Mr Cobbe.

> Secondly, the analysis of the law in *Cobbe*'s case was against the background of very different facts. The relationship between the parties in that case was entirely arm's length and commercial, and the person raising the estoppel was a highly experienced businessman. The circumstances were such that the parties could well have been expected to enter into a

contract, however, although they discussed contractual terms, they had consciously chosen not to do so. They had intentionally left their legal relationship to be negotiated, and each of them knew that neither of them was legally bound.

In these circumstances, I see nothing in the reasoning of Lord Scott in *Cobbe's* case which assists the defendants in this case. It would represent a regrettable and substantial emasculation of the beneficial principle of proprietary estoppel if they were artificially fettered so as to require the precise extent of the property the subject of the alleged estoppel to be strictly defined in every case. Concentrating on the perceived morality of the parties' behaviour can lead to an unacceptable degree of uncertainty of outcome, and hence I welcome the decision in *Cobbe's* case. However, it is equally true that focusing on technicalities can lead to a degree of strictness inconsistent with the fundamental aims of equity.

So it may be that a different approach to estoppel can be taken if the case involves ordinary people, as opposed to businessmen and women. The latter would be expected to know the law and not have to rely on equitable remedies such as those provided by proprietary estoppel. The strict decision in *Yeoman's Row Management Ltd v Cobbe* [2008] 1 WLR 1752 was followed in another 'business' case, *Crossco No 4 Unlimited v Jolan Ltd* [2012] 2 All ER 754.

6.3 Representation

The defendant must make a representation to the claimant, indicating that the claimant has some sort of right to the land, or at least acquiesce in the claimant's mistaken belief that they have a right to the land.

6.3.1 A representation of future rights

Re Basham [1986] 1 WLR 1498 was only a High Court case, but extended the scope of proprietary estoppel. As the judge, Nugee QC, said at 1511, *Basham* 'on its facts went beyond the facts of any reported case'. The plaintiff was not encouraged to believe that she had an existing right, such as an interest in land, but that she would be granted rights in future. Specifically she was promised that she would inherit a house, but Basham died without leaving any will. In what circumstances can such a promise be enforced?

● ***Re Basham*** [1986] 1 WLR 1498

Joan Bird had worked in family businesses and, with the help of her husband, looked after her stepfather, Henry Basham. This went on from 1936 until Basham's death in 1982. They had turned down other opportunities and possible jobs in order to do this. They had their own home and had never lived in Basham's cottage. They expected to be left the cottage in Basham's will, as he had said things such as 'You don't have to worry about money, you'll be all right' and 'Joan, you're to have the house'. Basham died intestate.

HELD: Edward Nugee QC at 1504:

> The factor which gives rise to the equitable obligation in the cases to which Nourse J. referred is B's receipt of the property on the faith of an understanding. In cases of proprietary estoppel the factor which gives rise to the equitable obligation is A's alteration of his position on the faith of a similar understanding.

At 1509:

> No case was cited to me, and I know of no case, which affords support for Mr Browne's main submission, that the belief on which A relies must be related to an existing right. Mr Browne accepted that this suggested requirement would have been satisfied if the plaintiff had been living with the deceased at the cottage, but he contended that the fact that she lived a short distance down the road made all the difference. In my judgment the question whether it is unconscionable for the deceased's personal representatives to assert a legal title to his property cannot turn on a factor of this kind.

At 1511:

> The present case has arisen solely out of the failure of the deceased to make the will which was necessary, in view of the absence of any blood relationship, in order that indisputable legal effect should be given to the expectations which he had encouraged in the plaintiff.

It is clear that Basham had wanted his stepdaughter to have his cottage: possibly he did not realize that his stepdaughter would not automatically inherit under the intestacy rules. It would be unconscionable for anyone else to receive the cottage.

6.3.2 Estoppel may restrict testamentary freedom

There have been a number of proprietary estoppel cases on the basis that the deceased made promises to leave property, which they did not keep, but in *Gillett v Holt* [2000] 2 All ER 298, the Court of Appeal further extended the doctrine. An estoppel was established even though Holt, who had promised to leave property to Gillett, was still alive and so capable of making a new will.

● *Gillett v Holt* [2000] 2 All ER 289

Holt was a wealthy farmer, who had no children. Gillett had worked for him since leaving school in 1956. He was treated as a son, rose to become farm manager, and was told repeatedly that he would inherit the farm. There were witnesses to these conversations and expert evidence that he had been paid less than would be expected as a farm manager. Gillett had also turned down other opportunities, because he expected to inherit the farm.

Holt befriended another young man Wood, then a trainee solicitor, and in 1994 Holt made a new will in favour of Wood, rather than Gillett.

HELD: The normal principle in English Law is that a will is **ambulatory** and so is always revocable. The High Court had thought this a significant factor and Holt was entitled to change his mind, but the Court of Appeal disagreed and thought that an estoppel was made out.

The court must look at all the factors.

Robert Walker LJ at 301:

> ...the doctrine of proprietary estoppel cannot be treated as subdivided into three or four watertight compartments. Both sides are agreed on that, and in the course of the oral argument in this court it repeatedly became apparent that the quality of the relevant assurances may influence the issue of reliance, that reliance and detriment are often intertwined, and that whether there is distinct need for a 'mutual understanding' may depend on how the

Ambulatory— literally movable or mobile, but here it means that the testator can always make a new will, which supersedes older wills.

other elements are formulated and understood. Moreover the fundamental principles that equity is concerned to prevent unconscionable conduct permeates all the elements of the doctrine. In the end the court must look at the matter in the round.

Gillett had clearly acted to his detriment and detriment did not necessarily have to be financial.

Holt owned more than one farm, so Gillett was awarded 'The Beeches', one of the farms, and approximately £100,000. This was the minimum equity required to do justice, took account of Gillett's long and devoted service, and would allow a clean break between the parties.

6.3.3 Acquiescence in the claimant's mistaken belief

It is not necessary for the defendant to make a representation to the claimant: acquiescence in the claimant's mistaken belief that they have a legal right over the land may be enough. This can be seen in the definitions of proprietary estoppel seen in *Ramsden v Dyson* (1866) LR 1 HL 129 and *Willmott v Barber* (1880) 15 Ch D 96 at 6.2. A good example can be seen in the more modern case of *Crabb v Arun District Council* [1976] Ch 179.

. . . .

● *Crabb v Arun District Council* [1976] Ch 179

Crabb needed access over Arun District Council's land to get to the road. Their negotiations over formal permission came to nothing, but Crabb and his vehicles continued to use two access points, with the knowledge of Arun. Arun built two gates. Crabb sold part of his land, containing one of the access points, then Arun closed the remaining gate and demanded £30,000 to reopen it.

HELD: Arun knew that Crabb intended to sell his land and led him to believe that he would be granted access. Crabb was encouraged to act to his detriment by selling the land. The remedy was for Arun to grant Crabb reasonable access to his land.

Proprietary estoppel cases are usually very fact-sensitive. Did the defendant really mean to promise the claimant an interest in the land and how did the claimant interpret what they were being told? In the end it depends who the court believes. In the following example, *Lissimore v Downing* [2003] 2 FLR 308, the court did not believe the claimant.

. . . .

● *Lissimore v Downing* [2003] 2 FLR 308

KK Downing, a rock guitarist with Judas Priest, invited Sarah Lissimore to live with him on his Astbury Estate. She stayed from 1993–2001 and alleged that he had promised her a share in the estate with phrases such as 'I bet you never thought all of this would be yours in a million years' and called her 'Lady of the Manor'. In return she claimed that she gave up her job, other opportunities, and carried out work on the estate.

HELD: The court preferred Downing's account, that he did not seriously mean to give her half his estate and that there was no estoppel.

Judge Norris QC at para 18:

It follows that I would accept [counsel for the claimant's] concession that the alleged statements to Miss Lissimore by Mr Downing during the relationship (that 'she would not want for anything', or that 'he would take care of her', or that 'she did not need to worry her pretty head about money', or that 'his other girlfriends had never wanted for anything', or that 'he had looked after his other girlfriends and she would be no different') do not found a proprietary estoppel. Such statements do not on their face relate to any specific property, they plainly do not amount to a representation which binds the whole of Mr Downing's property, and they are not expressed in terms which enable any objective assessment to be made of what is being promised. In this last respect they are to be contrasted with statements made to unpaid or underpaid workers or business partners, encouraged to work on because they would be 'treated right', and for whom a commensurate reward could be objectively assessed.

We saw in *Yeoman's Row Management Ltd v Cobbe* [2008] 1 WLR 1752 that ongoing negotiations about a business deal could not be an estoppel, because it was not possible to pin down a specific promise that the claimant would get a right to property. The representation must be unequivocal and clearly indicate the property interest 'promised'.

In the domestic context, representations do not have to be so precise in order to form the basis of a proprietary estoppel. In *Thorner v Major* [2009] 1 WLR 776, what mattered was how the representation could be reasonably understood by the claimant. A distinction could be drawn between commercial cases and domestic cases.

● *Thorner v Major and others* [2009] 1 WLR 776

The facts are given at 6.2.5 'Is there a distinction between business and domestic cases?'.

HELD: Lord Rodger at 786:

Even though clear and unequivocal statements played little or no part in communications between the two men, they were well able to understand one another. So, however clear and unequivocal his intention to assure David that he was to have the farm after his death, Peter was always likely to have expressed it in oblique language...What matters, however, is that what Peter said should have been clear enough for David, whom he was addressing and who had years of experience in interpreting what he said and did, to form a reasonable view that Peter was giving him an assurance that he was to inherit the farm and that he could rely on it.

Whether a representation has been made all depends upon the facts and the context of the case.

Lord Walker at 795:

In this case the context, or surrounding circumstances, must be regarded as quite unusual. The deputy judge heard a lot of evidence about two countrymen leading lives that it may be difficult for many city-dwellers to imagine—taciturn and undemonstrative men committed to a life of hard and unrelenting physical work, by day and sometimes by night, largely unrelieved by recreation or female company. The deputy judge seems to have listened carefully to this evidence and to have been sensitive to the unusual circumstances of the case.

The size of the farm fluctuated over the years, and the defendants had used this to argue that it was not clear what property had been 'promised' to Peter. It was held that the property had been clearly identified.

Lord Walker at 795–6:

In my opinion it is a necessary element of proprietary estoppel that the assurances given to the claimant (expressly or impliedly, or, in standing-by cases, tacitly) should relate to identified property owned (or, perhaps, about to be owned) by the defendant...Both Peter

KEY POINT
Whether a representation has been made depends upon what it is reasonable for the claimant to understand.

and David knew that the extent of the farm was liable to fluctuate (as development opportunities arose, and tenancies came and went). There is no reason to doubt that their common understanding was that Peter's assurance related to whatever the farm consisted of at Peter's death...

So there could be an estoppel despite the fact that there never were clear words promising the farm to David. Rather, it was understood by both of them that this would happen. Nor did it matter that the size of the farm fluctuated over the years; it was clear to both of them what was being promised.

thinking points

There is quite a contrast between the House of Lords' decisions in Yeoman's Row v Cobbe *and* Thorner v Major, *yet they are only a year apart and involve some of the same judges. Is it all down to the difference between business and commercial relations, or did the facts in* Cobbe *never indicate an estoppel?* Thorner *seems a return to the usual approach to estoppel. See Martin Dixon 'Proprietary Estoppel: A Return to Principle' [2009] Conv 260.*

6.4 Reliance

There has to be a link between the representation, the promise of the interest in land, and the claimant acting to their detriment. Did the claimant do what they did because they thought that they had a claim to the land? In the older cases, such as *Ramsden v Dyson* (1866) LR 1 HL 129, the situation would be something straightforward like the claimant thinking that they owned the land and spending money to build or improve a house there.

6.4.1 Why did the claimant act to their detriment?

In the more modern type of case, it might be harder to discover the motivation of the claimant. If we look back to *Gillett v Holt* [2000] 2 All ER 289 at 6.3.2 'Estoppel may restrict testamentary freedom', it is clear that 'reliance and detriment are often intertwined'. Once it is established that there is a clear representation and that the claimant acted to their detriment, it is likely that the claimant relied on the representation. The defence would have to disprove this and show that the claimant acted for a different motive.

• *Greasley v Cook* [1980] 1 WLR 1306

Doris Cooke was the maid to the Greasley family, looking after them, including the mentally ill Clarice, from 1948 onwards for no pay. She cohabited with Kenneth Greasley, and he and his brother Hedley had assured her that she had a home for life. When Kenneth died, Hedley told her to leave. His case was that Miss Cooke could not show that the reason that she stayed was because she thought she had a claim to the house.

HELD: Lord Denning MR at pages 1311–12.

There is a presumption that she did so, relying on the assurances given to her by Kenneth and Hedley. The burden is not on her, but on them, to prove that she did not rely on their assurances... Suffice it that she stayed on in the house, looking after Kenneth and Clarice, when otherwise she might have left and got a job elsewhere.

Doris Cooke was allowed to stay in the house as long as she wished.

6.4.2 People act from mixed motives

As we have seen, the courts have since abandoned a rigid insistence on the claimant proving the five requirements in *Willmott v Barber* (1880) 15 ChD 96. The courts now accept that a claimant's motives may be mixed, but one of their motives for acting as they did must be because they thought that they had an interest in the land.

. . . .

● ***Wayling v Jones*** [1995] 2 FLR 1029

Daniel Jones ran various café and hotel businesses. Paul Wayling worked for him in a number of capacities and lived with him as his homosexual companion. Jones paid Wayling pocket money and living expenses and promised to leave him his hotel. Wayling also bought some expensive equipment for the hotel, but Jones died without leaving the hotel to him in his will.

HELD: Balcombe LJ at 173:

Wayling was awarded the proceeds of sale of the hotel.

> He went on to find that the plaintiff suffered a detriment by not asking for, or receiving, higher wages and continuing to serve the deceased until his death.
>
> ... it is necessary that I should first set out the relevant legal principles:
>
> (1) There must be a sufficient link between the promises relied upon and the conduct which constitutes the detriment ...
>
> (2) The promises relied upon do not have to be the sole inducement for the conduct: it is sufficient if they are an inducement ...
>
> (3) Once it has been established that promises were made, and there has been conduct by the plaintiff of such a nature that inducement may be inferred then the burden of proof shifts to the defendant to establish that he did not rely on the promises.

KEY POINT
Proprietary estoppel applies when the claimant acts to their detriment, relying on the promise of another.

Wayling had acted to his detriment by not insisting on a proper wage and by buying the equipment. He did this because he thought that he would inherit the hotel. This is reliance and does not have to be the sole motivation. He would have left if the promise of the hotel had been withdrawn.

6.5 Detriment

6.5.1 Detriment as expenditure on land

The claimant must act to their detriment, relying on the representation made to them that they had some sort of legal right to the land concerned. In the older cases detriment would be expenditure on land, building on land, improvements to land, etc.

. . . .

● ***Dillwyn v Llewelyn*** (1862) 4 De GF & J 517

A father allowed one of his sons to occupy part of his land, signing a memorandum purporting to convey that land to the son. The son spent £14,000 building a house on that land, of which the father knew and approved. The father died, but all his land was left to his other sons.

HELD: Lord Chancellor, Lord Westbury at 521:

> So if A puts B in possession of a piece of land, and tells him, 'I give it to you that you may build a house on it,' and B on the strength of that promise, with the knowledge of A, expends a large sum of money in building a house accordingly, I cannot doubt that the donee acquires a right from the subsequent transaction to call on the donor to perform that contract and complete the imperfect donation which was made.

At 522:

> No one builds a house for his own life only, and it is absurd to suppose that it was intended by either party that the house, at the death of the son, should become the property of the father...I should be of opinion that it was the plain intention of the testator to vest in the son the absolute ownership of the estate.

The father had intended his son to have his own home, and because the son had believed him and spent a large sum of money on the land, it was only right that the son should have the full fee simple, despite the lack of proper legal formalities, which would have been a deed of conveyance, not just a piece of writing. (See 5.2.1 'Land' for further details on the legal formalities to transfer land.)

6.5.2 Detriment is an essential element of estoppel

It is generally considered that detriment is an essential part of proprietary estoppel. Lord Denning suggested to the contrary in *Greasley v Cooke* [1980] 1 WLR 1306 at 1311: 'There is no need for her to prove that she acted to her detriment or to her prejudice', but Lord Denning simply meant that detriment could be something other than the expenditure of money. (See 6.4.1 'Why did the claimant act to their detriment?' for the facts of *Greasley v Cooke*.)

6.5.3 Detriment need not involve spending money on land

Subsequent cases have insisted that detriment is required, but it need not be as narrowly defined as spending money on the land. It could involve caring for someone as in *Re Basham (Deceased)* [1986] 1 WLR 1498, or working for little or low pay as in *Gillett v Holt* [2000] 2 All ER 298, *Thorner v Major* [2009] 1 WLR 776, and *Wayling v Jones* (1993) 69 P & CR 170.

● *Gillett v Holt* [2000] 2 All ER 298

Robert Walker LJ at 308:

> The overwhelming weight of authority shows that detriment is required. But the authorities also show that it is not a narrow or technical concept. The detriment need not consist of the expenditure of money or other quantifiable financial detriment, so long as it is something substantial. The requirement must be approached as part of a broad inquiry as to whether repudiation of an assurance is or is not unconscionable in all the circumstances.

In this type of case the court must look at all the things that the claimant did for the defendant to decide whether there was sufficient detriment.

● *Re Basham (Deceased)* [1986] 1 WLR 1498

Judge Edward Nugee QC at 1505–6:

> It may be that none of these incidents, taken by itself, would be very significant, but the cumulative effect of them supports the view that the plaintiff and her husband subordinated their own interests to the wishes of the deceased. Mr Browne submitted that all this could be attributed to the plaintiff's natural love and affection for her stepfather; but in my judgment the plaintiff's acts went well beyond what was called for by natural love and affection for someone to whom she had no blood relationship, and both she and her husband made it very clear in their evidence that there was no great love and affection between her husband and the deceased, and that he was only willing to pay for meals that the plaintiff provided for the deceased and to work as he did in the garden of the cottage because of the expectation that the deceased's estate would in due course pass to the plaintiff.

6.5.4 Weighing up detriment against personal advantage

It may be that the claimant acted to their detriment, but also gained something from the use of the land. The court has to weigh up whether there was an overall detriment which deserves a remedy.

● *Henry v Henry* [2010] 1 All ER 988

Geraldine Pierre owned some land, jointly with a relative, Marie Mitchel, on part of which she allowed a relative, Gladys Henry, to build a house, live, and farm. A grandson of Gladys, Calixtus Henry, who was now about 50, lived with her from birth and took over the house when she died 30 years ago, living there with his own family. Geraldine promised Calixtus that if he farmed the land and looked after her he would be given a share of the land on her death. Instead, shortly before her death, she sold her land to another relative, Theresa Henry. Theresa argued that the land had been fairly sold to her and anyway Calixtus had been able to live rent free and enjoy the profits of the produce he sold. This satisfied the equity.

HELD: The Privy Council thought that Calixtus had acted to his detriment, contrary to the views of the original trial judge.

Sir Jonathan Parker at 999:

> But he did not attempt to weigh the disadvantages suffered by Calixtus Henry by reason of his reliance on Geraldine Pierre's promises against the countervailing advantages which he enjoyed as a consequence of that reliance. That is a process which, on principle, he should have undertaken (see *Jennings v Rice* [2002] EWCA Civ 159).

At 1002:

> Proportionality lies at the heart of the doctrine of proprietary estoppel and permeates its every application. The Board concludes that, in all the circumstances of the case, the appropriate relief in order to achieve the minimum equity required to do justice to Calixtus Henry is to award him one-half of Theresa Henry's undivided half share in the plot.

KEY POINT
The court must weigh up whether the detriment suffered outweighs any advantage gained and therefore deserves a remedy.

6.6 The remedy

6.6.1 The minimum equity to do justice

The basic principle is that the remedy should be 'the minimum equity to do justice', which was clearly explained in *Crabb v Arun District Council* [1976] Ch 179.

• *Crabb v Arun District Council* [1976] Ch 179

Lord Scarman at 193:

> First is there an equity established? Secondly, what is the extent of the equity, if one is established? And, thirdly, what is the relief appropriate to satisfy the equity?

At 198:

> There being no grant, no enforceable contract, no licence, I would analyse the minimum equity to do justice to the plaintiff as a right either to an easement or to a licence upon terms to be agreed.

In that case the remedy was pretty straightforward, to allow Crabb access to the highway. On other sets of facts it can be harder to work out what is the 'minimum equity'.

6.6.2 What the defendant promised

Sometimes what the defendant promised to the claimant can be granted and that would produce an equitable result. In *Thorner v Major* [2009] 1 WLR 776, Peter received the farm his cousin had promised him, in *Re Basham* [1986] 1 WLR 1498, Bird was given her stepfather's cottage, in *Wayling v Jones* (1993) 69 P & CR 170, Wayling was given the hotel his lover had promised him, and in *Dillwyn v Llewelyn* (1862) 4 De GF & J 517, Dillwyn was given the house his father, Llewelyn, had meant to give to him. This making good the promise approach does not always lead to consistent results, as seen in *Greasley v Cooke* [1980] 1 WLR 1306, where the claimant was only allowed to stay in the house for her lifetime instead of being granted the full fee simple. This case can be contrasted with *Pascoe v Turner* [1970] 2 All ER 945, where some would argue that fulfilling the promise meant that the plaintiff gained too much.

• *Pascoe v Turner* [1970] 2 All ER 945

Mr Pascoe bought a house in Camborne, Cornwall, where he lived with Mrs Turner. The legal estate was in his name, but after he left her for a new woman, he told her 'The house is yours and everything in it.' Mrs Turner only had about £1,000 left and she spent about £230 on the house from 1973 to 1976. Then Pascoe sought to recover the house.

HELD: Cumming-Bruce LJ at 952:

> ...the court must decide what is the minimum equity to do justice to her having regard to the way in which she changed her position for the worse by reason of the acquiescence and encouragement of the legal owner.

She had very little money left, whereas Pascoe was relatively well off. She should be left undisturbed by him.

Cumming-Bruce LJ at 953:

> Weighing such considerations this court concludes that the equity to which the facts in this case give rise can only be satisfied by compelling the plaintiff to give effect to his promise and her expectations. He has so acted that he must now perfect the gift.

So Mrs Turner received the full fee simple of the house that had once belonged to Pascoe. She had not contributed very much in financial terms compared to Pascoe, although it was a lot of money for her. In some cases the court has tried to make a rough calculation of what the detriment was worth, in order to decide upon the remedy.

6.6.3 The remedy should be in proportion to the detriment suffered

This might be a particularly appropriate approach where the defendant promised to reward the claimant in some way, but never made exactly clear what they were promising to give to them. We have already seen some examples.

In *Gillett v Holt* [2000] 2 All ER 298 (see 6.3.2 'Estoppel may restrict testamentary freedom'), Holt had promised Gillett a farm, but as Holt had more than one farm it was more appropriate to work out the approximate cost of his labour and sacrifice, and then devise a remedy.

This approach, of proportionality, was endorsed by the Privy Council in *Henry v Henry* [2010] 1 All ER 988 (see 6.5.4 'Weighing up detriment against personal advantage').

. . . .
● *Henry v Henry* [2010] 1 All ER 988

Sir Jonathan Parker at 1002:

> Proportionality lies at the heart of the doctrine of proprietary estoppel and permeates its every application. The Board concludes that, in all the circumstances of the case, the appropriate relief in order to achieve the minimum equity required to do justice to Calixtus Henry is to award him one-half of Theresa Henry's undivided half share in the plot.

The weighing up of how much the detriment is worth against what the claimant has gained from the relationship might lead to the conclusion that, although there is an estoppel, no remedy is required. The court has to look at the circumstances of both the claimant and the defendant to determine where the equity lies.

. . . .
● *Sledmore v Dalby* (1996) 72 P & CR 196

Sledmore owned a house in which her daughter and her husband, Dalby, lived. Dalby stopped paying rent in 1976, but paid for some major improvements to the property. His wife died, but Sledmore did not serve a notice to quit until 1990. She could no longer afford her old house and needed the house Dalby lived in for her own use. Dalby was in employment and lived in other accommodation with his new partner. Dalby's daughter lived there now.

HELD: Dalby had lived rent free for 20 years and the equity he had on the property had now expired. Sledmore was granted an order for possession.

The need for writing

6.7.1 Statutory writing requirements

Proprietary estoppel usually involves land, yet there is no writing, as most of the cases that we have seen in this chapter involve oral promises or assurances. Section 53(2) of the Law of Property Act 1925 and s. 2(5) of the Law of Property (Miscellaneous Provisions) Act 1989 both exclude resulting trusts and constructive trusts from the need for writing, but neither mention proprietary estoppels.

Law of Property (Miscellaneous Provisions) Act 1989

....

2 Contracts for sale etc. of land to be made by signed writing

(1) A contract for the sale or other disposition of an interest in land can only be made in writing and only by incorporating all the terms which the parties have expressly agreed in one document or, where contracts are exchanged, in each.

...

(4) And nothing in this section affects the creation or operation of resulting, implied or constructive trusts.

Law of Property Act 1925

....

53 Instruments required to be in writing

(2) This section does not affect the creation or operation of resulting, implied or constructive trusts.

6.7.2 Is proprietary estoppel excused from statutory writing requirements?

Old authority holds that proprietary estoppel is excluded from the writing requirement. As the equitable maxim has it: 'Equity will not permit a Statute to be used as an instrument of fraud.' (See 2.8 'Equity will not permit a statute to be used as an instrument of fraud'.)

....

● *Crabb v Arun District Council* [1976] Ch 179

Lord Denning MR at 187–8 quoting Lord Cairns LC in *Hughes v Metropolitan Railway Co* (1877) 2 App Cas 439 at 448:

> ...it is the first principle upon which all courts of equity proceed that it will prevent a person from insisting on his strict legal rights—whether arising under a contract, or on his title deeds, or by statute—when it would be inequitable for him to do so having regard to the dealings which have taken place between the parties.

And then Lord Denning himself at 188:

> Short of a binding contract, if he makes a promise that he will not insist upon his strict legal rights—then, even though that promise may be unenforceable in point of law for want of consideration or want of writing—then, if he makes the promise knowing or intending that the other will act upon it, and he does act upon it, then again a court of equity will not allow him to go back on that promise: *Central London Property Trust Ltd. v High Trees House Ltd.* [1947] KB 130...

6.7.3 Did the Law of Property (Miscellaneous Provisions) Act 1989 change the law?

The passing of s. 2(1) of the Law of Property (Miscellaneous Provisions) Act 1989, made it clear that all the terms of a contract for land had to be included. The old equivalent, s. 40 of the Law of Property Act 1925, allowed a memorandum or note rather than the actual contract and expressly preserved the old doctrine of part performance, which allowed the enforcement of oral contracts for land. The intention of the new Act was to abolish the doctrine of part performance. Section 2(5) of the 1989 Act exempts constructive and resulting trusts from the writing requirement, but there is no exemption for proprietary estoppel, which is not mentioned. This issue was considered in *Yaxley v Gotts* [2000] Ch 162.

. . . .

● *Yaxley v Gotts* [2000] Ch 162

Yaxley was a builder who saw a house with the potential for conversion into flats. He did not have the money to buy it, so he approached his friend, Brownie Gotts, to borrow the money. Brownie and he agreed that Brownie would buy the house, Yaxley would convert it, and in exchange Yaxley would get the ground floor of the property. Brownie's son Alan took on the project and bought the house with his own money. Yaxley did the conversion, but did not realize that Brownie was not the owner. Later, they fell out and Alan excluded Yaxley from the property and denied that he had any interest in the land. It was argued that any agreement that they might have made was not in writing and therefore unenforceable under the Law of Property (Miscellaneous Provisions) Act 1989.

HELD: The Court of Appeal examined the legislative history of the Law of Property (Miscellaneous Provisions) Act 1989, including a report of the Law Commission, and concluded that Parliament had intended to exempt proprietary estoppel from the Act.

Beldam LJ at 193:

> For my part I cannot see that there is any reason to qualify the plain words of section 2(5). They were included to preserve the equitable remedies to which the Commission had referred...
>
> In my view the provision that nothing in section 2 of the Act of 1989 is to affect the creation or operation of resulting, implied or constructive trusts effectively excludes from the operation of the section cases in which an interest in land might equally well be claimed by relying on constructive trust or proprietary estoppel.

The judges, in particular Robert Walker LJ, thought that this was also a constructive trust anyway, so it was clearly exempt under s. 2(5).

A few years later the House of Lords looked at the matter, but they were less sure that proprietary estoppel was exempt from the writing requirement.

• **Yeoman's Row Management Ltd v Cobbe**   [2008] 1 WLR 1752

The court thought that proprietary estoppel might threaten the certainty of contracts.

Lord Scott makes some interesting remarks to the effect that s. 2(1) of the Law of Property (Miscellaneous Provisions) Act 1989 requires there to be a written contract for land, and although s. 2(5) exempts constructive and resulting trusts from the writing requirement, there is no exemption for proprietary estoppel.

KEY POINT
Most authority indicates that writing is not required for a proprietary estoppel of land, but the point has not been finally decided.

At 1769:

> My present view, however, is that proprietary estoppel cannot be prayed in aid in order to render enforceable an agreement that statute has declared to be void ... Equity can surely not contradict the statute. As I have said, however, statute provides an express exception for constructive trusts.

In the following year, the House of Lords looked at proprietary estoppel again in *Thorner v Major* [2009] 1 WLR 776, but both parties agreed that there was no contract for land involved, so their Lordships did not have to make any decision on the s. 2(5) point.

6.8 Proprietary estoppel and constructive trusts

6.8.1 A proprietary estoppel and constructive trust could exist on the same facts

The difference between proprietary estoppel and constructive trusts has become increasingly small. Some of the cases that we have looked at, such as *Re Basham* [1986] 1 WLR 1498 (see 6.3.1 'A representation of future rights') and *Yaxley v Gotts* [2000] Ch 162 (see 6.7.3) also involved a constructive trust. The same facts can give rise to both, as was explained in *Yaxley*.

• **Yaxley v Gotts**   [2000] Ch 162

Robert Walker LJ at 176 and 177:

> But in the area of a joint enterprise for the acquisition of land (which may be, but is not necessarily, the matrimonial home) the two concepts coincide ...
>
> The oral bargain which the judge found to have been made between Mr Yaxley and Mr Brownie Gotts, and to have been adopted by Mr Alan Gotts, was definite enough to meet the test stated by Lord Bridge in Lloyds Bank plc v Rosset [1991] 1 AC 107, 132.

(See 18.4 'Sole name cases—acquiring a beneficial interest. The two categories in *Lloyds Bank v Rosset*' for *Lloyds Bank plc v Rosset*.)

6.8.2 A proprietary estoppel can be based on a representation

So if no oral agreement to share the land can be found, then it is unlikely to be a constructive trust. An estoppel is possible if something less, such as a representation, can be proved.

● **Southwell v Blackburn** [2014] EWCA Civ 1347

David Southwell bought a house, with the legal estate in his sole name, so that Catherine Blackburn and her two daughters could live with him. There was no common intention that they should share the beneficial interest in the house in equal shares, so there could not be a constructive trust. He did, however, reassure her that she would always have a home. She had given up a secure home, on which she had spent £15,000, to be with him and had spent about £4,000 on the new home.

HELD: The elements of an estoppel; representation and detrimental reliance, were present and it would be unconscionable not to give Mrs Blackburn a remedy. To compensate her for her loss of secure accommodation, Southwell was ordered to pay her £28,500, which was the amount that she had spent, updated for inflation.

6.8.3 Proprietary estoppel has a flexible remedy

It used to be said that a major difference between estoppel and constructive trust was that the remedy for estoppel was in the discretion of the court, whereas the remedy in a constructive trust must reflect the common intention of the parties. This distinction is no longer so clear cut, now that the Supreme Court in *Jones v Kernott* [2012] 1 AC 776 has said that it is possible to impute the common intention and award the parties fair shares. (See Chapter 18 'Trusts of the family home', particularly 18.8.3 '*Lloyds Bank v Rosset* and other cases').

6.8.4 Proprietary estoppel, constructive trust, resulting trust, and the family home

In cases that relate to the family home (see Chapter 18 'Trusts of the family home'), such as *Grant v Edwards* [1986] Ch 638 and *Lloyds v Rosset* [1991] 1 AC 107, it is stated that the principles of resulting trust, constructive trust, and proprietary estoppel combine together to form the common intention constructive trust. There does not seem much to be gained by arguing estoppel rather than common intention constructive trust in disputes over the family home. Cases such as *Southwell v Blackburn* [2014] EWCA Civ 1347 at 6.8.2 'A proprietary estoppel can be based on a representation' are rare and the claimant only gains an occupation right, rather than a share in the value of the home.

thinking points

There are similarities between constructive trusts and estoppels, but also differences. Often both occur or at least are argued in the same case, causing some confusion between the two. Yet they have separate origins and one is a trust, with the characteristics of a trust, and the other is not. Both estoppel and the constructive trust have been examined by the House of Lords in Stack v Dowden *[2007] 2 All ER 929, which concerned the family home and* Yeoman's Row Management Ltd v Cobbe *[2008] 1 WLR 1752, which concerned a business deal. Do the two concepts operate differently in different situations, or are they the same? See T Etherton 'Constructive Trusts and Proprietary Estoppel: The Search for Clarity and Principle' [2009] Conv 104.*

Conclusion

Proprietary estoppel provides a valuable means of enforcing informal transactions involving land. It means that promises are kept, the recipient's expectations are met, and those who have expended time, effort, and money, or in other words acted to their detriment, are rewarded. Because this is an equitable doctrine and any remedy is discretionary, the court is able to look at all the facts of the case and how all the parties involved, not just those before the court, are likely to be affected.

Flexibility, though, has its downside, as looking at the bare facts of a claim it is not always possible to tell whether an estoppel will succeed or not. This leads to much litigation, which is perhaps not a good thing, particularly when families are involved, which can be seen in many of the cases in this chapter.

Questions

Self-test questions

1   Define the basic requirements of an estoppel.

2   What is the difference between the definition of an estoppel in *Willmott v Barber* and *Taylor Fashions v Liverpool Victoria*?

3   What did *Yeoman's Row Management v Cobbe* decide?

4   What amounts to a representation?

5   What is the difference between a representation and acquiescence?

6   Who has to prove reliance?

7   Outline the different types of detriment that are possible.

8   What kind of remedy can be awarded if an estoppel is made out?

Discussion questions

1   Is it possible to define unconscionability?

2   Explain the difference between *Thorner v Major* and *Yeoman's Row v Cobbe*.

3   Is it possible accurately to define what is meant by detrimental reliance?

4   Does a proprietary estoppel escape the writing requirements of s. 2(5) of the Law of Property (Miscellaneous) Provisions Act 1989 and s. 53(2) of the Law of Property Act 1925?

5   What is the difference between a constructive trust and a proprietary estoppel?

Assessment question

Peter owned and ran a large farm, but only employed one full-time employee, David. Peter had no family of his own, so David often stayed in the farmhouse with Peter, even though David had a family of his own. Particularly as Peter got older, David also helped Peter around the house with domestic tasks.

In 2005 Peter sold part of the farm for building. David organized the sale and made sure that the legal work was done. Peter and David had informally agreed that they would share the proceeds, which were £1 million. Peter also told David: 'Thanks for helping me with the sale; sort out my affairs when I die and I will see you all right.' David thought that this meant that Peter would leave him the farm in his will, so David made no claim to a share of the money.

In 2010 Peter died without leaving any will. His only relative, a brother, Gareth, claims the farm and the £1 million.

David thinks that some of the farm, at least, and half of the £1 million should come to him and seeks your help.

Advise David.

Key cases

- *Crabb v Arun District Council* [1976] Ch 179 **(at 6.1.2, 6.3.3, 6.6.1, and 6.7.2)**

- *Yeoman's Row Management Ltd v Cobbe* [2008] 1 WLR 1752 **(at 6.1.2, 6.2.4, 6.2.5, and 6.7.3)**

- *Thorner v Major and others* [2009] 1 WLR 776 **(at 6.2.5 and 6.3.3)**

- *Gillett v Holt* [2000] 2 All ER 289 **(at 6.2.3, 6.3.2, 6.4.1, 6.5.3, and 6.6.3)**

- *Yaxley v Gotts* [2000] Ch 162 **(at 6.7.3 and 6.8.1)**

Further reading

Macfarlane and Robertson 'The Death of Proprietary Estoppel: A Critique of *Yeoman's Row Management Ltd v Cobbe*' [2008] *LMCLQ* 449

Is the decision in *Yeoman's Row* too strict on what is required for an estoppel?

M Dixon 'Proprietary Estoppel: A Return to Principle. A Commentary on *Thorner v Major*' [2009] *Conv* 260

The decision in *Thorner* was greeted with some relief, as it seemed a return to orthodoxy after *Yeoman's Row v Cobbe*.

T Etherton 'Constructive Trusts and Proprietary Estoppel: The Search for Clarity and Principle' [2009] *Conv* 104

The approaches to constructive trust and proprietary estoppel in *Yeoman's Row Management Ltd v Cobbe* and *Stack v Dowden*.

The disposal of property on death

Introduction

Although it might seem the easiest thing in the world to write a will, many people do not do so. This may be because of ignorance, a natural unwillingness to think about death, or sometimes because the person does not want the world or their family to know the true destination of their property. Although an Act of Parliament, the Wills Act 1837, lays down strict rules about how a will should be made and property disposed of after death, equity allows some exceptions to this. In the case of secret trusts and mutual wills, a promise has been made to the deceased to leave the property to a particular person. Equity regards breaking a promise as 'fraud' and will enforce such promises by imposing a trust on the person who holds the property. Death bed gifts (donatio mortis causa) involve a promise to hand over property, but the correct legal formalities are not completed. Equity will again enforce the promise by imposing a trust on the executors or administrators of the deceased's estate. All that the 'trust' means is that the property must be properly transferred to the intended donee.

7.1.1 General characteristics of wills

The obvious thing to do is to write a will. A valid will acts as both a transfer of property and a declaration of trust. If the deceased does not write a will, then the intestacy rules under the Administration of Estates Act 1925 apply—the property will go to the deceased's relatives.

A will is *ambulatory*, i.e. the testator, while still living, can always revoke his will and make a new one. The testator or testatrix has testamentary freedom in that they can leave their property to whom they like. Unlike many foreign legal systems, the testator/testatrix is not obliged to provide for spouse or children. The will takes effect upon the death of the testator/testatrix. There are strict rules relating to wills.

1. Wills Act 1837, s. 9 (as amended by the Administration of Justice Act 1982, s. 17). The will must be written, signed by the testator/testatrix, and the signature witnessed by two persons.
2. Wills Act 1837, s. 15. The witnesses to the signature cannot also be beneficiaries.
3. Wills Act 1837, s. 18. Marriage revokes previous wills. Divorce has a similar effect.
4. A will is a public document. After the testator/testatrix has died and the will has been admitted to probate, a copy of the will can be obtained and read by any member of the public. Wills are obtained from the Probate Registry, run by Her Majesty's Courts Service (to find the will of a deceased person see https://probatesearch.service.gov.uk/#wills).

7.1.2 The doctrine of incorporation by reference

● *In bonis (concerning the goods of) Smart* [1902] P 238

Smart made her will in 1895 and part of the will instructed her trustees to give certain articles to her friends. The will stated that a book or memorandum would be found with the will, specifying which article went to which friend. This book was prepared in 1898 or 1899.

In 1900 Smart made a **codicil**, which did not refer to the book.

HELD: Gorell Barnes J at 240:

> It seems to me that it has been established that if a testator, in a testamentary paper duly executed, refers to an existing unattested testamentary paper, the instrument so referred to becomes part of a will; in other words, it is incorporated into it; but it is clear that, in order that the informal document should be incorporated in the validly executed document, the latter must refer to the former as a written instrument then existing—that is, at the time of the execution—in such terms that it may be ascertained.

That meant that the book could not be considered as part of the will and that the directions in it had to be ignored.

The idea of doctrine of incorporation by reference is to try to prevent fraud. Anyone could produce a document and claim that it was the last wishes of the testator/testatrix. The fact that the document is referred to and identified in the will is some protection. Similarly, the testator/testatrix must specify what they want to happen to their property in their wills. They cannot just leave the property to the executors and state that they will supply the names of the beneficiaries later. There would be no witnesses and anyone could claim that the testator/testatrix had promised them the property.

Despite these considerations, equity has developed doctrines that allow the strict rules regarding wills to be circumvented. Common features of these separate doctrines are the ideas of respecting the testator's true intention and of enforcing promises that have been made to the testator.

Codicil—an amendment or addition to an earlier will. The codicil must be signed and have two witnesses just like the main will.

7.2 Secret trusts

7.2.1 The origins of the secret trust

The testator has left property by will to A, but A has in fact promised to give the property to B. Equity will impose a trust on A to ensure that he keeps his promise.

This is called a secret trust because the testator/testatrix does not want the identity of the true beneficiary to appear in the will, where anyone might read it. There are a number of reasons why someone would want to do this. In many of the cases, the 'secret beneficiary' was a 'mistress' or illegitimate child, in the days when this would have been a major social disgrace. The Statute of Mortmain 1736 made it impossible to leave land to the church, so some would try to evade it by leaving the land to a friend and asking them to give it to the church. In some of the more recent cases, the inspiration behind a secret trust seems to have been a desire to hide the identity of the true beneficiary from the taxman. Lastly, some people just seem to be ignorant of the requirement of a written will and try to dispose of their property orally.

A secret trust does not fully comply with the writing requirements of the Wills Act 1837, yet, from an early period, the courts have been willing to enforce the *oral* promise, in order to prevent fraud.

7.2.2 The difference between fully and half secret trusts

There are two distinct types of secret trust: fully secret and half secret. It is very important to distinguish between them, because the rules for the validity of the two types are different. In particular, the requirements for the communication of the secret trust to the secret trustees are not the same. *In Re Lucian Freud (Deceased)* [2014] EWHC 2577 (Ch) the court had to decide whether Freud, a famous artist, had created a fully secret or a half secret trust. The court did this by looking at the words that he used in his will.

● ***In Re Lucian Freud (Deceased)*** [2014] EWHC 2577 (Ch)

Paragraph 6 of Freud's 2006 will read:

> I GIVE all the residue of my estate (out of which shall be paid my funeral and testamentary expenses and my debts) and any property over which I have a general power of appointment to the said Diana Mary Rawstron and the said Rose Pearce jointly.

Rawstron and Pearce had been told that they were to hold the property on trust for beneficiaries, whose names Freud did not want to appear in his will. In a fully secret trust the trust is not mentioned in the will, it looks like an absolute gift to the people who have been told that they will be secret trustees. So this was a fully secret trust.

Freud had changed his mind, because in an earlier 2004 will, he had set up a half secret trust. In paragraph 1, Rawstron, a solicitor and Pearce, one of Freud's children, were named as executrices and trustees of the will. The old paragraph 6 read:

> I GIVE all the residue of my estate (out of which shall be paid my funeral and testamentary expenses and my debts) and any property over which I have a general power of appointment to my trustees ON TRUST to sell or retain it . . .

In a half secret trust the existence of the trust will be mentioned in the will.

KEY POINTS

- In a fully secret trust, there is no indication in the will that there is any trust at all, e.g. the will says 'To Richard and David absolutely'. In a half secret trust there is an indication that the persons named in the will cannot keep the property for themselves, e.g. 'To Richard and David for a purpose that I have made known to them'.

- In a fully secret trust communication must be before the death of the testator/testatrix.

- In a half secret trust communication must be before or at the time the will is made.

- Fully secret are the oldest type.

7.2.3 Fully secret trusts

The wording of the will indicates that property is left absolutely to the 'secret trustee'.

It is suggested, obiter dicta in *Stickland v Aldridge* (1804) 9 Ves 516, that a secret trust could apply in an **intestacy**, as it might be clear to the deceased which relative would inherit and the deceased could have made that relative promise to leave that property to another.

There are three main elements to form a valid secret trust.

7.2.4 Intention

The testator/testatrix must clearly intend a trust.

● ***McCormick v Grogan*** [1869] LR 4 HL 82

Abraham Craig, a linen merchant of Belfast, was dying of cholera and sent for his friend, William Grogan. He told Grogan that he had made a will long ago, leaving all his property to him. Grogan asked Craig, 'Is that right?' and Craig replied, 'It shall be no other way.' Grogan was told that he would find the will and a letter. Craig died shortly afterwards and the will and the letter were found. The letter asked Grogan to make various gifts to a large number of named persons. The letter, however, contained statements such as 'I do not wish you to act strictly to the foregoing instructions, but leave it entirely to your own good judgment to do as you think I would if living...' and 'I leave it to yourself to carry out the intentions as you may think best...' Grogan paid some of the beneficiaries, but not others, and one of those left out, McCormick, brought a test case.

HELD: Lord Hatherley LC at 94:

> The instructions on their very face appear to bear this interpretation, that it was the testator's intention to leave Mr Grogan sole and complete master of his property.

And at 95:

> ...I think the letter itself, and all the circumstances attending it, lead to the conclusion that it was the full intention of the testator, uninduced by anything except that it was his own wish so to deal with his property, and to leave the instructions simply as a guide which might assist him in the discretion which he would himself exercise.

Lord Westbury explained how a secret trust works at 97:

> The Court of Equity has, from a very early period, decided that even an Act of Parliament shall not be used as an instrument of fraud; and if in the machinery of perpetrating a fraud an Act of Parliament intervenes, the Court of Equity, it is true, does not set aside the Act of Parliament, but it fastens on the individual who gets a title under the Act, and imposes upon him a personal obligation, because he applies the Act as an instrument for accomplishing a fraud.

Craig had not intended a trust, but had instead made an outright gift of his property to Grogan.

As a trust is intended, the three certainties must also be satisfied for there to be a valid trust. (See Chapter 4 'Trusts and powers and the three certainties'.) This was confirmed by a modern Court of Appeal case.

● **Margulies v Margulies 2000 WL 362514** [1999–2000] 2 ITELR 641

Alexander Margulies had three children. His younger son, Stephen, alleged that his father had left all his property in a will to his elder son, Marcus, but had asked Marcus to give a third of the property to Stephen. The facts of the case are confusing, because there were, allegedly, several attempts to do this. A typical example was in 1982, when Alexander's solicitors made a note about his will, which read 'Everything to Marcus. Private instructions to him, to give whatever he thinks appropriate to Stephen and/or grandchildren.'

HELD: Nourse LJ at paras 15 and 16 (Westlaw report):

> I return to the first requirement of a secret trust, as stated by Peter Gibson LJ in *Kasperbauer v Griffith* [2000] 1 WTLR 333. What is needed is an intention by the testator to create a trust, satisfying the traditional requirement of the three certainties: certain language in imperative form; certain subject-matter; and certain beneficiaries. As to these, all of which must be established, I proceed on the footing that an arguable case has been shown in regard to certainty of beneficiaries, at any rate in the shape of Stephen himself.
>
> Viewed as a whole, this material falls far short of establishing that any relevant communication made by the father to Marcus was expressed in certain language in imperative form.
>
> In my view Stephen has failed to establish any arguable case as to certainty of subject-matter. Indeed, everything points to any instructions given or wishes expressed by the father as having been entirely unspecific as to the property to which they were to relate. That in itself is probably enough to defeat the claim for a secret trust or fiduciary power. But it must be added that the lack of specificity inevitably reflects on the instructions or wishes themselves, enforcing the conclusion that they cannot have been given or expressed in language in imperative form.

There must be certainty of intention, in that the testator/testatrix must clearly indicate to the 'secret trustee' that they want them to hold the property that they are leaving them on trust. The actual word 'trust' does not have to be used, but the intention must be clear. This was confirmed by the Canadian case *Chinn v Hanrieder* [2009] BCSC 635, where a fully secret trust of mineral rights was established. Testators are not expected to use legal words; the words that they use may be 'weak or even inapt'. As long as the intention to declare a trust is clear, then the courts may give effect to a secret trust. (See 4.7 'Certainty of intention' on certainty of intention and in particular *Gold v Hill* [1999] 1 FLR 54, which has some resemblances to a secret trust case.) There must also be certainty of subject matter: the trust property must be clearly specified. Lastly, there must be certainty of objects: the beneficiaries must be clearly identified.

7.2.5 Communication

Communication to the 'secret trustee' can be before or after the will is made. The secret trustee promises to carry out the wishes of the testator. It would be a fraud for the secret trustee to break his promise.

● **Moss v Cooper** [1861] 1 J & H 352

John Hill wanted to leave real property to charity, but he could not do this because of the Statute of Mortmain. So he made a new will in 1856 leaving his property to three named individuals. Hill gave instructions on his real wishes to one of them, Gawthorn, who passed this on to the other two.

HELD: Sir Page Wood VC at 367: There was no 'distinction between a will made on the faith of a previous promise, and a will followed by a promise'.

The communication must, however, be made before the death of the testator/testatrix.

. . . .
● *Wallgrave v Tebbs* (1855) 25 LJ Ch 241

William Coles made a will in 1850 leaving £12,000, freehold land in Chelsea, and a field in Earl's Court to Tebbs and Martin. In the same year, Coles wrote a letter expressing confidence in Tebbs and Martin, that they would use this property to build a church and help the poor. Tebbs and Martin did not know of the existence of this letter until after the death of Coles.

HELD: Wood VC at 247:

> Here there has been no promise or undertaking on the part of the legatee. The latter knew nothing of the testator's intention until after his death. Upon the face of the will, the parties take indisputably for their own benefit.

So a secret trust will fail if there is no communication. As there is no trust, the will takes effect and the persons to whom the property is left keep the property.

Communicating the secret trust by letter is quite a common practice, but the letter must actually be handed over to the secret trustee, before the death of the testator. (See also the half secret trust case *Re Keen* [1937] Ch 226 at 7.2.11 'Half secret trusts require communication before the will'.)

. . . .
● *Re Boyes* (1884) 26 ChD 531

George Boyes made a will leaving everything to his solicitor, Frederick Carritt, who was also made executor. Boyes had told Carritt that he was to hold the property on trust for a certain lady and child and would receive further directions. Carritt gave an undertaking that he would do this, but the further directions never came. After the death of Boyes a document was found telling Carritt to give everything to Nell Brown, except £25 for himself.

HELD: Kay J at 536:

> It may possibly be that he would be bound if the trust had been put in writing and placed in his hands in a sealed envelope, and he had engaged that he would hold the property given to him by the will upon the trust so declared although he did not know the actual terms of the trust.

The secret trustee needs to know that there is a trust and that they cannot keep the property for themselves, but the *name* of the beneficiary can be kept secret until the letter is opened, after the death of the testator.

Even though the secret trust had failed, Carritt could not keep the property for himself, because he had agreed to be a trustee.

> The Defendant, however, having admitted that he is only a trustee, I must hold...that he is a trustee of this property for the next of kin of the testator.

This was a resulting trust.

7.2.6 Acquiescence

The secret trustee must agree to carry out the trust, but does not actually have to accept, just not refuse. Unlike in standard contract law, the secret trustee's acceptance can be silent, rather than actively agreeing.

● *Moss v Cooper* (1861) 1 J & H 352

HELD: Sir Page Wood VC at 366:

> …I apprehend that, to fasten any trust upon an absolute bequest of property, it is necessary to prove knowledge on the part of the legatee of the intended trust, and acquiescence, either by words of consent or by silence, when the intention is communicated to them.

Lack of acquiescence was one of the reasons that a secret trust was not established in *McCormick v Grogan* (1869) LR 4 HL 82.

● *McCormick v Grogan* (1869) LR 4 HL 82

(See 7.2.4 'Intention'.) Grogan was told of the existence of a letter relating to Craig's will, but had no knowledge of its contents. So he could not very well agree to carry out the trust.

At 83:

> No assent was asked from Mr Grogan as to the contents of the letter.

Lord Westbury at 98 and 99:

> My Lords, it is impossible to hold that that amounts to a distinct promise, the breach of which would constitute a fraud; for you cannot constitute a fraud in this matter unless you find that there is a distinct and positive promise, the non-fulfilment of which brands the party with disgrace as having personally imposed on the testator.

7.2.7 A secret trust can even affect a person who did not make the promise

Usually the trust is imposed on the secret trustee, the person that made the promise to the testator/testatrix. The secret trust can also be imposed on others, to whom the secret trustee has left the property.

● *Ottaway v Norman* [1972] Ch 698

Harry Ottaway's will left his house and its contents to Miss Hodges, his housekeeper. He had asked that when she died she leave the house and its contents to his son, William, and

William's wife, Dorothy. Hodges had accepted her obligation, because her first will, in 1963, did this. Later, Hodges changed her mind and in a new will left the house to Mr Norman and his wife. Norman was also the executor of this will. William Ottaway claimed that Norman held the house on constructive trust for himself and Dorothy.

HELD: Brightman J at 711: He accepted that the three requirements of a secret trust, intention, communication, and acquiescence were made out. The Normans were bound by Hodges's promise.

> I am informed that there is no recent reported case where the obligation imposed on the primary donee is an obligation to make a will in favour of the secondary donee as distinct from some form of **inter vivos** transfer. But it does not seem to me that there can really be any distinction which can validly be taken on behalf of the defendant in the present case. The basis of the doctrine of a secret trust is the obligation imposed on the conscience of the primary donee and it does not seem to me that there is any materiality in the machinery by which the donor intends that that obligation shall be carried out.

The Normans had made no promise to Harry Ottaway and so had not acquired the property by fraud, i.e. breaking their promise. But Eva Hodges had not kept her promise, so the secret trust was imposed on them. So Eva Hodges was not free to leave her property to whoever she chose.

This restricts the general principle that a person has complete testamentary freedom, i.e. they can leave their property to whoever they like. (See 7.1.1 'General characteristics of wills'.) The same restriction can be seen in the doctrine of mutual wills. (See 7.3.2 'The mutual will is enforced by a 'floating trust''.)

7.2.8 Proof

It can be difficult to prove whether a secret trust actually exists or not. Even if the communication is in writing, the acceptance is likely to be oral. It is also quite possible that there are no witnesses. The older cases required a high standard of proof, before a trust would be imposed.

● *McCormick v Grogan* (1869) LR 4 HL 82

Lord Westbury at 97:

> Now, being a jurisdiction founded on personal fraud, it is incumbent on the Court to see that a fraud, a **malus animus**, is proved by the clearest and most indisputable evidence...direct proof, for the purpose of affixing the criminal character of fraud.

In more modern times, the courts simply required clear evidence.

● *Ottaway v Norman* [1972] Ch 698

Brightman J at 712:

> I do not think that Lord Westbury's words mean more than this: that if a will contains a gift which is in terms absolute, clear evidence is needed before the court will assume that the testator did not mean what he said.

The most recent ruling on this issue is in *Re Snowden* [1979] 2 All ER 172.

● **Re Snowden** [1979] 2 All ER 172

Megarry VC applied the normal civil standard of the balance of probabilities, but decided on the facts that a secret trust was not intended.

The balance of probabilities simply means that it is more likely that this happened than it did not.

7.2.9 Disclaiming the trust

It is thought that even after the secret trustee has accepted the trust, he/she can disclaim the trust.

● **Re Maddock** [1902] 2 Ch 220

Cozens-Hardy J at 231:

> Legatee—
> a person left
> personal property
> in a will.

> Now the so-called trust does not affect the property except by reason of a personal obligation binding the individual devisee or **legatee**. If he renounces and disclaims, or dies in the lifetime of the testator, the persons claiming under the memorandum can take nothing against the heir-at-law or next of kin or residuary devisee or legatee.

But the secret trustee must disclaim while the testator is still alive. That way the testator can make another will and find another secret trustee, who will carry out his or her wishes.

7.2.10 Half secret trusts

The wording of the will indicates that there is a trust. It took longer for the courts to accept that there could be secret trusts in these circumstances. They are not completely secret, because it says in the will that the trustees are holding the property for someone else. However, the identity of the beneficiary can be kept secret.

An early example can be found in the next case.

● **Re Fleetwood** [1880] 15 ChD 594

Elizabeth Fleetwood was ill in bed and about to die. James Beaumont made up a list of various people to whom he would give property. Elizabeth made a codicil to her will leaving all her property to James Beaumont 'to be applied as I have requested him to do'.

HELD: Hall VC at 607–8:

> In the argument before me it was said that the jurisdiction of the Court was altogether founded on personal fraud, the Court only depriving the legatee of what he would otherwise retain beneficially . . .
>
> . . . from which counsel have contended before me that where a trust appears on the will and the legatee can in no case take for himself, there can be no fraud, and therefore the doctrine does not apply.

I cannot treat either or both of those two cases…as establishing, contrary to the other authorities I have mentioned, that where trust is referred to on the face of the will, the Court will not give effect to the intended trust…

In a fully secret trust, if the secret trustee does not keep his promise, then he would keep the property for himself, as the will gives it to him absolutely. In a half secret trust, the secret trustee is named as a trustee in the will, so that he could not keep the property for himself. It was thought that this would mean that there was no 'fraud', so the courts would not enforce half secret trusts. Hall VC is saying that this theory is incorrect and the court will enforce half secret trusts.

The House of Lords agreed that half secret trusts could exist in *Blackwell v Blackwell* [1929] AC 318.

· ·

● ***Blackwell v Blackwell*** [1929] AC 318

The will of John Duncan Blackwell left £12,000 to five persons, to pay the income 'for the purposes indicated by me to them' and with the power to pay up to £8,000 of the capital 'to such person or persons indicated by me'. Before he made the will, Blackwell told the trustees orally that the money should go to a woman and his illegitimate son. Blackwell's widow and legitimate son challenged the validity of this trust and claimed the £12,000.

(Unlike a fully secret trust, if a half secret trust fails the secret trustees cannot keep the property for themselves, but must hold it on resulting trust for the estate of the testator. This is because the will states that they are trustees, so they cannot keep the property for themselves.)

HELD: Viscount Sumner at 334:

> The necessary elements, on which the question turns, are intention, communication and acquiescence. The testator intends his absolute gift to be employed as he and not as the donee desires; he tells the proposed donee of this intention and, either by express promise or by the tacit promise, which is signified by acquiescence, the proposed donee encourages him to bequeath the money in the faith that his intentions will be carried out.

At 335:

> For the prevention of fraud equity fastens on the conscience of the legatee a trust, a trust, that is, which would otherwise be inoperative; in other words it makes him do what the will in itself has nothing to do with; it lets him take what the will gives him and then makes him apply it, as the Court of conscience directs…

Even though the secret trustees can never keep the property for themselves, it would still be 'fraud' on the beneficiaries if they broke their promise, as explained by Lord Buckmaster at 329:

> It is, I think, more accurate to say that a testator having been induced to make a gift on trust in his will in reliance on the clear promise by the trustee that such trust will be executed in favour of certain named persons, the trustee is not at liberty to suppress the evidence of the trust and thus destroy the whole object of its creation, in fraud of the beneficiaries.

Viscount Sumner did express some doubts about the doctrine of secret trusts at 333–4:

> It is a grave thing to affirm a doctrine that violates the prescriptions of a statute and especially such a statute as the Wills Act, even though the error is of long standing…

but decided that it was too late now to abandon it at 340:

> ...I think that, in view of the subject-matter of these decisions and the length of time during which they have been acquiesced in, your Lordships may well in accordance with precedent refuse to overrule them lest titles should be rendered insecure and settlements, entered into in reliance on their authority, should now be disturbed.

The 'fraud' that causes the court to enforce a secret trust is not the secret trustee taking the property for himself, but failing to keep his promise to the testator.

7.2.11 Half secret trusts require communication before the will

An important difference between fully and half secret trusts is that with fully secret trusts communication must be made before the testator dies, but with half secret trusts communication must be before the will is made and must be in the form contemplated in the will.

This rule seems to date back to *Johnson v Ball* (1851) 5 De G & Sm 85.

● *Johnson v Ball* (1851) 5 De G & Sm 85

Lamb had cohabited with Mrs Johnson and they had had five children together. He wanted to provide for his children and he discussed this with the husbands of two of the children, Manners and Ball, who consented to his proposal. His will left an assurance policy to these two men and instructed them 'to hold the same upon the uses appointed by letter signed by them and myself'. The letter and the details were in fact provided *after* this will was made.

HELD: Sir James Parker VC at 90–1:

> The testator's language appears to point at some letter already signed by him and the trustees; but even supposing it to refer to a letter to be afterwards signed, it is impossible to give effect to any letter as a declaration by the testator of the trusts on which he had the policy to the trustees. To give them any such effect would be to receive, as part of the codicils to the will, papers subsequent in date to the will, which are unattested, and which have not been and could not be admitted to probate. A testator cannot by his will prospectively create for himself a power to dispose of his property by an instrument not duly executed as a will or codicil.

A basic principle of wills is that a will cannot be made which allows the testator to add to it and change it at a later date. (If the testator wants to do this he should make a new will.) The judge in this case thinks that communicating the half secret trust after the will does this and should therefore be forbidden. (See 7.1.2 'The doctrine of incorporation by reference'.)

Blackwell v Blackwell [1929] AC 318 accepts this rule without discussion.

● *Blackwell v Blackwell* [1929] AC 318

Viscount Sumner at 339:

> A testator cannot reserve to himself a power of making future unwitnessed dispositions by merely naming a trustee and leaving the purposes of the trust to be supplied afterwards, nor can a legatee give testamentary validity to an unexecuted codicil by accepting an indefinite

trust, never communicated to him in the testator's lifetime: Johnson v Ball (1851) 5 De G & Sm 85...To hold otherwise would indeed be to enable the testator to 'give the go-by' to the requirements of the Wills Act...

The communication before the will rule was confirmed and further explained in the next case.

. . . .

● *Re Keen* [1937] Ch 236

The will of Harry Augustus Keen included clause 5, which stated that:

> I give to the said Charles Arthur Cheshyre Hazelhurst and Edward Evershed the sum of £10,000...to be held upon trust and disposed of by them among such person, persons or charities as may be notified by me to them or either of them during my lifetime...

Before the will was made, Keen had given Evershed a sealed envelope containing the name of a lady. The envelope was not to be opened until after his death. Evershed understood that this was the notification under clause 5 and accepted it, although he did not know the contents of the letter.

HELD: Lord Wright MR at 242–3: There was sufficient notification.

> To take a parallel, a ship which sails under sealed orders, is sailing under orders though the exact terms are not ascertained by the captain till later. I note that the case of a trust put into writing which is placed in the trustees' hands in a sealed envelope, was hypothetically treated by Kay J as possibly constituting a communication in a case of this nature: *In re Boyes* 26 Ch D 531 at 536...The trustees had the means of knowledge available whenever it became necessary and proper to open the envelope.

(See 7.2.5 'Communication'.)

However, there was a problem with the wording of clause 5.

At 243:

> The words of the clause seem to me to refer only to something future and hypothetical, to something as to which the testator is reserving an option whether to do or not to do it.

At 246: This would be a

> reservation of a future power to change the trusts, in whole or in part. Such a power would involve a power to change a testamentary disposition by an unexecuted codicil and would violate s. 9 of the Wills Act.

Communication must be before the will is made.

At 247:

> The trusts referred to but undefined in the will must be described in the will as established prior to or at least contemporaneously with its execution.

There was yet another problem: the will said that communication would be in the future, but in fact it had already been made. This kind of inconsistency is not permitted.

At 248:

> But the objection remains that the notification sought to be put in evidence was anterior to the will and hence not within the language of clause 5, and inadmissible simply on that ground as being inconsistent with what the will prescribes.

The rule seems established: that communication must be made to the secret trustee before the will is made.

. . . .

● **Re Bateman** [1970] 1 WLR 1463

HELD: Pennycuick at 1467–8:

> Clause 7 has given rise to a good deal more difficulty. It will be remembered that the direction in that clause is to set aside a sum of £24,000 and pay the income 'to such persons and in such proportions as shall be stated by me in a sealed letter in my own handwriting addressed to my trustees'. Now those words are, on their plain meaning, future. There is no evidence as to whether a sealed letter had been written and addressed to the trustees by the testator at the date that he made his will. The only thing that does appear clear is that after his death some sealed letter, or at any rate some document, was in existence upon which the trustees acted. However, whatever the facts, the terms of the direction in clause 7 are plainly future.
>
> …it is really clear and not in dispute that once one must construe the direction as admitting of a future letter then the direction is invalid, as an attempt to dispose of the estate by a non-testamentary instrument.

The concern in half secret trusts is that later communication contravenes the Wills Act. We saw at 7.1.2 the doctrine of incorporation by reference. It is not permitted to make a will and say that the details will be supplied later. If a will refers to another document, that document must already be in existence. As a half secret trust is actually mentioned in the will itself, it is thought that these rules must be respected. A fully secret trust is not mentioned in the will, so there seems less need to respect these rules.

thinking points

Is this distinction in the communication rules for the two different types of secret trust logical? It does seem odd to have a different rule for fully secret and half secret trusts and makes this area of law even more confusing. The origins of the distinction seem to lie in Johnson v Ball *(1851) 5 De G & Sm 85, where the court thought that the doctrine of incorporation by reference applied to secret trusts. This seems odd, because secret trusts take effect outside the will, in a free-standing trust, so why should rules associated with wills apply? The rule of incorporation by reference applies to documents, but many secret trusts are oral. The rule that, in a half secret trust, communication must be before the will is made, has not been followed in other common law jurisdictions, such as Ireland and Australia. See Sheridan (1951) 67 LQR 314.*

7.2.12 Changes to the secret trust

Changes to the secret trust are permitted, as long as they are communicated in the proper way to the trustees. This allows the secret trustees to choose whether or not to accept the change.

● **Re Colin Cooper** [1939] Ch 811

The testator made a will and left £5,000 to two trustees. He communicated the secret trust to them before he made the will. He then made a new will which said that '[t]he sum of £5000 bequeathed to my trustees in the will now cancelled is to be increased to £10,000, they knowing my wishes regarding that sum'.

Unfortunately, the testator never told his trustees of the increase.

HELD: Greene MR at 817:

> In order that a secret trust might be made effective with regard to that added sum in my opinion precisely the same factors were necessary as were required to validate the original trusts, namely communication, acceptance or acquiescence, and the making of the will on the faith of such acceptance or acquiescence. None of these elements, as I have said were present.

The first £5,000 was held on secret trust. The second £5,000 was not, but as they were trustees, they could not keep the money, but held it on resulting trust, back for the estate of the testator.

KEY POINT If a half secret trust fails, the trustees hold the property on resulting trust. If a fully secret trust fails, the trustees keep the property. Except for *Re Boyes* (1884) 26 ChD 531.

7.2.13 Communication if there is more than one trustee

It may be that the testator leaves his property to two or more persons. If only one of these people is told of the secret trust, are the others bound by it? There are clear rules on this found in *Re Stead* [1900] 1 Ch 237.

● **Re Stead** [1900] 1 Ch 237

Maria Stead's will left property to Marsh and Andrew as executors and trustees. Marsh alleged that he had been told of a secret trust before the will was made, but Andrew had not.

HELD: Farwell J: There was not enough evidence that this communication had ever taken place, but if it had, the rules on communication were these.

If the secret trustees were tenants in common then only the trustee that had been told would be bound. The logic of this is that tenants in common have separate shares in the property.

If the secret trustees were joint tenants then it depended whether communication was before or after the will was made. If it was before, then all the joint tenants were bound. If it was after, then only the secret trustee that was told was bound. Joint tenants do not have individual shares in the property. The promise made before the will induces the gift. The gift is the whole property, so both are bound.

Farwell J did not think that the distinction between tenants in common and joint tenants was very logical, but felt bound by previous cases such as *Moss v Cooper* (1861) 1 J & H 352 (see 7.2.5 'Communication').

Secret trustees would usually be joint tenants. The will would simply say that the property went 'to A and B'. If they were tenants in common, there would be words indicating their separate shares. These words of severance would say something like, 'to A and B in equal shares' or 'two-thirds to A and one-third to B'.

thinking points

See Perrins [1972] 88 LQR 225. The distinction between joint tenants and tenants in common and communication before or after the will is not logical. It is possible that Farwell J misunderstood the older cases. The sole test should be whether the promise of one secret trustee induced the testator to make the gift in the will to them both. Secret trusts are based on the principle of fraud, breaking the promise to the deceased and the communication to one trustee rule should reflect that.

The cases above refer to fully secret trusts. Communication to one trustee only was found satisfactory in the half secret trust cases, *Blackwell v Blackwell* [1929] AC 318, and in the following case.

. . . .

● **Re Keen** [1937] Ch 236

Lord Wright MR at 248:

> That it was communicated to one trustee only and not to both would not, I think, be an objection (see Lord Warrington's observation in the *Blackwell* case).

The judge does not explain, so it is unclear whether the rule is different for half secret trusts. Communication must be before the will in a half secret trust anyway. If the will makes clear that all the secret trustees must be told, then if not all the secret trustees are told, the entire half secret trust fails, and the secret trustees hold on resulting trust for the estate of the deceased: *Re Spence* [1949] WBN 237.

7.2.14 What sort of trust are secret trusts?

Secret trusts are not part of the will. They take effect outside or 'dehors' (French for outside) the will.

. . . .

● **Blackwell v Blackwell** [1929] AC 318

Lord Warrington at 342:

> I think the solution is to be found by bearing in mind that what is enforced is not a trust imposed by the will, but one arising from the acceptance by the legatee of a trust, communicated to him by the testator, on the faith of which acceptance the will was made or left unrevoked, as the case might be.

This has the practical consequence that rules in the Wills Act 1837 do not apply to secret trusts.

● **Re Young** [1951] Ch 344

The testator made a half secret trust in which his wife agreed to give £2,000 to the testator's chauffeur, Thomas Cobb. The problem was that Cobb had witnessed the will and under s. 15 of the Wills Act 1837 he therefore could not receive a legacy under the will.

HELD: Danckwerts J at 350:

> The whole theory of the formation of a secret trust is that the Wills Act has nothing to do with the matter because the forms required by the Wills Act are entirely disregarded, since the persons do not take by virtue of the gift in the will, but by virtue of the secret trusts imposed upon the beneficiary, who does in fact take under the will.

Therefore, s. 15 did not apply.

Re Young was based on earlier cases, such as the next case.

● **Re Gardner (No 1)** [1920] 2 Ch 523

Elfrida Gardner had imposed a fully secret trust upon her husband, Herbert, by a memorandum drawn up in 1909. One of the executors had witnessed his agreement. The wife's property was left to her husband for life and the secret trust was that Herbert should divide the property amongst Elfrida's nephews and nieces, by will, when he died. (As she did not say *in the will* what would happen to her property after her husband died, this was a *partial intestacy*.)

Unfortunately, Herbert died only five days after his wife and did not do this.

HELD: The Court of Appeal accepted that this was a valid fully secret trust.

● **Re Gardner (No 2)** [1923] 2 Ch 230

Another problem was that one of the nieces was already dead and therefore predeceased Elfrida. Normally, if a beneficiary dies before the testatrix the gift in the will fails.

HELD: Romer J: The gift in the fully secret trust was valid. The trust was independent of the will.

At 233:

> The rights of the parties appear to me to be exactly the same as though the husband, after the memorandum had been communicated to him by the testatrix in the year 1909, had executed a declaration of trust binding himself to hold any property that should come to him upon his wife's partial intestacy upon trust as specified in the memorandum.

Romer J's words suggest that there is a declaration of trust when the secret trustee agrees to carry out the intention of the testator. This would suggest that a secret trust is an express trust. The requirement that there must be a clear intention on the part of the testator would also suggest that secret trusts are express trusts.

In contrast, particularly in the older cases, there is an emphasis that the secret trustee must keep his/her promise and to break it would be fraud and against 'conscience', e.g. *Blackwell v Blackwell* [1929] AC 318 at 7.2.10 and *McCormick v Grogan* (1869) LR 4 HL 82 at 7.2.8 'Proof'. This would suggest that secret trusts are constructive trusts. Unfortunately, judges have not expressed a view about which sort of trust they think secret trusts are. In *Ottaway v Norman* [1972] Ch 698 at 7.2.7 'A secret trust can even affect a person who did not make the promise', for example, the barristers for both sides state that they are dealing with constructive trusts, but this is not confirmed by the judge.

Does this debate actually have any practical consequences? If they were express trusts they would need to obey the normal formality rules for trusts. One of these is that a declaration of trust over land must be evidenced in writing: s. 53(1)(b) of the Law of Property Act 1925. (See 5.2.1 'Land'.)

● ***Re Baillie*** (1886) 2 TLR 660

There a half secret trust failed for lack of certainty of intention, but the judge also observed that there was a problem about the communication as it was oral and land was involved.

HELD: At 661:

> The point raised by Mr Theobald, that the Statute of Frauds applied so far as the realty was concerned, was a good one, because the trust was not indicated in writing.

No other secret trust cases involving land seem to have taken this writing point, e.g. *Ottaway v Norman* [1972] Ch 698, but then the judge would not think it relevant if it is a constructive trust and therefore exempt from the writing requirement under s. 53(2) of the Law of Property Act 1925.

It is possible to argue that fully secret trust cases are constructive, because they are based on fraud and not to allow the trust would allow the secret trustees to keep the property. On the other hand, under the half secret trust the secret trustee is identified as a trustee in the will, so can never keep the property for him/herself. Therefore, to break his or her promise could never be a fraud, and this type of trust must be based on intention and therefore an express trust.

thinking points

What type of trusts are secret trusts? Are they based on fraud? The earliest cases mention fraud as the basis for imposing the trust. The secret trustee is breaking his/her promise to the deceased testator and keeping the property for themselves. The fraud theory works less well with half secret trusts, where the secret trustee cannot keep the property for themselves, but it could be fraud, in the sense that the promise to the deceased testator is broken. If secret trusts are just ordinary trusts dehors the will, then they should obey all the normal formality and certainty rules for express trusts, which they do not always do. Perhaps secret trusts are just an anomaly that do not make any theoretical sense, but have to be tolerated because they have been in existence for a long time. See D Hodge 'Secret Trusts: The Fraud Theory Revisited' [1980] Conv 341.

 7.3 # Mutual wills

This is an equitable doctrine which was unconnected to secret trusts, but has some similarities. Here husband and wife make wills leaving their property to the same or similar people, typically their children or other close relatives. The spouses agree that they will never change their minds about this and, say, disinherit the children. The problem with this is that it is a basic principle of English law that, up until death, a person can always make a new will and it is the latest will that takes effect. (See 7.1.1 'General characteristics of wills'.) So equity devised a way of enforcing the agreement not to change the will.

7.3.1 A mutual will requires identical wills and a contract

● ***Dufour v Pereira*** (1769) 1 Dick 419

René Ranc and his wife, Camilla, made their **joint will** leaving a life interest in each other's property to the survivor of them and then on trust to a number of beneficiaries. René died first and his wife took possession of his property under his will. She used the property, together with her own, for a period of 16 or 17 years. Camilla made a new will leaving her estate to her daughter, Pereira. Dufour was a beneficiary under the original joint will and claimed the property.

HELD: Lord Camden LC at 421:

> It is a contract between the parties, which cannot be rescinded, but by the consent of both. The first that dies, carries his part of the contract into execution. Will the Court afterwards permit the other to break the contract? Certainly not.
>
> The defendant Camilla Rancer hath taken the benefit of the bequest in her favour by the mutual will; and hath proved it as such; she hath thereby certainly confirmed it; and therefore I am of opinion, the last will of the wife, so far as it breaks in upon the mutual will, is void.
>
> And declare, that Mrs Camilla Rancer having proved the mutual will, after her husband's death; and having possessed all his personal estate, and enjoyed the interest thereof during her life, hath by those acts bound her assets to make good all her bequests in the said mutual will; and therefore let the necessary accounts be taken.

KEY POINT
When a spouse dies, the agreement to make a mutual will becomes binding on the survivor.

Dufour v Pereira (1769) 1 Dick 419 sets out the basic requirements of a mutual will. The parties, usually a married couple, make very similar wills. Usually they would leave the property to each other and then to the same person or persons. Crucially, they would agree not to change their minds and this agreement not to revoke their will would form a contract.

Once the first spouse has died, the mutual will is binding. The surviving spouse cannot escape from what was agreed, even if, as here, the survivor lives on for another 17 years.

Joint will—the husband and wife make similar or identical wills. This could be in one document as in *Dufour* or, more usually, the husband and wife each make a separate will.

Mirror wills—the husband and wife make identical or near identical wills in separate documents.

For it to be a mutual will, the couple must also have an agreement not to revoke their joint will(s).

● ***Re Oldham*** [1925] Ch 75

In 1907 the husband and wife made nearly identical wills leaving their property to each other and then to the same beneficiaries. The husband died in 1914, the wife remarried and made a new will. She died in 1922 and a beneficiary under the 1907 will claimed.

HELD: Astbury J: The 1907 will was not binding, because there was no evidence that there was an agreement to make their wills irrevocable.

At 87:

> Of course it is a strong thing that these two parties came together, agreed to make their wills in identical terms and in fact so made them; but that is not sufficient evidence of an irrevocable interest.

The agreement not to revoke the will is often put into the wills themselves as a standard clause: 'That this be my last will and that I shall not amend or revoke my will after the death of my husband [or wife] if his [or her] will is then unamended and unrevoked'.

The agreement not to change the wills could exist outside the wills themselves, but either way if the agreement is not there, it is not a binding mutual will.

. . . .

● **Re Goodchild (Deceased)** [1997] 3 All ER 63

Joan and Dennis Goodchild made simultaneous wills each leaving their property to each other and then to their son, Gary. Joan died and Dennis remarried and made a new will leaving everything to his new wife. On the death of his father, Gary claimed under the original will. Friends of Joan and Dennis gave evidence that the couple thought that they had made a mutual will. Their solicitor gave evidence that they had not.

HELD: Leggatt LJ at 68:

> Faced with the conflict of evidence, I have to bear in mind that the onus of proof lies on the plaintiffs and that, as the cases show, there must be established evidence of a specific agreement outside their wills, not just some loose understanding or sense of moral obligation. I am satisfied that for the doctrine to apply there must be a contract at law.

KEY POINT
There must be an agreement not to change the will in order to make a mutual will binding.

Though it is a desirable practice for solicitors to put the agreement not to change the wills into the wills themselves it is possible for the contract not to revoke to exist outside the wills and even be oral, as seen in *Charles v Fraser* [2010] EWHC 2154 (Ch). This case was also unusual, because the couple who made the mutual will were sisters, not spouses.

. . . .

● **Charles v Fraser** [2010] EWHC 2154 (Ch)

Mabel and Ethel were widowed sisters who lived together in a house which they owned as joint tenants. In 1991 they both made wills leaving all their real and personal property to their sister. After the death of the survivor the property was to be sold and divided up into 40 shares to be distributed to 15 named beneficiaries. The sisters were careful to divide the 40 shares evenly between Ethel's family and friends, who received 20 shares, and Mabel's family and friends, who also received 20 shares. There was nothing in the wills themselves, or in any other documents, that indicated that this was a mutual will and that they promised not to revoke. Mabel died in 1995. In 2003 Ethel altered her will and amended the list of 15 beneficiaries. In 2006 she made another new will with a completely new beneficiary, Jill Fraser, a friend and neighbour, who was left all the real and personal estate. Ethel died in 2006 and Charles, on behalf of the beneficiaries of the 1991 will, claimed that the 1991 will should be enforced.

HELD: Jonathan Gaunt QC: There was an oral agreement not to revoke their wills attested by eight witnesses. This was supported by the terms of the wills and the close relationship of the sisters. The judge helpfully summarized the law on mutual wills at para 59:

I take the law on mutual wills to be as follows:

(i) Mutual wills are wills made by two or more persons, usually in substantially the same terms and conferring reciprocal benefits, following an agreement between them to make such wills and not revoke them without the consent of the other.

(ii) For the doctrine to apply there has to be what amounts to a contract between the two testators that both wills will be irrevocable and remain unaltered. A common intention, expectation or desire is not enough.

(iii) The mere execution of mirror or reciprocal wills does not imply any agreement either as to revocation or non-revocation.

(iv) For the doctrine to apply it is not necessary that the second testator should have obtained a personal financial benefit under the will of the first testator (albeit that in the present case Ethel had, of course, done so).

(v) It is perfectly possible for there to have been an agreement preventing revocability as to part of the residuary estate only, in which case the doctrine only applies to that part.

(vi) The agreement may be incorporated in the will or proved by extraneous evidence. It may be oral or in writing.

(vii) The agreement must be established by clear and satisfactory evidence on the balance of probabilities.

(viii) The agreement is enforced in equity by the imposition of a constructive trust on the property which is the subject matter of the agreement. The beneficiaries under the will that was not to be revoked may apply to the Court for an order that the estate is held on trust to give effect to the provisions of the old will.

It was points (vi) and (vii) that were crucial in this particular case; there was an oral agreement to abide by the terms of the original, 1991, will which would be enforced by imposing a constructive trust on Fraser.

7.3.2 The mutual will is enforced by a 'floating trust'

Section 18 of the Wills Act 1837 holds that a marriage revokes previous wills and, even if there is no remarriage, there is nothing to stop the survivor making a new will. Equity cannot overturn the legal will, but it can impose a trust on the survivor to respect the original agreement. This is a kind of 'floating trust' that comes into existence upon the death of the first spouse, and crystallizes upon the death of the second spouse. Because the survivor holds on trust and must leave the property to the agreed beneficiaries when he/she dies, there are some restrictions on what the survivor can do with the property, while still alive. These issues are considered in *Re Cleaver* [1981] 1 WLR 939.

●　*Re Cleaver* [1981] 1 WLR 939

This was an English case that adopted the views of Dixon J in an Australian case *Birmingham v Renfrew* (1937) 57 CLR 666 and compared the constructive trust used here with that used in the secret trust case *Ottaway v Norman* [1972] Ch 698. (See 7.2.7 'A secret trust can even affect a person who did not make the promise'.)

Dixon J at 682–3:

> I think the legal result was a contract between husband and wife. The contract bound him, I think, during her lifetime not to revoke his will without notice to her. If she died without altering her will, then he was bound after her death not to revoke his will at all. She on her part afforded the consideration for his promise by making her will. His obligation not to revoke his will during her life without notice to her is to be implied. For I think the express promise should be understood as meaning that if she died leaving her will unrevoked then he would not revoke his. But the agreement really assumes that neither party will alter his or her will without the knowledge of the other. It has long been established that a contract between persons to make corresponding wills gives rise to equitable obligations when one acts on the faith of such an agreement and dies leaving his will unrevoked so that the other takes property under its dispositions. It operates to impose upon the survivor an obligation regarded as specifically enforceable. It is true that he cannot be compelled to make and leave unrevoked a testamentary document and if he dies leaving a last will containing provisions inconsistent with his agreement it is nevertheless valid as a testamentary act. But the doctrines of equity attach the obligation to the property. The effect is, I think, that the survivor becomes a constructive trustee and the terms of the trust are those of the will which he undertook would be his last will.

Next, at 689:

> There is a third element which appears to me to be inherent in the nature of such a contract or agreement, although I do not think it has been expressly considered. The purpose of an arrangement for corresponding wills must often be, as in this case, to enable the survivor during his life to deal as absolute owner with the property passing under the will of the party first dying. That is to say, the object of the transaction is to put the survivor in a position to enjoy for his own benefit the full ownership so that, for instance, he may convert it and expend the proceeds if he chooses. But when he dies he is to bequeath what is left in the manner agreed upon. It is only by the special doctrines of equity that such a floating obligation, suspended, so to speak, during the lifetime of the survivor can descend upon the assets at his death and crystallise into a trust. No doubt gifts and settlements, inter vivos, if calculated to defeat the intention of the compact, could not be made by the survivor and his right of disposition, inter vivos, is, therefore, not unqualified. But, substantially, the purpose of the arrangement will often be to allow full enjoyment for the survivor's own benefit and advantage upon condition that at his death the residue shall pass as arranged.

Finally, at 690:

> But I do not see any difficulty in modern equity in attaching to the assets a constructive trust which allowed the survivor to enjoy the property subject to a fiduciary duty which, so to speak, crystallised on his death and disabled him only from voluntary dispositions inter vivos.
>
> I interject to say that Dixon J was there clearly referring only to voluntary dispositions inter vivos which are calculated to defeat the intention of the compact. No objection could normally be taken to ordinary gifts of small value.
>
> It is also clear from *Birmingham v Renfrew* (1937) 57 CLR 666 that these cases of mutual wills are only one example of a wider category of cases, for example secret trusts, in which a court of equity will intervene to impose a constructive trust. The judgment of Brightman J in *Ottaway v Norman* [1972] Ch 698 is to much the same effect.

KEY POINT

The agreement to make a mutual will is enforced by a constructive trust.

(See 7.2.7 'A secret trust can even affect a person who did not make the promise' for *Ottaway v Norman*.)

So, if there is a binding mutual will, the surviving spouse must not try to defeat the agreement made with his/her dead spouse by making a new will, or trying to dispose of the property while still alive. If he/she does, a constructive trust will be imposed on the property to try to prevent this. At the same time, the survivor is allowed reasonable expenditure, as he/she has to be able to live. The exact distinction between what would be reasonable expenditure and what would not is hard to define.

The scope of the constructive trust imposed on the property left in a mutual will came to be considered in *Olins v Walters* [2009] Ch 212, where the asset in dispute was a £1.5 million house in Mill Hill, London. The case had the unusual feature that one of the spouses was still alive and denied that he had ever agreed to a mutual will.

....

● *Olins v Walters* [2009] Ch 212

Mr and Mrs Walters had married in 1934 and made wills in 1988 in almost identical terms. They left their entire residuary estate to each other and then to their two daughters and grandchildren. In 1998 Olins, one of their grandsons and a solicitor, drafted a codicil to each will, which repeated the 1988 will, except that the interests going to the daughters and grandchildren were changed. The codicils also contained a clause 2 referring to a mutual will agreement that the couple had allegedly made. Mrs Walters died and Mr Walters, who had fallen out with Olins, denied that there was any mutual will agreement.

HELD (Court of Appeal): The evidence indicated that Mr and Mrs Walters had agreed to a mutual will. There was a contract and the fact that it did not go into detail about how the surviving spouse should deal with the property did not affect the binding nature of the mutual will. The court had only been asked to rule on whether there was a mutual will, not on what it obliged or did not oblige Mr Walters to do.

Mummery LJ at 219:

> On the judge's findings it was unclear what property was affected by the supposed constructive trust and what Mr Walters was entitled to do with the deceased's property, which had been left to him absolutely under the 1988 will, and even what he was entitled to do with his own property during the rest of his life. There was a range of possibilities as to the scope of the contract which the judge had failed to determine. Was Mr Walters prevented from dealing with the deceased's estate at all in his lifetime? Or did the constructive trust only extend to the part of the deceased's estate left when he died? Did it extend to his estate at the date of the deceased's death? Or as at the date of his death? What was the position in relation to the Mill Hill house? What, if anything, could be done in relation to it?

A constructive trust was imposed on Mr Walters. Its terms were laid down by the contract that formed the mutual will, but what exactly those terms were, might be the subject of future litigation.

Mummery LJ at 222:

> Disputes about the actual operation of the trust in practice usually turn on construction of the contract in all the relevant circumstances. Of course, the disagreements can be resolved without litigation, if all the beneficiaries are agreed and have legal capacity to do so. If not, the disputes can be determined on an application of the court by Mr Walters in proceedings to which those interested are made parties.

Olins v Walters [2009] Ch 212 confirms that there is a constructive trust, based on the contract between the couple that made the mutual will, but found it unnecessary to rule on how that trust bound Mr Walters. The exact obligation awaits further litigation.

7.3.3 Is there consideration for the contract?

The agreement between the spouses not to change their wills needs to have consideration to make it a legally binding contract. It was thought, from *Dufour v Pereira* (1769) 1 Dick 419, that the consideration was promising to leave their property to each other.

Although most mutual will cases involve the spouses leaving property to each other, this is not essential for there to be a binding contract and a valid mutual will.

. . . .
● *Re Dale* [1994] Ch 31

The couple made identical wills leaving everything to their son and daughter equally. The husband died and his widow made a new will leaving most of the property to her daughter. Then the widow died.

HELD: Morritt J: It was not necessary for the spouses to leave property to each other. Consideration could be provided by the promise not to change your will.

At 38:

> The performance of that promise by the execution of the will by the first testator is in my judgment sufficient consideration by itself.

This was supported by an alternative report of *Dufour v Pereira* Hargrave, Juridicial Arguments and Collections vol 2, 304 at 310:

> ...he that dies first, does by his death carry the agreement on his part into execution. If the other then refuses, he is guilty of fraud, can never unbind himself, and becomes a trustee of course. For no man shall deceive another to his prejudice.

7.3.4 Is the contract a contract for the sale of land?

Often, the property subject to a mutual will is land, typically the home of the couple. A mutual will involves a contract. Is that contract subject to the provisions of s. 2 of the Law of Property (Miscellaneous Provisions) Act 1989, which requires that contracts for the sale of land should be in writing and all the terms should be incorporated in one document? (See 5.2.1 'Land'.)

. . . .
● *Healey v Brown* [2002] WTLR 849

Mr and Mrs Brown executed mutual wills leaving 'All my share and interest in my flat known as 3 Phoenix Court...' to each other and then to Mrs Brown's niece, Jacqueline Healey. After Mrs Brown's death, Mr Brown broke the mutual will agreement by transferring the flat into the joint names of himself and his son, Paul Brown.

HELD: The mutual will was not binding because it depended upon the existence of a contract which had no legal effect. The clauses in Mr and Mrs Brown's two wills did not conform to the strict requirements of s. 2. It was clearly a contract for the sale of land, but it was not contained in one document and did not contain all the terms.

Instead, the court decided that there was a constructive trust, along the lines of the constructive trust in secret trusts, and the flat was held jointly by Paul Brown and Healey. (See 7.2.14 'What sort of trust are secret trusts?' and *Ottaway v Norman*.)

. . . .

Subsequent cases have not been enthusiastic about following the reasoning of *Healey v Brown* [2002] WTLR 849 and have taken the view, expressed in that case, that s. 2 of the Law of Property (Miscellaneous Provisions) Act 1989 only applies if land is expressly mentioned in the wills, as it was in *Healey v Brown* itself, with its mention of the flat. *Olins v Walters* [2009] Ch 212 also involved land, in that case a house, but the wills referred to 'residuary estate', and the judge 'resolved that tension by holding that the contract to make a will had to comply with the formalities requisite to dispose of the property actually described in the will (even though at death that property might have altered)': *Olins v Walters* [2007] EWHC 3060 (Ch), para 31 in the High Court. There was a valid mutual will, because land was not mentioned. In *Shovelar v Lane* [2012] 1 WLR 637, the Court of Appeal summarily dismissed the need for writing argument, in the words of Ward LJ at p. 653: 'They also took the bad point that section 2 of the Law of Property (Miscellaneous Provisions) Act 1989 applied.'

7.3.5 A mutual will can be revoked, while both spouses are still alive

It is clear from *Dufour* (1769) 1 Dick 419 onwards that it is possible to escape from the mutual will agreement while both the parties to the will, the husband and wife, are still alive. *Dufour* suggests that one spouse must give 'notice' to the other that he/she is changing his/her will. The case law suggests that notice is satisfied when the surviving spouse discovers that their dead spouse has changed their will. The survivor is no longer bound by their agreement and can leave the property to whomsoever they like.

. . . .

● *Re Hobley (Deceased)*   The Times 16 June 1997

Mr and Mrs Hobley executed mutual wills in 1975, leaving their property to the survivor and then to a number of common beneficiaries. A house was left to Mr Blythe. Later, Mr Hobley made a codicil revoking the devise to Blythe. His wife did not know that he had done this, but when he died in 1980 she would have discovered this from his will. In 1992 Mrs Hobley made a new will, leaving her property to different beneficiaries from the 1975 mutual will.

HELD:

> With some hesitation he had come to the conclusion that because of the unilateral alterations made to the mutual will by Mr Hobley's codicil Mrs Hobley was no longer bound to leave her estate . . . on the terms of the 1975 will . . .

7.3.6 What property is bound by the mutual will?

There are differences of opinion on this matter. The surviving spouse may live on for many years and acquire more property. Is this property bound by the promise in the mutual will?

Cases such as *Re Dale* [1994] Ch 31 and *Re Hobley* The Times 16 June 1997 state that the trust imposed by the mutual will includes all of the survivor's property, even property acquired after the death of the first spouse.

Re Hagger [1930] 2 Ch 190 states that the trust only affects the property that the survivor had at the time of the first death. *Healey v Brown* [2002] WTLR 849 states that the mutual will only affects property that the survivor inherits from the first to die.

The solution is for the original will and the agreement between the spouses to make clear which property is caught by the mutual will (see *Re Green* [1951] Ch 148). *Charles v Fraser* [2010] EWHC 2154 (Ch), which we saw earlier at 7.3.1 'A mutual will requires identical wills and a contract', confirms this, as does *Olins v Walters* [2009] Ch 212, which we saw at 7.3.2 'The mutual will is enforced by a 'floating trust'' and 7.3.4 'Is the contract a contract for the sale of land?'. Unfortunately, as *Olins* recognizes, the 'contract' between the couple often does not make things clear.

thinking points

Mutual wills raise many problems and if they are held to be valid can be difficult to enforce. There are disputes over the exact nature of the contract required to form the mutual will and also over what property is caught by the constructive trust that enforces the survivor's promise to the deceased. It would probably be necessary in most cases for the court to imply the terms of the contract between the couple, because they rarely state their wishes in express terms. The courts have had the opportunity to clarify some of the disputed issues in the recent cases of Olins v Walters *[2009] Ch 212 and* Healey v Brown *[2002] WTLR 849, but have not done so. See P Luxton 'Walters v Olin: Uncertainty of Subject Matter—An Insoluble Problem in Mutual Wills?' [2009] Conv 498.*

7.4 Donatio mortis causa: 'Death bed gifts'

7.4.1 An exception to the normal rules of property transfer

These are gifts made whilst living, but taking effect on death. They are unusual, in that these gifts do not obey the normal formality rules for wills, i.e. writing and witnesses (see 7.1 'Wills'), but nor do they obey the correct formalities for lifetime gifts, which might again involve writing, registration, etc. (See Chapter 5 'The formality requirements and incompletely constituted trusts'.)

Their odd nature was described in the following case.

● ***Re Beaumont*** [1902] 1 Ch 889

Buckley J at 892:

> . . . a singular form of gift. It may be said to be of an amphibious nature, being a gift which is neither entirely inter vivos nor testamentary. It is an act inter vivos by which the donee is to have the absolute title to the subject of the gift not at once, but if the donor dies. If the donor dies the title becomes absolute not under, but as against his executor. In order to make the gift valid it must be made so as to take complete effect on the donor's death.

If the donatio is valid, the donee applies to the executors, who complete the necessary formalities to transfer the property.

7.4.2 The three requirements for a valid 'donatio'

These are set out in most of the cases.

● **Re Craven** [1937] Ch 432

Farwell J at 426:

> Firstly, a clear intention to give, but to give only if the donor dies, whereas if the donor does not die then the gift is not to take effect and the donor is to have back the subject-matter of the gift.
>
> Secondly, the gift must be made in contemplation of death, by which is meant not the possibility of death at some time or other, but death within the near future, what may be called death for some reason believed to be impending.
>
> Thirdly, the donor must part with dominion over the subject matter of the donatio.

KEY POINTS

There are three requirements for a donatio:

- An intention to give if the donor dies.

- The donor must be expecting to die in the near future.

- The donor must part with dominion (control) over the gift.

7.4.3 Contemplation of death

The usual situation is when the donor is ill and fears that he/she might die.

● **Wilkes v Allington** [1931] 2 Ch 104

William Allington held a mortgage over the farm belonging to his nieces and nephew. In 1922 he had been diagnosed with cancer and had refused treatment.

At 106:

> …and from that time forward he regarded himself as a man under a sentence of death, and although he continued to carry on his farm, he remained seriously ill and had often to take to his bed.
>
> In August 1925 he was ill in bed and as he thought that he was dying he stated 'I…have instructed [the executor] to give you back that mortgage when I am gone; tear it up.' On December 11, 1927 he handed over the mortgage deeds and written on them was 'To be given up at death. W Allington'.

On 11 January 1928 he caught a chill, which turned into pneumonia, and he died on 23 January.

HELD: Lord Tomlin: There was a clear contemplation of death.

> That the man believed himself to be in the shadow of death I do not doubt: I think it is clear upon the evidence that he believed himself to be a doomed man.

At 110:

It did not matter that he in fact died from another cause, as in his own mind he still contemplated death. Nor did it matter that he died six weeks after handing over dominion of the mortgage and perhaps five months after forming his intention. If he had recovered from his illness, the gift would have been revoked.

A later case confirms that contemplation of death is subjective. It is not necessary to produce evidence that the donor was suffering from a life threatening illness.

● **Vallee v Birchwood** [2013] EWHC 1449

Wrodzimierz Bogusz was born in the Ukraine, but immigrated to England. His only daughter, Cheryle Vallee, had been adopted by her foster parents. Mr Bogusz owned a house, 2 Eldon Street, Reading, where his daughter visited him on 6 August 2003. He was unwell and coughing and told his daughter that he would not live until Christmas. Mr Bogusz gave Cheryle the title deeds to the house and the front door key and told her that he wanted her to have the house when he died. He continued to live in the house and died on 9 December 2003.

HELD: This was a valid donatio mortis causa.

> At paragraph 25: 'The question is not whether the donor had good grounds to anticipate his imminent demise or whether his demise proved as speedy as he may have feared but whether the motive for the gift was that he subjectively contemplated the possibility of death in the near future.'
>
> At paragraph 26: 'Most people would, I think, consider that a person who anticipated death within 5 months . . . was contemplating his "impending" death.'

7.4.4 Intention to give conditional upon death

A donatio is only effective once the donor has died. The donor might say something like 'Have my house when I am dead', or his intention might be ascertained from the circumstances of his illness and death.

● **Sen v Hedley** [1991] 2 WLR 1308

Nourse LJ at 431:

> Secondly, the gift must be made upon the condition that it is to be absolute and perfected only on the donor's death, being revocable until that event occurs and ineffective if it does not.

The donor can change his mind before death, say, by taking back the property as in *Bunn v Markham* (1816) 7 Taunt 224. Or if the donor recovers from his illness, the gift is also revoked: *Staniland v Willot* (1850) 3 Mac & G 664.

7.4.5 Delivery of dominion over the subject matter of the gift

Choses in action— a type of property that has no physical existence. A valuable personal right.

Something must be handed over or the means of access to the 'gift' must be given. With a chattel this would be easy, as the article itself could be handed over. With **choses in action** the document that gives evidence that it is the donor's property needs to be handed over. Here are some examples of what needs to be handed over.

Bank books

- ### *Re Weston* [1902] 1 Ch 680

Thomas Weston was ill in hospital and was visited by his fiancée, Helen Menzies. He told her that he wanted her to have his investment shares in a building society and his money in the Post Office Savings Bank, if anything should happen to him. He asked her to fetch the share certificate and the Post Office book and gave her the key to his bedroom drawer, where they were kept. She brought the documents to the hospital and he told her to keep them.

HELD: There was a donatio of the money in the Post Office. The book provided the means to deposit and withdraw money.

- ### *Birch v Treasury Solicitor* [1950] 2 All ER 1198

The donee was told to go to the donor's flat where her bank books would be found in a black bag. The donor said: 'I want you to take them home and keep them, and if anything happens to me I want you and Frank to have the money in the banks.'

HELD: This was a valid donatio.

At 311:

> Delivery must be made of 'the essential indicia ... of title, possession or production of which entitles the possessor to the money or property purported to be given'.

Keys

- ### *Re Lillingston* [1952] 2 All ER 184

The keys to a safety deposit box at Harrods were handed over. To be allowed to open the box, the donee would also need signed authorization from the deposit holder and the password.

HELD: This was sufficient delivery and the gift would be enforced.

- ### *Woodard v Woodard* [1995] 3 All ER 980

Leonard Woodard was in hospital, suffering from leukaemia, and while there he allowed his son Barrie to drive his car, an Austin Metro worth £3,900. So Barrie already had the car keys in his possession. Barrie visited his father and his father said 'You can keep the keys, I won't be driving it any more.' After his father's death, Barrie claimed that he had been given the car, but his mother disputed this.

HELD: There was a discussion over what Leonard had to hand over to Barrie to deliver dominion over the car and it was stated that: '[t]he log book is not a document of title to the car'. As Barrie already had a set of car keys, could there be delivery?

Dillon LJ at 984:

> The words of gift in such circumstances can operate to change the nature of the possession from possession as **bailee** to possession as donee, albeit in the present case as donee under a donatio mortis causa rather than under an immediate gift.

Bailment—Means that the person given the property, the bailee, has possession of the property. The bailor has a superior right and can retake possession. It is not intended that the bailee should keep the property.

Woodard v Woodard [1995] 3 All ER 980 is an unusual case, in that because of the facts (Barrie already had the car and the car keys) and the type of property (a car), there was nothing that Woodard senior could physically hand over to Woodard junior.

KEY POINT Handing over dominion over the gift is an essential part of donatio mortis causa. This could be a document, the property itself, or the means of gaining access to the property.

7.4.6 Can all types of property be the subject matter of a donatio?

Some cases, such as *Re Weston* [1902] 1 Ch 680 (see 7.4.5 'Delivery of dominion over the subject matter of the gift') hold that it is not possible to donatio shares. *Staniland v Willot* (1850) 3 Mac & G 664 said that it was possible to donatio shares in a public company, where registration could not be refused.

It was thought for a long time that it was not possible to make a death bed gift of land.

● *Duffield v Elwes* (1827) 1 Bli (NS) 497

Lord Eldon upheld the donatio of a mortgage, but doubted whether it was possible to have a donatio of land.

● *Sen v Headley* [1991] Ch 425

Margaret Sen had at one time lived with Mr Vivian Hewett and they remained close, such that she had keys to his house and was looking after it while he was ill in hospital with inoperable cancer of the pancreas. Three days before his death, Vivian told Margaret: 'The house is yours, Margaret. You have the keys. They are in your bag. The deeds are in the steel box.' Hewett then slipped some keys into her bag. One of the keys opened a cupboard in the house and another opened a steel box in that cupboard. In the box were the title deeds to the house. Margaret found them a day or two after his death.

HELD: Nourse LJ at 437:

> It cannot be doubted that title deeds are the essential indicia of title to unregistered land. Moreover, on the facts found by the judge, there was here a constructive delivery of the title deeds of 56, Gordon Road equivalent to an actual handing of them by Mr Hewett to Mrs Sen and it could not be suggested that Mr Hewett did not part with dominion over the deeds.

The court decided not to follow *Duffield v Elwes* (1827) 1 Bli (NS) 497.

At 440:

> Let it be agreed that the doctrine is anomalous. Anomalies do not justify anomalous exceptions. If due account is taken of the present state of the law in regard to mortgages and choses in action, it is apparent that to make a distinction in the case of land would be to make just

such an exception. A donatio mortis causa of land is neither more nor less anomalous than any other. Every such gift is a circumvention of the Wills Act 1837. Why should the additional statutory formalities for the creation and transmission of interests in land be regarded as some larger obstacle?

At 441:

We hold that land is capable of passing by way of a donatio mortis causa and that the three general requirements for such a gift were satisfied in this case.

This case suggests that all types of property, including land and shares, are capable of being the subject matter of a death bed gift. It is clear from subsequent cases that there can be a death bed gift of unregistered land. Handing over the title deeds to the donee is sufficient delivery of dominion and it does not matter that the donor continues to live in the house after the hand over: *Vallee v Birchwood* [2013] EWHC 1449 (Ch) and *King v Dubrey* [2014] EWCH 2083 (Ch).

> **thinking points**
> *It now seems clear that there can be a donatio of land, but the three cases all involve unregistered land, which is becoming increasingly rare. Delivery of dominion requires the hand over of the title deeds, but with registered land, there is only an entry on an electronic register, so what could be physically handed to the donee? This is also becoming a problem with other kinds of property, such as bank accounts and shares, where most transactions are now electronic. Will donatio mortis causa gradually die out, or should the requirements of delivery of dominion be adapted so hand over of documents is no longer required?*
> *See William Moffett 'Deathbed gifts in rude health: the recent case of Vallee v Birchwood.' [2014]* Trusts and Trustees *459.*
>
> *See Nicholas Roberts 'Donationes mortis causa in a dematerialized world' [2013]* Conveyancer *113.*

The rule in *Strong v Bird*

This is a rule that can seem strange and arbitrary in its effects. When a person dies his/her executor or administrator acquires the full legal and equitable estate in his/her property. (See 3.11 'Wills and intestacies'.) If there is more than one personal representative, each of them has the full legal and equitable estate. The situation that occurs in the following cases is that the donor attempts to make a gift, but does not complete the necessary formalities.

If the donee happens to be the deceased donor's executor or administrator it is accepted that the gift is completed, because the donee acquires the legal estate. In crude terms, the gift gets to the right person in the end and the intention of the donor is respected.

7.5.1 The original rule

● ***Strong v Bird*** (1874) LR 18 Eq 315

Bird borrowed £1,100 from his stepmother, Frances Bird. Frances lived in his house, paying rent, and she was going to be repaid by a reduction in her rent. £200 was repaid and then

Frances stated that she did not want any more repaid. Frances died and Bird was the sole executor under her will.

HELD: Sir G Jessel MR:

The normal legal position is that just saying to a person that they need not pay a debt has no legal effect, as there is no consideration and therefore no contract. However, this was different.

At 318:

> After her death he proved the will, and the legal effect of that was to release the debt in law, and therefore the condition which is required, namely, that the release shall be perfect at law, was complied with by the testatrix making him executor.

In effect, making Bird executor gave him the full legal estate in his stepmother's property, which was taken to include a gift of £900.

Some cases under this rule superficially resemble donatio mortis causa (see 7.4). The donor attempts to make a gift, but does not fulfil the proper formalities. Sometimes documents are handed over to the donee. Then the donor dies.

KEY POINT Three conditions must be satisfied for a valid death bed gift. There is only one condition for the rule in *Strong v Bird*. The donee must acquire the legal estate.

7.5.2 The rule is extended to imperfect gifts

● *Re Stewart* [1908] 2 Ch 251

Dr Stewart intended to give his wife three bonds, each worth £500. Shortly before his death, he handed his wife an envelope containing details of the bonds. He was unable to complete the transaction before his death. His wife was one of five executors.

HELD: Neville J at 254–5:

> I think it does, the case, in my opinion, being within the principle of *Strong v Bird*, which is a decision of the late Sir George Jessel that has remained unchallenged for upwards of thirty years and has been followed in several cases. It purports to lay down a principle of general application, and I think I am bound to apply that principle to the present case. The decision is, as I understand it, to the following effect: that where a testator has expressed the intention of making a gift of personal estate belonging to him to one who upon his death becomes his executor, the intention continuing unchanged, the executor is entitled to hold the property for his own benefit. The reasoning by which the conclusion is reached is of a double character— first, that the **vesting** of the property in the executor at the testator's death completes the imperfect gift made in the lifetime, and, secondly, that the intention of the testator to give the beneficial interest to the executor is sufficient to countervail the equity of beneficiaries under the will, the testator having vested the legal estate in the executor. The whole of the property in the personal estate in the eye of the law vesting in each executor, it seems to me immaterial whether the donee is the only executor or one of several; nor do I think the rule is confined to cases of the release of a debt owing by the donee.

Vesting—
here this means the transfer of the legal estate.

Dr Stewart had successfully made a gift of the bonds to his wife, because on his death she acquired the legal estate in them, as his executor, and this was what he intended.

KEY POINTS

For a gift under this rule to be effective:

- there must be a clear and continuing intention on the part of the donor;

- the donee must be an executor;

- the gift is still effective, even if there are other executors.

7.5.3 Land may pass under the rule in *Strong v Bird*

● ***Re James*** [1935] Ch 449

James James employed Sarah Maria James as his housekeeper. She was unpaid from 1905 until 1924, but he had stated that the house and furniture was to be hers on his death. His son, John James, allowed her to continue living there and handed over the title deeds. John died intestate in 1933 and Sarah was appointed as **administratrix**.

HELD: The house belonged to Sarah. She had the legal title as administratrix. It made no difference that this was land and she was an administratrix, not an **executrix**.

Administratrix—the female person appointed by the court to deal with the estate of a person who has died without making a will.

Executrix—the female person appointed in the will to carry out the deceased's instructions in the will, in particular to dispose of his/her property according to the will.

The rule was followed even though land was involved and Sarah was only an administratrix. Rather than being appointed as an executrix by the deceased, she had appointed herself.

7.5.4 The Rule in *Strong v Bird* continues to exist

Re Gonin [1977] 2 All ER 200 declined to follow the cases discussed earlier and expressed some scepticism that the rule could still apply. Despite these comments, the Court of Appeal confirmed that the rule was alive and well in *Royal College of Music v Harris*.

● ***Day v Harris, Arnold and Arnold, Royal College of Music v Harris*** [2013] EWCA Civ 191

A famous composer, Sir Malcolm Arnold, wanted to give some of his manuscripts and musical scores to his carer, Anthony Day. Arnold wrote a document in 1998, stating 'I would now like you to have these papers whilst I am still alive as a gift from me.' This was the incorrect method of transfer, for this type of property, chattels, because he did not deliver (hand over) the documents to Day, as most of them were in the custody of the Royal College of Music. Day was an executor of Arnold's will.

KEY POINT
The donee can also be an administratrix or administrator.

HELD: Lloyd LJ at paragraph 116:

> It could not be fully effective without delivery of the manuscripts, but it became a complete gift, by virtue of Strong v Bird.

(See 5.2.2 'Chattels, goods' for more details of this case.)

7.5.5 *Strong v Bird* and marriage settlements

A complicated example of the rule in *Strong v Bird* might be found in the next case.

. . . .

● **Re Ralli** [1964] 2 All ER Ch 288

The testator's will left his property to his wife for life and then to his two daughters, Helen and Irene. Helen made a marriage settlement and, as she had no children, the beneficiaries were the children of her sister, Irene. Helen had covenanted to settle after-acquired property on the trusts of this settlement, but she had never done this with the property that she inherited from her father's will. Helen died and her mother died. Calvocoressi, the husband of Irene, was the sole surviving trustee of the original will. Therefore, he held the legal estate in the share that Helen inherited from her father. But Calvocoressi was also trustee of the marriage settlement. For which trust did he hold the property?

HELD: Buckley J: Normally these after-acquired property clauses are not enforceable. (See 5.8 'Incompletely constituted trusts: covenants to settle property'.)

However, on considering *Strong v Bird* and *Re James* at 301:

> In my judgment the circumstance that the plaintiff holds the fund because he was appointed a trustee of the will is irrelevant. He is at law the owner of the fund, and the means by which he became so have no effect upon the quality of his legal ownership.
>
> It is for the defendants [those who claimed Helen's estate] to invoke the assistance of equity to make good their claim to the fund. To do so successfully they must show that the plaintiff cannot conscientiously withhold it from them. When they seek to do this, he can point to the covenant which, in my judgment, relieves him from any fiduciary obligation he would otherwise owe to the defendants as Helen's representative.

Calvocoressi held the property for the marriage settlement, not for those who claimed under Helen's will.

The logic of this decision seems to be that as the trustee already had the legal estate, he should hold the property from the father's will for the beneficiaries of the marriage settlement. As Helen had promised to transfer property to the marriage settlement she should not be allowed to claim it for herself. Therefore, nor should persons claiming through her, under her will. The criticism of this case and the rule in *Strong v Bird* is that expressed in *Re Gonin* [1977] 2 All ER 200, that it could just be a matter of chance who ends up with the legal estate.

thinking points

Is the rule in Strong v Bird *justifiable? Is it based on a misunderstanding of the original case?* Strong v Bird *involved the quite limited point of death releasing a debt. Later cases have extended this to gifts of land and, indeed, all types of property. It has also been applied to administrators, not just executors. Modern cases, such as* Re Gonin *[1977] 2 All ER 200, have doubted whether there really is precedent for this doctrine and whether it operates fairly, or just by chance. See G Kodilinye 'A Fresh Look at the Rule in* Strong v Bird' *[1982] Conv 14.*

Conclusion

Secret trusts, mutual wills, and death bed gifts are very old equitable doctrines. The rule in *Strong v Bird* is more recent, but not exactly modern. However, all four have many peculiarities. In secret trusts, the communication rules may not strike one as particularly logical. In mutual wills the difficulty is that the surviving spouse might live on for many years and be restricted in what they can do with their property. What exactly those restrictions are is unclear. The requirement that dominion must be delivered in death bed gifts is to modern minds a rather odd requirement, and it works differently for different kinds of property. The operation of the rule in *Strong v Bird* can sometimes be hard to spot: the intended donee happens to be an executor or administrator. These doctrines have their critics: see *Blackwell v Blackwell* [1929] AC 318 and *Re Gonin* [1977] 2 All ER 200. It might seem strange that a modern legal system should allow these exceptions from the requirement to make a will, but these doctrines have been around for a long time and the doctrine of precedent means that they are unlikely to be abandoned.

Questions

Self-test questions

1 What are the essential requirements of a secret trust?

2 What are the differences between fully secret and half secret trusts?

3 What are the requirements for a mutual will?

4 How is a mutual will enforced?

5 What are the three requirements of a donatio mortis causa?

6 How does the rule in *Strong v Bird* work?

Discussion questions

1 Is there any real justification for the difference in the communication rules for fully secret and half secret trusts?

2 What sort of trusts are secret trusts?

3 How does the floating trust in mutual wills and in *Ottaway v Norman* actually work?

4 Why is delivery of dominion necessary for a death bed gift?

5 Why does equity allow exceptions to be made to the normal law of wills?

Assessment question

John is a journalist who is about to go on an assignment in Iraq. He is only 30, so he has not made a will, but at the airport he suddenly realizes that Iraq is a dangerous place and he might be killed. So he tells his girlfriend, Carol, who is at the airport with him:

If I die in Iraq I want you to have my property. My house is yours. Here is the key to the front door. The solicitors dealt with the registration of title and the mortgage is kept by the bank. Ask them for the documents that you need.

Here is my credit card; use my money if I do not come back.

You are already looking after my car, the Porsche, while I am away. If I die, it is yours.

Six months later, John has finished his assignment in Iraq and goes on holiday in Turkey, where he is killed in a car crash. John has a brother, David, his only living relative, who claims all John's property.

Carol has applied for administration of John's estate and considers that she is entitled to his house, money, and car.

Advise Carol.

 # Key cases

- *Ottaway v Norman* [1972] Ch 698 **(at 7.2.7, 7.2.8, and 7.2.14)**

- *Blackwell v Blackwell* [1929] AC 318 **(at 7.2.10, 7.2.11, and 7.2.14)**

- *Re Keen* [1937] Ch 236 **(at 7.2.11 and 7.2.13)**

- *Re Gardner (No 2)* [1923] 2 Ch 230 **(at 7.2.14)**

- *Dufour v Pereira* (1769) 1 Dick 419 **(at 7.3.1 and 7.3.3)**

- *Re Cleaver* [1981] 1 WLR 939 including *Birmingham v Renfrew* (1937) 57 CLR 666 **(at 7.3.2)**

- *Wilkes v Allington* [1931] 2 Ch 104 **(at 7.4.3)**

- *Sen v Headley* [1991] Ch 425 **(at 7.4.6)**

- *Re Stewart* [1908] 2 Ch 251 **(at 7.5.2)**

 # Further reading

B Perrins 'Can You Keep Half a Secret?' (1972) 88 *LQR* 225
An examination of the communication rules in secret trusts.

D Hodge 'Secret Trusts: The Fraud Theory Revisited' [1980] *Conv* 341

Are secret trusts based on fraud or on the intention of the testator? Are they constructive trusts or express trusts?

LA Sheridan 'English and Irish Secret Trusts' (1951) 67 *LQR* 314

The different communication rules in fully and half secret trusts.

P Luxton 'Walters v Olin: Uncertainty of Subject Matter—An Insoluble Problem in Mutual Wills?' [2009] *Conv* 498

A consideration of two of the recent cases on mutual wills, *Walters v Olins* [2009] Ch 212 and *Healey v Brown* [2002] EWHC 1405.

W. Moffett 'Deathbed gifts in rude health: the recent case of *Vallee v Birchwood*.' [2014] *Trusts and Trustees* 459

What exactly is delivery of dominion over land? Does the concept still have any meaning?

N. Roberts 'Donationes mortis causa in a dematerialised world' [2013] *Conveyancer* 113

Donatio mortis causa relies upon the physical handover of documents, but in the modern world, electronic records are replacing documents. Should the law adapt to allow death bed gifts to continue?

G Kodilinye 'A Fresh Look at the Rule in *Strong v Bird*' [1982] *Conv* 14

Is the decision in *Strong v Bird* correct?

8

Resulting trusts

Learning objectives

This chapter will help you to:

- understand that a resulting trust returns property to the original or rightful owner
- distinguish between an automatic resulting trust and a presumed resulting trust
- distinguish clearly between the different presumptions of resulting trust and the presumption of advancement
- appreciate that these presumptions can be rebutted by evidence of the parties' true intentions
- understand that these presumptions may be out of place in the modern world and in need of reform.

Introduction

The idea of a resulting trust is that property returns or 'results back' to the original or rightful owner or settlor. It is not an express trust, in that the parties involved do not knowingly and intentionally create a resulting trust. Instead, the matter would have to go to court, where the judge would decide, on the evidence, whether a resulting trust had been created or not. Therefore, a resulting trust arises 'by operation of law'. Resulting trusts arise in a surprising number of situations, such as where an existing trust cannot, for some reason, carry on. Then the trust property is said to be held on resulting trust, which means that the property is to be returned to its original owner. This sounds straightforward, but often is not, because there may be many original owners, they may be hard to locate, and the size of the individual shares may be hard to calculate.

Another situation is when property is held legally in the name of A, but B considers that he has a strong claim to that property or to a share in that property. B can establish a claim in equity and then A, who holds the legal estate, becomes a resulting trustee, holding the equitable interest for B. A typical example is where B has paid for the property or at least paid part of the price. Such disputes can often arise between married or cohabiting couples, but these are now regarded as constructive trusts. Resulting trusts remain for commercial or business dealings of this nature. (See Chapter 18 'Trusts of the family home'.) 'Presumptions' also operate in resulting trusts: it is assumed that a certain legal situation exists unless there is evidence to the contrary, e.g. if two people contribute towards buying property, but it is legally in the name of only one of them, it is presumed that the property is held on resulting trust.

8.1 The two types of resulting trust

It is generally considered that there are two main types of resulting trust and this distinction goes right back to some of the earliest cases.

. . . .

● *Lloyd v Spillet* [1740] 2 Atk 148

Lord Hardwicke at 150:

> Why first when an estate is purchased in the name of one person, but the money or consideration is given by another; (2) or secondly. Where a trust is declared only as to part, and nothing said as to the rest, what remains undisposed of results to the heir at law.

The views of Megarry J have been influential here, in that he took these two categories and gave them names. The first category he called 'presumed resulting trusts' and the second category he termed 'automatic resulting trusts'.

● *Re Vandervell's Trusts (No 2)* [1974] Ch 269

Megarry J at 289:

> The distinction between the two categories of resulting trusts is important because they operate in different ways. Putting it shortly, in the first category, subject to any provisions in the instrument, the matter is one of intention, with the rebuttable presumption of a resulting trust applying if the intention is not made manifest. For the second category, there is no mention of any expression of intention in any instrument, or of any presumption of a resulting trust: the resulting trust takes effect by operation of law, and so appears to be automatic. What a man fails effectually to dispose of remains automatically vested in him, and no question of any mere presumption can arise. The two categories are thus of presumed resulting trusts and automatic resulting trusts.

8.2 The automatic resulting trust

There are various circumstances in which a trust can fail and the property must return to the settlors. There are also different ways of categorizing the cases on this and this is just one of several possible explanations.

8.2.1 Failure to declare a trust

Here there has been an attempt to establish an express trust. Typically the property has been properly transferred to the trustees, but the settlor or testator has neglected to tell them for whom they are holding the property. As it is a trust and they are trustees, the trustees cannot keep the property for themselves. Instead, the trustees hold the property on resulting trust for the original owner. This simply means that they must return the property to him or her.

● *Re Boyes* (1884) 26 ChD 531

George Boyes made a will leaving everything to his solicitor, Frederick Carritt, who was also made executor. Boyes had told Carritt that he was to hold the property on trust for a certain lady and child, and would receive further directions. Carritt gave an undertaking that he would do this, but the further directions never came. After the death of Boyes a document was found telling Carritt to give everything to Nell Brown, except £25 for himself.

HELD: Kay J at 536:

> It may possibly be that he would be bound if the trust had been put in writing and placed in his hands in a sealed envelope, and he had engaged that he would hold the property given to him by the will upon the trust so declared although he did not know the actual terms of the trust.

Carritt knew that there was a secret trust, but he did not know who the beneficiaries were, nor was he given any details in writing. So the secret trust failed, but Carritt could not keep the property for himself, because he had agreed to be a trustee.

> The Defendant, however, having admitted that he is only a trustee, I must hold...that he is a trustee of this property for the next of kin of the testator.

This was a resulting trust. (See 7.2.5 'Communication'.)

A more complicated example of a resulting trust can be seen in the celebrated *Vandervell* litigation.

. . . .

● *Vandervell v IRC* [1967] 2 AC 291

Mr Vandervell was subject to extremely high rates of tax, so he wanted to reduce his tax liability. He decided to give money to a charity, the Royal College of Surgeons, so that it could endow a Chair of Pharmacology. The National Provincial Bank held shares in Vandervell Products Ltd on trust for Mr Vandervell, who was the only beneficiary.

As he held the entire equitable interest in the shares he was perfectly entitled to instruct his trustees to transfer the shares to the Royal College of Surgeons.

His trustees transferred the legal estate in the shares to the Royal College.

So the Royal College of Surgeons held the shares both legally and equitably. The shares no longer belonged to Mr Vandervell.

Mr Vandervell wanted to have the ability to recover the shares from the Royal College of Surgeons, so the college had agreed to an **option** to allow the repurchase of the shares for £5,000. This agreement was with the Vandervell Trustees Ltd, who were the trustees of a number of Vandervell family trusts.

. . . .

Option—A contractual right to acquire property on payment of consideration. A contractual right is a form of property that has economic value and can be bought and sold, just like any other kind of property.

. . . .

The majority in the House of Lords decided that the trustees could not have the option for themselves, but must be held on trust. Mr Vandervell had neglected to declare the trusts on which the option was held so they were held back for him on resulting trust. Therefore, the IRC could successfully argue that he still had some form of beneficial interest in the shares and was still liable for tax on them.

Lord Wilberforce at 329:

> The conclusion on the facts found, is simply that the option was vested in the trustee company as a trustee on trusts, not defined at the time, possibly to be defined later. But the equitable, or beneficial interest, cannot remain in the air: the consequence in law must be that it remains in the settlor.

(See 5.3.2 'In two celebrated cases the court held that writing was not required'.)

8.2.2 Failure of the trust

A trust can fail for any number of reasons. For instance, the underlying purpose of the trust can disappear.

. . . .

● *Re Ames Settlement* [1946] Ch 217

When John Ames and Miss Hamilton married in 1908, John's father, Louis, the settlor, established a marriage settlement for them and transferred £10,000 to the trustees of the settlement. The trust had the standard terms of life interests for John Ames and Miss Hamilton, then to children of the marriage, and finally to the next of kin. In 1926 their marriage was dissolved as a nullity, the grounds being the husband's incapacity to consummate. The wife renounced her interest under the trust and remarried. The husband later gave up his own interest and died in 1945. The next of kin claimed their interests under the trust, but the father's personal representatives claimed that the money should return to the dead Louis's estate.

HELD: Vaisey J at 223:

> But that trust, with the other trusts, were all based on the consideration and contemplation of a valid marriage, and now that it has been judicially decided that there never was a marriage that trust cannot possibly form the foundation of a good equitable right. The settlor's representatives say that theirs is the better equity because the money was only parted with by their testator on a consideration which was expressed but which in fact completely failed. It seems to me that the claim of the executors of the settlor in this case must succeed.

(See 5.8.1 'Marriage settlements' for marriage settlements.)

As there had, legally, never been a marriage, there could not be a marriage settlement and the property returned, on resulting trust, to the estate of the original settlor.

When a trust is drafted, the draftsman tries to provide for all the possible events that could happen. It is possible for the draftsman to fail to foresee what actually happens.

. . . .

● *Re Cochrane* [1955] Ch 309

The husband and wife set up a trust, which stated that the income generated by the trust was to be paid to the wife, Emily, for life 'so long as she shall continue to reside with the said WJB Cochrane and shall remain faithful to him'. If she died, or the clause took effect, the income was to be paid to her husband. Ultimately the property went to their children, after the death of whichever of the husband and wife survived the longest. Unfortunately, events did not turn out as expected. The wife left the husband, which meant that her interest under the trust ended and the income was paid to him. Much later, in 1953, the husband died, but the property could not go to the children yet, as she was still alive. To whom was the income of the trust to be paid?

HELD: Harman J at 315–16:

> It is clear not only that something has been left out . . .
>
> The result of that is that the draftsman has failed to provide for the event which has happened. A resulting trust is the last resort to which the law has recourse when the draftsman has made a blunder or failed to dispose of that which he has set out to dispose of, but

that seems to have happened here, and until the death of the survivor I think that there is a resulting trust of the income of the fund in favour of the settlors in proportion to their several interests.

KEY POINT

If a trust fails, the property returns to the settlor(s) on a resulting trust.

The trust in *Cochrane* is rather technical and unusual in its wording, but it does show that, if even part of a trust cannot be carried out, the solution is to return that property, on resulting trust, to the original settlors.

8.2.3 Surplus after completion of purpose

A trust may be set up to achieve a particular purpose. What happens to the trust fund when that purpose has been achieved? If the person drafting the trust has thought the matter through properly then the trust will say what should happen to the surplus. Trusts are not always well drafted, so the court may have to decide what happens to any remaining funds and may use a resulting trust.

● *Re Trusts of the Abbott Fund* [1900] 2 Ch 326

Dr Abbott had two deaf mute daughters and when he died, in 1844, he left a trust fund to support them. By 1889 the money was exhausted and the last trustee had died. A Dr Fawcett raised a fund from friends to support the two ladies. By 1899 both daughters were dead, but there was £366.70 left in the fund. No provision had been made as to what to do with any left-over money.

HELD: Stirling J at 330: He decided that there should be a resulting trust for the subscribers to the fund.

> I cannot believe that it was ever intended to become the absolute property of the ladies so that they should be in a position to demand a transfer of it to themselves.

As the two sisters were dead they could have no further use for the money, so maybe it was logical to return the money to the original owners. The courts have usually come to a different decision in other 'maintenance' cases, when the beneficiaries are still alive.

● *Re Osoba* [1979] 1 WLR 247

Osoba put a trust in his will to maintain his widow, his mother, and 'for the training of my daughter Abiola up to university grade'. The widow and mother had died and Abiola had completed her education.

HELD: The fund was held jointly between the mother and the widow. When they died the entire fund went to Abiola.

This was explained well at first instance by Megarry VC ([1978] 1 WLR 791 at 796):

> If a trust is constituted for the assistance of certain persons by certain stated means there is a sharp distinction between cases where the beneficiaries have died and cases where they are still living. If they are dead, the court is willing to hold that there is a resulting trust for the donors; for the major purpose of the trust, that of providing help and benefit for the beneficiaries, comes to an end when the beneficiaries are all dead and so are beyond earthly help whether by the stated means or otherwise. But if the beneficiaries are still living, the

major purpose of providing help and benefit for the beneficiaries can still be carried out even after the stated means have all been accomplished, and so the court will be ready to treat the standard means as being indicative and not restrictive.

Trusts may be set up in quite informal ways and the organizers may not think through all the details. This is particularly the case when funds are swiftly raised in the wake of some sort of accident or disaster.

. . . .

● **Re Gillingham Bus Disaster Fund** [1958] Ch 300

On 4 December 1951 a squad of Royal Marine cadets was marching down a street in Gillingham, Kent. They were hit by an out-of-control bus, which killed 24 of them and injured others. The town clerk of Gillingham had a letter published in the *Daily Telegraph* stating that '[t]he Mayors of Gillingham, Rochester and Chatham have decided to promote a Royal Marine Cadet Corps Memorial Fund to be devoted, among other things, to defraying the funeral expenses, caring for the boys who may be disabled, and then to such worthy cause or causes in memory of the boys as the Mayors may determine'. Thousands of people from all over the country wrote letters of sympathy and some enclosed money. £9,000 was raised in all. Some of the donors could be identified, but some could not, particularly those who gave to street collections. There was a great deal of money left over, because the bus driver and his company accepted legal liability and damages were paid. 'Worthy causes' is too uncertain to be charitable (see 10.8 'Saving lives'), so the money could not be used for other charitable purposes. The Crown claimed the money as **bona vacantia**.

HELD: Harman J at 310:

> The general principle must be that where money is held upon trust and the trusts declared do not exhaust the fund it will revert to the donor or settlor under what is called a resulting trust. The reasoning behind this is that the settlor or donor did not part with his money absolutely out and out but only *sub modo* to the intent that his wishes as declared by the declaration of trust should be carried into effect. When, therefore, this has been done any surplus still belongs to him. This doctrine does not, in my judgment, rest on any evidence of the state of mind of the settlor, for in the vast majority of cases no doubt he does not expect to see his money back: he has created a trust which so far as he can see will absorb the whole of it. The resulting trust arises where that expectation is for some unforeseen reason cheated of fruition, and is an inference of law based on after-knowledge of the event.

At 314:

> In my judgment the Crown has failed to show that this case should not follow the ordinary rule merely because there were a number of donors who, I will assume, are unascertainable.
>
> The trustees must pay the money into court like any other trustee who cannot find his beneficiary. I conclude, therefore, that there must be an inquiry for the subscribers to this fund.

The approach of Harman J may be logical; the trust fails, so there must be a resulting trust and the trust funds must go back to the settlors, but it might be impracticable. Sometimes it can, as in this case, be very hard to find all the settlors. After gravestones had been purchased for some victims, £7,300 was left over and, as we have already seen, the trustees handed it over to the court for safekeeping. The money was still in a court bank account, uninvested, until 1991,

---

Bona vacantia—Latin—literally unoccupied property. More loosely translated it means ownerless goods. The government, or Crown, claims property that has no identifiable owner.

. . . .

. . . .

Sub modo—Latin—subject to a condition.

. . . .

when it was released and used to build a memorial to the dead boys. These kinds of difficulties are the reason why judges often prefer not to find a resulting trust, as in *Re Osoba* [1979] 1 WLR 247. What a judge can do very much depends upon the terms of the original trust, as far as those terms have been made clear.

8.2.4 Surplus in a pension fund

Companies often used to establish pension funds for their employees. Employees would pay part of their salaries into the fund and the employers would also make contributions for each employee. Commonly, these pension funds were set up as trusts with a trust deed and trustees. The deed would set out the terms of the trust, such as who would be paid a pension, how much, and when. A few years ago, in a favourable climate for investment, many pension schemes had surplus funds, in that they had more money than would ever be needed to pay pensions. Ideally, the terms of the trust would set out clearly what should happen to this surplus, but that was not always the case. The case below shows how the doctrine of resulting trust could be used to solve the dilemma.

● *Air Jamaica Ltd v Joy Charlton* [1999] 1 WLR 1399

Air Jamaica had a pension scheme for its employees, to which both the company and its employees contributed. When the airline was sold to the private sector there was a surplus of $400,000,000. Air Jamaica claimed a return of its contributions and the members of the scheme—employees, ex-employees, and pensioners—also claimed the return of their contributions. The Government of Jamaica also claimed the surplus as bona vacantia, on the grounds that neither the company nor the members had any right to the money. There was a problem in clause 4 of the trust deed, which stated: 'No moneys which at any time have been contributed by the company under the terms hereof shall in any circumstances be repayable to the company.'

HELD: Lord Millett at 1411:

> Prima facie the surplus is held on a resulting trust for those who provided it. This sometimes creates a problem of some perplexity. In the present case, however, it does not. Contributions were payable by the members with matching contributions by the company. In the absence of any evidence that this is not what happened in practice, the surplus must be treated as provided as to one half by the company and as to one half by the members.

The Crown tried to argue that clause 4 prevented the return of its contributions to the company.

At 1412:

> Consequently their Lordships think that clauses of this kind in a pension scheme should generally be construed as forbidding the repayment of contributions under the terms of the scheme, and not as a pre-emptive but misguided attempt to rebut a resulting trust which would arise dehors the scheme. The purpose of such clauses is to preclude any amendment that would allow repayment to the company.

The Crown also tried to argue that the members had received their pensions and were not entitled to anything further under the terms of the trust. The judge looked further into what the trust actually said: it said that if the trust was discontinued, any extra money should be used to provide additional benefits for the members.

> It is impossible to say that the members 'have received all that they bargained for'. One of the benefits they bargained for was that the trustees should be obliged to pay them additional benefits in the event of the scheme's discontinuance.

The members' share of the surplus should be divided pro rata among the members in proportion to the contributions made by each member without regard to the benefits each has received and irrespective of the dates on which the contributions were made.

Lord Millett managed to avoid clause 4 by interpreting it as only applying while the pension scheme was still running. It was to prevent the company 'robbing' the pension fund by claiming back their contributions. Now that the scheme was defunct, there was no harm in them having their money returned. It is very difficult to work out exactly how much to return to the members, so the court went for a simple calculation and did not deduct pensions paid out from their shares.

KEY POINT The failure of a trust may mean that the trust property is returned to the original settlors on resulting trust. What exactly is returned depends upon the terms of the trust.

thinking points

The courts may seem to come to contradictory decisions in the cases in this section. Is there really any coherent underlying theory? See CEF Rickett and R Grantham 'Resulting Trusts—The Nature of the Failing Trust Cases' (2000) 116 LQR 15. This article examines Air Jamaica Ltd v Joy Charlton [1999] 1 WLR 1399 *and considers the rival theories in* Re Vandervell's Trusts (No 2) [1974] Ch 269 *and* Westdeutsche Landesbank Girozentrale v Islington London BC [1996] AC 669 *that seek to explain how resulting trusts work. Which theory fits in best with the case law on this subject?*

8.3 The theory of resulting trusts

Now that we have seen a few examples of resulting trusts, it might be useful to examine some ideas about how they really work. We started at 8.1 'The two types of resulting trust' with Megarry VC's famous classification in *Vandervell v IRC* [1974] Ch 269, but not everyone agrees with his ideas. Some hold that all types of resulting trust are based on the 'intention' of the settlor or the parties involved. 'Intention' is meant in a specialized sense. It does not mean necessarily that the parties consciously intended to create a resulting trust, because they might well never have heard of resulting trusts or might not have expected events to turn out as they did. 'Presumed intention' means what they would have intended if they had thought about it. A clear statement of this theory can be found in the following leading trust case *Westdeutsche Landesbank Girozentrale v Islington London BC* [1996] AC 669.

· ·

● ***Westdeutsche Landesbank Girozentrale v Islington London BC*** [1996] AC 669

Lord Browne-Wilkinson at 708:

> Under existing law a resulting trust arises in two sets of circumstances: (A) where A makes a voluntary payment to B or pays (wholly or in part) for the purchase of property which is vested either in B alone or in the joint names of A and B, there is a presumption that A did not

intend to make a gift to B: the money or property is held on trust for A (if he is the sole provider of the money) or in the case of a joint purchase by A and B in shares proportionate to their contributions. It is important to stress that this is only a *presumption*, which presumption is easily rebutted either by the counter presumption of advancement or by direct evidence of A's intention to make an outright transfer...

(B) Where A transfers property to B *on express trusts*, but the trusts declared do not exhaust the whole beneficial interest:...*Barclays Bank v Quistclose Investments Ltd* [1970] AC 567.

Both types of resulting trust are traditionally regarded as examples of trust giving effect to the common intention of the parties. A resulting trust is not imposed by law against the intentions of the trustee (as is a constructive trust) but gives effect to his presumed intention. Megarry J in *Re Vandervell's Trusts (No 2)* [1974] Ch 269 suggests that a resulting trust of type (B) does not depend on intention but operates automatically. I am not convinced that this is right. If the settlor has expressly, or by necessary implication, abandoned any beneficial interest in the trust property, there is in my view no resulting trust: the undisposed of equitable interest vests in the Crown as bona vacantia: see *Re West Sussex Constabulary's Widows, Children and Benevolent (1930) Fund Trusts* [1971] Ch 1.

Some of the cases in 8.2 'The automatic resulting trust' suggest that the court is trying to approach the facts by looking for the intention of the testator/settlor. *Re Osoba* [1979] 1 WLR 247 would be a good example. But in other cases, such as *Vandervell v IRC* [1967] 2 AC 291, the intention of Mr Vandervell was to rid himself of his shares. The effect of the resulting trust was that he had to keep them.

The intention-based theory is useful in some situations such as in the *Quistclose*-type trusts, which have proved difficult to explain legally. (See 3.10 'Quistclose-type trusts'.)

. . . .

● *Barclays Bank v Quistclose* [1970] AC 567

Rolls-Razor owed money to its bankers Barclays. It was also unable to pay its shareholders. So Rolls-Razor borrowed money from Quistclose to pay dividends to the shareholders. This money was placed in a separate account at Barclays.

Rolls-Razor went into liquidation and the question was: who was entitled to the money in the separate account? Normally in a liquidation all the creditors receive a proportion of whatever property is left.

HELD: The money was for a special purpose and was therefore held on trust. That purpose had failed, so it went back to Quistclose on a resulting trust. It gained 'priority' over the claims of Barclays, as Barclays' claim was only a contractual one. (A debt is a contract.)

Lord Wilberforce at 580:

> That arrangements of this character for the payment of a person's creditors by a third person, give rise to a relationship of a fiduciary character or trust, in favour, as a primary trust, of the creditors, and secondarily, if the primary trust fails, of the third person, has been recognised in a series of cases over some 150 years.
>
> ...when the money is advanced, the lender acquires an equitable right to see that it is applied for the primary designated purpose...

Lord Wilberforce is saying that there is an express trust for the shareholders. That failed when the company went into liquidation, so there was a resulting trust to return the money to the original owners, or settlors, Quistclose.

That analysis raises all sorts of problems, so a new theory has gained prominence, where these situations are regarded as resulting trusts right from the start. This theory is much influenced by the book by Dr Chambers *Resulting Trusts* (Oxford: Oxford University Press, 1997), which was considered at 3.10 'Quistclose-type trusts'.

....

● *Twinsectra Ltd v Yardley* [2002] AC 164

Twinsectra had lent £1,000,000 to Mr Yardley for the purpose of buying land. He spent £357,720.11 of it on other purposes and so Twinsectra sued for its return. The £1 million had been advanced to Yardley's solicitor, Sims, who signed an undertaking that provided, among other things, that '[t]he loan monies will be utilised *solely* for the acquisition of property on behalf of our client *and for no other purpose*'. The question was whether this formed a trust.

HELD: Lord Millett states that there are problems with the traditional analysis from the original *Quistclose* case itself at 187:

> These passages suggest that there are two successive trusts, a primary trust for payment to identifiable beneficiaries, such as creditors or shareholders, and a secondary trust in favour of the lender arising on the failure of the primary trust. But there are formidable difficulties in this analysis, which has little academic support. What if the primary trust is not for identifiable persons, but as in the present case to carry out an abstract purpose? Where in such a case is the beneficial interest pending the application of the money for the stated purpose or the failure of the purpose?

The solution for Lord Millett is to say that the beneficiary must be the lender, right from the start. His conclusion is that it is a resulting trust.

At 193:

> A trust must have certainty of objects. But the only trust is the resulting trust for the lender. The borrower is authorised (or directed) to apply the money for a stated purpose, but this is a mere power and does not constitute a purpose trust.

At 192–3:

> The lender pays the money to the borrower by way of loan, but he does not part with the entire beneficial interest in the money, and in so far as he does it is held on a resulting trust for the lender from the outset.
>
> When the purpose fails, the money is returnable to the lender, not under some new trust in his favour which only comes into being on the failure of the purpose, but because the resulting trust in his favour is no longer subject to any power on the part of the borrower to make use of the money.

Lord Millett's argument is that the solicitor, Sims, is holding the loan on a resulting trust for Twinsectra, the beneficiary. Sims is allowed to use the money to buy land, but if he uses it for some other purpose, the resulting trust is still there and the money belongs in equity to Twinsectra. Lord Millett also advanced this theory in *Air Jamaica Ltd v Joy Charlton* [1999] 1 WLR 1399 considered at 8.2.4 'Surplus in a pension fund'.

....

● *Air Jamaica Ltd v Joy Charlton* [1999] 1 WLR 1399

Lord Millett at 1412:

> Like a constructive trust, a resulting trust arises by operation of law, though unlike a constructive trust it gives effect to intention. But it arises whether or not the transferor intended

to retain a beneficial interest—he almost always does not—since it responds to the absence of any intention on his part to pass a beneficial interest to the recipient. It may arise even where the transferor positively wished to part with the beneficial interest, as in *Vandervell v IRC* [1967] 2 AC 291.

This theory is based on an absence of intention in that the original owner never intends to transfer the property. So it is not surprising that it returns to that owner on a resulting trust.

KEY POINTS

There are perhaps three theories of resulting trust:

1. The Megarry J theory from *Re Vandervell's Trusts (No 2)* that there were two types of resulting trust, automatic and presumed.

2. The *Westdeutsche Landesbank Girozentrale v Islington London BC* [1996] AC 669 theory that all types of resulting trust are based on intention.

3. The Chambers/Millett theory that a resulting trust returns property to the original owner, subject to contractual rights in that property.

8.4 Presumed resulting trusts

These are only *presumed* resulting trusts, meaning that in certain situations the courts will conclude that there is a resulting trust, unless there is evidence that the parties involved intended some other arrangement. There are two types of presumed resulting trust. The first is a 'voluntary transfer' to another person and the other is a 'purchase in the name of another'.

8.4.1 Voluntary transfer to another

KEY POINT
When A gives property to B it is regarded as a resulting trust, with B holding the property on trust for A.

Here, A transfers the legal estate in some kind of property to B and B gives nothing in return. Legally we would say that B provides no consideration or, as equity puts it, B is a volunteer. Equity assumes that no one gets something for nothing and B is regarded as holding the property on resulting trust for A. That means, in effect, that B has to give the property back to A. This seems to go against common sense, but the original reason for this rule was to protect people against what we would nowadays call 'gold-diggers'.

. . . .

● *Fowkes v Pascoe* (1874–75) LR 10 Ch App 343

Sarah Baker, an elderly and wealthy woman, had transferred £7,000 into the name of a young man, John Pascoe, who was a relation of hers. He claimed that it was meant as a gift to him.

Sir G Jessel MR at 345:

> That is not only a rule of law, but a rule founded on sound policy and good sense. Those that allege that other people, especially in this position, give them large sums of money, must prove it, and prove to the satisfaction of a Court of Justice that they are entitled to that sum of money.

If A and B do not want there to be a resulting trust, they must make it clear that a gift is intended and that B can keep the property. That evidence would rebut the presumption of resulting trust.

It was thought at one time that Act of Parliament had altered this particular presumption of resulting trust.

Law of Property Act 1925

....

60   Abolition of technicalities in regard to conveyancing and deeds

(3) In a voluntary **conveyance** a resulting trust for the grantor shall not be implied merely by reason that the property is not expressed to be conveyed for the use or benefit of the grantee.

....
Conveyance—
the formal legal document, a deed, required to transfer the legal estate in land.
....

In fact, all that this subsection does is to simplify the wording used in a conveyance of land. The Supreme Court applied the presumption of resulting trust to land, without even considering s 60(3) in *Prest v Petrodel Resources Ltd* [2013] 3 WLR 1.

● *Prest v Petrodel Resources Ltd.*   [2013] 3 WLR 1

Mr and Mrs Prest were divorcing and Mrs Prest was seeking a financial settlement. She alleged that her husband had used offshore companies (PRL) to hold legal title to seven London houses, which, in reality, belonged beneficially to him. The houses had been transferred by Mr Prest to these companies for nominal sums, such as £1. Mr Prest failed to comply with court orders to disclose his financial position.

HELD: Equity presumes that if person A transfers property to B, and does not receive anything in return, A does not intend just to give their property away. Unless there is evidence to the contrary, B holds the property on resulting trust for A. This could be applied to Mr Prest: his companies held the houses on resulting trust for him and his wife could claim them.

> Lord Sumption at page 28: 'Since no explanation has been forthcoming for the gratuitous transfer of these properties to PRL, there is nothing to rebut the ordinary presumption of equity that PRL was not intended to acquire a beneficial interest in them.'

This was confirmed, obiter, by Eleanor King J. in a similar case *M v M (No 2)* [2013] EWCA 2354 at paragraph 173.

thinking point

Although Prest v Petrodel *seems a 'just' decision in that it tried to prevent the husband hiding his property from the court in a divorce case, it is arguable that the Supreme Court failed to fully think through the issues of principle at stake or to consider the previous case law. See Shah and Hitchens 'Fresh* Prest *juice: the consequences of the Supreme Court's landmark decision' (2014) 20* Trusts and Trustees *469.*

The presumption certainly applies to other kinds of property.

● **Re Vinogradoff** [1935] WN 68

In 1926 Mrs Vinogradoff transferred a £800 War Loan into the joint names of herself and her four-year-old granddaughter, Laura Jackson. Unsurprisingly, Laura did not give her granny anything in return. Later, the grandmother died. Did Laura own the War Loan?

HELD: Farwell J: Laura held the loan on resulting trust for the estate of Mrs Vinogradoff.

> The stock was not the property of the infant, but formed part of the estate of the testatrix.

8.4.2 Purchase in the name of another

The basic principle is that property is held on trust for the person or persons who put up the money, whoever's name the property is held on. The person or persons who hold the legal estate hold it on resulting trust for those who provide the money. This is not a new principle.

● **Dyer v Dyer** [1788] 2 Cox Eq Cases 92

Eyre CB at 93:

> The clear result of all the cases, without a single exception, is that the trust of a legal estate, whether freehold, copyhold, leasehold; whether taken in the names of the purchasers and others jointly, or in the name of others without that of the purchaser; whether in one name or several; whether jointly or successive, results to the man who advances the purchase money.

The principle lives on and was much used in cases where cohabiting couples are in dispute about their shares in the house that one or both of them purchased.

● **Tinsley v Milligan** [1994] 1 AC 340

Lord Browne-Wilkinson at 371:

> *Lloyds Bank plc v Rosset* [1991] 1 AC 107. The creation of such an equitable interest does not depend upon a contractual obligation but on a common intention acted upon by the parties to their detriment. It is a development of the old law of resulting trust under which, where two parties have provided the purchase money to buy a property which is conveyed into the name of one of them alone, the latter is presumed to hold the property on a resulting trust for both parties in shares proportionate to their contributions to the purchase price.

The resulting trust requires that the equitable interests are in proportion to the financial contribution made. So if Andrew and Bernadette buy a house together, the legal title is registered in Andrew's name only, but Andrew contributes £75,000 and Bernadette contributes £25,000, Andrew holds the legal estate on resulting trust for them both. Andrew has an equitable interest of three-quarters and Bernadette an equitable interest of one-quarter. If this sort of situation occurs in a cohabitation dispute, this is now regarded as a constructive trust: *Lloyds Bank v Rosset* [1991] 1 AC 107 (earlier), *Stack v Dowden* [2007] 2 All ER 929, and *Jones v Kernott* [2012] 1 AC 776. The practical differences are that in a constructive trust the court is not confined to only looking at financial contributions and is not bound to decide that the equitable interests are in strict proportion to the financial contributions. (See 18.9 'What sort of trust is this?') The presumption of resulting trust still remains in commercial cases, where it is not just a couple buying a home for themselves, but more a business proposition, e.g. *Laskar v Laskar* [2008] 1 WLR 2695.

KEY POINT The resulting trust is only a presumption. If there is evidence that the parties involved intended something different, the presumption will be rebutted, e.g. there is evidence that the parties agreed that one of them was not to have a share.

The presumption of advancement

8.5.1 The theory

In certain situations the court will presume that a resulting trust was not intended and, instead, a gift was. Advancement just means a gift. Again this is only a presumption and it can be displaced by evidence of what the parties really intended.

The thinking behind the presumption of advancement is that the person transferring the property intends to make an outright gift of the property to the person to whom they are transferring. They would do that because it would be a situation where they would have a legal obligation to support that person.

8.5.2 Transfer from husband to wife

A husband has a legal duty to support his wife financially; therefore, if he transfers property to her, it is presumed that he intends his wife to keep it. There is no presumption of resulting trust, because the husband does not expect to get the property back.

● ***Re Eykyn's Trusts*** (1877) 6 ChD 115

Malins VC at 118:

> The law of this court is perfectly settled that where a husband transfers money or other property into the name of his wife only, then the presumption is, that it is intended as a gift or an advancement to the wife absolutely at once ...

This presumption is somewhat old-fashioned in that it only applies to a transfer from husband to wife or from a man to the woman he is about to marry. It does not work in reverse and therefore does not apply to a transfer from a wife to a husband or to a transfer between a cohabiting couple.

8.5.3 Transfer from father to child

Fathers have a legal duty to support their children, so the presumption of advancement applies to any transfer of property from a father to a child. It is presumed to be a gift, unless there is evidence to the contrary to rebut the presumption.

● ***Bennet v Bennet*** (1879) 10 ChD 474

Ann Bennet transferred £3,000 to her son Philip. The son was in debt and insolvent. His trustee in bankruptcy claimed what he had left, while Ann claimed the return of her £3,000 on resulting trust. She argued that there could not be a presumption of advancement and the money was not a gift to her son.

HELD: Jessell MR at 476–7:

> A person **in loco parentis** means a person taking upon himself the duty of a father of a child to make a provision for that child.
>
> But the father is under that obligation from the mere fact of his being the father, and therefore no evidence is necessary to show the obligation to provide for his child, because that is part of his duty.
>
> But in our law there is no moral legal obligation—I do not know how to express it more shortly—no obligation according to the rules of equity—on a mother to provide for her child.

In loco parentis—Latin—in the place of the parent. It means anyone who has taken on the responsibilities of the father, though they are not the biological parent.

Fortunately there was a solution in this case, as there was clear evidence that the mother intended the money as a loan. She was able to proceed against the estate of her dead son for the return of the loan.

The presumption of advancement still does not apply if a mother transfers property to her son, even though the general law regarding the legal responsibilities of mothers is much changed from the 19th century.

KEY POINT The presumption of advancement means that the courts will assume that a transfer of property from a father to a child or from a husband to a wife is intended as a gift, unless there is evidence to prove the contrary.

233

8.6 The importance of the presumptions today

8.6.1 Rebutting the presumptions

The presumptions of resulting trust and advancement are only assumptions about what the parties to the transaction actually intended. If there is other evidence the courts will look at that evidence and may come to a different conclusion.

● ***Fowkes v Pascoe*** (1875) 10 Ch App 343

Mrs Baker was a wealthy woman with considerable investments in her own name. Mr Pascoe had lived with her and she provided for him. He was the son of her widowed daughter-in-law. Mrs Baker paid for £7,000 of annuities in their joint names. Mrs Baker died and her trustees claimed that the £7,000 was held by Pascoe on resulting trust for her estate.

HELD: The evidence showed that Mrs Baker intended a gift and this displaced the presumption of resulting trust. The dividends from the shares would be paid to Mrs Baker for her lifetime, but the shares would go to Pascoe on her death.

Mellish LJ at 352–3:

> In such a case, although the rule of law, if there was no evidence at all, would compel the Court to say that the presumption of trust must prevail, even if the Court might not believe that the fact was in accordance with the presumption, yet if there is evidence to rebut the presumption, then, in my opinion, the court must go into the actual facts. And if we are to go into the actual facts, and look at the circumstances of this investment, it appears to me utterly impossible, as the Lord Justice has said to come to any other conclusion than that the first investment was made for the purpose of gift and not for the purpose of trust.

Pascoe was her closest relation and, if she had wanted to make investments for herself, she would have done so in her own name.

There used to be restrictive rules of evidence, to the effect that a party could only put forward evidence of what happened at the time of the original transaction.

● *Shephard v Cartwright* [1955] AC 431

Viscount Simonds quoted from the then current edition of Snell's *Equity*.

At 445:

> The acts and declarations of the parties before or at the time of the purchase, or so immediately after it as to constitute a part of the transaction, are admissible in evidence either for or against the party who did the act or made the declaration…But subsequent declarations are admissible as evidence only against the party who made them, and not in his favour.

The rules of evidence have now been relaxed and the court may consider all the evidence that might reveal what the parties really intended.

● *Lavelle v Lavelle* [2004] 2 FCR 418

Lord Phillips MR at 419:

> Plainly, self-serving statements or conduct of a transferor, who may long after the transaction be regretting earlier generosity, carry little or no weight. But words or conduct more proximate to the transaction itself should be given the significance that they naturally bear as part of the overall picture. Where the transferee is an adult, the words or conduct of the transferor will carry more weight if the transferee is aware of them and makes no protest or challenge to them.

So the courts may still prefer evidence from near the time of the transaction, because people can change their minds later, particularly if they have made an over-generous gift or advancement! What the transferor says is particularly important. If they say 'this is a present for you', a gift is intended, but if they say that one day they will want the property back, it is a resulting trust.

8.6.2 The abolition of the presumption of advancement

Some judges are sceptical about how useful these presumptions really are in the modern world and would rather rely on the evidence, even if it is weak or contradictory.

● **Pettit v Pettit** [1970] AC 777

Lord Diplock at 824:

> It would in my view be an abuse of the legal technique for ascertaining or imputing intention to apply to transactions between the post-war generation of married couples 'presumptions' which are based upon inferences of fact which an earlier generation of judges drew as the most likely intentions of earlier generations of spouses belonging to the propertied classes of a different social era.

Pettit v Pettit was a dispute between a married couple. The later House of Lords case *Stack v Dowden* [2007] 2 AC 432 also took the view that the presumptions of advancement and indeed, resulting trust, had outlived their usefulness, at least as far as they applied to cohabiting couples.

● **Stack v Dowden** [2007] 2 AC 432

Baroness Hale at 455:

> The presumption of resulting trust is not a rule of law … [Quotes from Lord Diplock in *Pettit v Pettit* [1970] AC 777.] Equity, being concerned with commercial realities, presumed against gifts and other windfalls (such as survivorship). But even equity was prepared to presume a gift where the recipient was the provider's wife or child. These days, the importance to be attached to who paid for what in a domestic context may be very different from its importance in other contexts or long ago … The law has indeed moved on in response to changing social and economic conditions.

(See Chapter 18 'Trusts of the family home' for a further discussion of these two cases.)

Parliament also takes the view that the presumption of advancement is outdated and abolished it in the Equality Act 2010.

Equality Act 2010

198 Abolition of husband's duty to maintain wife

The rule of common law that a husband must maintain his wife is abolished.

199 Abolition of presumption of advancement

(1) The presumption of advancement (by which, for example, a husband is presumed to be making a gift to his wife if he transfers property to her, or purchases property in her name) is abolished.

(2) The abolition by subsection (1) of the presumption of advancement does not have effect in relation to—

   (a) anything done before the commencement of this section, or

   (b) anything done pursuant to any obligation incurred before the commencement of this section.

The reason for the legislation is that it offends the principle of equality, in that a husband is presumed to make gifts to his wife, but a wife is not presumed to make gifts to her husband. It will also enable the UK to comply with art. 5 of the 7th Protocol of the European Convention on Human Rights: 'Spouses shall enjoy equality of rights and responsibilities of a private law character between them … ' The Act will also abolish the presumption of advancement where a father transfers property to a child and this is presumed to be a gift. At the time of writing, this part of the Act had not been brought into force.

thinking points

Although the presumption of advancement between husband and wife looks old-fashioned and breaches the principle of equality, does it make sense also to abolish the presumption of advancement where a father transfers property to his children? If it is abolished, the presumption of resulting trust will apply instead with the result that the child holds on resulting trust for the father and cannot keep the gift. Surely this is not what the father intended? A better reform would have been to extend the presumption of advancement to mothers and their children, as has been done in other common law jurisdictions. See J Brightwell 'Good Riddance to the Presumption of Advancement' [2010] Trusts and Trustees *627.*

8.7 **Illegality**

Yet the presumptions still have their uses. Evidence which reveals an illegal purpose is not admissible in court. So if the evidence about the real intentions of the parties cannot be considered, the court may still have to rely on the presumptions of resulting trust and advancement.

The refusal to look at evidence of an illegal purpose is an old rule. It is examined earlier in the book in Chapter 2 'Maxims of equity' at 2.2.1 'He who comes to equity must come with clean hands'. It is important to realize that 'illegality' might just mean behaving badly and might not necessarily involve the commission of a criminal offence. The illegality doctrine is strongly associated with the leading Chancery judge, Lord Eldon.

• *Curtis v Perry* [1802] 6 Ves Jr 739

Nantes and Chiswell were business partners, who owned ships. The ships were in the sole name of Nantes. They had done this because Chiswell was a Member of Parliament and ships could not be used for government contracts, if they were owned by an MP.

HELD: Lord Eldon at 746a:

> The moment the purpose to defeat the policy of the law by fraudulently concealing, that this was his property, is admitted, it is very clear, he ought not to be heard in this court to say, that it is his property.

Because Chiswell could not produce his evidence, the ships belonged to Nantes.

Even in the modern age the courts might still refuse to look at evidence of an illegal purpose.

• *Tinker v Tinker* [1970] P 136

The husband conveyed property into his wife's name, in order to protect it from creditors, if a new garage business which he had purchased was not a success. The couple divorced and the husband claimed the return of 'his' property.

HELD: Lord Denning MR at 141:

> [The husband] found himself on the horns of a dilemma in that, as between himself and his wife, he wished to say that the property belonged to him, whereas, as between himself and his creditors, he wished to say that it belonged to her.

The presumption of advancement applied and the wife kept the property.

The House of Lords reconsidered this rule on illegality in *Tinsley v Milligan* [1994] 1 AC 340.

. . . .

● *Tinsley v Milligan* [1994] 1 AC 340

Stella Tinsley and Kathleen Milligan lived together as lovers for about four years and ran their home as a lodging house. This was a joint business venture and the house was paid for by the profits from the business. The house was registered in the name of Stella Tinsley, as the sole legal owner. This was done so that Milligan could claim benefits, such as housing benefit, from the Department of Social Security, by telling them that she was simply a lodger paying rent to Tinsley and had no stake in the business. Tinsley and Milligan separated, with Tinsley moving out and Milligan remaining. Tinsley sued for possession of the house, as she had the legal estate. Milligan claimed that she had a claim to half the house, based on a resulting trust, as she had contributed financially to the purchase of the house.

HELD: Lord Browne-Wilkinson at 376: He thought that the law in equity on resulting trusts and the common law relating to illegal contracts should be the same.

> I therefore reach the conclusion that, although there is no case overruling the wide principle stated by Lord Eldon, as the law has developed the equitable principle has become elided into the common law rule. In my judgment the time has come to decide clearly that the rule is the same whether a plaintiff founds himself on a legal or equitable title: he is entitled to recover if he is not forced to plead or rely on the illegality, even if it emerges that the title on which he relied was acquired in the course of carrying through an illegal transaction.
>
> As applied in the present case, that principle would operate as follows. Miss Milligan established a resulting trust by showing that she had contributed to the purchase price of the house and that there was a common understanding between her and Miss Tinsley that they owned the house equally. She had no need to allege or prove *why* the house was conveyed into the name of Miss Tinsley alone, since that fact was irrelevant to her claim: it was enough to show that the house was in fact vested in Miss Tinsley alone. The illegality only emerged at all because Miss Tinsley sought to raise it. Having proved these facts, Miss Milligan had raised a presumption of resulting trust. There was no evidence to rebut that presumption. Therefore Miss Milligan should succeed.

The logic of the judgment is simple: Milligan's claim is based on her financial contribution to buying the house. That raises a presumption of resulting trust and gives her a half share. Her defrauding the Social Security was a separate and irrelevant issue that had nothing to do with the basis of her claim. She did not, for instance, use Social Security money to pay for the house.

This decision has been criticized, as it appears to condone fraudulent behaviour. Lord Browne-Wilkinson was very careful to point out that what he was saying only applied to the presumption of resulting trust, not to the other presumption, that of advancement. If someone wanted to claim a resulting trust in an advancement case that person would have to produce evidence that an advancement was not intended. If the evidence disclosed an illegal purpose, it would not be accepted by the court. The whole point of *Tinsley v Milligan* [1994] 1 AC 340 is that Milligan did not have to produce any extra evidence; she could simply rely on the presumption of resulting trust.

Tinsley has been followed and again the court did not insist that the plaintiff (claimant) should have done nothing wrong, in order to succeed in his claim.

- -
● **Tribe v Tribe** [1996] Ch 107

Kim Tribe held most of the shares in a company, which leased shops selling ladies' wear in South Wales. Under the terms of the leases the landlord wanted him to carry out repairs to the shop premises. Kim decided to rid himself of the shares, so that he could claim that he had no money to carry out the repairs. He sold the shares to his son, David Tribe, for £78,000, only the money was never paid. The landlord relented and Kim did not have to repair the shops, but when he asked David to return the shares, David refused.

As David was his son, David was able to claim under the presumption of advancement. To disprove this, Kim had to rely on evidence of his illegal purpose to deceive the landlord.

HELD: Older cases, mentioned in *Tinsley v Milligan*, state that if a person voluntarily withdraws from his illegal purpose and does not carry it out, that purpose can still be used as evidence. Kim had not actually carried out his illegal purpose of deceiving the landlords. He did not need to, as they changed their minds about making him repair the shops. So he could put forward evidence that he did not mean to give the shares to his son as an outright gift, but expected them back at some time. David Tribe held on resulting trust for Kim Tribe.

Millett LJ at para. 136:

> I would hold that genuine repentance is not required. Justice is not a reward for merit; restitution should not be confined to the penitent. I would also hold that voluntary withdrawal from an illegal transaction when it has ceased to be needed is sufficient.

The presumption of advancement was rebutted by the evidence. Kim did not intend to make a gift of the shops to his son, David. Therefore, David held the property on resulting trust for his father.

This approach to illegality was followed in *Patel v Mirza* [2014] EWCA Civ 1047.

- -
● **Patel v Mirza** [2014] EWCA Civ 1047

Patel agreed with Mirza, that he, Patel, would pay Mirza £620,000 in exchange for 'insider' information, so that they could make illegal trades in Royal Bank of Scotland shares. Patel handed over the money, but Mirza never provided the information, so Patel wanted his money back.

HELD: Patel was entitled to his money back, because the illegal agreement was not going to be performed. He did not have to prove that he had changed his mind, repented and decided not to go through with the agreement.

Rimer LJ did not want to make any distinction between cases in which the illegal agreement was no longer needed (*Tribe*) and cases like this one where the illegal agreement could no longer be performed.

thinking points

The 'reliance principle', put forward in Tinsley v Milligan *[1994] 1 AC 340*, has proved controversial and so the Law Commission recommended in its report, 'The Illegality Defence' (Law Com 320), that the law should be changed. They recommended that 'illegality' should normally be ignored when considering whether a resulting trust has been established. If a trust is set up, or later used, in order to conceal a beneficiary's interest in the property, and this is done in connection with the commission of an offence, the beneficiary would still be able to rely on the normal legal right to enforce the trust.

The court would, however, have discretion to take account of the illegality and not enforce the trust. The government does not currently plan to enact these reforms.

See P Davies 'The Illegality Defence: Turning Back the Clock' [2010] Conv 282.

 # Conclusion

The phrase 'resulting trust' comes from the Latin *resalire*, which means to jump back. This is literally what happens with a resulting trust: the property is held on trust to be returned to the original or rightful owner. This seems to be a simple and useful concept and can be seen to work well in cases where a trust comes to an end and the property goes back to the original owners. A good modern example would be *Air Jamaica v Joy Charlton* [1999] 1 WLR 1399. Problems can be caused if the original owners cannot be found, as in *Re Gillingham Bus Disaster Fund* [1958] Ch 300, or it is uncertain whether the trust comes to an end or not. Contrast *Re Osoba* [1979] 1 WLR 247 and *Re Trusts of the Abbott Fund* [1900] 2 Ch 326.

The presumption of resulting trust, that if you put money into the purchase of property, you gain a proportionate share in that property, seems both fair and logical and can be seen operating in many cases today. The presumptions of voluntary transfer and advancement seem less helpful in the modern age. Legislative reform is planned. *Westdeutsche Landesbank Girozentrale v Islington London BC* [1996] AC 669 states that resulting trusts depend upon the intention of the parties, though it is hard to see that this applies in all the cases, such as in *Vandervell v IRC* [1967] 2 AC 291, where the resulting trust was the opposite of what Mr Vandervell intended.

 # Questions

Self-test questions

1   In what situations does an automatic resulting trust arise?

2   In what situations does a presumed resulting trust arise?

3   In what situations will it be presumed that an advancement has occurred?

4   Does an illegal purpose mean that evidence will not be considered by the court?

Discussion questions

1   Are resulting trusts based on the intention of the parties?

2   Do the presumptions of resulting trust and advancement still serve a useful purpose?

3   Should evidence of an illegal purpose be considered by the courts?

Assessment question

Alfonso makes the following gifts:

(a) £100,000 to the vicar of my local church 'to build and maintain a suitable tomb for me, to decorate the same with flowers, insofar as my trustees may legally do so';

(b) £100,000 to the British Anti-Vivisection Society, an unincorporated association. The gift is expressed to be, 'for the benefit and use of the members in their pursuit of the abolition of vivisection';

(c) £100,000 to Bernadette, a woman of 30, who has lived in his house since she was 20; and

(d) £100,000 to his friend Cedric to finance the university education of Cedric's three children, David, Edward, and Fiona. None of Cedric's children wishes to go to university.

Consider whether Alfonso has made valid gifts, or whether his money is held for him on resulting trust.

 # Key cases

- *Re Gillingham Bus Disaster Fund* [1958] Ch 300 **(at 8.2.3)**

- *Westdeutsche Landesbank Girozentrale v Islington London BC* [1996] AC 669 **(at 8.3)**

- *Twinsectra Limited v Yardley* [2002] AC 164 **(at 8.3)**

- *Fowkes v Pascoe* (1875) 10 Ch App 343 **(at 8.4.1 and 8.6.1)**

- *Tinsley v Milligan* [1994] 1 AC 340 **(at 8.4.2, and 8.7)**

 # Further reading

CEF Rickett and R Grantham 'Resulting Trusts. The True Nature of the Failing Trust Cases' (2000) 116 *LQR* 15
There appear to be contradictory decisions in these cases. Can unifying principles be found?

J Brightwell 'Good Riddance to the Presumption of Advancement' [2010] *Trusts and Trustees* 627
It is planned to abolish the presumption of advancement because it infringes the principle of equality between the sexes. But should parent to child advancement be abolished at the same time?

B Shah and E Hitchens 'Fresh *Prest* juice: the consequences of the Supreme Court's landmark decision' (2014) *Trusts and Trustees* 469.

Prest v Petrodel Resources [2013] 3 WLR 1 seems to use the presumption of resulting trust in a novel way in divorce cases, to prevent a husband concealing his assets from the court.

P Davies 'The Illegality Defence: Turning back the clock' [2010] *Conv* 282

Tinsley v Milligan was intended to reform the law on illegality, but has been much criticized. Would the proposed statutory reforms actually improve the situation?

9

Unincorporated associations and the beneficiary principle

Learning objectives

This chapter will help you to:

- understand that unincorporated associations have no legal personality

- understand why an unincorporated association cannot be a trust

- recognize that the members of an unincorporated association hold the property subject to a contract between themselves

- understand the beneficiary principle

- recognize the exceptions to the beneficiary principle.

Introduction

Unincorporated associations are a commonplace sort of organization, but they raise many legal problems. There are many clubs and societies that have not taken the trouble to incorporate and become companies. These are known as unincorporated associations and this means that, in the eyes of the law, they do not exist: they have no legal personality. Therefore, they cannot hold property in their own name. Some unincorporated associations own considerable property and it is usually thought that this must belong to the members of the association in some way. However, the form of that 'ownership' has never been finally resolved. Some cases consider that trustees of the association hold the association property on trust for the members of that association. Other cases consider that the unincorporated association's property is held on some form of contract between the members. The difficulties of a legal solution become particularly acute when an unincorporated association ceases to operate and is dissolved. If the association still has property, to whom it belongs may become a difficult question. Are the rights of the members determined by contract, the principles of trust law, or on some other basis? This chapter attempts to look at these problems, but be warned, there does not seem to be any definitive solution that can deal with all the legal and practical problems.

9.1 Unincorporated associations have no legal personality

The term unincorporated association is not used outside legal circles, but refers to a very common sort of organization. There are many clubs, societies, and organizations in this country which can include, for example, sports clubs, social clubs, student societies, political organizations, etc. Most of us are members of at least one unincorporated association, but the odd thing about these associations is that many of them have no formal legal status and are not recognized as existing by the law. The Court of Appeal took the opportunity to remind us of the peculiar characteristics of an unincorporated association in *R v L* [2009] 1 All ER 786, a case that involved a golf club.

● *R v L* [2009] 1 All ER 786

Hughes LJ at 790:

> There are probably almost as many different types of unincorporated association as there are forms of human activity. This particular one was a club with 900 odd members, substantial land, buildings, and other assets, and it had no doubt stood as an entity in every sense except the legal for many years. But the legal description 'unincorporated association' applies equally to any collection of individuals linked by agreement into a group. Some may be solid and permanent; others may be fleeting, and/or without assets. A village football team, with

no constitution and a casual fluctuating membership, meeting on a Saturday morning on a rented pitch, is an unincorporated association, but so are a number of learned societies with large fixed assets and detailed constitutional structures. So too is a fishing association and a trade union.

At common law, an unincorporated association is to be distinguished from a corporation, which has a legal personality separate from those who have formed it, or who manage it or belong to it...At common law, as the judge succinctly held, an unincorporated association has no legal identity separate from its members. It is simply a group of individuals linked together by contract. By contrast, the corporation, of whatever type, is a legal person separate from the natural persons connected with it.

The 'unincorporated' refers to the fact that the society, or whatever it is, has not been turned into a company. That is a simple process requiring registration and some legal formalities, but most societies and clubs never see the need to incorporate. If they did they would have 'legal personality' and be able to agree to contracts, hold property, etc. Most unincorporated associations carry on quite happily, without worrying about their exact legal status, but if they own valuable property or someone gives them valuable property, the association may get into all sorts of legal problems. Does the property belong to the members of the society or the society itself? But if the property belongs to the society there is a problem because, as far as the law is concerned, the society does not exist. How can property belong to something that does not exist?

Underhill and Hayton *Law Relating to Trusts and Trustees* (16th edn, London: Butterworths, 2003) at 123–4:

> Gifts to or in trust for unincorporated associations raise technical problems that will amaze or confound laymen wishing to benefit an association. The technical problems flow from the fact that an unincorporated association is not a legal person capable of owning property and of being the subject of legal rights and duties.

KEY POINT
An unincorporated association has no legal personality, therefore does not exist in law and cannot hold property, sue, or be sued.

Most unincorporated associations do not even realize that there is a legal problem with their very existence, but of course it only becomes a problem if a matter ends up in court.

9.2 Possible legal structures for unincorporated associations

9.2.1 An unincorporated association as a trust

Over the years the courts have come up with a number of solutions as to how an unincorporated association works legally. One idea is that trustees hold the property of the association on trust. Indeed many unincorporated associations have people designated as 'trustees' who look after the association's property.

● ***Re Drummond*** [1914] 2 Ch 90

Old boys—
Ex pupils of the school.

In his will, James Drummond left the residue of his estate to the Old Bradfordians' Club, London, which was a club for **old boys** of Bradford Grammar School. The money was to be used for such purposes as the committee of the club might determine, such as acquiring a club-house or providing scholarships.

HELD: Eve J at 97–8:

> Said that he could not hold … that the residuary gift … for the Old Bradfordians' Club was a gift to the members individually. There was, in his opinion, a trust, but there was abundant authority for holding that it was not such a trust as would render the legacy void as tending to a perpetuity … The legacy was not subject to any trust which would prevent the committee of the club from spending it in any manner they might decide for the benefit of the class intended. In his opinion, therefore, there was a valid gift to the club for such purposes as the committee should determine for the benefit of the old boys or members of the club.

Eve J does not provide any further explanation, as most of the case concerned other parts of the will, but there are several problems with his conclusion that this is a trust.

1. A trust must be for human beneficiaries (see 4.9 'Certainty of objects'). It is not possible to have a trust for a purpose, unless it is a charitable purpose (see 10.1.1 'Legal advantages'). Eve J does not say who the trust is for: whether it is to promote the purposes of the club or for the club members.

2. The rule against perpetuities. An equitable interest must vest within the perpetuity period. At the date of this case the perpetuity period was a life in being and 21 years. That meant that there should be no possibility that a member could join the club later than the death of an existing member and 21 years. If the club remained in existence for many years, that would be very possible. The policy, behind the perpetuity rule, is that property should be available to be bought and sold, or otherwise used and not be subjected to restrictions upon how it can be used for too long a period. No trust can last for longer than the perpetuity period, unless it is a charity (see 10.1.1 'Legal advantages' again). Eve J says that as the committee can do what they like with the money, there is no perpetuity problem. The money is not locked into the club for an indefinite period. That was not an uncommon approach to the perpetuity problem in trusts of unincorporated associations at that time.

9.2.2 The property of an unincorporated association is shared between the members

Many unincorporated associations were regarded as some sort of trust, until an important Privy Council case, in 1959, pointed out the errors in cases such as *Re Drummond* [1914] 2 Ch 90. (See 9.2.1 'An unincorporated association as a trust'.)

● ***Leahy v Attorney General for New South Wales*** [1959] AC 457

The will of Francis Leahy stated that his property, Elmslea, should be held upon trust 'for such order of nuns of the Catholic Church or the Christian Brothers as my executors and trustees shall select'. The problem was that some orders of nuns were charitable and some, the contemplative, were not. (See *Gilmour v Coats* [1949] AC 426 in 10.6.3 'Public benefit in the advancement of religion'.)

If the trustees gave 'Elmslea' to a contemplative order, then it could not be held by trustees for the purposes of the charity. The question was how could a non-charitable group of nuns hold the property?

HELD: Viscount Simonds at 477:

> 1. It arises out of the artificial and anomalous conception of an unincorporated society which, although it is not a separate entity in law, is yet for many purposes regarded as a continuing entity and, however inaccurately, as something other than an aggregate of its members. In

law a gift to such a society simpliciter (ie, where, to use the words of Lord Parker in *Bowman v Secular Society* [1917] AC 406, neither the circumstances of the gift nor the directions given nor the objects expressed impose on the donee the character of a trustee) is nothing else than a gift to its members at the date of the gift as joint tenants or tenants in common.

At 478:

If it is a gift to individuals, each of them is entitled to his distributive share (unless he has previously bound himself by the rules of the society that it shall be devoted to some other purpose).

2. At 478–9:

A gift can be made to persons (including a corporation) but it cannot be made to a purpose or to an object: so also, a trust may be created for the benefit of persons as cestuis que trust but not for the purpose or object unless the purpose or object be charitable.

3. At 484:

At the risk of repetition their Lordships would point out that, if a gift is made to individuals, whether under their own names or in the name of a society, and the conclusion is reached that they are not intended to take beneficially, then they take as trustees. If so, it must be ascertained who are the beneficiaries. If at the death of the testator the class of beneficiaries is fixed and ascertained or ascertainable within the limit of the rule against perpetuities, all is well. If it is not so fixed and not so ascertainable the trust must fail. Of such a trust no better example could be found than a gift to an Order for the benefit of a community of nuns, once it is established that the community is not confined to living and ascertained persons. A wider question is opened if it appears that a trust is not for persons but for a non-charitable purpose. As has been pointed out, no one can enforce such a trust.

But the rule as stated in *Morice v Bishop of Durham* [1804] 9 Ves 399 continues to supply the guiding principle.

(See 4.9.1 'Certainty of objects in fixed trusts' and 9.4.1 'The beneficiary principle' for the beneficiary principle.)

4. At 486:

It appears from the evidence that Elmslea is a grazing property of about 730 acres, with a furnished homestead containing 20 rooms and a number of outbuildings. With the greatest respect to those judges who have taken a different view, their Lordships do not find it possible to regard all the individual members of an order as intended to become the beneficial owners of such a property.

On the contrary, it seems reasonably clear that, however little the testator understood the effect in law of a gift to an unincorporated body of persons by their society name, his intention was to create a trust, not merely for the benefit of the existing members of the selected Order, but for its benefit as a continuing society and for the furtherance of its work.

Although this is quite a hard judgment to summarize, Viscount Simonds is making a series of valuable points about gifts to unincorporated associations. There are a number of ways of interpreting such gifts, but each of them has its problems and makes it difficult to make a valid gift to an unincorporated association.

1. Most people do not realize that an unincorporated association has no legal personality. As the association does not legally exist, a gift to such an association would usually be interpreted as a gift to be shared amongst the members of the association at the time of

the gift. The major problem with this is that there is nothing to stop members claiming their individual share and destroying the unincorporated association. A way of stopping this is to have rules of the society which prevent this.

2. Gifts can only be made to people or corporations. A trust must have beneficiaries, unless it is a charity, which can exist to promote a purpose. Other purpose trusts are not allowed, because there are no beneficiaries to enforce them. This beneficiary principle makes it difficult to make a gift to an unincorporated association.

3. If an unincorporated association is interpreted as a trust for the members, there are still two legal problems. All the beneficiaries must be 'ascertainable', in that it must be possible to compile a complete list of them. (See 4.9.1 'Certainty of objects in fixed trusts'.) It would be very difficult, if not impossible, to make such a list in clubs and societies where members continually leave and join. The perpetuity rule states that no equitable interest may vest later than a life in being and 21 years. The *existing* members are the lives in being. So if members are allowed to join in the future, which would be true of an order of nuns, as it would be of most unincorporated associations, the new members' interests might vest later than a life in being and 21 years, and the trust could last too long and break the perpetuity rule.

4. The gift of Elmslea to an order of nuns could not be interpreted as a gift to the individual members of the order. Leahy could not have intended that each nun could take an individual share of the farm. He must have intended a trust for members of the order, present and future. This broke the perpetuity rule under point 3 above, which could not be allowed and therefore the gift was invalid.

Later cases have accepted *Leahy v Attorney General for New South Wales* [1959] AC 457 as the law and its principles are well summarized in a case that was heard a couple of years later.

● ***Neville Estates Ltd v Madden and Others*** [1962] Ch 832

This case involved land held by Catford Synagogue. The synagogue promoted the Jewish religion and was held to be charitable. (See 10.6.3 'Public benefit in the advancement of religion'.)

Therefore, there was no legal problem: the trustees of the synagogue held the land on trust for the purpose of the advancement of religion. A purpose was allowed, as this was a charity. The judge discussed the position if this had *not* been a charity, but an unincorporated association.

HELD: Cross J at 849:

> I turn now at last to the legal issues involved. The question of the construction and effect of gifts to or in trust for unincorporated associations was recently considered by the Privy Council in *Leahy v Attorney General for New South Wales* [1959] AC 457. The position, as I understand it, is as follows. Such a gift may take effect in one or other of three quite different ways.
>
> [1] In the first place, it may, on its true construction, be a gift to the members of the association at the relevant date as joint tenants, so that any member can sever his share and claim it whether or not he continues to be a member of the association.
>
> [2] Secondly, it may be a gift to the existing members not as joint tenants, but subject to their respective contractual rights and liabilities towards one another as members of the association. In such a case a member cannot sever his share. It will accrue to the other members on his death or resignation, even though such members include persons who became members after the gift took effect. If this is the effect of the gift, it will not be open to objection on the score of perpetuity or uncertainty unless there is something in its terms or circumstances or in the rules of the association which precludes the

members at any given time from dividing the subject of the gift between them on the footing that they are solely entitled to it in equity.

[3] Thirdly, the terms or circumstances of the gift or the rules of the association may show that the property in question is not to be at the disposal of the members for the time being, but is to be held in trust for or applied for the purposes of the association as a quasi-corporate entity. In this case the gift will fail unless the association is a charitable body.

Cross J's solution [2] has proved the most popular, as it seems to take unincorporated associations out of the law of trusts and into the law of contract. As we shall see, for example in 9.2.5 'An unincorporated association can satisfy the beneficiary principle', it still leaves some unresolved questions.

9.2.3 The members of an unincorporated association have a contract between themselves

The second interpretation of a gift to an unincorporated association is the favoured one. Instead of thinking of the association as a trust it is thought of as a multi-party contract between the members of the association. The rules of the club or society form the terms of the contract and will probably prevent an individual claiming a share of the association's property.

This interpretation of the nature of unincorporated associations works well, as long as there is not a problem in the rules of the society. There may well be such a problem, as the people who draft the constitutions of societies and clubs may well lack knowledge of this specialized area of law.

One example of these problems is where there is no contract between the members.

● ***Conservative and Unionist Central Office v Burrell (Inspector of Taxes)*** [1982] 1 WLR 522

The Inland Revenue wanted to know whether the Conservative Party was an unincorporated association or not, as the Income and Corporation Taxes Act 1970 stated that unincorporated associations had to pay corporation tax.

HELD: Lawton LJ provided a definition of an unincorporated association at 525:

I infer that by 'unincorporated association' in this context Parliament meant two or more persons bound together for one or more common purposes, not being business purposes, by mutual undertakings, each having mutual duties and obligations, in an organisation which has rules which identify in whom control of it and its funds rests and upon what terms and which can be joined or left at will. The bond of union between the members of an unincorporated association has to be contractual.

No contract could be found.

At 525:

On the facts as found I can find nothing which links contractually and directly members of local constituency associations to Conservative members of the House of Commons representing their constituencies. The lack of a contractual link is even more clear in the case of peers who are members of the parliamentary party as long as they accept the Conservative Whip in the House of Lords.

At 527:

> There are no mutual understandings between all the members, no mutual rights and obligations and no rules governing control where it clearly lies, which is in the leader.

9.2.4 The property of an unincorporated association is the property of the leader

One of the other judges was concerned about who exactly held the funds if the Conservative Party was not an unincorporated association.

Brightman LJ explained the normal position with unincorporated associations at 529:

> If the party is rightly described as an unincorporated association with an identifiable membership bound together by identifiable rules, and Central Office funds are funds of the party, no problem arises. In that event, decided cases say that the contribution takes effect in favour of the members of the unincorporated association known as the Conservative Party as an accretion to the funds which are the subject matter of the contract which such members have made inter se: see, for example, *In re Recher's Will Trusts* [1972] Ch 526. If, however, the party is not an unincorporated association, that easy answer is not available.

(See 9.3.3 'Contract' for *Re Recher's Will Trusts*.)

The solution Brightman J came up with is that a donation to the party was just like giving money to a friend and telling the friend that the money must only be spent for a particular purpose. If the friend spends the money for another purpose, the friend can be sued. This is known as 'agency', which is one type of 'fiduciary relationship'. The same principle applies if a person donates money to the treasurer of the Conservative Party. The treasurer only has a 'mandate' to spend the money for the purpose of the party.

Brightman J is suggesting another way in which gifts to an unincorporated association can be held valid. It could simply be a gift to the treasurer or leader of the association, with an obligation to spend the money on the purposes of the association. This possibility is briefly mentioned in the leading case, *Leahy v Attorney General for New South Wales* [1959] AC 457 at 481, but there are doubts about how enforceable the 'obligation' really is. It clearly cannot be a trust, for the reasons explained in *Leahy* and what happens if the treasurer or leader changes?

9.2.5 An unincorporated association can satisfy the beneficiary principle

Conservative and Unionist Central Office v Burrell (Inspector of Taxes) [1982] 1 WLR 522 reveals that there are problems with both the contract and agency theories on how an unincorporated association works, so is the trust theory that we started with in *Re Drummond* [1914] 2 Ch 90 really so unworkable?

● *Re Denley's Trust Deed* [1969] 1 Ch 373

Charles Denley made a trust deed in 1936 which stated that 'the said land shall be maintained and used as and for the purpose of a recreation or sports ground primarily for the benefit of the employees of the company and secondarily for the benefit of such other person or persons (if any) as the trustees may allow...'. This was to be a recreation ground for employees of the Gloster Aircraft Co Ltd. The trustees had power to make rules and regulations as to how the ground should be used and contained a clause on how the trust would end if employees ceased to use the recreation ground. A 'perpetuity clause' was also inserted in the deed, which said that the trust would definitely end 21 years from the death of the last survivor of certain named persons, living at the date of the creation of the trust.

HELD: Goff J at 382–3:

> It was decided in *In re Astor's Settlement Trusts* [1952] Ch 534 that a trust for a number of non-charitable purposes was not merely unenforceable but void on two grounds; first, that it was not a trust for the benefit of individuals, which I will refer to as 'the beneficiary principle', and, secondly, for uncertainty. [See 9.4.1 'The beneficiary principle' for *Astor*.]
>
> I think there may be a purpose or object trust, the carrying out of which would benefit an individual or individuals, where that benefit is so indirect or intangible or which is otherwise so framed as not to give those persons any locus standi to apply to the court to enforce the trust, in which case the beneficiary principle would, as it seems to me, apply to invalidate the trust, quite apart from any question of uncertainty or perpetuity. Such cases can be considered if and when they arise. The present is not, in my judgment, of that character, and it will be seen that clause 2(d) of the trust deed expressly states that, subject to any rules and regulations made by the trustees, the employees of the company shall be entitled to the use and enjoyment of the land.

At 383–4:

> Where, then, the trust, though expressed as a purpose, is directly or indirectly for the benefit of an individual or individuals, it seems to me that it is in general outside the mischief of the beneficiary principle.

At 386:

> The trust in the present case is limited in point of time so as to avoid any infringement of the rule against perpetuities and, for the reasons I have given, it does not offend against the beneficiary principle; and unless, therefore, it be void for uncertainty, it is a valid trust.

As far as Goff J could see there was nothing wrong with this trust. It had identifiable beneficiaries, the employees of the company, who could enforce the trust if necessary and it did not infringe the perpetuity rule. So this is another possible way of interpreting an unincorporated association to be legally valid.

KEY POINT

An unincorporated association can be a valid trust, as long as it satisfies the beneficiary principle and a perpetuity period has been specified.

This solution may become more popular, following the reform of the perpetuity rule in the Perpetuities and Accumulations Act 2009. Section 5(1) changes the perpetuity period to 125 years and replaces all other perpetuity periods for trusts coming into force after the commencement of the Act. Under s. 7 it is possible to wait and see whether anyone's equitable interest vests later than the 125-year period. If anyone is likely to obtain their interest under the trust later than that period, they can be excluded under s. 8. These provisions should prevent most unincorporated associations breaking the perpetuity rule, if of course they are treated as trusts in the first place.

There is, however, one nagging legal problem remaining. In a 'normal trust' trustees would hold the land on trust for the beneficiaries. This means that, although the trustees hold the legal estate in the land, the beneficiaries hold the land in equity. This means that the beneficiaries are the real 'owners' of the land, and if they all agreed they could demand that the trustees end the trust and hand over the land to them: the rule in *Saunders v Vautier* (1841) 4 Beav 115. (See 14.1 'Adult beneficiaries'.)

The beneficiaries could then divide the proceeds of selling the land. This is not what the persons setting up the unincorporated association would want to happen, so usually they would insert rules to prevent this. Goff J recognized the problem (at 388) and thought that the beneficiaries could only enforce the trust by insisting that they could use the recreation ground or preventing the trustees from disposing of the land.

This does not, however, solve the problem of who holds the equitable interest in the land itself.

9.2.6 Do any of the legal structures for unincorporated associations work?

None of the possible legal solutions proposed for unincorporated associations solve all the problems. If they are, after all, trusts for the members, there is still the problem of the exact nature of each member's equitable interest as seen in *Re Denley's Trust Deed* [1969] 1 Ch 373 at 9.2.5 'An unincorporated association can satisfy the beneficiary principle' and of certainty of objects as seen in 9.2.2 'The property of an unincorporated association is shared between the members'.

The contract theory seems promising and J Warburton takes this to its logical conclusion in his book *Unincorporated Associations: Law and Practice* (2nd edn, London: Sweet & Maxwell, 1992) at 51, where he argues that there are no trusts at all in unincorporated associations and 'trustees' of the association are, in reality, merely custodians of the association's property, against whom the members merely have contractual rights. Unfortunately for this theory, most judgments accept that there are trustees holding on trust for the members in unincorporated associations. See for example, Walton J at 9.3.3 'Contract' *Re Bucks Constabulary Widows' and Orphans' Fund Friendly Society (No 2)* [1979] 1 WLR 936.

thinking points

Does the contract analysis work with all unincorporated associations? For it to work the unincorporated association must have rules, to form the contract between the members. Not all such associations have written rules and even those that do often have badly drafted rules that fail to cover all the possibilities, such as whether a member can sever and remove their share of the property when they leave the association. Another crucial omission from many rule books is who is entitled to the property of the unincorporated association, if the association ceases to exist. This is considered in the next section of this chapter. See P Matthews 'A Problem in the Construction of Gifts to Unincorporated Associations' [1995] Conv 302.

9.3 The dissolution of unincorporated associations

As we have seen, an unincorporated association can own considerable property. If the association ceases to exist, disputes can arise as to who owns that property. The solutions adopted in the cases vary greatly. Some judges start from the assumption that they are dealing with some sort of trust: then a solution based on resulting trust might seem appropriate. More commonly, nowadays, the judge would assume that the association was based on contract and try to find terms of the contract about the disposal of the society's funds on dissolution. In many cases the terms of the trust or the contract will not be clear as to what is to happen. Then the judge will have to interpret or imply terms in order to find a solution. If there is no owner of the funds they go to the Crown as bona vacantia.

9.3.1 Resulting trust

● *Re Printers and Transferrers Amalgamated Trades Protection Society* [1899] 2 Ch 184

This was a trade union and its purpose was to raise funds by means of weekly contributions in order to defend and support its members in obtaining reasonable wages. Printers, who were men, paid double the subscription of the transferrers, who were women. In return the printers received double the strike pay of the transferrers. Members could also be fined by the society, for breach of the rules. In 1898 the members passed a resolution to dissolve the society. There were 201 members at the time of dissolution and the society held £1,000, but there was no society rule as to what should happen to this money.

HELD: Byrne J at 189:

> Now, the true principle I think is to be found in this—that there is a resulting trust in favour of those who have contributed to these funds, and I think that the proper and legitimate way of dividing, therefore, will be in accordance with the amounts contributed by the existing members at the time of the passing of the resolution.

Byrne J decided not to calculate each member's share by taking into account what they might have received from the society in strike pay or lost in fines, 'on the ground of expense, loss, and delay that would thereby be occasioned'.

The members of the society had paid their contributions, and now that the society had ceased to exist it was logical to return the money that was left to them. This is seemingly a straightforward example of the resulting trust principles seen earlier in 8.4 'Presumed resulting trusts'.

● *Cunnack v Edwards* [1896] 2 Ch 679

In 1810 a number of people in Helston, Cornwall, formed a society, to which they made financial contributions in order to provide for their widows. The rules of the society stated that, if a man did not leave a widow, their contributions were not returned, but instead remained with the society. By 1879 all the members were dead and the last widow died in 1892, but the society had funds of £1,250. **Personal representatives** of some of the dead members claimed that this money should be returned to them. The High Court agreed that this was a resulting trust for them.

Personal representatives—executors or administrators who deal with the property of the deceased.

The Court of Appeal disagreed.

HELD: Lord Halsbury LC at 681:

> It was, as I shall have to repeat in another view of the case, a perfectly businesslike arrangement: each man contributed a certain sum of money to a common fund upon the bargain that his widow was to receive, upon terms definitely settled, a certain annuity proportionate to the time during which the husband had contributed to the common fund. There never was and there could never be any interest remaining in the contributor other than the right that his wife, if she survived him, should become entitled to a widow's portion thus provided. This was the final and exhaustive destination of all the sums contributed to the common fund. Under these circumstances, I am at a loss to see what room there is for the contention that there is a resulting trust.

So the £1,250 went to the Crown as bona vacantia, as there was no one else who had any claim to the money.

The difference between these two cases is firstly factual. In *Re Printers* [1899] 2 Ch 184 there were members alive who could claim the money, whereas in *Cunnack* [1896] 2 Ch 679 there was no one left to do so. Secondly, the judges could detect subtle differences in what was agreed. In *Cunnack* the agreement was only to pay the widows; the members never had any claim to the money for themselves. In *Re Printers* the members had agreed to provide benefits for themselves, so it was logical to return the money to them when the society ended.

The *Cunnack* case is also interesting because the judges seem to have regarded it as a contractual matter rather than a resulting trust.

KEY POINT
If the property of an unincorporated association is held on trust, then it is logical to return it to the members on the basis of resulting trust.

● ***Cunnack v Edwards*** [1896] 2 Ch 679

Rigby LJ at 689:

> The members were not cestuis que trust of the funds or of any part thereof, but persons who, under contracts or quasi-contracts with the society, secured for valuable consideration certain contingent benefits for their widows …

9.3.2 Contract and resulting trust

There is no such thing as a 'standard' unincorporated association, as they differ in their purposes, their rules, and how they raise money. This can present complex problems for a judge trying to unravel such an association. *Re West Sussex Constabulary's Widows, Children and Benevolent (1930) Fund Trusts* [1971] Ch 1 was an example of what is sometimes called an 'outward-facing' unincorporated association in that, although the members contributed to the fund, they took no benefit from it personally, but their widows and children did instead.

● ***Re West Sussex Constabulary's Widows, Children and Benevolent (1930) Fund Trusts*** [1971] Ch 1

Members of the West Sussex police subscribed to a fund to provide for widows and children of deceased members. Rule 10 provided that any member who left 'shall forfeit all claim against the fund'. Money was also raised from:

(a) entertainments, raffles, and sweepstakes;

(b) collecting-boxes;

(c) donations, including legacies.

In 1968 the West Sussex force was amalgamated with other police forces to form the Sussex Constabulary, but there was £40,000 in the fund. Were the members of the fund entitled to this money?

HELD: Goff J: His Lordship felt that this case was very similar to *Cunnack v Edwards* at 9.3.1 'Resulting trust'.

Concerning members' contributions at 10:

> Further, whatever the effect of the fund's rule 10 may be upon the contributions of those members who left prematurely, they and the surviving members alike are also in my judgment unable to claim under a resulting trust because they put up the money on a contractual basis and not one of trust.

> Accordingly, in my judgment all the contributions of both classes are bona vacantia, but I must make a reservation with respect to possible contractual rights.
>
> Those persons who died whilst still in membership cannot, I conceive, have any rights because in their case the contract has been fully worked out, and on a contractual basis I would think that members who retired would be precluded from making any claim by rule 10...The surviving members, on the other hand, may well have a right in contract...

(a) entertainments, raffles, and sweepstakes at 11:

> ...it appears to me to be impossible to apply the doctrine of resulting trust to the proceeds of entertainments and sweepstakes and such-like money-raising operations for two reasons: first, the relationship is one of contract and not of trust, the purchaser of a ticket may have the motive of aiding the cause or he may not; he may purchase a ticket merely because he wishes to attend the particular entertainment or to try for the prize, but whichever it may be, he pays his money as the price of what is offered and what he receives; secondly, there is in such cases no direct contribution to the fund at all; it is only the profit, if any, which is ultimately received and there may even be none.

(b) collecting-boxes at 13:

> I agree that all who put their money into collecting-boxes should be taken to have the same intention, but why should they not all be regarded as intending to part with their money out and out absolutely in all circumstances?

(c) donations, including legacies, at 16:

> Therefore, where, as in the present case, the object was neither equivocal nor charitable, I can see no justification for infecting the third category with the weaknesses of the first and second, and I cannot distinguish this part of the case from *In Re Abbott Fund Trusts* [1900] 2 Ch 326. [See 8.2.3 'Surplus after completion of purpose'.]
>
> And I make the following declarations: First, that the portion attributable to donations and legacies is held on a resulting trust for the donors or their estates and the estates of the respective testators; secondly that the remainder of the fund is bona vacantia.

Goff J decided that the basic arrangement of the fund was contractual and that the members had contracted to provide benefits for their widows and children, not for themselves. They were not entitled to anything else: particularly not to a return of their contributions. It is the same if someone buys a raffle ticket: it is a contract to compete for a prize. The buyer has not contracted for the return of their stake money, in some future, unspecified situation.

If a person puts money in a collection-box, they are not expecting to ever get their money back. It is unrealistic to see that as their intention. Goff J disagrees with *Re Gillingham Bus Disaster Fund* [1958] Ch 300 (see 8.2.3 'Surplus after completion of purpose').

The situation is different with a donation. Here the donor's intention can be identified, which is to help the fund and, if that is no longer possible, for his contribution to be returned.

As we are about to see, in 9.3.3 'Contract', the contract solution is usually preferred, but in some cases the unincorporated association may not have had any rules. This makes it difficult to find that there was a contract between the members. So the court may be driven back to using a resulting trust. In *Re St Andrews (Cheam) Lawn Tennis Club Trust* [2012] 1 WLR 3487, a resulting trust was used to return the land, used by the club, to the estate of Tweddle, who had originally funded the purchase.

9.3.3 Contract

Re West Sussex Constabulary's Widows, Children and Benevolent (1930) Fund Trusts [1971] Ch 1 is a complicated decision and most later cases have wanted a simpler solution to the problem of dissolving an unincorporated association than its mixture of contract, bona vacantia, and resulting trust. *Re Bucks Constabulary Widows' and Orphans' Fund Friendly Society (No 2)* [1979] 1 WLR 936 was not simply outward-facing, in that the members received benefits for themselves, so a decision that divided the remaining funds between surviving members may not seem unreasonable.

● *Re Bucks Constabulary Widows' and Orphans' Fund Friendly Society (No 2)* [1979] 1 WLR 936

This was a society open to serving members of the Buckinghamshire force. Members made contributions to the fund to provide for widows and orphans of deceased members and to help members who were ill. Most of the money was spent upon widows and orphans. The force merged with others to form the Thames Valley Force, but there was £40,000 left in the fund. The rules provided for dissolving the society, but not for what should be done with surplus funds.

HELD: Walton J at 952:

> …judicial opinion has been hardening and is now firmly set along the lines that the interests and rights of persons who are members of any type of unincorporated association are governed exclusively by contracts; that is to say the rights between themselves and their rights to any surplus assets. I say that to make it perfectly clear that I have not overlooked the fact that the assets of the society are usually vested in trustees on trust for the members. But that is quite a separate and distinct trust bearing no relation to the claims of the members inter se upon the surplus funds so held upon trust for their benefit.
>
> That being the case, prima facie there can be no doubt at all but that the distribution is on the basis of equality, because, as between a number of people contractually interested in a fund, there is no other method of distribution if no other method is provided by the terms of the contract…

At 953:

> The members are not entitled in equity to the fund, they are entitled at law. It is a matter, so far as the members are concerned, of pure contract, and, being a matter of pure contract, it is, in my judgment, as far as distribution is concerned, completely divorced from all questions of equitable doctrines.

KEY POINT
An unincorporated association may be dissolved on the basis of the contract between the members of the society.

This is a nice simple solution: split whatever is left between the members at the date of dissolution. The contractual term can be implied, and there is no need for a long and complicated inquiry into what members past and present had contributed to and received from the fund. The judge considered *West Sussex* [1971] Ch 1 at some length, but did not like the approach there.

There is a confusing aspect of these cases. They say that the contractual rights of the members are the important thing for dividing up the property, but also say that there are trustees holding the society's property on trust for the members. The *Bucks Fund* was registered as a Friendly Society and s. 49(1) of the Friendly Societies Act 1896 states that the property of a friendly society is held by trustees. Even if the unincorporated association is not a friendly society, if it owns land there is little alternative to having trustees to hold that land. It is also the easiest way of holding other types of property. We saw with *Leahy v Attorney General for New South Wales* [1959] AC 457 in 9.2.2 'The property of an unincorporated association is shared between the members' that there are two problems with trusts for the members of unincorporated associations, that of perpetuity and certainty. Membership is never static and members might join in the future and, in theory, at least, money could be tied up in the association for generations. The cases on dissolving unincorporated associations emphasize a practical solution to dissolving the corporation and do not dwell on the somewhat theoretical issue of whether the association had a proper legal existence in the first place.

Thousands of unincorporated associations exist and thousands of gifts are made to them. It would be unrealistic to say that these associations do not exist and no gifts can be made to them.

● *Re Recher's Will Trusts* [1972] Ch 526

Eva Recher made her will in 1957 and one of the gifts in it was to 'The Anti-Vivisection Society, 76 Victoria Street, London, SW1'. Unknown to her or her legal advisers, this society had merged with the National Anti-Vivisection Society in 1956. Eva died in 1962 and the issue was whether this gift could still take effect.

HELD: Brightman J at 536:

> It would astonish a layman to be told that there was a difficulty in his giving a legacy to an unincorporated non-charitable society which he had, or could have, supported without trouble during his lifetime. Yet this would be the position if the argument persuasively submitted on behalf of the third defendant represented the law of this country. For, on that argument, such a legacy is likely to fail for want of a beneficiary, or for remoteness, unless penned with unusual forethought and expertise.

At 539–40:

> The resultant situation, on analysis, is that the London and Provincial society represented an organisation of individuals bound together by a contract under which their subscriptions became, as it were, mandated towards a certain type of expenditure as adumbrated in rule 1 [the abolition of vivisection]. Just as the two parties to a bi-partite bargain can vary or terminate their contract by mutual assent, so it must follow that the life members, ordinary members and associate members of the London and Provincial society could, at any moment of time, by unanimous agreement (or by majority vote, if the rules so prescribe), vary or terminate their multi-partite contract. There would be no limit to the type of variation or termination to which all might agree. There is no private trust or trust for charitable purposes or other trust to hinder the process. It follows that if all members agreed, they could decide to wind up the London and Provincial society and divide the net assets among themselves beneficially. No one would have any **locus standi** to stop them so doing. The contract is the same as any other contract and concerns only those who are parties to it, that is to say, the members of the society.

Locus standi—
Latin—the right
to bring a case to
court.

> The funds of such an association may, of course, be derived not only from the subscriptions of the contracting parties but also from donations from non-contracting parties and legacies from persons who have died. In the case of a donation which is not accompanied by any words which purport to impose a trust, it seems to me that the gift takes effect in favour of the existing members of the association as an accretion to the funds which are the subject-matter of the contract which such members have made inter se, and falls to be dealt with in precisely the same way as the funds which the members themselves have subscribed. So, in the case

of a legacy, in the absence of words which purport to impose a trust, the legacy is a gift to the members beneficially, not as joint tenants or as tenants in common so as to entitle each member to an immediate distributive share, but as an accretion to the funds which are the subject-matter of the contract which the members have made inter se.

A strong argument has been presented to me against this conclusion, and I have been through most, if not all, of the cases which are referred to in *Leahy's Case* [1959] AC 457, as well as later authorities. It has been urged upon me that if the gift is not a purpose gift, there is no half-way house between, on the one hand, a legacy to the members of the London and Provincial society at the date of death, as joint tenants beneficially, and, on the other hand, a trust for members which is void for perpetuity because no individual member acting by himself can ever obtain his share of the legacy. I do not see why the choice should be confined to these two extremes. If the argument were correct it would be difficult, if not impossible, to make a straightforward donation, whether inter vivos or by will, to a club or other non-charitable association which the donor desires to benefit. This conclusion seems to me contrary to common sense.

And at 543:

In my judgment the London and Provincial society was dissolved on January 1, 1957, and the contract theretofore binding persons together, under the name and according to the rules on the London and Provincial Anti-Vivisection Society, was terminated.

Accordingly the gift in the will was void, as there was no longer anyone to whom to give the property.

Brightman J endorses the contract between the members theory of unincorporated associations. That means that the members can agree to end the contract and decide the terms on which the property is divided. That is a neat solution to the problem of how to dissolve an unincorporated association. Simply look at the rules, which form part of the contract, to which the members have agreed.

It is not, however, a completely convincing explanation of how an unincorporated association actually holds property. He dismisses *Leahy* [1959] AC 457 as contrary to common sense. If that case were followed literally it would be impossible to have unincorporated associations. Brightman J mentions that the rules of the London society state there are 'honorary trustees' holding the property 'upon trust to deal with the same as the committee direct', but does not go on to analyse how that trust connects with the contract between the members. Maybe he believes that there is not really a trust there at all, or, if there is, it is unimportant for practical purposes. In his view the contract between the members answers all legal problems.

KEY POINT
The property of an unincorporated association is held on a contract between the members.

9.3.4 A special kind of joint tenancy

The phrase 'unincorporated association' suggests that, to exist, an association must have at least two members, so what happens when there is only one member remaining? Are they entitled to any remaining property or has the association ceased to exist and the Crown is entitled to the property as bona vacantia? Just such a situation occurred in *Hanchett-Stamford v Attorney General* [2009] Ch 173, where Mrs Hanchett-Stamford was left claiming a very substantial value of land and stocks and shares.

. . . .

● ***Hanchett-Stamford v Attorney General*** [2009] Ch 173

The Performing and Captive Animals Defence League was founded in 1914, with the main purpose of making performances by animals illegal. Mr and Mrs Hanchett-Stamford joined the

League in the mid-1960s and acquired a house in Sidmouth, Devon, now worth £675,000, and a portfolio of stocks and shares valued at £1.77 million. Mr Hanchett-Stamford and a Mr Hervey held these assets as trustees, but Mr Hanchett-Stamford died in 2006, leaving Mrs Hanchett-Stamford as the sole surviving member. She wanted to give the property to a charity, the Born Free Association, but were the funds hers to give? The court held that the League was not a charity (see 10.9.3), therefore it was an unincorporated association.

HELD: Lewison J considered the earlier case law, in particular *Re Bucks Constabulary Widows' and Orphans' Fund Friendly Society (No 2)* [1979] 1 WLR 936 at 9.3.3 'Contract'. He agreed with Walton J's ultimate conclusion that the members' rights were based on contract, rather than in trust, and that any remaining assets should be shared equally between the surviving members. Lewison J disagreed with Walton J's remarks, suggesting that an association ceased to exist if it only had one member.

Walton J at 943:

> It may be that it will be sufficient for the society's continued existence if there are two members, but if there is only one the society as such must cease to exist. There is no association, since one can hardly associate with oneself or enjoy one's own society. And so indeed the assets have become ownerless.

Lewison J regarded this as obiter dicta, because *Re Bucks* did not actually involve only one surviving member. He thought it ridiculous that two surviving members could equally divide what was left, but if one of them dies, then everything goes to the Crown. *Cunnack v Edwards* [1896] 2 Ch 679, which we saw at 9.3.1 'Resulting trust', also ended in a decision of bona vacantia. Lewison J distinguished that case on the grounds that there were no surviving members there and the members only meant to provide for their widows not themselves and, so, expected nothing back. So the conclusion was that the property belonged to Mrs Hanchett-Stamford and therefore she could do what she liked with it.

Lewison J at 189:

> I consider that the League ceased to exist upon his [Mr Hanchett-Stamford's] death in January 2006, when its membership fell below two. Since Mrs Hanchett-Stamford is the sole surviving member of the League, she is, in my judgment, entitled to its assets.

More interestingly, Lewison J also explained how unincorporated associations work at 188:

> The thread that runs through all these cases is that the property of an unincorporated association is the property of its members, but that they are contractually precluded from severing their share except in accordance with the rules of the association; and that, on its dissolution, those who are members at the time are entitled to the assets free from any such contractual restrictions. It is true that this is not a joint tenancy according to the classical model; but since any collective ownership of property must be a species of joint tenancy or tenancy in common this kind of collective ownership must, in my judgment, be a sub-species of joint tenancy, albeit taking effect subject to any contractual restrictions applicable as between members ... The cases are united in saying that on a dissolution the members of a dissolved association have a beneficial interest in its assets, and Lord Denning goes as far as to say that it is a 'beneficial equitable joint interest'.

So this case takes the standard contract explanation as to how the members of an unincorporated association hold their property, but we might note the remarks of Lewison J, on joint tenancies, particularly where he quotes Lord Denning. If the members hold their property equitably, someone else must hold it legally, so there must be trustees of the unincorporated association, holding the property legally, on trust for the members. So we are back where we started with the problems raised by *Leahy v Attorney-General for New South Wales* [1959] AC 457 in 9.2.2 'The property of an unincorporated association is shared between the members'.

thinking points

The decision in Hanchett-Stamford v Attorney-General *[2009] Ch 173 seems to be a sensible decision on its facts. Who had a better right to the property than Mrs Hanchett-Stamford? S Baughen endorses the decision in 'Performing Animals and the Dissolution of Unincorporated Associations: The "Contract-holding Theory" Vindicated' [2010] Conv 216, but is critical of some of the reasoning by which it is reached. The article also examines the interplay of contract and trust law in unincorporated associations.*

9.4 Purpose trusts

As we saw in 9.2.1 'An unincorporated association as a trust' and 9.2.5 'An unincorporated association can satisfy the beneficiary principle', a trust must have human beneficiaries to enforce the trust against the trustees, should that become necessary. The only exception to that is charitable trusts, which do not have beneficiaries, but are enforced by the Attorney-General. (See 10.1.1 'Legal advantages'.)

Despite that general rule, there are a few types of trust that are allowed, despite the lack of a beneficiary.

9.4.1 The beneficiary principle

(See also 9.2.5 'An unincorporated association can satisfy the beneficiary principle'.) In the early 1950s, the courts reasserted the principle that a trust must have a beneficiary to enforce it. It was undesirable to have large sums of money tied up in vaguely worded trusts, which were not particularly useful to society. This was in contrast to charitable trusts, which were for the public benefit. (See Chapter 10 'Charitable trusts'.)

● *Re Astor's Settlement Trusts* [1952] Ch 534

Members of the Astor family set up a trust of most of the shares in the *Observer* newspaper, which they owned. There were a number of purposes, including promoting good understanding, sympathy, and cooperation between nations, the preservation of the independence and integrity of newspapers and the press, the promotion of high standards in journalism, etc. A perpetuity clause was inserted stating that the trust would not last longer than the lives of the children of Viscount Astor and King George VI, then living, and a period of 20 years.

It was accepted that this trust was not a charity.

HELD: Roxburgh J at 541–2:

> Prima facie, therefore, a trustee would not be expected to be subject to an equitable obligation unless there was somebody who could enforce a correlative equitable right, and the nature and extent of that obligation would be worked out in proceedings for enforcement.
>
> But if the purposes are not charitable, great difficulties arise both in theory and in practice. In theory, because having regard to the historical origins of equity it is difficult to visualize

the growth of equitable obligations which nobody can enforce, and in practice, because it is not possible to contemplate with equanimity the creation of large funds devoted to non-charitable purposes which no department of state can control, or in the case of maladministration reform.

At 547–8:

...the purposes must, in my judgment, be stated in phrases which embody definite concepts and the means by which the trustees are to try to attain them must also be prescribed with a sufficient degree of certainty.

The purposes must be so defined that if the trustees surrendered their discretion, the court could carry out the purposes declared...

And at 549:

But while I have reached my decision on two separate grounds, both, I think, have their origin in a single principle, namely, that a court of equity does not recognise as valid a trust which it cannot both enforce and control. This seems to me to be good equity and good sense.

KEY POINT A trust must have a beneficiary, because otherwise there is no one to enforce the trust against the trustees and ensure that it is carried out. Similarly the trust must be clear enough to enforce, e.g. how would the court know whether 'sympathy' was being promoted between nations?

thinking points

Perhaps the beneficiary principle is overrated. Re Denley has allowed a more flexible approach to the question of who may be a beneficiary and why could not the Attorney-General enforce purpose trusts as he/she enforces charitable trusts? If the courts were able to reconsider their rather old-fashioned ideas about what is and what is not charitable, as suggested by Lord Cross in Dingle v Turner *[1972] AC 601 (see 10.5.5 'Public benefit in the advancement of education'), then why should not purpose trusts that were deemed useful to society be allowed? See NP Gravells 'Public Purpose Trusts' (1977) 40 MLR 397.*

9.4.2 The exceptions to the rule

Old cases have allowed certain kinds of non-charitable purpose trusts and, because these precedents have stood for some time, the courts are now unwilling to overrule them.

• *Re Endacott, Deceased* [1960] Ch 232

The will of Albert Endacott stated: 'Everything else I leave to North Tawton Devon Parish Council for the purpose of providing some useful memorial to myself...' Was this gift valid?

HELD: Lord Evershed MR: It was decided that this gift was not a charity, but could it be valid in some other way?

At 245–6:

> I now turn to Mr Arnold's alternative argument based on the view that there is here a trust and a trust of a public character, but not a charitable trust. What he says is, that the trust is in line with the trusts which were rendered effective in those cases which I have called 'anomalous'…It will be found that they fall into the following groups:
>
> (1) trusts for the erection or maintenance of monuments or graves;
> (2) trusts for the saying of masses, in jurisdictions where such trusts are not regarded as charitable;
> (3) trusts for the maintenance of particular animals;
> (4) miscellaneous cases.
>
> Still, in my judgment, the scope of these cases…ought not to be extended. So to do would be to validate almost limitless heads of non-charitable trusts, even though they were not (strictly speaking) public trusts, so long only as the question of perpetuities did not arise; and, in my judgment that result would be out of harmony with the principles of our law. No principle perhaps has greater sanction or authority behind it than the general proposition that a trust by English law, not being a charitable trust, in order to be effective, must have ascertained or ascertainable beneficiaries.

Harman LJ at 250–1:

> …that though one knows there have been decisions at times which are not really to be satisfactorily classified, but are perhaps merely occasions when **Homer has nodded**, at any rate these cases stand by themselves and ought not to be increased in number, nor indeed followed, except where the one is exactly like another. Whether it would be better that some authority now should say those cases were wrong, this perhaps is not the moment to consider. At any rate, I cannot think a case of this kind, the case of providing outside a church an unspecified and unidentified memorial, is the kind of instance which should be allowed to add to those troublesome, anomalous and aberrant cases.

· · · · · · · · · · · · · · · ·

Homer nodded—even the best of us sometimes make mistakes. The 'Homer' referred to is the ancient Greek poet.

· · · · · · · · · · · · · · · ·

KEY POINT
Property should not be tied up in a trust to promote useless purposes.

Re Endacott, Deceased [1960] Ch 232 makes clear that certain categories of purpose trust can be allowed, because they always have been, but the categories should not be extended.

So the court would not allow Mr Endacott's memorial, but they did say that there were four exceptions to the 'beneficiary principle'.

9.4.3 Trusts for monuments or graves

It is possible to establish a trust to erect and/or maintain a grave. Such a trust has no living, human beneficiary, but the courts allow it, probably because it is common for testators and testatrixes to want to provide for this in their will. There are a number of cases that establish this point. Two examples reveal how this kind of trust works.

· ·

● ***Pirbright v Salwey*** [1896] WN 86

The testator expressed the desire to be buried in the same enclosure of a churchyard in which his child was buried. He left some investments to the rector and churchwardens of the church and specified that they should apply the interest and dividends in keeping up the enclosure and decorating it with flowers, for as long as the law for the time being permitted.

HELD: This was not a charitable trust, but was valid for a period of 21 years.

For the court in this case the main issue seems to have been the perpetuity rule, so they implied that this trust could only last for 21 years. This precedent was followed in *Re Hooper* [1932] 1 Ch 38.

● *Re Hooper* [1932] 1 Ch 38

The testator left money to his executors and trustees to provide, so far as they legally could do so, for the care and upkeep of certain graves, a vault, and certain monuments.

HELD: Maugham J at 39:

> This point is one to my mind of doubt, and I should have felt some difficulty in deciding if it were not for *Pirbright v Salwey*. That was a decision arrived at by Stirling J after argument by very eminent counsel. The case does not appear to have attracted much attention in textbooks, but it does not appear to have been commented upon adversely, and I shall follow it.

The period was limited to 21 years.

Although the Perpetuities and Accumulations Act 2009 will reform the rule against perpetuities, it is not intended that it should relax the rule for purpose trusts.

> **Perpetuities and Accumulations Act 2009**
>
> 18 Rule as to duration not affected
>
> This Act does not affect the rule of law which limits the duration of non-charitable purpose trusts.

Nowadays there is an easier way of maintaining a grave than establishing a trust. It is possible to make a contract with the local authority or burial authority to maintain a grave for a period not exceeding 99 years: s. 1 of the Parish Councils and Burial Authorities (Miscellaneous Provisions) Act 1970.

9.4.4 Trusts for the maintenance of particular animals

A trust to help animals in general might be charitable (see 10.9 'Animal welfare'), but a trust to look after an individual animal is not a charity. Many people are very fond of their pets and want to ensure that they are cared for after their death. So the law makes an exception to the normal rules, in order to allow this.

● *Pettingall v Pettingall* (1842) 11 LJ Ch 176

The testator made the following bequest in his will:

> Having a favourite black mare, I hereby bequeath, that at my death, £50 per annum be paid for her keep in some park in England and Wales; her shoes to be taken off, and she never be ridden or put in harness; and that my executor consider himself in honour bound to fulfil my wish…

HELD: Knight-Bruce VC at 177:

> The decree on this point ought to be, that £50 a year should be paid to the executor during the life of the mare, or until further order; he undertaking to maintain her comfortably; with liberty for all parties to apply.

The last part of the order is indicating that there are people to enforce the trust: the beneficiaries who inherit whatever is left after the mare has been cared for. There are, however, other animal cases where there was no one to enforce the trust.

● **Re Dean** (1889) 41 ChD 552

The testator gave his horses, ponies, and hounds to his trustees for a period of 50 years, if any of the said horses and hounds should so long live. His estate was charged with an annuity of £750 and the trustees were to use it in maintaining his horses and hounds and the buildings in which they lived.

HELD: North J at 556:

> Then it is said, that there is no cestui que trust who can enforce the trust, and that the court will not recognise a trust unless it is capable of being enforced by someone. I do not assent to that view. There is not the least doubt that a man may if he pleases, give a legacy to trustees, upon trust to apply it in erecting a monument to himself, either in a church or in a churchyard, or even in unconsecrated ground, and I am not aware that such a trust is in any way invalid, although it is difficult to say who would be the **cestuis que trust** of the monument. In the same way I know of nothing to prevent a gift of a sum of money to trustees, upon trust to apply it for the repair of such a monument. In my opinion such a trust would be good, although the testator must be careful to limit the time for which it is to last, because as it is not a charitable trust, unless it is to come to an end within the limits fixed by the rule against perpetuities, it would be illegal.

Cestuis que trust— beneficiaries

North J was certain that, although there was no one to enforce this trust, it could still be valid, as an exception to the normal rule, just as trusts to maintain tombs were allowed as an exception to the normal rule. He did show a concern for the perpetuity rule and it is wise for the testator or testatrix to insert a 'Royal Lives Clause', as in *Re Astor* [1952] Ch 534 (see 9.4.1), or a phrase such as 'for as long as the law allows', which the courts will interpret as 21 years.

9.4.5 Miscellaneous

There is an odd case called *Re Thompson* [1934] Ch 342, which seems to be a purpose trust, yet was allowed to stand.

● **Re Thompson** [1934] Ch 342

The testator left a legacy of £1,000 to his friend, Mr Lloyd, to be applied by him in such manner as he should think fit towards the promotion and furthering of fox-hunting and left the residue to Trinity Hall, University of Cambridge. The executors asked the court whether the legacy was valid.

HELD: Clauson J at 344:

> In my judgment the object of the gift has been defined with sufficient clearness and is of a nature to which effect can be given. The proper way for me to deal with the matter will be, not to make, as it is asked by the summons, a general declaration, but following the example of Knight Bruce VC in *Pettingall v Pettingall* (1842) 11 LJ Ch 176 to order that, upon the defendant Mr Lloyd giving an undertaking (which I understand he is willing to give) to apply

> the legacy when received by him towards the object expressed in the testator's will, the plaintiffs do pay to the defendant Mr Lloyd the legacy of £1000; and that, in case the legacy should be applied by him otherwise than towards the promotion and furthering of foxhunting, the residuary legatees are to be at liberty to apply.

The judge is convinced that this trust can be enforced either by the court, or Trinity Hall, holding Lloyd to his undertaking. The case also has vague similarities to *Re Dean* (1889) 41 ChD 552 at 9.4.4 'Trusts for the maintenance of particular animals', in that fox-hunting would involve horses and hounds.

It is probably unlikely that such a legacy would be left today, as the Hunting Act 2004 has heavily restricted fox-hunting, although it does not make gifts, as in *Re Thompson*, illegal.

9.4.6 Trusts for the saying of masses

It is a Roman Catholic practice to leave money so that masses can be said for the soul of the deceased. For centuries the courts refused to enforce such trusts, regarding them as 'superstitious uses'. They were finally allowed in *Bourne v Keane* [1919] AC 815, but were still not regarded as religious charities. They were regarded as non-charitable purpose trusts, until *Re Hetherington* [1990] Ch 1 accepted such trusts as charitable, as long as the public could attend the masses. (See 10.6.3 'Public benefit in the advancement of religion'.)

With changes in Roman Catholic doctrine, such trusts are likely to become increasingly rare anyway.

KEY POINT These categories of trusts for graves, animals, and other purposes are allowed, even though they do not comply with the normal rule that trusts must have a human beneficiary.

thinking points

Are purpose trusts really based on firm precedents? It might be noticed that in most of our preceding cases the courts have not been very enthusiastic about following the supposed precedents cited to them. See, for example, Re Endacott *at 9.4.2 'The exceptions to the rule'. Some of the other cases might well be based on a misunderstanding where the court became sidetracked on to issues such as the perpetuity rule or who could enforce the trust and neglected the central issue of whether such trusts should be allowed in the first place. The next time the issue comes to court the judge just finds it safer to follow the precedent, rather than consider whether it was right in the first place, as in, for example,* Re Hooper. *See LA Sheridan 'Trusts for Non-Charitable Purposes' [1953] Conv 46.*

The courts are determined that these categories will not be extended, as we have seen in *Re Astor's Settlement Trusts* [1952] Ch 534 and *Re Endacott, Deceased* [1960] Ch 232 at 9.4.1 'The beneficiary principle' and 9.4.2 'The exceptions to the rule'. This probably explains why the reforms to the rule against perpetuities, mentioned in 9.4.3 'Trusts for monuments or graves', have not been extended to this type of trust.

Conclusion

Unincorporated associations were once thought to be a kind of trust, as in *Re Drummond* [1914] 2 Ch 90. If the unincorporated association was dissolved, it would seem logical to return the property to the members of the association on resulting trust, as in *Re Printers* [1899] 2 Ch 184. Now it is thought simpler to approach unincorporated associations as a contract between the members. So the contract, found in the association's rules, determines what happens to the funds: *Re Recher's Will Trusts* [1972] Ch 526.

Unincorporated associations cannot be trusts, because there cannot be a trust for a purpose. There are exceptions to this, as shown in *Re Endacott, Deceased* [1960] Ch 232. These exceptions are, however, rare and tightly defined. The beneficiary principle remains a fundamental part of trust law.

Questions

Self-test questions

1 Why can an unincorporated association not hold property in its own right?

2 In what ways might the members of an unincorporated association hold property?

3 On what basis do the courts divide the property of a dissolved unincorporated association?

4 What exceptions do the courts allow to 'the beneficiary principle'?

Discussion questions

1 Does the theory of the contract between the members solve all the problems relating to the legal existence of an unincorporated association?

2 Why does a trust need beneficiaries?

Assessment question

One cannot, in law, speak of property being owned by an unincorporated association. The property must instead be owned by its members or, ... by some persons holding title to the property on their behalf.

G Moffat *Trust Law* (5th edn, Cambridge: Cambridge University Press, 2009) at 887

Consider the accuracy of the above statement.

Key cases

- *Leahy v Attorney General for New South Wales* [1959] AC 457 **(at 9.2.2, 9.3.3, and 9.3.4)**

- *Neville Estates Limited v Madden and Others* [1962] Ch 832 **(at 9.2.2)**

- *Re Denley's Trust Deed* [1969] 1 Ch 373 **(at 9.2.5)**

- *Re Bucks Constabulary Widows' and Orphans' Fund Friendly Society (No 2)* [1979] 1 WLR 936 **(at 9.3.3 and 9.3.4)**

- *Re Endacott, Deceased* [1960] Ch 623 **(at 9.4.2)**

Further reading

P Matthews 'A Problem in the Construction of Gifts to Unincorporated Associations' [1995] *Conv* 302

Do all unincorporated associations hold their property on a contract between the members? Do the rules of all unincorporated associations allow for this?

S Baughen 'Performing Animals and the Dissolution of Unincorporated Associations: The "Contract-holding Theory" Vindicated' [2010] *Conv* 216

The idea that the members of an unincorporated association hold its property according to the contractual rights between themselves solves some of the problems in this area. Not all the problems are solved, however, as they hold as beneficial joint tenants, so there must also be trustees holding on trust.

NP Gravells 'Public Purpose Trusts' (1977) 40 *MLR* 397

Purpose trusts are similar to charities in some ways. Why are they forbidden and charities allowed?

LA Sheridan 'Trusts for Non-Charitable Purposes' [1953] *Conv* 46

Why are some types of purpose trust allowed to infringe the beneficiary principle?

Charitable trusts

Learning objectives

This chapter will help you to:

- appreciate the legal advantages of charitable status
- understand the role of the Charity Commission
- appreciate that there is no overall definition of charity
- identify the four heads of charity: poverty, education, religion, and other purposes beneficial to the community
- understand that a charity must also be for the public benefit
- distinguish between the different public benefit requirements for different types of charity
- understand the basis of the cy-près doctrine.

Introduction

Normally, the law does not allow trusts for a purpose, e.g. a trust to repeal the Abortion Act 1967. A trust must have identifiable human beneficiaries (see 'Certainty of objects in fixed trusts' at 4.9.1 'Trusts and powers and the three certainties'), but charities are the exception. A charitable trust can be designed to achieve a purpose, e.g. to provide educational scholarships for the poor of south Bristol, but only certain purposes are regarded by the law as charitable. There is no overall definition of 'charity'; instead, the law has been built up bit by bit, case by case, over the centuries. The law can seem somewhat old-fashioned and not very logical, although judges, and the Charity Commissioners, have made great efforts to keep the law up to date and in step with modern social developments. It is a requirement that a charitable purpose must also be for 'the public benefit', which has two meanings. Firstly, it means that the intended charity must provide a useful service to the public. Secondly, the charitable benefits must be available to the general public and not just a select few. The meaning of public benefit changes in different types of charity and the courts are sometimes on their guard, to prevent wealthy individuals exploiting charitable status for its tax privileges. There are a number of 'Charity Acts', but even the Charity Act 2006 (now consolidated into the Charities Act 2011), which was intended as a reforming statute, did not change the old case law. The fear is that charities that have been valid for centuries might suddenly cease to be charitable, causing chaos to the voluntary sector and the practical problem of what to do with the billions of pounds of property dedicated to charitable purposes.

 ## 10.1 The advantages of charitable status

10.1.1 Legal advantages

A charity can be organized as a trust, but does not have to be. The charity could for instance incorporate and register as a company. Historically, however, charities were set up as trusts and many charities remain so today. As such, charitable trusts are treated differently from ordinary, private trusts. They are not affected by the third of the three certainty rules (see 4.9 'Certainty of objects'). There is no need for there to be identifiable beneficiaries who, if necessary, could enforce the trust in court. This is also considered at 9.4.1 as 'The beneficiary principle'.

● *Morice v Bishop of Durham* [1805] 9 Ves 399

Sir William Grant MR at 405:

> Every other trust must have a definite object. There must be somebody, in whose favour the court can decree performance. But it is now settled, upon authority, which it is too late to controvert, that, where a charitable purpose is expressed, however general, the bequest shall not fail on account of the uncertainty of the object: but the particular mode of application will be directed by the King in some cases, in others by this court.

So it is perfectly possible to have a charitable trust to relieve 'the poor of Bristol'. It would not be possible to identify all the beneficiaries and it does not matter that 'poor' is a fairly vague definition.

If there are any problems with the administration of the charity, the Attorney General can take the trustees to court. Nowadays the Charity Commissioners would do this on behalf of the Attorney General.

If it is unclear to whom the charitable funds should go, the doctrine of cy-près comes into play (see 10.11 'The cy-prés doctrine'). Historically the courts would assign the funds to another similar charity. Nowadays this is done by the Charity Commission.

It is not usually legal to set up a trust that lasts forever, which is known as perpetual duration. The maximum time is a lifetime plus 21 years or 80 years, whichever is the longer, though this has increased to 125 years under the Perpetuities and Accumulations Act 2009. Anyway, the perpetuity rule does not apply to charitable trusts, which can last for any length of time.

269

10.1.2 Tax advantages

Charities enjoy various tax privileges, which can make charitable status an attractive financial proposition.

Charities would usually own property, which would produce income such as rents or dividends. They do not have to pay income tax if this money is applied for charitable purposes. When people donate money to charity, if they **covenant** to do so, the charity can reclaim the tax on the donation.

....
Covenant—
a legally binding
promise, made in a
deed.
....

Donations to charities during the donor's life are exempt from capital transfer tax and, when the donor dies, from inheritance tax. Charities are also exempt from capital gains tax and stamp duty.

Charitable premises can claim an 80 per cent reduction in non-domestic rates. Charities do not have to pay value added tax on the goods that they supply, if those goods are made by beneficiaries of the charity.

These tax exemptions might explain the caution of judges in granting charitable status to new charities, but it is seldom discussed in judgments. See the notable exception of Lord Cross of Chelsea in *Dingle v Turner* [1972] AC 601 at 624 at 10.4.2 'Public benefit and the relief of poverty'.

10.2 The Charity Commission

This body was originally established in 1853, but is now governed by the Charities Act 2011. It acts on behalf of the Crown but is independent of 'the direction or control of any Minister of the Crown or other government department' (s. 13, 2011 Act). The new Act sets out the Commission's objectives, which are defined in:

Charities Act 2011

. . . .

Section 14 The Commission's objectives

(3) Those objectives are defined as follows—

1. The public confidence objective is to increase public trust and confidence in charities.
2. The public benefit objective is to promote awareness and understanding of the operation of the public benefit requirement.
3. The compliance objective is to promote compliance by charity trustees with their legal obligations in exercising control and management of the administration of their charities.
4. The charitable resources objective is to promote the effective use of charitable resources.
5. The accountability objective is to enhance the accountability of charities to donors, beneficiaries and the general public.

This leads on to the functions of the Commission.

Charities Act 2011

. . . .

Section 15 The Commission's general functions

(1) The Commission has the general functions set out in subsection (2).

(2) The general functions are—

1. Determining whether institutions are or are not charities.
2. Encouraging and facilitating the better administration of charities.
3. Identifying and investigating apparent misconduct or mismanagement in the administration of charities and taking remedial or protective action in connection with misconduct or mismanagement therein.

Appeals against the Commission's decision on charitable status go to the Tribunal system, First Tier, then Upper Tier. There is a further appeal to the Court of Appeal.

KEY POINT

The Charity Commission decides whether an organization is charitable or not. It is only if there is disagreement with their decision that the matter goes to court.

10.3 The legal definition of charity

10.3.1 The Preamble

The Mediaeval Church provided most of the services that we nowadays regard as charitable, namely religion, education, helping the poor, and caring for the old and sick. After the

Reformation in the early 16th century, other bodies and persons provided some of these services. At the start of the following century, an Act of Parliament laid out what was then regarded as charitable.

Preamble to the Statute of Charitable Uses 1601

. . . .

...some for relief of aged, impotent and poor people, some for the maintenance of sick and maimed soldiers and mariners, schools of learning, free schools and scholars in Universities, some for the repair of bridges, ports, havens, causeways, churches, sea-banks, and highways, some for the education and preferment of orphans, some for or towards relief, stock or maintenance for houses of correction, some for the marriages of poor maids, some for supportation, aid and help of young tradesmen, handicraftsmen and persons decayed, and others for the relief or redemption of prisoners and captives, and for aid or ease of any poor inhabitants concerning payment of fifteens, setting out of soldiers and other taxes...

Although this was repealed by the Charities Act 1960, it is still regarded as our starting point for the definition of charity.

. . . .

● *Morice v Bishop of Durham* (1805) 9 Ves 399

Sir William Grant MR at 405:

> Those purposes are charitable which that statute enumerates or which by analogies are deemed within its spirit and intendment.

Some things in the Preamble now look very outdated, as society has changed. For instance 'the marriages of poor maids' simply means providing a dowry (payment of money to a husband), so that an unmarried woman ('maid'), who was poor, could marry. This is a practice, which although still common in parts of the world, is now unusual in Western society.

So judges and the Charity Commission start with the Preamble and try to find a similar case to the new charity being proposed. The process is explained in *Scottish Burial Reform and Cremation Society v Glasgow Corporation* [1968] AC 138.

. . . .

● *Scottish Burial Reform and Cremation Society v Glasgow Corporation* [1968] AC 138

The House of Lords had to decide whether the provision of cremation for a fee, by a non-profit making organization, was charitable.

HELD: It was charitable.

Lord Reid at 147:

> The Preamble specifies a number of objects which were then recognised as charitable. But in more recent times a wide variety of other objects have come to be recognised as also being charitable. The courts appear to have proceeded first by seeking some analogy between an object mentioned in the preamble and an object with regard to which they had to reach a decision and then they appear to have gone further and to have been satisfied if they could find an analogy between an object already held to be charitable and the new object held to be charitable.

Lord Wilberforce at 154:

> The purposes in question, to be charitable, must be shown to be for the benefit of the public, or the community, in a sense or manner within the intendment of the preamble to the statute 43 Eliz. 1, c. 4. The latter requirement does not mean quite what it says; for it is now accepted that what must be regarded is not the wording of the preamble itself, but the effect of decisions given by the courts as to its scope, decisions which have endeavoured to keep the law as to charities moving according as new social needs arise or old ones become obsolete or satisfied.

What the court means by analogy is that if a new charitable purpose is similar to something listed in the Preamble, it is accepted. The process can be taken further by then saying that something is similar to that newly accepted charitable purpose and is in turn charitable. Examples are given in the following case.

● *Incorporated Council of Law Reporting for England and Wales v Attorney General* [1972] Ch 73

Russell LJ at 87–8:

> Of this approach perhaps the most obvious example is the provision of crematoria by analogy with the provision of burial grounds by analogy with the upkeep of churchyards by analogy with the repair of churches.
>
> I can understand it when you say that the preservation of sea walls is for the safety of lives and property, and therefore by analogy the voluntary provision of lifeboats and fire brigades are charitable.

The proposed charity must be exclusively charitable. It cannot be for non-charitable purposes as well as charitable purposes.

● *Helena Partnerships Ltd. (formerly Helena Housing Ltd.) v Revenue and Customs Commissioners* [2012] 4 All ER 111

A housing association could provide housing for the poor and would be charitable. If it was also doing non-charitable things it would lose its charitable status.

Lloyd LJ at 144:

> Paragraph (f) extends to providing services to housing associations and other voluntary associations connected with housing. Such bodies are not necessarily charitable, so this assistance need not be of a charitable nature . . . that would not confine operations pursuant to para (f) to that which is exclusively and necessarily charitable.

(A fuller account of this case can be found at 10.7 'Other purposes beneficial to the community'.)

10.3.2 The four heads of charity

The courts have simplified the task of deciding upon charitable status by summarizing the main types, or 'heads' of charity. This was first done in *Morice v Bishop of Durham* (1805) 9 Ves 399 (see 10.1.1 'The advantages of charitable status' and 10.3.1 'The Preamble') but is best explained in the next case.

● **Commissioners for Special Purposes of Income Tax v Pemsel** [1891] AC 531

Lord Macnaghten at 583:

> How far then, it may be asked, does the popular meaning of the word 'charity' correspond with its legal meaning? 'Charity' in its legal sense comprises four principal divisions: trusts for the relief of poverty; trusts for the advancement of education; trusts for the advancement of religion; and trusts for other purposes beneficial to the community, not falling under any of the preceding heads.

KEY POINTS

The main types of charity are for:

• the relief of poverty;

• the advancement of education;

• the advancement of religion; and

• other purposes beneficial to the community.

However, we should not follow these categories too slavishly, as many charities do not fit neatly into just one of the four categories.

● **Scottish Burial Reform and Cremation Society v Glasgow Corporation** [1968] AC 138

Lord Wilberforce at 154:

> Lord Macnaghten's grouping of the heads of recognised charity in Pemsel's case is one that has proved to be of value and there are many problems which it solves. But three things may be said about it, which its author would surely not have denied: first that, since it is a classification of convenience, there may well be purposes which do not fit neatly into one or other of the headings, secondly, that the words used must not be given the force of a statute to be construed; and thirdly, that the law of charity is a moving subject which may well have evolved even since 1891.

10.3.3 The 'twelve heads of charity'

The Charities Act 2011 improves upon this description, by defining 'charity', or rather listing 12 charitable purposes:

Charities Act 2011

Section 3 *Descriptions of purposes*
(a) the prevention or relief of poverty;
(b) the advancement of education;

(c) the advancement of religion;

(d) the advancement of health or the saving of lives;

(e) the advancement of citizenship or community development;

(f) the advancement of the arts, culture, heritage or science;

(g) the advancement of amateur sport;

(h) the advancement of human rights, conflict resolution or reconciliation or the promotion of religious or racial harmony or equality and diversity;

(i) the advancement of environmental protection or improvement;

(j) the relief of those in need by reason of youth, age, ill-health, disability, financial hardship or other disadvantage;

(k) the advancement of animal welfare;

(l) the promotion of the efficiency of the armed forces of the Crown, or of the efficiency of the police, fire and rescue services or ambulance services;

(m) any other purposes within subsection.

'Any other purposes' includes recreational trusts (see 10.10 'Sport and recreation') under s. 5 of the Act and purposes that are analogous to or within the spirit of (a) to (l) or analogous to or within the spirit of purposes that have been recognized as charities in England and Wales. The Charities Act 2011 is not the radical departure from the past that it may seem, as the extra purposes were all already recognized under the fourth head of charity. It may help to clarify some difficult, borderline cases, as we shall see later in the chapter.

10.3.4 Public benefit

Each head of charity must also contain an element of 'public benefit'. It is difficult to define exactly what this means, but it seems to contain two major elements. First, it must be thought that the charitable services provided are socially useful. Secondly, the charitable benefits must be available to the general public. The public benefit required differs in the different heads of charity and can even be different for different types of charity within each head of charity.

● *Gilmour v Coats* [1949] AC 426

Lord Simonds at 449:

> It would not therefore be surprising to find that, while in every category of legal charity some element of public benefit must be present, the court had not adopted the same measure in regard to different categories, but accepted different standards in different branches.

This was confirmed in *R (Independent Schools Council) v Charity Commission for England and Wales, Attorney-General v Charity Commission and the Independent Schools Council* [2012] 1 All ER 127

At 138:

> ...the law has developed differently in relation to different 'heads' of charitable endeavour. Care must be taken in applying the law established in one area to another area, particularly when the same words are used to describe similar, but not identical concepts.

An example can be found in the following case.

....

● *Incorporated Council of Law Reporting for England and Wales v Attorney General* [1972] Ch 73

The question was whether the production of a system of law reports was charitable or not. Did it just benefit a small and usually affluent section of society, the legal professions?

HELD: This was charitable, either under the second head, the advancement of education, or the fourth head, general purposes beneficial to the public.

Sachs LJ at 95:

> Does it benefit a sufficiently wide section of the community? As satisfactory administration of the law in practice depends on there being a proper system of law reporting, it can well be said that the whole community benefits from the purposes of the council: but even if the benefits were confined to those who have to make judicial decisions and to the members of the legal profession advising clients and appearing for them in court, none the less a sufficiently large section of the community would derive the relevant benefits.

KEY POINT
Every charity must also be for the public benefit.

10.3.5 The Charities Act 2011 and public benefit

Section 4 of the Charities Act 2011 requires that all charities, under whichever head or purpose they fall, must demonstrate that they are 'for the public benefit'. Before the 2006 Act, it had been thought that it could be presumed that the old-established categories of poverty, education, and religion would be for the public benefit. Thinking that the law had been changed, the Charity Commission began investigating whether sectors such as fee-paying schools and private hospitals really were for the public benefit. This was challenged in court and the courts held that the law had not been changed. There never had been any presumption of public benefit and all charities had to prove that they were for the public benefit. The confusion had been caused by what we saw in 10.3.4 'Public benefit'. There are two aspects of public benefit, social usefulness and availability to the public, and how these are defined differs depending upon the type of charity being considered.

It has always been permissible for charities to charge for their services, as long as the charity is non-profit making. (See at 10.7.1 'Aged, impotent, and sick' *Joseph Rowntree Memorial Trust v Attorney General* [1983] Ch 159 and at 10.7.2 'Public benefit in charities to relieve the aged and impotent' *Re Resch's Will Trusts* [1969] 1 AC 514.)

KEY POINT
Charitable benefits do not have to be provided for free.

....

● *Scottish Burial Reform and Cremation Society v Glasgow Corporation* [1968] AC 138

Lord Reid at 147–8:

> In the present case the appellants make a charge for the services which they provide. But it has never been held that objects, otherwise charitable, cease to be charitable if beneficiaries are required to make payments for what they receive . . . But no authority and no reason has been put forward for holding that . . . the objects and activities of the non-profit-earning charitable organisation cease to be charitable.

This was confirmed by the Upper Tribunal in *R (Independent Schools Council) v Charity Commission for England and Wales, Attorney-General v Charity Commission and the Independent Schools Council* [2012] 1 All ER 127. The judges also explained how the two aspects of public benefit, social usefulness and availability to the public, worked in the advancement of education.

● *R (Independent Schools Council) v Charity Commission for England and Wales, Attorney-General v Charity Commission and the Independent Schools Council* [2012] 1 All ER 127

The Charity Commission had stated that fee-charging schools had to provide a certain percentage of their places for free or scholarship students, in order to satisfy the public benefit requirement.

HELD: This guidance over-simplified the legal position.

There never had been a presumption that education was for the public benefit. At 157:

> The irony of our analysis, however, is that the 2006 Act itself really makes little, if any, difference to the legal position of the independent schools sector. But what the 2006 Act has done is to bring into focus what it is that the pre-existing law already required, and what the law now requires by way of the provision of benefit and to whom it must be provided.

Education was accepted as being socially useful and so passed the first requirement of public benefit. At 162:

> Educational trusts of an ordinary sort are seen as being for the public benefit in the first sense because of the value to society of having an educated population. It is no more and no less of benefit to the community in the case of a rich person than a poor person.

A charity must not exclude the poor, but it can charge fees for the services that it provides. At 182:

> This conclusion is based on the proposition that a trust which excludes the poor cannot be a charity . . . an institution may be a charity even though it charges, without any element of subsidy at all, for its services . . .

Public benefit in the second sense, availability to the public, could be direct, indirect, or of benefit to the wider community. At 143:

> Given the very wide range of potential charitable purposes, it is obvious that some charities have purposes which have the primary effect of conferring direct benefits on certain individuals, while other charities have purposes which confer benefit on the public, whether individually or collectively, much more indirectly. An educational charity such as a school is a clear example of the first class of charity, while a charity for the advancement of animal welfare is a clear example of the second class. A trust for maintaining a bridge is somewhere in between: it is of direct benefit to those who use it but of indirect benefit to the relevant community. Mr Pearce has put forward a terminology which we have found useful in illuminating the subject and we adopt it in this judgment. It distinguishes the following three types of benefit. (a) Direct benefits: benefits to persons whose needs it is a purpose of the charity to relieve which are received by such persons as recipients of the main service which the charity provides. (b) Indirect benefits: benefits to persons whose needs it is a purpose of the charity to relieve which are received by such persons otherwise than as recipients of the main service that the charity provides. (c) Wider benefits: benefits other than direct and indirect benefits which are received by the community at large from the activities of the charity.

The tribunal then explained how these definitions of public benefit applied to fee-charging schools. At 186:

> Those benefits include some or all of the following:
>
> (a)   provision of scholarships and bursaries;

(b)   arrangements under which students from local state schools can attend classes in sub-
      jects not otherwise readily available to them;

(c)   sharing of teachers or teaching facilities with local state schools;

(d)   making available (whether on the internet or otherwise) teaching materials used in the
      school;

(e)   making available to students of local state schools other facilities such as playing fields,
      sports halls, swimming pools or sports grounds;

(f)   making those last facilities available to the community as a whole.

Category (a) is a direct benefit. Categories (b) to (e) will be direct or indirect benefits, depending on the precise constitution of the school. They might also be wider benefits.

Category (f) does not count as public benefit because it is not 'the provision of education'.

It was up the trustees of the charity to decide whether they were meeting the public benefit requirement. The tribunal could not lay down any hard and fast rule, and the Charity Commission guidance would have to be redrafted. At 191:

> b) The second approach is to apply a more fact-sensitive assessment. It is to look at what
> a trustee, acting in the interests of the community as a whole, would do in all the circum-
> stances of the particular school under consideration and to ask what provision should be
> made once the threshold of benefit going beyond the de minimis or token level had been
> met . . .

The very nature of this approach means that it is not possible to be prescriptive about the nature of the benefits which a school must provide to the poor nor the extent of them. It is for the charity trustees of the school concerned to address and assess how their obligations might best be fulfilled in the context of their particular circumstances.

KEY POINT A charity must be for the public benefit. This means that it must be socially useful. It also means that the services that the charity provides must be available to the public, either directly to the recipients of the charitable services or indirectly to the wider public.

thinking points

*Some thought that the Charities Act 2006 (now 2011) radically changed the law by requiring
all charities to prove that they actually were for the public benefit.* Independent Schools
Commission v Charity Commission for England and Wales *[2012] 1 All ER 127 shows that
this is not so; charities always had to prove this and the law has not changed. The case does attempt
to explain what public benefit is and comes up with four key elements. These are public benefit
in the first sense, public benefit in the second sense, the proposition that a charity may not exclude
the poor, and lastly, a duty to carry out the charity's purposes in a way that is for the public benefit.
The judges discovered that previous cases did not clearly decide the law and so had to come to their
own conclusions on what it should be. Unfortunately, although the case was clear that independent
schools did not necessarily have to provide scholarships to satisfy the public benefit, it did not make
clear what those schools had to do so as not to exclude the poor and satisfy the public benefit
requirement. See Mary Synge 'Independent Schools Commission v Charity Commission for England
and Wales' (2012) 75 MLR 624.*

10.4 The relief of poverty

10.4.1 The definition of poverty

KEY POINT
The courts have previously accepted that no absolute definition of poverty is possible.

The first problem is to define what is meant by 'poverty'. The Preamble just refers to the relief of poor people, and as G Cross has remarked at (1956) 72 *LQR* 187 at 206–7: 'Poverty is a vague word which has meant different things at different times and in different places.' The Charity Commission suggests substituting 'people on low incomes' as a more modern equivalent of 'the poor' and even provides a definition: those households living on less than 60 per cent of average income or people living at or below the level of income support. It remains to be seen whether this definition is accepted.

● ***Re Coulthurst*** [1951] Ch 661

The will of the testator left a fund to be applied

> to or for the benefit of such…of the…widows and orphaned children of deceased officers and deceased ex-officers of Coutts & Co…as the bank shall in its absolute discretion consider by reason of his her or their financial circumstances to be most deserving of such assistance.

HELD: This was a valid charity.

Evershed MR at 666:

> It is quite clearly established that poverty does not mean destitution; it is a word of wide and somewhat indefinite import; it may not unfairly be paraphrased for present purposes as meaning persons who have to 'go short' in the ordinary acceptation of that term, due regard being had to their status in life, and so forth.

Coutts and Co are a very prosperous bank, but it is possible that the widows and orphans of ex-employees could be poor and the trustees could use their discretion to choose only the poor.

● ***Re Gardom*** [1914] 1 Ch 662

The will of Eliza Gardom set up a trust for the maintenance of a temporary house of residence for ladies of 'limited means'.

HELD: This was acceptable as a charity for the relief of poverty.

Eve J at 668:

> It is true that ladies of limited means are not destitute, and that the expression 'limited means' may vary in its signification according to the standard by which the means are measured, but these arguments provoke the rejoinder that there are degrees of poverty less acute than abject poverty or destitution, but poverty nevertheless…In other words the objects to be benefited by the bequest are ladies too poor to provide themselves with a temporary home without outside assistance.

Here the provision of housing was regarded as within the relief of poverty.

The court, however, must be satisfied that the benefits of the charity are aimed exclusively at the poor. In *Helena Partnerships Ltd v Revenue and Customs Commissioners* [2012] 4 All ER 111, housing was provided for tenants, only some of whom were poor. This was fatal to charitable status. (See 10.7 'Other purposes beneficial to the community' for more on this case.)

● ***Re Sanders' Will Trusts*** [1954] Ch 265

A codicil to the will established funds 'to provide or assist in providing dwellings for the working classes and their families resident in the area of Pembroke Dock . . . or within a radius of 5 miles therefrom'.

HELD: Harman J: The phrase 'working classes' did not necessarily indicate poor people and therefore this trust was not charitable.

Whether the trust is actually aimed at the poor can depend upon all the circumstances.

● ***Re Niyazi*** [1978] 1 WLR 910

Niyazi left property, which turned out to be worth £15,000, for 'the construction of or as a contribution towards the cost of a working men's hostel' in Famagusta, Cyprus.

HELD: Megarry VC at 915:

He felt that *Re Sanders* could be distinguished.

> The word 'hostel' has to my mind a strong flavour of a building which provides somewhat modest accommodation for those who have some temporary need for it and are willing to accept accommodation of that standard in order to meet the need. When 'hostel' is prefixed by the expression 'working men's', then the further restriction is introduced of the hostel being intended for those with a relatively low income who work for their living, especially as manual workers.
>
> The money is given for the purpose 'of the construction of a working men's hostel in Famagusta, Cyprus'. £15,000 will not go very far in such a project . . .

At 916:

> The other consideration is that of the state of housing in Famagusta. Where the trust is to erect a building in a particular area, I think it is legitimate, in construing the trust, to have some regard to the physical conditions existing in that area. Quite apart from any question of the size of the gift, I think that a trust to erect a hostel in a slum or in an area of acute housing need may have to be construed differently from a trust to erect a hostel in an area of housing affluence or plenty. Where there is a grave housing shortage, it is plain that the poor are likely to suffer more than the prosperous, and that the provision of a 'working men's hostel' is likely to help the poor and not the rich.
>
> In the result, then, I hold that the trust is charitable.

KEY POINT
It is common to restrict a charity to a particular area. The type of area could be very relevant to whether the trust is deemed charitable.

Sometimes testators or settlors attempt to establish charities with very restrictive provisions as to who is eligible. This can be fatal to charitable status, if it is not made clear that the main objective of the charity is to help the poor.

● **Re Gwyon** [1930] 1 Ch 255

The testator attempted to set up the 'Gwyon's Boys Clothing Foundation' which was to provide 'knickers' (short trousers, often called knee breeches or knickerbockers) to boys aged between five and 15 in Farnham and District. There were a number of conditions for a boy to be eligible for his knickers. They must not be supported by any other charity, must not receive poor relief, must not be black, and when they returned the knickers, in order to obtain a new pair, it must still be possible to read 'Gwyon's Present', which was printed on the waistband!

HELD: Eve J at 260:

Charitable status was rejected. The very poorest were ineligible, which might be acceptable in itself, but the conditions of the gift could include the wealthy, which was not acceptable.

> . . . it does not follow that a gift to all and sundry in a particular locality and not expressed to be for the poor ought to be construed as evidencing an intention to relieve poverty.

Poverty can be relieved by gifts of money, provision of housing, provision of clothes, food, furniture, family help, or indeed, help in obtaining work.

10.4.2 Public benefit and the relief of poverty

It is assumed that relieving poverty is a socially useful thing to do and the normal requirement that the benefit of the charity should be available to the public or a section of the public does not apply.

● **Re Scarisbrick** [1951] Ch 622

The testatrix's will provided that, the residue of her estate should be held upon trust 'for such relations of my said son and daughters as in the opinion of the survivor of my said son and daughters shall be in needy circumstances'.

HELD: Jenkins LJ at 650:

> Accordingly, in the view I take, this is a trust for the relief of poverty in the charitable sense amongst the class of relations described, and, being a trust for the relief of poverty, is in view of the exception above stated, not disqualified from ranking as a legally charitable trust by the circumstances that its application is confined to a class of relations (albeit a wide class), with the result that its potential beneficiaries do not comprise the public or a section thereof under the decisions to which I have referred.
>
> I am accordingly of opinion that as the law now stands the trust in question should be upheld as a valid charitable trust for the relief of poverty.
>
> I think the true question in each case has really been whether the gift was for the relief of poverty amongst a class of persons, or rather . . . a particular description of poor, or was merely a gift to individuals, albeit with relief of poverty amongst those individuals as the motive of the gift, or with a selective preference for the poor or poorest amongst those individuals.

This was acceptable, because the trustee could select amongst the category of poor relatives. If the gift gave the property to the poor relatives as an absolute gift then it would be a private trust and not a charity.

Charities for poor relations are such an established exception to the normal approach to public benefit, that even more borderline cases have been accepted, such as the following example.

. . . .

● **Re Segelman** [1996] Ch 171

The will of Gerald Segelman set up a trust for 21 years, for poor and needy members of his relations, naming six individuals and their issue. At the time of the trial there were 26 members of the class.

HELD: Chadwick J at 190: Over the 21 years the class of relations would increase as children were born. Not all the members of the class were poor. They were 'comfortably off', although they might need a 'helping hand' from time to time. However, it was still a charity.

> The basis for disqualification as a charitable gift must be that the restricted nature of the class leads to the conclusion that the gift is really a gift to the individual members of the class. In my view, the gift in clause 11 of the will is not of that character. The gift with which I am concerned has, in common with the gift which the Court of Appeal had to consider in *Re Scarisbrick*, the feature that the class of those eligible to benefit was not closed upon the testator's death. It remained open for a further period of 21 years. During that period issue of the named individuals born after the death of the testator will become members of the class...
>
> It follows that I am satisfied that a gift to the poor and needy of the class of persons set out in the second schedule to the will falls on the charitable side of the line, wherever that line has to be drawn.

The exception even extends to poor employees of a company.

. . . .

● **Dingle v Turner** [1972] AC 601

Frank Dingle established a trust in his will to pay pensions to poor employees of E Dingle and Co Ltd, who were aged or incapacitated. The company had over 600 employees and a substantial number of ex-employees.

HELD: This fell within the poverty exception.

At 615: Lord Cross of Chelsea observed that the definition of public benefit was different under the Education Head of Charity. (See 10.5.5 'Public benefit in the advancement of education'.)

He urged a reconsideration of public benefit, which would take account of the fiscal benefits of charitable status, i.e. tax saving. (See 10.1.2 'Tax advantages'.)

This particular case, however, fell within the poverty exception, where public benefit was treated differently.

At 623:

> But the 'poor members' and the 'poor employees' decisions were a natural development of the 'poor relations' decisions and to draw a distinction between different sorts of 'poverty' trusts would be quite illogical and could certainly not be said to be introducing 'greater harmony' into the law of charity. Moreover, though not as old as the 'poor relations' trusts 'poor employees' trusts have been recognised as charities for many years; there are now a large number of such trusts in existence; and assuming, as one must, that they are properly administered in the sense that benefits under them are only given to people who can be fairly said to be, according to current standards, 'poor persons', to treat such trusts as charities is not open to any practical objection.

Even if fiscal benefits were taken into account, this would not be an important consideration in trusts to relieve poverty.

At 625:

> In the field of poverty the danger is not so great as in the field of education—for while people are keenly alive to the need to give their children a good education and to the expense of doing so they are generally optimistic enough not to entertain serious fears of falling on evil days much before they fall on them. Consequently the existence of company 'benevolent funds' the income of which is free of tax does not constitute a very attractive 'fringe benefit'. This is a practical justification—though not, of course, the historical explanation—for the special treatment accorded to poverty trusts in charity law.

Lord Cross did not want to remove charitable status from trusts that had been operating for some time to help the poor, particularly as there was no evidence that charities to relieve poor employees were being abused to gain tax advantages.

We saw in 10.3.5 'The Charities Act 2011 and public benefit' that some thought that s. 3 of the Charities Act 2006 (now s. 4 of the Charities Act 2011) changed the law, by requiring all categories of charity, including charities for the relief of poverty, to prove that they were for the public benefit. In this category of charity it is unnecessary to prove that its benefits are available to the general public. Did s. 3 change this?

● *Attorney-General v The Charity Commission for England and Wales* [2012] WTLR 977

The law was not changed by the 2006 Act. There were two aspects of the public benefit requirement. Firstly, all charities must be 'socially useful'. This was an essential requirement of charitable status and poverty charities would usually fulfil this requirement. The second aspect, that the benefits of the charity must be available to the public or a section of the public, had never been satisfactorily decided in previous cases on charities for the relief of poverty. There seemed to be two opinions: either that poverty charities used a different and wider definition of what was available to the public or that they were exempt from the public availability requirement. Interpreting the case law was not helped by some cases failing to distinguish clearly between the two aspects of public benefit. The tribunal decision was that charities for the relief of poverty were exempt from the requirement to be available to the public or a section of the public.

HELD: Warren J, para 64:

> The 2006 Act has not, in our judgment, changed that. The 'public benefit' as that term was understood for the purposes of the law of charity required, *in the context of a trust for the relief of poverty*, only that public benefit in the first sense should be shown. Of course, a trust for the relief of poverty might be one which is also for the public benefit in the second sense because the class of potential beneficiary is, on my view, a sufficient section of the community. But it does not follow from that consideration that every trust for the relief of poverty must be for the public benefit in the second sense.

Apart from trusts for the *relief* of poverty, there are also trusts for the *prevention* of poverty. Does the same public benefit rule apply to them? The tribunal thought that in most types of charity for the prevention of poverty it would.

Para 79:

> In addition, it is to be noted that section 2(2)(a) [Charities Act 2006] combines 'prevention' and 'relief' into a single 'description of a purpose' to use the terminology of the Act—'the prevention or relief of poverty'. We take this as some indication that, for the future at least,

Parliament saw no real distinction between prevention and relief, although we acknowledge that these two purposes could be pursued independently. Accordingly, the drafting supports the conclusion that, just as it is not necessary to demonstrate public benefit in the second sense in the case of relief of poverty, it is not necessary to demonstrate it in the case of prevention of poverty.

KEY POINT Under the poverty head, public benefit is treated differently from under the other heads of charity. Trusts to relieve relatives, employees, or other limited groups, connected to the settlor or testator are acceptable.

The advancement of education

10.5.1 Education includes teaching and research

The Preamble of 1601 mentions 'schools of learning, free schools and scholars in Universities' (see 10.3.1 'The Preamble'), so education has always been regarded as charitable. Most forms of teaching would be regarded as the advancement of education.

● *Re British School of Egyptian Archaeology* [1954] 1 All ER 887

This school discovered knowledge about ancient Egypt, published on this subject, and trained students in excavation.

HELD: Harman J at 890:

> I cannot doubt that this was a school for the diffusion of a certain branch of knowledge, namely, knowledge of the ancient past of Egypt, and that the school has a direct educational purpose, namely to train students in that very complicated branch of knowledge known as Egyptology. On that view, the school is clearly a charity.

Research would also be charitable, as long as the research was communicated to the general public.

● *Re Hopkins Will Trusts* [1965] Ch 669

The testatrix left part of her estate to establish 'The Francis Bacon Society'. Its objects were to find the 'Bacon–Shakespeare manuscripts', to study the works of Francis Bacon, and 'to encourage the general study of evidence in favour of Francis Bacon's authorship of the plays commonly ascribed to Shakespeare'.

[Sir Francis Bacon was an eminent lawyer and scientist of the Elizabethan and early Stuart period, living at the same time as William Shakespeare.]

HELD: Wilberforce J at 680:

> I think, therefore that the word, 'education' as used by Harman J in *Re Shaw* [1957] 1 WLR 729 must be used in a wide sense, certainly extending beyond teaching, and that the requirement is that, in order to be charitable, research must either be of educational value to

the researcher or must be directed as to lead to something which will pass into the store of educational material, so as to improve the sum of communicable knowledge in an area which education may cover—education in this last context extending to the formation of literary taste and appreciation...

At 681:

I accept that research of a private character, for the benefit only of the members of a society, would not normally be educational—or otherwise charitable...but I do not think that the research in the present case can be said to be of a private character for it is inherently inevitable and manifestly intended, that the result of any discovery should be published to the world.

There was no doubt about the value of such research.

At 679:

Accepting, as I have the authority of Lord Simonds for so doing, that the court must decide each case as best it can, on the evidence available to it, as to benefit, and within the moving spirit of decided cases, it would seem to me that a bequest for the purpose of search, or research, for the original manuscripts of England's greatest dramatist (whoever he was) would be well within the law's conception of charitable purposes. The discovery of such manuscripts, or of one such manuscript, would be of the highest value to history and to literature.

KEY POINT
Education is not confined to teaching and research, but can also include museums, art galleries, and even zoos. Education can include fun!

● **Re Lopes** [1931] 2 Ch 130

Lopes left money in her will towards the upkeep of the London Zoological Gardens. The objects of the London Zoological Society were 'the advancement of zoology and animal physiology and the introduction of new and curious subjects of the animal kingdom'. The next of kin questioned whether the zoo was a charity, as food and amusements were also provided.

HELD: Farwell J: It was an educational charity, as the food and amusement were provided in aid of the main charitable objective.

At 136–7:

It must widen the mind and outlook of every one to see, in the flesh, animals now becoming scarce in many parts of the world, which otherwise they might not see at all.

It may also be necessary, in order to attract younger persons to be educated, that some form of amusement such as riding on animals, should be provided. A ride on an elephant may be educational. At any rate it brings the reality of the elephant and its uses to the child's mind, in lieu of leaving him to mere book learning. It broadens his mind, and in that sense is educational.

KEY POINT A charity may include purposes that are not charitable, as long as the main purpose of the trust is charitable. These other purposes are known as satellite or ancillary purposes.

10.5.2 Education includes the advancement of culture

- *Re Shaw's WT* [1952] Ch 163

The widow of the famous playwright, George Bernard Shaw, left funds for

> the bringing of the masterpieces of fine art within the reach of the people of Ireland of all classes in their own country…The teaching, promotion and encouragement in Ireland of self-control, elocution, oratory, deportment, the arts of personal contact of social intercourse, and the other arts of public, private, professional and business life…

HELD: Vaisey J at 172:

> [It was]…a sort of finishing school for the Irish people. I think that 'education' includes not only teaching, but the promotion and encouragement of these arts and graces of life which are, after all, perhaps the finest and best part of the human character. It is education of a desirable sort, and which, if corrected and augmented and amplified by other kinds of teaching and instructing might have most beneficial results.

10.5.3 The value of the education provided

As education is so widely defined, the court may need to make a judgment on the value of the education provided and whether it is worthwhile. Expert evidence may be called upon.

- *Re Pinion* [1965] Ch 85

The will of Arthur Pinion required that his studio at 22a Pembridge Villas, Notting Hill should be kept intact and offered to the nation. The National Trust refused to take his collection of pictures, furniture, china, glass, and *objets d'art*. The charitable status of his bequest was challenged.

HELD: Harman LJ concluded that the collection was worthless and had no educational value. He made a number of observations from 105–7.

> It would appear that a gift to an established museum is charitable…A school for prostitutes or pickpockets would obviously fail.
>
> Where a museum is concerned and the utility of the gift is brought in question it is, in my opinion, and herein I agree with the judge, essential to know at least something of the quality of the proposed exhibits in order to judge whether they will be conducive to the education of the public. So I think with a public library, such a place if found to be devoted entirely to works of pornography or of a corrupting nature, would not be allowable. Here it is suggested that education in the fine arts is the object.
>
> However that may be, there is a strong body of evidence here that as a means of education this collection is worthless. The testator's own paintings, of which there are over 50, are said by competent persons to be in an academic style and 'atrociously bad' and the other pictures without exception worthless.
>
> I can conceive of no useful object to be served in foisting upon the public this mass of junk. It has neither public utility nor educative value.

The testator or settlor might think that the education that they are providing is worthwhile, but the court decides whether it actually is. It is not the personal opinion of the judge that matters, but what the evidence shows, as there is 'an accepted canon of taste on which the court must rely'. So in a subsequent case, a trust to promote the musical works of a well-known and well-respected composer did not cause so much difficulty and was granted charitable status.

● **Re Delius** [1957] Ch 299

Roxburgh J at 306:

> I do not find it necessary to consider what the position might be if the trusts were for the promotion of the works of some inadequate composer. It has been suggested that perhaps I should have no option but to give effect even to such a trust. I do not know, but I need not investigate that problem, because counsel who have argued before me have been unanimous in the view that the standard of Delius's work is so high that that question does not arise in the present case.

If the education proposed appears a little strange, the courts may deny charitable status. Charitable status cannot be used to force the testator's eccentric views upon the public. This is regarded as mere 'propaganda'.

● **Re Shaw's Will Trusts** [1957] 1 WLR 729

The will of the playwright, George Bernard Shaw, left money to:

(i) ascertain by inquiry how much time and money could be saved by a new British alphabet of 40 letters;

(ii) translate 'Androcles and the Lion' [a play by GBS] into the new language and advertise this by sending copies to public libraries. This would be an example of how good the new alphabet would be.

HELD: Harman J at 738:

> The research and propaganda enjoined by the testator seem to me merely to tend to the increase of public knowledge in a certain respect, namely, the saving of time and money by the use of the proposed alphabet. There is no element of teaching or education combined with this, nor does the propaganda element in the trust tend to more than to persuade the public that the adoption of the new script would be a good thing and that, in my view, is not education. Therefore I reject this element.

At 740:

> I do not see how mere advertisement and propaganda can be postulated as being beneficial.

At 742:

> It seems to me that the objects of the alphabet trusts are analogous to trusts for political purposes, which advocate a change in the law. Such objects have never been considered charitable.

KEY POINT
The court may decide that the 'education' provided is not worthwhile and therefore deny charitable status.

10.5.4 Political purposes

Trusts to promote a political purpose cannot have charitable status. The courts do not wish to be drawn into conflict with Parliament or the government. Nor do the courts wish to assess whether a change in the law would be beneficial or not. Political purposes could arise under any of the heads of charity, but it is most likely under the education head or the fourth head.

287

● **Bowman v Secular Society** [1917] AC 406

The Secular Society, as the name suggests, campaigned against religion.

HELD: Lord Parker at 442:

> Now if your Lordships will refer for a moment to the society's memorandum of association you will find that none of its objects, except, possibly, the first, are charitable. The abolition of religious tests, the disestablishment of the Church, the secularisation of education, the alteration of the law touching religion or marriage, or the observation of the Sabbath, are purely political objects. Equity has always refused to recognise such objects as charitable ... a trust for the attainment of political objects has always been held invalid, not because it is illegal, for every one is at liberty to advocate or promote by any lawful means a change in the law, but because the court has no means of judging whether a proposed change in the law will or will not be for the public benefit, and therefore cannot say that a gift to secure the change is a charitable gift.

The well-respected charity, Amnesty International, fell foul of this restriction, as some of its objects were deemed political.

● **McGovern v Attorney General** [1981] Ch 321

The objects of the Amnesty International Trust were:

A The relief of needy persons, such as prisoners of conscience and the relatives and dependants of prisoners of conscience

B To secure the release of prisoners of conscience

C The abolition of torture and inhuman and degrading treatment or punishment

D Research into human rights

E Dissemination of such research.

HELD: Slade J: A, D, and E were charitable, but B and C were too political and, as they were the main objects of the trust, the whole trust was void as a charity.

At 340:

> Trusts for political purposes falling within the spirit of this pronouncement include, inter alia, trusts of which a direct and principal purpose is either (i) to further the interests of a particular political party; or (ii) to procure changes in the laws of this country; or (iii) to procure changes in the laws of a foreign country; or (iv) to procure a reversal of government policy or of particular decisions of governmental authorities in this country; or (v) to procure a reversal of government policy or of particular governmental authorities in a foreign country.

Trying to change government policy was also too political for charitable status.

A good example of a clearly political trust can be found in the next case.

● *Southwood v Attorney General* **(2000)** 80 P & CRD 34

A trust called the Project on Demilitarisation (PRODEM) was established with the main object of 'the advancement of the education of the public in the subject of militarism and disarmament and related fields'. Its activities were to campaign against militarism, military interventions in foreign countries, and the activities of NATO.

HELD: Chadwick LJ:

> On the basis of his finding that the purpose of Prodem was to challenge the current policies of Western governments the judge was bound to hold, as he did, that the Charity Commissioners had been right to refuse to recognise the trusts declared by the 1994 deed as charitable. That was not, as the judge made clear, because those policies were unchallengeable—or because to challenge them was in any way unlawful or improper—but because the court cannot determine (and should not attempt to determine) whether policies adopted by the government of the United Kingdom and other Western governments are or are not for the public benefit.

thinking points

Is this approach unduly restrictive? Why should not charities be able to criticize government policy? The older authorities on political purposes and charities took the view that charities could not challenge existing laws, because that would conflict with the supremacy of Parliament: National Anti-Vivisection Society v IRC *[1948] AC 31. This was taken further in* McGovern v Attorney-General, *where Amnesty International were not allowed to criticize the laws or policies of foreign governments, in case it might damage the relations of the UK with that government. Surely that was not that likely? Similarly, requiring Amnesty International to prove that what it did benefited the public in the UK, set too high a bar, as many UK charities working abroad would find it hard to prove exactly how their activities benefited people in the UK. See R Nobles 'Politics, Public Benefit and Charity' (1982) 45 MLR 704.*

Discussion of political issues can have charitable status, if it is unbiased. Trying to publicize one point of view and persuade the public that it is right is, however, not charitable.

● *Re Koeppler* [1986] Ch 423

The will of Sir Heinrich Koeppler left money to a conference centre known as Wilton Park. The conferences were attended by representatives of major Western nations in order to exchange views on political, economic, and social issues of common interest.

The conferences discussed subjects that were recognized academic subjects in higher education and encouraged 'an exchange of views in a manner familiar in places of higher education'.

HELD: Slade J at 437–8:

> ...the concept of education is now wide enough to cover the intensive discussion process adopted by Wilton Park in relation to a somewhat special class of adults, persons influencing opinion in their own countries, designed (as I was told Sir Heinrich put it) to dent opinions and to fertilise ideas.
>
> ...the activities of Wilton Park are not of a party political nature. Nor, so far as the evidence shows, are they designed to procure changes in the laws or governmental policy of this or

any other country: even when they touch on political matters, they constitute, so far as I can see, no more than genuine attempts in an objective manner to ascertain and disseminate the truth.

Campaigning charities may have to redraft their objects so as to avoid being regarded as 'political' and losing their charitable status. Some charities divide themselves into separate organizations: one which provides charitable services and another which does not have charitable status, but campaigns for political change.

KEY POINTS

Political objects are not charitable. 'Political' means:

- supporting a political party;
- trying to change the law;
- trying to change government policy.

The Charities Act 2011 restates but appears not to change the law.

Charities Act 2011, s. 3(1)(h)

. . . .

(h) the advancement of human rights, conflict resolution or reconciliation or the promotion of religious or racial harmony or equality and diversity [are regarded as charitable].

10.5.5 Public benefit in the advancement of education

The benefits of a trust must be available 'for the benefit of the community or an appreciably important class of the community' for the trust to be a charity.

As we saw at 10.3.5 'The Charities Act 2011 and public benefit', in *R (Independent Schools Council) v Charity Commission for England and Wales, Attorney-General v Charity Commission and the Independent Schools Council* [2012] 1 All ER 127, public benefit has two aspects. Firstly, the object of the charity must be deemed socially useful, and education is so regarded, and secondly, the educational charity must provide benefits to the general public. Charging fees to attend the school does not lose charitable status, as long as the poor are not excluded. Providing scholarships and sharing facilities and teachers with state schools are two examples of how a fee-charging school might provide benefit to the general public.

There must be no 'personal nexus'—the beneficiaries must not be defined by their relationship to a particular individual or individuals. This rule was propounded in *Re Compton* [1945] Ch 123.

. . . .
● *Re Compton* [1945] Ch 123

Compton's will provided funds to be applied forever to provide for the education of the lawful descendants of HC Compton, Weyland Powell, and William, Earl of Sandwich.

HELD: This was a family trust to pay for the education of the children of the Compton, Powell, and Montague families. It could not be a charity, because the beneficiaries were defined by reference to a personal relationship.

> In the case of many charitable gifts it is possible to identify the individuals who are to benefit, or who at any given moment constitute the class from which the beneficiaries are to be selected. This circumstance does not, however, deprive the gift of its public character. Thus, if there is a gift to relieve the poor inhabitants of a parish the class to benefit is readily ascertainable. But they do not enjoy the benefit, when they receive it, by virtue of their character as individuals but by virtue of their membership of the specified class. In such a case the common quality which unites the potential beneficiaries into a class is essentially an impersonal one. It is definable by reference to what each has in common with the others, and that is something into which their status as individuals does not enter. Persons claiming to belong to the class do so not because they are AB, CD and EF, but because they are poor inhabitants of the parish …
>
> It seems to me that the same principle ought to apply when the claimants, in order to establish their status, have to assert and prove, not that they themselves are AB, CD and EF, but that they stand in some specified relationship to the individuals AB, CD and EF, such as that of children or employees. In that case, too, a purely personal element enters into and is an essential part of the qualification, which is defined by reference to something, ie, personal relationship to individuals or an individual which is in its essence non-public.

(See 10.4.2 'Public benefit and the relief of poverty'. Charities to relieve poverty do not insist that there is no personal nexus between the testator/settlor and the objects of the charity.)

However, the personal nexus test has been followed in other education cases and can be taken to be the law.

● ***Oppenheim v Tobacco Securities Trust Co*** [1951] AC 297

John and Elizabeth Phillips established a trust to produce income for the education of the children of employees or former employees of British-American Tobacco Co Ltd. The number of employees exceeded 110,000.

HELD: This was a private trust, not a charity.

Lord Simonds at 305:

> Before I turn to the authorities I will make some preliminary observations. It is a clearly established principle of the law of charity that a trust is not charitable unless it is directed to the public benefit. This is sometimes stated in the proposition that it must benefit the community or a section of community.

At 306:

> The difficulty arises where the trust is not for the benefit of any institution either then existing or by the terms of the trust to be brought into existence, but for the benefit of a class of persons at large. Then the question is whether that class of persons can be regarded as such a 'section of the community' as to satisfy the test of public benefit. These words 'section of the community' have no special sanctity, but they conveniently indicate first, that the possible [I emphasize the word 'possible'] beneficiaries must not be numerically negligible, and secondly, that the quality which distinguishes them from other members of the community, so that they form by themselves a section of it, must be a quality which does not depend on their relationship to a particular individual. It is for this reason that a trust for the education of members of a family or, as in *In re Compton* [see earlier], of a number of families cannot be regarded as charitable. A group of persons

may be numerous but, if the nexus between them is their personal relationship to a single propositus or to several propositi, they are neither the community nor a section of the community for charitable purposes.

I come, then, to the present case where the class of beneficiaries is numerous but the difficulty arises in regard to their common and distinguishing quality. That quality is being children of employees of one or other of a group of companies. I can make no distinction between children of employees and the employees themselves.

Lord MacDermott disagreed with this 'personal nexus' test and found it impossible to lay down any general rule. He thought that it was a valid charitable trust.

At 314:

> Until comparatively recently the usual way of approaching an issue of this sort, at any rate where educational trusts were concerned, was, I believe, to regard the facts of each case and to treat the matter very much as one of degree …
>
> If it is still permissible to conduct the present inquiry on these broad if imprecise lines, I would hold with the appellant. The numerical strength of the class is considerable on any showing. The employees concerned number over 110,000, and it may reasonably be assumed that the children, who constitute the class in question, are no fewer.

At 318:

> It was conceded in the course of the argument that, had the present trust been framed so as to provide for the education of the children of those engaged in the tobacco industry in a named county or town, it would have been a good charitable disposition, and that even though the class to be benefited would have been appreciably smaller and no more important than is the class here. That concession follows from what the Court of Appeal has said. But if it is sound and a personal or impersonal relationship remains the universal criterion I think it shows, no less than the queries I have just raised in indicating some of the difficulties of the problem, that the Compton [see earlier] test is a very arbitrary and artificial rule.

This personal/impersonal test has also been criticized in the poverty charity case *Dingle v Turner* [1972] AC 601 on the grounds that, first, it was a very difficult test to apply and, secondly, it was odd to have different tests for poverty and education. (This case can also be found at 10.4.2 'Public benefit and the relief of poverty'.)

. . . .

● *Dingle v Turner* [1972] AC 601

Lord Cross of Chelsea at 623–5:

> That reasoning—based on the distinction between personal and impersonal relationships—has never seemed to me very satisfactory and I have always if I may say so—felt the force of the criticism to which my noble and learned friend Lord MacDermott subjected it in his dissenting speech in Oppenheim. For my part I would prefer to approach the problem on far broader lines. The phrase a 'section of the public' is in truth a vague phrase which may mean different things to different people. In the law of charity judges have sought to elucidate its meaning by contrasting it with another phrase: 'a fluctuating body of private individuals'. But I get little help from the supposed contrast for as I see it one and the same aggregate of persons may well be describable both as a section of the public and as a fluctuating body of private individuals. The ratepayers of the Royal Borough

of Kensington and Chelsea, for example, certainly constitute a section of the public; but would it be a misuse of language to describe them as a 'fluctuating body of private individuals'? After all, every part of the public is composed of individuals and being susceptible of increase or decrease is fluctuating. So at the end of the day one is left where one started with the bare contrast between 'public' and 'private'. No doubt some classes are more naturally describable as sections of the public than as private classes while other classes are more naturally describable as private classes than as sections of the public. The blind, for example, can naturally be described as a section of the public; but what they have in common—their blindness—does not join them together in such a way that they could be called a private class. On the other hand, the descendants of Mr Gladstone might more reasonably be described as a 'private class' than as a section of the public, and in the field of common employment the same might well be said of the employees in some fairly small firm. But if one turns to large companies employing many thousands of men and women most of whom are quite unknown to one another and to the directors the answer is by no means so clear. One might say that in such a case the distinction between a section of the public and a private class is not applicable at all or even that the employees in such concerns as I.C.I. or G.E.C. are just as much 'sections of the public' as the residents in some geographical area. In truth the question whether or not the potential beneficiaries of a trust can fairly be said to constitute a section of the public is a question of degree and cannot be by itself decisive of the question whether the trust is a charity. In answering the question whether any given trust is a charitable trust the courts—as I see it—cannot avoid having regard to the fiscal privileges accorded to charities. As counsel for the Attorney General remarked in the course of the argument the law of charity is bedevilled by the fact that charitable trusts enjoy two quite different sorts of privilege. On the one hand, they enjoy immunity from the rules against perpetuity and uncertainty and though individual potential beneficiaries cannot sue to enforce them the public interest arising under them is protected by the Attorney General. But that is not all. Charities automatically enjoy fiscal privileges which with the increased burden of taxation have become more and more important and in deciding that such and such a trust is a charitable trust the court is endowing it with a substantial annual subsidy at the expense of the taxpayer. Indeed, claims of trusts to rank as charities are just as often challenged by the revenue as by those who would take the fund if the trust was invalid. It is, of course, unfortunate that the recognition of any trust as a valid charitable trust should automatically attract fiscal privileges, for the question whether a trust to further some purpose is so little likely to benefit the public that it ought to be declared invalid and the question whether it is likely to confer such great benefits on the public that it should enjoy fiscal immunity are really two quite different questions. The logical solution would be to separate them and to say—as the Radcliffe Commission proposed—that only some charities should enjoy fiscal privileges. But, as things are, validity and fiscal immunity march hand in hand and the decisions in the Compton [1945] Ch 123 and Oppenheim [1951] AC 297 cases were pretty obviously influenced by the consideration that if such trusts as were there in question were held valid they would enjoy an undeserved fiscal immunity. To establish a trust for the education of the children of employees in a company in which you are interested is no doubt a meritorious act; but however numerous the employees may be the purpose which you are seeking to achieve is not a public purpose. It is a company purpose and there is no reason why your fellow taxpayers should contribute to a scheme which by providing 'fringe benefits' for your employees will benefit the company by making their conditions of employment more attractive.

The dissentients Lords MacDermott and Cross disliked the 'personal nexus' test favoured by the majority and instead proposed no definite test. A judge should look at all the factors, such as the possible number of beneficiaries, whether it is a 'tax dodge', and, overall, would the proposed charity actually provide benefits to the public? Despite these criticisms, the personal nexus test continues not to apply to poverty charities: *Attorney-General v The Charity Commission* [2012] WTLR 977. (See 10.4.2 'Public benefit and the relief of poverty'.)

thinking points

Is the 'personal nexus' test easy to understand and apply? Or do you prefer the approach of Lords MacDermott and Cross, that no single test should be used? Looking at whether an employer is trying to provide 'fringe benefits' to attract employees or is trying to, say, genuinely help the poor might prove just as difficult as the existing law. The personal nexus rule does not apply to charities to help the poor, but that is hard to justify logically. Maybe it benefits us all because society is relieved of the need to support a few poor people, which is the same argument used to justify the charitable status of private hospitals in Re Resch, *that there are a few less sick people for state hospitals to look after. It does not seem a very substantial public benefit. See T Watkins 'Charity: The Purport of Purpose' (1978) 42 Conv 277.*

KEY POINT
An education charity is not for the public benefit if it is only providing benefits for the members of a family or employees of a company.

As can be seen from *Oppenheim* [1951] AC 297, educational charities often provide funds for scholarships. These must be available to the general public and not restricted to employees of a company.

Re Koettgen [1954] Ch 252 illustrates that a preference for employees of a particular company may be acceptable, as long as the funds are offered to the general public first. However, if the majority of the charitable funds are in fact given to the children of company employees, that is unacceptable. There is insufficient public benefit: *IRC v Educational Grants Association* [1967] Ch 123.

10.6 The advancement of religion

10.6.1 The definition of religion

The 1601 Preamble only refers to 'the repair of churches', but despite this trusts to promote Christianity have always been charitable. This is explained in *Bowman v The Secular Society* [1917] AC 406.

. . . .

● ***Bowman v The Secular Society*** [1917] AC 406

Charles Bowman's will left property to the Secular Society Limited. The Secular Society's main object was:

> To promote, in such ways as may from time to time be determined, the principle that human conduct should be based upon natural knowledge, and not upon super-natural belief, and that human welfare in this world is the proper end of all thought and action.

The issue was whether such a gift was legal or whether to question religion was blasphemy and therefore unlawful. The House of Lords decided that disputing religion in a rational, serious manner was not blasphemy. Their Lordships also considered the law relating to religious charities.

HELD: Lord Parker of Waddington at 448–9: He considered the history of religious trusts and explained that before the Reformation 'that form of Christianity now called Roman Catholic was undoubtedly within the rule'. After the Reformation Anglican Christianity replaced it and it was only gradually that other forms of Christianity were recognized. First it was non-conformists, but it was not until the 19th century that Roman Catholicism was accepted again. Jewish religious charities were not recognized until 1846.

> It would seem to follow that a trust for the purpose of any kind of monotheistic theism would be a good charitable trust.

This definition of 'monotheistic theism' has been elaborated on in later case law.

● *Re South Place Ethical Society (Barralet v AG)* [1980] 1 WLR 1565

The society had originally been a Unitarian chapel, but had changed in 1887 to an ethical society. 'The objects of the society are the study and dissemination of ethical principles and the cultivation of a rational religious sentiment.' It held Sunday meetings and lectures, at Conway Hall, which were open to the public. The trustees asked the court whether the society was a religious charity.

HELD: Dillon J at 1572: The court adopted a definition of religion from the *Oxford English Dictionary.*

> A particular system of faith and worship. Then: 'Recognition on the part of man of some higher unseen power as having control of his destiny, and as being entitled to obedience, reverence, and worship.'

The court also took a definition of worship from *R v Registrar General, ex p Segerdal* [1970] 2 QB 697 at 709:

> Worship I take to be something which must have some at least of the following character-istics: submission to the object worshipped, veneration of that object, praise, thanksgiving, prayer or intercession.

At 1571:

> Religion, as I see it, is concerned with man's relations with God, and ethics are concerned with man's relations with man. The two are not the same...

The study and promotion of ethical principles is not religion, but could be educational and therefore qualify as charitable under the education head or the fourth head.

At 1576:

> I turn therefore to the objects of the society, as set out in its rules. The first part of the objects is the study and dissemination of ethical principles. Dissemination, I think, includes dissemi-nation of the fruits of the study, and I have no doubt that that part of the objects satisfies the criterion of charity as being for the advancement of education.

KEY POINT
A charity could be valid under more than one head of charity.

It is not enough to encourage the members of a society to lead a good and virtuous life; there must also be 'advancement' of the religion, some sort of reaching out to the rest of the public.

● *United Grand Lodge v Holborn BC* [1957] 1 WLR 1080

A Freemasons' Lodge was held not to be charitable. The 'Volume of the Sacred Law' (the Bible in Christian countries, the Koran in Moslem ones) is recommended to masons.

HELD: Donovan J at 1090:

> When one considers the work done by organizations which admittedly do set out to advance religion, the contrast with masonry is striking. To advance religion means to promote it, to spread its message ever wider among mankind; to take some positive steps to sustain and increase religious belief; and these things are done in a variety of ways which may be comprehensively described as pastoral and missionary. There is nothing comparable to that in masonry. This is not said by way of criticism. For masonry really does something different. It says to a man, 'Whatever your religion or your mode of worship, believe in a Supreme Creator and lead a good moral life.' Laudable as this precept is, it does not appear to us to be the same thing as the advancement of religion. There is no religious instruction, no programme for the persuasion of unbelievers, no religious supervision to see that its members remain active and constant in the various religions they may profess, no holding of religious services, no pastoral or missionary work of any kind.

KEY POINT A religion requires a god, worship of that god, and active promotion of the religion.

10.6.2 When is a 'religion' unacceptable?

A religion might have few followers and be thought to have no truth by others, but that does not matter if it meets the general definition of a religion explained in 10.6.1 'The definition of religion'. Unlike under the education head, the court does not assess whether the religion has any value or question the validity of the beliefs. It is not possible for a court to decide whether what someone believes is true or not.

That means that religions with few followers and with beliefs that may seem foolish or misguided by outsiders may be granted charitable status. The cases concern different denominations of Christianity.

● *Re Watson* [1973] 1 WLR 1472

This was a gift in a will 'for the continuance of the work of God as it has been maintained by Mr HG Hobbs and myself since 1942 by God's enabling...in propagating the truth as given in the Holy Bible'. This was a group consisting of just a few families in Long Melford, Suffolk.

HELD: Despite expert evidence that the intrinsic worth of these teachings were nil, it was accepted as a charity.

A more recent example can be found in *Le Cren Clarke (Funnell v Stewart)* [1996] 1 WLR 288.

● *Le Cren Clarke (Funnell v Stewart)* [1996] 1 WLR 288

Miss Le Cren Clarke had run a small religious healing movement at her home in Hastings for 30 years or so. There would be healing sessions three to four times a week, which involved the laying on of hands, prayers, and meditation.

HELD: There would also be a religious service once a week. Although these sessions only involved between six and twelve people, members of the public were welcome to attend. The religious beliefs were within the Christian tradition and this met the definition of a religious charity.

The court does not make decisions upon whether a religion is 'worthwhile' or not, but a religion that was 'subversive of all morality' would not be granted charitable status.

. . . .

● **Thornton v Howe** (1862) 31 Beav 14

Joanna Southcott (or Southcote) was a domestic servant in Exeter and a Methodist, who then claimed that she was a prophetess and gathered many followers, who were known as 'Southcottians' or 'British Israelites'. At the age of 64, she claimed that she was pregnant and would give birth to a son, Shiloh, prophesied in the book of Genesis as a redeemer of Judah. Instead she died. She also left a box, which was only to be opened in a time of national crisis, in the presence of all the bishops of England. It was opened in 1927, in the presence of one bishop, and contained a few papers and a lottery ticket (not the winning number). A follower, Essam, left money to the trustee, Howe, to pay for 'the printing, publishing and propagation of the sacred writings of the late Joanna Southcote'.

HELD: Sir John Romilly MR at 18: Read her writings and came to a conclusion that it was a religious charity.

> She was, in my opinion, a foolish, ignorant woman, of an enthusiastic turn of mind...

At 19–21:

> ...the Court of Chancery makes no distinction between one sort of religion and another.
>
> Neither does the court, in this respect, make any distinction between one sect and another. It may be that the tenets of a particular sect inculcate doctrines adverse to the very foundations of all religion, and that they are subversive of all morality. In such a case, if it should arise, the Court will not assist the execution of the bequest, but will declare it to be void...But if the tendency were not immoral, and although this Court might consider the opinions sought to be propagated foolish or even devoid of foundation, it would not, on that account, declare it void...
>
> In truth, though her works are in a great measure incoherent and confused, they are written obviously with a view to extend the influence of Christianity.

The judgment gives no clue as to what would be regarded as an 'immoral' religion, but a concern at the time about the Southcottians, and other similar cults, was that they practised sex outside marriage and encouraged followers to leave their families and jobs to join the cult.

KEY POINT
Charitable status is denied to a religion that is immoral or subversive of all morality.

The cases generally assume that the religious charities that they will encounter are Christian and there are few cases that consider non-Christian religions. The Charity Commissioners grant charitable status to all the major world religions, such as Hinduism, Sikhism, Islam, Judaism, and Buddhism. Some of these religions do not quite fit the strict definition of religion given earlier in the chapter, as they may have no god, or many gods. The Charities Act 2011 attempts to clarify the situation.

Charities Act 2011, s. 3(2)
. . . .

(a) in paragraph (c) 'religion' includes—

   (i) a religion which involves belief in more than one god, and

   (ii) a religion which does not involve belief in a god.

This was a case that decided whether a Scientology Church was a 'place of meeting for religious worship', which was required by the Places of Worship Registration Act 1855, in order for a valid marriage to be celebrated there. It was not about whether the Church was a charity.

Lord Toulson commented upon the meaning of section 3(2) above at paragraph 55:

> That definition removes uncertainty created by Dillon J's judgment in *South Place Ethical Society* (see 10.6.1) about whether religious charitable trusts exclude faiths such as Hinduism and Buddhism...it is a further indication that the understanding of religion in today's society is broad.

His Lordship also considered that a religion does not necessarily have to include a belief in a Supreme Being. At para 57:

> For the purposes of PWRA, I would describe religion in summary as a spiritual or non-secular belief system, held by a group of adherents, which claims to explain mankind's place in the universe and relationship with the infinite, and to teach its adherents how they are to live their lives in conformity with the spiritual understanding associated with the belief system. By spiritual or non-secular I mean a belief system which goes beyond that which can be perceived by the senses or ascertained by the application of science. I prefer not to use the word 'supernatural' to express this element, because it is a loaded word which can carry a variety of connotations. Such a belief system may or may not involve belief in a supreme being, but it does involve a belief that there is more to be understood about mankind's nature and relationship to the universe than can be gained from the senses or from science.

The Church of Scientology does not currently enjoy charitable status, so it remains to be seen whether that will be reconsidered in the light of Lord Toulson's comments.

10.6.3 Public benefit in the advancement of religion

Although a religious charity provides benefits for the followers of that religion, what benefits does it provide for the wider society? It has to provide some, or it will not be charitable. The public must have some access to the benefits of the religion.

● *Gilmour v Coats* [1949] AC 426

Evelyn Coats declared a trust of £500 for the Roman Catholic Carmelite Priory in Notting Hill, London. The Prioress, Ethel Gilmour, asked the court whether this was a charity. Cardinal Griffin, the Roman Catholic Archbishop of Westminster, gave evidence that these nuns were a contemplative order, who were strictly enclosed in their convent, devoting their lives to the contemplation of God and penance. Contemplative orders could be distinguished from active orders, which went out into the world teaching, nursing the sick, and tending to the poor. The cardinal argued that the Carmelite nuns provided benefit to the wider public in three ways.

1. Their prayers were on behalf of all mankind and drew down the grace of God.
2. Their lives, dedicated to prayer, set a good example for the rest of society.
3. Any female Roman Catholic, with a vocation, could become a nun, so this was rather like an education charity, where only some students can enter a school.

HELD: The House of Lords rejected all these arguments, because it considered itself bound by earlier cases that denied such religious orders charitable status.

1. It is, no doubt, true that the advancement of religion is, generally speaking, one of the heads of charity. But it does not follow from this that the court must accept as proved whatever a particular church believes. The faithful must embrace their faith believing where they cannot prove: the court can act only on proof. A gift to two or ten or a hundred cloistered nuns in the belief that their prayers will benefit the world at large does not from that belief alone derive validity any more than does the belief of any other donor for any other purpose...

2. I turn to the second of the alleged elements of public benefit, edification by example and I think that this argument can be dealt with very shortly. It is in my opinion sufficient to say that this is something too vague and intangible to satisfy the pre-scribed test.

At 448–9:

3. It is a trite saying that the law is life, not logic. But it is, I think, conspicuously true of the law of charity that it has been built up not logically but empirically. It would not, there-fore be surprising to find that, while in every category of legal charity some element of public benefit must be present, the court had not adopted the same measure in different categories, but had accepted one standard in regard to those gifts which are alleged to be for the advancement of education and another for those which are alleged to be for the advancement of religion, and it may be yet another in regard to the relief of poverty. To argue by a method of syllogism or analogy from the category of education to that of religion ignores the historical process of the law.

It could not be proved that the benefit of their prayers and the example of their lives was beneficial to the public. The court would not accept that becoming a nun was just like winning a scholarship to a school.

If these Carmelite nuns had been an active order, going out into the community, they would have provided public benefit and be a charity: *Cocks v Manners* (1871) LR 12 Eq 574.

Another way of providing public benefit is to allow the public access to religious services.

● *Re Hetherington* [1990] Ch 1

The will of Mrs Hetherington left £2,000 to the Roman Catholic Bishop of Westminster for masses to be said for the souls of her husband, parents, sisters, and self.

At one time such masses had been illegal as a 'superstitious use', but had been permitted in the 20th century. But were they charitable?

HELD: Sir Nicolas Browne-Wilkinson VC at 12:

The celebration of a religious rite in public does confer a sufficient public benefit because of the edifying and improving effect of such celebration on the members of the public who attend.

The celebration of a religious rite in private does not contain the necessary element of public benefit since any benefit by prayer or example is incapable of proof in the legal sense, and any element of edification is limited to a private, not public, class of those present at the celebration.

(See 9.4.6 'Trusts for the saying of masses'.)

As we have seen, religious charities must hold some kind of services, but in some religions, only the members of the congregation attend. This still satisfies the requirement of public benefit, because the congregation goes out into the world and mixes with the public. Presumably, this sets a good example.

....

● **Neville Estates v Madden** [1962] Ch 832

The trustees of Catford Synagogue wanted to sell some land. An issue arose as to whether the trusts of the synagogue were charitable. The synagogue had a list of members who were entitled to attend services there. Other members of the public, even Jewish members, could not.

HELD: Cross J at 852:

His Lordship distinguished *Gilmour v Coats* (in 10.6.3).

> The two cases, however, differ from one another in that the members of the Catford Synagogue spend their lives in the world, whereas the members of a Carmelite Priory live secluded from the world.
>
> But the court is, I think, entitled to assume that some benefit accrues to the public from the attendance at places of worship of persons who live in this world and mix with their fellow citizens. As between different religions the law stands neutral, but it assumes that any religion is at least likely to be better than none.

KEY POINT Public benefit requires that the religion is available to the general public. Either the public can attend religious services, or the followers of the religion go out into the world.

10.7 Other purposes beneficial to the community

The fourth head of charity is a very broad category, containing all sorts of different kinds of charity. Some can be traced back to the 1601 Preamble (see 10.3.1 'The Preamble') and some are modern developments reflecting the changes in society since the early 17th century. Although this category of charity might seem very broad, the courts will not recognize a new type of 'charity', unless it bears some relationship to existing types. It is not enough for the purpose to be for the benefit of the public, it must also be 'within the spirit and intendment of the Preamble'.

....

● **Helena Partnerships Ltd. (formerly Helena Housing Ltd.) v Revenue and Customs Commissioners** [2012] 4 All ER 111

Helena Partnerships was a registered social landlord, which took over council housing from St. Helens Metropolitan Borough Council. Some of its tenants were in need, but others were not. It also provided other housing services, such as selling houses and managing properties for house owners. Helena was non-profit making, but was it a charity?

HELD: The answer was no. Just because what Helena did was for the public benefit or of general public utility, did not necessarily mean that it was charitable.

Lloyd LJ at 134:

> It is not sufficient to assert, or even for the relevant constituent document to stipulate, that the activities or operations of the body in question are to be undertaken for the benefit of the community. More is required. The purpose or purposes must be of the right kind, falling within the spirit and intendment of the preamble, directly or by analogy.

Providing housing for poor tenants would be charitable, but the partnerships' other activities were not.

At 145:

> First, I do not consider that the provision of housing accommodation, otherwise than for those in some relevant charitable need, is a purpose within the spirit and intendment of the preamble, either directly or by analogy with any other purpose which has been so recognized ... there is also a substantial element of benefit to individuals, which cannot be regarded as only subordinate to the achievement of the benefit to the community.

10.7.1 Aged, impotent, and sick

Impotent—
does not have its modern meaning of sexually incapable. It means disabled or ill.

The Preamble refers to the relief of 'aged, **impotent** and poor people, some for the maintenance of sick and maimed soldiers and mariners'. The recipients of the charity do not have to be aged, impotent, *and* poor. They could simply be old or ill.

The Preamble must be read disjunctively. The beneficiaries do not have to be aged and poor or impotent and poor.

● *Re Robinson* [1951] Ch 198

The will of John Robinson gave his residuary estate to 'old people over sixty-five years of Hazel Slade near Hednesford to be given as my trustees think best'.

HELD: Vaisey J at 200–1:

> I think that, according to the proper construction of the will, the gift is to the old people direct as a class, not as a class of individuals, but as a group of people, who are, within the Statute of Elizabeth, qualified not by poverty, sickness or impotence, but by age. It has recently been held by Danckwerts, J, that that statute brings within the ambit of 'charity' those who satisfy any one of the three qualifications of age, impotence and poverty. He took that view in *In re Glyn Will Trusts* [1950] WN 373, and I followed that decision in *In re Bradbury* [1950] WN 558. In that case the testator directed that her residuary fund should be applied for the maintenance of an aged person or persons in a nursing home approved by her trustees. There again, although I conceive that the aged person in a nursing home may be a person not at all in need of any sort of pecuniary assistance, I nevertheless held, following the decision in *In re Glyn Will Trusts* [1950] WN 373, that it was a good charitable gift.
>
> Here I think that the old people over sixty-five years in a particular parish are a class of persons just as much objects of charity, having regard to the preamble of the statute, as the poor of the parish or the sick of the parish.

So the beneficiaries need only be old, they do not need to be poor as well.

There can also be charities for the disabled, who, also, do not need to be poor as well.

● **Re Lewis** [1955] Ch 104

Mark Lewis left a will, which included the following disposition: 'I leave to 10 blind girls Tottenham residents if possible the sum of £100 each. I leave to each of 10 blind boys Tottenham residents if possible the sum of £100 each.'

HELD: Roxburgh J at 108:

> Mr Gibson's argument was to this effect: prima facie, when the statute speaks of 'aged, impotent, and poor' it must envisage three classes: (1) aged, (2) impotent, (3) poor. But he argued that ... it was necessary not to read the words disjunctively, but to say that 'poor' was an essential ingredient in each class.

But Roxburgh J did not agree at 109:

> Fortunately for me, my path is very much easier. There is no case which suggested that in the case of impotent persons, the statute should not be read properly, that is to say, disjunctively, so as to constitute impotent persons as a class per se.

Although the charity need not be aimed at the poor, it must relieve need. A children's home would normally be charitable, but not if it goes beyond relieving need.

● **Re Cole** [1958] Ch 877

This was a gift for the general benefit and general welfare of children in a county council run home.

HELD: These purposes were too wide to be regarded as charitable.

Romer J at 888:

> Nevertheless I cannot regard the provision of television sets, etc, for the benefit of such persons as juvenile delinquents and refractory children in Southdown House as coming within any conception of charity which is to be found in the preamble. If it were, then I suppose a gift to provide the inmates of a Borstal institution with amenities would be charitable which would appear to me to be an impossible contention.

At that date, televisions were a rare and luxury item. Children could be looked after, but should not be given luxuries. The point is better explained in a more modern case, concerning relief of the aged.

● **Joseph Rowntree Memorial Trust v Attorney General** [1983] Ch 159

The charity sold long lease housing, designed for their needs, to the elderly. The elderly were defined as 65 for men and 60 for women. The Charity Commission had refused charitable status.

HELD: Gibson J at 171:

> Second, essential to the charitable purpose is that it should relieve aged, impotent and poor people. The word 'relief' implies that the persons in question have a need attributable to their condition as aged, impotent or poor persons which requires alleviating, and which those

persons could not alleviate, or would find difficulty in alleviating, themselves from their own resources. The word 'relief' is not synonymous with 'benefit'.

Mr Nugee stresses that any benefit provided must be related to the needs of the aged. Thus a gift of money to the aged millionaires of Mayfair would not relieve a need of theirs as aged persons.

These were charitable schemes.

In *Rowntree* [1983] Ch 159, the housing was sold at near market value and it is not unusual for charities to charge fees for their services. This is acceptable as long as the charity is non-profit making.

● ***Joseph Rowntree Memorial Trust v Attorney General*** [1983] Ch 159

Peter Gibson J at 176:

> The fourth objection was that the schemes were a commercial enterprise capable of producing a profit for the beneficiary. I have already discussed the cases which show that the charging of an economic consideration for a charitable service that is provided does not make the purpose in providing the service non-charitable, provided of course that no profits accrue to the provider of the service.

10.7.2 Public benefit in charities to relieve the aged and impotent

Looking after the sick also qualifies as charitable. Even private hospitals can be charitable, as long as they are non-profit making.

● ***Re Resch's Will Trusts*** [1969] 1 AC 514

The will of Edmund Resch left AUS$8,000,000 'to the sisters of Charity for a period of 200 years or for so long as they shall conduct St Vincent's Private Hospital'. The sisters ran the 82-bed private hospital adjacent to a 500-bed public hospital. The private hospital was opened to help meet the pressing demand for hospital beds and give those patients who desired it more privacy and comfort.

HELD: Lord Wilberforce at 540:

[Medical care for the sick is charitable.]

> A gift for the purposes of a hospital is prima facie a good charitable gift. This is now clearly established both in Australia and in England, not merely because of the use of the word 'impotent' in the preamble to 43 Eliz. C4, though the process of referring to the preamble is one often used for reassurance, but because the provision of medical care for the sick is, in modern times, accepted as a public benefit suitable to attract the privileges given to charitable institutions.

[Can a charity that charges for its services provide public benefit?]

> Disqualifying indicia may be either that the hospital is carried on commercially, ie, with a view to making profits for private individuals, or that the benefits it provides are not for the public, or a sufficiently large class of the public to satisfy the necessary tests of public character.

At 541–2:

[1. Non-profit making]

> As regards these purposes, it appears, from the evidence already summarised, that the making of profits for the benefit of individuals is not among them. The most that is shown is that, on a cash basis, and without making such adjustments as would be required for commercial accounting, a net surplus is produced over the years which in fact has been largely applied, though not exclusively for hospital purposes.

Their Lordships turn to the second objection. This, in substance, is that the private hospital is not carried on for purposes 'beneficial to the community' because it provides only for persons of means who are capable of paying the substantial fees required as a condition of admission.

At 544:

[2. The poor are not excluded]

> It would be a wrong conclusion to state that a trust for the provision of medical facilities would necessarily fail to be charitable merely because by reason of expense they could only be made use of by persons of some means. To provide, in response to public need, medical treatment otherwise inaccessible but in its nature expensive, without any profit motive, might well be charitable: on the other hand to limit admission to a nursing home to the rich would not be so. The test is essentially one of public benefit, and indirect as well as direct benefit enters into the account. In the present case, the element of public benefit is strongly present. It is not disputed that a need exists to provide accommodation and medical treatment in conditions of greater privacy and relaxation than would be possible in a general hospital and as a supplement to the facilities of a general hospital. This is what the private hospital does and it does so at, approximately, cost price. The service is needed by all, not only by the well-to-do. So far as its nature permits it is open to all; the charges are not low, but the evidence shows that it cannot be said that the poor are excluded: such exclusion as there is, is of some of the poor—namely, those who have (a) not contributed sufficiently to a medical benefit scheme or (b) need to stay longer in the hospital than their benefit will cover or (c) cannot get a reduction of or exemption from the charges. The general benefit to the community of such facilities results from the relief to the beds and medical staff of the general hospital, the availability of a particular type of nursing and treatment which supplements that provided by the general hospital and the benefit to the standard of medical care in the general hospital which arise from the juxtaposition of the two institutions.

KEY POINT

There is public benefit because the poor can attend the private hospital and the private hospital helps provide a better service at the connected public hospital.

Section 4 of the Charities Act 2011 requires all charities to demonstrate that they are for the public benefit.

The approach to public benefit in *Re Resch* [1969] 1 AC 514, is confirmed as correct in the advancement of education case, *R (Independent Schools Council) v Charity Commission for England and Wales, Attorney-General v Charity Commission and the Independent Schools Council* [2012] 1 All ER 127. (See 10.3.5 'The Charities Act 2011 and public benefit'.)

KEY POINT

Charities may charge for the services that they provide. But the charity must be non-profit making and must not exclude the poor.

The Charities Act 2011 confirms that the type of charities recognized in this section remain charitable.

Charities Act 2011, s. 3(1)

....

(j) the relief of those in need by reason of youth, age, ill-health, disability, financial hardship or other disadvantage.

10.8 Saving lives

The Preamble allows for 'the repair of bridges, ports, havens, causeways, churches, sea-banks, and highways'. (See 10.3.1 for The Preamble.) The repair of sea walls prevents flooding, which saves lives. By extension this has been taken to mean that various kinds of rescue service are entitled to charitable status, because they also save lives. The fire brigade was accepted in *Re Wokingham Fire Brigade Trusts* [1951] Ch 373 and so have the Royal National Lifeboat Institution and mountain and cave rescue services. Charities can also be established to help the victims of natural disaster and war, but care must be taken not to go beyond just relieving 'need' as in *Joseph Rowntree* in 10.7.1 'Aged, impotent, and sick'. An example can be found in *Re Gillingham Bus Disaster Fund* [1959] Ch 62, where 24 Royal Marine cadets were killed by a bus. The public raised money to help them, but it could not be a charity, because after the dead were buried and the injured treated, free by the National Health Service, there was no further 'need' to be relieved. (See 8.2.3 'Surplus after completion of purpose'.)

Patriotic gifts to help the armed forces (*Re Gray* [1925] Ch 362) or even 'unto my country England to and for—own use and benefit absolutely' (*Re Smith* [1932] 1 Ch 153), have been held to be charitable.

Once again, the Charities Act 2011 attempts to give guidance.

> **Charities Act 2011, s. 3(1)**
> ....
>
> (l) the promotion of the efficiency of the armed forces of the Crown, or of the efficiency of the police, fire and rescue services or ambulance services.

10.9 Animal welfare

Charities for the benefit of animals are the most numerous and most popular type of charity in the present day UK. Yet they are not mentioned in the 1601 Preamble, nor is it easy to see how they benefit the human public. The courts have developed two arguments for allowing animal charities.

10.9.1 Animals useful to mankind

If a trust aids domesticated animals, that helps humans and can therefore be for the public benefit. As early as 1857, the courts held that a bequest 'for the establishment of a hospital in which animals, which are useful to mankind, should be properly treated and cured, and the nature of their diseases investigated, with a view to public advantage' was charitable: *University of London v Yarrow* (1857) 1 De G & J 72. This was further explained in *Re Douglas* (1887) 35 ChD 472.

....

● **Re Douglas** (1887) 35 ChD 472

The will of Elizabeth Douglas left £100 to a 'Home for Lost Dogs', amongst other charities.

HELD: Kay J at 478–9:

> It seems to me that all the reasoning in the case of the University of London v Yarrow applies distinctly to show that that is a charity. It is quite true that attending a sick canary, or a sick dog, or sick animal, may not be itself within the meaning of charity, but when an institution is referred to which is for the benefit of domestic animals, that is so far a benefit to the human species who are served by the domestic animal, that the institution itself may well be treated as a charity, as an institution founded for the charitable purpose of assisting those animals which are useful to mankind, and which are commonly called domestic animals. And of all animals useful to mankind, and of all animals to which people have a strong attachment, I am sure one need not have lived long in the world to know that dogs hold the foremost place.

10.9.2 To reduce the pain and suffering of animals

The definition of animal charities was then extended to include trusts that reduced the suffering of animals.

. . . .

● *Re Wedgwood* [1914] 1 Ch 113

Frances Wedgwood established a secret trust 'for the protection of animals' or 'for the protection and benefit of animals'. The testatrix had indicated that the humane slaughtering of animals was one of the purposes that she had in mind, but she had not restricted her gift to domestic animals.

HELD: Lord Cozens-Hardy MR at 117:

> Apart from authorities which are binding upon us, I should be prepared to support the trust on the ground that it tends to promote public morality by checking the innate tendency to cruelty.

The other two judges elaborated on this, e.g. Swinfen Eady LJ at 122:

> It is a gift for a general public purpose beneficial to the community. A gift for the benefit and protection of animals tends to promote and encourage kindness towards them, to discourage cruelty, and to ameliorate the condition of the brute creation, and thus to stimulate humane and generous sentiments in man towards the lower animals, and by these means promote feelings of humanity and morality generally, repress brutality, and thus elevate the human race.

These charities benefit the *human* public, because they make them better people.

10.9.3 Public benefit in animal charities

However, not all trusts aimed at helping animals qualify as charitable. *Re Grove-Grady* [1929] 1 Ch 557 did not fall neatly under helping domestic animals or reducing cruelty to animals, so it did not gain charitable status.

. . . .

● *Re Grove-Grady* [1929] 1 Ch 557

The will of Sarah Grove-Grady left money to establish 'The Beaumont Animals Benevolent Society', which would provide 'a refuge or refuges for the preservation of all animals, birds or

KEY POINT
To be a charity the trust must either help domestic animals or reduce cruelty to animals.

other creatures not human' living on the land or that might be brought to the land 'to be safe from molestation or destruction by man'. The society was to be run by **anti-vivisectionists** and those opposed to 'all sport involving the pursuit or death of any stag, deer, fox, hare, rabbit, bird, fish or any other animal'.

HELD: The trust did not protect the animals from cruelty, which could be inflicted by the other animals in the refuge.

Lord Hanworth MR at 573–4:

> The fox and the rabbit, birds of all sorts with the stoat and the weasel and rats as neighbours, and hawks and crows as spectators, are to live and enjoy themselves after their kind. The struggle for existence is to be given free play...
>
> The one characteristic of the refuge is that it is free from the molestation of man, while all the fauna within it are to molest and harry one another.

Nor did the trust help animals useful to man. In fact, it might help animals that hindered mankind.

In argument at 560:

> A trust to preserve pests is not charitable.

Russell LJ at 585–6:

There was no public benefit.

> If the trust is carried out according to its tenor, no animal within the area may be destroyed by man no matter how necessary that destruction may be in the interests of mankind or in the interests of other **denizens** of the area or the interests of the animal itself; and no matter how painlessly such destruction may be brought about. It seems to me impossible to say that the carrying out of such a trust necessarily involves benefit to the public. Beyond perhaps hearing of the existence of the enclosure the public does not come into the matter at all. Consistently with the trust the public could be excluded from entering the area or even looking into it.

KEY POINT Public benefit in an animal charity requires helping animals useful to man, reducing cruelty to animals, which makes mankind better or at least allowing public access.

As we saw in 10.5.1 'Education includes teaching and research', in *Re Lopes* [1931] 2 Ch 130, zoos can be educational charities, but they allow public access. Public attitudes may have changed since *Grove-Grady* in 1929. Hunting is less popular with the public and certain forms of hunting are illegal, under the Hunting Act 2004. The Charities Act 2011 appears to allow animal charities without public access.

Charities Act 2011, s. 3(1)

(i) the advancement of environmental protection or improvement;

...

(k) the advancement of animal welfare.

Subsection (k) was considered in *Hanchett-Stamford v Attorney General* [2008] 4 All ER 323. Advancing animal welfare is charitable, but an organization with an objective of trying to change the law is not charitable.

- ● ***Hanchett-Stamford v Attorney General*** [2009] Ch 173

The Performing and Captive Animals Defence League was an organization with the objective of making the use of animals for public performances and in films illegal, on the grounds that it was cruel to train the animals to perform. In 1949 the Inland Revenue had declined to treat it as a charity, because following *National Anti-Vivisection Society v IRC* [1948] AC 31, its principal objects were to change the law and that meant that it did not have charitable status. That case held that, if the courts sanctioned charities that were trying to change the law, that might bring the courts into conflict with the legislature and the courts had to assume that the law was right as it stood. Besides, animal experiments were for the public benefit, as the suffering caused to animals was outweighed by the benefits to humans of scientific and medical advances. Did the Charities Act 2006 change the law, because s. 2(2)(k) lists 'the advancement of animal welfare' as a charitable purpose?

HELD: Lewison J: This subsection did not change the existing law, as promoting animal welfare was already regarded as charitable, but trying to change the law was not.

At 181–2:

> The 2006 Act has not changed the fundamental principle that if one of the objects or purposes of an organisation is to change the law, it cannot be charitable.

At 180: That does not stop a charity promoting or opposing changes in the law but, 'an organisation set up for the purpose of changing the law cannot be a charity'.

(See also 10.5.4 'Political purposes'.)

10.10 Sport and recreation

10.10.1 'Mere sport'

Sport, by itself, was not regarded as charitable, and does not feature in the 1601 Preamble. The reasons why are explained in *Re Nottage* [1895] 2 Ch 649.

- ● ***Re Nottage*** [1895] 2 Ch 649

Charles Nottage left a will which contained a bequest to the Yacht Racing Association of Great Britain to constitute a trust fund to buy a cup, 'The Nottage Cup', to be awarded to the most successful yacht of the season. The purpose was to encourage the sport of yacht racing.

HELD: This was not charitable.

Lopes LJ at 656:

> I am of the opinion that a gift the object of which is the encouragement of a mere sport or game primarily calculated to amuse individuals apart from the community at large, cannot upon the authorities be held to be charitable, though such a sport or game is to some extent beneficial

> to the public. If we were to hold the gift before us to be charitable, we should open a very wide door, for it would be difficult to say that gifts for promoting bicycling, cricket, football, lawn tennis, or any other outdoor game were not charitable for they promote the health and bodily well-being of the community.

The objection to this sport being charitable is that ocean-going yacht racing is a sport in which only the wealthy can indulge. Giving it charitable status and tax concessions hardly helps the rest of society. There is also the problem of where to draw the line. Which sports should be granted charitable status and which should be denied? If football was given charitable status, should it be granted to darts or hunting and shooting and fishing?

10.10.2 Sport as part of education

Sport can, however, be charitable as part of the education of the young. The young need healthy, outdoor exercise.

. . . .

● *Re Mariette* (1915) 2 Ch 284

The bequest was to provide courts for the playing of Eton fives and squash rackets at Aldenham School.

HELD: This was charitable.

Eve J at 288:

> No-one of sense could be found to suggest that between [the ages of 10–19] any boy can be properly educated unless at least as much attention is given to the development of his body as is given to the development of his mind . . . To leave 200 boys at large and to their own devices during their leisure hours, would not be educating, but would probably result in their quickly relapsing into something approaching barbarism.

Other sports have been accepted as being capable of contributing to the educational development of the young.

. . . .

● *Re Dupree's Deed Trusts* [1945] Ch 16

A prize was provided for an annual chess tournament for boys and young men up to 21 in the City of Portsmouth. A schoolteacher gave evidence that chess was a game of skill and educational. The trustees were schoolteachers.

HELD: Evidence was accepted that the playing of chess had educational value.

Not all sports could be regarded as contributing to the education of the young, but judges could make decisions as required on whether a 'sport' qualified for charitable status.

Vaisey J at 20:

> I think that the case before me may be a little near the line, and I decide it without attempting to lay down any general propositions. One feels, perhaps, that one is on a rather slippery slope. If chess, why not draughts? If draughts, why not bezique, and so on, through to bridge and whist, and, by another route, to stamp collecting and the acquisition of birds' eggs? Those pursuits will have to be dealt with if and when they come up for consideration in connection with the problem whether or not there is in existence an educational trust.

The provision of sporting facilities or encouragement of sport does not have to be confined to a particular educational establishment.

. . . .

● *IRC v McMullen* [1981] AC 1

A Football Association Youth Trust was established for

> the organisation and provision of facilities which will enable and encourage pupils of
> schools and universities in any part of the United Kingdom to play association football
> or other games or sports and thereby to assist in ensuring that due attention is given to
> the physical education and development of such pupils as well as to the development and
> occupation of their minds ...

HELD: The House of Lords decided that this was charitable.

Lord Keith of Kinkel at 21:

> A trust for the mere promotion of a particular sport or sports does not qualify as charitable
> under this head: *In re Nottage* [1895] 2 Ch 649. On the other hand a gift to a particular
> educational establishment for the purpose of improving the sporting facilities available
> to the pupils there does so qualify: *In re Mariette* [1915] 2 Ch 284. In the present case the
> purpose of the trust is plainly to improve the sporting facilities, particularly as regards the
> playing of association football, available to pupils undergoing formal courses of education
> at schools and universities in the United Kingdom. It has long been recognised that the
> provision of such facilities tends to promote the success of formal education processes
> with which it is associated. In my opinion the link which by this trust deed is required to
> be established between the facilities to be provided and persons undergoing courses of
> formal education at schools and universities must necessarily lead to the conclusion that
> the trust is for the promotion of education, and that its purposes are therefore exclusively
> charitable.

The Charities Act 2011 s. 3(1)(g) states that 'the advancement of amateur sport' is a
charitable purpose. There is a definition in s. 3(2)(d): 'in paragraph (g), "sport" means
sports or games which promote health by involving physical or mental skill or exertion.'
There is nothing to say that the sporting charity needs to be educational and restricted to
the young. The Charity Commission accepted 'Hitchin Bridge Club' as a charity, because
bridge involved 'mental skill and exertion', that was particularly beneficial to the health of
older people. It also satisfied the public benefit requirement below, because anyone could
attend and the fees charged were low. <https://www.gov.uk/government/publications/
hitchin-bridge-club>

10.10.3 Sport and public benefit

The provision of parks and playing fields for open-air recreation is considered to be charitable.

. . . .

● *Re Hadden* [1932] 1 Ch 133

Hadden left a will to provide open-air recreation for as many working people as possible, in
Nottingham, by the provision of playing fields or gymnasia.

HELD: This was charitable, as it was not to promote mere 'sport', but would contribute to the
health and welfare of the working classes.

The difference between this and cases such as *Re Nottage* (1895) 2 Ch 649, is that the charity is open to all. Similarly, village halls have charitable status, as they are available to the whole community.

It is quite common to make a charity only available to the inhabitants of a town or district.

● ***Verge v Somerville*** [1924] AC 496

This involved a Repatriation Fund for soldiers returning to New South Wales, Australia.

Lord Wrenbury at 499:

> The inhabitants of a parish or town, or any particular class of such inhabitants, may, for instance, be the objects of such a gift, but private individuals, or a fluctuating body of private individuals, cannot.

Where the facilities are only provided for a limited group of the public, there may not be enough public benefit for charitable status.

● ***Williams Trustees v IRC*** [1947] AC 447

Sir Howell Williams set up an institute and meeting place in London known as

> The London Welsh Association for the benefit of Welsh people resident in or near or visiting London with a view to creating a centre in London for promoting the moral social spiritual and educational welfare of Welsh people and fostering the study of the Welsh language and of Welsh history literature music and art.

'Welsh people' were defined as people born, educated, or at any time domiciled in Wales or people of Welsh descent. The institute had premises in London where classes were held, but there were also cards, dances, sports, and other social events.

HELD: The Institute did not fall within any definition of charity.

Lord Normand at 460:

> In the present case the decision of the commissioners was that, while certain features of the institute conformed to the idea of charity, they were not so dominating nor was the general character of the institute such as effectively to distinguish if from an ordinary social club. In my opinion this conclusion is amply supported by the facts and is well founded in law.

Even if it had been a charity, there was doubt over whether there was enough public benefit.

Lord Simonds at 457–8:

> …the principle has been consistently maintained, that a trust in order to be charitable must be of a public character. It must not be merely for the benefit of particular private individuals.
>
> But the difficulty of finding the community in the present case, when the definition of 'Welsh people' in the first deed is remembered, would not I think be less than that of finding the community of Jews in *Keren Kayemeth le Jisroel v IRC* [1932] AC 650.

This was a House of Lords case and formed a precedent for subsequent cases.

● **IRC v Baddeley** [1955] AC 572

The Stratford Newtown Methodist Mission had some land, with a church, lecture room, and store, and the trustees were to use this property for the promotion of the religious, social, and physical well-being of persons resident in West Ham and Leyton. This was to be done by providing religious services, instruction, social and physical training, and recreation for residents, who were, in the opinion of the leaders of the church, members or likely to become members of the Methodist Church and were of insufficient means otherwise to enjoy these advantages.

HELD: This was not a charity. It was not educational or religious, nor did it relieve poverty.

Under the fourth head the House of Lords was bound by its previous decision in *Williams*. The Methodist Mission was also a social club rather than a charity. There was also no public benefit.

Viscount Simonds at 591:

> For here is a slippery slope. In the case under appeal the intended beneficiaries are a class within a class; they are those of the inhabitants of a particular area who are members of a particular church; the area is comparatively large and populous and the members may be numerous. But, if the trust is charitable for them, does it cease to be charitable as the area narrows down and the numbers diminish? Suppose the area is confined to a single street and the beneficiaries to those whose creed commands few adherents: or suppose the class is one that is determined not by religious belief but by membership of a particular profession or by pursuit of a particular trade.

At 592:

> But I think that … the difficulty has sometimes been increased by failing to observe the distinction, which I hinted at earlier in this opinion, between a form of relief extended to the whole community yet by its very nature advantageous only to the few and a form of relief accorded to a selected few out of a larger number equally willing and able to take advantage of it.
>
> For example, a bridge which is available for all the public may undoubtedly be a charity and it is indifferent how many people use it. But confine its use to a selected number of persons, however numerous and important: it is then clearly not a charity.
>
> Who has ever heard of a bridge to be crossed only by impecunious Methodists?

KEY POINT
Public benefit in recreational charities means that the charitable benefits should be available to the whole community.

Lord Reid dissented. He considered that this was a trust to provide recreation and that was charitable. More importantly he differed in his interpretation of public benefit. He did not see why the public benefit requirement should differ in the Four Heads of Charity. Following *Verge v Somerville,* he could not see why Methodists in West Ham and Leyton could not be a 'particular class of the community'.

The decisions in *Baddeley* [1955] AC 572 and *Williams* [1947] AC 447 brought into question the charitable status of a number of existing institutions, such as the Women's Institute and Boys' Clubs, so Parliament intervened.

> **Charities Act 2011, Section 5 Recreational and similar trusts**
>
> (1) Subject to the provisions of this Act, it shall be and be deemed always to have been charitable to provide, or assist in the provision of, facilities for recreation or other leisure-time occupation, if the facilities are provided in the interests of social welfare.

> Provided that nothing in this section shall be taken to derogate from the principle that a trust or institution to be charitable must be for the public benefit.
>
> (2) The requirement in subsection (1) that the facilities are provided in the interests of social welfare cannot be satisfied if the basic conditions are not met.
>
> (2A) The basic conditions are—
>
>   (a) that the facilities are provided with the object of improving the conditions of life for the persons for whom the facilities are primarily intended; and
>
>   (b) that either—
>
>   (i) those persons have need of the facilities by reason of their youth, age, infirmity or disability, poverty, or social and economic circumstances, or
>
>   (ii) the facilities are to be available to the members of the public at large or to male, or to female members of the public at large.
>
> (3) Subject to the said requirement, subsection (1) of this section applies in particular to the provision of facilities at village halls, community centres and women's institutes, and to the provision and maintenance of grounds and buildings to be used for the purposes of recreation or leisure-time occupation and extends to the provision of facilities for those purposes by the organising of any activity.

This section, originally enacted in 1958, causes almost as many problems of interpretation as it was designed to solve. It is arguable that it does not change the position of a trust aimed at the Welsh or at East Ham Methodists. Neither group qualifies as the whole of society and neither group is distinguished by poverty, youth, etc. as required by the Act. In *IRC v McMullen* [1979] 1 WLR 130, the Court of Appeal thought that the Act required the recreational trust to be aimed at a 'deprived' group (see 10.10.2 'Sport as part of education'). The House of Lords corrected this misapprehension in *Guild v IRC* [1992] 2 AC 310.

. . . .

● **Guild v IRC** [1992] 2 AC 310

This was a bequest to a sports centre in North Berwick, which was open to the whole community.

HELD: Lord Keith of Kinkel at 322–3:

> I would therefore reject the argument that the facilities are not provided in the interests of social welfare unless they are provided with the object of improving the conditions of life for persons who suffer from some form of social disadvantage. It suffices if they are provided with the object of improving the conditions of life for members of the community generally.
>
> The leading characteristics of the sports centre lie in the nature of the facilities which are provided there and the fact that those facilities are available to the public at large.

thinking points

'Whether trusts for the furtherance of sport and the playing of games are charitable is complicated.' According to Re Nottage *the furtherance of sport by itself is not charitable, but if it is coupled with education it is:* Re Mariette. *Exercise in the open air, available to all is charitable (*Re Hadden*), but if it is restricted to Methodists it is not:* Re Baddeley.

After that decision the Recreational Charities Act 1958 was passed to try to safeguard the charitable status of social clubs and other organizations. Unfortunately, it was interpreted as only saving the charitable status of bodies that provided services to the 'deprived'. This was disputed in the Scottish case, Guild v IRC, *which considered that charitable status was enjoyed, as long as the facilities were provided to the public as a whole. In Canada,* Re Nottage *has been reconsidered in* Re Laidlaw *(1985) 13 DLR (4th) 491. We now live in a sedentary society and surely physical exercise is for the public benefit? 'Amateur sport' should be encouraged and this would seem to be recognized by s. 3(1))(g) of the Charities Act 2006. See J Hopkins 'Trusts for the Advancement of Sport—Recreational Charities Act 1958' [1992] CLJ 429.*

The cy-près doctrine

10.11.1 When cy-près applies

A trust might be a valid charity, but it may be impossible for that charity actually to run. Section 62 of the Charities Act 2011 recognizes a number of situations where this is so. The charity may be impossible, impracticable, unsuitable, or ineffective. The original purpose may have been fulfilled, the area or the original beneficiaries may have ceased to be suitable, or it may be better to combine the charity with another charity, etc. A common problem is that property is left to a charity that no longer exists or in some cases never existed.

Under the Charities Acts 1985 and 1993, small charities are encouraged to merge with larger charities. 'Schemes', as they are called, used to be devised by the courts, but now this is done by the Charity Commission.

One of the problems with charities is that they can last for hundreds of years, so what was a good charitable purpose at the time becomes outdated. An example can be seen in *Re Campden Charities* (1881) 18 ChD 310.

. . . .

● *Re Campden Charities* [1881] 18 ChD 310

Viscount and Viscountess Campden left land in Shepherds Bush and Kensington that produced an annual income of £10. Half was to be given to the poor and needy (of good life and conversation) of Kensington and the other half was to pay for a boy of the parish to be apprenticed. This was in 1651, when Shepherds Bush and Kensington were rural villages. By the date of the case they were part of London and the land produced an income of £2,200.

The Charity Commission drew up a scheme to spend the money more widely. Some was to be spent on the poor hurt in accidents and the provision of pensions. Apprenticeships were still to be provided, but there were also to be scholarships and the education of deaf and dumb children.

HELD: Jessel MR at 323:

Cy-près—
French—near
to or close to.

> …the scheme is made in pursuance of what is commonly called the **cy-près** doctrine, and, in cases like this, it is applied where, from lapse of time and change of circumstances, it is no longer possible beneficially to apply the property left by the founder or donor in the exact way in which he has directed it to be applied, but it can only be applied beneficially to similar purposes by different means.

The cy-près doctrine

313

A more modern example can be seen where a religious charity had split and some followers of that religion no longer wished to worship with the others. The charity owned buildings, such as temples and churches, and these could be divided between the different factions. The 'scheme' has to reflect the spirit and intention of the original gift.

● **White and others v Williams and others** [2010] PTSR 1575

The trustees of the Bibleway Church UK held a number of churches, which were used by local congregations. There was a schism in the Church, which divided into two factions. The Lewisham congregation decided to leave entirely and establish itself as the Tabernacle Ministries of Great Britain, but wanted the church they used to be transferred to them.

HELD: It was no longer suitable or acceptable for the Lewisham congregation to remain under the control of Bibleway, who were not sympathetic to their beliefs. The original spirit and intention of the gift, which must be respected, was that the local congregation should have somewhere to worship, so the church building was transferred to the Tabernacle trustees.

The law makes a distinction between subsequent failure and initial failure.

> **KEY POINT**
> Cy-près means that the charitable property is given to a similar charity to reflect, as far as possible, the original intention of the settlor or testator.

10.11.2 Subsequent failure

This is where the property has been given to a valid, operating charity that then ceases to operate or exist, or for some other reason (see 10.11.1 'When cy-près applies') cannot be continued. In cases of subsequent failure, the charitable property has been dedicated to charity and is always applied to another similar charity.

● **Phillips v The Royal Society for the Protection of Birds** [2012] EWHC 618 (Ch)

The will of Vera Spear left money to 'The New Forest Owl Sanctuary Ltd' (NFOS). Mrs Spear died on 5 January 2007, but NFOS had ceased to operate by 13 July 2006. It had been removed from the register of charities on 17 August 2006, but NFOS was not dissolved as a company until 6 February 2007.

HELD: Para 27:

> This case is therefore one of supervening failure, that is to say one where the gift was effective at the date of death to impress the funds with the charitable purpose intended to be given effect to through NFOS, but which cannot now be carried through in that manner by reason of NFOS having subsequently ceased to exist.

Mrs Spears' property was given to charity on the date of her death, 5 January 2007. The charity did not fail until a month later, so her property remained charitable, and did not revert back to her relatives.

10.11.3 Initial failure

This is where the charity failed from the start, usually the date of death of the testator or testatrix. It can sometimes be difficult to determine whether it is a case of initial or subsequent failure, as illustrated in *Kings v Bultitude* [2010] EWHC 1795 (Ch).

● **Kings v Bultitude** [2010] EWHC 1795 [Ch]

Mrs Schroder died in 2008 and left the residue in her will to 'the Trustee of the Ancient Catholic Church of the Good Shepherd at present meeting at Rockwood Road, London N16... for the general purposes of the said Church'. The Primate of this Church, which was a breakaway Roman Catholic church, had been Mr Schroder, the husband of the deceased, who had run the Church until his death in 1985. Then Mrs Schroder ran it, conducting services for a very small congregation until her death, when the Church ceased to operate. A number of questions had to be answered to decide whether her residue could be given to another, similar charity, cy-près.

HELD: Proudman J:

Was her gift charitable in the first place? It was a charity for the advancement of religion.

Is this a case of initial failure? Yes, it was a case of initial failure.

> It seems to me that Mrs Schroder was essential to the activities of the Church and without her it ceased to exist.

So the charity ceased to exist at the moment her will took effect. In contrast, Mrs Schroder had kept bank accounts for the Church, which still had money in them. These accounts had been given to the Church when it was still a going concern and used by it, so this was a case of subsequent failure. The bank account money could be applied cy-près.

So her residue could only go to charity if that was her general charitable intention.

> Moreover there is nothing in the Will to indicate a general charitable intention which might save the gift... The Will contains no other charitable gift.

If it is a case of initial failure, as seen in *Kings*, the courts have to be satisfied that the testator would not have minded his/her property going to another, similar charity.

This is known as discovering the 'general charitable intention', sometimes called the 'paramount charitable intention'. If that is found, then the gift can be applied cy-près, to similar charitable purposes. On the other hand, if the gift is very specific, in that the testator/testatrix wanted that charity and no other, there can be no general charitable intention.

A specific charitable intent

These cases are examples of gifts that were so specific that the court felt unable to give the property to another charity. So the consequence is that the gift goes back to the estate of the deceased, or falls into residue as it is called. It would go to whoever is named in the will or the next of kin.

● **Re Rymer** [1895] 1 Ch 19

Horatio Rymer had a legacy of £5,000 in his will 'to the rector for the time being of St Thomas's Seminary for the education of priests in the diocese of Westminster'. When Rymer made his will the seminary was in existence, but, by the time that he died in 1893 and his will took effect, the Westminster seminary had closed and the students had transferred to a seminary near Birmingham.

HELD: This was a gift to this particular seminary, so there was no general charitable intent and could be no cy-près.

Lindley LJ at 34:

> I quite agree that in coming to that conclusion you have to consider whether the mode of attaining the object is only machinery, or whether the mode is not the substance of the gift. Here it appears to me the gift to the seminary is the substance of the whole thing. It is the object of the testator. I think that is plain from the language used.

The legacy went back into the residue of Rymer's estate. Rymer had chosen one particular seminary and no other.

A similar conclusion was reached in *Re Spence (Deceased)* [1979] Ch 483.

● **Re Spence (Deceased)** [1979] Ch 483

The testatrix made her will in 1968 and left half the residue to 'the Old Folks' Home at Hillworth Lodge, Keighley for the benefit of the patients'. The home closed in 1971 and the testatrix died in 1972.

HELD: Megarry J at 493:

> If a particular institution or purpose is specified, then it is that institution or purpose, and no other, that is to be the object of the benefaction.
>
> It is otherwise where the testator has been unable to specify any particular charitable institution or practicable purpose, and so although his intention of charity can be seen, he has failed to provide any way of giving effect to it.

Ms Spence only intended to benefit this particular old people's home, not old people's homes in general.

A general charitable intent

The court tries to interpret the intention of the testator/testatrix from the will. Did he or she just want to give to charity and was not too concerned to which one? There are a number of things that the court can look for to decide that there was a general charitable intent.

A gift to a charity that never existed indicates general charitable intention. The testator/testatrix could not have really minded which 'charity' benefitted, if he or she did not check which one was receiving the gift.

● **Re Harwood** [1936] Ch 285

The testatrix made her will in 1925, leaving £200 to the Wisbech Peace Society, £300 to the Peace Society of Belfast, and £300 to the Peace Society of Dublin. The testatrix died in 1934. The Wisbech Peace Society had existed, but did not exist by that date. There was no record of any Peace Society ever having existed in Belfast. It was said that there had been a Dublin Peace Society, but it had ceased to exist many years before.

HELD: There was no general charitable intent with regard to the Wisbech Society.

Farwell J at 287:

> Here the testatrix had gone out of her way to identify the object of her bounty. In this particular case she has identified it as being 'the Wisbech Peace Society Cambridge (which is a branch of the London Peace Society).' Under those circumstances, I do not think it is open to me to hold that there is in this case any such general charitable intent as to allow the application of the cy-près doctrine.

On the other hand, the Belfast Society had never existed. Therefore, there was general charitable intent and the £300 could be applied cy-près.

At 288:

> I think that she had a desire to benefit any society which was formed for the purpose of promoting peace and was connected with Belfast. Beyond that, I do not think that she had any very clear idea in her mind.

The same applied to the Dublin Society.

At 289:

> ...her ideas as to any particular society which she desired to benefit by this gift were extremely vague; her one idea seems to have been to benefit any society whose object was the promotion of peace which was connected with Dublin. Under those circumstances, there never having been any society which exactly answers the description in the will, this again is a case where the doctrine of cy-près applies.

Gifts to unincorporated associations indicate general charitable intention. If the gift was to an incorporated body, such as a company, there would be nothing to stop that company using those funds for general company purposes, which might not be charitable: *Phillips v The Royal Society for the Protection of Birds* [2012] EWHC 618 (Ch). That might be taken to indicate a lack of general charitable intention.

. . . .

● *Re Finger's Will Trusts* [1972] Ch 286

There were a number of named charities including the National Radium Commission and the National Council for Maternity and Child Welfare. Both had ceased to exist between the date of the will and the date of death.

HELD: Goff J: There was a distinction made between incorporated and unincorporated institutions in a previous case, which was binding on the court.

If the institution was unincorporated, it was assumed that there was a general charitable intention. This was the case with the National Radium Commission, so there could be cy-près.

However, if the institution was incorporated, it was assumed that it was a gift to that institution and no other. The National Council for Maternity and Child Welfare was incorporated, but the evidence indicated general charitable intention.

> The judge found the distinction illogical and looked at the other evidence, which showed a general charitable intent. The testatrix had given her whole estate to charity as she had no relatives to whom to leave her money. The National Council for Maternity had actually been a coordinating body for other charities, so the testatrix could not have meant her money to go just to the one charity and no other.

Generally, the courts prefer to find a general charitable intention if they can. If the rest of the will is charitable, particularly if the same kind of charity is chosen, that tends to indicate general charitable intention.

● **Re Satterthwaite's Will Trusts** [1966] 1 WLR 277

In 1952 Phyllis Satterthwaite made her will, announcing that she hated all human beings and wished to leave her estate to animal charities. Nine were selected from the London telephone book. One, the London Animal Hospital, had existed, but was not a charity and had ceased to operate under that name at about the time that the testatrix made her will.

HELD: There was a general charitable intention.

Russell LJ at 286:

> Here I have no doubt from the nature of the other dispositions by the testatrix of her residuary estate that a general intention can be discerned in favour of charity through the medium of kindness to animals.

It is important to note that cy-près can only apply if the gift is charitable in the first place.

> **KEY POINT**
> A finding of general charitable intent means that the charitable gift can be reassigned to another charity.

● **Re Jenkins Will Trusts** [1966] Ch 249

The testatrix divided her property into seven equal parts. Six were to go to charitable institutions, but the seventh was to go 'to the British Union for the Abolition of Vivisection to do all in its power to urge and get an Act passed prohibiting unnecessary cruelty to animals'.

HELD: The seventh gift was not charitable and could not be given by cy-près to another charity. The other six charitable gifts did not make this one charitable.

Anti-vivisection trusts want to change the law to prevent experiments on live animals. This is not charitable, as it is deemed political (see *National Anti-Vivisection Society v IRC* [1948] AC 31 and 10.5.4 'Political purposes').

A non-charitable gift cannot be turned into a charitable one by cy-près.

> **KEY POINT**
> Cy-près only applies to a gift that falls within the four heads of charity.

10.11.4 Amalgamation and merger of charities

It is always possible that cy-près will not be needed if the charity continues in another form. The gift can just go to the new 'merged' charity (see Diagram 10.1).

● **Re Faraker** [1912] 2 Ch 488

Mrs Faraker died in 1911 leaving a legacy to 'Mrs Bailey's Charity, Rotherhithe'.

In 1756 'Hannah Bayly's Charity' had been established for the benefit of poor widows resident in Rotherhithe. In 1905 the Charity Commissioners had amalgamated the Bayly Charity, with other Rotherhithe charities. The new charity was for the relief of poverty generally, and did not specifically mention widows. Widows who had received pensions from the Bayly Charity continued to be paid.

Diagram 10.1

*'General
charitable intent'*

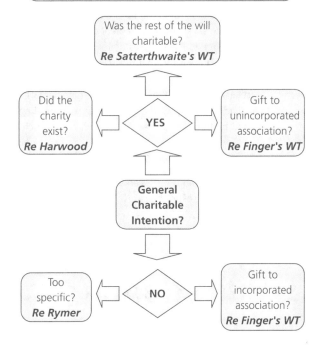

In cases of intital failure, when will the courts *tend* to find the General Chartitable Intention necessary to apply the funds cy-près?

Was the rest of the will charitable?
Re Satterthwaite's WT

Did the charity exist?
Re Harwood

YES

Gift to unincorporated association?
Re Finger's WT

General Charitable Intention?

Too specific?
Re Rymer

NO

Gift to incorporated association?
Re Finger's WT

HELD: Cozens-Hardy MR at 493:

> Hannah Bayly's Charity is not extinct, it is not dead, and I go further and say it cannot die.
>
> Subject to that lawful alteration by competent authority [the Charity Commission] of the objects, Hannah Bayly's Charity is not extinct, it exists just as much as it did when the testatrix died in 1756.

Farwell LJ at 495:

> In the present case there is no question of a cy-près execution. Nobody suggests that there has been a failure of poor widows in Rotherhithe.

The Bayly Charity continued to carry out its work as part of another charity.

 # Conclusion

Charity law is not logical, but has been built up case by case. Therefore, you need to know these cases. It is hard to identify consistent underlying concepts and principles. Each area of charity law has its own distinctive features, which do not necessarily apply to other areas of charity law. Charities for the relief of poverty must only help the poor, not the rich, yet there is no definition of poverty. There is no real public benefit requirement for poverty charities, which can even be restricted to the testator's or settlor's relatives. The advancement of education is widely defined to include the promotion of culture, so the courts may have to decide whether the education provided is of any value. Similarly, if a charity becomes too 'political', it will be in danger of losing its charitable status. An educational charity must be available to the public, to satisfy the requirement of public benefit, yet schools that charge high fees retain charitable status. The only restriction is that education must not be confined to relatives or employees. The advancement of religion is clearly defined, but in a rather old-fashioned and restrictive way. The courts are not very willing to be drawn into a debate about the merits of a particular religion, yet to satisfy the requirement of public benefit the religion must be open to all. The last category of charity, other purposes beneficial to the community, has had to be updated by the Charities Act 2011, as it covers such a vast range of purposes. Here, public benefit is very restrictively defined and seems to require the charitable services to be available to the whole community.

Lastly, cy-près stands out as an area without any underlying principle and all that we can say, is, once again, look at the cases!

? Questions

Self-test questions

1 What advantages does charitable status give?

2 What purposes are regarded as charitable?

3 What does the requirement of public benefit mean?

4 In what ways may a charity relieve poverty?

5 What are the public benefit requirements in a poverty charity?

6 What is the advancement of education?

7 What is the personal nexus rule?

8 When will a trust be regarded as too political to qualify for charitable status?

9 What is the advancement of religion?

10 How can a religion be for the public benefit?

11 How can the 'need' of the aged, disabled, and sick be relieved?

12 Is it permissible to charge for a charitable service?

13 How is animal welfare defined for charitable purposes?

14 Is sport charitable?

15 What does the cy-près doctrine allow the Charity Commissioners to do?

16 What is the difference between subsequent and initial failure?

17 How is a general charitable intent identified?

Discussion questions

1 Is it possible to come up with an overall definition of charity?

2 Does the Charities Act 2011 help to define 'charitable purposes' and public benefit?

3 Should the public benefit requirement differ for different types of charity?

4 Is the definition of religion outdated?

5 Why should 'political trusts' be denied charitable status?

Assessment question

Tom is a famous actor and a follower of the teachings of Old Mother Hubbard, a self-proclaimed prophetess, who claimed that she would give birth to the returning Jesus Christ, but died, without doing so, in 1985. Tom establishes the following trusts:

(a) £1 million to hold an annual public ceremony to commemorate the death of Old Mother Hubbard, to sing hymns in her praise, and pray to her;

(b) £5 million to open a school for the children of followers of Old Mother Hubbard, where they will be educated according to her teachings;

(c) £6 million to provide housing for poor and needy followers of Old Mother Hubbard; and

(d) £10 million to open a public park in her memory, where young people can play sports.

Advise Tom.

 # Key cases

- *Commissioners for Special Purposes of Income Tax v Pemsel* [1891] AC 531 **(at 10.3.2)**

- *Independent Schools Commission v Charity Commission for England and Wales* [2012] 1 All ER 127 **(at 10.3.4 and 10.3.5)**

- *Re Gardom* [1914] 1 Ch 662 **(at 10.4.1)**

- *Dingle v Turner* [1972] AC 601 **(at 10.1.2, 10.4.2 and 10.5.5)**

- *Re Hopkins* [1965] Ch 669 **(at 10.5.1)**

- *Re Pinion* [1965] Ch 85 **(at 10.5.3)**

- *McGovern v Attorney General* [1981] Ch 321 **(at 10.5.4)**

- *Oppenheim v Tobacco Securities Trust Co* [1951] AC 297 **(at 10.5.5)**

- *Bowman v Secular Society* [1917] AC 406 **(at 10.5.4 and 10.6.1)**

- *Thornton v Howe* (1862) 31 Beav 14 **(at 10.6.2)**

- *Gilmour v Coats* [1949] AC 426 **(at 10.3.4 and 10.6.3)**

- *Re Resch* [1969] 1 AC 514 **(at 10.3.5 and 10.7.2)**

- *Re Grove-Grady* [1929] 1 Ch 557 **(at 10.9.3)**

- *IRC v McMullen* [1981] AC 1 **(at 10.10.2 and 10.10.3)**

- *IRC v Baddeley* [1955] AC 572 **(at 10.10.3)**

- *Re Rymer* [1895] 1 Ch 19 **(at 10.11.3)**

- *Re Harwood* [1936] Ch 285 **(at 10.11.3)**

- *Re Faraker* [1912] 2 Ch 488 **(at 10.11.4)**

 # Further reading

M Synge 'Independent Schools Commission v Charity Commission for England and Wales' (2012) 75 *MLR* 624.

The *Independent Schools* case attempts to define what the public benefit requirement means in the advancement of education, but does it do this satisfactorily?

R Nobles 'Politics, Public Benefit and Charity' (1982) 45 *MLR* 704

In the light of the Amnesty International case, *McGovern v AG*, when can a charity engage in politics?

J Hopkins 'Trusts for the Advancement of Sports—Recreational Charities Act 1958' [1992] *CLJ* 429

Does this Act solve the problem of what is public benefit in a recreational charity?

<https://www.gov.uk/government/organisations/charity-commission>

This is the website of the Charity Commission and contains up-to-date information on what is regarded as charitable.

11

The duties of trustees: with special reference to investment

Learning objectives

This chapter will help you to:

- understand that trustees have a duty to make money—to invest for profit
- understand that trustees owe a duty of reasonable care and skill
- appreciate that trustees may now make any kind of investment
- recognize that trustees must take advice
- understand that trustees are liable for loss caused by breach of duty
- appreciate that trustees may hire agents to assist them in performing their duties
- understand that agents must be selected and supervised with reasonable care and skill.

Introduction

Trustees have always had a duty to invest the trust funds to provide an income for the beneficiaries and to maintain or, indeed, increase the value of the trust. Before the Trustee Act 2000, the type of investments trustees could make was heavily regulated by law. After that Act trustees have far greater freedom to make different types of investment. Trustees, however, are still controlled by a basic duty to take reasonable care and skill in all their decisions. Similarly, the Trustee Act 2000 encourages trustees to employ 'agents', people with specialized skills, to run the investment policy of the trust. Yet, again, the trustees must recruit and supervise these agents with reasonable care and skill.

11.1 What is investment?

Although it is not laid down by statute, it has long been clear that the trustees have a duty to invest the trust property. This is illustrated by the next case.

● **Cowan v Scargill** [1985] Ch 270

The pension scheme for miners had ten trustees, five appointed by the employers, the National Coal Board, and five appointed by the employees' trade union, the National Union of Mineworkers. Scargill and the four other NUM trustees wanted the trust to invest in such a way that it protected the coal mining industry, for example by investing in Britain and avoiding energy industries which were in direct competition with coal. This was opposed by Cowan and the four other NCB trustees and they applied to the court.

HELD: Sir Robert Megarry VC at 286–7:

> I turn to the law. The starting point is the duty of the trustees to exercise their powers in the best interests of the present and future beneficiaries of the trust, holding the scales impartially between different classes of beneficiaries. The duty of the trustees towards their beneficiaries is paramount. They must, of course, obey the law; but subject to that, they must put the interests of their beneficiaries first.
>
> When the purpose of the trust is to provide financial benefits for the beneficiaries, as is usually the case, the best interests of the beneficiaries are normally their best financial interests. In the case of a power of investment, as in the present case, the power must be exercised so as to yield the best return for the beneficiaries, judged in relation to the risks of the investments in question; and the prospects of the yield of income and capital appreciation both have to be considered in judging the return from the investment.

KEY POINTS

• The duty of trustees is to make money;

• To balance the conflicting interests of the beneficiaries.

Investment has not been defined by statute, but the *Oxford English Dictionary* meaning of 'investment' was accepted in *Re Wragg* [1919] 2 Ch 58 at 64 as 'to employ money in the purchase of anything from which interest or profit is expected'.

This means that there is a vast range of things that trustees can do with trust property. It might be considered that there are two basic types of investment.

11.1.1 Loans at a rate of interest

This could be something as simple as putting money in a building society or bank deposit account, which pays interest. For a trust it would be purchasing what are known as government or local authority 'stocks'. These are fixed blocks or units, say, £100, which pay a guaranteed, fixed rate of interest. These are very safe investments, as it is very unlikely that the government will be unable to pay the interest, but the rate of interest is low, so they are not that profitable. Alternatively, the trustees might lend money on a mortgage. The rate of interest would be quite good and if the mortgagee cannot repay the loan, the trustees may foreclose and obtain the land. Hence this is known as a 'secured loan'. Another type of secured loan is a debenture, where the trustees lend money to a company. If the company cannot pay, the trustees have a claim against the assets of the company, which might be machinery, plant, the goods produced, or even intellectual property rights.

11.1.2 Participation in a profit-making enterprise

These are various kinds of shares in a company. When a company is formed it declares that it has a certain amount of capital. People and other companies buy 'shares' in this capital. This means that if the company does well the value of these shares goes up, but if it does badly it goes down. If the company is profitable it pays out a dividend or annual profit on all its shares.

If the trustees do not consider that they have the knowledge to invest in shares on their own account, it is possible to buy investments such as unit trusts, where the company selling the unit trusts does the buying and selling of shares on behalf of its clients. Nowadays there are all kinds of investments. Some trust funds have been known to buy paintings, antiques, or even stamp collections, in the hope that they will go up in value!

Whatever happens, trustees cannot just leave money in a current bank account (s. 11 Trustee Act 1925). They must try to use it to make a profit.

The historical background

The 'old law' as in s. 1 of the Trustee Act 1925 restricted trustees' powers of investment to safe investments such as stocks and mortgages on land. Buying land itself was forbidden, as, historically, property prices have gone down as much as they have gone up: *Re Power* [1947] 2 All ER 282.

Because of these restrictions, many trusts were drafted to give the trustees much wider powers of investment. These express powers of investment have the effect of excluding the statutory powers. This is still common practice today.

Even by the 1960s the law on trustees' investments seemed too restrictive. Shares, which produced a much better return, were forbidden. So, the Trustee Investment Act 1961 widened the investment powers of trustees by permitting investment in shares. However, investment powers were still restricted, in order to protect the beneficiaries from the trustees losing the trust fund in risky investments.

In Schedule I the Act listed the types of investment that trustees were permitted to make. In some ways this made things simple for trustees: if the investment was not listed, they were not permitted to make it.

Part I was called the 'narrower range without advice' and this included really safe investments such as putting the trust money in an interest-bearing account in a bank. As this was the kind of thing that an ordinary person might do, the trustees did not need to seek expert advice from someone like a financial adviser before doing this.

Part II was called the 'narrower range with advice' and included slightly more risky investments such as stocks and loans on mortgage and debenture. Because of the added risk, expert advice was required here.

Part III was called the 'wider range with advice' and this was the real innovation, as it allowed trusts to invest in shares. Even so, this power was still heavily restricted so as not to endanger the trust fund. According to Part IV of the Schedule, the company had to be one quoted on the UK Stock Exchange, have a share capital of at least £1,000,000, which had been fully paid for by the shareholders, and to have paid a dividend for each of the preceding five years.

Even more importantly, a maximum of half the trust fund could be invested in the wider range. This was to ensure that at least half the fund was kept in 'safe' investments.

Later, in 1996, as there did not seem to be any great risk to the beneficiaries' money, the maximum proportion that could be invested in shares was raised to three-quarters.

By the 1980s, the 1961 Act was thought outdated. The Law Reform Committee called for reform in 1984 (Cmd 8733). This was endorsed by a leading trusts judge, Megarry VC in *Trustees of the British Museum v Attorney General* [1984] 1 All ER 337. Many large trusts, such as the British Museum charity, had long ago 'opted out' of the Trustee Investment Act 1961 and had their own express powers of investment enabling their trustees to invest outside the UK and in non-stock exchange listed companies.

Reform came, first for pension fund trusts in the Pensions Act 1995, then for trusts of land in the Trusts of Land and Appointment of Trustees Act 1996. Finally, following the Law Commission No 260 (1999) report on Trustees' Powers and Duties, a new Trustee Act was enacted in 2000.

KEY POINT
In the past trustees were restricted to a statutory list of permitted investments. Investment in shares was limited.

11.3   The Trustee Act 2000

11.3.1   The modern investment power for trustees

This broke with the past by freeing the trustees from any restrictions on the kind of investments that they could make. According to the Trustee Act 2000, s. 3(1):

> ... a trustee may make any kind of investment that he could make if he were absolutely entitled to the assets of the trust.

This means that the trustees can invest in anything that they like. The old lists of permitted investments are gone. There is no statutory definition of investment, so we fall back on the case law such as *Re Wragg* [1919] 2 Ch 58 and *Cowan v Scargill* [1984] 2 All ER 750 mentioned in 11.1 'What is investment?'.

11.4 The duty of care

Instead of protecting the beneficiaries by restricting the investments that could be made by the trustees, it was made clear that the trustees had a duty of care. According to the Trustee Act 2000, s. 1(1):

> Whenever the duty under this subsection applies to a trustee, he must exercise such care and skill as is reasonable in all the circumstances, having regard in particular—
>
> (a) to any special knowledge or experience that he has or holds himself out as having, and
>
> (b) if he acts as a trustee in the course of a business or profession, to any special knowledge or experience that it is reasonable to expect of a person acting in the course of that kind of business or profession.

Section 1(1)(b) is based on earlier case law, which recognized that trustees would have a higher duty of care if they were professional trustees who charged for their services.

● ***Bartlett v Barclays Bank Trust Company Limited*** [1980] Ch 515 at 534

Brightman LJ:

> I am of the opinion that a higher duty of care is plainly due from someone like a **trust corporation** which carries on a specialised business of trust management. A trust corporation holds itself out in its advertising literature as being above ordinary mortals. With a specialist staff of trained trust officers and managers, with ready access to financial information and professional advice, dealing with and solving trust problems day after day, the trust corporation holds itself out, and rightly, as capable of providing an expertise which it would be unrealistic to expect and unjust to demand from the ordinary prudent man or woman who accepts, probably unpaid and sometimes reluctantly from a sense of family duty, the burdens of trusteeship. Just as, under the law of contract, a professional person possessed of a particular skill is liable for a breach of contract if he neglects to use the skill and experience which he professes, so I think that a professional corporate trustee is liable for breach of trust if a loss is caused to the trust fund because it neglects to exercise the special care and skill which it professes to have.

KEY POINT
Professional trustees owe a higher duty of care.

Trust corporation—a company that can act as a trustee. Most banks offer this service and there are many companies specifically formed to act as trustees. (See 13.2.4 'Trust corporations'.)

The basic duty of care was developed in the 19th century in cases such as the following.

● *Learoyd v Whiteley* [1886] LR 33 ChD 347

Learoyd and Carter were trustees for Elizabeth Whiteley and her children. They had power to invest in mortgages and so lent £3,000 at 5 per cent, secured on a freehold brickfield, both the land and the equipment. They employed experienced local valuers, who reported that the brickfield was good security for a loan of £3,500. Unfortunately, it proved to be a poor investment, as the brickfield went out of business. The beneficiaries sued the trustees to restore their loss.

HELD: They were held liable, because they should have avoided 'hazardous and speculative' investments. A general duty of care was laid down.

Lindley LJ at 355:

> ...care must be taken not to lose sight of the fact that the business of the trustee, and the business which the ordinary prudent man is supposed to be conducting for himself, is the business of investing money for the benefit of persons who are to enjoy it at some future time, and not for the sole benefit of the person entitled to the present income. The duty of a trustee is not to take such care only as a prudent man would take if he had only himself to consider; the duty rather is to take such care as an ordinary prudent man would take if he were minded to make an investment for the benefit of other people for whom he felt morally bound to provide. That is the kind of business the ordinary prudent man is supposed to be engaged in; and unless this is borne in mind the standard of a trustee's duty will be fixed too low.

On appeal *Learoyd v Whiteley* (1887) 12 App Cas 727 Lord Watson added, at 733:

> Business men of ordinary prudence may, and frequently do, select investments which are more or less of a speculative character; but it is the duty of a trustee to confine himself to the class of investments which are permitted by the trust, and likewise to avoid all investments of that class which are attended with hazard.

NB: The key to this case is that a brickfield is a 'depreciating asset'. The more clay that is dug out to make bricks, the less the field is worth. This is not suitable for a trust where long-term investments are usually required.

KEY POINTS

- The duty of care for a trustee is to act as a man of ordinary prudence.

- This is now restated in the Trustee Act 2000 as 'a duty to exercise such care and skill as is reasonable in the circumstances'.

Schedule 1 to the 2000 Act makes clear that the duty of care applies to investment duties, acquiring land, and employing agents. In particular, in relation to agents, the duty of care applies to:

(a) selecting the person who is to act;

(b) determining any terms on which he is to act; and

(c) preparation of a policy statement under s. 15 (see 11.11 'What is investment?').

Investment: advice and selection

As we saw earlier, the most important change in the Act is that the trustees can now invest in anything that they want. This is called 'the general power of investment'. The trustees cannot, however, do just as they please; they are under a duty of care, as we have seen, and there are a number of restrictions in the Act designed to protect the property of the beneficiaries.

11.5.1 The standard investment criteria

The trustees must have regard to the 'standard investment criteria' which are based on the old s. 6(1) of the Trustee Investment Act 1961 and modern portfolio theory. This means that they must not put all the trust funds in one investment. They must spread the investments, and how they do this depends upon the size of the trust fund and the number and type of the beneficiaries. They must also not be complacent, and should regularly check whether the investments are still profitable and still suitable.

Trustee Act 2000, s. 4

....

(2) A trustee must from time to time review the investments of the trust and consider whether, having regard to the standard investment criteria, they should be renewed.

(3) The 'standard investment criteria' are

    (a) whether a particular type of investment is suitable for the trust and whether the investment proposed is a suitable example of that type...

    (b) the need for diversification, in so far as it is appropriate to the circumstances of the trust.

....

● *Jeffery v Gretton* [2011] WTLR 809

Mrs Beken left a valuable old house on trust for her three children. The trustees did not sell the house, but tried to repair it themselves from 2002 to 2008. One of the beneficiaries, Mrs Jeffrey, claimed that the delay was a breach of trust.

HELD: Blohm QC agreed.

> Para. 69: 'However, a trustee who fails to exercise a power that he ought to exercise will be in a breach of trust. A trustee owes his beneficiaries a duty to review the trust holding from time to time—see Section 4(2) Trustee Act 2000...and if appropriate to alter the investment of the trust...
>
> In these circumstances a failure to review investments within a reasonable time would be a breach of the trustees' statutory duty. It would be all the more so if the trustees positively decided not to review their investments, or as a matter of policy not to effect any change to the investments.'

Despite the breach of trust, Mrs Jeffery could not prove that it caused her any loss. The house could have been sold for £610,000 in 2002, but was actually sold for £885,000 in 2007,

11.5.2 When trustees must seek investment advice

Trustees may not be professional and they might not be experts on investment, so they must seek expert advice.

Under s. 5 of the Trustee Act 2000, before investing, a trustee must obtain and consider proper advice. This also applies to reviewing existing investments and complying with the standard investment criteria. Proper advice is from a person who is reasonably believed to be qualified to give it by his ability in and practical experience of financial and other matters relating to the proposed investment.

In *Jeffery v Gretton* [2011] WTLR 809 (see 11.5.1) the trustees also failed to take any advice on investing the trust property.

● *Jeffery v Gretton* [2011] WTLR 809

Blohm QC at para. 72:

> I conclude that a decision by trustees to carry out works on the scale carried out over a period of six years, without taking professional advice, was in breach of the duties owed by the trustees to the beneficiaries. They should have taken professional advice on the merits of their plan to retain the property for what was going to be a very substantial length of time.

But:

Trustee Act 2000, s. 5

(3) The trustee need not obtain such advice if he reasonably concludes that in all the circumstances it is unnecessary or inappropriate to do so.

Expert advice would usually be from someone registered to give it, such as under the Financial Services and Markets Act 2000. The expertise required would depend upon what sort of investment was contemplated. For instance, land would need a surveyor; buying paintings would require an art expert!

The trustees need not seek advice if they are financial experts themselves or if the investment is so small that it is not worth paying for advice.

NB: The trustees still have their duty of care and so must exercise reasonable care and skill when deciding whether or not to seek advice. Even if they do seek advice, this does not automatically protect them from liability. They still have a duty of care in deciding whether to accept it or not, as can be seen from *Learoyd v Whiteley* (1886) LR 33 ChD 347 at 11.4 'The duty of care'.

KEY POINTS

Trustees must:

- Select the right investment.
- Diversify.
- Seek expert advice.

11.6 Excluding the Act

Settlors are still free to make their own arrangements for investment when they establish a trust. Many do and put in their own instructions on how they want the trustees to invest.

Section 6 makes it clear that the investment powers in the Act can be restricted or excluded by the trust instrument.

Trust instrument—the document that sets out the terms of the trust, identifies the trust property, specifies the beneficiaries and their beneficial interests, and names the trustees.

Even the duty of care can be excluded by the **trust instrument**. Some trusts contain clauses protecting the trustees from some kinds of legal liability if they are sued by the beneficiaries. An example can be seen in *Armitage v Nurse*.

● *Armitage v Nurse* [1997] 2 All ER 705

The following clause was held to protect the trustees unless it could be shown that they had committed fraud:

> No trustee shall be liable for any loss or damage which may happen to Paula's fund or any part thereof or the income thereof at any time or from any cause whatsoever unless such loss or damage shall be caused by his own actual fraud . . .

(See 15.6.1 'Trustee exemption clauses'.)

11.7 Effect of the Act

Section 7 states that these new investment powers apply to trusts created before or after this Act, unless there is something in the trust itself that excludes this Act, as we have just seen, or the trust is governed by another statutory regime for investment (e.g. pension funds, which are governed by the Pensions Acts 1995 and 2004).

11.8 Acquisition of land

Formerly this was not generally allowed, unless the trust was a trust of land and governed by the Trusts of Land and Appointment of Trustees Act 1996.

> **Trustee Act 2000, s. 8**
>
> (1) A trustee may acquire freehold or leasehold land in the United Kingdom
>
> (a) as an investment,
>
> (b) for occupation by a beneficiary, or
>
> (c) for any other reason.

It might be noted that this power is not restricted just to investment purposes; the trustees might, for instance, wish to buy a house for a beneficiary.

As before, the power to buy land can be restricted or excluded by the trust instrument and it applies to trusts created before or after this Act.

thinking points

In Victorian times, the courts developed the 'prudent businessman' test, in cases such as Learoyd v Whiteley *and* Speight v Gaunt, *to ascertain the duty of care when trustees chose investments for the trust. That was at a time when trustees had to choose investments from a list of authorized investments. The prudent businessman test survives in the legal systems of a number of countries, but how well does it work in an era where investment choice is near unlimited and portfolio theory prevails?*

See P Panico 'Trustee Investment Powers in International Trust Law' [2009] Trusts and Trustees 96.

11.9 The liability of trustees

11.9.1 The duty of reasonable care and skill

The trustees have a general duty of care, and if they do not fulfil it they will be liable to restore the trust fund for the beneficiaries. It is clear that they are not liable for every minor mistake, nor are they liable if they have taken reasonable care and skill and an investment still loses money. Trustees cannot be held responsible if there is a general recession.

● ***Re Chapman*** [1896] 2 Ch 763

The will of James Chapman required the trustees to invest in mortgages secured on farmland. The trustees were farmers themselves, so did not seek expert advice. There had been a prolonged agricultural depression and the value of agricultural land had continued to fall. Were the trustees liable for the fall in value of the investments? Should they have perhaps foreclosed on the mortgages and sold the land in order to recover their loan?

HELD: The trustees were not liable.

Lopes LJ at 778:

> A trustee who is honest and reasonably competent is not to be held responsible for a mere error in judgment when the question which he has to consider is whether a security of a class authorized, but depreciated in value, should be retained or realized, provided he acts with reasonable care, prudence, and circumspection.

KEY POINTS

- A trustee who acts honestly and with reasonable care will escape liability.

- This is the case even if the trust loses money.

In contrast we can consider the case of *Bartlett v Barclays Bank (No 1)* [1980] Ch 515, where the trustees were found liable.

● **Bartlett v Barclays Bank (No 1)** [1980] Ch 515

Barclays Bank was the trustee of a trust for the Bartlett family. The trust investment was 99.8 per cent of the shares in Bartletts Trust Ltd, a family company that rented properties. Money was needed to pay estate duty (now called inheritance tax). Merchant bankers advised the board of the company and the trustees that the company should invest in property development, to which the trustees agreed. The company invested in two projects, one of which at Guildford was successful. The second, involving land near the Old Bailey, caused a large loss, because the company bought land at a high price, hoping to obtain planning permission, but failed to do so. The trustees were not consulted about these developments, nor did they have a director on the board of Bartletts Trust Ltd. They were content to receive only the information received by all shareholders.

HELD: The trustees were liable for breach of trust, because they had not acted as ordinary prudent men of business. They should have insisted on receiving more information and acted upon that information.

Brightman J at 532:

> The prudent man of business will act in such manner as is necessary to safeguard his invest-ment. He will do this in two ways. If facts come to his knowledge, which tell him that the com-pany's affairs are not being conducted as they should be, or which put him on inquiry, he will take appropriate action. Appropriate action will no doubt consist in the first instance of inquiry of and consultation with the directors, and in the last but most unlikely resort, the convening of a general meeting to replace one or more directors. What the prudent man of business will *not* do is to content himself with the receipt of such information on the affairs of the company as a shareholder ordinarily receives at annual general meetings. Since he has the power to do so, he will go further and see that he has sufficient information to enable him to take a responsible decision from time to time either to let matters proceed as they are proceeding, or to intervene if he is dissatisfied.

This did not necessarily mean that the trustees should have insisted that one of them was a director on the board, but they should have found out what was being discussed at board meetings.

And at 534–5:

> Had the bank been in receipt of more frequent information it would have been able to step in and stop, and ought to have stopped, the board embarking on the Old Bailey project. That project was imprudent and hazardous and wholly unsuitable for a trust whether undertaken by the bank direct or through the medium of its wholly owned company. Even without the regular flow of information, which the bank ought to have had, it knew enough to put it on inquiry. There were enough obvious points at which the bank should have intervened and asked questions.

Similarly trustees could be liable for failing to take the necessary action.

At 546:

> Wilful default by a trustee in this context means a passive breach of trust, an omission by a trustee to do something which, as a prudent trustee, he ought to have done—as distinct from an active breach of trust, that is to say, doing something which the trustee ought not to have done.

Bartlett can be contrasted with *Nestlé v National Westminster plc*, where the trustees were not found liable. Although they could have done better, they had not actually done anything wrong.

● **Nestlé v National Westminster Bank plc** [1993] 1 WLR 1260

This case involved a trust established by Georgina Nestlé's grandfather. When the trust fund ended and the capital finally came to her, she complained to the courts that it was not as much as she had expected. She claimed that she would have had more than £1 million if it had been properly invested, but instead she inherited £269,203. Before her, the previous beneficiaries, her father and uncle, had also complained to the trustees, the National Westminster Bank plc, that their incomes would be more if different investment policies had been followed. She could show that the trustees had not reviewed the investment portfolio between 1922 and 1959 and that the trustees had not realized the full extent of their investment powers. They had invested in bank and insurance firm shares, when they could have diversified more.

HELD: Leggatt LJ outlined the legal duties of trustees regarding investment at 1282:

> There is no dispute about the nature of the bank's duty. It was, as Lindley LJ has expressed it, a duty 'to take such care as an ordinary prudent man would take if he were minded to make an investment for the benefit of other people for whom he felt morally bound to provide': *Re Whiteley* (1886) 33 ChD 347 at 355. The trustee must have regard 'not only to the interests of those who are entitled to the income, but to the interests of those who will take in future': per Cotton LJ at 350. 'A trustee must not choose investments other than those which the terms of his trust permit': *Speight v Gaunt* (1883) 9 App Cas 1 at 19 (Lord Blackburn). So confined the trustee must avoid all investments of that class which are attended with hazard': *Learoyd v Whiteley* (1887) 12 App Cas 727 at 733 (Lord Watson). The power of investment 'must be exercised so as to yield the best return for the beneficiaries, judged in relation to the risks of the investments in question; and the prospects of the yield of income and capital appreciation both have to be considered in judging the return from the investment': *Cowan v Scargill* [1985] Ch 270 at 287.
>
> It is common ground that a trustee with a power of investment must undertake periodic reviews of the investments held by the trust. In relation to this trust, that would have meant a review carried out at least annually, and whenever else a reappraisal of the trust portfolio was requested or was otherwise requisite.

Miss Nestlé had to prove that the trustees had caused a loss to the trust.

At 1283:

> In this context I would endorse the concession of Mr Nugee for the bank that 'loss' will be incurred by a trust fund when it makes a gain less than would have been made by a prudent businessman.

The judge looked at the investments made and considered expert evidence, and accepted that (at 1284–5):

> ...the bank did no less than expected of it up to the death of the testator's widow in 1960...
>
> No testator, in the light of this example, would choose this bank for the effective management of his investment. But the bank's engagement was as a trustee; and as such, it is to be judged not so much by success as by absence of proven default. The importance of preservation of a trust fund will always outweigh success in its advancement. Inevitably, a trustee in the bank's position wears a complacent air, because the virtue of safety will in practice put a premium on inactivity. Until the 1950s active management of the portfolio might have been seen as speculative, and even in these days such dealing would have to be notably successful before the expense would be justified. The very process of attempting to achieve a balance, or (if that be old-fashioned) fairness, as between the interests of life-tenants and those of a

remainderman inevitably means that each can complain of being less well served than he or she ought to have been. But by the undemanding standard of prudence the bank is not shown to have committed any breach of trust resulting in loss.

KEY POINTS

- So in *Bartlett* a risky, but potentially very lucrative, investment was tried. It went wrong, so the trustees were liable.

- In *Nestlé* they took no risks and so escaped liability.

11.9.2 The extent of trustees' liability

The consequences of a breach of trust are severe for the trustees. They are personally liable and must restore the trust fund to what it would have been but for their breach.

● ***Bartlett v Barclays Bank (No 2)*** [1980] Ch 515

Brightman J at 535:

> I hold that the bank failed in its duty whether it is judged by the standard of the prudent man of business or of the skilled trust corporation. The bank's breach of duty caused the loss, which was suffered by the trust estate. If the bank had intervened as it could and should have that loss would not have been incurred. By 'loss', I mean the depreciation, which took place in the market value of the BT shares, by comparison with the value, which the shares would have commanded if the loss on the Old Bailey project had not been incurred, and reduction of dividends through loss of income. The bank is liable for the loss so suffered by the trust estate, except to the extent that I shall hereafter indicate.

The meaning of the order made by Brightman J was disputed and the matter came back to court for Brightman, now a Lord Justice of Appeal, to explain further. Barclays Bank was disputing the valuation of the shares by saying that they should be valued according to what they were worth in 1974, when the Bartlett trust ended, rather than at their 1978 value when the shares were finally sold. Similarly, the bank wanted to value each beneficiary's shareholding separately. This too would mean that they were worth less than if they were all valued together, because together they would give control over the company. Barclays also wanted to deduct the tax that the plaintiffs would have had to pay on their shares. Brightman LJ disagreed with the arguments of the bank and gave the Bartletts the benefit of the full valuation. He said at 543:

> In my judgment such an approach is unrealistic and wrong. As I have said, the obligation of the defaulting trustee is essentially that of restitution. It was plain from the evidence, and I hold, that a beneficiary properly advised would not have sold his shareholding on its own and without regard to its value as a proportion of the total assets of the company. The unwinding of the Old Bailey speculation removed an impediment to such en bloc realisation, and the sale to Phoenix followed very shortly thereafter. I reject the defendant's submissions.

And at 545:

> My reasoning is this: the obligation of a trustee who is held liable for breach of trust is fundamentally different from the obligation of a contractual or tortious wrongdoer. The trustee's obligation is to restore to the trust estate the assets of which he has deprived it.

The liability of trustees for breach of trust generally was reconsidered in the House of Lords case that follows.

● **Target Holdings v Redfern** [1996] 1 AC 421

Target Holdings lent £1,525,000 to Crowngate, so that Crowngate could buy a commercial property. Target lost money because the property was massively overvalued and was only worth £500,000. Redferns were the solicitors in the transaction and had held the money, which was only to be released upon the completion of the conveyance. This is regarded as a trust (held for Target) and is standard practice for solicitors. Unfortunately, Redferns had released the money too early, before completion, and this was a breach of trust.

HELD: Redferns was not liable, as its breach of trust had not caused the loss to Target. The loss was caused by the overvaluation, which was not the responsibility of Redferns.

The court made a distinction between 'traditional' trusts, intended to provide for a family, and commercial cases such as this one. There was no right to have a client account at a solicitors reconstituted, when the breach had not caused any loss.

There is no suggestion in the judgment that this is intended to change the liability of trustees for the investments that they make.

Lord Browne-Wilkinson said at 434:

> The basic right of a beneficiary is to have the trust duly administered in accordance with the provisions of the trust instrument, if any, and the general law. Thus, in relation to a traditional trust where the fund is held in trust for a number of beneficiaries having different, usually successive, equitable interests (e.g. A for life with remainder to B), the right of each beneficiary is to have the whole fund vested in the trustees so as to be available to satisfy his equitable interest when, and if, it falls into possession. Accordingly, in the case of a breach of such a trust involving the wrongful paying away of trust assets, the liability of the trustee is to restore to the trust fund, often called 'the trust estate', what ought to have been there.
>
> The equitable rules of compensation for breach of trust have been largely developed in relation to such traditional trusts, where the only way in which all the beneficiaries' rights can be protected is to restore to the trust fund what ought to be there. In such a case the basic rule is that a trustee in breach of trust must restore or pay to the trust estate either the assets, which have been lost to the estate by reason of the breach, or compensation for such loss. Courts of Equity did not award damages but, acting in personam, ordered the defaulting trustee to restore the trust estate: see *Nocton v Lord Ashburton* [1914] AC 932, 952, 958, per Viscount Haldane LC. If specific restitution of the trust property is not possible, then the liability of the trustee is to pay sufficient compensation to the trust estate to put it back to what it would have been had the breach not been committed: *Caffrey v Darby* (1801) 6 Ves 488; *Clough v Bond* (1838) 3 M & C 490. Even if the immediate cause of the loss is the dishonesty or failure of a third party, the trustee is liable to make good that loss to the trust estate if, but for the breach, such loss would not have occurred: see Underhill and Hayton, *Law of Trusts & Trustees* 14th edn (1987) pp 734–6; In re Dawson, decd.; *Union Fidelity Trustee Co Ltd v Perpetual Trustee Co Ltd* [1966] 2 NSWR 211; *Bartlett v Barclays Bank Trust Co Ltd (Nos 1 and 2)* [1980] Ch 515. Thus the common law rules of remoteness of damage and causation do not apply. However there does have to be some causal connection between the breach of trust and the loss to the trust estate for which compensation is recoverable, viz the fact that the loss would not have occurred but for the breach: see also *In re Miller's Deed Trusts* [1978] 75 LSG 454; *Nestlé v National Westminster Bank plc* [1993] 1 WLR 1260.

But Lord Browne-Wilkinson was unwilling to extend this approach to the special situation of this case where the solicitors were only temporarily holding the money on trust until it could be paid to the seller.

Lord Browne-Wilkinson was making a distinction between the traditional family trust, where funds were dedicated to provide for that family, and trusts used in commercial dealings. He was not suggesting that rules about causation of damage should change for these family trusts, which would always involve investment. It does highlight, however, the punitive consequences of breach of duty for trustees: full restoration of the trust fund. *Target Holdings v Redfern* [1996] 1 AC 421 has been confirmed by the Supreme Court in *AIB Group (UK) plc v Mark Redler & Co Solicitors* [2014] 3 WLR 1367. (See 15.3 'Equitable compensation'.)

Ethical investment

Some private persons prefer not to invest in industries of which they morally disapprove. These industries might include things such as military industries, gambling, alcohol, or even newspapers. We have already seen that the duty of trustees is to make money for their beneficiaries, so could trustees adopt an 'ethical investment' policy? On a superficial reading the case law might suggest that they cannot, but the point the judges are making is subtler than that. In *Cowan v Scargill* [1985] Ch 270, which we saw at the start of this chapter (see 11.1 'What is investment?'), it was made clear that trustees' normal duty was to make money from the trust investments and secure the best financial return for the beneficiaries, without putting the trust fund at risk. This was the 'first point' that Megarry VC made.

· ·

● *Cowan v Scargill* [1985] Ch 270

HELD: Megarry VC at 287–8:

> This leads me to the second point, which is a corollary of the first. In considering what investments to make trustees must put on one side their own personal interests and views. Trustees may have strongly held social or political views. They may be firmly opposed to any investment in South Africa or other countries, or they may object to any form of investment in companies concerned with alcohol, tobacco, armaments or many other things. In the conduct of their own affairs, of course, they are free to abstain from making any such investments. Yet under a trust, if investments of this type would be more beneficial to the beneficiaries than other investments, the trustees must not refrain from making the investments by reasons of the views that they hold.

Megarry VC was ruling that the mineworkers' proposed investment policy would be unlawful. The purpose of this trust was to provide pensions for *retired* miners, their widows, and children. What they wanted was financial benefits from the trust and that they got their pensions paid. Whether the coal industry survived or not was not relevant to this trust.

He was not, however, saying that ethical investment was always unlawful.

At 288 he said:

> Third, by way of caveat I should say that I am not asserting that the benefit of the beneficiaries which a trustee must make his paramount concern inevitably and solely means their financial benefit, even if the only object of the trust is to provide financial benefits. Thus if the

only actual or potential beneficiaries of a trust are all adults with very strict views on moral and social matters, condemning all forms of alcohol, tobacco and popular entertainment, as well as armaments, I can well understand that it might not be for the 'benefit' of such beneficiaries to know that they are obtaining rather larger financial returns under the trust by reason of investments in those activities than they would have received if the trustees had invested the trust fund in other investments. The beneficiaries might well consider that it was far better to receive less than to receive more money from what they consider to be evil and tainted sources.

What Megarry VC meant by these last remarks was explained in a subsequent case.

● ***Harries v Church Commissioners*** [1992] 1 WLR 1241

The Church Commissioners are the trustees of the Church of England. They already had an ethical investment policy and already avoided investments in armaments, gambling, alcohol, tobacco, and newspapers. Harries, who was the Bishop of Oxford, wanted an even more ethical policy, which would promote the Christian faith.

HELD: Nicholls VC at 1247:

> Trustees may, if they wish, accommodate the views of those who consider that on moral grounds a particular investment would be in conflict with the objects of the charity, so long as the trustees are satisfied that course would not involve a risk of significant financial detriment.

And at 1249:

> The commissioners' investment policy is set out in their annual report for 1989...As regards our Stock Exchange holdings this means that we do not invest in companies whose main business is armaments, gambling, alcohol, tobacco and newspapers.

And at 1250:

> It will be seen, therefore, that the commissioners do have an 'ethical' investment policy.
>
> As I understand the position, the commissioners have felt able to exclude these items from their investments despite the conflicting views on the morality of holding those items as investments because there has remained open to the commissioners an adequate width of alternative investments.

KEY POINT

Ethical investment is legal as long as the profit motive is not neglected.

thinking points

The Law Commission gave guidance on this area of law. Trustees may not impose their own ethical views on the beneficiaries. They must ensure that the beneficiaries share their ethical concerns and not risk significant financial detriment. Environmental, social, or governance concerns might affect a company's long-term profitability, which would be a financial factor of which the trustees should take account. Does this advice go far enough to promote ethical business practices?

See 'Fiduciary Duties of Investment Intermediaries' particularly the Appendix 'Is it Always About the Money' Law Commission No. 350 <http://lawcommission.justice.gov.uk/areas/fiduciary_duties.htm>.

11.11 Delegation

11.11.1 The old case law

Trustees may not want or be able to carry out all the functions of running a trust. They may wish to employ people like solicitors, accountants, or investment specialists and pay them for their services out of the trust fund. Long before there were any Acts of Parliament on this subject the courts had permitted this.

There was an attempt to codify this case law in the Trustee Act 1925.

Trustee Act 1925

. . . .

Section 23

(1) Trustees may...instead of acting personally, employ and pay an agent...to do any act required in execution of the trust...*and shall not be responsible for the default of any such agent* if employed in good faith.

Section 30

(1) A trustee shall be chargeable only for money and securities actually received by him...and shall be answerable only for his own...defaults and not for those of any other trustee, nor for any banker, broker, or other person with whom any trust money or securities may be deposited...nor for any other loss, unless the same happens through his own wilful default.

The curious wording of s. 23 caused problems. The section was probably intended to widen the situations in which trustees could employ agents. But if it is read literally (see the italicized words above), it seems to excuse the trustees from all liability for what the agent does unless the trustee knows that the agent was at fault or just does not care what the agent is doing. This was not at all the position under the previous law, where the trustees had to behave as ordinary prudent men of business. (See 11.4 'The duty of care'.)

. . . .

● *Re Vickery* [1931] 1 Ch 572

The executor of Mrs Vickery's will, Stephens, a missionary, was ignorant of business affairs, so he employed a solicitor to administer the estate. Unknown to Stephens, the solicitor, Jennens, had once been suspended from practice. After a year of inaction by the solicitor and the warnings of the beneficiaries, the sons of Mrs Vickery, Stephens replaced Jennens with another solicitor. By then it was too late, for Jennens had absconded with the estate of about £300.

HELD: Maugham J did not use the 'ordinary prudent man of business' test, but instead relied on the words of the Act, which excused the executor from liability.

At 581:

> It is hardly too much to say that it revolutionizes the position of a trustee or executor so far as regards the employment of agents. He is no longer required to do any actual work himself, but he may employ a solicitor or other agent to do it, whether there is any real necessity for the employment or not.

> No doubt he should use his discretion in selecting an agent, and should employ him only to do acts within the scope of the usual business of the agent; but, as will be seen, a question arises whether even in these respects he is personally liable for a loss due to the employment of the agent unless he has been guilty of wilful default.

And at 583–4:

> But for the reasons which I have given I think that, where an executor employs a solicitor or other agent to receive money belonging to the estate in reliance on s. 23 (1) ..., he will not be liable for a loss of the money occasioned by misconduct of the agent unless the loss happens through the wilful default of the executor, using those words as implying, as the Court of Appeal have decided, either a consciousness of negligence or breach of duty, or recklessness in the performance of a duty.

This proved to be a controversial decision, academically at least, and it was one of the stated objectives of the Trustee Act 2000 to make it clear that trustees would be liable for the actions of their agents.

11.11.2 Trustee functions that can be delegated

The Trustee Act 2000 attempts to clarify what trustees can delegate and how they should supervise and control what their 'agents' do. This applies to situations where the trustees *collectively* delegate their functions. *Individual* trustees wishing to delegate their functions still use s. 25 of the Trustee Act 1925.

Nowadays many trustees would wish to employ 'professionals' to carry out investment functions, and the Act is designed to encourage this by making the legal position clearer.

The old view was that trustees could not delegate their decisions on the distribution of property or decisions of a fiduciary nature, such as the selection of investments. These distinctions were not very clear. The new law states what *cannot* be delegated.

Trustee Act 2000, s. 11

In non-charitable trusts the trustees may authorise any person to exercise any or all of their delegable functions as their agent. They *cannot* delegate:

(a) any function relating to the way trust assets should be distributed,

(b) any power to decide on fees or payments out of the income or capital,

(c) any power to appoint trustees,

(d) any power to delegate in the trust instrument.

Therefore, trustees *can* delegate anything else, such as investment decisions.

You may note that crucial decisions on the distribution of trust property to beneficiaries, such as decisions on 'pay-outs' to beneficiaries (a) or maintenance or advancement (b), cannot be delegated to agents. (See Chapter 12 'Maintenance and advancement and protective trusts' for maintenance and advancement.)

Charitable trusts are treated differently and here trustees are told which functions they *can* delegate. These are:

1. any function consisting of carrying out a decision taken by the trustees;

2. any function relating to the investment of assets of the trust, including land;

KEY POINT
Trustees are
allowed to
delegate
investment
decisions.

3. any function relating to the raising of funds for the trust, unless these are the profits of a trade which is an integral part of carrying out the trust's charitable purpose.

Therefore, charitable trustees can delegate investment and fundraising functions, but not decisions upon how the trust money should be distributed.

11.11.3 The terms upon which agents are employed

Under s. 12 a trustee can be an agent, but a beneficiary cannot. If there are two or more agents they must exercise their function jointly.

Section 14 states that trustees are permitted to pay the agent(s) and to set the terms. The Act recognizes that the trustees may have to agree to terms, which are not to the advantage of the trust, because no agent would otherwise take the work, i.e. the agent is allowed to appoint a substitute, the agent is allowed to restrict his liability, or the agent might have a conflict of interest.

If the agent is engaged in 'asset management functions', i.e. investment, acquisition of property, or management of trust property, the trustees must draw up an agreement, evidenced in writing, with the agent. This would include a 'policy statement' to which the agent must agree. This statement is guidance for the agent upon how to act in the best interests of the trust.

It is anticipated that the 'policy statement' would cover matters such as ethical investment, types of investment permitted, income yield, capital growth, etc.

KEY POINTS

- There must be a written agreement between the trustees and the agent.

- There must also be a 'policy statement' to guide the agent on how to invest the trust funds.

The Act then goes on to detail how trustees may appoint nominees and custodians under broadly similar conditions. In all these situations the trustees still retain liability for the actions of nominees, custodians, and agents.

11.11.4 Trustees must supervise their agent

Section 21 allows the trust instrument to exclude or restrict the trustees' liability. (See 11.6 'Excluding the Act'.) Otherwise, the Act applies:

Under s. 22 the trustees must check what their agents, custodians, or nominees are doing and if they discover a problem must act.

Trustee Act 2000, s. 22

(1) The trustees

  (a) must keep under review the arrangement under which the agent . . . acts and how those arrangements are being put into effect,

  (b) if circumstances make it appropriate to do so, must consider whether there is a need to exercise any power of *intervention* that they have, and

  (c) if they consider that there is a need to exercise such a power, must do so.

This would seem to give statutory approval to the old case of *Rowland v Witherden*.

Witherden was one of the trustees of a trust for the Rowland family. In 1838 the trustees employed a solicitor, Jenner, and handed over the trust funds to him, so that he could invest the trust funds on a mortgage loan. Jenner did not do this, but kept the money for himself. As he regularly paid what seemed to be the interest on the loan to Mrs Rowland, it was not until 1847 that the trustees discovered what had really happened.

HELD: The trustees were liable. They had not made sufficient checks on the solicitor. Accepting his assurances was not enough; they should have at least checked that there actually was a mortgage deed.

This principle is reinforced by the rest of s. 22(2) and (4) of the Trustee Act 2000.

KEY POINT

The trustees must check what the agent is doing and intervene if necessary.

Trustee Act 2000, s. 22

. . . .

(2) Trustees have:

    (a) a duty to consider whether there is any need to revise or replace the policy statement made for the purposes of section 15,

    (b) if they consider that there is a need to revise or replace the policy statement a duty to do so, and

    (c) a duty to assess whether the policy statement . . . is being complied with.

. . .

(4) Power of intervention includes—

    (a) a power to give directions to the agent . . .

    (b) a power to revoke the authorisation or appointment.

11.11.5 The liability of the trustees for their agent

Section 23 of the Trustee Act 2000 repeals the old ss. 23 and 30 of the Trustee Act 1925, which as interpreted in *Re Vickery* [1931] 1 Ch 572 (see 11.11.1 'The old case law') excused trustees from most of their liability when employing agents. The idea now is, put simply, that the 'duty of care' in s. 1 of the 2000 Act applies.

Trustee Act 2000, s. 23

. . . .

(1) A trustee is not liable for any act or default of the agent, nominee or custodian unless he has failed to comply with the duty of care applicable to him . . .

    (a) when entering into the arrangements under which the person acts as agent . . . ,

    (b) when carrying out the duties of review under s. 22.

(2) The same applies if the agent etc. is allowed to use a substitute.

Some older case law gives useful guidance upon how the trustees might conduct the employment of agents with 'reasonable care and skill'.

● *Speight v Gaunt* (1883–84) LR 9 App Cas 1

Gaunt was made a trustee in the will of Speight. He was authorized by the trust to invest in municipal corporations, but unfortunately he knew nothing about the technical side of investment. So Gaunt went to the firm of stockbrokers that Speight had used in his lifetime and employed Cooke. Gaunt handed over trust funds to Cooke, but Cooke did not make the investments and took £15,000 from the trust. The money could not be recovered from Cooke, because he was now bankrupt, so was Gaunt responsible for the loss?

The court had accepted evidence that a person experienced in investment would have realized what Cooke was really doing, but that there was nothing that an 'ordinary prudent man of business' would have detected.

HELD: The House of Lords accepted that Gaunt was not liable for the loss. Employing an agent to invest and handing over trust money to the agent were both the 'usual mode of conducting business'. Gaunt had at all times acted with 'reasonable care and prudence'.

Earl of Selborne LC at 4:

> In the early case of *Ex parte Belchier*, before Lord Hardwicke, it was determined that trustees are not bound personally to transact such business connected with or arising out of the proper duties of the trust, as, according to the usual mode of business of a like nature, persons acting with reasonable care and prudence on their own account would ordinarily conduct through mercantile agents;
>
> and that when, according to the usual and regular course of business, moneys receivable or payable ought to pass through the hands of such mercantile agents, that course may properly be followed by trustees, though the moneys are trust moneys;
>
> and that if, under such circumstances, and without any other misconduct or default on the part of the trustees, a loss takes place through any fraud or neglect of the agents employed, the trustees are not liable to make good such loss.

KEY POINT
The trustees must supervise their agent with reasonable care and skill.

The trustees cannot just employ anybody to make investment decisions. They must use reasonable care and skill to select a suitably qualified person.

343

● *Fry v Tapson* (1885) 28 Ch 268

The trustees lent money secured on the mortgage of a house in Toxteth Park, Liverpool. The trustees had used solicitors to arrange this and they, in their turn, had employed a valuer who received a commission when he found a suitable property. The valuer had given the house a glowing report, although the valuers were not local and there was no evidence that they had ever visited Liverpool. The mortgage loan could not be repaid and the house was not worth enough to cover the loan. The trust lost £5,000.

KEY POINT
A suitable agent must be selected with reasonable care and skill.

HELD: The trustees were liable for the loss caused by their breach of trust. The agents that they employed, the solicitors, were not employed in their 'ordinary course of business'. Selling the house and selecting a valuer were not normal tasks for a solicitor. A 'prudent man of business' would not have used a valuer who had a financial stake in having his recommendation accepted, nor was his report a proper report.

thinking points

The Trustee Act 2000 might seem like a pretty radical overhaul of the law on trustee investments, but it is in fact built on the principles of the older case law. The law has had to be adapted to recognize that trusts are no longer just used to provide for a family and that investment opportunities are international. A comprehensive review of all parts of the Trustee Act 2000 can be found in LM Clements 'Bringing Trusts into the Twenty-First Century' [2004] 2 Web JCLI.

11.12 Information for the beneficiaries

When the Trustee Bill was proceeding through Parliament, there were attempts to amend it in order to give more protection to the beneficiaries. These attempts failed. The beneficiaries have limited rights to information from the trustees and the trustees do not have to explain or justify their decisions to the beneficiaries. The reason for this is that the courts wish to protect trustees from being 'harassed' by the beneficiaries, otherwise no one would want to be a trustee!

Under s. 22(4) of the Trustee Act 1925 the trustees may pay out of trust funds for the trust accounts to be audited and examined by an independent accountant. There are similar provisions in s. 13 of the Public Trustee Act 1906, where the beneficiaries have the right to see audited accounts of the trust fund. This is extended in the traditional case law to the right to see 'trust documents'.

11.12.1 The beneficiaries have the right to see trust documents

● ***Re Londonderry's Settlement*** [1965] Ch 918

This was a trust that was established by the 7th Marquis of Londonderry to provide for his family. Under the terms of the trust, the trustees were allowed to distribute the income to the family, appoint to the family and finally distribute the capital among the family and end the trust. They decided to divide the capital among the family. The daughter of the Marquis, Lady Helen Maglona Walsh, was dissatisfied with her share and that of her children. She wanted to know how the trustees had made their decision, so she asked to see various documents, which would have revealed the shares given to other beneficiaries.

HELD: The beneficiaries had the right to see 'trust documents', but the trustees were not obliged to give reasons for their decisions.

Harman LJ explained why at 928–9:

> I have found this a difficult case. It raises what in my judgment is a novel question on which there is no authority exactly in point although several cases have been cited to us somewhere near it. The court is really required here to resolve two principles that come into conflict, or at least apparent conflict. The first is that, as the defendant beneficiary admits, trustees exercising a discretionary power are not bound to disclose to their beneficiaries the reasons actuating them in coming to a decision. This is a long-standing principle and rests largely I think on the view that nobody could be called upon to accept a trusteeship involving the exercise of

a discretion unless, in the absence of bad faith, he were not liable to have his motives or his reasons called in question either by the beneficiaries or by the court. To this there is added a rider, namely that if trustees do give reasons, their soundness can be considered by the court.

Lady Walsh was entitled to see written summaries of the state of the fund (valuations) and letters from the solicitors to the trustees. She was not allowed to see the trustees' letters to other beneficiaries. An older case, which stated that trust documents belonged to the beneficiaries, was quoted, but not fully endorsed, as the phrase 'trust document' was not defined.

● **O'Rourke v Darbishire** [1920] AC 581

Lord Wrenbury at 626–7:

If the plaintiff is right in saying that he is a beneficiary and if the documents are documents belonging to the executors as executors, he has a right of access to the documents which he desires to inspect upon what has been called in the judgments in this case a proprietary right. The beneficiary is entitled to see all trust documents because they are trust documents and because he is a beneficiary. They are in this sense his own. Action or no action, he is entitled to access to them.

11.12.2 Beneficiaries have no automatic right to information

The names of the trustees are not something that the general public is entitled to know. A beneficiary might be entitled to this information, but as the following case illustrates, it is not an automatic right.

● **Re Murphy's Settlements** [1998] 3 All ER 1

John Murphy thought that he might be a beneficiary under various trusts established by his father, also called John Murphy, and his mother. To find out, he wanted to know the names and addresses of the trustees. His father would not tell him.

HELD: This was a discretionary trust, but the judge thought that his request was reasonable, and as he was one of the children it was likely that he was a beneficiary.

The Privy Council reconsidered the rights of beneficiaries to information in the following case.

● **Schmidt v Rosewood Trust** [2003] 3 All ER 76 (PC)

This case was an appeal from the Isle of Man and involved 'offshore trusts' set up there by directors of the Russian oil company Lukoil. Like many of these trusts it was designed with maximum secrecy. The settlors were companies and a network of companies held the trust property, so it would be hard for anyone to discover what property was actually held on trust. These were discretionary trusts with very wide categories of beneficiaries amongst whom the trustees could choose. Vitali Schmidt had been one of the directors of Lukoil, but had died in 1996. His son, Vadim Schmidt, was trying to recover his and his father's share of these trusts and wanted to see various trust documents.

HELD: The Privy Council found in his favour, but remitted the case to the Isle of Man for the court there to rule on exactly which documents he could see. They were unwilling to lay down any general rule as to what a beneficiary could see and did not think that there was any 'proprietary right' to 'trust documents'.

Lord Walker at 91:

> Their Lordships consider the more principled and correct approach is to regard the right to seek disclosure of trust documents as one aspect of the court's inherent jurisdiction to supervise, and if necessary to intervene in, the administration of trusts. The right to seek the court's intervention does not depend on entitlement to a fixed and transmissible beneficial interest. The object of a discretion (including a mere power) may also be entitled to protection from a court of equity, although the circumstances in which he may seek protection, and the nature of the protection he may expect to obtain, will depend upon the court's discretion.

The court would have to take all the circumstances into account.

At 93:

> There are three such areas in which the court may have to form a discretionary judgment: whether a discretionary object (or some other beneficiary with only a remote or wholly defeasible interest) should be granted relief at all; what classes of documents should be disclosed, either completely or in a redacted form; and what safeguards should be imposed (whether by undertakings to the court, arrangements for professional inspection, or otherwise) to limit the use which may be made of documents or information disclosed under the order of the court.

In other words, the Privy Council was unwilling to recognize that beneficiaries had any general right to information, perhaps because this was a discretionary trust. The beneficiaries have a right to see basic trust information, such as the accounts, as we saw in *Re Londonderry's Settlement* [1965] Ch 918, but even there they were not entitled to see information that might indicate how the trustees exercised their discretion, because, as we shall see in 11.12.3 'Trustees are not obliged to give reasons for their decisions', the trustees are not obliged to give reasons to the beneficiaries for their decisions. Discretionary trusts are common nowadays and settlors often give the trustees a 'letter of wishes', on how they want their trustees to exercise their discretion. Can the beneficiaries see the letter of wishes? This was considered in *Breakspear v Ackland* [2009] Ch 32.

● ***Breakspear v Ackland*** [2009] Ch 32

Towards the end of his life, Basil Dunning, the father, settled a discretionary trust for his children and third wife. He included a 'letter of wishes' that he had given to the trustees. Some of the children wanted to see this document but, after taking legal advice, the trustees refused, on the grounds that it would cause family discord to reveal its contents.

HELD: Briggs J: It would be unusual to refuse to allow beneficiaries to see the trust instrument.

At para 60:

> The trust deed is a document which confers and identifies the trustees' powers. There is, in principle, nothing confidential about the existence and precise boundaries of those powers.

The letter of wishes was, however, different, as the trustees' discretionary decisions, about appointing trust property to beneficiaries, might well be based upon it. It should remain confidential.

Briggs J at para 24:

> ...that the process of the exercise of discretionary dispositive powers by trustees is inherently confidential exists for the benefit of beneficiaries rather than merely for the protection of trustees.

If the beneficiaries wanted to see the letter of wishes, against the view of the trustees, the beneficiaries would have to show that the trustees' decisions were in bad faith or unfair. If the trustees gave reasons for their decision not to disclose the letter, as the trustees had done here, then the court could examine those reasons. The judge accepted their reasons for non-disclosure of the letter of wishes.

KEY POINTS

- *Londonderry* is to be preferred in most types of trust: the beneficiaries have a right to see the basic trust documentation.

- *Schmidt* applies to discretionary trusts where there are many beneficiaries who might receive nothing under the trust.

(See Chapter 4 'Trusts and powers and the three certainties' for discretionary trusts.)

11.12.3 Trustees are not obliged to give reasons for their decisions

The thinking behind non-disclosure is that the trustees are not obliged to give reasons to the beneficiaries or explain to them why they have taken particular decisions. This has been long established in the case law.

● ***Re Beloved Wilkes Charity*** [1851] 3 Mac & G 440

This was a charitable trust under which the trustees were to select a boy to be educated at Oxford in preparation for him to become a Minister of the Church of England. The trust stated that they should select a boy from four named parishes if a fit and proper candidate could be found there. In fact they selected a boy who did not come from these parishes after his brother, a Minister, had sought assistance from the trustees. The trustees did not give any reason for their choice.

HELD: The trustees did not have to give a reason and the plaintiff would have to produce some evidence of bad motives.

Lord Truro LC at 448:

> The duty of supervision on the part of this Court will thus be confined to the question of the honesty, integrity and fairness with which the deliberation has been conducted, and will not be extended to the accuracy of the conclusion arrived at, except in particular cases. If, however,...trustees think fit to state a reason, and the reason is one which does not justify their conclusion, then the Court may say that they have acted by mistake and in error, and that it will correct their decision; but if, without entering into details, they simply state, as in many cases it would be most prudent and judicious for them to do, that they have met and considered and come to a conclusion, the Court has then no means of saying that they have failed in their duty, or to consider the accuracy of their conclusion.

Trustees are not obliged to give a reason, but if they do, the courts can examine the reason given. The rule that trustees are not obliged to give reasons has been confirmed in the modern case law, even in a case involving a pension fund.

● *Wilson v Law Debenture Trust Corp plc* [1995] 2 All ER 337

Wilson and Clarke were employees of Chloride and members of the company pension scheme. The company was sold to CMP Batteries and the trustees of the pension scheme, Law Debenture, transferred enough money to cover employees' past service to CMP's pension scheme. Law Debenture had also built up a considerable surplus in the Chloride fund and did not transfer it to the new scheme. Wilson and Clarke questioned this decision and wanted to see the trust documents for an explanation.

HELD: The court refused to order disclosure and cited *Re Londonderry* and *Re Beloved Wilkes* with approval. A quotation from *Re Londonderry* was adopted:

Salmon LJ [1965] Ch 918 at 936:

> Nothing would be more likely to embitter family feelings and the relationship between the trustees and members of the family than that the trustees should be obliged to state their reasons for the exercise of the powers entrusted to them. It might indeed well be difficult to persuade any persons to act as trustees were a duty to disclose their reasons, with all the embarrassment, arguments and quarrels that might ensue, added to their present not inconsiderable burdens.

KEY POINT So in conclusion we could say that the trustees are left to run the trust in the best interests of the beneficiaries, but the trustees do not have to explain to the beneficiaries what they are doing or justify the choices they have made to them. It is thought that it is best to allow the trustees to do their work without interference by the beneficiaries.

There is a very limited exception to this in the Trusts of Land and Appointment of Trustees Act 1996, which provides for trustees to consult the beneficiaries. It only applies to trusts involving land as the subject matter and can be excluded in the trust document (the 'disposition').

Trusts of Land and Appointment of Trustees Act 1996

11 Consultation with beneficiaries

(1) The trustees shall in the exercise of any function relating to land subject to the trust—

    (a) so far as practicable, consult the beneficiaries of full age and beneficially entitled to an interest in possession in the land, and

    (b) so far as consistent with the general interest of the trust, give effect to the wishes of those beneficiaries, or (in case of dispute) of the majority (according to the value of their combined interests).

(2) Subsection (1) does not apply—

    (a) in relation to a trust created by a disposition in so far as provision that it does not apply is made by the disposition,

    (b) in relation to a trust created or arising under a will made before the commencement of this Act, . . .

> **thinking points**
>
> Schmidt v Rosewood *seems to say that what the beneficiaries can see is in the discretion of the trustees. It is argued that this does not change their right to see basic information, such as the trust instrument and the trust accounts, as in* Re Londonderry. *Gavin Lightman argues that more emphasis should be placed on the beneficiaries' rights to see information, because otherwise they cannot properly enforce the trust against the trustees. They should even be allowed to see 'letters of wishes', contrary to the later decision of* Breakspear v Ackland. *See G Lightman 'The Trustees' Duty to Provide Information to Beneficiaries' [2004]* Private Client Business *23.*

 # Conclusion

The trustees have a basic duty to invest the trust property. That duty is not defined by statute, although the case of *Cowan v Scargill* [1985] 1 Ch 270 provides some guidance. The Trustee Act 2000 now contains most of the law on this subject, repealing older legislation such as the Trustee Investment Act 1961. The trustees must use reasonable care and skill as they carry out their investment duties and can make any kind of investment as though the property was their own. This is a marked contrast with the older legislation which strictly limited the types of investment that trustees could make. Bear this in mind when reading the older cases. Trustees must obtain suitable advice and can employ professional investment advisers to help them in their tasks. Delegating to agents has been modernized and, hopefully, simplified by the Trustee Act 2000 and rids us of the problem caused by the old case of *Re Vickery* [1931] 1 Ch 572. Last, but not least, many settlors stipulate their own rules for investment, when they establish a trust, and can 'opt out' of the Act. So if you are looking at a real trust document it will probably contain detailed clauses on how the trustees should invest, which may be different from what is explained in this chapter.

 # Questions

Self-test questions

1 What is the duty of care of the trustees under the common law and under the Trustee Act 2000?

2 What types of property may trustees invest in?

3 When should trustees seek advice?

4 What other duties do trustees have when selecting investments?

5 When can a trustee employ an agent?

6 How should a trustee supervise an agent?

7 What does a trustee have to tell a beneficiary?

Discussion questions

1 Consider whether there is enough guidance in the Trustee Act 2000 for non-professional trustees to be able to invest in a manner that is both profitable and does not endanger the trust property.

2 Does the law give sufficient rights to beneficiaries? What sort of rights should beneficiaries have?

3 Is the liability that trustees have for their agents now clearly defined in law?

Assessment question

Greta has the life interest in her family trust, the Cadbury Trust. The remainder is shared between her brothers and sisters and their children.

Greta is dissatisfied with the income that she receives from the trust of £100,000 per year. She asks the trustees for more information on how the trust fund is invested and why it is producing so little income for her. Tim and Tom, the trustees, send her a copy of the trust accounts, but refuse to give Greta any other information.

Greta learns from the accounts that all the trust fund is invested in shares in the family property company, Cadbury and Co, and in a house, Cadbury House, where her mother, Dolores, lives. Dolores is not a beneficiary of the trust.

Greta also learns that Phillip, a solicitor who has been banned from legal practice, in fact undertakes the running of the trust, including investment decisions.

Greta thinks that the trustees are not running the trust correctly and seeks your advice.

Advise Greta.

Key cases

- *Cowan v Scargill* [1985] 1 Ch 270 **(at 11.1 and 11.10)**

- *Re Whiteley* (1887) 12 App Cas 727 (at 11.4)

- *Bartlett v Barclays Bank (No 1)* [1980] Ch 515 **(at 11.4, 11.9.1, and 11.9.2)**

- *Nestlé v National Westminster Bank plc* [1993] 1 WLR 1260 **(at 11.9.1)**

- *Speight v Gaunt* (1883) 22 ChD 727 **(at 11.11.5)**

- *Re Beloved Wilkes* (1851) 3 Mac & G 440 **(at 11.12.3)**

Further reading

P Panico 'Trustee Investment Powers in International Trust Law' [2009] *Trusts and Trustees* 96
How well does the 'prudent businessman' test survive in the world of internationalized investment and portfolio theory?

LM Clements 'Bringing Trusts into the Twenty-First Century' [2004] 2 *Web JCLI*
A comprehensive review of all parts of the Trustee Act 2000.

'Fiduciary Duties of Investment Intermediaries' particularly the Appendix 'Is it Always About the Money' Law Commission No. 350 <http://lawcommission.justice.gov.uk/areas/fiduciary_duties.htm>
Trustees may take account of ethical concerns when they invest, as long as they do not forget the primary objective of making money for the beneficiaries.

G Lightman 'The Trustees' Duty to Provide Information to Beneficiaries' [2004] *Private Client Business* 23
The provision of information by trustees to their beneficiaries is at the heart of the trust relationship.

12

Maintenance and advancement and protective trusts

Learning objectives

This chapter will help you to:

- recognize an express power of maintenance
- understand the statutory powers of maintenance in s. 31 of the Trustee Act 1925
- appreciate that adult beneficiaries have a right to be maintained
- understand what an accumulation is
- appreciate that there must be income from which to maintain
- understand that the courts have a power to order maintenance
- understand the meaning of advancement
- understand the statutory powers of advancement in s. 32 of the Trustee Act 1925
- recognize an express power of advancement
- appreciate that an advancement is for the benefit of the beneficiary
- recognize that protective trusts are for the protection of spendthrift and improvident beneficiaries.

Introduction

Trusts often include many beneficiaries, some of whom will only become entitled to the property, maybe at some distant date in the future. Again the beneficiary may have to satisfy a contingency to become entitled to the property, e.g. reach the age of 21, marry, etc. So well-drafted trusts give the trustees powers to help the beneficiaries financially before the interests of the beneficiaries vest (become fully entitled) in possession.

KEY POINT A 'contingency' literally means something that might happen. In trusts it is common to insert contingencies or conditions that beneficiaries must meet in order to qualify for the property. Examples might include reaching a certain age, marrying, or taking up a particular profession.

These powers to aid the beneficiaries financially are so common that they were given statutory form in ss. 31 and 32 of the Trustee Act 1925. Maintenance is the power to pay money to the beneficiaries out of the trust income: s. 31. Advancement is the power to give part of the capital to the beneficiary: s. 32. If the testator wishes to exclude these statutory powers and provide for something different, he can do so by the words of the trust. This is allowed by the Trustee Act 1925, s. 69.

(1) This Act, except where otherwise expressly provided, applies to trusts including, so far as this Act applies thereto, executorships and administratorships constituted or created either before or after the commencement of this Act.

(2) The powers conferred by this Act on trustees are in addition to the powers conferred by the instrument, if any, creating the trust, but those powers, unless otherwise stated, apply if and so far only as a contrary intention is not expressed in the instrument, if any, creating the trust and have effect subject to the terms of that instrument.

KEY POINT The provisions of the 1925 Act apply to all trusts, whether they were created before or after the Act, unless the trust states that these powers are not to apply.

Maintenance and advancement can also be utilized to attempt to reduce tax liability. Inheritance tax has to be paid when a person inherits property on death. This is at the rate of 40 per cent on any amount above £325,000. Married couples and couples in a civil partnership may combine their allowances and leave £650,000 without their heirs having to pay inheritance tax on the estate.

To avoid inheritance tax it can be wise to give property away to children or grandchildren seven years or more before death. One way of doing this was to set up a maintenance and accumulation trust. Typically, the property would be invested and the profits accumulated until the children were 25. The trustees would have power to pay maintenance to the children. This was changed in the 2006 Budget, when a maximum age of 18 was stipulated for such trusts, reducing their popularity.

12.1 Maintenance

The original idea was to grant the trustees the power to provide for the daily needs of the beneficiary out of the trust income.

12.1.1 Express powers of maintenance

It is common for there to be an express power of maintenance in a trust, which may differ from the statutory scheme.

● ***Re Peel*** [1936] Ch 161

Lieutenant Owen Peel married Violet Jardine, and Major Hugh Peel, his father, covenanted that he would pay £1,000 a year to the trustees if Owen Peel died in his (Hugh's) lifetime. The trust was to pay to Violet until she died or remarried and then 'to or for the benefit of the children or child for the time being living of the said intended marriage'. While the children were under age, the trustees had power to pay for their 'maintenance, education or benefit in such manner as the trustees should think fit'. The marriage was dissolved in 1920 and they had one child. Owen died in 1925 and Violet remarried in 1929.

The trustees did not want to pay maintenance to the child.

HELD: The trust clearly stated that it was for the 'benefit' of the child once Violet remarried. Therefore, the trustees had no discretion to withhold maintenance, unlike under the statutory scheme.

Eve J at 164:

> I think the trust is a compulsory one, to apply the whole fund for the maintenance, education and benefit of the infant for any or more of such purposes and thus the trustees have no power to retain any part of the fund for the purposes they suggest.

Here the trust made maintenance of the child compulsory, unlike the statutory scheme, where maintenance is at the discretion of the trustees (see 12.1.3 'The statutory power of maintenance').

12.1.2 Exclusion of maintenance

The possibility of maintenance can be completely excluded by the words of the trust.

● ***Re Delamere*** [1984] 1 All ER 584

A settlement by the Honourable Ruth Mary Clarisse Delamere gave the trustees **power to appoint** in favour of her children, grandchildren, and great-grandchildren. The trustees appointed to six grandchildren, the Cunningham-Reids, in 'equal shares absolutely'.

HELD: The word 'absolutely' meant that the property was completely theirs. The grandchildren had all the capital and all the income that it produced. This gave the trustees no discretion to withhold some income for accumulations and to provide some to them as maintenance.

. . . .

Power of appointment—A beneficiary, or sometimes a trustee, is given the power to choose who inherits the property next. They would name the person appointed in their will or perhaps in a deed while they are still alive. (See 4.1.1 'Powers of appointment'.)
. . . .

Maintenance is not possible in a discretionary trust. (See 4.1.3 'Discretionary trust'.)

. . . .

● ***Re Vestey's Settlement*** [1951] Ch 209

Baron Vestey established a trust for his brother, Sir Edmund Vestey. The terms were that the:

> [t]rustees should pay or apply the income of the fund unto and in such manner for the support and benefit of the wife of Sir Edmund Vestey his children and two grandsons and their issue at and for such times in such shares in such manner and upon any such terms or conditions whatsoever as Edmund's trustees in their discretion shall from time to time think proper and so that the same shall in no case give any right of continued or future receipt or enjoyment of any income or the employment thereof.

The trustees had thought that they had a power to maintain the children.

HELD: As this was a discretionary trust the children did not have individual equitable interests. Therefore, s. 31 did not apply. (See the wording of s. 31 in 12.1.3 'The statutory power of maintenance', where it refers to interests, vested or contingent.) The trust also clearly says what is to happen to the income, indicating that maintenance is not intended by the settlor.

KEY POINT
The statutory power of maintenance does not apply in a discretionary trust.

12.1.3 The statutory power of maintenance

> **Trustee Act 1925, s. 31**
> . . . .
>
> (1) Where any property is held by trustees in trust for any person for any interest whatsoever, whether vested or contingent, then, subject to any prior interests or charges affecting that property—
>
> (i) during the infancy of any such person, if his interest so long continues, the trustees may, at their sole discretion, pay to his parent or guardian, if any, or otherwise apply for or towards his maintenance, education or benefit, the whole or such part if any, of the income of that property as the trustees may think fit . . . .

The trustees have a discretion to pay maintenance to the child's parent or guardian to provide the child with education, living expenses, and any other things that would benefit the child. The trustees could also pay for these things directly, bypassing the parents. 'Infant' used to mean a person under the age of 21, but the Family Law Reform Act 1969 reduced this to 18. Trusts established before that date still keep the age of 21, so it is probable that there are still some trusts in operation with the higher age: *Begg-MacBrearty (Inspector of Taxes) v Stilwell (Trustee)* [1996] 4 All ER 205.

The trustees have discretion on whether to give any money at all and how much. Section 31(1)(ii) used to give the trustees guidance upon how the trustees should exercise their discretion. They had to have regard to the age and requirements of the infant and to take account of any other resources that the child might have, such as money from his/her parents or (say) another trust and keep some sort of proportion between the different funds being used to maintain the child, but that part of the Act was repealed by the Inheritance and Trustees Powers Act 2014. The aim is to remove restraints on the discretion of the trustees.

● ***Fuller v Evans*** [2000] 1 All ER 636

Fuller had created accumulation and maintenance trusts for the benefit of his two children. Each of the children had a life interest and then their property went to their children and remoter issue. The property was to be accumulated for 21 years. While the children were under 21 the trustees had power to pay the whole or part of the income for the maintenance, education, or benefit of the children. Clause 12(c) prohibited the trustees from exercising their powers 'in such manner that the settlor may become entitled either directly or indirectly to any benefit in any manner or in any circumstances whatsoever'. On Fuller's divorce, a consent order was made requiring him to pay the children's maintenance and school fees. The trustees proposed using their maintenance powers to pay the school fees and maintenance. Was this allowed, as it relieved Fuller of his responsibilities?

HELD: Lightman J at 639:

> ...clause 12 did not preclude the trustees from exercising the power conferred upon them by reason of any incidental, and unintended, conferment of relief on the settlor. This conclusion of course does no more than leave it open to the trustees to exercise a discretionary power to make provision for the education and maintenance of the two children out of the settlement funds. The trustees could only exercise that power if they considered that to do so was in the best interests of the beneficiaries despite the existence of the consent order and the obligations of the settlor thereunder. The trustees must have regard to the settlor's obligations to provide for the beneficiaries' maintenance and education when undertaking the decision-making process, but the existence of that obligation is no more than a consideration to which due weight must be given (consider section 31(1)(i)(b) of the Trustee Act 1925). If the trustees reach the conclusion that it is in the best interests of the beneficiaries to make such provision out of trust funds, they are free to do so.

KEY POINT

The purpose of maintenance powers is to benefit the child beneficiaries.

The courts do not interfere with the discretionary decision of trustees unless they grossly misuse their powers. (See *Re Pauling's Settlement Trusts* [1964] Ch 303 in the Advancement section of this chapter at 12.3 'The exercise of discretion'.)

Section 31(1) gives guidance to the trustees on how to exercise their discretion. They do not have to pay the beneficiary all the income, but 'shall have regard to the age of the infant and his requirements and generally to the circumstances of the case, and in particular to what other income, if any, is applicable for the same purposes...'.

12.1.4 Duty to maintain an adult beneficiary

Once the beneficiary is an adult the trustees have a duty to pay maintenance, which means that the income generated by the property goes to the beneficiary. This is the case even if the beneficiary has yet to reach a contingency, e.g. the trust says 'to Ruth upon marriage'. Ruth receives the income upon reaching 18, whether she is married or not. When Ruth marries she meets the contingency and her equitable interest becomes vested in interest. She may have to wait for other beneficiaries to die before she actually gets her share of the trust property, i.e. her interest becomes vested in possession. The point of maintenance is that she can be paid the income generated by her share of the trust property when she turns 18. Whether she ever marries or ever actually succeeds to the trust property remains unknown and in the future.

> **Trustee Act 1925, s. 31**
> ....
>
> (1) (ii) if such person on attaining the age of 18 years has not a vested interest in such income, the trustees shall henceforth pay the income of that property and of any accretion thereto under subsection (2) of this section to him, until he either attains a vested interest therein or dies, or until failure of his interest.

KEY POINTS

- The statutory scheme requires that maintenance should be paid to adult beneficiaries.

- The settlor or testator may exclude the statutory scheme and make his own arrangements, as we saw earlier in the Introduction, and in 12.1.1 'Express powers of maintenance' and 12.1.2 'Exclusion of maintenance'.

....

● *Re Turner* [1937] Ch 15

Robert Turner made his will, which gave his residuary estate to such children of his late son Charles as should attain 28 years. There was an express power of maintenance while they were infants, but also a *power* to pay income to such of the children as attained 21. The trustees were to accumulate the surplus.

HELD: The wording chosen by the testator clearly excludes the statutory *duty* to pay income. It left it in the discretion of the trustees.

Turner did not want compulsory maintenance for his children, once they reached the age of majority, but he wanted it left to his trustees' discretion.

12.1.5 Accumulations

The trustees might not use up all the income in maintaining the beneficiaries while they are children, so the trustees are instructed to invest this surplus.

> **Trustee Act 1925, s. 31**
> ....
>
> (2) During the infancy of any such person, if his interest so long continues, the trustees shall accumulate all the residue of that income by investing it, and any profits from so investing it from time to time in authorised investments...

Then the question arises of who should receive these 'accumulations'. The rest of the subsection explains. If the beneficiary has a vested interest, i.e. one where he/she does not have to meet any condition to become entitled, then he/she receives the accumulations on reaching the age of majority of 18 or marrying or entering into a civil partnership below that age. The beneficiary also receives the accumulations, if he/she has to meet a contingency to become fully entitled to the property and the contingency is to reach 18, marry, or enter a civil partnership. When beneficiaries meet the contingency they are entitled to the accumulations.

In any other situation the accumulations fall back into the main capital of the trust. This would be, for example, if the beneficiary died before the age of 18 or the contingency is not marriage or reaching 18.

12.1.6 There must be income from which to maintain

If we had a simple trust such as 'to A for life, remainder to the children of A', A would be receiving the income on the trust property, which would be invested (see Chapter 11 'The duties of trustees: with special reference to investment') and when A died the capital would go to the children. In more complicated trusts, the basic pattern would be the same: some beneficiaries would receive the income and, maybe, different beneficiaries would eventually receive the capital. For maintenance to be possible there must be income available from which to maintain. So we have to think that each individual equitable interest is carrying with it its own piece of income. The phrase used is that they 'carry intermediate income'.

Therefore, maintenance is not possible if there is a discretionary trust (see *Re Vestey* [1951] Ch 209 at 12.1.2), as all the income is distributed under the discretionary trust. As Jenkins LJ put it at 223, 'The whole of the intermediate income is exhausted by the discretionary trust...'.

Section 31 refers to the power to maintain being 'subject to any prior interests' (see 12.1.3 'The statutory power of maintenance'). This means that if there is a prior life interest there can be no maintenance. In the example at the beginning of this section, all the maintenance would be paid to A, leaving none available for the children.

KEY POINT
Prior life interests mean that there can be no maintenance.

With other, more complex, trusts it is necessary to decide whether there is any intermediate income to allow maintenance for the particular beneficiary being considered. Fortunately, an Act of Parliament has intervened and stipulates that most kinds of property gift carry intermediate income.

> **Law of Property Act 1925, s. 175**
>
> ....
>
> A contingent or future **specific** devise or **bequest** of property, whether real or personal, and a contingent residuary devise of freehold land and a specific or **residuary devise** of freehold land to trustees upon trust for persons whose interests are contingent or executory shall, subject to the statutory provisions relating to accumulations, carry the intermediate income of that property from the death of the testator, except so far as such income, or any part thereof, may be otherwise expressly disposed of.

....

Specific—The property is identified.

Residuary—What is left of the deceased's property when debts, taxes, and identified gifts have been paid.

Devise—Land is left in a will.

Bequest—Personal property is left in a will.

Pecuniary legacy—A sum of cash left in a will.

....

Even with the definitions, s. 175 seems pretty incomprehensible. It covers most kinds of property gift, but the wishes of the testator might mean that it does not apply. A nice illustration of how the section works can be seen in *Re McGeorge* [1963] Ch 544.

● *Re McGeorge* [1963] Ch 544

Reginald McGeorge died in 1961 leaving a will, clause 4 of which was considered by the court. He devised some identified agricultural land to his daughter, Helen Ratcliff, and a **pecuniary legacy** to his son, Thomas McGeorge, equal in value to a valuation of the agricultural land. The testator added 'that the aforesaid devise and pecuniary legacy shall not take effect until after the death of my said wife should she survive me'. The court was asked to decide whether the gifts to the daughter and son carried the intermediate income.

HELD: Cross J at 550:

> No doubt arises with regard to the legacy. A deferred legacy, such as I have construed the legacy to the son to be, does not carry interest until the date fixed for payment.

Legacies are not mentioned in s. 175 and the will clearly states that the son is not to receive it until after the death of his mother.

A 'future specific devise', which covers the land left to the daughter, is mentioned in s. 175, but this is excluded by the express words of the will.

At 552–3:

> ... a will containing such a gift expresses a contrary intention within section 69(2) which prevents the section 31 from applying. By deferring the enjoyment of the devise until after the widow's death the testator has expressed the intention that the daughter shall not have the immediate income.

Put more simply, it was clearly not the intention of the testator that his children should receive any income from their gifts, until their mother died. As stated in the Introduction to this chapter, it is always possible for the person establishing the trust to use s. 69(2) of the Trustee Act 1925 to make their own arrangements for maintenance.

12.1.7 Contingent pecuniary legacies

Section 175 of the Law of Property Act 1925 does not mention contingent pecuniary legacies as carrying the intermediate income either. These are sums of money left in a will, subject to a condition, e.g. £10,000 to Johnny if he attains the age of 30.

Generally, no maintenance is possible. This is based on the presumed intention of the testator or testatrix: they just wanted the beneficiary to have the cash sum, *if* they met the condition.

● *Re Raine* [1929] 1 Ch 716

Annie Raine died in 1926 leaving a will in which she left £2,000 to Sydney Stansfield and £100 to Sylvia Stansfield, her godchildren, when they reached the age of 21. Everything else was left to her sister-in-law. When Annie died, Sydney was 9 and Sylvia was 14. Could any maintenance be paid to them while they waited to become adults?

HELD: Eve J: Section 175 did not apply and there was nothing in the will to set aside any funds to provide for maintenance.

There is an exception to this, where the will is made by the parent. It is assumed that the parent would want to maintain his/her child.

Trustee Act 1925, s. 31
. . . .

(3) This section applies in the case of a contingent interest only if the limitation or trust carries the intermediate income of the property, but it applies to a future or contingent legacy by the parent of, or a person standing in loco parentis to, the legatee, if and for such period as, under the general law, the legacy carries interest for the maintenance of the legatee…

● **Re Abrahams** [1911] 1 Ch 108

The father's will left £15,000 to each son who attains 25 and a further £15,000 when they attained 30.

HELD: The exception did not apply as the age stipulated as a contingency was not 21. The in loco parentis idea only applies to maintaining children, those under 21 (now 18).

thinking points

Section 31 of the Trustee Act 1925 has been criticized by Sir Raymond Evershed in Re Vestey's Settlement *[1950] Ch 209 at 215: 'The language…I confess, is by no means easy to follow, nor does it seem to me that the section has been put together in a way which makes the task of apprehending its effect as easy as it might be.' The main problem is contingent pecuniary legacies and whether they carry the income out of which maintenance can be paid. See BS Ker (1953) 17 Conv 275, who carefully examines the case law on this subject.*

12.1.8 The power of the courts to award maintenance

It may be that the trustees cannot or will not give maintenance to the beneficiaries. In that situation it is possible to apply to the courts. The courts have a discretion to order maintenance. There is an old 'inherent' jurisdiction meaning that it is so ancient that it is not possible to identify the earliest case. An example can be found in *Wellesley v Wellesley*.

● **Wellesley v Wellesley** (1828) 2 Bli 124

The Honourable Tylney Long Wellesley had separated from his wife and was living 'in an adulterous union' with another woman in France. His wife died and his children were being cared for by her sisters. He wanted to recover them. There was a marriage settlement to provide for Wellesley, his wife, and children.

(See 5.8.1 'Marriage settlements'.) HELD: The courts had an ancient jurisdiction to make sure that children were properly cared for. They were acting on behalf of the Crown as **parens patriae**.

In that capacity the court agreed to make the children **wards of court**, because of Wellesley's bad conduct, which included 'encouraging the children in the vice of swearing'. The court also ordered that the trustees paid maintenance to the children out of the marriage settlement.

Parens patriae—Latin—father of the country.

Ward of court—The child is placed under the protection of the court.

There is also a very widely drafted statutory power, which would allow the court to order the payment of maintenance out of the income or the capital of a trust.

> **Trustee Act 1925, s. 53**
>
> (1) Where an infant is beneficially entitled to any property the court may, with a view to the application of the capital or income thereof for the maintenance, education, or benefit of the infant, make an order 'conveying the property, transferring the property, the dividends or income' as the court may think fit.

12.2 Advancement

12.2.1 The meaning of advancement

It is likely in most trusts that some of the beneficiaries might have to wait a considerable time before they become entitled to their share. If we take a simple trust such as 'to A for life, remainder to her children that attain the age of 25', the children have to wait for their mother to die *and* meet the age contingency, before they receive their share. Trusts often contain a power of advancement to let the beneficiaries have some of their share, before the date that they become entitled.

The leading case defines the meaning of advancement.

● *Pilkington v IRC* [1964] AC 612

Viscount Radcliffe at 634:

> The word 'advancement' itself meant in this context the establishment in life of the beneficiary who was the object of the power or at any rate some step that would contribute to the furtherance of his establishment.
>
> Typical instances of expenditure for such purposes under the social conditions of the 19th century were an apprenticeship or the purchase of a commission in the army or of an interest in business. In the case of a girl there could be an advancement on marriage...Advancement had, however, to some extent a limited range of meaning, since it was thought to convey the idea of some step in life of permanent significance, and accordingly, to prevent uncertainties about the permitted range of objects for which moneys could be raised and made available, such words as 'or otherwise for his or her benefit' were often added to the word 'advancement'. It was always recognised that these added words were 'large words'...

An example of a typical 'advancement' can be found in *Re William's WT*.

● *Re William's WT* [1953] Ch 138

According to the terms of the will, payments could be made to the son on attaining the age of 35 'for the purpose of starting my said son in business or for the advancement of any business with which he may be concerned'. The son was a doctor and wanted an advance to buy a house for use both as a residence and for his practice.

HELD: An advance could be made. 'Business' included the medical profession and the house would advance his prospects as a doctor.

Advancements have also been permitted if the beneficiary feels a 'moral obligation' to donate money to charity.

● *Re Clore's Settlement Trusts* [1996] 1 WLR 955

When he turned 21, a beneficiary asked for one-seventh of his eventual fund, so that he could donate it to a family charitable foundation.

HELD: Pennycuick J: This was permissible. The improvement of the material situation of the beneficiary is not confined to his direct financial situation, but could include the discharge of certain moral or social obligations, particularly in relation to provision for family and dependants.

At 959:

> If the obligation is not to be met out of the capital of the trust fund, he would have to meet it out of his own pocket, if at all. Accordingly, the discharge of the obligation out of the capital of the trust fund does improve his material situation.

The amount to be advanced was not 'excessive'.

In a more recent case, an advancement for charitable giving was not granted. The difference was in the amount of money that was being advanced: practically the whole trust fund would be advanced and other beneficiaries would see their share of the trust cut down.

● *X and Another v A and Others* [2006] 1 WLR 741

This was a marriage settlement for the wife, children, and grandchildren. The trustees had power to advance the whole trust fund, £3.1 million, to the wife. She proposed that the trustees should do this, save for £750,000 kept back for the family, so that she could donate it to charity.

HELD: Hart J: There must be objective evidence that a moral obligation to give to charity actually exists. There was ample evidence here: the family were Christians, had set up a charitable trust, and previously donated large sums.

However, the advancement was refused, as the amount was too great.

At 753:

> No such case goes anywhere near recognising the existence of a moral obligation of the extent in question here.

And at 754:

> ...the trustees should have asked themselves whether it was proper to make it given the fact that it would severely cut down...the interests of those entitled to capital under the settlement.

KEY POINTS

- 'Advancement' is widely defined. It usually means the improvement of the material position of the beneficiary.

- The addition of 'benefit' means that wider considerations can be taken into account.

thinking points

See DWM Waters 'The "New" Power of Advancement' [1958] 22 Conv 413. Waters considers the case law on express powers of advancement and the statutory formulation in s. 32 of the Trustee Act 1925. He observes that the words 'or benefit' vastly extend the power. Advancements can now be made even if there is no financial need on the part of the beneficiary. The courts may also authorize advancements for the 'benefit' of an infant under s. 53 of the Trustee Act 1925. Although an extended power of advancement is a great advantage to the trustees, such a wide power should be approached with caution.

12.2.2 The statutory power of advancement

As with maintenance, all trusts now contain a power for the trustees to advance. Section 32 applies to all trusts created after 1925.

Trustee Act 1925, s. 32

(1) Trustees may at any time or times pay or apply any capital money subject to a trust or transfer or apply any other property forming part of the capital of the trust property, for the advancement or benefit, in such manner as they may, in their absolute discretion, think fit, of any person entitled to the capital of the trust property or of any share thereof, whether absolutely or contingently on his attaining any specified age or on the occurrence of any other event, or subject to a gift over on his death under any specified age or on the occurrence of any other event, and whether in possession or in remainder or in reversion, and such payment, transfer or application may be made notwithstanding that the interest of such person is liable to be defeated by the exercise of a power of appointment or revocation, or to be diminished by the increase of the class to which he belongs.

This is a very wide power and the trustees may advance money to any beneficiary of the trust, no matter how unlikely it is that he/she might actually inherit.

● **Re Garrett** [1934] Ch 477

Among other provisions, the will of William Garrett left property to his daughter, Mrs Croft, for life and after her death to her children. There was a contingency that they should survive her *and* reach 21 to become entitled. She wanted an advance so that she could pay school fees for her daughter.

HELD: The fact that there was a double contingency here made no difference to the power of advance. Mrs Croft consented to the advance being made. Insert blue dotted line below this line to indicate end of case.

Section 32 does lay down some restrictions on the power to advance capital money to the beneficiary:

1. The consent in writing of the prior life interest or other interest, who must be of full age, is needed. This is because if part of the capital is advanced, the income produced by the capital will decrease, reducing the income of the life interest. Mrs Croft in *Re Garrett* [1934] Ch 477 (see 12.2.2 'The statutory power of maintenance') is an example.

2. The entire share of the beneficiary can be advanced. For trusts created before 1 October 2014, half the eventual share can be advanced. The law was changed by the Inheritance and Trustees' Powers Act 2014.

3. When the beneficiary eventually becomes entitled to their share in the capital, the advance that they have already had is deducted from it. This is known as the equitable doctrine of 'hotchpot'.

A final restriction on the power to make advances can be found in s. 32(2): 'This section does not apply to capital money arising under the Settled Land Act 1925.' Settled land is fairly rare nowadays and there is no legal restriction on advancing all other types of land.

● **Re Collard's Will Trusts** [1961] Ch 293

Under her father's will, property was held for Margaret Rees on protective trusts for life and then to her children. She had one son, John, and was too old to have any more. The value of her share was £74,112 and she wanted the trustees to advance him a farm, which he already farmed, worth £20,000. He had already had £9,788 in advances.

HELD: Buckley J at 301:

> In the present case, the farm has been recently valued by qualified valuers at £20,000, and an advance of £20,000 would be within the financial limit of the power of advancement which the trustees at present have, having regard to the value of the elder daughter's settled share. So far as I can see, there would be nothing wrong in the trustees making an advance in cash to her son of £20,000 and subsequently selling the farm to him for £20,000. In those circumstances, it seems to me that the court need not insist on that process having gone through: and that the right view is that the trustees have power to convey the farm to the son and treat that conveyance as an advancement to him of its market value.

12.2.3 Express powers of advancement

Using s. 69(2) of the Trustee Act 1925, the settlor or testator can totally exclude the power to make advances if he/she wishes.

- *Bernstein v IRC* [1961] Ch 399

William Bernstein set up a trust with instructions that income should be accumulated during his life and after his death should go to his wife and any children that they might have.

HELD: Section 32 was excluded, as he wanted an accumulation of the income until his death.

Lord Evershed at 414:

> On a fair reading of the instrument in question it could be said that the application of the power would be inconsistent with the purpose of the instrument.
>
> In this case it is quite apparent that the whole object of the instrument was to build up a capital sum which would be paid to the beneficiary or her children, if any, upon the settlor's death.

It is also possible to modify the statutory powers. It was quite common, before the Inheritance and Trustees' Powers Act 2014 was passed, for the trust to allow the advancement of a beneficiary's entire estate rather than have it restricted to half, as it was in the old law.

- *Henley and Another v Wardell and Others* The Times 29 January 1988

The will of Francis Wardell set up a trust where his property went to his wife for life and then the capital was to be shared between his sons Geoffrey and John. The will contained a clause 10 which stated that 'to the intent that the powers given to trustees by section 32 of the Trustee Act 1925 shall be enlarged so as to permit my trustees in their absolute and uncontrolled discretion to advance at any time the whole of any expectant or presumptive share to any of my children or any infant beneficiary . . .'.

The trustees valued the whole fund at £155,000 and had advanced £608 and £614 for school fees and then £77,500 to Geoffrey. So the amount advanced was nearly his entire share. The widow of the testator had signed away half her life interest to John Phibbs, who did not consent to the advances.

Were the advances invalid?

HELD: The size of the advance was acceptable, but the need for the consent of the prior interest had not been altered, so the advances were invalid.

That showed that the only purpose of the enlargement of the powers was as to the size of the share that could be advanced and did not do away with the need for consents as provided for by s. 32(1)(c).

12.2.4 The advance need not be made directly to the beneficiary

In many cases the beneficiaries will still be children. This does not prevent the trustees advancing trust capital to them, as their consent is not needed, as long as it is for their 'benefit'. 'Advance' does not necessarily mean that the beneficiaries receive the property earlier than they would under the trust. It has the technical meaning of setting the beneficiaries up in life or otherwise benefiting them. Advances are often made for tax reasons, particularly to avoid inheritance tax. In many of the cases, therefore, the Inland Revenue (now HM Revenue and Customs) was one of the parties.

● *Pilkington v IRC* [1964] AC 612

By his will dated 14 December 1934 William Pilkington directed his trustees to invest his residuary estate and hold the fund upon trust in equal shares for his nephews and nieces. These beneficiaries held for life on protective trust and then the fund went to their children. One nephew, Richard Pilkington, and the trustees wanted to make an advance of half her eventual share to his daughter, Penelope Pilkington, who was five years old. The reason was to save estate duty (now inheritance tax) and to reduce his own tax burden. So, as the prior interest he gave consent, but the trustees were uncertain whether they could do this and the Inland Revenue opposed it.

Penelope was not to receive the property outright, but it was to be held on a new trust for her. Maintenance could be paid until she was 21; then she would receive all the income, but she would not become entitled to the capital until she was 30. If she died before the age of 30 the property was to go to any children that she might have.

HELD: Viscount Radcliffe, in the House of Lords, answered a series of objections to the advancement.

1. It was argued that this was not an 'advance' because Penelope would have to wait until she was 30 to get her property.

    Lord Radcliffe replied that that was a confusion of meanings. 'Advance' meant to receive the property earlier, but 'advancement' did not mean that.

At 635:

> It means any use of the money which will improve the material situation of the beneficiary.

2. It was objected that her money should not be 'tied up in the proposed settlement'.

Again, Lord Radcliffe disagreed at 636:

> Anyone can see, I think, that there can be circumstances in which, while it is very desirable that some money should be raised at once for the benefit of an owner of an expectant or contingent interest, it would be very undesirable that the money should not be secured to him under some arrangement that will prevent him having the absolute disposition of it. I find it very difficult to think that there is something at the back of section 32 which makes such an advancement impossible.

There were advantages in not allowing a beneficiary to have full control of their money.

3. It was argued that Penelope had not consented to or asked for this advancement.

Lord Radcliffe said that this was not necessary at 637–8:

> But if application and consent were necessary requisites of advancement that would cut out the possibility of making any advancement for the benefit of a person under age, at any rate without the institution of court proceedings and formal representation of an infant.

A child cannot legally consent, so to insist on this would make it impossible to make advancements to children.

4. Others might benefit incidentally from the advance, such as her future children if she died before the age of 30.

Lord Radcliffe did not think that this mattered at 636:

> But if the disposition itself, by which I mean the whole provision made, is for her benefit, it is no objection to the exercise of the power that other persons benefit incidentally as a result of the exercise.

5. A tax saving did not relate to Penelope's personal needs, as she was five years old and probably not very interested in tax questions.

Lord Radcliffe rejected this argument too at 640:

> And, if the advantage of preserving the funds of a beneficiary from the incidence of death duty is not an advantage personal to that beneficiary, I do not see what is.

6. So it looked as if the proposed advancement was valid, except for the last objection, which was successful.

The resettlement on Penelope infringed the rule against perpetuities.

(A further explanation of the rule against perpetuities is outside the scope of this book.)

KEY POINT Despite this perpetuity problem, this important case did establish, at the highest level of court, that advancements to avoid tax were permissible and that the advancement did not have to go directly to the beneficiary. It could for instance be resettled on another trust.

---

thinking points

This decision might seem to extend the concepts of advancement and benefit too far, but was welcomed by most practitioners in the field. The words 'or benefit' in the Act allow the trustees greater flexibility to promote the financial gain of the beneficiary. Pilkington v IRC *was the first time that the courts allowed the advancement to be put on a protective or discretionary trust, rather than given as a lump sum to the beneficiary. See FR Crane (1963) 67* Conv *65.*

12.2.5 The courts' power to authorize advancements

As with maintenance, the courts can also order advancements under s. 53 of the Trustee Act 1925 and under their inherent jurisdiction.

The exercise of discretion

Despite their wide discretion, trustees must consider carefully before they award maintenance or grant an advance and ensure, as far as they reasonably can, that the money actually does go for the benefit of the beneficiary. They should guard against, for instance, the money being taken by the parents. These problems are illustrated by *Re Pauling's Settlement Trusts*.

● *Re Pauling's Settlement Trusts* [1964] Ch 303

Miss Pauling, an heiress, had married a naval officer, Commander Younghusband, 'who had almost no fortune at all'. To prevent the misuse of her fortune it was put into a trust for her for life and then to the children that she might have. The trust contained a power of advancement to the children of up to half their presumptive share. The parents were in constant financial difficulty and, at the instigation of the Commander, they systematically used advancements to the children to solve their financial problems. These included the purchase of a house on the Isle of Man, furniture for that house, a house in Chelsea, and paying off a loan to her mother.

Coutts and Co were the trustees, but also bankers to the mother. They and lawyers, who were consulted, do not appear to have appreciated that there was anything wrong in this. When the children realized that these advancements might have been illegal, they sued the trustees for the return of £29,160 of their estimated £70,000 fortune.

HELD: Willmer LJ at 333–4:

1. Coutts and Co, the trustees, had not exercised the advancement power properly.

> ...the parties to a settlement intend the normal trusts to take effect, and that a power of advancement be exercised only if there is some good reason for it. That good reason must be beneficial to the person to be advanced; it cannot be exercised capriciously or with some other benefit in view. The trustees, before exercising the power, have to weigh on the one side the benefit to the proposed advancee, and on the other hand the rights of those who are or may hereafter become interested under the trusts of the settlement.
>
> On the other hand, if the trustees make the advance for a particular purpose which they state, they can quite properly pay it over to the advancee if they reasonably think they can trust him or her to carry out the proposed purpose. What they cannot do is to prescribe a particular purpose, and then raise and pay the money over to the advancee leaving him or her entirely free, legally and morally, to apply it for that purpose or to spend it in any way he or she chooses, without any responsibility on the trustees even to inquire as to its application.

2. Coutts and Co was also a bank, concerned about Mrs Younghusband's overdraft, so it was guilty of a conflict of interest.

At 341:

> Even at this early stage they wholly failed to exercise any powers or duties as trustees, and thought of themselves as bankers to the commander and the mother.

3. Section 61 of the Trustee Act 1925 allows the court to relieve trustees of their liability (see 15.6.4 'Section 61 of the Trustees Act 1925').

Trustee Act 1925, s. 61

If it appears to the court that a trustee...is or may be personally liable for any breach of trust...but has acted honestly and reasonably, and ought fairly to be excused for the breach of trust and for omitting to obtain the directions of the court in the matter in which he committed such breach, then the court may relieve him either wholly or partly from personal liability for the same.

This did not help the bank avoid liability.

At 339:

> Where a banker undertakes to act as a paid trustee of a settlement created by a customer, and so deliberately places itself in a position where its duty as a trustee conflicts with its interest as a banker, we think that the court should be very slow to relieve such a trustee under the provisions of the section.

4. Normally, it is not necessary for a beneficiary to consent to an advancement, but if it is an improper advance then consent would give the trustee a defence. The children were over 21 and had consented to the advancements. This did not let the bank escape liability because it was deemed that the children were still under parental control and therefore there was undue influence.

At 337:

> In our judgment the question is one of fact and degree. One begins with a strong presumption in the case of a child just 21 living at home, and this will grow less and less as the child goes out in the world and leaves the shelter of the home. Nevertheless, the presumption normally lasts only a 'short' time after the child has attained 21.

However, the children were emancipated from parental control for the later advancements and it was decided that they could consent to them.

This meant that the bank only had to restore the money for the earlier advancements to the beneficiaries.

KEY POINTS

- There must be good reason for an advancement.

- An advancement is for a particular purpose and the trustees have a responsibility to ensure that it is spent for that purpose.

- Trustees must ensure that they have no conflict of interest and duty.

Protective trusts

12.4.1 The purpose of a protective trust

KEY POINT
The purpose of a protective trust is to protect the debtor and his family from their creditors.

It might have been noticed earlier in the chapter that sometimes property is settled in what is called a 'protective trust', e.g. *Pilkington v IRC* [1964] AC 612 at 12.2.4. A protective trust is a trust designed to protect the beneficiary from the consequences of getting into debt. Usually, the beneficiary has a life interest, which ends as soon as they do anything that might put them into debt. Then the property is held on a discretionary trust for the beneficiary, spouse, and children. Because the beneficiary no longer has any equitable interest, there is nothing that the creditors can proceed against. Under the discretionary trust, none of the beneficiaries has individual equitable interests either, again leaving the creditors with nothing to proceed against. Such trusts became so common that a statutory formula was enacted in s. 33 of the Trustee Act 1925. Now all that a testator or settlor has to do to create a protective trust is to use the words 'protective trust' in the trust instrument and s. 33 will apply, e.g. *Re Wittke* [1944] Ch 166: 'Under protective trusts for the benefit of my sister'.

12.4.2 How a protective trust works

It is desirable for the life interest to be 'determinable' and words such as 'while', 'during', 'until', and 'as long as' should be used. This sets out how long the life interest will last. 'Conditional' life interests, where a condition ends the life interest, are undesirable, because any attempts to restrict a beneficiary's ability to sell or alienate property is void, as against the policy of the law.

● *Rochford v Hackman* [1852] 9 Hare 475

> … if Richard Rochford should in any manner sell, assign, transfer, incumber or otherwise dispose of or anticipate his share or any part thereof, then, immediately after such alienation, sale, assignment, transfer or disposition, the bequest in trust for Richard Rochford should cease, determine and become utterly void.

HELD: at 601:

> Lord Eldon in that judgment, first observes that a disposition to a man until he shall become bankrupt, and after his bankruptcy over, is quite different from an attempt to give to him for life, with a proviso that he shall not sell or alien; and the distinction between the two cases is obvious.

To modern readers this distinction is not obvious, but s. 33 maintains the idea that a determinable life interest should be used.

Trustee Act 1925, s. 33

(1) Where any income, including an annuity or other periodical income payment, is directed to be held on protective trust for the benefit of any person (in this section called 'the principal beneficiary') for the period of his life or for any less period, then, during that period (in this section called the 'trust period') the said income shall, without prejudice to any prior interest, be held on the following trusts, namely—

(i) Upon trust for the principal beneficiary during the trust period or until he, whether before or after the termination of any prior interest, does or attempts to do or suffers any act or thing, or until any event happens, other than an advance under any statutory or express power, whereby, if the said income were payable during the trust period to the principal beneficiary absolutely during that period, he would be deprived of the right to receive the same or any part thereof, in any of which cases, as on the termination of the trust period, whichever first happens, this trust of the said income shall fail or determine;

(ii) If the trust aforesaid fails or determines during the subsistence of the trust period, then, during the residue of that period, the said income shall be held upon trust for the application thereof for the maintenance or support, or otherwise for the benefit, of all or any of the other or others of the following persons (that is to say)—

(a) the principal beneficiary and his or her spouse or civil partner, if any, and his or her children or more remote issue, if any; or

(b) if there is no spouse or civil partner or issue of the principal beneficiary in existence, the principal beneficiary and the persons who would, if he were actually dead, be entitled to the trust property or the income thereof or to the annuity fund, if any, or arrears of the annuity, as the case may be;

as the trustees in their absolute discretion, without being liable to account for the exercise of such discretion, think fit.

The objective is to protect the 'principal beneficiary' from his/her creditors.

The 'principal beneficiary' holds the life interest. As soon as he/she consents to, or any circumstances arise under which any of his/her income is payable to some other person (e.g. he/she gets into debt), then the life interest determines (ends) and a discretionary trust comes into existence. Under this trust the trustees have discretion to pay the income to the principal beneficiary, spouse, and children for their maintenance, support, or benefit.

The principal beneficiary's consent to an advance would mean that some of the capital of the trust was paid to a beneficiary. With less capital, the principal beneficiary 'would be deprived of the right to receive...part' of the income, but this does not count as an 'act or thing' which would determine his or her life interest and therefore 'trigger' the discretionary trust. See s. 31(1)(i) earlier, 'other than an advance under any statutory or express power'.

12.4.3 Determining events

It may seem unfair that a beneficiary should be protected from his/her creditors, but there is a restriction that settlors cannot protect themselves from the consequences of their own bankruptcy by setting up a protective trust.

● ***Re Burroughs-Fowler*** [1916] 2 Ch 251

Fowler put a protective trust into his marriage settlement in 1905, but this did not prevent his trustee in bankruptcy taking his life interest and offering it for sale in 1915. Bankruptcy had not ended Fowler's life interest.

If *someone else* had set up the protective trust for Fowler, it would have worked and his interest would have ended—'determined'—upon his bankruptcy.

An unusual example of a protective trust protecting a beneficiary can be seen in *Re Gourju's Will Trusts*.

● ***Re Gourju's Will Trusts*** [1943] Ch 24

Mrs Gourju had a life interest under a protective trust established by her husband's will. She lived in Nice, France, which was occupied by the Germans in the Second World War. Under wartime legislation, payments of the income of the trust could no longer be paid to enemy territory. The Custodian of Enemy Property wanted to claim this income.

HELD: The protective trust took effect, as an event had happened which deprived her of the income. Her life interest ended and the property was held on a discretionary trust. The trustees undertook to accumulate the income until the end of the war, when they would be able to pay it to Mrs Gourju.

This case illustrates the purpose of a protective trust, to protect the interests of the principal beneficiary.

Under the Matrimonial Causes Act 1973, the courts have power to alter the provisions of a trust when a couple divorces. It is thought that this does not end the determinable interest.

● ***General Accident v IRC*** [1963] 1 WLR 1207

The principal beneficiary was ordered to pay £750 per annum out of his income to his former wife.

HELD: Donovan LJ: This did not determine his life interest.

At 1218:

> Looking at the matter broadly, it is not easy to perceive why an order of the court made under the authority of a statute should come within the scope of section 33, or what useful purpose is served if it does. The section is intended as a protection to spendthrift or improvident or weak life tenants. But it can give (as is admitted) no protection against the effect of a court order such as was made here. Furthermore, if such an order involves a forfeiture much injustice could be done.

If the decision had been to the contrary the wife would have got nothing, because her ex-husband's life interest would have ceased and there would have been nothing from which to order maintenance.

12.4.4 Protecting the beneficiary

Once the 'forfeiture' has occurred a discretionary trust arises. The trustees may pay to any of the beneficiaries, including the principal one, as in *Re Gourju* [1943] Ch 24. If the beneficiary has serious financial problems, it may be wise for the trustees to pay directly for the goods and services that the beneficiary requires, rather than give the beneficiary money of his/her own. That way it is kept out of the hands of creditors.

● *Re Coleman* (1888) 39 ChD 443

Cotton LJ at 451:

> If the trustees were to pay an hotel keeper to give him a dinner he would get nothing but the right to eat a dinner, and that is not property which could pass by assignment or bankruptcy.

Conclusion

Trusts are not just a simple mechanism of holding property, e.g. for A for life, remainder for her children, but complex schemes to provide for a family, when what exactly will happen cannot be foreseen. Maintenance makes sure that there is money to feed, clothe, house, and educate children. Maintenance also ensures that a beneficiary can have some money while they wait to inherit, which could be a long time. It can be the most tax efficient way of moving money from one generation of a family to another. Advancement means that a trustee can also give the beneficiary part of their share before they become fully entitled to it. This might be so that the beneficiary can set up in business, start in a profession, have their school fees paid, donate to charity, or even minimize tax liability.

A heavy burden rests on the trustees. They must not just do what the beneficiaries ask or parents tell them to do, but exercise their discretion reasonably and properly.

Protective trusts also protect beneficiaries, but this time from their own mistakes. This type of trust ensures that a family is provided for, even if the mother or father is reckless with money.

As with most trust arrangements, settlors or testators do not have to be content with the statutory scheme, but can customize and personalize their trust. It is their money after all (see Table 12.1).

Table 12.1

A comparison— the statutory scheme

Maintenance	Advancement
Maintenance, education, or benefit of the beneficiary.	Advancement or benefit of beneficiary.
In the discretion of the trustees.	In the discretion of the trustees.
Payments from the *income* of the trust.	Payments from the *capital* of the trust.
Payments to the parents or guardian of the child beneficiary. Or to persons providing service for child, e.g. education.	Payments to the beneficiary directly, if an adult. Or to persons providing services for the beneficiary. Or to parents or guardian if the beneficiary is still a child.
The beneficiary can have any type or equitable interest, vested or contingent. If it is contingent, it must carry the intermediate income.	The beneficiary can have any type of equitable interest, vested or contingent.
If there is a prior life interest there can be no maintenance.	Prior life interest must give consent in writing and must be an adult to do this.
The trustees may pay maintenance as they see fit.	The trustees must not advance more than half of the beneficiary's eventual share. This is deducted when the beneficiary eventually inherits their share.
The beneficiary is *entitled* to maintenance when they become an adult (18).	The rights of the beneficiary do not change when they become an adult. The payment of an advance is still in the *discretion* of the trustees.

Questions

Self-test questions

1 What does s. 69(2) of the Trustee Act 1925 allow settlors and testators to do?

2 What is the purpose of maintenance?

3 When should trustees grant maintenance?

4 Why are contingent pecuniary legacies a problem?

5 What does 'advancement or benefit' mean?

6 What are the conditions that have to be satisfied before an advancement can be made?

7 To what extent should trustees check on how maintenance and advancements are spent?

8 In a protective trust, what happens to the trust fund upon a determining event?

Discussion questions

1 Is the statutory maintenance scheme in s. 31 easy to operate and understand?

2 Do the trustees' powers to maintain excuse the parents from their duties?

3 Do advancement and benefit have too wide a meaning?

4 Is a protective trust fair to the creditors of the principal beneficiary?

Assessment question

Emmanuel leaves two trusts in his will, in order to provide for his family after his death.

The first trust is known as 'The Family Trust' and its terms are: 'To my wife Sheila for life, remainder to my children, if they reach the age of 25 and qualify as a barrister.'

The second trust is called 'The Children's Trust' and its terms are that the children have life interests, and the trust property is to be accumulated and paid to the children when they reach 21. There is an express term including the statutory power of maintenance in s. 31 of the Trustee Act 1925.

The children have various financial problems and ask the trustees, Tim and Tom, for financial assistance. Alfred is 24 and has just qualified as a solicitor. He wants £100,000 from 'The Family Trust' to establish himself in practice as a solicitor. Belinda is 11 and wants to go to a school where she can train for an acting career. She seeks payment of her school fees from 'The Children's Trust'. Cyril is 19 and wants money from both trusts to pay for his 'playboy' lifestyle. Their mother is not content with the income from her life interest and wants the trustees to grant her money to help pay for the living expenses of her children, all of whom still live at home.

Advise Tim and Tom.

Key cases

- *Fuller v Evans* [2000] 1 All ER 636 **(at 12.1.3)**

- *Pilkington v IRC* [1964] AC 612 **(at 12.2.1 and 12.2.4)**

- *Re Pauling's Settlement Trusts* [1964] Ch 303 **(at 12.3)**

Further reading

BS Ker 'Trustees' Powers of Maintenance' (1953) 17 *Conv* 273
An examination of how s. 31 works and the tricky topic of intermediate income.

DWM Waters 'The "New" Power of Advancement' (1958) 22 *Conv* 413
Explains the meaning of advancement by looking at s. 32 and at express powers.

FR Crane (1963) 27 *Conv* 65
A note explaining the leading case of *IRC v Pilkington*.

The appointment of trustees

Learning objectives

This chapter will help you to:

- understand who is eligible to be a trustee
- understand how trustees are appointed and replaced
- appreciate what makes a trustee unsuitable for his/her office.

Introduction

It is essential for a trust to have trustees. They hold and safeguard the trust property and have complex duties to perform, so it is essential that they are carefully chosen. (See Chapter 11 'The duties of trustees: with special reference to investment' and Chapter 12 'Maintenance and advancement and protective trusts'.) Perhaps surprisingly, there are very few legal rules about who can be a trustee, but this is easily explained, as a trust is a private arrangement created by the settlor or testator. The settlor/testator decides what he or she wants and the courts are unwilling to interfere, unless it is not possible for the trust to run or the property of the beneficiaries is under threat from the trustees. The settlor/testator lays down in the trust instrument who will be the trustees and who has the power to replace them if that becomes necessary. There are elaborate statutory provisions on the appointment and replacement of trustees, but these only apply if the settlor/testator has failed to specify what he or she wants in the trust instrument.

 ## 13.1 The general duties of trustees

Trustees must follow the terms of the trust, act exclusively in the interest of the trust, and generally do their best for the beneficiaries. They are not entitled to make any personal profit from the trust, compete in business with the trust, or even use knowledge acquired during their work as a trustee for their own personal benefit. They are personally liable for any loss caused by dishonesty or inefficiency. Trustees do not even get paid for their work, unless there is a clause in the trust instrument authorizing payment. (See 16.2 'General application of constructive trust', and 16.3 'Unauthorized transactions' for the fiduciary nature of trusteeship.)

KEY POINT
The settlor or testator is free to select whoever they wish as trustee.

So why would anyone want to be a trustee? The trustee could often be a relative or friend of the settlor or testator, who feels obliged to act as a trustee. There are also many professional trustees, who will want to charge for their services. Nowadays it would be more usual to appoint professional trustees. Traditionally, the 'family solicitor' would often agree to be a trustee, but there are also trust corporations. Banks and insurance companies usually have specialist trustee departments and, nowadays, there are also many companies formed specifically to act as trustees.

 ## 13.2 Who may be a trustee?

13.2.1 Ordinary trustees

Any human individual can be a trustee. The only exception would be minors. Originally this was anyone under 21, but since s. 1 of the Family Law Reform Act 1969 this has been anyone under 18. Section 20 of the Law of Property Act 1925 makes the appointment of a minor as a trustee void. If that happens, a replacement trustee could be appointed using s. 36 of the Trustee Act 1925 (see 13.5 'The appointment of trustees'). A minor certainly could not be a trustee of land, because trustees hold the legal estate in land and under s. 1(6) of the Law of Property Act 1925 a minor cannot hold the legal estate in land.

KEY POINT
A minor (child) cannot be a trustee of an express trust.

Nevertheless, it is thought possible for a minor to become a trustee if a resulting trust or a constructive trust is imposed by the court. Admittedly this is on the authority of just one High Court case.

. . . .

● **Re Vinogradoff** 1935 WN 68

In 1926 Mrs Vinogradoff transferred a £800 War Loan into the joint names of herself and her four-year-old granddaughter, Laura Jackson. Unsurprisingly, Laura did not give her granny anything in return. Later, the grandmother died. Did Laura own the War Loan?

HELD: Farwell J: Laura held the loan on resulting trust for the estate of Mrs Vinogradoff.

> The stock was not the property of the infant, but formed part of the estate of the testatrix.

(See 8.4.1 'Voluntary transfer to another' for further information on this type of resulting trust.)

It is not really a problem if a child is declared to be a resulting trustee, as unlike in an express trust, they have no duties to perform. All that a resulting trust means is that the property returns to the original owner, Mrs Vinogradoff in the earlier example.

13.2.2 The number of trustees

There must be at least one trustee and there is a maximum number if the trust property is land. Section 34(2) of the Trustee Act 1925 states that a maximum of four trustees can hold the legal estate in land. If more than four trustees are appointed, only the first four named hold the legal estate. There is also, in effect, a minimum number of trustees where land is involved. It is more convenient to have two trustees. If the land is sold, the money must be paid to at least two trustees (s. 27(2) of the Law of Property Act 1925) and there must be a minimum of two trustees to give a valid receipt for the money received (s. 14(2) of the Trustee Act 1925). Similarly, there must be at least two trustees if the purchaser is to **overreach** the interests of the beneficiaries (s. 2(1) of the Law of Property Act 1925).

. . . .

Overreaching—the purchaser only wants to buy the legal estate in the land and does not want to be concerned with who might be the beneficiaries of the trust and what interests they might hold in the property. So, if the purchaser buys from two trustees, the purchaser is not bound by any claims that the beneficiaries might have to the land: Instead, the beneficiaries may claim against the seller of the land for their share of the purchase price.

. . . .

For other types of property, apart from land, there are no rules on the maximum number of trustees.

KEY POINT There is no maximum and no minimum number for trustees, unless the trust property is land. For land, there is a maximum of four and it is advisable to have a minimum of two trustees.

13.2.3 Unanimity

It is better to have more than one trustee, because each trustee can keep an eye on what the other trustees are doing and this may help to reduce fraud or incompetence. The rule is that trustees must be unanimous about any decisions that they take, which means that it is inadvisable to a have a large number of trustees, as if they fail to agree nothing gets done. A testator or settlor can provide for majority voting, by writing this into the trust instrument if he or she wishes. Majority voting is also allowed in pension trusts and charitable trusts, where it is common to have a large number of trustees. (See for example *Re Coates to Parsons* (1886) 34 ChD 370 at 13.5.2 and *Cowan v Scargill* [1985] Ch 270 at 13.11.2 'Removal of trustees by the court is rare'.)

13.2.4 Trust corporations

Trust corporations are commonly used as trustees, either alone or jointly with ordinary trustees. A trust corporation, however, would usually be a sole trustee. This would seem to have advantages, as there would be no need to replace dead or retiring trustees and a large corporation should have the money to compensate for any breach of trust that might occur. A trust corporation can even act alone in selling land, without the problems seen in 13.2.2 'The number of trustees'. On the other hand, trust corporations may charge a lot for their services and, unlike ordinary trustees, they can charge for their services even if there is no charging clause in the trust instrument. This is under s. 29 of the Trustee Act 2000.

In order to protect the public, there are minimum requirements for a trust corporation. These are found in the Public Trustee (Custodian Trustee) Rules 1975 (SI 1975/1189):

The corporation must

(i) be constituted under the law of the UK or of any other Member State of the EU; and

(ii) be empowered by its constitution to undertake trust business in England and Wales; and

(iii) have one or more places of business in the UK; and

(iv) have an issued **share capital** of not less than £250,000, of which not less than £100,000 has been paid up in cash.

. . . .

Share capital—when a company is formed its promoters decide what value of shares the company will have and will be offered for sale. £250,000 indicates that the company will have a reasonable amount of money behind it. The paid up in cash requirement indicates that the shareholders have actually paid for their shares.

. . . .

13.2.5 The public trustee

The office of Public Trustee was created by the Public Trustee Act 1906, and is a type of trust corporation, with the same advantages mentioned in 13.2.4 'Trust corporations'. Nowadays, the Public Trustee is part of the office of the Official Solicitor. As the Public Trustee is part of government, the government will pay compensation if it is necessary. The original reason for establishing the Public Trustee in 1906 was to provide a trustee for small value estates and this is still true today, as the Public Trustee cannot refuse to act just because the value of the trust is small.

> **Public Trustee Act 1906, s. 2**
> ....
> (3) The public trustee may decline, either absolutely or except on the prescribed conditions to accept any trust, but he shall not decline to accept any trust on the ground only of the small value of the trust property.

Administrator—
the person appointed by the court to deal with the estate of a person who has died without making a will.

The Public Trustee can be appointed in the same way as an ordinary trustee and also holds the property of a person who has died intestate, until an **administrator** can be appointed. The Public Trustee provides an 'effective executor and trustee service of last resort'.

The Public Trustee cannot, however, act as the trustee of a charitable trust.

13.2.6 Custodian trustees

The idea of a custodian trustee is that the custodian trustee keeps the trust property and the documents of title safe, while the 'managing trustees' conduct the daily running of the trust. Ordinary trustees, i.e. private individuals, cannot be custodian trustees. Instead, trust corporations, the Public Trustee, and the Official Custodian for Charities act as custodian trustees. A custodian trustee cannot also be a managing trustee. Custodian trustees would normally be appointed if the trust was a large one and the advantage is that, if the managing trustees change, the trust property does not have to be vested in each newly appointed managing trustee. (See 13.9 'The vesting of the legal estate in the trustees'.)

Custodian trustees act upon the instructions of the managing trustees.

13.2.7 Judicial trustees

The High Court may appoint judicial trustees. This is usually done when the administration of the trust has broken down or the trust faces problems such as complex litigation. Normally, if a trust faces problems, those with the power to appoint trustees (see 13.5 'The appointment of trustees') would appoint a professional, such as a trust corporation, to deal with those problems. The court steps in if, for some reason, this cannot happen and will appoint a fit and proper person, usually a solicitor, bank, or accountant, as judicial trustee. (See 13.11.1 'The removal of trustees to protect the beneficiaries' *Carvel Foundation v Carvel* [2007] 4 All ER 81 for an example.) A beneficiary, trustee, or settlor can apply to the court asking for the appointment of a judicial trustee.

> **Judicial Trustee Act 1896, s. 1**
> ....
> (1) Where application is made to the court by or on behalf of the person creating or intending to create a trust, or by or on behalf of a trustee or beneficiary, the court may, in its discretion, appoint a person (in this Act called a judicial trustee) to be a trustee of the trust, either jointly with any other person or as a sole trustee, and, if sufficient cause is shown, in place of all or any existing trustees.

The judicial trustee, who is often a sole trustee, acts under the supervision of the court and can also obtain informal directions from the court. Nevertheless, a judicial trustee has all the powers of an ordinary trustee and is paid by the trust in the normal way.

● **Re Ridsdel** [1947] Ch 597

HELD: Jenkins J at 605:

> ...the object of the Judicial Trustees Act 1896, as I understand it, was to provide a middle course in cases where the administration of the estate by the ordinary trustees had broken down and it was not desired to put the estate to the expense of a full administration. In those circumstances, a solution was found in the appointment of a judicial trustee, who acts in close concert with the court and under conditions enabling the court to supervise his transactions. I cannot think that it was intended to complicate the matter by prohibiting such a trustee from exercising any discretion without first going to the court and asking for directions.

13.3 'The court will not allow a trust to fail for want of a trustee'

The title of this section is one of the maxims of equity (see Chapter 2 'Maxims of equity') and indicates that the death of a trustee does not prevent the continuation of a trust.

When a settlor establishes a trust he or she would usually appoint the trustees at the same time. It is normal to do this by a **deed** and make the trustees parties to the deed. The deed has the advantage of vesting the trust property in the trustees. (See 13.9 'The vesting of the legal estate in the trustees'.)

Deed—a formal legal document, that has to be signed, witnessed, and **delivered**.

Delivered—the person making the deed must hand it over to the person to whom it grants rights, with the intention that it is legally binding.

It is perfectly permissible for the settlor to appoint himself/herself as a trustee.

When a testator establishes a trust it is usual for the will to name persons to act as **executors** of the deceased's estate. The will might also name trustees, which could be the same people as the executors. If they are different people, when the executors have finished administering the estate, they must formally transfer the property to the trustees. (See 13.9 'The vesting of the legal estate in the trustees'.) If no trustees are named, or they are already dead by the time the testator dies, then the executors hold the property as trustees until new trustees can be appointed.

Executor—the persons appointed in the will to carry out the deceased's instructions in the will, in particular to dispose of his/her property according to the will.

It is usual to appoint more than one trustee, in order to take advantage of the right of survivorship. The trustees hold the legal estate of the trust property as joint tenants, meaning that their shares are undivided. If one trustee dies, the surviving trustee or trustees take on all the rights and liabilities over the trust property: s. 18(1) of the Trustee Act 1925.

When the last surviving trustee dies, the executors of that trustee take over as trustees, until replacement trustees are appointed: s. 18(2) of the Trustee Act 1925. If the last trustee has not

KEY POINT
The right of survivorship means that, if a trustee dies, the remaining trustees can continue the trust.

made a will, the Public Trustee (see 13.2.5 'The public trustee') holds the trust property until new trustees are appointed.

Even if trustees disclaim the trust (see 13.4 'Disclaimer'), the trust still continues with the settlor or executors of the testator holding as trustees.

13.4 Disclaimer

The general principle is that no one can be compelled to accept the office of trustee against their will. We are of course considering express trusts here. Many resulting and constructive trustees are unwilling to be trustees, but are forced to become trustees by order of the court. (See Chapter 8 'Resulting trusts' and Chapter 16 'Constructive trusts'.)

Someone who has been appointed as a trustee, but does not want the role, should ideally disclaim as soon as possible. A good way of doing this is for the trustee to draw up a deed stating that he/she does not want to act as a trustee. This avoids any confusion, because once a trustee carries out any trustee duties this will probably be regarded as accepting the office of trustee. Total inaction can also be regarded as disclaiming, but this would be a risky strategy to adopt for someone who definitely did not want to be a trustee. This can be seen by contrasting the following two cases.

● ***Re Clout and Frewer's Contract*** [1924] 2 Ch 230

The testator drew up his will in 1870 leaving his **residuary** real and personal property to his three trustees, his wife Emma, Honton, and Crick. These three were also named as his executors. The testator died in 1872. Emma applied for **probate**, had the property formally transferred to her, and sold the leasehold property and bought other investments, as instructed by the will. Honton and Crick did nothing and in 1890 Honton died. In 1897 Emma died and, as she died intestate, her new husband became the administrator of her estate. He appointed two new trustees replacing Emma, Honton, and Crick. Years later the question arose whether it had been possible to replace Crick in this way.

Residue—the normal legal term used to describe anything that is left after specific bequests in a will.

Probate—the executors of the will prove to the court that the document really is the will of the deceased. Unless the will is disputed, this is just a routine, administrative matter.

HELD: Lord Buckmaster: Crick had disclaimed his trusteeship and therefore it was possible to replace him.

At 236:

> In the present case Crick survived the testator for nearly thirty years without proving, acting, or applying for or receiving his official legacy. In the circumstances I think that is sufficient evidence that he never intended to act, and disclaimed the trusts.

Crick did absolutely nothing and had therefore disclaimed.

In contrast, even quite minor actions taken by a trustee might be regarded as acceptance of the post.

Frank Holder was a farmer and made his will in 1956. By it he appointed as executors and trustees, his wife Mrs Holder, his daughter Barbara Campbell, and his younger son Victor Holder. The property consisted of two farms and the trustees were instructed to sell them and divide the proceeds between Mrs Holder and their ten children, which made 11 equal shares. Victor had helped his father farm the land and in the final years of his father's life had taken over both farms. Frank Holder died in August 1959 and Mrs Holder hired solicitors to act for the executors, who obtained the signatures of all three executors to open an executor's bank account. In order to pay tax and to pay for the funeral, cheques for £600 were drawn on the account and the executors also claimed on the deceased's insurance policies. Mrs Holder instructed a local estate agent to value the farms and Victor carried on farming the land. Victor then decided that he wanted to buy the farms and so, in August 1960, he drew up a deed renouncing his executorship.

Victor did this because there is a rule that forbids trustees or executors from buying trust property. See 16.2.3 'Unauthorized activities of trustees occasioning breach of trust'.

Victor bought the farms at a public auction, for what was thought to be a fair price.

In 1963 his older brother, Frank, who lived in one of the farmhouses and stood to be evicted, questioned the legality of the sale and sought to have it set aside.

HELD: Victor had accepted that, as he had already acted as an executor, he could not disclaim.

Harman LJ at 391:

> It was admitted at the bar in the court below that the acts of Victor were enough to constitute intermeddling with the estate and that his renunciation was ineffective. On this footing he remained a personal representative, even after probate had been granted to his co-executors, and could have been obliged by a creditor or a beneficiary to re-assume the duties of an executor.

At least one of the judges had his doubts.

Danckwerts LJ at 397:

> The three grounds that were relied on are so technical and trivial and not really the acts of Victor, who really simply complied with the directions of Mrs Holder, that in my opinion they should not have the effect of preventing a renunciation of probate by an executor. However, it was conceded at the hearing that the renunciation was invalid and, accordingly, we must act on that admission and the effect that it has in regard to the position of an executor. In my view this was a mistake.

KEY POINTS

- *Re Clout* and *Holder* indicate that the safest course for a trustee who does not want to be one is to disclaim by deed as soon as possible, before they do anything connected with the trust.

- If a trustee does not disclaim at the outset, he or she can later on retirement. (See 13.10 'The retirement of trustees'.)

- The difference is that retirement later on would need the agreement of his or her fellow trustees and anyone else who has the power to appoint trustees.

13.5 The appointment of trustees

As we saw in 13.3 '"The court will not allow a trust to fail for want of a trustee"', the trustees are usually appointed by the original settlor or testator, but trustees often need to be replaced. This is governed by s. 36 of the Trustee Act 1925.

13.5.1 Express powers

The trust instrument will often say who has the power to appoint new trustees.

> **Trustee Act 1925, s. 36**
> ....
>
> 1(a) The person or persons nominated for the purpose of appointing new trustees by the instrument, if any, creating the trust; . . .

It could be the settlor, a beneficiary, an existing trustee, or, indeed, anyone. Quite often the person nominated only has the power to appoint trustees in certain situations. This is illustrated by the following case.

● **Re Wheeler and de Rochow** [1896] 1 Ch 315

A trust was set up to provide for the marriage of Mr Rochow to Mrs Wheeler. The trust contained an express appointment clause:

> . . . it shall be lawful for the said AE De Rochow and ES Wheeler or the survivor of them . . . by any deed or deeds, to appoint any other person or persons to supply the place of the trustee or trustees respectively so dying, desiring to be discharged, or refusing, declining, or becoming incapable to act as aforesaid.

One of the trustees, Wynne, was bankrupt, but had absconded and could not be found. Mrs Wheeler was dead, so Rochow tried to appoint Sewell as a replacement trustee.

HELD: Rochow did not have the power to do this, as Wynne was 'unfit' to be a trustee, not 'incapable'.

Kekewich J at 322:

> Those considerations lead me to the conclusion that, inasmuch as the event which has occurred, namely, the bankruptcy of Mr Wynne (who whether or not he may be unfit by reason of his bankruptcy, is certainly unfit by reason of his having absconded), is not within the power contained in the settlement,

The court might have to identify the person with the power to appoint trustees.

● **Shergill v Khaira** [2014] 3 All ER 243

A religious charity for a Sikh sect was established by the 'First Saint'. The trust deed stated that he or his successor could remove and appoint trustees. A dispute arose in the sect over who his true successor was.

KEY POINT

If there is an express power to appoint new trustees, this takes priority over the other powers to appoint trustees in s. 36.

HELD: At 261j:

> The courts have jurisdiction to determine disputes over the ownership, possession and control of property held on trusts for religious purposes.

This meant that the court might have to 'adjudicate upon matters of religious doctrine and practice' in order to decide who the successor was.

13.5.2 The surviving or continuing trustees

If there is no express power to appoint trustees, then the other trustees have the power to replace a trustee.

Trustee Act 1925, s. 36

. . . .

(1) (b) If there is no such person, or no such person able and willing to act, then the surviving or continuing trustees or trustee for the time being...

...

(8) ...a continuing trustee include[s] a refusing or retiring trustee...

Trustees who do not want to act, or wish to retire, can appoint their replacements and indeed it is standard practice for refusing or retiring trustees to participate in appointing their replacements.

The subsection seems to say that all the trustees must concur in the new appointment(s), but taken literally this could cause problems if a trustee is unwilling to cooperate. The court will allow the other trustees to go ahead without him or her.

. . . .
● ***Re Coates to Parsons*** (1886) 34 ChD 370

The Methodist Chapel at Thrapston, Northamptonshire, had 11 trustees, hence the strange case name. One trustee was dead and another, Dearlove, had been outside the UK for 12 months. The nine remaining trustees appointed a new trustee, without the cooperation of Dearlove.

HELD: North J at 377:

> I hold, therefore, that under the terms of the Act the nine trustees, who were clearly continuing trustees, were competent to make the appointment, unless it were shown that the person who had been absent for so long, and in whose place there was a clear right to substitute a new trustee, was willing and competent to act. This has not been shown, and it seems to me, therefore, that the first objection, namely, that WR Dearlove ought to have concurred in making the appointment, is not established.

13.5.3 The personal representatives of the last surviving trustee

If all the trustees are dead, then their personal representatives have the power to appoint new trustees.

> **Trustee Act 1925, s. 36**
>
> . . . .
>
> (1) (b) . . . or the personal representatives of the last surviving or continuing trustee;
>
> . . .
>
> (4) Personal representatives mean the executors who have proved the will or the administrators.

. . . .

● *Re Higginbottom* [1892] 3 Ch 132

After the death of Joseph Higginbottom, in 1834, it was held that his will appointed his son, John Higginbottom, and Edward Lees as trustees. Lees had died and Higginbottom died in 1853, making his wife, Sarah Higginbottom, his executor. Sarah died in 1885 and she made her daughter, Mary Jane Broadbent, her executor. Mary Jane wanted to appoint new trustees, but this was opposed by five-sixths of the beneficiaries, who had their own choice of trustees.

HELD: Kekewich J at 135:

> Mary Jane Broadbent, the legal personal representative of the last surviving executor of the testator's will, insists that, she being willing to exercise such powers as are vested in her by statute or otherwise, including that of appointing new trustees, no order for the appointment of new trustees can properly be made by the court.
>
> The non-interference by the court with the legal power of appointment of new trustees is established by several cases . . .

KEY POINT
Section 36 states who can appoint new trustees. The court will not normally interfere with the choices made.

Mary Jane's statutory right to appoint new trustees outweighed the wishes of the beneficiaries. The court has no desire to become unnecessarily involved in the running of a trust, unless it is absolutely necessary in order to protect the beneficiaries.

So it is only in extreme cases that the court will override the wishes of the person given the power of appointment in the trust. In *Thomas Jones, Ian Firkin-Flood and others v Daniel Firkin-Flood, Louise Firkin-Flood* [2008] EWHC 2417 (Ch) (see 13.11.1 'The removal of trustees to protect the beneficiaries'), the trustees had shown themselves unfit to act. One of those trustees, Ian Firkin-Flood, had the express power to replace trustees. The court could, if necessary, override his wishes because the power to replace trustees 'is a fiduciary power rather than a beneficial right, and thereby subject to the supervision and control of the court' (at para 296).

13.5.4 Section 36(1) is a replacement power

This subsection only allows the replacement of trustees. The subsection has been interpreted in a very literal way, as illustrated in *Adams & Co International Trustees Ltd v Theodore Goddard (A Firm)* [2000] WTLR 349.

. . . .

● *Adam & Co International Trustees Ltd v Theodore Goddard (A Firm)* [2000] WTLR 349

Two trustees tried to retire and appoint a single trustee to replace them.

HELD: Evans-Lombe J:

> A single trustee could not replace two trustees under a true construction of s. 36, and the second retiring trustee could only achieve a discharge under the retirement provisions contained in s. 39.

(See 13.10 'The retirement of trustees' for retirement of trustees under s. 39.)

thinking points

Is the decision in Adam & Co International Trustees Ltd *unduly restrictive? The Trustee Act 1925 is a consolidating Act, bringing together parts of older legislation. It contains anomalies, such as new trustees must be appointed in writing under s. 36, but by a deed under s. 39. The decision in* Adams *was an unwelcome surprise for many practitioners, as s. 36 had been used to reduce the number of trustees and there was a fear that it would render previous appointments of trustees invalid. Section 36 cannot be used in the way it was in* Adams, *because the section says that the new trustee is appointed 'in place of' the old trustee so, on a literal interpretation, Evans-Lombe J is correct. See F Barlow 'The Appointment of Trustees: A Disappointing Decision' [2003] Conv 15.*

The wording of s. 36(1), 'in the place of', which can be seen at 13.5.5 'The situations in which a trustee may be replaced', indicates that s. 36 is a power to *replace* trustees.

Under the Trustee Act 1925, trustees are allowed to retire, but they must be replaced by other trustees. Section 37(1)(c) states that:

> a trustee shall not be discharged from his trust unless there will be either a trust corporation or at least two individuals to act as trustees to perform the trust.

We can see another example of literal interpretation of the Trustee Act 1925 in *Jasmine Trustees Ltd v Wells and Hind (A Firm)* [2007] 3 WLR 810.

● *Jasmine Trustees Ltd v Wells and Hind (A Firm)* [2007] 3 WLR 810

Major-General Coaker and Mrs Coaker were trustees and purported to retire and be replaced as trustees by the Investment Bank of Ireland and Mr Thornton.

HELD: Mann J: The word 'individuals' had to be given its normal meaning. It meant human individual. That meant that either two human beings had to be appointed as the replacement trustees *or* a trust corporation. A human being *and* a trust corporation were not permitted by the literal wording of the Act.

At 821:

> ...individuals in section 37(1)(c) means natural persons.

That meant that the new 'trustees' had never been properly appointed. They were 'trustees de son tort', as they had acted, thinking that they were trustees. Their basic duty was to safeguard the trust property and hand it over to the beneficiaries or properly appointed trustees.

At 827:

> The trustee de son tort will be obliged to hold the property for, and to account to, the beneficiaries, but on the other side of the coin will not have the powers of the trustee conferred by the settlement.

Trustees de son tort do not have the powers of properly appointed trustees. It is more a question of their liability to return the property to its rightful owners.

Making someone liable as a trustee de son tort is a type of constructive trust. See Chapter 16 'Constructive trusts' and particularly 16.4.1 'Who is a trustee de son tort?'

13.5.5 The situations in which a trustee may be replaced

Trustee Act 1925, s. 36
. . . .

(1) Where a trustee, either original or substituted, and whether appointed by a court or otherwise, is dead, or remains out of the United Kingdom for more than 12 months, or desires to be discharged from all or any of the trusts or powers reposed in or conferred on him, or refuses or is unfit to act therein, or is incapable of acting therein, or is an infant, then, subject to the restrictions imposed by this Act on the number of trustees—appointors [mentioned in 13.5.1 'Express powers' to 13.5.3 'The personal representatives of the last surviving trustee'] may, by writing, appoint one or more other persons (whether or not being the persons exercising the power) to be a trustee or trustees in the place of the trustee so deceased, remaining out of the United Kingdom, desiring to be discharged, refusing, or being unfit or being incapable, or being an infant, as aforesaid.

Dead

According to s. 36(8), this includes 'the case of a person nominated trustee in a will but dying before the testator'.

12 months outside the UK

The 12-month period has to be continuous.

. . . .

● **Re Walker** [1901] 1 Ch 259

There were two trustees, Summers and Mrs Walker. Summers went abroad in April 1899 and, on 1 June 1900 Walker tried to replace him.

HELD: Farwell J: Summers had returned to London for one week in November, when he saw the trust solicitors and transacted some trust business. Therefore, the statutory power to replace him did not apply.

A trustee can be removed against his will under this section.

The trustees of Stoneham's settlement were his widow, his son, Stoneham, and Crosthwaite. The widow and Stoneham had been outside the UK for more than 12 months, so Crosthwaite replaced them, against the wishes of Stoneham.

HELD: Danckwerts J at 63:

> Stoneham, as it seems to me, is a person who can be removed under the statutory power whether he agrees or not. It seems to me that the words of section 36(1) are plain in that respect, and I do not understand the doubts...

Nor was Stoneham's agreement required to the new appointments.

At 64:

> It seems to me, therefore, that this decision does not fetter the view which I should otherwise be disposed to take of the proper construction of the section, and I come to the conclusion quite plainly that a trustee who is removed against his will is not a refusing or retiring trustee, not, at any rate, in the case of a trustee removed because of his absence outside the United Kingdom for consecutive periods of more than 12 months.

Desires to be discharged

As we saw in 13.5.4 'Section 36(1) is a replacement power', this section can be used as a way for a trustee to retire, as long as a replacement is appointed: *Adams & Co International Trustees Ltd v Theodore Goddard (A Firm)* [2000] WTLR 349.

The other method of retiring is to use s. 39. (See 13.10 'The retirement of trustees'.)

Refuses to act

As we saw in 13.4 'Disclaimer', a trustee can disclaim if they do it before carrying out any trustee actions, otherwise they will be regarded as refusing to act and could be replaced.

Unfit to act

An example can be seen in 13.5.1 'Express powers', where a trustee was bankrupt: *In Re Wheeler and de Rochow* [1896] 1 Ch 315.

Incapable of acting

This might be through illness, old age, or mental disorder.

Section 36(3) adds that if a trust corporation is dissolved, it is deemed incapable of acting and can be replaced.

Infant

We saw in 13.2.1 'Ordinary trustees' that an infant could not be a trustee.

Trust instrument

As s. 36(2) makes clear, the trust instrument may include additional powers to replace trustees.

> **Trustee Act 1925, s. 36**
> ....
>
> (2) Where a trustee has been removed under a power contained in the instrument creating the trust, a new trustee or new trustees may be appointed in the place of the trustee who is removed, as if he were dead, or, in the case of a corporation, as if the corporation desired to be discharged from the trust, and the provisions of this section shall apply accordingly, but subject to the restrictions imposed by this Act on the number of trustees.

13.6 The appointment of additional trustees

Before the 1925 Act, trustees were only appointed as replacements for the existing trustees. Extra trustees could only be appointed if the trust instrument allowed it. Section 36(6) of the Trustee Act 1925 allows for the appointment of additional trustees, up to an overall maximum of four.

> **Trustee Act 1925, s. 36**
> ....
>
> (6) Where, in the case of any trust, there are not more than three trustees—
>   (a) the person or persons nominated for the purpose of appointing new trustees by the instrument, if any, creating the trust; or
>   (b) if there is no such person, or no such person able and willing to act, then the trustee or trustees for the time being;
>
>   may, by writing, appoint another person or other persons to be an additional trustee or additional trustees, but it shall not be obligatory to appoint any additional trustee, unless the instrument, if any, creating the trust, or any statutory enactment provides to the contrary, nor shall the number of trustees be increased beyond four by virtue of any such appointment.

It can be seen from the wording of the subsection, 'another person…', that the appointor cannot appoint himself as trustee.

13.7 The appointment of trustees by the beneficiaries

13.7.1 The beneficiaries could not appoint trustees

Traditionally, the beneficiaries were not permitted to appoint the trustees unless the trust instrument allowed this. It was thought that if beneficiaries had this power it would interfere with the vital discretion of the trustees to take decisions in the best interests of the trust. (See 11.12 'Information for the beneficiaries'.)

● ***Re Brockbank*** [1948] Ch 206

The will of Joseph Brockbank set up a trust for his wife and five children. There were two trustees, Ward and Bates. Ward and the beneficiaries wanted Ward to retire and both trustees to be replaced by a sole trustee, the trust corporation, Lloyds Bank Ltd. Bates refused to agree.

HELD: Vaisey J at 208–9:

> The power of nominating a new trustee is a discretionary power, and, in my opinion is no longer exercisable and, indeed, can no longer exist if it has become one of which the exercise can be dictated by others. But then it is said that the beneficiaries could direct the trustees to transfer the trust property either to themselves absolutely, or to any other person or persons or corporation, upon trusts identical with or corresponding to the trusts of the testator's will. I agree…

At 212:

> To appoint a bank, who charge an acceptance fee, who charge a withdrawal fee and who charge an income fee, as a trustee of the trust, of which all that remains to be done is to pay the income to a lady of eighty-three years and on her death to divide the capital, seems to me to be a very improvident way of dealing with the position.

The beneficiaries cannot tell the trustees who to appoint as replacements. There is nothing, however, to stop the beneficiaries all agreeing to end the trust and set up a new trust, with new trustees, if they want to do so. This is known as the rule in *Saunders v Vautier* (1841) 4 Beav 115. (See 14.1 'Adult beneficiaries'.)

The judge goes on to warn the beneficiaries that replacing trustees can be expensive, as they might need to compensate the old trustees and there could be tax liabilities. He also reminds them that trust corporations may charge high fees.

13.7.2 Beneficiaries are given the power to appoint trustees

The Trusts of Land and Appointment of Trustees Act 1996 changed this position and allowed all the beneficiaries to replace the trustees.

Trusts of Land and Appointment of Trustees Act 1996

19 Appointment and retirement of trustee at instance of beneficiaries

(1) This section applies in the case of a trust where—
  (a) there is no person nominated for the purpose of appointing new trustees by the instrument, if any, creating the trust, and
  (b) the beneficiaries under the trust are of full age and capacity and (taken together) are absolutely entitled to the property subject to the trust.
(2) The beneficiaries may give a direction or directions of either or both of the following descriptions—
  (a) a written direction to a trustee or trustees to retire from the trust, and

(b) a written direction to the trustees or trustee for the time being, (or, if there are none, to the personal representative of the last person who was a trustee) to appoint by writing to be a trustee or trustees the person or persons specified in the direction.

(5) This section has effect subject to the restrictions imposed by the Trustee Act 1925 on the number of trustees.

It can be seen that this power has limitations. Subsection (1)(a) indicates that it can be excluded by the trust instrument. Subsection (1)(b) states that all the beneficiaries must be in agreement and that all of them must be of full age. It might be rare for all the beneficiaries to agree, as seen in *Re Higginbottom* [1892] 3 Ch 132 in 13.5.3 'The personal representatives of the last surviving trustee'.

The Trusts of Land and Appointment of Trustees Act 1996 also allows the beneficiaries to replace trustees with mental disorders, if no one else is willing and able to do so.

KEY POINT
Beneficiaries can replace their trustees, but all the beneficiaries must be in agreement, of full age, and mentally capable.

> **Trusts of Land and Appointment of Trustees Act 1996**
> . . . .
> 20 Appointment of substitute for incapable trustee
>
> (1) This section applies where—
>   (a) a trustee is incapable by reason of mental disorder of exercising his functions as a trustee,
>   (b) there is no person who is both entitled and willing and able to appoint a trustee in place of him under section 36(1) of the Trustee Act 1925, and
>   (c) the beneficiaries under the trust are of full age and capacity and (taken together) are absolutely entitled to the property subject to the trust.
> (2) The beneficiaries may give . . . a written direction . . .

> ***thinking points***
> *Does s. 19 of TOLATA 1996 give beneficiaries too much power over their trustees? The scheme in the Trustee Act 1925 does not allow beneficiaries to remove and replace trustees and, generally, under trust law beneficiaries are not entitled to tell trustees what to do, because otherwise trustees might be rendered incapable of exercising their discretion (see 11.12 'Information for the beneficiaries'). TOLATA 1996 seems to change this, but in fact the s. 19 power can be excluded by the settlor or testator and, as all the beneficiaries have to agree, it may not add much to the beneficiaries' existing power under* Saunders v Vautier *(see 3.6.7 'Bare trusts' and 14.1 'Adult beneficiaries'). There may be technical problems with s. 19, as it does not say what happens if a trustee refuses to comply or specify the exact mechanism of retirement. Would the trustee need to retire under s. 39? (See 13.10 'The retirement of trustees'.) See M Keppel-Palmer 'Discretion No More?' (1996) 146 NLJ 1779.*

13.8 The appointment of trustees by the court

The court has an ancient common law power and a statutory power to appoint new trustees to a trust.

13.8.1 The courts' power in s. 41 of the Trustee Act 1925

> **Trustee Act 1925**
>
> . . . .
>
> 41 Power of court to appoint new trustees
>
> The court may, whenever it is expedient to appoint a new trustee or new trustees, and it is found inexpedient difficult or impracticable so to do without the assistance of the court, make an order appointing a new trustee or new trustees either in substitution for or in addition to any existing trustee or trustees, or although there is no existing trustee.
>
> In particular and without prejudice to the generality of the foregoing provision, the court may make an order appointing a new trustee in substitution for a trustee who is incapable, by reason of a mental disorder within the meaning of the Mental Health Act 1983, of exercising his functions as trustee or is a bankrupt, or is a corporation which is in liquidation or has been dissolved.

This section mentions replacing trustees who are mentally disordered, bankrupt, or a dissolved corporation, but, in fact, the court has a general power to replace trustees for any reason.

The court will not use this power against the wishes of those who have the power under s. 36 to appoint. (See *Re Higginbottom* [1892] 3 Ch 132 at 13.5.3 'The personal representatives of the last surviving trustee'.)

The court is also reluctant to overrule the choice made by the statutory appointors, if the trustees seek the approval of the court for their choice of trustees.

. . . .

● *Richard v The Hon AB Mackay* [1997] 11 TLI 23

This was an English trust, with English trustees, and it was proposed to appoint trustees in Bermuda.

HELD: Millett J:

> Where, however, the transaction is proposed to be carried out by the trustees in exercise of their own discretion, entirely out of court, the trustees retaining their discretion and merely seeking the authorisation of the court for their own protection, then in my judgment the question that the court asks itself is quite different. It is concerned to ensure that the proposed exercise of the trustees' power is lawful and within the power and that it does not infringe the trustees' duty to act as ordinary, reasonable and prudent trustees might act, but it requires only to be satisfied that the trustees can properly form the view that the proposed transaction is for the benefit of beneficiaries or the trust estate.

KEY POINT
Court selection of trustees is a last resort.

(See 14.5.3 'Export of the trust' on the appointment of trustees abroad.)

13.8.2 The selection of trustees by the court

Where, however, the statutory appointors were in disagreement, the court was willing to appoint a trustee. The judge also gave useful guidance on how trustees should be selected.

Sir CR Tempest set up a trust in his will, but one of the trustees had died before he did. The surviving trustee, Fleming, and one of the Tempest beneficiaries, had the power under the will to appoint a new trustee. Tempest wanted to appoint Petre, but this was opposed by Fleming, because Petre was connected with a branch of the family with whom Sir CR Tempest had not been on friendly terms.

HELD: Sir GJ Turner LJ at 487–90: The court had a discretion and there were three main principles upon which that discretion would be exercised. These three principles were applied to Petre.

> It was said in argument, and has been frequently said, that in making such appointments the Court acts upon and exercises its discretion; and this, no doubt, is generally true; but the discretion that the court has and exercises in making such appointments, is not, as I conceive, a mere arbitrary discretion, but a discretion in the exercise of which the Court is, and ought to be, guided by some general rules and principles, and, in my opinion, the difficulty which the Court has to encounter in these cases lies not so much in ascertaining the rules and principles by which it ought to be guided, as in applying those rules and principles to the varying circumstances of each particular case. The following rules and principles may, I think safely be laid down as applying to all cases of appointment by the Court of new trustees.
>
> First, the Court will have regard to the wishes of the persons by whom the trust has been created, if expressed in the instrument creating the trust, or clearly to be collected from it. I think this rule may be safely laid down, because if the author of the trust has in terms declared that a particular person, or a person filling a particular character, should not be a trustee of the instrument, there cannot, as I apprehend, be the least doubt that the Court would not appoint to the office a person whose appointment was so prohibited, and I do not think that upon a question of this description any distinction can be drawn between express declarations and demonstrated intention.
>
> Another rule which may, I think, safely be laid down is this—that the Court will not appoint a person to be trustee with a view to the interest of some of the persons interested under the trust, in opposition either to the wishes of the testator or to the interests of others of the cestuis que trusts. I think so for this reason, that it is of the essence of the duty of every trustee to hold an even hand between the parties interested under the trust. Every trustee is duty bound to look to the interests of all, and not of any particular member or class of members of his cestuis que trusts.
>
> A third rule which, I think, may safely be laid down, is—that the Court in appointing a trustee will have regard to the question, whether his appointment will promote or impede the execution of the trust, for the very purpose of the appointment is that the trust may be better carried into execution.

Petre was not acceptable under any of the three principles.

> First, as to the wishes of this testator, it is impossible, I think, to read this will without being fully satisfied that the great object and purpose of the testator was to exclude Mr Charles Henry Tempest not only from all interest in, but from all connection with his estate... Is it then consistent with this purpose of the testator that a trustee should be appointed who, upon the evidence before us, I cannot doubt is the nominee of Mr Charles Henry Tempest, and is proposed for the purpose of carrying into effect his wishes and intentions?

Then, as to the second ground, the objection to the appointment of Mr Petre seems to me to be still more decisive. The evidence, in my opinion, very plainly shows that Mr Petre has been proposed as trustee, and has accepted that office, with a view to his acting in the trust in the interests of some only of the objects of it, and in opposition to the wishes of the testator, and not with a view to his acting as an independent trustee for the benefit of all the objects of the trusts, and I do not hesitate to say that, in my opinion, this fact is alone sufficient to prevent us from confirming his appointment.

The third and remaining ground of objection to the appointment of Mr Petre is, I think, open to more difficulty. On the one hand, there cannot, I think, be any doubt that the Court ought not to appoint a trustee whose appointment will impede the due execution of the trust...Upon the facts of this case, however, it seems to me that the objections taken by Mr Fleming to the appointment of Mr Petre were and are well founded, and upon the whole case, therefore, my opinion is, that the order under appeal, so far as it appoints Mr Petre, ought to be discharged.

Lord Camoys was appointed trustee in his place.

It must be emphasized that the court does not want to be involved in appointing trustees if it can be avoided. There have to be very strong reasons for not appointing a trustee, for the court to become involved. For illustration, a brief obiter dictum on fitness to be a trustee can be found in the following case. Even the infirm could make a perfectly satisfactory trustee.

● *Hanchett-Stamford v Attorney General* [2008] 4 All ER 323

Mrs Hanchett-Stamford had suffered 'a stroke which deprived her of her power of speech and her mobility' and required her to move to a nursing home. She had now regained her speech and planned to move back home, where she would need support, but not constant medical attention. She had understood the court proceedings.

Lewison J at 339:

She had a good grasp of past events, and understood the questions that were put to her... Ms. Bevan, her solicitor, said that she had been impressed with Mrs Hanchett-Stamford's grasp of the implications of these proceedings and said that, with advice, Mrs Hanchett-Stamford would make a capable co-trustee. I have no reason to disagree.

KEY POINTS

- The *court* will take three factors into account when appointing a trustee:

  1. the wishes of the settlor or testator;

  2. the trustee must serve the interests of *all* the beneficiaries;

  3. the trustee must not impede the execution of the trust.

- A settlor, testator, or appointor is free to appoint any trustee that they wish. The factors above are not binding on them but simply good advice.

13.9 The vesting of the legal estate in the trustees

In a trust the trustees hold the legal estate in the trust property, so it is important that the trust property is properly 'vested' in them. This means that the legal formalities for that particular type of property must be completed, in order to transfer the legal estate to them. (See Chapter 5 'The formality requirements and incompletely constituted trusts'.)

As we have seen, trustees can be replaced, so it would be inconvenient to have to go through the formalities to transfer the legal estate each time there was a new trustee. So, under s. 40 of the Trustee Act 1925, if the new trustee is appointed by deed the legal estate will automatically vest in the new trustee. After 1925, any deed of appointment will automatically do this, without the need for any special form of words.

Trustee Act 1925

....

40 Vesting of trust property in new or continuing trustees

(1) Where by a deed a new trustee is appointed to perform any trust, then—

    (a) if the deed contains a declaration by the appointor to the effect that any estate or interest in any land subject to the trust, or in any chattel so subject, or the right to recover or receive any debt or other thing in action so subject, shall vest in the persons who by virtue of the deed become or are the trustees for performing the trust, the deed shall operate, without any conveyance or assignment, to vest in those persons as joint tenants and for the purposes of the trust the estate interest or right to which the declaration relates; and

    (b) if the deed is made after the commencement of this Act and does not contain such a declaration, the deed shall, subject to any express provision to the contrary therein contained, operate as if it had contained such a declaration by the appointor extending to all the estates interests and rights with respect to which a declaration could have been made.

Section 40 does not apply to all types of property, for subsection (4) exempts mortgages, leases with covenants, and stocks and shares. For those types of property, the full formalities will have to be completed to transfer the legal estate in the trust property to the trustee.

KEY POINT

Appoint trustees by deed, because that vests the legal estate in them.

Neither does s. 40 apply to trusts set up in a will. The executors will need formally to transfer the trust property to the trustees.

If we look back to 13.5.5 'The situations in which a trustee may be replaced', s. 36(1) says that replacement trustees can be replaced in 'writing', but it is better to use a deed, because that will vest the legal estate in them.

13.10 The retirement of trustees

We have seen that trustees can be replaced under s. 36 of the Trustee Act (see 13.5 'The appointment of trustees') and by the court under s. 41 (see 13.8 'The appointment of trustees by the court'). The beneficiaries can also instruct a trustee to retire under

s. 19 of the Trusts of Land and Appointment of Trustees Act 1996 (see 13.7.2 'Beneficiaries are given the power to appoint trustees'). Trustees can, however, voluntarily retire without being replaced, as long as there are at least two trustees or a trust corporation remaining. The retiring trustee needs the agreement of his fellow trustees and anyone with the power to appoint trustees.

Trustee Act 1925

· ·

39 Retirement of trustee without a new appointment

(1) Where a trustee is desirous of being discharged from the trust, and after his discharge there will be either a trust corporation or at least two persons to act as trustees to perform the trust, then, if such trustee as aforesaid by deed declares that he is desirous of being discharged from the trust, and if his co-trustees and such other person, if any, as is empowered to appoint trustees, by deed consent to the discharge of the trustee, and to the vesting in the co-trustees alone of the trust property, the trustee desirous of being discharged shall be deemed to have retired from the trust, and shall, by the deed, be discharged therefrom under this Act, without any new trustee being appointed in his place.

As with s. 40 in 13.9 'The vesting of the legal estate in the trustees', a *deed* is once again required.

13.11 The removal of trustees

As a last resort the court has the power to remove a trustee. Usually a trustee could be removed using s. 36 of the Trustee Act 1925, s. 19 of the Trusts of Land and Appointment of Trustees Act 1996, or the voluntary retirement provisions under s. 39 of the Trustee Act 1925. The court also has a replacement power under s. 41 of the Trustee Act 1925, but if none of these powers seems appropriate, the court can always fall back on its inherent jurisdiction to control trusts and remove a trustee.

13.11.1 The removal of trustees to protect the beneficiaries

· ·

● ***Letterstedt v Broers*** (1883–84) LR 9 App Cas 371

Jacob Letterstedt died in 1862, when his only daughter was eight years old. His will instructed his executors to run his brewery business and give his daughter four-sixths of the profit when she was 25 years old. There were originally three executors, but two of them died, not long after Jacob, leaving the Board of Executors of Cape Town (a trust corporation) as the sole executor. Miss Letterstedt was unhappy with the way that they had run the brewery business, accused them of charging too much, 10 per cent, and concealing this in the accounts. She wanted her money restored to her and the board to be removed as trustees.

HELD: Lord Blackburn: The board of executors had accepted the trusts and so were to be regarded as trustees. His Lordship noted that such cases were rare, as normally where there were disagreements with the beneficiaries the trustees voluntarily resigned.

At 387:

> In exercising so delicate a jurisdiction as that of removing trustees, their Lordships do not venture to lay down any general rule beyond the very broad principle above enunciated, that their main guide must be the welfare of the beneficiaries. Probably it is not possible to lay down any more definite rule in a matter so essentially dependent on details often of great nicety. But they proceed to look carefully into the circumstances of the case.

And at 389:

In the court below, the board had opposed Miss Letterstedt's 'perfectly reasonable inquiry' into their financial conduct.

> It is quite true that friction or hostility between trustees and the immediate possessor of the trust estate is not of itself a reason for the removal of the trustees. But where the hostility is grounded on the mode in which the trust has been administered, where it has been caused wholly or partially by substantial overcharges against the trust estate, it is certainly not to be disregarded.
>
> Looking therefore at the whole circumstances of this very peculiar case, the complete change of position, the unfortunate hostility that has arisen, and the difficult and delicate duties that may yet have to be performed, their Lordships can come to no other conclusion than that it is necessary, for the welfare of the beneficiaries, that the Board should no longer be trustees.

Letterstedt is still accepted as the leading authority on the removal of trustees and has been applied to the removal of a personal representative as well.

● ***Thomas and Agnes Carvel Foundation v Carvel and Another*** [2007] 4 All ER 81

Thomas and Agnes had made mutual wills, leaving their property to each other for life and then to the Thomas and Agnes Carvel Foundation, a non-profit making foundation that they had established. Thomas died first, bringing the mutual will agreement into effect, but Agnes made a new will leaving her property to a different not-for-profit corporation, the Carvel Foundation. A niece, Pamela Carvel, was the only executor of the will of Agnes, but she made her own claim for £8 million against the estate of Agnes and did not inform the Thomas and Agnes Carvel Foundation of legal proceedings related to her claim. This Foundation claimed that the mutual will agreement meant that the property of Agnes was held on trust for them and they wanted Pamela Carvel removed.

(See 7.3 'Mutual wills'.)

HELD: Lewison J: Agreed that this was a trust and cited *Letterstedt* with approval.

At 96:

> Lord Blackburn cited as the guiding principle to the jurisdiction to remove trustees as being 'the welfare of the beneficiaries', Mr Barlow submitted:
>
> Pamela has wholly disregarded this principle. Her every act has been calculated to promote her own personal interests and to prejudice those of the foundation. She is in a position of irreconcilable conflict with the principal beneficiary of Agnes' estate and her hostility to the foundation renders it quite impossible for her to fulfil her fiduciary duties. Her position as personal representative is untenable. She should be removed.

I agree. I will order Pamela to be removed as personal representative. The foundation has proposed that Mr Guy Greenhous, a solicitor and partner in Radcliffes Le Brasseur, be appointed as personal representative (or judicial trustee).

A trustee must promote the interests of the trust, which means that there will be a conflict of interest if the trustee has claims to trust property also claimed by a beneficiary. The conflict here was so serious that a judicial trustee had to be appointed. (See 13.2.7 'Judicial trustees'.)

Following on from the leading case of *Letterstedt v Broers* [1883–84] LR 9 App Cas 371, the High Court emphasized that it was not necessary to prove wrongdoing or dishonesty for the court to order the removal of trustees. Lack of capacity was enough, and when appointing new trustees the court should have regard to the welfare of the beneficiaries and the circumstances of the trust.

● ***Thomas Jones, Ian Firkin-Flood and others v Daniel Firkin-Flood, Louise Firkin-Flood*** [2008] EWHC 2417 (Ch)

The will of Douglas Firkin-Flood left trusts for his three children, Ian, Daniel, and Louise. The trustees were Ian, the eldest son, Jones, the family solicitor, and two long-serving employees of the Flood businesses, Levy and Bramley. Daniel and Louise claimed that Ian was gaining too large a share of their father's trusts and sought the removal of the trustees.

HELD: Biggs J: The trustees were in breach of trust.

At para 239:

> I regret to have to say that the facts as I have found them reveal not merely a number of isolated breaches of trust by the Trustees, but rather a total abdication of their duties by all of them...

The other three trustees had let Ian run the trust on his own, failed to supervise Ian or the companies that the trust owned, failed to invest, and failed to compile accounts.

The professional trustee, Jones, did not 'provide appropriate advice and guidance to his lay colleagues'.

Because of this, the trustees had to be removed by the court.

At para 285:

> The present case is not one of dishonesty or even of deliberate breach and only to a limited extent one involving a breach of aspects of the duty of fidelity. It is pre-eminently a case of want of capacity, or, as I would prefer to put it, of unfitness. The Trustees have, quite simply, amply demonstrated their collective unfitness to be trustees of the Trust.

There was still important business of the trust to transact, as the trust funds had to be distributed to the beneficiaries. Levy would be kept on, as a link to the family should be maintained and two professional trustees nominated by Louise and Daniel should also be appointed.

At para 292:

> In my judgment, the governing criterion, consistent with the need to have regard first and foremost to the interests of the beneficiaries, is to constitute a body of trustees who will be able with the minimum of expense and dissention, and in particular with as little as possible

further assistance from the court, to restore the administration of the Trust to a basis capable of commanding the confidence and respect of all its beneficiaries, and dealing impartially with their separate claims to consideration for distribution.

---

thinking points

The choice of suitable trustees is an important decision for the settlor or testator. As we saw in 13.2 'Who may be a trustee?' there are few legal restrictions upon who may be appointed, but the case law, such as Re Tempest *and* Letterstedt v Broers, *does give some guidance on what not to do. It is not advisable to appoint trustees who favour the interests of one beneficiary over another or their own interests or who are incompetent or dishonest. Other than that it is up to the settlor or testator. See C Bell 'Some Reflections on Choosing Trustees' (1988)* Trust Law and Practice 86.

13.11.2 Removal of trustees by the court is rare

As suggested in *Letterstedt v Broers* (1883–84) LR 9 App Cas 371, removing the trustees would be a last resort. Even if the trustees are guilty of a breach of trust, the court will not remove them if it will not promote the welfare of the beneficiaries.

....

● ***Re Wrightson*** [1908] 1 Ch 789

The will of Francis Wrightson left his property to his wife for life and then to be divided equally between his nine children. The trustees had invested the trust money by lending it on a mortgage, but had not completed the proper formalities, such as a deed, a valuation of the property, or proper accounts. The solicitors had admitted the breach of trust and made good any loss from their own money. Mrs Wrightson was now dead.

HELD: Warrington J at 802:

> Is it necessary here, having regard to the welfare of the beneficiaries and for the protection of this trust, to remove the trustees? At the present moment nothing remains for the trustees to do except to wind up the estate; the testator's widow is dead; the whole of the estate is divisible amongst a number of persons who are *sui juris*.

And at 803:

> ... but, having regard to the fact that the Court now has the power of seeing that the trust is properly executed, to the fact that a large proportion of the beneficiaries do not require the trustees to be removed, and further (and this is of great importance), to the extra expense and loss to the trust estate which must be occasioned by the change of trustees, I think it would not be for the welfare of the cestuis que trust generally, or necessary for the protection of the trust estate, that these trustees should be removed.

The trustees should not be removed, as their remaining duties were simple and to do so would cause expense. The court might prefer to advise trustees on how to run the trust, rather than go to the trouble of removing and replacing them.

Sui juris—
a Latin phrase which means that the persons referred to have full legal capacity, i.e. they are of full age and are not mentally disordered.

399

● *Cowan v Scargill* [1985] Ch 270

The pension fund for coal miners was a trust, with five trustees appointed by the National Union of Mineworkers and five trustees appointed by the National Coal Board. The mineworker trustees wanted to adopt an investment policy for the trust, which protected the British coal industry. This was held to be unlawful, as trustees should pursue purely financial considerations when investing the money of beneficiaries.

HELD: Megarry VC at 296–7:

> Accordingly, subject to what may be said when I have concluded the judgment, I propose to make suitable declarations.
>
> It is important to get this large trust back on the rails; and it may help to do this if at this stage the court refrains from giving directions or making any coercive orders, whether under the inherent jurisdiction or otherwise, and remains in the background while the normal operation of the scheme is being re-established. It is very much to be hoped that there will be no need to consider the exercise of the court's inherent power to remove trustees.

KEY POINTS

- The court will only remove trustees in order to protect the welfare of the beneficiaries or to preserve trust property.

- Removing and replacing trustees is expensive for the trust.

Conclusion

The choice of trustees is important. The settlor or testator may choose private persons, professionals, or trust corporations. Those establishing elaborate and wealthy trusts may choose sophisticated arrangements, such as the use of a custodian trustee, whereas small trusts may end up with the Public Trustee.

Under s. 36 of the Trustee Act 1925, there should always be someone able to appoint new trustees, either named persons (appointors), the trustees themselves, or the personal representatives of the last surviving trustees.

Trustees, who do not want to continue being trustees, can step down voluntarily. They can disclaim right at the start or have themselves replaced under s. 36 or resign, without being replaced, under s. 39.

If all the beneficiaries agree, they can replace their trustees under s. 19 of the Trusts of Land and Appointment of Trustees Act 1996.

Trusts are private arrangements, so the courts do not interfere in the appointment of trustees unless there is no other alternative. The courts do have an inherent power to appoint and replace trustees and a statutory power to appoint under s. 41 of the Trustee Act 1925, but the courts are cautious about how they use these powers.

Questions

Self-test questions

1 Are any qualifications required to become a trustee?

2 How many trustees can be appointed?

3 How does someone refuse to be a trustee?

4 Who appoints trustees?

5 When can a trustee be replaced?

6 When can the beneficiaries replace their trustees?

7 When would the court intervene to replace trustees?

8 How should the legal estate be conveyed to the trustees?

9 How can a trustee retire?

10 In what circumstances would the court remove a trustee?

Discussion questions

1 What are the qualifications and personal qualities that a settlor or testator should look for in a trustee?

2 Should the beneficiaries have more control over the appointment and removal of the trustees?

3 Should the courts exercise more control over the appointment and removal of trustees?

Assessment question

Jacob sets up a trust in his will to provide an income for his wife and his four children. His will names two executors: his brother Edward and Jacob's son George, who are also named as trustees. Unfortunately, Jacob dies young, when his son George is only ten years old. Edward proceeds to administer Jacob's estate and then carry out the terms of the trust. The trust property consists of land and shares.

Jacob's widow, Anne, and her adult children, Richard, Susan, and Timothy, are dissatisfied with the way that the trust is being run. They consider that Edward is endangering the trust property by making risky business deals and, also, that he is favouring George in his distribution of the trust income. They want Edward and George to resign as trustees and be replaced by a trust corporation.

The trust, set out in the will, says nothing about who has the right to appoint new trustees. Edward refuses to resign.

Advise Anne and her four children.

Key cases

- *Holder v Holder* [1968] Ch 353 **(at 13.4)**

- *Re Wheeler and de Rochow* [1896] 1 Ch 315 **(at 13.5.1 and 13.5.5)**

- *Re Higginbottom* [1892] 3 Ch 132 **(at 13.5.3 and 13.7.2)**

- *Re Tempest* (1865–66) LR 1 Ch App 485 **(at 13.8.2)**

- *Letterstedt v Broers* (1883–4) LR 9 App Cas 371 **(at 13.11.1 and 13.11.2)**

Further reading

F Barlow 'The Appointment of Trustees: A Disappointing Decision' [2003] *Conv* 15
The power in s. 36 of the Trustee Act 1925 to appoint trustees.

M Keppel-Palmer 'Discretion No More?' (1996) 146 *NLJ* 1779
The power of the beneficiaries to replace trustees.

C Bell 'Some Reflections on Choosing Trustees' (1988) *Trust Law and Practice* 86
Criteria for selecting trustees.

14

Variation of trust

Learning objectives

This chapter will help you to:

- understand the meaning of 'variation'
- appreciate the importance of taxation in this area
- understand the rule in *Saunders v Vautier*
- understand when the court may consent for beneficiaries under the Variation of Trusts Act 1958.

Introduction

Variation means changing the terms of the trust. The trustees and beneficiaries are bound by the terms of the trust and to disregard these terms is a breach of trust. (See Chapter 15 'Breach of trust'.)

If the trust is drafted correctly then it should have enough flexibility to deal with future events. That is why many trusts are discretionary or contain powers of appointment. (See Chapter 4 'Trusts and powers and the three certainties'.) It is even possible for a settlor to insert a power of revocation, which allows him or her to revoke or undo the trust.

A trust can last for a long time; under the rule against perpetuities this could be say two generations, which might be 80 years or more. In that time tax laws can be changed by Parliament, potential beneficiaries can fail to be born, or beneficiaries can die unexpectedly, wrecking tax saving plans. If flexibility has not been built into the trust, a variation of trust may be desirable.

If we took as our example a very simple trust, such as: 'to Richard for life, to his wife for life (if she survives him), remainder to their children', even this could cause problems. What if Richard never marries? What if he in fact has no children? Although no inheritance tax is payable when Richard dies and his wife inherits, it would be when the children inherit.

Currently, inheritance tax is 40 per cent of any amount above £325,000. Married couples and couples in civil partnerships can combine their tax allowance to leave £650,000, without paying inheritance tax.

Inheritance tax is charged when property is inherited on death and also covers property given away within seven years before death. This tax was first introduced in 1894, when it was known as estate duty. The before death period has changed over the years.

14.1 Adult beneficiaries

If all the beneficiaries are adults they can just agree to end the trust, or set up a new trust. This is laid down in the famous rule in *Saunders v Vautier* (1841) Cr & Ph 240.

● *Saunders v Vautier* (1841) Cr & Ph 240

Under this trust the property was to be accumulated until the beneficiary reached the age of 25. When he reached the age of majority, then 21, nowadays 18, he decided to end the trust and take the property.

He could do this because he was the only beneficiary. Normally it is not so easy, as there is usually more than one beneficiary. These beneficiaries may disagree, be children, or may not even be born yet or may be unidentifiable.

The rule in *Saunders v Vautier* (1841) Cr & Ph 240 is often misunderstood. The beneficiaries may only instruct the trustees to end the trust and hand over the trust property to them if absolutely all the beneficiaries agree. This includes beneficiaries who are yet to be born or ascertained, so in many trusts the rule will be inoperable.

. . . .

● *Thorpe v Revenue and Customs Commissioners* [2009] Pens LR 139

Mr Thorpe had a pension scheme held in trust for himself, his wife, and dependants. His wife had died and he had no children, so he asked the pension trustees to transfer the trust fund to him, as the sole beneficiary, under the rule in *Saunders v Vautier*.

HELD: at para 14:

> … it is fundamental to the application of the rule that the beneficiaries must be together entitled to the whole of the beneficial interest. In my judgment, it is clear that the rule can have no application where there are potential beneficiaries not yet in existence, however remote their interests might be or however unlikely it might be that those beneficiaries should come into existence.
>
> The Appellant accepted that there was a theoretical possibility that he might remarry or that he might have dependants within the meaning of the rules of the Scheme.

So Mr Thorpe could not end the trust, because it was possible, though unlikely, that there could be other beneficiaries.

Even if the beneficiaries are able to use the rule in *Saunders v Vautier* (1841) Cr & Ph 240, they cannot truly vary the trust, as shown in the following case.

. . . .

● *Stephenson v Barclays Bank Trust Co Ltd* [1975] 1 WLR 882

Here there were only two, adult, beneficiaries, Richard and Charles.

HELD: This still did not give the beneficiaries the right to instruct the trustees upon how to carry out their duties while the trust continues. Nor could they override the existing trust. All that they could do was to instruct the trustees to hand over the property to them and then they could establish a new trust if they wished.

14.2 Powers to vary a trust

The courts have various powers to change the terms of the trust in specific situations.

14.2.1 Matrimonial Causes Act 1973

Under s. 24, the court may vary the trusts of divorcing couples.

● **Ulrich v Ulrich** [1968] 1 WLR 180

The couple divorced and although the house was legally in the name of Kenneth Ulrich, because of his wife's financial contribution, the court decided that, in equity, the couple held as tenants in common. (See Chapter 18 'Trusts of the family home'.) On divorce the court could alter or vary this trust.

HELD: Lord Denning MR at 188:

> The husband and wife were tenants in common sharing equally, but there is a power in the court to vary to do what is fair in the circumstances. I think that the husband should have the whole of his half share. The wife's half share should be applied for the child, or part for the child and part for the wife.

Prest v Petrodel Resources Ltd. [2013] 3 WLR 1

Mr and Mrs Prest were divorcing and Mrs Prest was seeking a financial settlement. She alleged that her husband had used offshore companies (PRL) to hold legal title to seven London houses, which, in reality, belonged beneficially to him. The houses had been transferred by Mr Prest to these companies for nominal sums, such as £1.

HELD: The Supreme Court decided that companies held the houses on resulting trust for Mr Prest. (See 3.3 'What trusts are used for' and 8.4.1 'Voluntary transfer to another'. for resulting trusts.) Therefore the court could order that the houses be transferred to his wife.

Baroness Hale at para. 84:

> I agree that this appeal should succeed, on the basis that the properties in question were held by the respondent companies on trust for the husband. As he is beneficially entitled to them, they fall within the scope of the court's power to make transfer of property orders under section 24(1)(a) of the Matrimonial Causes Act 1973. It also means that the court has power to order that the companies, as bare trustees, transfer these properties to the wife.

The same now applies to civil partnerships: Civil Partnerships Act 2004, s. 72, Scheds 5–7. The courts do not yet have the power to vary the constructive trusts established by cohabiting couples. (See Chapter 18 'Trusts of the family home'.)

14.2.2 Mental Capacity Act 2005

Under s. 18(1)(h), the Court of Protection may vary trusts for patients suffering from mental disorders.

14.2.3 Trustee Act 1925

There are powers to vary trusts under the Trustee Act 1925 in order to benefit infants or children, as we would now call them.

> **Trustee Act 1925**
>
> ·
>
> 53 Vesting orders in relation to infants' beneficial interests
>
> Where an infant is beneficially entitled to any property the court may, with a view to the application of the capital or income thereof for the maintenance, education, or benefit of the infant, make an order...

Saving tax would generally be regarded as for the 'benefit of the infant'.

· ·

● **Re Meux** [1958] Ch 154

The Gilmour family had a trust where the property descended in a tail male, i.e. it went to the eldest son down the generations. This would have led to a large inheritance tax bill (then called estate duty), each time the property went to the next son.

HELD: The court allowed this trust to be ended and a new trust to be established for the infant, David Gilmour. Tax saving was for his benefit.

> **Trustee Act 1925**
>
> ·
>
> 57 Power of court to authorise dealings with trust property
>
> (1) Where in the management or administration of any property vested in trustees, any sale, lease, mortgage, surrender, release, or other disposition, or any purchase, investment, acquisition, expenditure, or other transaction, is in the opinion of the court expedient, but the same cannot be effected by reason of the absence of any power for that purpose vested in the trustees by the trust instrument, if any, or by law, the court may by order confer upon the trustees, either generally or in any particular instance, the necessary power for the purpose...

Older cases, such as *Anker-Petersen v Anker-Petersen* [1991] 16 LS Gaz 32 and the House of Lords case, *Chapman v Chapman* [1954] AC 429 (see 14.2.5 'The inherent power of the court'), had decided that the power of the court to change a trust under s. 57 Trustee Act 1925 was limited to administrative changes, such as widening trustees' investment powers, and did not extend to varying the beneficial interests. The Variation of Trusts Act 1958 granted that power to the courts, but proceedings under that Act can be slow and expensive because of the need to obtain the consent of all the identifiable adult beneficiaries and to decide that the change would be for the benefit of the infant, unborn, and future beneficiaries. This approach was modified in *Southgate v Sutton* [2011] EWCA 637.

· ·

● **Southgate v Sutton** [2011] EWCA 637

A trust fund was shared between the families of four brothers. This caused a problem for the family of one brother, the Southgate family, who had moved to the US. They had to pay more tax because the trust fund was in pounds sterling, rather than US dollars. The obvious solution was to divide ('partition') the fund into two separate dollar and sterling funds, but this would mean setting up two separate trust funds.

HELD: The Court of Appeal confirmed that it was possible to use s. 57 to alter beneficial interests, as long as this was incidental to the main purpose of solving a problem in the management and administration of the trust. The trustees had no other means of solving this administrative difficulty.

14.2.4 Settled Land Act 1925

Settled land was a system for keeping land in the same family. The land descended from one eldest son to the next, who only held the property for their lifetimes, which limited their ability to dispose of the property. Settled land could cause tax problems, as we saw in the Introduction. The family line could die out or the trustees might not want the next heir to inherit, as we see in our unusual example: *Hambro v Duke of Marlborough* [1994] Ch 158. Therefore, the legislation contained a power for the court to authorize variations of trust.

Settled Land Act 1925

. . . .

64 General power for the tenant for life to effect any transaction under an order of the court

(1) Any transaction affecting or concerning the settled land, or any part thereof, or any other land (not being a transaction otherwise authorised by this Act, or by the settlement) which in the opinion of the court would be for the benefit of the settled land, or any part thereof, or the persons interested under the settlement, may, under an order of the court, be effected by a tenant for life, if it is one which could have been validly effected by the absolute owner.

. . . .

● *Hambro v Duke of Marlborough* [1994] Ch 158

By a 1706 Act of Parliament, Blenheim Palace had been left on an entail for the Dukes of Marlborough. The eldest son, the Marquis of Blandford, stood to inherit next. The trustees and the current duke wanted to change the trust, because the marquis was unbusiness-like and immature, and receiving psychological treatment for a drug problem. They did not want him to have the power to sell Blenheim when he became duke, so they wanted a **protective trust** instead.

HELD: The court interpreted the section widely. 'Any transaction... for the benefit of the settled land' would allow this change. Changing the equitable interest of an adult beneficiary was very unusual, but justifiable in these special circumstances. (See 14.4 'For whom does the court consent?'. Under the Variation of Trusts Act 1958, it is not thought possible to override the wishes of adult beneficiaries.)

. . . .

Protective trust—a trust where the main beneficiary, here the Marquis of Blandford, holds the property for life, until he is declared bankrupt or gets into debt, etc. Then his life interest ends and the trustees hold the property on a discretionary trust for the former life interest, spouse, and children. A protective trust is well named, because it protects a beneficiary from the consequences of getting into debt. (See Chapter 12 'Maintenance and advancement and protective trusts'.)

14.2.5 The inherent power of the court

The court has some powers, derived from old case law rather than statute, to permit changes to the terms of a trust. This can be done if there is an emergency, a child's interests are at stake, or if there is a dispute between beneficiaries that needs to be resolved (this last is called 'the compromise jurisdiction').

● *Re New* [1901] 2 Ch 534

The New, Leavers and Morley Trusts needed changes to their investment powers. They all had shares in the Wollaton Colliery Co Ltd, which was reconstructing and wished to issue **debentures**. The trusts had no power to make this kind of investment.

HELD: Romer J at 545:

> In a case of this kind, which may reasonably be supposed to be one not foreseen or anticipated by the author of the trust, where the trustees are embarrassed by the emergency that has arisen and the duty cast upon them to do what is best for the estate, and the consent of all the beneficiaries cannot be obtained by reason of some of them not being sui juris or in existence, then it may be right for the Court, and the Court in a proper case would have jurisdiction, to sanction on behalf of all concerned such acts on behalf of the trustees as we have above referred to.

Re New [1901] 2 Ch 534 is an example of the 'emergency jurisdiction'; the court could alter the investment powers of the trust to meet the 'unforeseen' situation.

The courts came to the conclusion, however, that this inherent power did not give them the jurisdiction to rearrange the equitable interests of a trust, particularly if it was being done merely to save tax.

● *Chapman v Chapman* [1954] AC 429

The planned variation was to reduce the risk of death duties for infant beneficiaries. The House of Lords refused to approve the variations. The legal position was well summarized in the Court of Appeal.

Lord Evershed [1953] Ch 218 at 266:

> We would point out, therefore, that it was no part of the functions of Her Majesty's court to recast settlements from time to time, merely with a view to tax avoidance, even if they had the power to do so, which, in our opinion, they have not.

This was a most inconvenient ruling as the main aim of most variations of trust is to avoid or reduce tax, particularly inheritance tax.

So Parliament enacted the Variation of Trusts Act 1958.

Debenture—
a loan secured on the assets of a company. If the loan is not repaid, the assets can be sold by the person who made the loan.

KEY POINT
Before 1958, there were only limited powers to vary a trust.

14.3 Variation of Trusts Act 1958

This Act gives the court the power to authorize wide-ranging changes to an existing trust. This is called an 'arrangement'.

> **Variation of Trusts Act 1958, s. 1**
>
> . . . .
>
> (1) Where property, whether real or personal, is held on trusts arising, whether before or after the passing of this Act, under any will, settlement or other disposition, the court may, if it thinks fit, by order approve on behalf of . . . [see 14.4 'For whom does the court consent?'] . . . any arrangement (by whomsoever proposed, and whether or not there is any other person beneficially interested who is capable of assenting thereto) varying or revoking all or any of the trusts, or enlarging the powers of the trustees of managing or administering any of the property subject to the trusts.

14.3.1 What is an arrangement?

The original trust should not be completely abandoned, but can be considerably altered.

. . . .

● **Re Ball's Settlement Trusts** [1968] 1 WLR 899

The original settlement, established by James Ball, gave the property to him for life and then stated he had a power of appointment by his will to give the property to his two sons and their families, with a stipulation that neither family should get more than half. The problem with this trust was that if the sons inherited on the death of James Ball they would have to pay what is now called inheritance tax. (See the Introduction to this chapter.) So the proposed 'arrangement' was to split the trust fund in half and establish two separate trusts for each of the sons and their families. If they received the property now, the tax burden would be much reduced.

HELD: Megarry J at 905:

> If an arrangement changes the whole substratum of the trust, then it may well be that it cannot be regarded merely as varying the trust. But if an arrangement, while leaving the substratum, effectuates the purpose of the trust by other means, it may still be possible to regard that arrangement as merely varying the original trusts, even though the means employed are wholly different and even though the form is completely changed.

Permission for the variation was granted, because although the form of the trusts was completely changed, the substance remained. The property of James Ball was equally divided between his two sons and their families.

14.3.2 Is an arrangement a disposition of an equitable interest?

A technical point has been raised as to whether the alteration of the beneficial interests, which can be part of a variation of trust, counts as 'a disposition of an equitable interest' for the purposes of s. 53(1)(c) of the Law of Property Act 1925 (see 5.3). If this was so it would need to be made in writing and could be taxable in itself.

This was thought not to be the situation in *Re Holmden's ST* [1968] AC 685.

. . . .

● ***Re Holmden's ST*** [1968] AC 685

The arrangement is regarded as an agreement of the beneficiaries to vary the trust.

For whom does the court consent?

The court consents for the beneficiaries that cannot consent for themselves. Different categories of beneficiaries are set out in the Variation of Trusts Act 1958.

> **Variation of Trusts Act 1958**
>
> . . . .
>
> 1 Jurisdiction of courts to vary trusts
>
> (1) Where property, whether real or personal, is held on trusts arising, whether before or after the passing of this Act, under any will, settlement or other disposition, the court may if it thinks fit by order approve on behalf of—
>
> (a) any person having, directly or indirectly, an interest, whether vested or contingent, under the trusts who by reason of infancy or other incapacity is incapable of assenting, or
>
> (b) any person (whether ascertained or not) who may become entitled, directly or indirectly, to an interest under the trusts as being at a future date or on the happening of a future event a person of any specified description or a member of any specified class of persons, so however that this paragraph shall not include any person who would be of that description, or a member of that class, as the case may be, if the said date had fallen or the said event had happened at the date of the application to the court, or
>
> (c) any person unborn, or
>
> (d) any person in respect of a discretionary interest of his under a protective trust...
>
> Provided that except by virtue of paragraph (d) of this subsection the court shall not approve an arrangement on behalf of any person unless it would be for the benefit of that person.

Section 1(1)(a) covers child beneficiaries who are unable to consent to changes in the trust until they reach their majority. It also includes other beneficiaries incapable of giving their own consent such as those suffering from mental incapacity.

Section 1(1)(c) covers beneficiaries of the trust who are yet to be born. For example, a trust might state that the beneficiaries are 'the children of Richard'. While Richard is still alive we cannot identify all these beneficiaries, as some could still be born.

Section 1(1)(d) covers a protective trust. The court may consent on behalf of the family members covered by the discretionary trust. (See 14.2.4 'Settled Land Act 1925' and 12.4 'Protective trusts'.)

14.4.1 The meaning of s. 1(1)(b)

Category (b) of beneficiaries has caused some problems. It has often been held that it does not apply, in that it does not give the court power to consent on behalf of those who could consent for themselves.

....

● *Knocker v Youle* [1986] 1 WLR 934

Charles McMahon Knocker had set up a trust that seemed to cover all the possibilities of beneficiaries dying. The income went to his daughter, Augusta Youle, for life and then to whomever she appointed. If she failed to appoint, then the income went to her brother, Charles Knocker, and then to whomever he appointed. If both Augusta and Charles failed to appoint, then the property went to the settlor's wife, Mildred, for life, then to her four sisters and if the sisters were dead to the sisters' children. The wife and her sisters were dead, but there were 17 children living in Australia, who, of course, were cousins of Augusta and her brother Charles.

Both Augusta and Charles junior had made wills, so they had appointed. They wanted a variation of trust, but the Australian cousins would not consent.

HELD: The cousins had identifiable beneficial interests; they were living and were over the age of majority. They were not covered by subsection (b), which says, 'may become entitled'. They were already entitled. It did not matter that it was most unlikely that they would ever actually inherit anything under the trust. Their actual consent was needed and the court could not consent on their behalf.

Subsection (b) seems to cover what is sometimes called the 'spectral spouse'. The beneficiary could marry, but as he has not done so yet, there is no way of knowing who it might be and therefore no way of gaining the spouse's consent.

....

● *Re Steed's Will Trusts* [1960] Ch 407

(This case also appears at 14.5.1 'The wishes of the settlor/testor'.)

Property was left on protective trust to Gladys Sandford for her life, after that to those whom she should appoint and in default of appointment to her next of kin. It could not be known who the next of kin were because Gladys might marry. The court was asked to consent under the subsection on behalf of any future husband.

As it was a protective trust, consent under subsection (d) was also necessary.

Another case also held that the second part of the subsection did not help much either.

....

● *Re Suffert's Settlement* [1961] Ch 1

Nor could the court consent for the statutory next of kin, because once Suffert had died it was known who they were.

thinking points

What categories of beneficiaries are covered by category (b)? The subsection allows the court to give permission to a variation of trust on behalf of those who may become entitled to an interest under the trust. As held in Knocker v Youle, *it does not cover those who already have an equitable interest under the trust, even if the interest is contingent and exceedingly remote. The actual consent of these beneficiaries is required. This may be inconvenient for practitioners in this area of law and may not have been the intention of Parliament when enacting this section. Previous case law, such as* Re Suffert's Settlement, *does not seem to have understood the section in this way. See J Riddall 'Does It or Doesn't It? Contingent Interests and the Variation of Trusts Act 1958' [1987] Conv 144.*

14.4.2 Adult beneficiaries

The court cannot consent for adult beneficiaries. Their actual consent must be obtained.

● ***Re Berry*** [1966] 1 WLR 1515

The trust here was to the Right Honourable Sheila, Countess of Birkenhead, for life. If she became a widow the property would be held on protective trust. The remainder went to her children, who were Frederick William Robin Smith and Juliet Margaret Smith. Both were adults. If the children died before their mother and failed to appoint, then the property would go to various nephews and nieces.

To avoid estate duty (now called inheritance tax), a variation was proposed. The main proposals were that the countess would lose her life interest in exchange for 75 per cent of the trust property. Twenty-four per cent would go to present and future children if they attained the age of 21 or married. The other 1 per cent was allocated to the nephews and nieces.

The court's consent was needed on behalf of nieces and nephews who were still children—subsection (a); unborn children or nephews and nieces—subsection (c) and interests under the protective trust—subsection (d).

HELD: Stamp LJ: There was no need to decide whether the beneficiaries under (d) gained any benefit from the variation, as that was not a statutory requirement.

One per cent was enough for the nephews and nieces, as it was most unlikely that they would actually inherit.

Lady Birkenhead's share was over large, but the court did not have to consent on behalf of Frederick and Juliet, as they were adults and had consented for themselves.

At 1518:

> I think I can approve the arrangement on behalf of those on whose behalf I am asked to approve it, if I make it clear that I am not approving the arrangement as representing a fair bargain between Lady Birkenhead as tenant for life and her children. About that I express no opinion. I approve the variation on behalf of those persons on whose behalf I am asked to approve it.

413

Adult beneficiaries must give their consent to the court to permit a variation of trust. In what form must that consent be given? The courts of Jersey, where a similar system of variation of trust exists, looked at this question in *Mubarak v Mubarak* [2008] JRC 136.

● *Mubarak v Mubarak* [2008] JRC 136

Mr and Mrs Mubarak were engaged in prolonged divorce litigation in England. A trust for the family was established in Jersey and in that trust, Mr Mubarak was allowed to add and remove beneficiaries. He removed his wife, but as part of the divorce proceedings in England, he was required to reinstate her. Mr Mubarak wrote to the trustees in Jersey to that effect.

HELD: Mr Mubarak had freely given his consent to the variation.

The fact that Mr Mubarak was obeying an English court order did not invalidate his consent.

14.5 What is benefit?

The court may only authorize a variation of trust if it is for the *benefit* of the beneficiaries. The Act does not define benefit, so it has been left to the courts to interpret.

14.5.1 The wishes of the settlor/testator

The wishes of the settlor/testator might be taken into consideration, but they are not conclusive.

● *Re Steed's Will Trusts* [1960] Ch 407 (This case also appears at 14.4.1.)

The property was held on protective trust. The trustees wished to sell a farm, which was part of the trust property, on which Gladys's brother lived. Gladys wanted to stop the sale. To do this she asked the court to vary the trust, so that her life interest was absolute and she, rather than the trustees, would have the power to sell or not to sell.

HELD: Lord Evershed MR at 421: The court refused to give consent.

> It was part of the testator's scheme, made as I think manifest by the language which I have read from the clauses of the will, that it was the intention and desire of the testator that this trust should be available for the plaintiff so that she would have proper provision made for her throughout her life, and would not be exposed to the risk that she might if she had been handed the money, part with it in favour of another individual about whom the testator felt apprehension, which apprehension is plainly shared by the trustees.

Here the court did abide by the wishes of the testator, to protect Gladys from her brother.

It is possible though, that the court will go against the wishes of the testator/settlor.

● *Goulding v James* [1997] 2 All ER 239

The will of Violet Froud left her estate to her daughter, June, for life with the remainder to the son of the daughter, Marcus Goulding, on attaining the age of 40. If Marcus died before June or before reaching 40, then the property would go to the children of Marcus, living at Marcus's death. Because of fears over inheritance tax, a variation was proposed. Forty-five per cent would go to June, 45 per cent would go to Marcus, and 10 per cent to the grandchildren.

Marcus was 32 and living in an artistic community in Nantucket, New England. There was evidence that Violet did not want Marcus to have the money until he was older and considered him a 'free spirit'.

Marcus had no children, so the court was being asked to consent on behalf of the unborn (subsection (c)).

HELD: It was clearly for the benefit of these possible children to minimize the tax liability, so consent was granted. This outweighed the supposed wishes of the testatrix. In *Re Steed* [1960] Ch 407, benefit was less important, because the main category of beneficiary were those under a protective trust, where the court does not have to consider benefit.

---

thinking points

Should the courts disregard the wishes of the testator/settlor? The decision in Goulding v James *does not sit very easily with* Re Steed's Will Trusts. *This may be because, although thousands of variation cases are decided in chambers, few are reported. 'As a result, although there is an accumulated body of judicial practice among judges and counsel in the Chancery Division, very little of this has filtered down to the law reports.' The problem is whether the court is bound to respect the intention of the settlor or not. After* Re Weston, *the courts are not restricted to just considering the financial benefits of the proposed variation for each beneficiary. So the courts are forced into an awkward balancing exercise; the wishes of the settlor/testator against a wide conception of 'benefit', which might involve many considerations. See P Luxton 'Variation of Trusts: Settlors' Intentions and the Consent Principle in* Saunders v Vautier' (1997) 60 MLR 719.

'Benefit' can mean different things in different contexts. The court decides whether the proposed arrangement is for the benefit of *all* the beneficiaries for whom they are consenting.

14.5.2 Tax saving

Most cases involve trying to minimize tax liabilities. The courts require actuarial evidence. This means that they look at the likelihood of a person actually inheriting and value his share accordingly. For instance, in *Goulding v James* [1997] 2 All ER 239, at 14.5.1 'The wishes of the settlor/testor', the actuarial value of the children's share was only 1.85 per cent of the fund. This was because they were not even born yet and they would only inherit if, after they were born, their father died soon afterwards. For a youngish man like Marcus, this was unlikely to happen. A full explanation of actuarial valuations is outside the scope of this book.

Tax planning can go wrong, if beneficiaries die in the wrong order. The court ignores possibilities and looks at the probabilities.

. . . .

● **Re Holt** [1969] 1 Ch 100 [This case also appears at 14.5.4 'Moral and social benefit'.]

Megarry J at 122:

> … in exercising the jurisdiction under the Act of 1958, the court must, on behalf of those persons for whom it was approving the arrangement, take the sort of risk, which an adult would be prepared to take.

This principle was stated more fully in the following case.

● **Re Cohen** [1965] 1 WLR 1229

Here the trust in question was for the grandchildren alive at the death of, as it turned out, Eliot Eliot-Cohen. The variation wanted to get rid of the death condition by stating a fixed date of 30 June 1973. The evidence was that it was most unlikely that Eliot would be alive at that date. Initially the variation was refused, because it was just possible that grandchildren could be born after that date while Eliot was alive and would therefore become disentitled. The variation was approved when the trustees agreed to hold some money back for this possibility.

HELD: Stamp J at 1236:

> In my judgment, the court has to be satisfied in the case of each individual infant that on balance the proposed variation is for his benefit. Similarly, in my judgment, the court must be satisfied that the proposed variation is for the benefit of any individual person who may hereafter come into existence and become interested under the trusts of the settlement.
>
> The court does not have to be satisfied that by the effect of a proposed variation each individual infant is bound to be better off than he would otherwise have been, but that that infant is making a bargain which is a reasonable one and one which an adult would be prepared to make.

KEY POINTS

- The variation must be for the benefit of *all* the possible beneficiaries, for whom the court is consenting.

- The basis of the court's consent is whether the proposed variation is a reasonable bargain to which an adult would consent.

14.5.3 Export of the trust

This is where the trust is relocated in a foreign jurisdiction. New trustees would be appointed, located in that country. Normally this is allowed.

● **Re Seale's Marriage Settlement** [1961] Ch 574

The whole family, who were the beneficiaries of the trust, moved to Canada. This was to be their permanent residence.

HELD: Buckley J at 579:

> The evidence establishes to my satisfaction that the husband and wife intend to continue to live in Canada, that their children who are living in Canada and have been brought up as Canadians are likely to continue to live in Canada, and that it will be for the general advantage of all the beneficiaries that the administrative difficulties and the difficulties of other kinds which result from the fact that it is an English settlement and the beneficiaries all reside in Canada should be brought to an end; and I am satisfied that the arrangement is sensible and advantageous for all concerned.

Similarly, a variation was allowed in *Re Windeatt* [1969] 1 WLR 692, where the court was satisfied that the move was genuine and permanent. The family had lived in Jersey for 19 years.

Moving to a 'tax haven' can be popular, particularly when tax rates were very high in the UK. The court might refuse consent for a variation, if it considers that it is solely motivated by tax considerations.

● *Re Weston* [1969] 1 Ch 223

Stanley Weston made two settlements in 1964, one for each of his sons. They were for the sons for life, then to the sons' children. Because of the high taxation in the UK, in 1967 they all moved to Jersey and applied to appoint Jersey trustees.

HELD: Lord Denning MR refused at 245–6:

> The court should not consider merely the financial benefit to the infants or unborn children, but also their educational and social benefit. There are many things in life more worthwhile than money. One of these things is to be brought up in this our England, which is still 'the envy of less happier lands'. I do not believe it is for the benefit of children to be uprooted from England and transported to another country simply to avoid tax.
>
> The only thing that Jersey can do for them is to give them an even greater fortune. Many a child has been ruined by being given too much. The avoidance of tax may be lawful, but it is not yet a virtue. The Court of Chancery should not encourage or support it—it should not give its approval to it—if by so doing it would imperil the true welfare of the children, already born or yet to be born. There is one thing more. I cannot help wondering how long these young people will stay in Jersey. It may be to their financial interest at present to make their home there permanently. But will they remain there once the capital gain is safely in hand, clear of tax? They may well change their minds and come back to enjoy their untaxed gains. Is such a prospect really for the benefit of the children? Are they to be wanderers over the face of the earth, moving from this country to that, according to where they can best avoid tax? I cannot believe that to be right. Children are like trees: they grow stronger with firm roots.

Harman LJ at 246:

> This is an essay in tax avoidance naked and unashamed.

Although Lord Denning's judgment is both forceful and entertaining, it should not be misunderstood. It is not saying that trusts cannot be moved abroad, for genuine and permanent moves abroad are allowed. Nor is it saying that variation for tax purposes is not allowed; after all, most variation cases involve this. What it is saying is that 'benefit' is such a wide word that the court can take into account non-financial benefit, particularly where children are involved.

(See also 13.8.1 'The courts' power in s. 41 of the Trustee Act 1925'.)

KEY POINT
The court may also consider non-financial benefit.

14.5.4 Moral and social benefit

A consideration of the wider issues of 'benefit' might lead the courts to deprive a beneficiary of their beneficial interest.

● *Re CL* [1969] 1 Ch 587

A psychiatric patient had a life interest, which produced an income of £7,000, of which £6,500 went in tax.

HELD: A variation gave the money to her adopted daughter, without compensation to the mother. This was justified, as it is what the mother would have done herself, if she were of sound mind.

The court might find it desirable to postpone an inheritance.

● **Re T** [1964] Ch 158

A child would become entitled to a quarter of a fund on reaching 21 or marrying, then another quarter on the death of her mother and yet another quarter on the death of a sibling. The daughter was about to reach 21, but the mother did not want her to become entitled and so applied for a variation of trust.

HELD: The court eventually accepted the variation proposed and put the property for Miss T on protective trust. They viewed her as 'alarmingly immature and irresponsible as regards money'.

● **Re Holt** [1969] 1 Ch 100 (This case also appears at 14.5.2.)

Under the original trust, the children became entitled at the age of 21. The proposed arrangement was to change this to 30. The main reason was to save tax, but the judge found it desirable for other reasons.

HELD: Megarry J at 121:

> I should however, state that I fully concur in the view taken by Mrs Walsh that, speaking in general terms, it is most important that young children should be reasonably advanced in a career and settled in life, before they are in receipt of an income sufficient to make them independent of the need to work.

A similar approach was taken in *Wright v Gater* [2011] EWHC 2881 (Ch), although the judge stressed that, as all the factors affecting 'benefit' for a child had to be taken into account, there could hardly be binding 'precedents' in this area of law.

● **Wright v Gater** [2011] EWHC 2881 (Ch)

Rory's grandfather and father died when he was only three years old, so that he inherited £514,600. Under the Administration of Estates Act 1925, the estate would be held on trust for Rory until he reached 18. His mother Ellen sought a variation of trust, so that he did not become rich too young.

HELD: Norris J: The court had to decide whether the variation was for the benefit of Rory. Benefit did not necessarily have to be financial and the court might ask itself the question whether a prudent adult would accept the proposed change.

Para 15:

> I do not consider that these cases...*Re T's Settlement Trusts* [1964] Ch 158, *In Re Holt's Settlement* [1969] 1 Ch 100, *Re CL* [1969] 1Ch 587 or *Re Remnant* [1971] Ch 560, warrant the conclusion that the Court should regard postponement of vesting beyond the age of majority as 'beneficial' in principle. I think in each case the Court will have to be persuaded that a variation incorporating such a feature is justified on the facts of a particular case; perhaps because of the proven personal characteristics of the beneficiary; or perhaps because of the size of

the fund, the circumstance in life of the beneficiary, the family context in which the existing trusts will be implemented or some similar feature (the list is not exhaustive) gives rise to risks which any reasonable person would regard as real, and to which the proposed variation provides a sufficient and proportionate response.

If the money was invested until Rory was 18 that would give him unrestricted access to about £750,000 when he turned 18, and that would be a risk in a family unaccustomed to wealth and without a father's influence. The solution was to vary the trust 'to introduce Rory gradually to control of his wealth', although not as gradually as his mother wanted, who favoured an age of 30. Rory would get the income at 18, 10 per cent of the fund at 21, and the balance at 25.

A very good example of non-financial criteria being taken into account can be found in *Re Remnant's Settlement Trusts* [1970] 1 Ch 560.

● *Re Remnant's Settlement Trusts* [1970] 1 Ch 560

This involved a trust where the beneficiaries had to be adherents of a particular religion in order to be entitled. The trust was for the children of two sisters, Dawn Hooper and Merrial Crosthwaite, but the interests were subject to forfeiture if a child became a Roman Catholic or married a Roman Catholic. If that happened the property would go to the children of the other sister. Dawn's children were Protestant and Merrial's were Roman Catholic. The two families applied to delete the forfeiture provision.

HELD: The variation was allowed, even though it was obviously not for the financial benefit of Dawn's children.

Pennycuick J decided that he should take a broad view of what was benefit and disregard the wishes of the testator. He regarded this kind of forfeiture clause as undesirable.

At 566:

> Obviously a forfeiture provision of this kind might well cause very serious dissension between the families of the two sisters.

At 567:

> It remains to consider whether the arrangement is a fair and proper one. As far as I can see, there is no reason for saying otherwise, except that the arrangement defeats this testator's intention. That is a serious but by no means conclusive consideration. I have reached the clear conclusion that these forfeiture provisions are undesirable in themselves in the circumstances of this case and that an arrangement involving their deletion is a fair and proper one.

thinking points

Some cases are a mixture of financial and non-financial benefit. How do the courts balance the two? Re Remnant's Settlement Trusts *went further than* Re Weston. *It did not just consider the educational and social benefit of the beneficiaries, but wider family issues, and gave little weight to the wishes of the settlor/testator. The same approach can be seen in* Re CL. *But how does a judge weigh financial gain for the beneficiaries against other, hard to quantify, considerations? Could decisions become too subjective? 'In view of the awesome width of the court's present discretion, it will be regrettable if judges underestimate the importance of precedent.' See R Cotterill 'The Requirement of "Benefit" under the Variation of Trusts Act 1958' (1971) 34 MLR 98.*

Conclusion

Variation of trust is quite a common practice, because it is impossible for the testator or settlor to foresee everything that might happen. The beneficiaries themselves can agree to change the trust, but only if all of them are identifiable, adult, and consenting. Most trusts will contain beneficiaries who are yet to be born, so it is quite unusual for this procedure to be used. Therefore, the trustees and beneficiaries have to apply to the court. The court may give consent for those unable to consent for themselves. The usual reason for an application to vary is to save tax, but as we have seen in this chapter, it can be for other reasons.

? Questions

Self-test questions

1 Why is a variation of trust ever required?

2 How does the rule in *Saunders v Vautier* work?

3 Why was the Variation of Trusts Act 1958 necessary?

4 For whom can the court consent under this Act?

5 What is benefit?

Discussion questions

1 Should the courts allow beneficiaries to avoid tax?

2 Does s. 1(1)(b) of the Variation of Trusts Act 1958 have any identifiable meaning?

3 Is the requirement of benefit too vague?

Assessment question

Tommy and his wife, Anthea, have life interests in a family trust, which was established by Tommy's father. The remainder is shared equally between their children, on condition that they remain members of the Orthodox Jewish faith.

The family lives in London. Tommy and Anthea are shocked by the crime in the city and resent the high rates of tax that they have to pay in England. They want to move to the Isle of Man and relocate the trust there, replacing the trustees with trustees resident in the Isle of Man. Tommy and Anthea believe that they will pay less tax in the Isle of Man, but they have not researched the matter yet. They have four children, but three of them have expressed no interest in the Orthodox Jewish faith, so they want to delete the condition in the trust requiring their children to remain in that faith. Instead, they want to insert a condition that the children do not become entitled until they are 25 years old.

Cyril, the eldest child, is 22 and opposes the proposed variations of trust, as he wants to remain in London.

Bernard is 16 and an Orthodox Jew, so he opposes the variation that would remove the religious condition in the trust.

The youngest two children, Dolores and Edna, are 14 and 13 respectively and are happy to agree to whatever their parents want.

Advise Tommy and Anthea on whether the court will give permission for their proposed variations.

 # Key cases

- *Knocker v Youle* [1986] 1 WLR 934 **(at 14.4.1)**
- *Re Berry* [1966] 1 WLR 1515 **(at 14.4.2)**
- *Re Cohen* [1965] 1 WLR 1229 **(at 14.5.2)**
- *Re Weston* [1969] 1 Ch 223 **(at 14.5.3)**
- *Re Remnant* [1970] 1 Ch 560 **(at 14.5.4)**

 # Further reading

P Luxton 'Variation of Trusts: Settlors' Intentions and the Consent Principle in *Saunders v Vautier*' (1997) 60 *MLR* 719
This considers how permissible it should be for the court to disregard the wishes of the settlor/testator and the consent of beneficiaries.

R Cotterill 'The Requirement of "Benefit" under the Variation of Trusts Act 1958' (1971) 34 *MLR* 98
How do the courts balance financial and non-financial benefit?

J Riddall 'Does It or Doesn't It? Contingent Interests and the Variation of Trusts Act 1958' [1987] *Conv* 144
The problems of interpreting s. 1(1)(b).

15

Breach of trust

Learning objectives

This chapter will help you to:

- understand that a trustee must act with reasonable care and skill
- understand the fiduciary nature of a trustee's duty
- understand the nature of equitable compensation
- appreciate the extent of a trustee's liability to the beneficiaries
- recognize a trustee exemption clause
- understand when the statutory period of limitation applies.

Introduction

The office of trustee is a difficult one. The trustee must dedicate himself or herself to running the affairs of the trust and promoting the interests of the beneficiaries at the expense of his or her own interests. Earlier chapters of this book illustrate some of these duties, such as Chapter 11 on the duty to invest the trust property and Chapter 12 on the discretion to pay maintenance and advance capital to the beneficiaries. If things go wrong and trust property is lost, the trustees may have to restore the trust property. This chapter will look at the basis of trustee liability and the ways in which trustees might defend or protect themselves from legal action. The seeming strictness of the trustees' duties is described in the following extract.

● *Head v Gould* [1898] 2 Ch 250 (This case also appears at 15.4.2 'When a trustee can escape liability' and 15.4.4 'The liability of retiring trustees'.)

Kekewich J at 268–9:

> It is the duty of trustees to protect the funds entrusted to their care, and to distribute those funds themselves or hand them over to their successors intact, that is, properly invested and without diminution, according to the terms of the mandate contained in the instrument of trust. This duty is imposed on them as long as they remain trustees and must be their guide in every act done by them as trustees. On retiring from the trust and passing on the trust estate to their successors…they are acting as trustees, and it is equally incumbent on them in this ultimate act of office to fulfil the duty imposed on them as at any other time. If therefore they neglect that duty and part with the property without due regard to it, they remain liable and will be held by the court responsible for the consequences properly traceable to that neglect.

KEY POINT
Trustees must preserve and protect the trust fund.

15.1 The trustees' duty of care

15.1.1 The standard of care

Case law had decided that trustees owed a duty of care to their beneficiaries in how they managed the trust. The standard was that the trustee must run the trust as an ordinary prudent man of business would run similar affairs of his own. If the trustee did not meet this standard he or she would be liable for the loss.

● *Learoyd v Whiteley* (1886) LR 33 ChD 347

Lindley LJ at 355:

> The duty of a trustee is not to take such care only as a prudent man would take if he had only himself to consider; the duty rather is to take such care as an ordinary prudent man would

take if he were minded to make an investment for the benefit of other people for whom he felt morally bound to provide. That is the kind of business the ordinary prudent man is supposed to be engaged in; and unless this is borne in mind the standard of a trustee's duty will be fixed too low.

Learoyd concerned investment, but the duty to act as a reasonable businessman extends to the other duties of trustees.

Professional trustees have a higher duty of care, as they are expected to use their specialist skills for the benefit of the trust and to reflect the fact that they charge for their services.

● *Bartlett v Barclays Bank Trust Company Limited* [1980] Ch 515

Brightman LJ at 534:

> I am of the opinion that a higher duty of care is plainly due from someone like a trust corporation which carries on a specialised business of trust management.
>
> ...so I think that a professional corporate trustee is liable for breach of trust if a loss is caused to the trust fund because it neglects to exercise the special care and skill which it professes to have.

The trustees' duty of care is given statutory form in the Trustee Act 2000.

Trustee Act 2000, s. 1

(1) Whenever the duty under this subsection applies to a trustee, he must exercise such care and skill as is reasonable in all the circumstances, having regard in particular—

   (a) to any special knowledge or experience that he has or holds himself out as having, and

   (b) if he acts as a trustee in the course of a business or profession, to any special knowledge or experience that it is reasonable to expect of a person acting in the course of that kind of business or profession.

KEY POINT A trustee must act with reasonable care and skill. What is reasonable is judged by the trustee's knowledge, experience, or professional skills. (See Chapter 11 'The duties of trustees: with special reference to investment'.)

15.2 The fiduciary nature of trusteeship

Trustees are also fiduciaries and this brings with it a series of very strict duties. The consequences of being a fiduciary are explained in the following case.

· ·

● *Bristol and West Building Society v Mothew* [1998] Ch 1

Millett LJ at 18:

> A fiduciary is someone who has undertaken to act for or on behalf of another in a particular matter in circumstances which may give rise to a relationship of trust and confidence.
>
> The distinguishing obligation of a fiduciary is the obligation of loyalty. The principal is entitled to the single-minded loyalty of his fiduciary. This core liability has several facets. A fiduciary must act in good faith; he must not make a profit out of his trust; he must not place himself in a position where his duty and his interest may conflict; he may not act for his own benefit or the benefit of a third person without the informed consent of his principal. This is not intended to be an exhaustive list, but it is sufficient to indicate the nature of fiduciary obligations.

This is a restatement of the older *Bray v Ford* [1896] AC 44. (See Chapter 16 where the fiduciary duty is examined in greater detail at 16.2 'General application of constructive trust'.)

Fiduciary duties can apply in many walks of life and the courts often have to remind people of the strict nature of these duties.

· ·

● *Imageview Management v Jack* [2009] 2 All ER 666

Kelvin Jack was Trinidad and Tobago's international goalkeeper. He agreed that Imageview would act as his agent and that company negotiated a two-year playing contract for him with Dundee United, for which Imageview received 10 per cent of his salary.

Imageview also agreed with Dundee United, that Dundee would pay Imageview £3,000 for negotiating a work permit for Mr Jack. Jack did not know about this other agreement and when he found out about it he stopped paying the 10 per cent to Imageview.

HELD: Imageview were in breach of their fiduciary duty as an agent.

Jacob LJ at 669:

> …Imageview in negotiating a deal for itself had a clear conflict of interest. Put shortly, it is possible that the more it got for itself, the less there would or could be for Mr. Jack. Moreover it gave Imageview an interest in Mr Jack signing for Dundee as opposed to some other club where no side deal for Imageview was possible.
>
> There is no answer to this. The law imposes on agents high standards. Footballers' agents are not exempt from these. An agent's own personal interests come entirely second to the interest of his client. If you undertake to act for a man you must act 100%, body and soul, for him. You must act as if you were him. You must not allow your own interest to get in the way without telling him. An undisclosed but realistic possibility of a conflict of interest is a breach of your duty of good faith to your client.
>
> That duty should not cause an agent any problem. All she or he has to do to avoid being in breach of duty is to make full disclosure.

This case reiterates the strict duties laid down in *Bray v Ford* [1896] AC 44.

KEY POINT The fiduciary duty means that trustees must not make a profit from their trustee position, must not buy trust property, must not use knowledge that they gain from their position for personal advantage, and generally must promote the interests of the beneficiaries above their own interests.

Equitable compensation

15.3.1 The traditional duty to restore the trust fund

If trustees breach their duty, either by failing to act as ordinary prudent men of business or failing to act properly as fiduciaries, the consequences are severe for the trustees. They are personally liable and must restore the trust fund to what it would have been but for their breach. This is an old remedy from the Court of Chancery, but even in 1915, which was in living memory (1873) of when Chancery had been a separate court, there was some uncertainty amongst the lawyers of how this was different from ordinary common law damages.

● *Nocton v Lord Ashburton* [1914] AC 932

Viscount Haldane LC at 952:

> Moreover, its [the Court of Chancery] remedies were more elastic. Operating **in personam** as a court of conscience it could order the defendant, not, indeed, in those days, to pay damages as such, but to make restitution, or to compensate the plaintiff by putting him in as good a position pecuniarily as that in which he was before the injury.

In personam—Latin and literally means against the person. The Court of Chancery used to order parties to do something, such as to return property and if they did not do it they were punished for contempt of court. This might involve fines, imprisonment, or seizure of assets.

At 956–7:

> Courts of Equity had jurisdiction to direct accounts to be taken, and in proper cases to order the solicitor [in that case a solicitor, Nocton, was being sued] to replace property improperly acquired from the client, or to make compensation if he had lost it by acting in breach of a duty which arose out of his confidential relationship to the man who had trusted him.

A good example of a traditional trust case is *Clough v Bond* (1838) 3 My & Cr 491. The breach of trust does not have to *cause* the loss for the trustee to be liable.

● *Clough v Bond* [1838] 3 My & Cr 491

Emily Bond and her brother, Thomas Dixon, held property on trust for Louisa Clough. When Emily was pregnant, her husband, John Bond, took over the running of the trust. Bond and Dixon put the money into Child & Co's bank, in their joint names. John Bond died and Dixon was able to steal the money and leave the country. Emily Bond was liable for a breach of trust because she should have added her name to the bank account. Then Dixon would not have been able to sign for the money by himself and steal it.

HELD: Lord Cottenham LC at 494:

> The principle of the court is to charge persons in the situation of trustees as parties to the breach of trust, wherever they have acted irregularly, and the irregularity, however well-intended, has in the result enabled their trustees to commit a breach of trust, or has been, however remotely, the origin of the loss.

At 496:

> …yet if that line of duty be not strictly pursued, and any part of the property be invested by such personal representative in funds or upon securities not authorised, or be put within the control of persons who ought not to be entrusted with it, and a loss be thereby eventually sustained, such personal representative will be liable to make it good, however unexpected the result, however little likely to arise from the course adopted, and however free such conduct may have been from any improper motive.

In the old-fashioned sort of trust it is easy to see how equitable compensation would have worked. The trust would probably be very specific about what property should be held on trust. It might, for instance, be the house and land and possessions of a wealthy family. If any of this property went missing the trustees had to return it to the beneficiaries or replace the value of it, if it could not be returned. The trustees would also have to return any profit that either was made with the property or might have been made. Similarly, trusts used to specify what property the trustees could invest in. If the trust instrument did not do this, the general law laid down a limited list of permitted trustee investments. So if, for example, trustees were only allowed to invest by lending money secured on a mortgage, if they invested in shares they would have to sell the shares, replace them with a mortgage and replace any money lost to the trust.

15.3.2 Equitable compensation in the modern age

In a modern trust, the trust property is more likely to be an ever-changing mixture of all types of property, shares, stocks, land, bonds, etc., so it is harder to identify what was definitely trust property and say that it must be replaced if the trustees fail to carry out their duties correctly. In some cases, however, it can be seen how the equitable compensation is assessed.

. . . .
● *Bartlett v Barclays Bank (No 2)* [1980] Ch 515

Barclays Bank was the trustee of a trust for the Bartlett family. The main investment of the trust was shares in the Bartlett family company. Barclays made a disastrous attempt to involve this company in property development, which failed when planning permission was not obtained.

HELD: Brightman J at 535:

> I hold that the bank failed in its duty whether it is judged by the standard of the prudent man of business or of the skilled trust corporation. The bank's breach of duty caused the loss, which was suffered by the trust estate. If the bank had intervened as it could and should have that loss would not have been incurred. By 'loss', I mean the depreciation, which took place in the market value of the BT shares, by comparison with the value, which the shares

> would have commanded if the loss on the Old Bailey project had not been incurred, and reduction of dividends through loss of income. The bank is liable for the loss so suffered by the trust estate, except to the extent that I shall hereafter indicate.

At 545:

> My reasoning is this: the obligation of a trustee who is held liable for breach of trust is fundamentally different from the obligation of a contractual or tortious wrongdoer.

KEY POINT The trustee's obligation is to restore to the trust estate the assets of which he has deprived it.

Equitable compensation here was to restore the value of the company that had been lost.

15.3.3 Difficulties in assessing the level of compensation

The difficulty of establishing the level of equitable compensation in a modern trust can be seen in *Nestlé v National Westminster Bank plc* [1993] 1 WLR 1260.

● **Nestlé v National Westminster Bank plc** [1993] 1 WLR 1260

This case involved a trust established by Georgina Nestlé's grandfather. When the trust fund ended and the capital finally came to her, she complained to the courts that it was not as much as she had expected. She claimed that she would have had more than £1 million if it had been properly invested, but instead she inherited £269,203. Before her, the previous beneficiaries, her father and uncle, had also complained to the trustees, the National Westminster Bank plc, that their incomes would be more if different investment policies had been followed. She could show that trustees had not reviewed the investment portfolio between 1922 and 1959 and that the trustees had not realized the full extent of their investment powers. They had invested in bank and insurance firm shares, when they could have diversified more.

HELD: Leggatt LJ: Miss Nestlé had to prove that the trustees had caused a loss to the trust.

At 1283:

> In this context I would endorse the concession of Mr Nugee for the bank that 'loss' will be incurred by a trust fund when it makes a gain less than would have been made by a prudent businessman.

The judge looked at the investments made and considered expert evidence, and accepted at 1285:

> But by the undemanding standard of prudence the bank is not shown to have committed any breach of trust resulting in loss.

It is difficult for the court to be drawn into arguments of what *might* have happened if the trustees had made different choices of investment. Just because trustees did not make the *best* choice of investment does not make them in breach of trust. They only have to make *reasonable* choices, to live up to the standard of an ordinary, prudent man of business.

15.3.4 Should the test of liability be causation?

The liability of trustees for breach of trust generally was reconsidered in a House of Lords case. In certain situations, the principles of equitable compensation could lead to a result that looks unfair.

● *Target Holdings v Redfern* [1996] 1 AC 421

Target Holdings lent £1,525,000 to Crowngate, so that Crowngate could buy a commercial property. Target lost money because the property was massively over-valued and was only worth £500,000. Redferns were the solicitors in the transaction and had held the money, which was only to be released upon the completion of the conveyance. It is standard practice for the solicitors to hold the purchase money before completion and the solicitors are regarded as holding the money on trust. Unfortunately, Redferns had released the money too early, before completion, and this was a breach of trust.

HELD: Redferns were not liable, as their breach of trust had not caused the loss to Target. The loss was caused by the over-valuation, which was not the responsibility of Redferns.

The court made a distinction between 'traditional' trusts, intended to provide for a family, and commercial cases such as this one.

Lord Browne-Wilkinson at 434:

> The basic right of a beneficiary is to have the trust duly administered in accordance with the provisions of the trust instrument, if any, and the general law. Thus, in relation to a traditional trust where the fund is held in trust for a number of beneficiaries having different, usually successive, equitable interests (e.g. A for life with remainder to B), the right of each beneficiary is to have the whole fund vested in the trustees so as to be available to satisfy his equitable interest when, and if, it falls into possession. Accordingly, in the case of a breach of such a trust involving the wrongful paying away of trust assets, the liability of the trustee is to restore to the trust fund, often called 'the trust estate', what ought to have been there.
>
> The equitable rules of compensation for breach of trust have been largely developed in relation to such traditional trusts, where the only way in which all the beneficiaries' rights can be protected is to restore to the trust fund what ought to be there. In such a case the basic rule is that a trustee in breach of trust must restore or pay to the trust estate either the assets, which have been lost to the estate by reason of the breach, or compensation for such loss. Courts of Equity did not award damages but, acting in personam, ordered the defaulting trustee to restore the trust estate: see *Nocton v Lord Ashburton* [1914] AC 932, 952, 958, per Viscount Haldane LC. If specific restitution of the trust property is not possible, then the liability of the trustee is to pay sufficient compensation to the trust estate to put it back to what it would have been had the breach not been committed: *Clough v Bond* (1838) 3 M & C 490. Even if the immediate cause of the loss is the dishonesty or failure of a third party, the trustee is liable to make good that loss to the trust estate if, but for the breach, such loss would not have occurred: *Bartlett v Barclays Bank Trust Co Ltd (Nos 1 and 2)* [1980] Ch 515. Thus the common law rules of remoteness of damage and causation do not apply. However there does have to be some causal connection between the breach of trust and the loss to the trust estate for which compensation is recoverable, viz. the fact that the loss would not have occurred but for the breach: *Nestlé v National Westminster Bank plc* [1993] 1 WLR 1260.

But Lord Browne-Wilkinson was unwilling to extend this approach to the special situation of this case.

At 435:

> Thus, even applying the strict rules so developed in relation to traditional trusts, it seems to me very doubtful whether Target is now entitled to have the trust fund reconstituted. But in my judgment it is in any event wrong to lift wholesale the detailed rules developed in the context of traditional trusts and then seek to apply them to trusts of quite a different kind. In the modern world the trust has become a valuable device in commercial and financial dealings. The fundamental principles of equity apply as much to such trusts as they do to the traditional trusts in relation to which those principles were originally formulated. But in my judgment it is important, if the trust is not to be rendered commercially useless, to distinguish between the basic principles of trust law and those specialist rules developed in relation to traditional trusts which are applicable only to such trusts and the rationale of which has no application to trusts of quite a different kind.

Target v Redfern was confirmed by the Supreme Court in AIB Group (UK) plc v Mark Redler & Co Solicitors [2014] 3 WLR 1367, where the solicitors were, once again, holding a mortage advance on trust, until the transaction was completed.

● **AIB Group (UK) plc v Mark Redler & Co Solicitors** [2014] 3 WLR 1367

A bank, the AIB Group, agreed to lend Mr and Mrs Sondhi £3.3 million to be secured by a first legal charge on their home. A condition was that they must pay back another first legal charge of £1.5 million in favour of Barclays Bank plc, which was already secured on their home. The solicitors, Mark Redler, failed to discharge all of this first mortgage, leaving £309,000 still owing to Barclays. The Sondhis defaulted on their mortgage and their home was sold for £1.2 million, although AIB had accepted a valuation of £4.25 million. AIB were only able to recover £867,697, because Barclays had to be paid first. AIB sued Redlers for the full amount of loss on the loan of £3.3 million, which was £2.5 million, claiming that Redlers had to restore the trust fund.

HELD: The Bank was only entitled to the amount by which it suffered loss. This was the £309,000, over which they had failed to obtain security.

Lord Toulson at 1384:

> There are arguments to be made both ways, as the continuing debate among scholars has shown, but absent fraud, which might give rise to other public policy considerations that are not present in this case, it would not in my opinion be right to impose or maintain a rule that gives redress to a beneficiary for loss which would have been suffered if the trustee had properly performed its duties.

Even if AIB had obtained a charge for the full £3.3 million, they would still have lost most of their money, because the house was only worth £1.2 million. The only loss was the £300,000 or so, on which Barclays had first claim.

Lord Reed at 1400–1:

> Following that approach . . . the model of equitable compensation, where trust property has been misapplied, is to require the trustee to restore the trust fund to the position it would have been in if the trustee had performed his obligation.

> The measure of compensation should normally be assessed at the date of trial, with the benefit of hindsight. The foreseeability of loss is generally irrelevant, but the loss must be caused by the breach of trust, in the sense that it must flow directly from it.

It follows that the liability of a trustee for breach of trust, even where the trust arises in the context of a commercial transaction which is otherwise regulated by contract, is not generally the same as liability in damages for tort or breach of contract. Of course, the aim of equitable compensation is to compensate: that is to say, to provide a monetary equivalent of what has been lost as a result of a breach of duty. At that level of generality, it has the same aim as most awards of damages for tort or breach of contract.

Those structural similarities do not however entail that the relevant rules are identical... As courts around the world have accepted, a trust imposes different obligations from a contractual or tortious relationship, in the setting of a different kind of relationship. The law responds to those differences by allowing a measure of compensation for breach of trust causing loss to the trust fund which reflects the nature of the obligation breached and the relationship between the parties. In particular... where a trust is part of the machinery for the performance of a contract, that fact will be relevant in considering what loss has been suffered by reason of a breach of trust.

KEY POINT

A trustee is only liable for the loss caused by his breach of trust.

The *AIB v Mark Redler* case explains *Target Holdings v Redfern* [1996] 1 AC 421 by saying that the older case was not making a clear distinction between how loss should be determined in commercial and family trust cases. There is only one duty of equitable compensation, but how it works depends upon the type of trust, whether there are also contractual obligations and, most importantly, which type of trustee duty has been breached. For example, in *Bristol and West Building Society v Mothew* [1998] Ch 1, at 15.3.5 'The trustees' liability for lack of reasonable care and skill', the trustees had made a negligent statement, so that particular breach of duty might be treated in a similar way to the tort of negligence. If, say, the trustees stole the trust fund that would be treated differently and the trustees would be required to restore the whole fund. (See 11.9 'The liability of trustees'.)

> **thinking points**
>
> Should *Target Holdings v Redfern* [1996] 1 AC 421 become the test for liability in all breach of trust cases? Lawyers have increasingly used equitable doctrines and remedies in the commercial world, where previously they would have been content with the common law of tort and contract. Common law lawyers do not always fully understand equity. The fiduciary duty has become increasingly important, but it is not just one all-encompassing duty. There are at least three distinct categories of fiduciary relationship. These are the relationship of trust and confidence, influence, and, thirdly, confidentiality. The judgment in *Target Holdings Ltd v Redferns* is rather an oversimplification, to say that equitable principles do not apply to a commercial trust. Properly understood, the principles of equitable accounting are subtler than that. Accounts can be taken on the basis of wilful default, which roughly accords with common law negligence or on the basis of falsifying the account, which would have been applicable in *Target*. The trustee has misapplied trust money and must replace that money with his own. The trustee is not liable for the loss, but is liable to restore trust property. See Sir Peter Millett 'Equity's Place in the Law of Commerce' (1998) 114 LQR 214.

15.3.5 The trustees' liability for lack of reasonable care and skill

We saw in 15.1 'The trustees' duty of care' that the trustees have a duty of reasonable care and skill. Traditionally if they breached this duty of care it would be treated in the same way as the more serious breach of a fiduciary duty, dealt with in 15.2 'The fiduciary nature of trusteeship'. Both, it was held, gave rise to equitable compensation, as explained in 15.3 'Equitable compensation'. Nowadays, many would distinguish between lack of care and skill and a full-blown breach of trust. Breach of trust should lead to the trustees having to restore the trust fund, but lack of care and skill should be treated like common law damages. Did the lack of care and skill cause any loss and how much loss did that lack of care actually cause?

• *Bristol and West Building Society v Mothew* [1998] Ch 1

Millett LJ at 17:

> Although the remedy which equity makes available for breach of the equitable duty of skill and care is equitable compensation rather than damages, this is merely the product of history and in this context is in my opinion a distinction without a difference. Equitable compensation for breach of the duty of skill and care resembles common law damages in that it is awarded by way of compensation to the plaintiff for his loss. There is no reason in principle why the common law rules of causation, remoteness of damage and measure of damages should not be applied by analogy in such a case. It should not be confused with equitable compensation for breach of fiduciary duty, which may be awarded in lieu of rescission or specific restitution.

(See Chapter 19 'Equitable remedies'.)

thinking points

Equity always had its own approach to monetary remedies against the trustees, known as equitable accounting and now under the broad heading of equitable compensation. Equitable compensation includes several different remedies and this article attempts to explain these remedies and compare them to the better known common law equivalents. Sir Peter Millett mentions two main types of monetary remedy, in his article mentioned at 15.3.4 'Should the test of liability be causation?' and in Bristol and West Building Society v Mothew. In the article they are referred to as Substitutive Compensation and Compensatory Damages. Equity, however, can also award Disgorgement Damages, as in Attorney-General v Blake [2001] 1 AC 268 and Restitutionary Damages, as in Tang Man Sit v Capacious Investments Ltd [1996] AC 514. Equity has yet to find an equivalent to the common law's Punitive Damages. See S Elliott and J Edelman 'Money Remedies against Trustees' (2004) 18 TLI 116.

15.4 The liability of individual trustees

Trustees do not act and decide individually nor do they take majority votes on decisions, unless it happens to be a charitable or pension trust. They should act and decide unanimously: *Re Mayo* [1943] Ch 302. Sometimes that is not quite what happens, because (say) one trustee is much more active than the others and takes it upon him or herself to run the trust.

(See 13.2.3 'Unanimity'.)

15.4.1 A 'sleeping' trustee is liable for the actions of the other trustees

An old authority, *Townley v Sherborne* (1643) J Bridge 35, holds that a trustee is not liable for the faults of other trustees, but it is not quite as simple as that.

It is the duty of a trustee personally to run the trust, and part of that duty is to observe what the other trustees are doing and intervene if they are doing something wrong. Doing nothing or very little can itself be a breach of trust.

● *Bahin v Hughes* (1886) LR 31 ChD 390

In his will, Robert Hughes made his three daughters trustees of a trust for Mrs Bahin and her children. Eliza Hughes 'managed the business as the acting trustee'. She reinvested some of the trust funds on a mortgage of leasehold houses and money was lost. One of the other trustees, Mrs Edwards, claimed that it was all the fault of Hughes and that Hughes should pay. The third trustee, Mrs Burden, did not appear in the case.

HELD: Cotton LJ at 394: As far as the beneficiaries were concerned all the trustees were liable.

> We feel no doubt that the cestui que trust is entitled to redress as against the trustees, and therefore consider both that the wife of Mr Edwards and himself, as well as Mr and Mrs Burden, were answerable.

(The events in this case were before the Married Women's Property Act 1884 allowed married women to hold their own property.)

> …and in my opinion it would be wrong to raise a distinction as regards the liability of Mr Edwards. He is answerable for the same breach of trust, and is not to be differently treated from the other trustees in the matter.

Fry LJ pointed out that there were sound reasons for not allowing a trustee to escape liability by blaming the other trustee or trustees for what had gone wrong.

At 398:

KEY POINT
All the trustees must act for the benefit of the trust.

> In my judgment the courts ought to be very jealous of raising any such implied liability as is insisted on, because if such existed it would act as an opiate upon the conscience of the trustees; so that instead of the cestui que trust having the benefit of several acting trustees, each trustee would be looking to the other or others for a right of indemnity, and so neglect the performance of his duties. Such a doctrine would be against the policy of the court in relation to trusts.

433

15.4.2 When a trustee can escape liability

It would only be in limited circumstances that a trustee could escape liability.

● *Bahin v Hughes* (1886) LR 31 ChD 390

Cotton LJ again at 395–6:

KEY POINT
For one trustee to take all the blame, that trustee must take the trust property or be the only trustee guilty of fraud.

> …but so far as cases have gone at present, relief has only been granted against a trustee who has himself got the benefit of the breach of trust, or between whom and his co-trustees there has existed a relation, which will justify the court in treating him as solely liable for the breach of trust.

Therefore, in order to escape liability, a trustee would have to prove that his or her fellow trustees had taken the trust property for themselves or had taken a bribe. Even where one trustee is a solicitor and the other is not, the non-solicitor cannot place all the blame on the other trustee, just because he is a solicitor and is presumed to know more about the law.

● **Head v Gould** [1898] 2 Ch 250

(This case can also be found in the Introduction and at 15.4.4 'The liability of retiring trustees'.)

The trustees were a solicitor, Gould, and a young beneficiary, Miss Adelaide Head. All the trust property had been used up to help her mother, Mrs Head, with her debt problems. Miss Head's younger brother complained to the court that his share of the trust had gone.

HELD: Kekewich J at 265:

> ...I do not myself think that Byrne J or any other judge ever intended to hold that a man is bound to indemnify his co-trustee against loss merely because he was a solicitor, when that co-trustee was an active participator in the breach of trust complained of, and is not proved to have participated merely in consequence of the advice and control of the solicitor.

It will be hard for trustees to show that they are not to blame for the breach of trust of the other trustees.

15.4.3 The trustees' liability to the beneficiaries

From the point of view of the beneficiaries, the trustees are said to have *joint and several liability*. This means that the trustees are all equally liable. The beneficiaries can sue them all or just one of them and he or she has to reimburse the full amount. The one that has been successfully sued would then seek to recover what he had paid from his fellow trustees.

Normally the court would hold that all the trustees were equally liable, unless it could be shown that one trustee was solely to blame. That trustee would have to indemnify the other trustees, as explained in *Head v Gould* [1898] 2 Ch 250 at 15.4.2 'When a trustee can escape liability'. It is also possible under s. 2 of the Civil Liability (Contribution) Act 1978 for the court to apportion the contribution between the trustees as is 'just and equitable'.

Civil Liability (Contribution) Act 1978, s. 2

....

(1) ...such as may be found by the court to be just and equitable having regard to the extent of that person's responsibility for the damage in question.

(2) ...the court shall have power in any such proceedings to exempt any person from liability to make contribution, or to direct that the contribution to be recovered from any person shall amount to a complete indemnity.

KEY POINT
The beneficiaries can recover their loss from one or all of the trustees.

15.4.4 The liability of retiring trustees

If a trustee retires, he or she is not usually liable for breaches of trust committed after his or her retirement, unless implicated in them.

● **Head v Gould** [1898] 2 Ch 250 (This case can also be found in the Introduction and at 15.4.2. 'When a trustee can escape liability')

Clapp and Houlditch were the trustees of the Head family marriage settlements. They felt that they had done all that they could to help Mrs Head with her financial problems and volunteered to stand down in favour of others, who might be prepared to advance her more money from the trust. Were they liable for what the new trustees Gould and Miss Head did subsequently?

HELD: Kekewich J at 272–3:

I cannot blame Messrs Houlditch and Clapp for the appointment which they made, nor do I think that they had any reasonable ground for believing, or that they believed, that the trust would be otherwise than secure in the hands of their successors.

At 273–4:

...in order to make a retiring trustee liable for a breach of trust committed by his successor you must show, and show clearly, that the very breach of trust which was in fact committed was not merely the outcome of the retirement and new appointment, but was contemplated by the former trustee when such retirement and appointment took place.

To make the retiring trustees liable for breaches of trust committed by the new trustees, it is necessary to prove that the old trustees had reasonable grounds for believing the new trustees would commit a breach of trust.

The criminal liability of trustees

Trustees hold the legal estate in the trust property, but if they take trust property they are guilty of theft. The trust property belongs to the beneficiaries.

> **Theft Act 1968**
> ....
> 1(1) A person is guilty of theft if he dishonestly appropriates property belonging to another with the intention of permanently depriving the other of it ...
> 5(2) Where property is subject to a trust, the persons to whom it belongs shall be regarded as including any person having a right to enforce the trust, and an intention to defeat the trust shall be regarded accordingly as an intention to deprive of the property any person having that right.

● ***R v Clowes and Another (No 2)*** [1994] 2 All ER 316

Clowes and Naylor ran a group of companies called the Barlow Clowes Group, which encouraged investors to send their money to them, for the group to invest on their behalf. The group's promotional literature gave many assurances about the safety and profitability of the investments that would be made, e.g. 'All moneys received are held in a designated clients account and the clients are the beneficial owners of all securities purchased on their behalf'. Clowes and Naylor did not invest the money as promised, but took it from the account and used it for their own purposes.

HELD: Watkins LJ:

The wording used indicated that the investors' funds were held on trust.

At 325:

> As to segregation of funds, the effect of the authorities seems to be that a requirement to keep moneys separate is normally an indicator that they are impressed with a trust . . .

Clowes and Naylor may not have had the legal knowledge to realize that this was a trust, but they had still acted dishonestly in taking the money.

At 330–1:

> However, dishonesty is an ingredient of many offences and does not necessarily depend upon a correct understanding by an accused of all the legal implications of the particular offence with which he is charged. The test is that laid down by this court in *R v Ghosh* [1982] QB 1053, namely whether the accused was acting dishonestly by the standards of ordinary and decent people and, if so, whether he himself must have realised that what he was doing was, by those standards, dishonest.

At 336:

KEY POINT
If a trustee dishonestly appropriates trust property, it is theft.

> Thus at the moment Naylor removed the £19,000 he was taking something in which the investors had an equitable interest. What was taken falls in our view four square within the definition of property belonging to another under s. 5(1) of the 1968 Act.

(See 16.4.3 'What is dishonesty?', where this criminal law test is used to establish civil liability for assisting in a breach of trust in *Twinsectra v Yardley* [2002] 2 AC 164.)

15.6 Protection of trustees

There are a number of things that trustees can do to protect themselves from being sued or to reduce their liability.

15.6.1 Trustee exemption clauses

When the trust is established it is quite common to insert a clause into the trust instrument that protects the trustees from being sued by the beneficiaries. If this was not done, many trustees would refuse to be appointed and this is particularly the case with professional trustees.

● *Armitage v Nurse* [1997] 2 All ER 705

A trust for Paula Armitage contained clause 15, which was a standard clause in trusts:

> No trustee shall be liable for any loss or damage which may happen to Paula's fund or any part thereof or the income thereof at any time or from any cause whatsoever unless such loss or damage shall be caused by his own actual fraud . . .

Paula claimed that the trustees had not maintained the value of the trust property.

HELD: Millett LJ at 711:

> In my judgment cl. 15 exempts the trustee from liability for loss or damage to the trust property no matter how indolent, imprudent, lacking in diligence, negligent or wilful he may have been, so long as he has not acted dishonestly.

The Privy Council looked at the issue of trustee exemption clauses in the Guernsey case of *Spread Trustee v Hutcheson* [2012] 1 All ER 251. They confirmed the views of Millett LJ in *Armitage v Nurse*, that it was permissible for trustees to exclude liability for negligence, even gross negligence, but not for breach of trust. There was a clear distinction between trustees' core fiduciary duties, which could not be excluded, and their duty of reasonable care and skill, which could.

. . . .

● *Spread Trustee v Hutcheson* [2012] 1 All ER 251

Lord Clarke at 271:

> Yet it is common ground, that is a failure to act with reasonable care and skill, can lawfully be excluded under both Guernsey customary law and English law . . . the Board concludes that under the customary law of Guernsey the parties could lawfully agree that the liability of the trustee arising out of its negligence or gross negligence was excluded.

The phrase 'wilful misconduct' was sometimes used in trustee exemption clauses to the effect that this was liability that could not be excluded. The Privy Council agreed with Millett LJ that this phrase, when used in a trustee exemption clause, meant a breach of trust.

Lord Clarke at 269:

> The Board [of the Privy Council] agrees with counsel for the trustee that English law is clear that in this class of case it is not permissible to exclude wilful misconduct as described by Millett LJ in the above passage.

The meaning of 'dishonesty' in the context of trustees' civil liability has caused the courts particular difficulty. *Walker v Stones* [2000] 4 All ER 412 attempts to define the meaning of 'dishonesty'.

. . . .

● *Walker v Stones* [2000] 4 All ER 412

Sir Christopher Slade at 444:

> A person may in some cases act dishonestly, according to the ordinary use of language, even though he genuinely believes that his action is morally justified. The penniless thief, for example, who picks the pocket of the multi-millionaire is dishonest even though he genuinely considers the theft is morally justified as a fair redistribution of wealth and that he is not therefore dishonest.

This means that the trustees cannot excuse themselves by saying that they thought that they were doing the right thing. Their conduct has to be judged by a reasonable standard. The test is objective, not subjective. (See 16.4.3 'What is dishonesty?'.)

The wide protection given to trustees by exemption clauses has been criticized by the Law Commission (Trustee Exemption Clauses (2003) Law Com CP 171), but Parliament has not

KEY POINT
An exemption clause can protect trustees from liability unless they act dishonestly.

legislated on the area. Instead, a code of practice has been adopted, under which potential trustees should warn customers of any exclusion clauses in their terms of business, before agreeing to become trustees.

thinking points

The decision in Spread Trustee v Hutcheson *is not as clear-cut as it might seem. As it is a Privy Council decision, dealing with Guernsey law, it is not, strictly speaking, a precedent for England and Wales. Two of the judges dissented and there was not total agreement upon whether 'gross negligence' could be excluded under a trustee exemption clause. Millet LJ in* Armitage v Nurse *had thought that it could, but what exactly is 'gross negligence'? Is it an extreme form of lack of reasonable care and skill, in which case it might well be excluded, or is it equivalent to bad faith or breach of fiduciary duty, in which case it should not be excluded? See Kelry CF Loi 'Gross negligence and trustee exemption clauses in the Privy Council: Spread Trustee v Hutcheson' [2011]* Conveyancer and Property Lawyer *521.*

15.6.2 Consent of the beneficiaries

The trustees might be able to establish that the beneficiary or beneficiaries consented to the breach of trust. Indeed, the beneficiaries may have instigated the breach of trust.

The court will examine whether the beneficiary freely consented and whether the beneficiary understood to what he was consenting.

● ***Re Pauling's Settlement Trusts*** [1964] Ch 303

Miss Pauling, an heiress, had married a naval officer, Commander Younghusband, 'who had almost no fortune at all'. To prevent the misuse of her fortune it was put into a trust for her for life and then to the children that she might have. The trust contained a power of advancement to the children of up to half their presumptive share. Advancements allow beneficiaries to have part of their share of the trust, before they become fully entitled to it. (See 12.3 'The exercise of discretion'.)

The parents were in constant financial difficulty and, at the instigation of the commander, they systematically used advancements to the children to solve their financial problems. The children were advanced money by the trustees, but in fact the parents took it and used it to purchase a house on the Isle of Man, furniture for that house, a house in Chelsea, and to pay off a loan to the mother.

Coutts & Co was the trustee, but also the banker to the mother. The bank and lawyers, who were consulted, do not appear to have appreciated that there was anything wrong in parents taking the children's advances. When the children realized that these advancements might have been illegal, they sued the trustees for the return of £29,160 of the estimated £70,000 fortune. The case went to the Court of Appeal.

HELD: Willmer LJ at 334:

1.   Coutts & Co had not exercised the advancement power properly, in allowing the parents to spend the children's money. This was a breach of trust.

> What they cannot do is to prescribe a particular purpose, and then raise and pay the money over to the advancee leaving him or her entirely free, legally and morally, to apply it for that purpose or to spend it in any way he or she chooses, without any responsibility on the trustees even to inquire as to its application.

2. However, the trustee had a defence, in that the beneficiaries had consented to the breach of trust.

Willmer LJ at 335:

> But in the circumstances of this case it is clear to us that if the bank can establish a valid request or consent by the advanced beneficiary to the advance in question, that is a good defence on the part of the bank to the beneficiary's claim, even though it be plain that the advance was made in breach of trust.

3. There was, however, the problem of *undue influence*. The children were over 21 and had consented to the advancements, but this did not let the bank escape liability because it was deemed that the children were still under parental control and therefore subject to undue influence.

Willmer LJ at 337:

> In our judgment the question is one of fact and degree. One begins with a strong presumption in the case of a child just 21 living at home, and this will grow less and less as the child goes out in the world and leaves the shelter of the home. Nevertheless, the presumption normally lasts only a 'short' time after the child has attained 21.

However, the children were emancipated from parental control for the later advancements and it was decided that they could consent to them.

This meant that the bank only had to restore the money for the earlier advancements to the beneficiaries.

The court looks at all the circumstances of the consent, in order to come to a fair and equitable solution.

. . . .

● *Re Pauling's Settlement Trusts* [1964] Ch 303

Wilberforce J at 108 in the High Court:

> The court has to consider all the circumstances in which the concurrence of the *cestui que trust* was given with a view to seeing whether it is fair and equitable that, having given his concurrence, he should afterwards turn around and sue the trustees: that, subject to this, it is not necessary that he should know what he is concurring in is a breach of trust, provided that he fully understands what he is concurring in, and it is not necessary that he should himself have directly benefited by the breach of trust.

KEY POINT
To escape liability, the trustees must prove that the beneficiaries freely consented to the breach of trust.

The children did not personally benefit from the advances, their parents did. They were judged to have freely consented to the final advances of £5,350, which went straight into their parents' bank account because, by that date, they were old enough to know to what they were consenting.

15.6.3 Impounding the beneficiaries' interests

As we saw in 15.3 'Equitable compensation' and 15.4 'The liability of individual trustees', the trustees must restore the loss to the trust. If, however, the beneficiaries consented to the breach of trust, the court may go further and allow the trustees to reclaim the loss to the trust from the equitable interests of the beneficiaries.

The courts possess an ancient, inherent power to do this, which was expanded by Act of Parliament.

> **Trustee Act 1925, s. 62**
> ....
> Where a trustee commits a breach of trust at the instigation or request or with the consent in writing of a beneficiary, the court may, if it thinks fit, make such order as to the court seems just, for impounding all or any part of the interest of the beneficiary in the trust estate by way of indemnity to the trustee or persons claiming through him.

For instance, in *Re Pauling's Settlement Trusts* [1964] Ch 303, at 15.6.2 'Consent of the beneficiaries', the court allowed the trustees to reclaim part of the loss from the life interests of the parents, Commander Younghusband and the former Miss Pauling. Once again the court looks at all the circumstances before deciding whether to impound an equitable interest.

....
● ***Bolton v Curre*** [1895] 1 Ch 544

There was a marriage settlement for Mr and Mrs Blood, to which Mr Blood had brought mortgages on his estates in Ireland and Mrs Blood property which was sold and invested in Great Western Railway stock. Mr Blood needed money, so he requested the trustees to sell the GWR stock and give him the proceeds in cash. Mrs Blood gave her written consent. Later, new trustees required the old trustee, Bolton, to make good this loss. Bolton's representative claimed the life interests of Mr and Mrs Blood.

HELD: Romer J at 550–1:

> For these reasons I hold that the trustees' right to have the interest of Mr Blood impounded is established, and that the life interest must be impounded accordingly.
>
> I have next to consider the life interest of Mrs Blood... Now, that lady has done nothing in the matter of the breach of trust but consent in writing to the change of investment. She did not instigate the change; she did not in fact know that the new investment was in breach of trust, or was improper in any way. Under these circumstances, in the exercise of my judicial discretion I shall not order... that the trustees may impound her life interest.

Mrs Blood did not realize what she was consenting to and was deemed to be under the influence of her husband, so it would be unjust to take away her equitable interest.

KEY POINT
The trustees may take a beneficiary's interest in order to repay money lost through a breach of trust, if it is just in all the circumstances to do so.

15.6.4 Section 61 of the Trustee Act 1925

Even if a breach of trust is established, the court may excuse a trustee from liability if the trustee can show that he has acted honestly and reasonably.

> **Trustee Act 1925, s. 61**
> ....
> If it appears to the court that a trustee, whether appointed by the court or otherwise, is or may be personally liable for any breach of trust, whether the transaction alleged to be a breach of trust occurred before or after the commencement of this Act, but has acted honestly and reasonably, and ought fairly to be excused for the breach of trust and for omitting to obtain the directions of the court in the matter in which he committed such breach, then the court may relieve him either wholly or partly from personal liability for the same.

The trustees argued this defence in *Re Pauling's Settlement Trusts* [1964] Ch 303, at 15.6.2 and 15.6.3, but the court was reluctant to allow it, because of the serious breach of duty by the trustees.

. . . .

● ***Re Pauling's Settlement Trusts*** [1964] Ch 303

The trustee, Coutts & Co, was also a bank, concerned about Mrs Younghusband's overdraft, so it was guilty of a conflict of interest.

Willmer LJ at 341:

> Even at this early stage they wholly failed to exercise any powers or duties as trustees, and thought of themselves as bankers to the commander and the mother.

Section 61 of the Trustee Act 1925 did not help the bank avoid liability.

Willmer LJ at 339:

> Where a banker undertakes to act as a paid trustee of a settlement created by a customer, and so deliberately places itself in a position where its duty as a trustee conflicts with its interest as a banker, we think that the court should be very slow to relieve such a trustee under the provisions of the section.

As we saw in 15.4.1 'A "sleeping" trustee is liable for the actions of the other trustee', an inactive trustee will not be excused liability, even under s. 61, as he will not be regarded as acting honestly and reasonably. Acting honestly is not enough, the trustee must also act reasonably to be excused liability.

. . . .

● ***Lloyds TSB Bank Plc v Markandan & Uddin (a firm)*** [2012] 2 All ER 884

Mr Davies obtained a loan of £742,500 from the Cheltenham and Gloucester Building Society to buy a property. He instructed Markandan and Uddin as his solicitors, and Cheltenham and Gloucester also employed them and handed over the money to them. They held it on trust, on the standard terms, not to release it until completion. A firm calling themselves Deen Solicitors claimed to act for the vendors of the property and persuaded Markandan and Uddin to hand over the money. In fact, Deen were fraudsters and stole the money.

HELD: Markandan and Uddin were in clear breach of trust for releasing the money. Although they were honest, as they were not involved in the fraud, they did not act reasonably. They released the money before completion and failed to check whether the solicitors they dealt with really existed. So they could not be excused.

Rimer LJ at 903:

> It is, therefore, the discretionary power under s. 61 that provides the key to the claimed unfairness of holding a solicitor liable for breach of trust in circumstances such as the present. The careful, conscientious and thorough solicitor, who conducts the transaction by the book and acts honestly and reasonably to it in all respects but still does not discover the fraud, may still be held to have been in breach of trust for innocently parting with the loan money to a fraudster. He is, however, likely to be treated mercifully by the court on his s. 61 application. M&U's conduct of the transaction was, however, found to fall short of the standard that merited such mercy.

In contrast the solicitors escaped liability in *Nationwide Building Society v Davisons Solicitors* [2012] EWCA Civ 1626.

....

● ***Nationwide Building Society v Davisons Solicitors*** [2012] EWCA Civ 1626

Davisons were acting for a Mr Patel purchasing a house from Shansun Naher Begum. A Mr BK Gill, of a firm called Rothschild, claimed to be acting for Begum. Davisons had not previously dealt with Rothschild, so they followed procedure by checking the websites maintained by the Law Society and Solicitors Regulation Authority. These showed that a Mr B. K. Gill was a solicitor working for Rothschild in Birmingham and Small Heath. On the basis of that, Davisons handed over the purchase money to Rothschild. It turned out that although Mr B. K. Gill was a real solicitor and Rothschild were a real firm, they did not have a branch in Small Heath. An impostor had placed the false information on the SRA website.

HELD: Davisons had acted in breach of trust, but ought to be excused liability under section 61.

Sir Andrew Morrit, Chancellor at para 48:

> The section only requires [the solicitor] to have acted reasonably. That does not, in my view, predicate that he has necessarily complied with best practice in all respects … It is seldom help-ful to compare conduct found to be reasonable or not in one case with that of another; but the factual similarity of this appeal with that in *Lloyds TSB Bank Plc v Markandan & Uddin (a firm)* justifies pointing out that the conduct of the solicitors in that case … was quite different from that relied on in this case. In my view [the solicitor] did, in all the circumstances, act reasonably.

A solicitor is entitled to rely on the accuracy of an official Solicitors Regulatory Authority website.

A trustee who does nothing will probably not succeed with a s. 61 defence.

....

● ***Re Second East Dulwich 745th Starr Bowkett Building Society*** (1899) 79 LT 726

The building society was wound up and Streeter was one of the trustees of the deed of dissolution. He tried to blame the other trustees for the losses.

HELD: Kekewich J at 727:

> …he states that, being co-trustee with Pearce he knew nothing of the books, he trusted to Pearce, and never inquired how matters went on. He signed document after document without inquiry as Pearce told him, and swore an affidavit which he did not understand … It seems to me that a man who accepts such a trusteeship, and does nothing, swallows wholesale what is said by his co-trustee, never asks for explanation, and accepts flimsy explanations, is dishonest.

A trustee who does his or her job conscientiously and properly may succeed with the s. 61 defence.

....

● ***Re Evans (deceased)*** [1999] 2 All ER 777

David Evans died intestate in 1987. His daughter, Lillian Westcombe, acted as administrator and distributed the estate in 1990. She could not locate her brother, also David Evans, with whom she had lost contact in 1962, so on legal advice, she took out a missing beneficiary insurance policy to pay him his share of the estate, if he ever turned up. David reappeared in

1994 and claimed his share, plus interest. The insurance policy only paid the capital sum, not interest as well.

HELD: Richard McCombe QC at 789:

> …to act on legal advice is not a 'passport to relief' under s. 61, but…it is important to have regard to the nature of the estate, the circumstances of the defaulting representative and his or her actions in the light of the advice received. This…was a relatively small estate, the representative was a lay person unaccustomed to problems of this nature who was at all times willing to abide by the advice of solicitors…She was never advised to consider interest.

At 790:

> In these circumstances, I am prepared to relieve the defendant against the plaintiff's claim to interest to which he is otherwise entitled…

The 'trustee', Lillian, had done all that she reasonably could in the circumstances and her breach of trust was relatively minor.

KEY POINT
If a trustee has acted honestly and reasonably the court may excuse liability under s. 61 of the Trustee Act 1925.

thinking points

To escape liability, the trustee must show not only that they acted both honestly and reasonably, but also that they 'ought fairly to be excused'. This enables the court to look at all the facts and the effect of the breach of trust on all the parties involved. So individual cases depend very much on their facts, but some general principles can be extracted from the case law. 'For example, nearly all the English cases demonstrate that the judges are prepared to use the section freely, and welcome it as a release from having to hold people liable for having to live up to unattainable ideals.' See LA Sheridan 'Excusable Breaches of Trust' (1955) 19 Conv 420.

15.7 Limitation

15.7.1 The time limits for commencing an action

Disputes about breach of trust can be very long running. Trustees can raise a limitation defence: that the breach was so long ago that they cannot be sued now.

It is undesirable to have litigation about events that happened long ago, as a fair trial becomes difficult. Witnesses' memories fade and documents become lost. Besides, people are entitled to conduct their affairs without the risk that someone will question the legality of what they did many years before. Because of this there are statutory time limits within which a court action must be commenced. The general time limit is six years from the right of action accruing, i.e. when the alleged unlawful act occurred. This applies to torts, contract, and breach of trust. For claims against the estate of a dead person, the time limit is 12 years.

Limitation Act 1980

2 Time limit for actions founded on tort

An action founded on tort shall not be brought after the expiration of six years from the date on which the cause of action accrued.

5 Time limit for actions founded on simple contract

An action founded on simple contract shall not be brought after the expiration of six years from the date on which the cause of action accrued.

21 Time limit for actions in respect of trust property

(3) Subject to the preceding provisions of this section, an action by a beneficiary to recover trust property or in respect of any breach of trust, not being an action for which a period of limitation is prescribed by any other provisions of this Act, shall not be brought after the expiration of six years from the date on which the right of action accrued.

22 Time limit for actions claiming personal estate of a deceased person

Subject to section 21(1) and (2) of this Act—

(a) no action in respect of any claim to the personal estate of a deceased person or to any share or interest in any such estate (whether under a will or on intestacy) shall be brought after the expiration of 12 years from the date on which the right to receive the share or interest accrued;

These time limits provide a defence for trustees if they are sued for a breach of trust, but there are two major exceptions which allow a beneficiary to sue a trustee without the hindrance of any set time limit.

15.7.2 There is no statutory time limit for fraud or to recover trust property

Limitation Act 1980, s. 21

(1) No period of limitation prescribed by this Act shall apply to an action by a beneficiary under a trust, being an action—

(a) in respect of any fraud or fraudulent breach of trust to which the trustee was a party or privy; or

(b) to recover from the trustee trust property or the proceeds of trust property in the possession of the trustee, or previously received by the trustee and converted to his use.

'Fraud' means that the beneficiary has to prove that the trustee was dishonest (*Armitage v Nurse* [1997] 2 All ER 705), which might prove difficult. (See 15.6.1 'Trustee exemption clauses'.) Just proving that the trustee has taken trust property would seem easier.

Section 38 of the Limitation Act 1980 defines 'trustee' by adopting the same definition as in the Trustee Act 1925:

Trustee Act 1925, s. 68

(17) ... the expressions 'trust' and 'trustee' extend to implied and constructive trusts ...

Therefore, the existence of a constructive trust can extend the period of limitation.

● *James v Williams* [1999] 3 All ER 309

William and Violet Warren lived in and owned a cottage in Cornwall. William died in 1971 and Violet died in 1972, but neither of them left a will. Their son, also called William, lived with them and just carried on living there, without going through any legal formalities such as administering their estates. As there were no wills, the property should have been divided into three equal shares, for William and his sisters, Thirza and Mary.

William died in 1993 and he had made a will, leaving the cottage to his sister, Thirza. The other sister, Mary, claimed her third share, but she seemed to be outside the time limits of the Limitation Act 1980.

HELD: Sir Stephen Brown:

At 313:

> The plaintiff submitted that the definition of 'trust' in the Trustee Act 1925 makes it clear that the word 'trust' in s. 21 of the 1980 Act included a constructive trust. She went on to submit that a constructive trust arose in this case with a result that the limitation period did not start to run against her claim.

There was a constructive trust dating back to 1971 or 1972, when William unlawfully took possession of the land.

At 315:

> As a general rule a constructive trust attaches by law to property which is held by a person in circumstances which would be inequitable to allow him to assert full beneficial ownership of the property.

At 316:

> It follows that the defendant's title is that of a constructive trustee with the result that the plaintiff's case is not statute barred.

William was regarded as a real trustee, because he actually held the trust property so his sister, Mary, could sue under s. 21(1)(b) of the Limitation Act 1980 and avoid the six-year time limit. He was not the same kind of constructive trustee as explained in *Central Bank of Nigeria v Williams* [2014] 2 All ER 489 at 15.7.3 in the following section.

15.7.3 The limitation period applies if it is not a 'true' trust

Alleging that there is a constructive trust might seem a clever way of avoiding the statutory time limits, but the courts are wary of claimants who pretend that there is a constructive trust, when their case is really based on 'simple contract'.

● *Paragon Finance v DB Thakerar & Co* [1999] 1 All ER 400

Paragon were mortgage lenders and had lent money to purchasers of flats in London's Docklands in 1990. Thakerar was a firm of solicitors, who acted for Paragon and the purchasers. The flats were bought at an inflated valuation and Paragon lost money. Paragon sued the solicitors for breach of contract and also claimed a breach of fiduciary duty. They argued that the solicitors knew of the inflated valuation and should have told them. To get round the six-year time limit Paragon tried to argue that fiduciaries had similar duties to trustees and s. 21(1) would apply. (See Chapter 16 'Constructive trusts' at 16.2.1 'Abuse of fiduciary position' and 16.2.2 'What is fiduciary relationship?' for fiduciaries.)

HELD: Millett LJ at 408–9: He explained that there were two types of trust and the second type were not 'true trusts', and therefore the six-year time limit would apply.

> Regrettably, however, the expressions 'constructive trust' and 'constructive trustee' have been used by equity lawyers to describe two entirely different situations. The first covers those cases already mentioned, where the defendant, although not expressly appointed as trustee, has assumed the duties of a trustee by a lawful transaction which was independent and preceded the breach of trust and is not impeached by the plaintiff. The second covers those cases where the trust obligation arises as a direct consequence of the unlawful transaction which is impeached by the plaintiff.
>
> In the first class of case, however, the constructive trustee really is a trustee. He does not receive the trust property in his own right but by a transaction by which both parties intend to create a trust from the outset and which is not impugned by the plaintiff.
>
> The second class is different. It arises when the defendant is implicated in a fraud... In such a case he is traditionally though I think unfortunately described as a constructive trustee and said to be 'liable to account as constructive trustee'. Such a person is not in fact a trustee at all, even though he may be liable to account as if he were. He never assumes the position of a trustee, and if he receives the trust property at all it is adversely to the plaintiff by an unlawful transaction which is impugned by the plaintiff.

Thakerar never held trust property for Paragon and therefore fell into the second category; the allegation was that they were implicated in a fraud.

At 414:

> There is a case for treating fraudulent breach of trust differently from other frauds, but only if what is involved really is a breach of trust. There is no case for distinguishing between an action for damages for fraud at common law and its counterpart in equity based on the same facts merely because equity employs the formula of constructive trust to justify the exercise of the equitable jurisdiction.

This was really a case about breach of contract and should not be treated as a trust.

Subsequent cases have followed and developed this distinction between two types of trust, where claimants have tried to avoid the limitation period by claiming the existence of a constructive trust.

● **Coulthard v Disco Mix Club** [1999] 2 All ER 457

Coulthard did work for Tony Prince of Radio Luxembourg, 'beat-mixing' various records, which is 'the technique of linking two different sound recordings so that the beat is not disrupted on the dance floor'. They had various agreements in the early 1980s and Coulthard alleged that Prince had never given him his rightful share of the profits. Some years later, after Coulthard had qualified as a barrister, he sued, claiming that they had had a fiduciary relationship and that there had been a breach of trust.

KEY POINT

A trust involves a trustee holding trust property for the beneficiary from the outset.

HELD: at 480:

> What *Paragon Finance v DB Thakerar & Co* [1999] 1 All ER 400 makes clear is that the critical boundary in these cases lies between those cases where the defendant is a true trustee (be it of an express trust or a constructive trustee) and those where he is not. In...Mr Coulthard and Mr Prince's relationship, the relationship is not that of trustee and beneficiary. The touchstone of a true trusteeship is trust property.

Prince never held property on trust for Coulthard, and therefore this was a contract case and barred by the six-year limit.

This approach was confirmed in *Central Bank of Nigeria v Williams* [2014] 2 All ER 489, which also involved second category constructive trusts, based on knowing receipt and dishonest assistance. (See 16.4 'Liability of third parties (strangers) in constructive trusts' for this type of constructive trust.)

KEY POINT
The statutory limitation period cannot be avoided by claiming that a party to a contract is also a fiduciary, nor by suing knowing receipt or dishonest assistance constructive trustees.

● ***Central Bank of Nigeria v Williams*** [2014] 2 All ER 489

> Dr Williams claimed that his trustee had taken $6,020,190 from him with the assistance of the Central Bank of Nigeria. This had occurred in 1986. Section 21(1)(a) Limitation Act 1980 does not apply any limitation period to a 'trustee'. If the Bank was a constructive trustee, were they a 'trustee' according to the meaning of this section?

HELD: The majority of the Supreme Court did not think that this type of constructive trustee was a real trustee and therefore the normal six-year limitation period applied.

Lord Sumption at page 506:

> The essence of a liability to account on the footing of knowing receipt is that the defendant has accepted trust assets knowing that they were transferred to him in breach of trust and that he had no right to receive them. His possession is therefore at all times wrongful and adverse to the rights of both the true trustees and the beneficiaries. No trust has been reposed in him. He does not have the power or duties of a trustee, for example with regard to investment or management. His sole obligation of any practical significance is to restore the assets immediately.

15.7.4 Limitation periods for future beneficiaries

A trust can have many beneficiaries and they are not all bound by the same limitation period.

Limitation Act 1980, s. 21

(3) [The beneficiary is subject to a six year time limit] then:

For the purposes of this subsection, the right of action shall not be treated as having accrued to any beneficiary entitled to a future interest in the trust property until the interest fell into possession.

The six-year period does not start to run until the beneficiary actually becomes entitled to his or her share of the trust. The reason is that beneficiaries are not likely to go to court until they are actually entitled to receive their share.

● *Cattley v Pollard* [2007] 2 All ER 1086

The breaches of trust had occurred between 1987 and 1996, but the court action, 'the Second Proceedings', was commenced in 2005, more than six years after these events.

Under the trust there were nine nephews and nieces with life interests under the trust fund, but they had 17 children who would not become entitled to their shares until their parents died.

HELD: Richard Sheldon QC:

At 1109:

> It follows that the last subparagraph of s. 21(3) applies to the Second Proceedings. Time has not begun to run as regards the beneficiaries with a future interest in the estate and the second proceedings are therefore not time barred.

The six-year period did not begin for the children until their parents died and they inherited.

KEY POINT
Time only begins to run against a beneficiary when their interest comes into possession.

The effect of this decision is that trustees could be sued many years after the breach of trust, by beneficiaries who finally come into possession of their equitable interest under the trust.

15.7.5 The doctrine of laches

Section 21(1) of the Limitation Act 1980 might be taken to suggest that there is no limitation period for a beneficiary suing a trustee for fraud or for the return of trust property. There is no statutory limit, but equity has always had its own approach to deciding whether too much time has elapsed for the beneficiary to sue the trustee. These are the linked doctrines of laches, acquiescence, and delay. Nowadays the court would take a flexible approach and look at all the circumstances.

● *Cattley v Pollard* [2007] 2 All ER 1086

Richard Sheldon QC refers to a recent case.

At 1119:

> In *Green v Gaul* [2006] EWCA Civ 1124, what was described as the modern approach to the defences of laches, acquiescence and estoppel was set out. Preconceived formulas derived from earlier cases were discouraged.
>
> The inquiry should require a broad approach, directed to ascertaining whether it would in all the circumstances be unconscionable for a party to be permitted to assert his beneficial right.
>
> Unconscionability depends on all the circumstances but, for the doctrine of laches to apply, would usually require some form of unconscionable conduct on the part of the claimants. Delay alone is unlikely to be sufficient for the doctrine to apply unless coupled with conduct on the part of the claimant which would make it inequitable for him to enforce the claim.

If the beneficiary delays too long before starting the case, the trustee will have a defence. Twenty years was once suggested as a rough maximum. If the beneficiary consents to what the trustee has done, or gives the impression that consent has been given, this too could give the trustee a defence. Even after 38 years a claim might be allowed, particularly if the claimant never consented to what the defendant had done and the court is satisfied that there will be no injustice to the defendant. As mentioned earlier, the court takes a flexible approach and does not wish to be bound by technical rules.

A claim to the court must be brought within a reasonable time. Equity has a flexible approach and looks at all the factors in the case.

● **Fisher v Brooker** 2009 WL 2207452

Fisher had composed and played the organ part on the original recording of the 1967 pop hit 'A Whiter Shade of Pale' by the group Procol Harum. Thirty-eight years later, he claimed copyright for his contribution and his rightful share of future royalties. The leader of Procol Harum, Brooker, defended the claim by saying that it would be unfair to the defendants for Fisher to bring his case after this lengthy delay.

HELD: Their Lordships did not wish to make fine distinctions between the doctrines of laches, estoppel, and acquiescence.

Lord Neuberger at para 62:

> Thirdly, laches and estoppel are well-established equitable doctrines. However, at least in a case such as this, I am not convinced that acquiescence adds anything to estoppel and laches. The classic example of proprietary estoppel, standing by whilst one's neighbours builds on one's land believing it to be his property, can be characterised as acquiescence— see per Oliver J in *Taylor Fashions Ltd v Liverpool Victoria Trustees Ltd* [1982] 1 QB 133, 151. Similarly, laches, failing to raise or enforce an equitable right for a long period, can be characterised as acquiescence.

At para 63:

> …one would expect the respondents to succeed in estoppel only if they could show that they reasonably relied on his having no such claim, that they acted on that reliance, and that it would be unfairly to their detriment if he was now permitted to raise or to enforce such a claim.

Fisher had never renounced his claim and said that he would not sue.

At para 64:

> Although I would not suggest that it is an immutable requirement, some sort of detrimental reliance is usually an essential ingredient of laches, in my opinion.

At para 79:

> …laches only can bar equitable relief, and a declaration as to the existence of a long-term property right, recognised as such by statute, is not equitable relief…They cannot show any prejudice resulting from the delay, and, even if they could have done so, they have no answer to the judge's finding…that the benefit they obtained from the delay would outweigh any such prejudice.

Brooker had enjoyed the royalties for 38 years. It was not unfair to allow Fisher to bring his claim now, particularly as he was asserting a legal, not an equitable, right.

(See Chapter 6 'Proprietary estoppel' for further information on the doctrine of estoppel.)

Conclusion

The law on breach of trust is designed to protect the beneficiaries. They can sue the trustees for failing to run the trust to the standard of the ordinary prudent man of business and also if the trustees fail to pursue the interests of the beneficiaries with a single-minded devotion. Liability for the trustee means that they have to restore the trust fund for what it would have been, but for their breach of trust. Even a trustee who had little to do with the breach of trust will find it hard to escape liability and, even if the beneficiaries have consented to the breach, the trustees may still be liable on the grounds that the beneficiaries did not fully understand to what they were consenting (see *Re Pauling's Settlement Trusts* [1964] Ch 303). The trustees may even find themselves sued and found liable, under s. 21(1) of the Limitation Act 1980, many years after the breach of trust occurred. The trustees' lot is not a happy one, so that is why a potential trustee might only accept the office if there is an exemption clause in the trust.

Questions

Self-test questions

1 What is the trustee's duty of care?

2 What are the obligations of a fiduciary?

3 Explain the principles of equitable compensation.

4 When is a trustee liable for a breach of trust committed by his fellow trustees?

5 What is the effect of a trustee exemption clause?

6 When does the consent of the beneficiaries excuse the trustees from their breach of trust?

7 How can a trustee show that they have acted honestly and reasonably?

8 In what circumstances does the six-year limitation period apply?

Discussion questions

1 Trustees have different duties of care, according to their knowledge, experience, and professional qualifications. Are these workable distinctions?

2 Should equitable compensation be determined by principles of causation, as suggested in *Target v Redferns* [1996] 1 AC 421?

3   Should all trustees be held equally liable for breaches of trust?

4   Is it acceptable for an exemption clause to protect a trustee from being sued?

5   Do beneficiaries really have enough legal knowledge to consent to a breach of trust?

6   Should a six-year limitation period apply to all breaches of trust?

Assessment question

The Bartleby Family Trust holds various rented flats and houses on trust for Mrs Bartleby for life, remainder to be shared equally between her children. Mrs Bartleby wants more income and asks the trustees, Tim and Teresa, to provide it. Tim and Teresa decide that the only way that they can provide extra income is to sell some of the flats and houses. They seek expert advice from the trust's solicitor and bank, who both advise against doing this. However, Mrs Bartleby is insistent that she needs the money and her twin children, Bill and Ben, who are just 18, agree. All three Bartlebys give their written consent to the sale to Tim and Teresa. Teresa does not want to go against the expert advice, but she decides not to oppose the wishes of Tim and the Bartlebys. In 1990 the trustees sell half the houses that the trust owns and give the money to Mrs Bartleby.

In 2006 Mrs Bartleby dies and the trust fund goes to Bill and Ben. They are appalled to discover that the trust is worth very little and sue Tim and Teresa.

Advise Tim and Teresa on the likely success of Bill and Ben's action.

 Key cases

- *Head v Gould* [1898] 2 Ch 250 **(at Introduction, 15.4.2, and 15.4.4)**
- *Target Holdings v Redferns* [1996] 1 AC 421 **(at 15.3.4)**
- *Bahin v Hughes* (1886) LR 31 ChD 390 **(at 15.4.1 and 15.4.2)**
- *Re Pauling's Settlement Trusts* [1964] Ch 303 **(at 15.6.2–15.6.4)**
- *Paragon Finance v DB Thakerar & Co* [1999] 1 All ER 400 **(at 15.7.3)**

 Further reading

P Millett 'Equity's Place in the Law of Commerce' (1998) 114 *LQR* 214
How the old equitable principles fit into the modern commercial world.

S Elliott and J Edelman 'Money Remedies against Trustees' (2004) 18 *TLI* 116
The difficult subject of equitable compensation.

KCF Loi 'Gross negligence and trustee exemption clauses in the Privy Council: Spread Trustee v Hutcheson' 2011 *Conveyancer and Property Lawyer* 521

Trust instruments commonly contain clauses that protect the trustees from legal liability. What is the effect of these clauses and should they be allowed?

L Sheridan 'Excusable Breaches of Trust' (1955) 19 *Conv (NS)* 420

A survey of the old case law on s. 61 of the Trustee Act 1925.

16

Constructive trusts

Learning objectives

This chapter will help you to:

- define a constructive trust
- understand the circumstances that give rise to a constructive trust
- appreciate the different approaches to constructive trust
- appreciate the different views on the future of constructive trusts
- understand the nature and function of constructive trusts.

Introduction

Constructive trusts arise mainly through the operation of the law rather than by the actual conduct of the parties. As will be recalled from previous chapters, a trust arises either when parties formally comply with prescribed legal requirements, such as setting their intention on paper, or orally when parties manifest a clear intention that they want to engage in a trust relationship. This is not so with constructive trusts. A constructive trust usually arises when a court infers or implies its existence from circumstances surrounding the conduct of one or both parties. Constructive trust can be said to be one area where the maxim 'equity looks at the intent rather than the form' is most useful. A person can become a constructive trustee when it is his least intention to be so. Yet, despite the fact that a constructive trust is a creation of the law, few concepts have proved more controversial. The application of constructive trust varies widely; its province is contentious, and its future sustainability remains largely uncertain. To some, constructive trust is a remedial measure resorted to by courts in circumstances that otherwise would have left someone to benefit from fraud. To others, constructive trust is simply an institutional mechanism that enables the court to bind a party to a transaction or dealing to which he has not consented to being a trustee, if not doing so may lead to unconscionable profiting from one's unfair dealing. Most English courts take the latter approach. This chapter studies the meaning, nature, and approaches to constructive trusts and discusses the various circumstances in which constructive trust might emerge.

16.1 Definition

16.1.1 An imprecise term

● **Carl-Zeiss Stiftung v Herbert Smith (No 2)** [1969] 2 Ch 276

Edmund Davies LJ at 300:

> English law provides no clear and all embracing definition of a constructive trust. Its boundaries have been left perhaps deliberately vague, so as not to restrict the court by technicalities in deciding what the justice of a particular case may demand.

It seems therefore deliberate that English courts do not define constructive trust so as to afford it adaptability. Now, let us consider some examples of how the concept has been described.

● **Paragon Finance plc v DB Thakerar & Co** (1999) 3 All ER 309

Millett LJ at 400:

>...arises by the operation of law where the facts are such that it would be unconscionable for an owner to deny that another person has acquired a beneficial interest in his property.

This shows that constructive trust is not created by people, but through the operation of law.

● **Muschinki v Dodds** (1985) 62 ALR 429

Deane J at 451:

>...as a remedial institution which equity imposes regardless of actual or presumed agreement or intention (and subsequently protects) to preclude the retention or assertion of beneficial ownership to property to the extent that such retention or assertion would be contrary to equitable principle.

● **HKN Invest OY v Incortrade PVT Ltd** (1993) 3 IR 152

Costello J at 162:

>...the principle of [constructive trust] is that where a person who holds property in circumstances which in equity and good conscience should be held or enjoyed by another he will be compelled to hold the property in trust for another.

It does not matter what definition of constructive trusts one holds. What is important is the rationale for constructive trusts.

● **Re Montagu's Settlement Trusts** [1987] Ch 264

Sir Robert Megarry VC at 277:

>...in determining whether a constructive trust has been created, the fundamental question is whether the conscience of the recipient is bound in such a way as to justify equity in imposing a trust on him.

In *Beatty v Guggenheim Exploration Co* 122 NE 378 (NY 1919), Cardozo J said that:

>a constructive trust is the formula through which the conscience of equity finds expression. When...the holder of the legal title may not in good conscience retain the beneficial interest, equity converts him into a trustee.

In *Stephen James Thomas v FWT Holdings Limited* (Judgment 9 July 2009), CIV 2008-485-120 (High Court of New Zealand), DI Gendall J observes, at para 28, that:

>[t]o succeed in a constructive trust claim, the claimant must establish that it would be unconscionable for the respondent to assert an exclusive beneficial interest in the properties because the respondent's conscience requires the recognition of the applicant's beneficial claim.

thinking points

From the various definitions stated earlier, what is the main objective of constructive trust? It does not matter what definition one ascribes to constructive trust. What is important is to reflect the fact that constructive trust is an arrangement which basically aims at averting injustice from occurring simply because of lack of compliance with some legal formality. See David R Lawson and F Ladson Boyle 'Constructive Trust' (1992) 4(2) Probate Practice Reporter.

16.2 General application of constructive trust

Constructive trust applies to a wide variety of situations. It applies to occasions when formal legal requirements have not been complied with; it is sometimes applied to prevent the abuse of fiduciary relationships by trustees. Often, constructive trust is applied to entitle a spouse of a marriage to beneficial interest that he or she is not otherwise entitled to under the common law.

● ***In Matter of the Estate of McKim*** 807 P2d 215 (NM 1991)

The defendant and his spouse married in 1981, agreeing that property owned by each prior to the marriage and acquired by each subsequent to the marriage would remain separate property. When the wife's corporation experienced financial difficulty, she conveyed its properties to her husband in consideration of his paying the balance on a loan secured by the properties. Subsequently, to avoid foreclosure of the properties by his wife's mortgagee and the Internal Revenue Service (IRS), the husband took out additional loans and executed a new property agreement with his wife that designated the properties as his separate property. Before his death in 1986, the husband attempted to convey the properties to his wife, requesting deeds from his title insurer and attorney but not signing them. The estate rejected the widow's claim against the estate for recovery of the properties. Upholding the trial court's decision that the estate held the properties as constructive trustee for the widow, the Supreme Court reviewed the circumstances that might result in a constructive trust. Relying on the *Restatement (Second) of Trusts* s. 44 and the *Restatement of Restitution* s. 182, it stated that the mere existence of a fiduciary or confidential relationship, regardless of the lack of abuse of this relationship, is adequate to justify finding that a transferee of property is a constructive trustee when retention of the property would result in the transferee's unjust enrichment. It found that the trial court was correct in holding that a fiduciary relationship was established between the decedent and his spouse when the properties were transferred to the decedent, although neither the decedent nor his spouse intended for him to receive a beneficial interest in the property, and that the estate would be unjustly enriched if allowed to retain the properties.

See Chapter 18 'Trusts of the family home' on the trust of the family home for a fuller discussion of this application of constructive trust. For now, let us consider the more rampant and common use of constructive trust, which is to prevent someone in a fiduciary relationship to the beneficiary of a trust from profiting from the position.

16.2.1 Abuse of fiduciary position

The prevention of abuse of fiduciary position is one of the most important applications of constructive trust in England and, indeed, as will be seen later, it is one area that almost completely blurs the distinction between institutional and remedial approaches to the constructive trust.

16.2.2 What is fiduciary relationship?

According to Finn (*Fiduciary Obligations* (Sydney: Law Book Co, 1977) 1), a fiduciary 'is, simply, someone who undertakes to act for or on behalf of another in some particular matter or matters. It is immaterial whether the undertaking is gratuitous. And the undertaking may be officiously assumed without request.' Finn further observes that 'the category of cases in which fiduciary obligations and duties arise from the circumstances of the case and the relationship of the parties is no more closed than the categories of negligence at common law' (Finn 'The Fiduciary Principle' in TG Youdan (ed) *Equity, Fiduciaries and Trusts* (Toronto: Carswell, 1989) 1–4).

Traditional categories of fiduciaries

Fiduciary relationships can occur in a number of scenarios. The most common fiduciary relationships exist between trustees and beneficiaries, agents and principals, directors and companies, and partners and co-partners. However, these categories are not mutually exclusive. For instance, the 'directors and companies' category could easily fit into an instance of 'trustee and beneficiary'.

thinking points

What distinguishes a fiduciary relationship from any other type of relationship? The golden rule of trust is that fiduciaries cannot use their position to personally benefit themselves. This rule is premised on the fact that fiduciaries, by virtue of their positions, have a great access to vital information about the trusts they retain and the beneficiaries of such trusts. This position is different from, for example, a mere contractual relationship between a buyer and a seller where such access is not common or usual, and the fact that the seller knows a lot about the buyer does not necessarily prejudice the latter in a typical commercial transaction. In short, it is the lopsided nature of the relationship between a fiduciary and a beneficiary that remarkably distinguishes fiduciary relationship from all other types of relations. See Jensen Darren 'Prescription and Proscription in Fiduciary Obligations' (2010) (21)2 King's LJ 333–54.

16.2.3 Unauthorized activities of trustees occasioning breach of trust

The golden rule of trust is that a trustee cannot take advantage of his position to make unauthorized profit from the trust or use the trust to his advantage in any other manner. It is a strict rule. The defences of good faith, lack of knowledge, or morally upright conduct do not vary the rule. This rule was laid down on 31 October 1726 in *Keech v Sandford* (1726) 2 Eq Cas Arb 741.

....

● ***Keech v Sandford*** (1726) 2 Eq Cas Arb 741

The lease of a market was devised to a trustee for the benefit of an infant. Before the expiration of the lease, the lessors refused to renew to the infant, as a result of which the trustee renewed for himself.

HELD: Lord King C:

> I must consider this as a trust for the infant; for I very well see, if a trustee, on the refusal to renew, might have a lease to himself, few trust estates would be renewed to *cestui que* use; though I do not say there is a fraud in this case, yet he should rather have let it run out, than to have had the lease to himself. This may seem hard, that the trustee is the only person of all mankind who might not have the lease: but it is very proper that rule should be strictly pursued, and not in the least relaxed; for it is very obvious what would be the consequence of letting trustees have the lease, on refusal to renew to *cestui que use*. So decreed, that the lease should be assigned to the infant, and that the trustee should be indemnified from any covenants comprised in the lease, and an account of the profits made since the renewal.

The rationale behind the rigidity of the fiduciary rule is succinctly laid down by Lord Herschell in the following case.

● ***Bray v Ford*** [1896] AC 44

> It is an inflexible rule of the court of equity that a person in a fiduciary position … is not, unless otherwise expressly provided [in the terms of the person's fiduciary duties], entitled to make a profit; he is not allowed to put himself in a position where his interests and duty conflict. It does not appear to me that this rule is, as had been said, founded upon principles of morality. I regard it rather as based on the consideration that, human nature being what it is, there is danger, in such circumstances, of the person holding a fiduciary position being swayed by interest rather than duty, and thus prejudicing those whom he was bound to protect. It has, therefore, been deemed expedient to lay down this positive rule.

The rule in *Keech v Sandford* is particularly difficult because it is applicable even, as with that case itself, if the lessor refuses to renew the lease; thereby, without renewing it for the trustee, the lease would expire. However, where only one of the many interested persons obtains a renewal, that person does not automatically enter a fiduciary relationship with those others for the purpose of the renewed lease.

● ***Re Biss*** [1903] 2 Ch 40

A lessee of a property died intestate, leaving a widow and three children, one being an infant. The widow and her two adult children, one of whom was a son, administered her husband's estate and continued to carry on the business under the existing annual tenancy. The widow and the son each applied to the lessor for a new lease for the benefit of the estate, which he refused to grant to the widow but which he granted to the son 'personally' for three years at a still further increased rent.

The administratrix applied to have the new lease treated as having been taken by the son for the benefit of the estate, and for an account of the rents and profits received by him.

The court held that it is not automatic that if someone who is only partly interested in an old lease obtains its renewal if he holds it on behalf of others. A person renewing is only held to be a constructive trustee of the new lease if, in respect of the old lease, he occupied some special position by virtue of which he owed a duty towards the other persons interested. For instance, in the case of a renewal by a partner of a partnership lease, or by a mortgagee of a mortgaged lease, it is deemed that the new lease forms part of the original lease.

At 63 in *Re Biss*, Roler LJ held that the infant who obtained the renewal was not in a fiduciary position in respect of the matter and owed no duty to anyone in respect of it. He was not guilty of fraud or concealment and had not used any right that a court of equity can recognize as belonging to other persons to enable him to obtain the lease.

thinking points

Do you think the strict nature of the Keech v Sandford *principle makes sense in an age of commercial exigency? Striking a balance between the protection of a beneficiary and a trust or trust investment is at the core of doctrinal debate about the decision in* Keech v Sandford. *On the one hand, one understands the reasoning of Lord King C in that case and Lord Herschell in* Bray v Ford *about the need to prioritize the duty of a trustee above their interest. Whether one agrees with the rule in* Keech v Sandford, *it is important to stress that that is the golden rule of trust, although the rule has been recently relaxed, especially with regard to commercial activities. See Matthew Harding 'Dual Listed Companies: Understanding Conflicts of Interest for Directors' [2002]* University of New South Wales LJ *34 and (2002) 25(2)* University of New South Wales LJ *594; PD Finn's review of WR McComas, MR Davison, and DM Gonski* The Protection of Trade Secrets *(London: Butterworths, 1981) in (1982)* Sydney L Rev *728.*

● ***Protheroe v Protheroe*** [1968] 1 All ER 1111 (CA)

A husband and wife acquired a leasehold dwelling-house as their matrimonial home. The leasehold was transferred into the name of the husband alone but it was not in dispute that the lease was held by the husband on trust for himself and the wife in equal shares. In March 1964 the husband left the home; in July the wife presented a petition for divorce, and in October 1964 the husband purchased the freehold reversion in the matrimonial home for £200 which he borrowed from a building society. The leasehold was worth separately £2,450, but the freehold would fetch £3,950. Was the wife entitled to a half share in the freehold of the matrimonial home?

HELD: The wife was entitled equally with the husband to the net proceeds of sale of the freehold of the matrimonial home, since, as the husband had held the leasehold as trustee, the freehold reversion was regarded in equity as having been acquired on the same trusts as the leasehold was held; the husband, however, was entitled to be reimbursed the purchase price of the freehold reversion and the expenses in connection with its acquisition.

A party who is held liable in constructive trust on the authority of *Keech v Sandford* is entitled to a lien on the property for the expenses incurred on the renewal.

● ***Bradford v Brownjohn*** [1868] 3 Ch App 711

A tenant for life of leaseholds for years determinable on lives, obtained, before his estate for life has come into possession, the grant of a reversionary term determinable on a new life, and to commence after the determination of the old term. He came into possession, and afterwards died, having possessed the estate during part of the term created by the new grant.

HELD: The amount to be paid by the remainderman in respect of the fine and expenses of renewal was to be ascertained by reference to the actual enjoyment of the tenant for life, and compound interest to be computed on the proportion attributable to the remainderman up to the death of the tenant for life, and simple interest from that time until payment.

- The rule in *Keech v Sandford* is strict and it does not matter whether fraud is intended or not.

- The main requirement for applying *Keech v Sandford* is fiduciary relationship.

- The rule in *Keech v Sandford* does not apply invariably to anyone having some kind of relationship with others interested in property. It has to be a fiduciary relationship.

16.3 Unauthorized transactions

The application of constructive trust to unauthorized transactions specifically concerns areas such as solicitors using their offices to make money or profits from property subject to trust, agents of estates receiving bribes, and representatives of governments abusing their office to commit crimes.

16.3.1 Solicitor/trusts

The *locus classicus* of this category is *Boardman v Phipps* [1967] 2 AC 46, the facts of which are fully set out here.

• **Boardman v Phipps** [1967] 2 AC 46

The residuary estate of a testator, who had died in 1944, included 8,000 shares in a private company, which had an issued share capital of 30,000 shares. The trustees of the testator's will were, in 1956, his widow (who was then senile), a married daughter, and an accountant. The beneficial trusts of the testator's residuary estate were for its division, subject to an annuity to his widow and his children, of whom the respondent was one and was entitled to 5/18ths of the estate. At all material times the appellant, B, acted as solicitor for the trustees and for his co-appellant, P, a son of the testator. In 1956 B and the accountant trustee decided that the position of the company was unsatisfactory and that something must be done to improve it. Towards the end of 1956 B and P attended the company's annual general meeting with proxies obtained from two trustees, the accountant and the daughter. They attended as representing the estate. Shortly after this meeting B and P decided, with the knowledge of the two trustees, to endeavour to obtain control of the company by themselves purchasing shares. The trustees had no power to invest trust moneys in shares of the company. B, purporting to act on behalf of the trustees as a shareholder, obtained information from the company concerning the price at which shares had changed hands. The negotiations for acquisition of shares were prolonged and passed through three phases. During the second phase, from April 1957 to October 1958, B obtained much information from the company by purportedly acting on behalf of the trustees. In November 1958 the widow trustee died. Ultimately, on 10 March 1959 (in the third phase of negotiations) an agreement for the sale of 14,567 shares of the company to B and P was signed and by the end of July 1959, they had acquired (with other purchases) 21,986 shares of the company. A considerable profit subsequently accrued from capital distributions on these shares. The appellants had acted honestly throughout. They appealed from a decision affirming an order declaring that they held 5/18ths of the shares on trust for the respondent and directing an account of profits and an inquiry into what should be allowed to B and P or either of them for their work and skill in obtaining the shares. On this appeal it was not contended that B and P had obtained the informed consent of the respondent beneficiary to their purchase of the shares of the company.

HELD: (1) Although the mere use of knowledge or opportunity coming to a trustee or agent in the course of the trusteeship or agency did not necessarily render him accountable for profit from its use, yet in the present case, as both the information which satisfied B and P that purchase of the shares would be a good investment and the opportunity to bid for them came to B and P as a result of B's acting or purporting to act on behalf of the trustees for certain purposes (although not for the particular purpose of bidding), B and P were constructive trustees of 5/18ths of the 21,986 shares in the company for the respondent and were liable to account to him for the profit thereon accordingly; (2) there should be an inquiry as to what sum was proper to be allowed to B and P or either of them in respect of their or his work and skill in obtaining the shares and the profits thereon, such payment to be on a liberal scale.

> ### thinking points
>
> *Query: Do you think that this is a plausible application of the rule in* Keech v Sandford? *The application of the* Keech v Sandford *principle in the* Boardman *case shows the dangers inherent in a strict application of the rule, especially in commercial contexts. There is no doubt that the decision of the fiduciary in this case to invest in the concerned company was solely motivated by the need to prevent the company from collapsing, an investment which the trustees themselves were not keen to make. See G Jones 'Unjust Enrichment and the Fiduciary's Duty of Loyalty' (1968) 84* LQR *472.*

Lord Upjohn, while agreeing with the majority of the court in *Boardman v Phipps*, cautioned against a slavish application of *Keech v Sandford*. His Lordship agreed with the general principle of *Keech v Sandford*, and its affirmation, by Lord Herschell in *Aberdeen Ry Co v Blaikie Brothers* [1843–60] All ER 249, where:

. . . .
● ***Aberdeen Ry Co v Blaikie Brothers*** [1843–60] All ER Rep 249

Lord Cranworth LC at 252:

> …and it is a rule of universal application that no one having such duties to discharge shall be allowed to enter into engagements in which he has or can have a personal interest conflicting or which possibly may conflict with the interests of those whom he is bound to protect.

Nevertheless, Lord Upjohn picked on the phrase 'possibly may conflict' used by Lord Cranworth to argue a different application of the rule in *Keech v Sandford*:

> The phrase 'possibly may conflict' requires consideration. In my view it means that the reasonable man looking at the relevant facts and circumstances of the particular case would think that there was a real sensible possibility of conflict; not that you could imagine some situation arising which might, in some conceivable possibility in events not contemplated as real sensible possibilities by any reasonable person, result in a conflict.

Some writers have argued that Lord Upjohn should have considered also the statement of Lord Selborne LJ in *Barnes v Addy* (1874) 9 Ch 244 at 251:

● **Barnes v Addy** (1874) 9 Ch 244

Lord Selborne LJ at 251:

> It is equally important to maintain the doctrine of trusts which is established in this court, and not to strain it by unreasonable construction beyond its due and proper limits. If a defendant has breached his fiduciary duty of loyalty he is liable in respect of any profits he has received: there is no requirement that the profit was obtained 'by virtue of his position'.

On one hand, *Boardman v Phipps* seems an insensible application of *Keech v Sandford* given that the solicitors involved afforded the trust the opportunity to make the investment, and it was only in light of the failure of that that they decided to make it themselves. On the other hand, making an exception of the nature that Lord Upjohn canvassed for in *Boardman v Phipps* could have opened a floodgate.

---

thinking points

Suppose Boardman had intimated to the trustees and the beneficiaries that he intended to acquire shares for himself in light of the inability of the Phipps family to acquire those shares, could this have led to authorized profit so as to make him avoid liability? It is possible that courts will show more leniency towards fiduciaries which make profit from their positions if such fiduciaries make a full disclosure of their intention to make investments in respect of the trust and where the fiduciary's interest is not in conflict with that of the trust in the circumstances. A determination of the situations in which the court will show a greater flexibility in applying the rule in Keech v Sandford *will often depend on the category of fiduciaries involved. See JC Shepherd 'Towards a Unified Concept of Fiduciary Relationship' (1981) 97 LQR 51.*

● **Queensland Mines v Hudson** (1977) 18 ALR 1

Mr Hudson was the managing director of the plaintiff company, thus standing in an unquestionable fiduciary relationship to the latter. After learning of some new mining opportunities, he informed the company of these but the company decided not to pursue this development. However, both the company and the board of directors were fully aware of the defendant's intention to pursue the opportunity himself. Mr Hudson resigned from the company, pursued the mining opportunity, and made profits. The company then tried to recover some of Mr Hudson's profits.

HELD: There was no conflict of interest between his duty and the company, he having fully disclosed his intentions prior to resigning from the company.

● **Industrial Development Consultants Ltd v Cooley** [1972] 2 All ER 162

The facts of this case are somewhat similar to those of *Queensland Mines*. The defendant, who was previously the chief architect for the West Midlands Gas Board, was a managing director of the plaintiff. The plaintiff's success was largely in the private sector and it was anxious to enter the public sector. Because of the defendant's connections and contacts in the gas industry the chairman of the group offered the defendant the post of managing director of the plaintiff. The defendant accepted and the appointment took effect from 5 February 1968. Within days of joining the plaintiff the defendant embarked on negotiations with the

Eastern Gas Board in an effort to discharge his duty to the plaintiff. In 1968 the Eastern Gas Board was contemplating building four depots and had not decided whether to farm out the work to other architects or do the work itself. The plaintiff was interested in this work and with the aid of the defendant it attempted to get at least one of the depots. That attempt failed. It became evident that the Eastern Gas Board disliked the set-up of the plaintiff's organization and was not prepared to deal with the plaintiff in any capacity. The board made it clear that it was only interested in employing the defendant privately and that it did not want any trouble with his employers. The defendant feigned illness and resigned from his company in order to join the new company.

HELD: While the defendant was managing director of the plaintiff a fiduciary relationship existed between him and the plaintiff; accordingly, information which came to him while he was managing director and which was of concern to the plaintiff was information which it was his duty to disclose to the plaintiff. He was under a duty therefore to disclose all information which he received in the course of his dealings with the gas board. Instead, he had embarked on a deliberate course of conduct which had put his personal interests as a potential contracting party with the gas board in direct conflict with his pre-existing and continuing duty as managing director to the plaintiff. He was therefore in breach of his fiduciary duty to the plaintiff in failing to pass on to the plaintiff all the relevant information received in the course of his dealings with the gas board and in guarding it for his own personal purposes and profit.

16.3.2 Bribes

Until recently, the rule governing the effect of bribes and other corrupt practices was laid down in *Lister & Co v Stubbs* (1850) 45 ChD 1.

. . . .

● *Lister & Co v Stubbs* [1850] 45 ChD 1

The plaintiff, a manufacturing company, employed the defendant, who was its foreman, to buy for it certain materials which it used in its business. The defendant, under a corrupt bargain, took from one of the firms from which products were purchased by him for the plaintiff large sums by way of commission, some of which he invested. The plaintiff brought an action against the defendant to recover the moneys so paid to him, claiming to be entitled to follow such moneys into the investments and moved for an injunction to restrain the defendant from dealing with the investments or for an order directing him to bring the moneys and the investments into court.

HELD: The relationship between the defendant and the plaintiff was that of debtor and creditor, and not that of trustee and *cestui que trust*, and that the plaintiff was not entitled to the order.

It does seem that this case does not lay down a general rule by which a bribe cannot be recovered, but rather limits or delineates the category of those who can be said to be in a fiduciary relationship with a company for the purpose of liability for bribes.

Many other cases have followed *Lister v Stubbs*.

. . . .

● *Powell & Thomas v Evans Jones & Co* [1905] 1 KB 11

Agents, who were employed for commission to procure an advance of money for their principals, employed for that purpose, with the assent of the principals, a sub-agent, on the footing that he should share the commission with them. The sub-agent was aware that the agents were acting in the matter for their principals. He succeeded in procuring the advance of the required amount from a company. Without the knowledge of the agents or their principals, the sub-agent received from the company a commission for introducing the business to it.

The principal then sought to recover the commission from the sub-agent.

HELD: The court must decline to make any further declaration of right with regard to such sums other than that the sub-agent would become indebted in respect of them to the principals when and if he received them.

But note in this case that the court already held that there was a fiduciary relationship between the director and the company. The court only refused to extend that relationship to those who were not directors of the company.

● *Regal (Hastings) Ltd v Gulliver* [1942] 1 All ER 378

This case involved a bona fide transaction involving the directors and certain other persons in a relationship with a company. The question arose as to whether money can be recovered from the directors and these individual persons including a solicitor of a subsidiary company.

HELD: The chairman of the board of directors, because he did not take the shares beneficially, was not liable to repay the profit made by those who took the shares from him, as the latter were not in a fiduciary relationship with the company. Since Garton was not a director of the appellant company he was not in a fiduciary relationship with it, and was not liable to make any repayment. Moreover, he took the shares at the express request of the directors of the appellant company.

KEY POINTS

* *Regal* clearly continued the trend laid down in *Lister v Stubbs* that unless the defendant is in a clear fiduciary relationship with the claimant, he will not be liable to refund money received even if it was received inappropriately.

* The rule in *Lister v Stubbs*, and all its permutations, has been criticized extrajudicially. See Sir P Millett 'Remedies: The Error in *Lister v Stubbs*' in P Birks (ed) *The Frontiers of Liability* (Oxford: Oxford University Press, 1994) vol 1 at 56. Also, several judicial authorities have departed from *Lister v Stubbs*.

* The new rule is that where a trustee accepts a bribe and is thus in breach of his fiduciary relationship, he is held to be a constructive trustee for the bribe. His liability also extends to profits made in investing the bribe and property acquired through it.

● *AG for Hong Kong v Reid* [1994] 1 All ER 1

Mr Reid, a solicitor and New Zealand national, joined the legal service of the Government of Hong Kong and became successively Crown counsel, deputy Crown Prosecutor, and ultimately Acting Director of Public Prosecutions. In the course of his career Mr Reid, in breach of the fiduciary duty which he owed as a servant of the Crown, accepted bribes as an inducement to him to exploit his official position by obstructing the prosecution of certain criminals. He was arrested, pleaded guilty to offences under the Prevention of Bribery Ordinance, and was sentenced on 6 July 1990 to eight years' imprisonment and ordered to pay the Crown the sum of $HK12.434 million, equivalent to $NZ2.435 million, being the value of assets then controlled by him which could only have been derived from bribes. No part of the sum of $HK12.434 million has been paid by Mr Reid.

HELD: When a fiduciary accepted a bribe as an inducement to betray his trust he held the bribe in trust for the person to whom he owed the duty as fiduciary; and if property representing the bribe increased in value, the fiduciary was not entitled to retain any surplus in excess of the initial value of the bribe because he was not allowed by any means to make a profit out of a breach of duty.

On the nature of the relationship between an employee and his employer company—which *Lister v Stubbs* had held was not fiduciary—Lord Templeman stated (at 9) that:

> The decision in *Lister & Co v Stubbs* is not consistent with the principles that a fiduciary must not be allowed to benefit from his own breach of duty, that the fiduciary should account for the bribe as soon as he receives it and that equity regards as done that which ought to be done. From these principles it would appear to follow that the bribe and the property from time to time representing the bribe are held on a constructive trust for the person injured. A fiduciary remains personally liable for the amount of the bribe if, in the event, the value of the property then recovered by the injured person proved to be less than that amount.

The court defined (at 2) a bribe as:

> ...a secret benefit which the fiduciary derived from trust property or obtained from knowledge which he acquired in the course of acting as a fiduciary and he was accountable under a constructive trust for that secret benefit to the person to whom the fiduciary duty was owed as soon as the bribe was received, whether in cash or in kind, under the equitable principle that equity considered as done that which ought to have been done. If property representing the bribe increased in value or if a cash bribe was invested advantageously the false fiduciary was accountable not only for the original amount or value of the bribe but also for the increased value of the property representing the bribe since otherwise he would receive a benefit from his breach of duty.

Clearly, the court was influenced here by consideration of public policy rather than the necessity of law (at 4):

> Bribery is an evil practice which threatens the foundations of any civilised society. In particular, bribery of policemen and prosecutors brings the administration of justice into disrepute. Where bribes are accepted by a trustee, servant, agent or other fiduciary, loss and damage are caused to the beneficiaries, master or principal whose interests have been betrayed. The amount of loss or damage resulting from the acceptance of a bribe may or may not be quantifiable. In the present case the amount of harm caused to the administration of justice in Hong Kong by Mr Reid in return for bribes cannot be quantified.

● *Reading v AG* [1951] AC 507

A sergeant in the British Army on active service abroad consented on several occasions to accompany civilian lorries transporting illicit spirits to specified destinations. He always wore military uniform in order to avoid inspection of the goods by the police, and for his services he received in all £20,000. The military authorities took possession of several thousand pounds found in his hands, and he was tried by court-martial and convicted of conduct prejudicial to good order and military discipline. After his release from prison he claimed, by petition of right, the return of the amount seized.

HELD: Viscount Jowitt LC and Lord Porter: He could not recover the money. The official position held by this soldier, which enabled him to earn the money by its use, gave the Crown, his master, the right to the money so earned as money had and received, even though it was earned by a criminal act and even though the Crown suffered no loss. The Crown was also entitled to the money on the separate and independent ground that a fiduciary relationship existed between the soldier and it.

It is interesting to consider how Sir Hartley Shawcross AG, JP Ashworth, and Henry Fisher for the Crown (at 512) sought to distinguish between an agent having a fiduciary relationship with his master and one that may not be presumed so.

> The Crown does not ask the House to enlarge any principle of law and does not submit that it is in a different position from any other master. The uniform of a servant of the Crown is, however different from the livery of a chauffeur; it clothes him with a different authority and is a very special asset. A soldier is under a duty to wear it in a way that is consistent with good order and discipline. The broad principle is that arising from the servant's relationship with his master; his duty is to serve the interests of his master and use the status conferred on him for the purposes of his master.

● ***Chan v Zacharia*** (1984) 53 ALR 417

The High Court of Australia forcefully enunciated the modern principle on liability for a bribe.

At 433:

> Stated comprehensively in terms of the liability to account, the principle of equity is that a person who is under a fiduciary obligation must account to the person to whom the obligation is owed for any benefit or gain (i) which has been obtained or received in circumstances where a conflict or significant possibility of conflict existed between his fiduciary duty and his personal interest in the pursuit or possible receipt of such a benefit or gain or (ii) which was obtained or received by use or by reason of his fiduciary position or of opportunity or knowledge resulting from it. Any such benefit or gain is held by the fiduciary as constructive trustee (see *Keith Henry & Co Pty Ltd v Stuart Walker & Co Pty Ltd* (1958) 100 CLR 342 at 350). That constructive trust arises from the fact that a personal benefit or gain has been so obtained or received and it is immaterial that there was no absence of good faith or damage to the person to whom the fiduciary obligation was owed.

thinking points

- *Is there a difference to be made between bribes taken by a normal employee (even if he is a foreman as in* Lister v Stubbs*) and a director of the public prosecutor acting on behalf of a government?*
- *Suppose that Mr Reid was a clerk in the Crown Office and not a DPP, do you think the decision would and/or should have been different?*
- *On what basis could a bribe be held in constructive trust if the Crown could not have had any legitimate expectations of bribes, and what is the rationale for holding profits originating from the investment of bribes as belonging in constructive trust?*
- *Was this case not decided on the principle that the law would not allow anyone to benefit from his fraud?*
- *What is the nature of the proprietary right the Crown has in a bribe? An ordinary employee who receives a bribe does not do so as a fiduciary and as such may not be treated as a constructive trustee of his boss for the money received. The boss may however have a personal claim against such an employee if, for instance, the latter receives the bribe in the ordinary course of his duty. The position*

of a fiduciary is different from this since the latter occupies a position of privilege. Even if there is no proprietary right over the bribe, it suffices that on the ground of public policy the fiduciary is denied the right to benefit from his fraud. See Matthew Harding 'Dual Listed Companies: Understanding Conflicts of Interest for Directors' [2002] University of New South Wales LJ *34 and (2002) 25(2)* University of New South Wales LJ *594.*

It must not be supposed that there was no movement towards the new rule. Indeed, as far back as the 19th century, courts have enunciated this rule before the Court of Appeal decision in *Lister v Stubbs*.

● ***Fawcett v Whitehouse*** (1829) 1 Russ & M 132, 39 ER 51

The defendant, Whitehouse, intending to enter into partnership with the plaintiffs Shand and Fawcett, negotiated for the grant of a lease by a landlord to the partnership. The landlord paid Whitehouse £12,000 for persuading the partnership to accept the lease.

HELD: Leach VC:

> Whitehouse was bound to obtain the best terms possible for the intended partnership … and that all he did obtain will be considered as if he had done his duty and had actually received the £12,000 for the new partnership, as upon every equitable principle he was bound to do. I am of opinion, therefore, that this is what must be called in a court of equity a fraud on the part of the defendant. It was in fact selling his intended partner for £12,000 … (See 1 Russ & M 132 at 149, 39 ER 51 at 58.)

The extent to which a company director can now be held accountable for money made by virtue of him being a director was recently touched upon by an English court.

● ***Sinclair Investments (UK) Ltd v Versailles Trade Finance Ltd (in Administrative Receivership) and others*** [2010] EWHC 1614

The facts of the case are very complex and the decision related to only an aspect of the entire case. In a nutshell, the Versailles Group collapsed in January 2000. Its business was discovered to be little but a fraudulent scam. Those who invested in the company did so through another company, Trading Partners Ltd (TPL), one of the directors of which was Mr Carl Cushnie, who was also a director of the Versailles company. Both investors and lenders lost heavily when Versailles collapsed, but some assets were recovered. These assets included £28.6 million shares sold by Mr Cushnie as part of his shareholding at the top of the market. One of the questions before the court was concerning the liability of Mr Cushnie as a director of TPL.

HELD: Unless the company can show that the director made the unauthorized profit by the use of company property, he would not be liable as a constructive trustee for the company. This was clearly a less stringent position than the *Boardman v Phipps* rule whereby merely using one's position as a director was a ground of liability.

In the instant case, Justice Lewison said, at para 81, that:

> [t]he fiduciary duty relied on in the present case is a duty owed by Mr Cushnie to TPL. The unauthorised profit is a profit realised by Mr Cushnie on the sale of shares in VGP. So far as the evidence goes Mr Cushnie acquired those shares before TPL was even incorporated. But

at any rate his initial acquisition of the shares could not, in my judgment, have amounted to an acquisition of property that belonged in any sense to TPL. Before his sale of those shares he did not owe trustee-like duties in relation to that specific property. It follows, in my judgment, that the claim by TPL to the profit realised by Mr Cushnie on a sale of those shares is a claim based on the transaction which gave rise to those profits...and gives rise to a personal remedy only.

KEY POINTS

- It is essential that there is a fiduciary relationship between the culprit and his betrayed employer.

- It does not seem that the person in breach must be a director of a company or someone in a significant position. What is required is that he is in some fiduciary relationship with the company. A caretaker who knows where keys to the company's safe are may be in a fiduciary relationship whereas an ex officio chairman of the company may not necessarily be.

- The present state of the law seems to be rooted in public policy and political correctness, all of which frown on bribes and corrupt practices in all forms.

- Liability extends to profits made by investing the bribe which are, in addition to the bribe, recoverable.

Liability of third parties (strangers) in constructive trusts

One of the most delicate issues in a constructive trust is that liability for constructive trusts extends to people who are not immediately concerned by the transaction warranting a constructive trust, but are held liable either because they dishonestly assist in the commissioning of the breach or they knowingly receive trust property.

The principle is laid down by Lord Selborne LC in *Barnes v Addy* (1874) 9 Ch App 244.

● ***Barnes v Addy*** (1874) 9 Ch App 244

Lord Selborne at 251:

> Those who create a trust clothe the trustee with a legal power and control over the trust property, imposing on him a corresponding responsibility. That responsibility may no doubt be extended in equity to others who are not properly trustees, if they are found either making themselves trustees *de son tort*, or actually participating in any fraudulent conduct of the trustee to the injury of the *cestui que trust*. But, on the other hand, strangers are not to be made constructive trustees merely because they act as the agents of trustees in transactions within their legal powers, transactions, perhaps of which a court of equity may disapprove, unless those agents receive and become chargeable with some part of the trust property, or unless they assist with knowledge in a dishonest and fraudulent design on the part of the trustee.

A, the surviving trustee of a fund, in exercise of a power in the settlement, appointed B sole trustee of half the fund. B misapplied the fund transferred to him and became bankrupt. Having advised A against the appointment, A's solicitor prepared the deeds of appointment and indemnity and introduced him to a broker for the purpose of selling out some of the stock to pay some costs to which it was liable. B employed another solicitor, who warned B's wife of the risk attending the proposed transaction, but settled the deed of indemnity on her behalf.

HELD: In a suit by B's children, seeking to make A and the two solicitors responsible for the fund which was lost, the court ruled that since neither of the solicitors had any knowledge of, or any reason to suspect, a dishonest design in the transaction, and as the fund had not passed into their hands, the action must fail.

- **Barnes v Addy** (1874) 9 Ch App 244

James LJ:

> I most cordially concur in the general principle with which the Lord Chancellor began his judgment. I have long thought, and more than once expressed my opinion from this seat, that this court has in some cases gone to the very verge of justice in making good to cestuis que trust the consequences of the breaches of trust of their trustees at the expense of persons perfectly honest, but who have been, in some more or less degree, injudicious. I do not think it is for the good of cestuis que trust, or the good of the world, that those cases should be extended. In this, if I may respectfully say so, I entirely agree.

16.4.1 Who is a trustee de son tort?

- **Mara v Browne** (1896) 1 Ch 199

AL Smith LJ at 209:

> Now, what constitutes a trustee *de son tort*? It appears to me if one, not being a trustee and not having authority from a trustee, takes upon himself to intermeddle with trust matters or to do acts characteristic of the office of trustee, he may thereby make himself what is called in law a trustee of his own wrong—i.e. a trustee *de son tort*, or, as it is also termed, a constructive trustee.

- **Taylor v Davies** [1920] AC 636

Viscount Cave:

> …these persons, though not originally trustees, had taken upon themselves the custody and administration of property on behalf of others; and though sometimes referred to as constructive trustees, they were, in fact, actual trustees, though not so named.

16.4.2 Dishonest assistance

A third party who has nothing to do with a trust relationship can be liable in equity for a breach of trust. It does not matter that such a person has never been in possession or receipt of the trust property concerned or that the assistance he renders is not in furtherance of an act which is itself dishonest. What matters is that the assistance given by the third party is dishonest. Once this is proved, his liability could be to restore the trust property or make good the loss to the beneficiary.

The foundation of dishonest assistance for third party liability for the breach of trust was laid down in *Barnes v Addy*. Here the question was whether the solicitors of a party who misappropriated funds held on trust were liable for the breach of the trust. It was held that the solicitors did not knowingly assist in the breach of the trust. Lord Selborne LC insisted that for liability to arise the third party must have assisted in the line of dishonest duty. That means that the trustee must have acted dishonestly for the dishonest assistance rendered by the third party to occasion the latter's liability. In the instant case of the solicitors, it was the first time dishonesty had been laid down as a condition for liability in this type of situation.

The court considered the basis for third party liability laid down in *Barnes v Addy*.

● *Royal Brunei Airlines v Tan* [1995] 2 AC 378

Royal Brunei Airlines appointed Borneo Leisure Travel (BLT) to act as its general travel agent. BLT was required to account to the airline for all amounts received from sales of tickets and received commission on sales and, under the terms of the agreement, all moneys received by the company for sales on behalf of the airline were the property of, and to be held in trust for, the airline and were to be paid to it within 30 days. Clearly, BLT was supposed to keep the airline's money in a separate account. In fact, the money was paid into an ordinary account, and used to relieve BLT's cash flow problems. Tan was managing director and principal shareholder of BLT, and knew that its use of the money in this way was unauthorized. Tan was sued (as a knowing assister) because BLT had gone into arrears and become insolvent. Tan argued that he had not assisted in a fraudulent breach of trust, because BLT had not acted dishonestly.

HELD: The liability of the third party depended on the dishonesty of that party, and that the breach of trust (which was, of course, a prerequisite for accessory liability) need not itself be a dishonest and fraudulent breach of trust by the trustee. On the facts, however, both the trustee and the third party had acted dishonestly, the latter by causing or permitting the trustee to apply money in a way he knew was not authorized by the trust. Tan was dishonest, but so was BLT, since in effect Tan was the company.

Thus, *Royal Brunei* changed the requirement for holding a third party liable for breach of trust by holding, contrary to the principle in *Barnes v Addy*, that dishonesty of the third party was a sufficient ground for holding him liable even if the company has been honest. Thus, the approach in *Barnes v Addy* that third parties cannot be liable was rejected.

Explaining the rationale for dishonest assistance, Lord Nicholls states (at 385) that:

> [i]f the liability of the third party is fault-based, what matters is the nature of his fault, not that of the trustee. In this regard dishonesty on the part of the third party would seem to be sufficient basis for his liability, irrespective of the state of mind of the trustee who is in breach of trust. It is difficult to see why, if the third party dishonestly assisted in breach, there should be a further prerequisite to his liability, namely that the trustee also must have been acting dishonestly. The alternative view would mean that a dishonest third party is liable if the trustee is dishonest, but if the trustee did not act dishonestly that of itself would excuse the dishonest party. That would make no sense.

(See 15.5 'The criminal liability of trustees' for the criminal liability of trustees.)

Here, Lord Nicholls rejected the principle in *Barnes v Addy* that the trustee must have acted dishonestly for the defendant's dishonest assistance to give rise to liability. His Lordship was of the view that all that was required was that the third party acts dishonestly, although in all likelihood, that would mean the trustee must have acted dishonestly.

Lord Nicholls at 392:

> Drawing the threads together, their Lordships' overall conclusion is that dishonesty is a necessary ingredient of accessory liability. It is also sufficient ingredient. A liability in equity to make good resulting loss attaches to a person who dishonestly procures or assists in a breach of trust or fiduciary obligation. It is not necessary that, in addition, the trustee or fiduciary was acting dishonestly.

16.4.3 What is dishonesty?

● **Walker v Stones** [2000] 4 All ER 412

Sir Christopher Slade at 444:

> A person may in some cases act dishonestly, according to the ordinary use of the language, even though he genuinely believes that his action is morally justified. The penniless thief, for example, who picks the pocket of the multi-millionaire is dishonest even though he genuinely considers the theft is morally justified as a fair redistribution of wealth and that he is not therefore being dishonest.

In *Twinsectra v Yardley* [2002] 2 All ER 377, the House of Lords considered the subjective and objective perspectives on dishonesty.

● **Twinsectra v Yardley** [2002] 2 All ER 377

> Whilst in discussing the term 'dishonesty' the courts often draw a distinction between subjective dishonesty and objective dishonesty, there are three possible standards which can be applied to determine whether a person has acted dishonestly. There is a purely subjective standard, whereby a person is only regarded as dishonest if he transgresses his own standard of honesty, even if that standard is contrary to that of reasonable and honest people. This has been termed the 'Robin Hood test' and has been rejected by the courts. As Sir Christopher Slade stated in *Walker v Stones* [2001] 2 WLR 623, [2000] Lloyds Rep PN 864 at 877 of the latter report para 164…
>
> Secondly, there is a purely objective standard whereby a person acts dishonestly if his conduct is dishonest by the ordinary standards of reasonable and honest people, even if he does not realise this. Thirdly, there is a standard which combines an objective test and a subjective test, and which requires that before there can be a finding of dishonesty it must be established that the defendant's conduct was dishonest by the ordinary standards of reasonable and honest people and that he himself realised that by those standards his conduct was dishonest. I will term this 'the combined test'.

The House of Lords endorsed the objective and subjective tests of dishonesty in *Twinsectra*. However, in *Barlow Clowes International Ltd (in Liquidation) v Eurotrust International Ltd* [2005] UKPC 37, Lord Hoffmann rejected the bases on which the reasoning of the House, especially the arguments of Lord Hutton, which tended to the mental state of the third party when determining the extent of his knowledge in the dishonest assistance. Lord Hoffmann thought that Lord Hutton's rationale 'may have encouraged a belief…that the *Twinsectra* case had departed from the law as previously understood and invited inquiry not merely into the defendant's mental state about the nature of the transaction in which he was participating but also into his view about generally acceptable standards of honest conduct' (at 15).

In *Abou-Rhaman v Abacha* [2005] EWHC 2662 (QB), three principles to determining the test of dishonesty were laid down. These are that:

1. a defendant's knowledge of the relevant transaction is such that it renders his participation contrary to normally acceptable standards of honest conduct;

2. such a state of mind may involve knowledge that he cannot participate…or may involve suspicions combined with a conscious decision not to make enquiries which might result in knowledge; and

3. it is not necessary for the claimant to show that the person assisting knew of the existence of a trust or fiduciary relationship or that the transfer of the claimant's moneys involved a breach of that trust or fiduciary relationship. It is sufficient that he should have entertained a clear suspicion that this was the case.

In *William and the Central Bank of Nigeria* (2014) UKSC 10, the UK Supreme Court distinguished between knowing (dishonest) assistance and knowing receipt. After the Supreme Court had determined that the Central Bank of Nigeria was not a trustee of the money subject of litigation, it had to determine whether, despite this fact, the Central Bank, being a stranger to the trust in question, could be held responsible for the trust property under any circumstances. The UK Supreme Court held that, at para 35, that:

> the ancillary liability of a stranger to the trust arises independently of any fraud on the part of the trustee. This has always been recognised in the case of ancillary liabilities on the footing of knowing receipt. A liability on that basis does not require proof of any dishonesty on anyone's part. Knowing assistance is different. It is based on fraud. But it is now clear that that knowing assisters are liable on account of their own dishonesty, irrespective of the dishonesty of the trustees…

thinking points

Do you think the reasoning of Lord Nicholls is convincing? What would become of an innocent volunteer if he could be liable without the liability of the wrongdoing trustee himself? The liability of a person for dishonest assistance is not premised upon the dishonesty of a trustee or beneficiary. This has the practical advantage of delinking the 'wrongdoings' of the trustee or beneficiary, on the one hand, from that of a third party who renders dishonest assistance. One good consequence is that the trust property in respect of which a dishonest assistance has been rendered will always be protected even where the trustee or beneficiary has been mistaken in dealing with the property. See Susan Barkehall-Thomas 'Defining (or Refining) the Meaning of Dishonesty after Twinsectra' (2006) Singapore J Legal Studies 459–64.

16.4.4 Knowing receipt of trust money or property

A person who receives trust property with the knowledge that the property has been dealt with in a manner inconsistent with the trust may be liable for breach of the trust. This is known as knowing receipt. Thus, for a person to be liable in knowing receipt, the property must have been transferred to him in breach of the trust or a fiduciary duty and the transferee must have knowledge that the assets are traceable to a breach of duty (see Hoffmann LJ in *El Ajou v Dollar Land Holdings* [1994] 2 All ER 685 at 700).

● *Re Loftus* [2005] EWHC 406

Lawrence Collins J at 172:

> The main purpose of seeking to establish constructive trust liability on the basis of knowing receipt is when the alleged constructive trustee has disposed of the property so that a personal remedy for its value is sought against him.

As with the dishonest assistance, it is necessary to establish what 'knowing' is for the defendant to be liable in knowing receipt. In *Baden v Société Générale pour Favoriser le Développement du Commerce et de l'Industrie en France SA* [1983] BCLC 325 at 407, Gibson J enumerated five distinct scenarios that could constitute knowledge. These are:

1. actual knowledge;
2. wilfully closing one's eyes to the obvious;
3. knowledge of the circumstances which could have put an honest and reasonable man on notice;
4. knowledge of circumstances as to prompt an honest and reasonable man towards inquiry; and finally
5. wilful and reckless failure to make such inquiries as an honest and reasonable man would make.

There have been several views on what constitutes knowledge under the 'knowing receipt' category. Examples of views offered included by Megarry VC in *Re Montague's Settlement* [1987] Ch 264, in which his Lordship underscored the problem about formulating a close principle of knowledge or laying any categorical precedent. Thus, the attempt has been made to unify the several theories of knowledge and collapse everything under one head, which, in *Bank of Credit and Commerce International (Overseas) Limited v Akindele* [2001] Ch 437, Nourse LJ referred to as the 'conscionability test'. As his Lordship stated, 'all that is necessary is that the recipient's state of knowledge should be such as to make it unconscionable for him to retain the benefit of the receipt' (at 437). However, this test is imprecise and it is difficult to calibrate what constitutes conscionability in given circumstances.

16.5 Nature of constructive trust

Constructive trusts can either be institutional or remedial.

16.5.1 Institutional constructive trust

A constructive trust is institutional when it is not regarded as automatically providing a remedy to a wronged party.

● *Westdeutsche Landesbank Girozentrale v Islington LBC* [1996] AC 669

Lord Browne-Wilkinson at 714:

> Under an institutional constructive trust, the trust arises by operation of law as from the date of the circumstances which give rise to it: the function of the court is merely to declare

that such trust having arisen (including the possibility of unfair consequences to third parties who in the interim have received the trust property) is also determined by rules of law, under a discretion.

Thus, the court does not decree the existence of a remedy simply because of the wrongful conduct of the defendant. What the court does is to recognize a situation as giving rise to a constructive trust whereby the wrongful party is then held to be a constructive trustee for the wronged party after a careful consideration of the matter under substantive law, as opposed to a mere application of the court's discretion.

● ***Springette v Defoe*** [1992] 2 FLR 388 (CA)

The parties, who were cohabitants, purchased a council flat in their joint names. They had obtained a reduced rate of 40 per cent of the total market value because the plaintiff had lived there for 11 years. They took out a mortgage and contributed to the house in equal shares, although it was not specified what interest they each possessed in the house. The question then arose as to how the court should determine the beneficial interest of the parties in the property.

HELD: Dillon LJ:

> ...the common intention must be founded on evidence such as would support a finding that there is an implied or constructive trust for the parties in proportions to the purchase price. The court does not as yet sit, as under a palm tree, to exercise a general discretion to do what the man in the street, on a general view of the case, might regard as fair...

● ***Lonhro plc v Al-Fayed (No 2)*** [1992] 1 WLR 1

Millett LJ at 12:

> ...it is a mistake to suppose that in every situation in which a constructive trust arises the legal owner is necessarily subject to all the fiduciary obligations and disabilities of an express trustee.

16.5.2 Effect of constructive trust

Whether a constructive trust is perceived as institutional or remedial has implications for its effects on the transaction concerned. The following extracts provide some guidance.

Parker and Mellows *The Modern Law of Trusts* (7th edn, London: Sweet & Maxwell, 1998) 268–9:

> ...the moment at which the constructive trust takes effect will determine the extent to which the rights of the constructive beneficiary will be binding upon third parties, whether the general creditors of the constructive trustee or any person to whom the property which forms the subject matter of the constructive trust has been transferred. It seems to be generally accepted that, in the absence of any kind of judicial order to the contrary, a constructive trust will take effect from the moment at which the conduct which has given rise to its imposition occurs.

Alastair Hudson *Equity & Trusts* (4th edn, London: Cavendish, 2005) 425:

> [The court, by declaring a constructive trust] in truth is recognising that that trust has existed *ever since* the unconscionable action of the trustee which brought it into effect: the constructive trust does not come into effect from the date of the court order award... For example, if it is found that a constructive trust ought to have arisen in January, but the constructive trustee goes into insolvency in March and a court makes an order recognising the proprietary constructive trust only in May, the order recognising the constructive trust will declare that the constructive trust came into existence automatically in January, and therefore that the proprietary rights of the beneficiaries pre-date the insolvency in March. If the constructive trust operated in the same manner as proprietary estoppel, that is prospectively from the date of the court order, granting whatever remedy the court considered appropriate in its discretion... then it could not protect the beneficiaries against the constructive trustee's insolvency...

Retrospective effect of institutional constructive trust

One major consequence of the institutional approach is that the trust so determined is retrospective in effect. (See Lord Browne-Wilkinson in the *Westdeutsche* case at 714.)

● ***Re Sharpe (a bankrupt)*** [1980] 1 All ER 198, [1980] 1 WLR 219

In 1975 Mr Sharpe purchased a property for £17,000 with the help of £12,000 lent to him by his aunt as part of an arrangement whereby the aunt was to live with the debtor and his wife in the property and they were to look after her. Mr Sharpe became bankrupt and a receiving order was made against him on 27 April 1978. Despite the fact that the trustees contacted her to clarify the nature of the loan, there was no response from Mr Sharpe's aunt. But after the date of the contract, however, she made a claim to the property, claiming either a beneficial interest under a resulting trust by virtue of the loan or alternatively a right under an irrevocable licence to occupy the property until repayment of the loan. The trustee in bankruptcy claimed possession of the property against the debtor and his aunt. The questions arose (i) whether the aunt had any interest in the property and (ii) if so, whether it was binding on the trustee in bankruptcy.

HELD: Browne-Wilkinson J at 225:

> The aunt's irrevocable licence was not merely a contractual licence but arose under a constructive trust and as such conferred on her an interest in the property binding on the trustee in bankruptcy.

On the important question of when precisely the right of the defendant arises, counsel for the trustee in bankruptcy argued that since Sharpe's aunt had 'failed to put forward her claim until after the trustee had contracted to sell the property to an innocent third party, notwithstanding two enquiries as to whether she had a claim. Accordingly, he said, it would not be equitable to grant her an interest under a constructive trust at this time.'

Lord Browne-Wilkinson rejected this argument:

> I cannot accept that argument in that form. Even if it be right to say that the courts can impose a constructive trust as a remedy in certain cases (which to my mind is a novel concept in English law), in order to provide a remedy the court must first find a right which has been infringed. So far as land is concerned an oral agreement to create any interest in it

must be evidenced in writing: see the Law of Property Act 1925, s. 40. Therefore if these irrevocable licences create an interest in land, the rights cannot rest simply on an oral contract. The introduction of an interest under a constructive trust is an essential ingredient if the plaintiff has any right at all. Therefore in cases such as this, it cannot be that the interest in property arises for the first time when the court declares it to exist. The right must have arisen at the time of the transaction in order for the plaintiff to have any right the breach of which can be remedied.

● ***Westdeutsche Landesbank Girozentrale v Islington London Borough Council***
[1996] AC 669

The parties entered into a ten-year interest rate swap agreement starting on 18 June 1987 based on a notional principal sum of £25 million. Additionally, the plaintiff bank as the fixed-rate payer paid the defendant council as the floating-rate payer a lump sum of £2.5 million. Pursuant to the agreement, the council made 'interest' payments in December 1987, June and December 1988, and June 1989 to the bank totalling £1,354,474.07. On 1 November 1989 the Divisional Court of the Queen's Bench Division held in an unrelated case that interest rate swap transactions by local authorities were ultra vires. Following that decision, the council made no more payments. The bank brought an action against the council claiming repayment of the balance of the £2.5 million amounting to £1,145,525.93 plus interest from 18 June 1987. The judge gave judgment for the bank for the principal sum plus compound interest from 1 April 1990. The Court of Appeal dismissed an appeal by the council and allowed a cross-appeal by the bank against the judge's rejection of 18 June 1987 as the date from which interest should run.

HELD: The bank should recover simple interest only as from 18 June 1987, the date of accrual of its cause of action.

KEY POINTS

- This line of cases suggests that unlike under express trusts—where the obligations of trustees are determined through the express terms of the trusts—the obligations of the constructive trustee are determined by the circumstances warranting the trust.

- Under the institutional approach, the role of the court can be said to be merely declaratory, i.e. it simply recognizes a trust that has arisen by the operation of law.

- Institutional constructive trusts are retroactive because it is not the court that creates this kind of trust: it merely declares its existence. If it declares its existence, it then means that the trusts had existed much earlier before the case came to court.

16.5.3 Remedial constructive trust

A remedial constructive trust is the direct opposite of the institutional constructive trust in that it does not arise directly from the transaction between the individual claimants, but rather it is created by the court as a measure of justice after the event. (See *Re Goldcorp Exchange Ltd (in receivership)* [1995] 1 AC (Lord Mustill) at 99.)

● **Westdeutsche Landesbank Girozentrale v Islington London Borough Council** [1996]
AC 669

Lord Browne-Wilkinson at 714:

> A remedial constructive trust, as I understand it, is different. It is a judicial remedy giving rise
> to an enforceable equitable obligation: the extent to which it operates retrospectively to the
> prejudice of the third parties lies in the discretion of the court.

● **Re Polly Peck International plc (in administration) (No 2)** [1998] 3 All ER 812

Nourse LJ:

> In referring to a remedial constructive trust, I mean an order of the court granting, by way
> of remedy, a proprietary right to someone who, beforehand, had no proprietary right.

16.5.4 Origin and rationale of remedial constructive trust

Remedial constructive trusts are popular in America, although they are thought to be championed by Canada. (See *Pettkus v Becker* (1980) 117 DLR (3d) 257; *Sorochan v Sorochan* (1986) 29 DLR (4th) 1 (Supreme Court of Canada); *Peter v Beblow* (1993) 101 DLR (4th) 621; see also *Halsbury's Laws of England* at 588.) In the *Restatement of the Law of Restitution* (American Law Institute, 1937), the remedial constructive trust was described thus:

> Where a person holding title to property is subject to an equitable duty to convey it to another
> on the ground that he would be unjustly enriched if he were permitted to retain it, a constructive trust arises.

● **Betty v Guggenheim Exploration Co** 255 NY 380 (1919)

Cardozo J at 386:

> A constructive trust is the formula through which the conscience of equity finds expression. When property has been acquired in such circumstances that the holder of the legal
> title may not in good conscience retain the beneficial interest, equity converts him into a
> trustee.

● **Pettkus v Becker** (1980) 117 DLR (3d) 257

Rosa Becker and Lothar Pettkus were together in a common law relationship for 19 years. Over this period Pettkus ran a successful beehive operation. When the relationship fell apart Becker attempted to claim half of the beehive business. She claimed that since her income went towards supporting Pettkus while he got his beehive business off the ground, she was entitled to a share in the business. In the alternative, she argued that there was a constructive trust of the assets which belonged to her on the basis of unjust enrichment.

HELD: Brian Dickson, Chief Justice of Canada: There were three requirements for finding a constructive trust: there must be (i) an enrichment, (ii) a corresponding deprivation, and (iii) the absence of any juristic reason for the enrichment. In this case, Dickson found that the requirements were satisfied and held that Becker was entitled to half the assets. He held that:

> …where one person, in a relationship tantamount to spousal, prejudices herself in the reasonable expectation of receiving an interest in property, and the other person in the relationship freely accepts benefits conferred by the first person in circumstances where he knows or ought to have known of that reasonable expectation, it would be unjust to allow the recipient of the benefit to retain it.

But this does not mean that unjust enrichment always automatically gives rise to constitutive constructive trust. See *Korkontzillas v Soulos* (1997) 146 DLR (4th) 214.

● *Peter v Bedlow* (1993) 101 DLR (4th) 621

The plaintiff agreed to live with the defendant in a house if she would take care of the house and children. They lived together for 12 years, but they were never married. The defendant worked full time, although the plaintiff only worked part time. They later separated, with the whole house going to the plaintiff. There was an action for unjust enrichment.

HELD: An unjust enrichment accrued to the plaintiff by retaining the whole house and the court reallocated the house to the defendant.

NB: The fact that the house was reallocated to the defendant underlines the power of the court to determine the effect of a constructive trust under the remedial category.

KEY POINTS

* Under the remedial approach, what matters in determining whether a constructive trust exists or not 'depends on the presence or absence of unjust enrichment, not on the presence or absence as against whether there can be a case under specific categories as with the English jurisdiction'. (See also Parker and Mellows at 275–6.)

* But it does not mean that unjust enrichment per se automatically leads to a remedial constructive trust.

16.5.5 Remedial trust is not automatically retrospective

Unlike institutional constructive trust, the effect of a remedial constructive trust is not automatically retrospective but rather, as Lord Browne-Wilkinson stated in the *Westdeutsche* case, is determined by the court.

● *Halifax Building Society v Thomas and Another* [1996] Ch 217 (CA)

The first defendant, Thomas, fraudulently obtained a mortgage advance from a building society to finance the purchase of a flat on the condition that the mortgage should be security for 'all moneys which may be or become owing by the borrower to the society on any account'. After making some payments of interest under the mortgage, the borrower defaulted. The society obtained an order for possession against him and thereafter, as mortgagee, sold the flat and recouped the mortgage debt. The surplus realized on the sale was put into a suspense account by the society, which sought a declaration that it was entitled to retain the surplus for its own use and benefit.

HELD: Peter Gibson LJ at 229:

> [The borrower's] unjust enrichment could not be treated as having been gained at the society's expense; that, since the wrongdoing of the borrower could not translate the society into the owner of the entire beneficial interest in the property when the mortgage had not been set aside, the borrower was not a constructive trustee of the surplus for the society and consequently section 105 of the Act of 1925 required the society to hold the surplus in trust for the borrower; and that, accordingly, the borrower had been entitled to the surplus immediately before the making of the confiscation and charging orders.

Thus, in this case, the defendant's wrong did not automatically amount to benefit (or remedy) for the plaintiff. Note also that the court was not prepared to accept that the wrongdoing of the defendant automatically resulted in remedy to the plaintiff. (See *Sinclair v Brougham* [1914] AC 398, which was the earlier position on the effect of constructive trust.)

....

● ***Re Polly Peck International plc (in administration) (No 2)*** [1998] 3 All ER 812

The applicants claimed to own immovable property in the northern part of Cyprus, which had been declared by the Turkish Cypriot authorities to be the Turkish Republic of Northern Cyprus. Following the Turkish invasion of Cyprus, the properties had been expropriated. Under purported legislation, immovable property and land in the Republic (the owners of which were no longer present) was declared to be the immovable property of the Republic, which was to be entitled to lease it and make grants for long periods. The applicants contended that their property had been, with knowledge of the wrongs committed against them and their property, illegally occupied and exploited without their authority by direct or indirect subsidiaries of PPI, or by persons acting for, or at the direction of, the company's administrators. The applicants applied for leave, pursuant to s. 11(3)(d) of the Insolvency Act 1986, to commence proceedings by way of writ against PPI and its administrators, claiming, inter alia, that an undisclosed substantial sum received by the administrators represented the profits and proceeds of wrongdoing by PPI, which had been unjustly enriched at the applicants' expense. They claimed that that sum was subject to a 'remedial constructive trust' for their benefit. PPI opposed the application, contending that the proposed action was bound to fail on the ground, inter alia, that the claim was misconceived and failed to disclose any serious arguable case. The judge granted the application, holding that, although the draft statement of claim faced 'formidable obstacles', it did disclose a serious arguable claim for a remedial constructive trust against PPI. PPI appealed.

HELD: The order sought by the applicants would require an English court *retrospectively* to impose on the assets of an insolvent company in administration in England a 'remedial constructive trust' giving them a proprietary interest in those assets and as such, would operate to exclude those assets from pari passu distribution by the administrators among the unsecured creditors of the company. There was, accordingly, no prospect that the court would grant the order sought. The appeal would therefore be allowed (see 822h, 823d, 826j–p, 827g, 830c and d, and 831d). (See also, however, *Ocular Sciences Ltd v Aspect Vision Care Ltd* [1997] RPC 289 at 411–16, where the constructive trust appears to have been regarded as a remedy, although on the facts no trust was imposed: the imposition of a constructive trust is part of the equitable armoury of the court: Laddie J at 416.)

Remedial constructive trust is largely discretionary in that it is the court, not the law, that fixes its operation, both in terms of parties' obligations and the time of its operation. (See *Westdeutsche Landesbank Girozentrale v Islington London Borough Council* [1996] AC 669 case.)

16.5.6 Current trends in the English courts: a move towards remedial constructive trust?

As stated earlier, English courts have traditionally adopted the institutional approach towards constructive trusts, seeing no reason or justification, as it were, to allow a person entitlement to proprietary rights in a property to which he is not otherwise entitled by virtue of his being wronged by another.

Attempts have been made in the past, however, towards embracing remedial trusts in England.

● ***Hussey v Palmer*** [1972] 3 All ER 744

The facts of this case are closer to resulting trusts than constructive trusts. The plaintiff agreed to move in to live with the defendant, her son-in-law, upon the sale of her own house. Owing to the small size of the defendant's house, the plaintiff paid for an extension to be built, but had to move out later because of differences between her and her son-in-law. Was she entitled to make a claim for the money she had lent to him to build the extension and what was the extent of her beneficial interest in the house?

HELD: In the circumstances of the present case the court should impose or impute a resulting trust for the plaintiff by which the son-in-law held the house on terms which gave the plaintiff an interest in the house proportionate to the £607 she had put into it in paying for the extension, even if (Phillimore LJ) the transaction was a loan, as that would not be inconsistent with it also involving a resulting trust.

Lord Denning's separate judgment in this case, apart from signalling what was then considered as the English court's preparedness to embrace 'remedial constructive trusts', reveals many more significant aspects of (i) the relationship between constructive and resulting trusts and (ii) the discretionary power of the court to fix the time in which a remedial constructive trust becomes effective. According to his Lordship, it does not matter whether it is called a resulting trust or a constructive trust.

> If there was no loan, was there a resulting trust? And, if so, what were the terms of the trust? Although the plaintiff alleged that there was a resulting trust, I should have thought that the trust in this case, if there was one, was more in the nature of a constructive trust; but this is more a matter of words than anything else. The two run together. By whatever name it is described, it is a trust imposed by law whenever justice and good conscience require it. It is a liberal process, founded on large principles of equity, to be applied in cases where the defendant cannot conscientiously keep the property for himself alone, but ought to allow another to have the property or a share in it. The trust may arise at the outset when the property is acquired, or later on, as the circumstances may require. It is an equitable remedy by which the court can enable an aggrieved party to obtain restitution. It is comparable to the legal remedy of money had and received which, as Lord Mansfield said, is very beneficial and, therefore, much encouraged. Thus we have repeatedly held that, when one person contributes towards the purchase price of a house, the owner holds it on a constructive trust for him, proportionate to his contribution, even though there is no agreement between them, and no declaration of trust to be found, and no evidence of any intention to create a trust.

In *Re Sharpe (a bankrupt), ex p the Trustee of the Bankrupt v Sharpe and Another* [1980] 1 All ER 198, Lord Browne-Wilkinson also contemplated the possibility of the remedial constructive trust developing in England. His Lordship had to consider the time when the operation of the constructive trust started.

● **Re Sharpe (a bankrupt), ex p the Trustee of the Bankrupt v Sharpe and Another** [1980] 1 All ER 198

Lord Browne-Wilkinson at 203: In January 1975 the debtor purchased a property for £17,000 with the help of £12,000 lent to him by his aunt as part of an arrangement whereby the aunt was to live with the debtor and his wife in the property and they were to look after her. On 27 April 1978 a receiving order was made against the debtor. On 30 April his trustee in bankruptcy contracted to sell the property with vacant possession to a purchaser for £17,000. Prior to the contract the trustee twice wrote to the aunt asking whether the £12,000 was a gift or a loan and if it was a loan whether any consideration or security had been given for it, but she did not reply to the letters, probably because of her old age and bad health. After the date of the contract, however, she made a claim to the property, claiming either a beneficial interest under a resulting trust by virtue of the loan or alternatively a right under an irrevocable licence to occupy the property until repayment of the loan. The trustee in bankruptcy claimed possession of the property against the debtor and his aunt. The questions arose (i) whether the aunt had any interest in the property and (ii) if so, whether it was binding on the trustee in bankruptcy. Counsel argued:

> …the time to decide whether to grant such a remedy is when the matter comes before the court in the light of the then known circumstances. In the present case those circumstances are that the debtor is a bankrupt and Mrs Johnson has failed to put forward her claim until after the trustee has contracted to sell the property to an innocent third party, notwithstanding two enquiries as to whether she had a claim. Accordingly, it would not be equitable to grant her an interest under a constructive trust at this time.

HELD: Lord Browne-Wilkinson:

> I cannot accept that argument in that form. Even if it be right to say that the courts can impose a constructive trust as a remedy in certain cases (which to my mind is a novel concept in English law), in order to provide a remedy the court must first find a right which has been infringed.

The attempt to extend the development of the 1970s and 1980s into the 1990s backfired and the idea of the remedial constructive trust developing in England suffered a retrogression.

● **Halifax Building Society v Thomas and Another** [1996] Ch 217 (CA) (For the facts of the case see [1996] Ch 229)

This was a case before an English court. However, the plaintiff argued that it was beneficially entitled under a constructive trust imposed on the defendant in accordance with the US *Restatement of Restitution* (see earlier). The Court of Appeal responded that:

> English law has not followed other jurisdictions where the constructive trust has become a remedy for unjust enrichment

and

declined to extend the law of constructive trusts in order to prevent a fraudster benefiting from his wrong.

16.5.7 The future of remedial trust in England

- *Metall und Rohstoff AG v Donaldson Lufkin & Jenrette Inc* [1989] 3 All ER 14, [1990] 1 QB 391

The Court of Appeal, after quoting from *Snell's Principles of Equity* (28th edn, London: Sweet & Maxwell, 1982) 193 and Goff and Jones *The Law of Restitution* (3rd edn, London: Sweet & Maxwell, 1986) 78, said at 57:

While we have had the benefit of very full argument on almost all other aspects of the law involved in this case, we have neither heard nor invited comprehensive argument as to the circumstances in which the court will be prepared to impose a constructive trust de novo as a foundation for the grant of an equitable remedy by way of account or otherwise. Nevertheless, we are satisfied that there is a good arguable case that such circumstances may arise and, for want of a better description, will refer to a constructive trust of this nature as a 'remedial constructive trust'.

In the *Westdeutsche* case (cited earlier, at 716), Lord Browne-Wilkinson appeared to have been influenced by *Metall* dictum to found the justification for the decision of Goulding J in *Chase Manhattan Bank v Israel-British Bank (London)*. Here, after observing that a 'bank that paid the same sum twice rather than once to another bank could maintain an equitable proprietary claim against it' (see Parker and Mellows at 278) his Lordship noted that 'the retention of remedial constructive trust, if introduced into English law, may provide a more satisfactory road forward'.

Despite this ray of hope, a new era of reluctance has resurfaced in the English courts' attitude towards remedial constructive trusts.

- *Re Polly Peck International plc (in administration) (No 2)* [1998] 3 All ER 812

Rattee J:

Later cases do not, in my view, take the matter of remedial constructive trusts any further than the statements quoted above.

- *Re Goldcorp Exchange Ltd (in receivership)* [1994] 2 All ER 806

Although Lord Mustill was prepared to countenance 'remedial restitutionary rights', he argued at 826–7 that:

...remedial restitutionary rights may prove in the future to be a valuable instrument of justice.

His Lordship felt that this could not

be brought to bear on the present case.

Writing extrajudicially, Sir Peter Millett observed that the remedial constructive trust is 'a counsel of despair which too readily concedes the impossibility of propounding a general rationale for the availability of proprietary remedies' (see [1995–6] *King's College LJ 1*).

....

● *El Ajou v Dollar Land Holdings plc* [1993] 3 All ER 717

Millett J at 733–4, having referred to the requirement of a *fiduciary relationship* in order to establish a right to trace in equity, made it clear that reliance was being placed not 'on some new model remedial constructive trust, but an old-fashioned institutional resulting trust'.

> Although...Lord Mustill in *Re Goldcorp Exchange Ltd (in receivership)* [1994] 2 All ER 806, [1995] 1 AC 74 and Lord Browne-Wilkinson in *Westdeutsche Landesbank Girozentrale v Islington London BC* [1996] 2 All ER 961, [1996] AC 669 have accepted the possibility that the remedial constructive trust may become part of English law, such observations, being both obiter and tentative, can only be of limited assistance when the question has to be decided, as it does here. There being no earlier decision, we must turn to principle. In doing so, we must recognise that the remedial constructive trust gives the court a discretion to vary proprietary rights. You cannot grant a proprietary right to A, who has not had one before-hand, without taking some proprietary right away from B. No English court has ever had the power to do that, except with the authority of Parliament; cf *Chapman v Chapman* [1954] 1 All ER 798, [1954] AC 429.

Although this statement is often cited to represent the contemporary attitude of the English court to the issue of remedial constructive trust, Nourse LJ's statement was often short-circuited. Nourse LJ actually flashed a ray of hope when he declared:

> But it is said that, although that may be the law today, it may not be the law tomorrow. If the Supreme Court of Canada can develop the law so as to permit the court to vary proprietary rights without legislative authority, why cannot the House of Lords do likewise? At least, it is said, there must be a real prospect that they will, and so the applicants ought to be allowed to bring their action.

For more cases that rejected the remedial constructive trust approach, see *Burns v Burns* [1984] Ch 317 and *Ashburn Anstalt v Arnold* [1989] Ch 1.

 # Conclusion

There is no doubt that the constructive trust is a very complex area of equity and trust, but it is a very important area as well. Constructive trusts are applied to a wide variety of situations and to that extent they are a formidable tool in the court of equity. As we have seen, different jurisdictions have different approaches towards the constructive trust, but what is really important is not whether one sees constructive trusts as institutional or remedial but whether constructive trusts perform such a useful function as to justify their continued retention as part of the legal system of the land. In this respect, considering the extremely crucial position that constructive trusts occupy, it seems reasonable to hope that they will continue to be a part of the English legal system for quite some time to come.

 # Questions

Self-test questions

1 Who is a fiduciary and why is a fiduciary relationship different from any other kind of relationship?

2 Who are trustees de son tort and on what bases can they be held liable for a breach of trust?

3 Explain the terms 'institutional' and 'remedial' constructive trusts.

4 What are dishonest assistance and knowing receipt, and how do these differ?

5 How would you define a constructive trust?

Discussion questions

1 Do you think the English courts should adopt the remedial constructive trust in light of its utility or should they simply carry on as if the concept can never be accommodated under the English legal system?

2 What would you think makes one nature of the constructive trust more advantageous than the other?

3 Do you think the explanation given by Millett J in *El Ajou* for the difference between an action for recovery of profits made from an abuse of fiduciary position (which does make such cases look like remedial constructive trusts) and institutional constructive trusts, which his Lordship claimed is the rationale for such cases, is convincing?

4 How would you distinguish between the test of dishonest assistance laid down in the *Barnes v Addy* and *Royal Brunei* cases?

5 Is there a great difference between the retrospective effect of constructive trusts under institutional and remedial constructive trusts in light of the fact that, under the institutional approach, it is the circumstances of the transaction that fix the time of effect whereas, under the remedial approach, it is the court, through its discretion, that fixes the effect?

Assessment question

James, a trustee for the Randolph estate, decided to use some of the trust money to build a private business for himself because he honestly believed that the slowdown in the property market in the UK meant that if he bought some property now, he would make a large profit in a few years and be able to pay back the trust. So he went to John, his good friend and banker, and told him that he needed the money to sort out his personal problems, which John knew about and sympathized with. John invested the money and lost heavily. A few years later, Thomas and Jan, both beneficiaries under the trust, sued James and John to make good the loss.

Advise John.

 # Key cases

- *Carl-Zeiss Stiftung v Herbert Smith (No 2)* [1969] 2 Ch 276 **(at 16.1)**

- *Keech v Sandford* (1726) 2 Eq Cas Arb 741 **(at 16.2.3 and 16.3.1)**

- *Boardman v Phipps* [1967] 2 AC 46 **(at 16.3.1)**

- *AG for Hong Kong v Reid* [1994] 1 All ER 1 **(at 16.3.2)**

- *Lister & Co v Stubbs* (1850) 45 ChD 1 **(at 16.3.2)**

- *Royal Brunei Airlines v Tan* [1995] 2 AC 378 **(at 16.4.2)**

 # Further reading

AJ Oakley (ed), Parker and Mellows *The Modern Law of Trusts* (7th edn, London: Sweet & Maxwell, 1998)
Discussion on various approaches to constructive trust.

AJ Oakley *Constructive Trusts* (3rd edn, London: Sweet & Maxwell, 1997)
The nature of constructive trust.

J Darren 'Prescription and Proscription in Fiduciary Obligations' (2010) 21(2) *King's LJ* 333–54
M Harding 'Dual Listed Companies: Understanding Conflicts of Interest for Directors' [2002] *University of New South Wales LJ* 34 and (2002) 25(2) *University of New South Wales LJ* 594
G Jones 'Unjust Enrichment and the Fiduciary's Duty of Loyalty' (1968) 84 *LQR* 472
For the nature of fiduciary obligations.

David R Lawson and F Ladson Boyle 'Constructive Trust' (1992) 4(2) *Probate Practice Reporter*
For the application of constructive trusts.

JC Shepherd 'Towards a Unified Concept of Fiduciary Relationship' (1981) 97 *LQR* 51
On the different categories of fiduciaries and the move to harmonize them under one concept.

S Barkehall-Thomas 'Defining (or Refining) the Meaning of Dishonesty after Twinsectra' (2006) *Singapore J Legal Studies* 459–64
On third party liability.

WG Hart 'The Development of the Rule in *Keech v Sandford*' (1905) 21 *LQR* 258
For an early overview of the rule in *Keech v Sandford*.

17

Tracing

Learning objectives

This chapter will help you to:

- understand that tracing is the process by which trust assets that have been removed from a trust can be identified
- appreciate that common law tracing is restricted to unmixed property
- recognize that equitable tracing requires there to be a trust or fiduciary relationship
- understand that equitable tracing allows tracing into mixed funds
- appreciate that equitable tracing ceases when the trust property can no longer be identified
- understand that tracing is possible against an innocent volunteer.

Introduction

Tracing is a very old remedy in the law, both common law and equity, and is based on a very simple principle, that if your property is taken you should be able to recover it, as long it is still identifiable. As we shall see, this deceptively simple idea has been applied to all sorts of property, from bags of gold, to money in a bank account, stocks and shares, and even really modern types of property such as speculating on the future price of potatoes. The key issue in tracing is evidential: is it still possible to prove that this was once your property? There is also the issue of competing claims to the same property to be considered. It is important not to view tracing in isolation from the remedies generally available in equity. Chapter 16 'Constructive trusts' could usefully be read in conjunction with this chapter.

What is tracing?

17.1.1 A definition of tracing

Tracing is a proprietary remedy, where the claimant shows that he or she has a right to specific property in the hands of the defendant. As a remedy, it can have advantages over personal remedies such as suing for damages. If the defendant is bankrupt or, if the defendant is an insolvent company, the tracing claimant takes priority over the other creditors. In other words, the tracer takes their piece of property first and the other claimants divide up what is left. As we shall see, if the piece of property has gone up in value, the tracer will be able to claim that increase. Tracing might be used when there is no other remedy, as it can be used against an **innocent volunteer**, someone who has done no wrong, but just happens to be in possession of the tracer's property. The idea of tracing is that the claimant is pursuing an identifiable item of property, as it changes hands and perhaps changes form. A useful definition of tracing can be found in the leading case of *Foskett v McKeown and Others* [2001] 1 AC 102.

. . . .

Innocent volunteer—volunteer means that the person has provided no consideration. Innocent means that they are unaware that they have received someone else's property.

. . . .

. . . .

● *Foskett v McKeown and Others* [2001] 1 AC 102

Lord Millett at 127–8:

> The process of ascertaining what happened to the plaintiff's money involves both tracing and following. These are both exercises in locating assets which are or may be taken to represent an asset belonging to the plaintiffs and to which they assert ownership. The processes of following and tracing are, however, distinct. Following is the process of following the same asset as it moves from hand to hand. Tracing is the process of identifying a new asset as the substitute for the old. Where one asset is exchanged for another, a claimant can elect whether to follow the original asset into the hands of the new owner or to trace its value into the new asset in the hands of the same owner. In practice his choice is often dictated by the

circumstances…Tracing is thus neither a claim nor a remedy. It is merely the process by which a claimant demonstrates what has happened to his property, identifies its proceeds and the persons who have handled or received them, and justifies his claim that the proceeds can properly be regarded as representing his property.

So tracing involves looking at the evidence and deciding whether the claimant's property can still be identified. Then the claimant can decide what remedy to pursue to get their money back. In common law tracing, he or she might claim a common law remedy such as that for money had and received or conversion. If it is equitable tracing a constructive trust might be claimed or a **charge** might be imposed on the property. (See 16.4 'Liability of third parties (strangers) in constructive trusts' for this type of constructive trust.) Choosing the most advantageous remedy to pursue is known as the doctrine of election.

. . . .

A charge—the defendant is obliged to pay the sum or the claimant can have the property sold and take what they are owed from the proceeds. A mortgage is a type of charge.
. . . .

As we will see from the case law examples later in this chapter, the claimant has another decision to make, apart from the remedy sought. As Lord Millett explains earlier, he or she must also decide which asset, and thus which defendant, to pursue, as their property might have passed through many hands and changed into several different forms. The choice is likely to be dictated by who is most likely to be able to pay.

thinking points

Lord Millett's statement 'Tracing is thus neither a claim nor a remedy' may seem rather confusing. Tracing is just a means to find the property; the remedies, such as constructive trust, by which it may be recovered, are another matter. These remedies, and how they relate to each other and the two forms of tracing, are considered by Lord Millett in P Millett 'Tracing and the Proceeds of Fraud' (1991) 107 LQR 71.

17.1.2 Common law and equitable tracing

Both the common law and equity allow tracing, but different rules apply in each system. The chief difference is that the common law does not allow tracing to continue once the property has become mixed with other property. Equity does allow tracing into what is called a 'mixed fund', but for equitable tracing to be allowed the property must have been taken from a trust, or at least a fiduciary relationship. (See Chapter 16 'Constructive trusts' for examples of fiduciary relationships.)

This split came into being because of the historical difference between the common law courts and the Court of Chancery, which administered equity. (See Chapter 1 'The birth of equity and trusts' for a general account.) Some have questioned whether two different systems of tracing, with two different systems of rules, serve a very useful purpose today. Chief among those critics was Professor Birks, who was quoted, with approval, by Lord Steyn in *Foskett v McKeown and Others* [2001] 1 AC 102.

. . . .

● *Foskett v McKeown and Others* [2001] 1 AC 102

Lord Steyn at 113:

In arguing the merits of the proprietary claim counsel for the purchasers from time to time invoked 'the rules of tracing'. By that expression he was placing reliance on a corpus of supposed rules of law, divided into common law and equitable rules. In truth tracing is a process of identifying assets: it belongs to the realm of evidence. It tells us nothing about legal or equitable rights to the assets traced. In a crystalline analysis Professor Birks ('The Necessity of a Unitary Law of Tracing', essay in Making Commercial Law, Essays in Honour of Roy Goode (1997), pp 239–258) explained, at p 257, that there is a unified regime for tracing and that 'it allows tracing to be cleanly separated from the business of asserting rights in or in relation to assets successfully traced'. Applying this reasoning Professor Birks concludes, at p 258:

> that the modern law is equipped with various means of coping with the evidential difficulties which a tracing exercise is bound to encounter. The process of identification thus ceases to be either legal or equitable and becomes, as is fitting, genuinely neutral as to the rights exigible in respect of the assets into which the value in question is traced. The tracing exercise once successfully completed, it can then be asked what rights, if any, the plaintiff can, on his particular facts, assert. It is at that point that it become relevant to recall that on some facts those rights will be personal, on others proprietary, on some legal, and on others equitable.

I regard this explanation as correct.

Lord Millett agreed at 128:

> Given its nature, there is nothing inherently legal or equitable about the tracing exercise. There is thus no sense in maintaining different rules for tracing at law and in equity. One set of tracing rules is enough.

Despite this, even Lord Millett conceded that *Foskett v McKeown* should be decided on the basis of the rules of equitable tracing, since it clearly involved a trustee taking property from a trust. So the distinction between common law and equitable tracing remains, until a court decides otherwise.

KEY POINT
There are two types of tracing: common law and equitable. Although criticized academically, the distinction remains.

17.2 Common law tracing

This is a process recognized as far back as the Middle Ages and the type of property envisaged would have been a chattel, such as a bag of gold. If someone takes their gold, the claimant is entitled to recover it.

....

● *Ex parte Cooke* (1876) 4 ChD 123

Bramwell JA at 128:

> But if this payment were made by a bag of gold which the broker put into his strong box, and then misapplied part of the money, leaving the rest in the bag, there would be no doubt that what was so left could be claimed as the money of the client.

17.2.1 The property may change its form

It does not matter if the property becomes another kind of property; as long as it can still be identified, it can still be traced. The classic statement of this principle can be found in *Taylor v Plumer* (1815) 3 M & S 562.

● **Taylor v Plumer** [1815] 3 M & S 562

Sir Thomas Plumer wanted his stockbroker, Walsh, to invest some money for him in exchequer bonds. He allowed Walsh to withdraw £22,000 of his money from the bank, but Walsh only spent £6,500 of it in buying the bonds. With the rest he bought US investments and gold bullion and was apprehended at Falmouth, where he was trying to board a ship for the USA.

HELD: Plumer recovered his property, even though it had changed into another form of property.

Lord Ellenborough at 574:

> It makes no difference in reason or law into what other form, different from the original, the change may have been made, whether it be into that of promissory notes for the security of the money which was produced by the sale of the goods of the principal, or into other merchandise, for the product of or substitute for the original thing still follows the nature of the thing itself, as long as it can be ascertained to be such, and the right only ceases when the means of ascertainment fail, which is the case when the subject is turned into money, and mixed and confounded in a general mass of the same description. The difficulty which arises in such a case is a difficulty of fact and not of law, and the dictum that money has no earmark must be understood in the same way; i.e. as predicated only of an undivided and undistinguished mass of current money. But money in a bag or otherwise kept apart from other money, guineas, or other coin marked, if the fact were so, for the purpose of being distinguished and so far ear-marked as to fall within the rule on this subject.

So property can be changed into another kind of property, say shares could be used to buy gold bullion, and it can still be traced. If it is mixed up with someone else's property it cannot, for then equitable tracing is needed. We might note that Lord Ellenborough does not think that money can be traced, because one sum of £22,000 is exactly like any other sum of £22,000. There is nothing to identify it, unless it is kept separate, for instance in a bag.

In later cases, the courts recognized that it was possible to trace money at common law, as long as the sum sought was not mixed with other money.

● **Banque Belge pour l'Étranger v Hambrouck** [1921] 1 KB 321

Hambrouck took £6,000 from his employer by drawing cheques on his employer's bank account at the Banque Belge. Hambrouck paid the money into his bank, Farrow's Bank, and then paid some of it to the woman he lived with, Spinoghe, which she paid into a deposit account at London Joint City and Midland Bank. At the time the fraud was discovered she had £315 in her account, which the Banque claimed.

HELD: The Banque succeeded as, although the money had passed through several bank accounts, it could still be identified. Spinoghe had not mixed it with any money of her own.

Atkins LJ at 335–6:

KEY POINT
Unmixed money in a bank account can be traced at common law.

> On these principles it would follow that as the money paid into the bank can be identified as the product of the original money, the plaintiffs have the common law right to claim it, and can sue for money had and received. In the present case less difficulty than usual is experienced in tracing the descent of the money, for substantially no other money has ever been mixed with the proceeds of the fraud.

Common law tracing may still be a useful remedy today, despite the restriction on tracing into mixed funds. It was used in *Lipkin Gorman v Karpnale Ltd* [1991] 2 AC 548, where a claim in constructive trust had failed. (See 16.4 'Liability of third parties (strangers) in constructive trusts'.) Norman Cass was a partner at a firm of solicitors, who stole money from the clients' accounts, which he gambled at the Playboy Club. His overall losses were £154,695 and Lipkin Gorman attempted to recover them from the club.

. . . .

● *Lipkin Gorman v Karpnale Ltd* [1991] 2 AC 548

Cass had taken the money from Lipkin's bank account. A bank account is a kind of property, a chose in action, which represents the bank's debt to their client. This had become money, then gambling chips, which Cass used at the Playboy Club.

HELD: The House of Lords agreed that Lipkin could trace.

Lord Templeman put it very simply at 563:

> My conclusion is that the club has no right to retain stolen money received by the club from the thief.

Lord Goff gave a more technical explanation at 573–4:

> The relationship of the bank with the solicitors was essentially that of debtor and creditor; and since the client account was at all material times in credit, the bank was the debtor and the solicitors were its creditors. Such a debt constitutes a chose in action, which is a species of property: and since the debt was enforceable at common law, the chose in action was legal property belonging to the solicitors at common law.
>
> There is in my opinion no reason why the solicitors should not be able to trace their property at common law in that chose in action, or in any part of it, into its product, i.e. cash drawn by Cass from their client account at the bank. Such a claim is consistent with their assertion that the money so obtained by Cass was their property at common law.

17.2.2 The property may increase in value

The principle behind tracing is that the claimant is attempting to recover his or her property and it does not matter if it has changed into another kind of property. So if the new type of property increases the value of the original property, who is entitled to the profit, the original owner, or the person who just happens to hold the property now? The answer given in *Jones (FC) & Sons v Jones* [1996] 3 WLR 703 was that the original owner should have the increased value.

. . . .

● *Jones (FC) & Sons v Jones* [1996] 3 WLR 703

A partnership lawfully loaned £11,700 to Mrs Jones, wife of one of the partners. She invested the money in potato futures and ended up with £49,860, which she placed in a separate bank account, unmixed with her own money. It turned out that the partnership was bankrupt and that the loan should not have been made. The Official Receiver sought to recover the money.

HELD: The Court of Appeal agreed that the Official Receiver could have all the money. Nourse LJ endorsed this approach on a broad principle of conscience at 714:

> In my view the defendant cannot in conscience retain the profit any more than the original £11,700. She had no title to the original. She could not have made the profit without her use of it. She cannot, by making a profit through the use of money to which she had no title, acquire some better title to the profit.

KEY POINT
In common law tracing the claimant takes the benefit of any increase in value of the property.

The defendant never had any right to the property, so if they happen to make a profit with it, the profit also belongs to the original owner.

17.3 Equitable tracing

17.3.1 The need for a trust or fiduciary relationship

Equitable tracing can only take place if the property sought has been subject to a trust or, at least a fiduciary relationship. As we saw in 17.1.2 'Common law and equitable tracing', this has been questioned, but remains the rule.

● ***Re Diplock*** [1948] Ch 465

Caleb Diplock left a will which stated that the residue of his property should be held on trust 'for such charitable institutions or other charitable and benevolent objects in England as my executors may in their absolute discretion select'. It was held to be invalid as a charity, but the executors had already distributed £203,000 to 139 charities. Caleb's next of kin were now entitled to the property, so it was necessary for the executors to try to recover as much property as they could from the charities.

HELD: Lord Greene MR at 530:

> …equity may operate on the conscience not merely of those who acquire a legal title in breach of some trust, express or constructive, or of some other fiduciary obligation, but of volunteers provided that as a result of what has gone before some equitable proprietary interest has been created and attached to the property in the hands of the volunteer.

'Volunteer' just means that a person has given no consideration in return for the property that they have received. In *Diplock* the volunteers had not done anything wrong, because they did not know that the charity part of the trust was invalid and that the executors should not have given them any property. Tracing was still available against them and the beneficiaries of the trust should be allowed to pursue and recover their property.

The need for a trust or fiduciary relationship is a crucial requirement for equitable tracing and makes it distinct from common law tracing. The other distinction is that equitable tracing is available to trace into a mixed fund.

● ***Agip (Africa) Ltd v Jackson and Others*** [1991] Ch 547

Agip were an oil company based in Tunisia. Their chief accountant, Zdiri, altered the names on payment orders and diverted millions of dollars to a number of companies registered in England, France, and the Isle of Man, managed by Jackson. The payments went through a bank in London and New York. It could be shown that the money ended up with Jackson and tracing was still possible, even though Agip's money had been thoroughly mixed up with other money.

Fox LJ at 566:

> Both common law and equity accepted the right of the true owner to trace his property into the hands of others while it was in an identifiable form. The common law treated property as identified if it had not been mixed with other property. Equity, on the other hand, will follow money

into a mixed fund and charge the fund. There is, in the present case, no difficulty about the mechanics of tracing in equity. The money can be traced through the various bank accounts to Baker Oil and onwards. It is, however, a prerequisite to the operation of the remedy in equity that there must be a fiduciary relationship which calls the equitable jurisdiction into being. There is no difficulty about that in the present case since Mr Zdiri must have been in a fiduciary relationship with Agip. He was the chief accountant of Agip and was entrusted with the signed drafts or orders upon Banque du Sud.

It was recognized as long ago as 1880, in *Re Hallett's Estate* (1879–80) LR 13 ChD 696, that equitable tracing could extend to a fiduciary relationship.

. . . .

● *Re Hallett's Estate* (1879–80) LR 13 ChD 696

Hallett was a solicitor, who had a client, Mrs Cotterill. He had for many years been entrusted with her investments which he managed on her behalf, buying and selling, collecting the dividends, and paying them over to her.

HELD: Fry J: Although Hallett was not formally appointed as a trustee for Mrs Cotterill, his actions made him a fiduciary.

At 702:

It has been argued that Mr Hallett was a trustee for Mrs Cotterill. In that view I cannot concur; but it appears to me that he was solicitor for her, that he was agent for her, and that he was bailee for her. I think, therefore, that he stood in what has been called a fiduciary relation towards her.

Agents, working for a principal, are in a fiduciary relationship. Therefore the agent should not make a profit from their position that has not been authorized by their principal. This could be an undisclosed commission or a bribe. The agent must not place himself in a position where his duty to his principal conflicts, particularly by acting for both sides in a business deal, without getting permission from his principal. It is clear that the agent must hand over any unauthorized profits to their principal. However, it was not clear whether this was a personal liability of equitable compensation or whether the agent holds the profit on constructive trust for the principal. If it is the latter, claimants can trace and follow that profit as it passes through other persons' hands. After several hundred years of differing legal opinions, the matter was finally settled in *FHR European Ventures v Cedar Capital Partners* [2014] UKSC 45. (See also Chapter 16 'Constructive trusts' and, in particular, 16.3.2 'Bribes'.)

. . . .

● *FHR European Ventures v Cedar Capital Partners* [2014] UKSC 45

European Ventures bought the Monte Carlo Hotel for 211.5 million euros. Cedar acted for both sides in the transaction and received 10 million euros commission from Monte Carlo. European Ventures did not know about Cedar's 'Exclusive Brokerage Agreement' with Monte Carlo and wanted to recover the 10 million euros, in whoever's hands it now was. Were they able to trace?

HELD: Lord Neuberger: European Ventures could trace the 10 million euros:

At paragraph 46: 'The considerations of practicality and principle...support the...case, namely that a bribe or secret commission accepted by an agent is held on trust for his principal.'

At paragraph 44: '...it appears to be just that a principal whose agent has obtained a bribe or secret commission should be able to trace the proceeds of the bribe or commission into other assets and to follow them into the hands of knowing recipients.'

17.3.2 Tracing into a mixed fund

An old and rather quaint example can be seen in a Canadian case, *Jones v De Marchant* (1916) 28 DLR 561, where the tracer was able to recover their property and the property with which it was mixed.

● *Jones v De Marchant* [1916] 28 DLR 561

A husband used 18 beaver skins that belonged to his wife and four beaver skins of his own and had them made up into a coat, which he gave to his mistress. The mistress was an innocent volunteer, in that she did not know that the skins belonged to his wife.

HELD: The wife was entitled to recover the whole coat. The mistress had no claim, because any claim that she might have had derived from the wrongdoer, the husband. The coat was an entirely new asset and not just the product of mingling the 22 skins. The coat could hardly be divided and the two ladies could not be expected to share it.

More modern cases are not likely to involve chattels, like beaver skins, but choses in action, such as bank accounts and shares, which are easily transferred and mixed together. Equitable tracing is still possible, but the remedy is likely to be the imposition of a charge or a constructive trust.

● *El Ajou v Dollar Land Holdings plc* [1994] 2 All ER 685

El Ajou was a wealthy businessman living in Saudi Arabia. His was the largest loss of many victims of a massive share fraud carried out in Amsterdam by three Canadians. Some of the proceeds passed through Geneva, Gibraltar, Panama, and Geneva (again) and ended up in London, invested with Dollar Land Holdings to develop property at Nine Elms in Battersea.

HELD: There were many other victims of the fraud and other investors in the development project, but the Court of Appeal accepted the view of Millett J, in the court below, that £1.3 million of El Ajou's money could still be identified.

Millett J at [1993] 3 All ER 717, 738:

> The plaintiff can follow his money through these various transactions, but the relevant asset capable of being identified as having been received by DLH is an interest in the site corresponding to the payment of the deposit.

DLH knew that this money was the product of fraud and so a constructive trust could be imposed. (See 16.4 'Liability of third parties (strangers) in constructive trusts'.)

17.3.3 The wrongdoer spends his own money first

It is quite likely that the person who has taken the trust money will have mixed it with his or her own money. The beneficiaries of the trust get the first claim to the money, because it is not right that a person who has removed money should profit from their own wrong.

● **Re Hallett's Estate** (1879–80) LR 13 ChD 696

Hallett was a solicitor who was the trustee of his own marriage settlement. He took £770.52 from that trust and paid it into his own bank account. Hallett was also a fiduciary for a client, Mrs Cotterill, and he took £1,804.30 from her and also paid it into his bank account. Hallett died and left £3,029.75 in that account. Some of the money in the account was his own, mixed up with the money of the two trusts. Who should have the first claim to this money?

HELD: Court of Appeal: It had to be assumed that Hallett spent his own money first and what was left could be claimed first by the two trusts. Fortunately, there would be enough money in the account to satisfy both the trust claims. This approach was to be preferred to the rival approach laid down in *Clayton's Case* (1816) 1 Mer 572. (See 17.3.6 'The first in, first out rule: the rule in *Clayton's Case*'.)

Jessell MR at 727–8:

> When we come to apply that principle to the case of a trustee who has blended trust moneys with his own, it seems to me perfectly plain that he cannot be heard to say that he took away the trust money when he had a right to take his own money … Could he say that he had actually drawn out anything but his own money? His money was there, and he had a right to draw it out, and why should the natural act of simply drawing out the money be attributed to anything except to his ownership of money which was at his bankers.

Re Hallett's Estate (1879) 13 ChD 696 was applied in *Sinclair Investments (UK) Ltd v Versailles Trade Finance Ltd* [2011] 4 All ER 335. If the fiduciary has mixed the trust property with his own property, then the claimant can take it all, unless the defaulting fiduciary can prove that the property actually belongs to them.

● **Sinclair Investments (UK) Ltd v Versailles Trade Finance Ltd** [2011] 4 All ER 335

Cushnie had moved the property taken from the fiduciary relationship around his network of companies. The defence was that it could not now be identified, being hopelessly mixed up with other property, but the Court of Appeal did not agree.

Lord Neuberger at 367:

> I do not doubt the general principle, reiterated by Lord Millett in Foskett v McKeown [2000] 1 AC 102, that if a proprietary claim is to be made good by tracing, there must be a clear link between the claimant's funds and the asset or money into which he seeks to trace. However, I do not see why this should mean that a proprietary claim is lost simply because the defaulting fiduciary, while still holding much of the money, has acted particularly dishonestly or cunningly by creating a maelstrom. Where he has mixed the funds held on trust with his own funds, the onus should be on the fiduciary to establish that part, and what part, of the mixed fund is his property.

The principle here is that the wrongdoer should not profit from his own wrong, but in many situations there would no longer be enough money left in (say) a bank account to satisfy a trust's claim. As we saw in 17.1 'What is tracing?', the claimant can choose who to pursue for their money and they might look elsewhere than the bank account.

● **Re Oatway** [1903] 2 Ch 356

Lewis Oatway was a solicitor, whose financial misdemeanours were revealed when he died insolvent in 1902. He and Maxwell Skipper were the trustees of the will of Charles Skipper, father of Maxwell. They made a £3,000 advance from the trust to Maxwell, secured by a mortgage given by Oatway to Maxwell. Oatway sold the mortgaged property, which brought him £7,000. He put it in his bank account and then used £2,137.61 from it to buy shares in the Oceana Company. The rest of the money in the account was spent, leaving £77.66. The trust sought to recover the £3,000 that had been wrongly advanced to Maxwell Skipper.

Joyce J: The money could be followed into the bank account and then into the shares purchased with that money. The trust could have a charge of £3,000 over the shares. That way some of the money could be recovered and Oatway did not profit from his wrong.

At 360:

> ... when any of the money drawn out has been invested, and the investment remains in the name or under the control of the trustee, the rest of the balance having been afterwards dissipated by him, he cannot maintain that the investment which remains represents his own money alone, and that what has been spent and can no longer be traced and recovered was the money belonging to the trust.

Though *Re Hallett's Estate* (1879–80) LR 13 ChD 696 and *Re Oatway* [1903] 2 Ch 356 look dissimilar, the basic principle underlying them is the same. The wrongdoer, who takes from the trust, should not be allowed to profit from their wrong and the beneficiaries should be given every opportunity to follow and recover their property.

17.3.4 The rule of the lowest intermediate balance

As we have seen in *Re Hallett's Estate* (1879–80) LR 13 ChD 696, money can be traced into a bank account, but only if the money can still be shown to be there. If the sum in the bank account falls below the amount taken from the trust fund, it is presumed that the trust money has been paid out. This might seem strange, but the logic of tracing is that a specific item of property, like a bag of gold, is being pursued. It goes into the bank account and then out again. The tracer has to follow it to its new destination, as in *Re Oatway* [1903] 2 Ch 356, at 17.3 'Equitable tracing'.

. . . .

● ***Roscoe v Winder*** [1915] Ch 62

Wigham bought the goodwill of the business of John Roscoe (Bolton) Ltd and agreed to collect the debts owing to them and pay them over to Roscoe. He collected all the debts, £623.42, and paid £455.95 of them into his own, personal bank account. Wigham then spent the money in his account, until he had £25.90 left. Then he paid into the account his own money, until he had £358.27 when he died. Could Roscoe claim back the £455.95 that had been taken from them from what was left in the bank account?

HELD: Sargant J: Because of the terms of the agreement, Wigham held the debts on trust for Roscoe, but Roscoe could not have the £358.27, because only £25.90 of their money was left in the account. Their money came into the account and was presumed to leave it, when Wigham spent the money in the account.

Sargant J at 68:

> So that, although the ultimate balance at the debtor's death was about £358 there had been an intermediate balance of only £25 18s. The result of that seems to me to be that the trust moneys cannot possibly be traced into this common fund, which was standing

to the debtor's credit at his death, to an extent of more than £25 18s., because, although prima facie under the second rule in *In re Hallett's Estate* any drawings out by the debtor ought to be attributed to the private moneys which he had at the bank and not to the trust moneys, yet, when the drawings out had reached such an amount that the whole of his private money part had been exhausted, it necessarily followed that the rest of the drawings must have been against trust moneys. There being on May 21, 1913, only £25 18s., in all, standing to the credit of the debtor's account, it is quite clear that on that day he must have denuded his account of all the trust moneys there—the whole £455 18s. 11d.—except to the extent of £25 18s.

When Wigham subsequently put money into the account it was not money from Roscoe, but his own money. It could not be shown that Wigham intended to replace the money he had taken from Roscoe.

Sargant J at 69:

I think it is impossible to attribute to him that by the mere payment into the account of further moneys, which to a large extent he subsequently used for purposes of his own, he intended to clothe those moneys with a trust in favour of the plaintiffs.

Re Hallett's Estate (1879–80) LR 13 ChD 696 could not be used, because unlike in that case, the trust money was no longer in the wrongdoer's bank account.

17.3.5 Tracing into overdrawn bank accounts

The same approach, as in *Roscoe v Winder* [1915] Ch 62, is taken if an attempt is made to trace into an overdrawn bank account. The logic is that the trust money has been spent and has gone elsewhere and that is where the tracer must look. It is also not possible to trace into the general assets of the bank or to try what is sometimes called 'backwards tracing', which is where the account holder overdraws to buy something and then immediately gets back into credit with the misappropriated trust funds. The trust cannot claim the purchased asset.

. . . .
● ***Bishopsgate Investment Management Ltd v Homan and Others*** [1995] Ch 211

Bishopsgate were the trustees of pension funds for the employees of the Maxwell group of companies. On the unexpected death of Robert Maxwell in 1991, it was discovered that very large amounts of money from the pension funds had been taken and paid into various Maxwell companies and the National Westminster Bank. The Maxwell bank accounts at the National Westminster were overdrawn. Was it possible to trace the pension fund money into them?

HELD: Dillon LJ (Court of Appeal): In an earlier case, *Space Investments Ltd v Canadian Imperial Bank of Commerce Trust Co (Bahamas) Ltd* [1986] 1 WLR 1072, Lord Templeman had suggested that, where the bank account was overdrawn, it might be possible to trace into the general assets of the bank. This was only an obiter remark and was rejected in a subsequent case and in this one.

At 220:

But that was rejected in *In re Goldcorp Exchange Ltd.* [1995] 1 A.C. 74 because equitable tracing, though devised for the protection of trust moneys misapplied, cannot be pursued through an overdrawn and therefore non-existent fund.

KEY POINT
For tracing to be possible the sum of money sought must be identifiable either as a separate fund or part of a mixed fund.

Leggatt LJ rejected the idea of 'backwards tracing' at 221:

> As Buckley L.J. said in *Borden (U.K.) Ltd. v. Scottish Timber Products Ltd.* [1981] Ch 25, 46: 'it is a fundamental feature of the doctrine of tracing that the property to be traced can be identified at every stage of its journey through life . . .'
>
> For the same reason there can be no equitable remedy against an asset acquired *before* misappropriation of money takes place, since ex hypothesi it cannot be followed into something which existed and so had been acquired before the money was received and therefore without its aid.

17.3.6 The first in, first out rule: the rule in *Clayton's Case*

This is a rule that only applies to current, active bank accounts. It is applicable when more than one trust is trying to trace into the same bank account and there is not enough money left in the account to satisfy all the claims. Hence it did not apply in *Re Hallett's Estate* (1879–80) LR 13 ChD 696, because there was enough money to satisfy both claims there, nor in *Re Oatway* [1903] 2 Ch 356, because there was only one trust claiming. The rule originates from the collapse of a bank, where customers tried to reclaim their money from what was left, but the rule has been applied when two or more trusts trace against a bank account.

● ***Clayton's Case, Devaynes v Noble*** [1816] 1 Mer 572, [1814–32] All ER Rep 1

Grant MR at 608:

> In such a case, there is no room for any other appropriation than that which arises from the order in which the receipts and payments take place, and are carried into the account. Presumably, it is the sum first paid in, that is first drawn out. It is the first item on the debit side of the account, that is discharged, or reduced, by the first item on the credit side.

If you imagine looking at a bank statement, the rule can be understood. If you look at Diagram 17.1, the money from Trust A comes in on 10 March and appears on the credit side of the account. So when the payments out on the debit side are made on 12 and 13 March it is assumed that they come from Trust A. Trust B's money, which came into the account later, is regarded as still remaining in the bank account and so the £1,000 which is left belongs to Trust B. This result might seem arbitrary and unfair, and so was reconsidered in *Barlow Clowes International Ltd v Vaughan* [1992] 4 All ER 22.

Diagram 17.1
Clayton's Case

Trust B has the £1,000 left

Payments in. Credit	Payments out. Debit
10 March £1,000 Trust A	
11 March £1,000 Trust B	
	12 March £500 shares
	13 March £500 shares

● **Barlow Clowes International Ltd v Vaughan** [1992] 4 All ER 22

Barlow Clowes was a company registered in Gibraltar which took deposits from customers, held them upon trust, and promised to invest the deposits and make a healthy profit for the investors. In fact, most of the money was taken by the owners of the company. After the company collapsed the 11,000 investors were owed over £115 million and they sought to trace it into various assets, such as **gilt-edged stock**, a yacht, and various bank accounts.

Gilt-edged stock— also known as gilts. These are fixed interest loan securities issued by the UK government. They are regarded as particularly safe investments.

HELD: Court of Appeal: The issue was whether the rule in *Clayton's Case* applied. The court thought that it should not, for a number of reasons. This was not a case where individual deposits had been put into a bank account, but one where they had all been mixed together in a common fund. The rule in *Clayton's Case* was the basic rule.

Dillon LJ at 33:

> None the less the decisions of this court, in my judgement, establish and recognise a general rule of practice that *Clayton's Case* is to be applied when several beneficiaries' moneys have been blended in one bank account and there is a deficiency. It is not, in my judgement, for this court to reject that long established general practice.

However, it was just a rule of convenience and the court was not bound to apply it if it would lead to injustice. They would not apply it here.

Woolf LJ at 42:

> For the reasons I have expressed, the approach, in summary, which I would adopt to resolving the issues raised by this appeal are as follows:
>
> 1. While the rule in Clayton's Case is *prima facie* available to determine the interests of investors in a fund into which their investments have been paid, the use of the rule is a matter of convenience and if its application in particular circumstances would be impracticable or result in injustice between the investors it will not be applied if there is a preferable alternative.
> 2. Here the rule will not be applied because this would be contrary to either the express or inferred or presumed intention of the investors. If the investments were required by the terms of the investment contract to be paid into a common pool this indicates that the investors did not intend to apply the rule. If the investments were intended to be separately invested, as a result of the investments being collectively misapplied by BCI a common pool of the investments was created. Because of their shared misfortune, the investors will be presumed to have intended the rule not to apply.
> 3. As the rule is inapplicable the approach which should be adopted by the court depends on which of the possible alternative solutions is the most satisfactory in the circumstances. If the North American solution is practical this would probably have advantages over the **pari passu** solution. However the complications of applying the North American solution in this case make the third solution the most satisfactory.

Pari passu—Latin—literally means spread out equally. The depositors share out what is left in proportion to what was taken from them. In Diagram 17.1 it would mean that an equal amount was taken from Trust A and Trust B, so they should share what was left equally. That would mean that they received £500 each, instead of under the rule in *Clayton's Case*, Trust B taking everything that was left; the whole £1,000.

The Court of Appeal also rejected the more complex 'rolling charge' method of calculating each depositor's share. With 11,000 claimants it would be very difficult to calculate the amount each one was owed using the *Clayton* or rolling charge approach. So the only sensible approach was to divide up what was left proportionally.

Woolf LJ at 35 describes how rolling charge works:

> The second solution for resolving the claims of the investors among themselves is the rolling charge or North American solution ('North American' because it is the solution adopted or favoured in preference to the rule in Clayton's Case in certain decisions of the courts in the United States and Canada because it is regarded as being manifestly fairer). This solution involves treating credits to a bank account made at different times and from different sources as a blend or cocktail with the result that when a withdrawal is made from the account it is treated as a withdrawal in the same proportions as the different interests in the account (here of the investors) bear to each other at the moment before the withdrawal is made.

So the solution was to share out what was left of the depositors' money in proportion to what was taken from them, but the rule in *Clayton's Case* remains for current bank accounts.

thinking points

Clayton's Case *is actually an exception to the usual approach in tracing where 'the basic principle is that each innocent contributor has an equal equity so that each will share pari passu (i.e. rateably), neither having priority over the other'. Ideas on what is fair have changed and the rule now seems outdated. 'Priority in time, although once seen as a convenient basis for allocation of payments between competing contestants, is now viewed as anomalous and irrational.' It is arguable that it is a rule confined to banking and should never have been imported into tracing. See, for example, the view of Leggatt LJ in* Barlow-Clowes *on this. The courts will try to avoid using the rule in* Clayton's Case, *if they possibly can, as seen in* Barlow-Clowes *and* Russell-Cooke Trust Co v Prentis (No 1) [2003] 2 All ER 478, *a similar case where investors' money was pooled in a bank account. It seems, however, that the rule remains for 'competing beneficial claims to a mixed fund in a running account', if there are no factors in the case to displace it. See M Pawlowski 'The Demise of the Rule in* Clayton's Case' [2003] Conv 339.

17.3.7 Increases in value

Tracing means that the claimant pursues the asset taken from the trust as it changes hands and changes form. Can the tracer take the benefit if the asset happens to increase in value? We have seen at 17.2.2 'The property may increase in value' in *Jones (FC) & Sons v Jones* [1996] 3 WLR 703 that the answer in common law tracing is yes. Should the approach be the same in equitable tracing? The question was considered in *Re Tilley's Will Trusts* [1967] Ch 1179.

● *Re Tilley's Will Trusts* [1967] Ch 1179

Mrs Tilley was the trustee of a trust for herself for life and then equally for her son and her daughter. She took £2,237 of the trust capital and over the years thoroughly mixed it up with her own money, in her own bank account. The bank granted her a considerable overdraft facility, for the time, of £22,000. Over the years, she bought and sold houses and by the time of her death had accumulated an estate worth £94,000. The daughter's personal representatives claimed that half of this profit belonged to them, as it had been made using the trust money.

HELD: The claimant can claim an asset bought with trust money or enforce a charge over it to repay the money taken from the trust. The charge can be enforced even if the asset is bought partly with trust money and partly with the defendant's own money.

Ungoed-Thomas J at 1189:

> For the defendants it has been rightly admitted that if a trustee wrongly uses trust money to pay the whole of the purchase price in respect of the purchase of an asset a beneficiary can elect either to treat the purchased asset as trust property or to treat the purchased asset as security for the recouping of the trust money. It was further conceded that this right of election by a beneficiary also applies where the asset is purchased by a trustee in part out of his own money and in part out of the trust moneys, so that he may, if he wishes, require the asset to be treated as trust property with regard to that proportion of it which the trust moneys contributed to its purchase.

This principle would allow the claimant to take a share of any profit made with the trust property.

Ungoed-Thomas J at 1193:

> If, of course, a trustee deliberately uses trust money to contribute with his own money to buy property in his own name, then I would see no difficulty in enabling a beneficiary to adopt the purchase and claim a share of any resulting profits.

However, the claimant could not share in the £94,000 here, because the judge decided that it was the large overdraft facility that allowed Mrs Tilley to build up her estate from buying and selling houses. The £2,237 taken from the trust was not used to buy the houses. Therefore, the claimants were only entitled to the return of half of £2,237.

The principle, that increases in value could be recovered via equitable tracing, was recognized in *Re Tilley's Will Trusts*, but held not to be applicable on the facts of that case. Tracers were finally allowed to take the increase in value of their property in the House of Lords case, *Foskett v McKeown and Others* [2001] 1 AC 102.

● *Foskett v McKeown and Others* [2001] 1 AC 102

Murphy was a property developer in Portugal, and Foskett and 219 other clients paid over £2.6 million, with the agreement that building plots would be developed for them. This money was held on trust, but Murphy never carried out the development. He used £20,440 of this money to pay the last two of five annual premiums of a life insurance policy on his life. In 1991 Murphy committed suicide and the life insurance death benefit paid out £1 million. The question was whether the £1 million should go to his three children or whether the property clients could trace their £20,440 into the death benefit.

HELD: House of Lords, 3–2 majority.

Lord Browne-Wilkinson set the scene nicely at 106:

> My Lords, there are many cases in which the court has to decide which of two innocent parties is to suffer from the activities of a fraudster. This case, unusually, raises the converse question: which of two innocent parties is to benefit from the activities of the fraudster.

The purchasers' money had been used to pay for the insurance policy and that had produced the payout of £1 million. Therefore, they were entitled to share in what their property had produced.

Lord Browne-Wilkinson at 110:

> I do not myself quibble at the description of it being 'a windfall' on the facts of this case. But this windfall is enjoyed because of the rights which the purchasers enjoy under the law of property. A man under whose land oil is discovered enjoys a very valuable windfall but no one suggests that he, as owner of the property, is not entitled to the windfall which goes with his property right.

Lord Millett explained the basic principle of tracing, where the claimant was entitled to assets purchased with their money, or a proportionate share of the asset.

At 131:

> Accordingly, I would state the basic rule as follows. Where a trustee wrongfully uses trust money to provide part of the cost of acquiring an asset, the beneficiary is entitled *at his option* either to claim a proportionate share of the asset or to enforce a **lien** upon it to secure his personal claim against the trustee for the amount of the misapplied money. It does not matter whether the trustee mixed the trust money with his own in a single fund before using it to acquire the asset, or made separate payments (whether simultaneously or sequentially) out of the differently owned funds to acquire a single asset.

Lien—a right to keep possession of property belonging to another person until a debt owed by that person is discharged (*Oxford English Dictionary*).

Therefore, the claimants were entitled to a proportionate share of the insurance payout.

At 134:

> It follows that, if a claimant can show that premiums were paid with his money, he can claim a proportionate share of the policy... In principle the plaintiffs are entitled to the insurance money which was paid on Mr Murphy's death in the same shares and proportions as they were entitled in the policy immediately before his death.
>
> Where A misappropriates B's money and uses it to buy a winning ticket in the lottery, B is entitled to the winnings. Since A is a wrongdoer, it is irrelevant that he could have used his own money if in fact he used B's. This may seem to give B an undeserved windfall, but the result is not unjust.
>
> The application of these principles ought not to depend on the nature of the chose in action. They should apply to a policy of life assurance as they apply to a bank account or a lottery ticket.

KEY POINT
In equitable tracing, claimants can take the increase in value of their asset.

So the claimants were entitled to a share in the death benefit proportionate to the amount of premium that they had contributed. That would be two-fifths of the £1,000,000 insurance payout.

The minority judges, Lord Steyn and Lord Hope, thought that the insurance policy was already secured by the payment of the first three premiums, so the last two premiums did not produce the £1 million payout. Therefore, the property purchasers were only entitled to the return of their £20,440.

thinking points

Foskett v McKeown and Others is a controversial decision. The judges were divided on what the claimants should recover and it might seem unfair that Murphy's children were deprived of part of their inheritance, when they had done nothing wrong. The case raises the issue of why there should be any difference between common law and equitable tracing (see 17.1.2 'Common law and equitable tracing'), but then leaves the old law intact. The interaction between tracing and restitution is also raised as in Lipkin Gorman v Karpnale Ltd *[1991] 2 AC 548 (see 17.2.1 'A definition of tracing'), but left unresolved. These issues are considered by G Virgo in 'Vindicating Vindication: Foskett v McKeown Reviewed' in AS Hudson (ed)* New Perspectives in Property Law, Obligations and Restitution *(London: Cavendish, 2003).*

17.4 Tracing against volunteers

17.4.1 Bona fide purchaser for value without notice

Tracing is not possible against a person who pays for the traced property and does not know that the property has been taken from a trust or fiduciary relationship. This is explained in *Foskett v McKeown and Others* [2001] 1 AC 102.

● *Foskett v McKeown and Others* [2001] 1 AC 102

Lord Millett at 127:

> A beneficiary of a trust is entitled to a continuing beneficial interest not merely in the trust property but in its traceable proceeds also, and his interest binds every one who takes the property or its traceable proceeds except a bona fide purchaser for value without notice. In the present case the plaintiffs' beneficial interest plainly bound Mr Murphy, a trustee who wrongfully mixed the trust money with his own and whose every dealing with the money (including the payment of the premiums) was in breach of trust. It similarly binds his successors, the trustees of the children's settlement, who claim no beneficial interest of their own, and Mr Murphy's children, who are volunteers. They gave no value for what they received and derive their interest from Mr Murphy by way of gift.

A similar approach is taken in common law tracing, as can be seen in our example *Banque Belge pour l'Etranger v Hambrouck* [1921] 1 KB 321 in 17.2.1 'The property may change its form', where Spinoghe could not defeat the tracing claim of the bank because the money was a gift from her lover, Hambrouck, and she gave no consideration in return.

The question of what may count as 'value' was considered in *Independent Trustee Services Ltd v GP Noble Trustees Ltd and others* [2012] 3 All ER 210.

● *Independent Trustee Services Ltd v GP Noble Trustees Ltd and others* [2012]
    3 All ER 210

Mr Morris had dishonestly assisted in taking £52 million from an occupational pension scheme. He and his wife were divorcing and the court had ordered him to pay her £1.481 million. This was equivalent to a contract for which his wife had given consideration, the settlement of her claims against him. Subsequently she sought a better settlement and the court set aside its order. The trustees of the pension scheme claimed that the £1.481 million came from the pension scheme and sought to trace against her and seek its return.

HELD: The setting aside of the court order meant that she had given no consideration.

Lloyd LJ at 246:

> In those circumstances it seems to me that the setting aside of District Judge Black's order was relevant both in principle and in practice to the position as between Mrs Morris and ITS thereafter. Before the order of Moylan J she was able to assert and establish that she was a bona fide purchaser for value without notice. Afterwards she could not do so, because the transaction under which she had given value had been set aside and was of no effect; as between her and the other party, Mr Morris, it was as if it had not happened.

The counter argument, that the equitable tracing claim was knocked out forever by the original court order and could not revive, was rejected.

Therefore, the money could be recovered from Mrs Morris.

Patten LJ at 232:

> The task of this court is simply to determine whether Mrs Morris has a defence to any tracing claim on the basis that she received the £1.481 million as a bona fide purchaser for value without notice. To that end, the order should simply declare that ITS is beneficially entitled to the traceable proceeds of the £1.481 million.

This 'equity's darling' defence was given further consideration in *Armstrong DLW GmbH v Winnington Networks Ltd.* [2012] 3 All ER 425. The judgment gave some thought to the meanings of 'good faith' and 'notice'.

● ***Armstrong DLW GmbH v Winnington Networks Ltd*** [2012] 3 All ER 425

Armstrong held 21,000 carbon emission allowances, also called European Union Allowances (EUAs), in a registry based in Germany. These allowances were stolen by a company called Zen Holdings, who sold them on to Winnington. Armstrong sought to recover their EUAs and in their defence Winnington argued that they did not know that they were stolen.

HELD: Stephen Morris QC at 486–7: The meaning of 'notice'.

> Winnington deliberately and consciously chose to take the risk that the EUAs did not belong to Armstrong . . . In this way, by not awaiting an answer to the inquiries, Winnington was either 'wilfully shutting [their] eyes to the obvious' or at the very least 'wilfully and recklessly failing to make such inquiries as an honest and reasonable man would make'. Put another way, Winnington's knowledge fell within, at least *Baden* type (3), because Winnington wilfully and recklessly failed to make such *further* inquiries as an honest and reasonable man would have made in the circumstances then pertaining.

(See 16.4 'Liability of third parties [strangers] in constructive trusts' for *Baden v Société Générale* [1992] 4 All ER 161.)

'Good faith' is not the same as honesty. A person could be in bad faith by doing something that is not actually dishonest.

At 452–3, quoting from *Niru Battery Manufacturing Co v Milestone Trading Ltd* [2004] QB 985:

> In my view it [good faith] is capable of embracing a failure to act in a commercially acceptable way and sharp practice of a kind that falls short of outright dishonesty as well as dishonesty itself.

The conclusion was that Winnington were not in good faith and had notice that the EUAs were stolen. There were suspicious circumstances which should have led them to ask questions.

The Court of Appeal also tried to define the meaning of 'notice' in *Sinclair Investments (UK) Ltd v Versailles Trade Finance Ltd* [2011] 4 All ER 335. (See 17.3.1 'The need for a trust or fiduciary relationship'.)

....

● *Sinclair Investments (UK) Ltd v Versailles Trade Finance Ltd* [2011] 4 All ER 335

Lord Neuberger at 362:

> In this case, it appears to me that the question which the judge had to determine was whether, on the facts known to the banks as at the three dates ... above, a reasonable person with their attributes (i.e. those of a responsible large bank, with the benefit of highly experienced insolvency practitioners as their appointed administrative receivers) should either have appreciated that a proprietary claim probably existed or should have made inquiries or sought advice, which would have revealed the probable existence of such a claim.

17.4.2 Innocent volunteers

As we have just seen in *Foskett v McKeown and Others* [2001] 1 AC 102 at 17.3.7 'Increases in value', those who have given nothing in return for the property that they have received, volunteers, are defeated by the claims of the wronged beneficiaries, who have had their property stolen. It might become more complicated than that, when, for example, the innocent volunteers have mixed up the trust property with their own property. Some basic principles were laid down in *Re Diplock* [1948] Ch 465. The question is who is to take priority: who gets first claim to the money if there is not enough to satisfy all the claims?

....

● *Re Diplock* [1948] Ch 465

Caleb Diplock left a will which stated that the residue of his property should be held on trust; 'for such charitable institutions or other charitable and benevolent objects in England as my executors may in their absolute discretion select'. It was held to be invalid as a charity, but the executors had already distributed £203,000 to 139 charities. Caleb's next of kin were now entitled to the property, so it was necessary for the executors to try to recover as much property as they could from the charities.

HELD: Lord Greene MR at 539:

> [1] Where one claimant is a person in a fiduciary relationship to another and has mixed moneys of that other with moneys of his own, that other takes priority. The same result follows where a person taking that other claimant's money from the person in a fiduciary relationship, with notice that it is money held in a fiduciary capacity, proceeds to mix it with money of his own.
>
> [2] Where the contest is between two claimants to a mixed fund made up entirely of moneys held on behalf of the two of them respectively and mixed together by the fiduciary agent, they share pari passu, each being innocent.
>
> [3] Where the moneys are handed by way of transfer to a person who takes for value without notice, the claim of the owner of the moneys is extinguished just as all other equitable estates or interests are extinguished by a purchase for value without notice.
>
> [4] In the case, however, of a volunteer who takes without notice, e.g., by way of gift from the fiduciary agent, if there is no question of mixing, he holds the money on behalf of the true owner whose equitable right to the money still persists as against him.

> [5] On the other hand, if the volunteer mixes the money with money of his own, or receives it mixed from the fiduciary agent, he must admit the claim of the true owner, but is not precluded from setting up his own claim in respect of the moneys of his own which have been contributed to the mixed fund. The result is that they share pari passu.

[1] Tracers take priority over wrongdoers. (See *Re Hallett's Estate* (1879–80) LR 13 ChD 696 at 17.3.3 'The wrongdoer spends his own money first'.)

[2] If there is more than one tracer into the mixed fund, their claims are treated equally. (See *Barlow Clowes International Ltd v Vaughan* [1992] 4 All ER 22 at 17.3.5 'Tracing into overdrawn bank accounts'.)

[3] A bona fide purchaser for value without notice is able to defeat a tracing claim. (See 17.4.1 'Bona fide purchaser for value without notice'.)

[4] Innocent volunteers have no defence against a tracing claim. (See *Foskett v McKeown and Others* [2001] 1 AC 102 at 17.4.1 'Bona fide purchaser for value without notice' also.)

[5] In *Re Diplock* itself, the charities had mixed 'Diplock money' with their own resources. They were entitled to keep their own resources, but had to return the 'Diplock money'. If some of the money had been spent and was irrecoverable, the charities and the Diplock claimants would share what was left in the proportions in which they had contributed. So, for example, if a charity had £20,000, received £5,000 from Diplock and there was £10,000 left, the proportions would be four-fifths for the charity and one-fifth for Diplock, giving the charity £8,000 and the tracer £2,000.

17.4.3 The change of position defence

In some situations it would be very difficult for an innocent volunteer to return trust money and might be unfair to make them do so. Such a situation occurred in *Re Diplock* [1948] Ch 465.

. . . .

● *Re Diplock* [1948] Ch 465

Some of the Diplock money had been paid to hospitals and a school, and they had used the money to improve their buildings or erect other buildings on their land.

HELD: Lord Greene MR: The only way that the hospitals could return the trust money would be to sell the buildings and divide the proceeds. Buildings in the middle of a hospital complex are not very saleable and they could hardly be expected to sell the whole hospital, so the claim for return of trust property would be denied.

At 548:

> In the absence of authority to the contrary our conclusion is that as regards the Diplock money used in these cases it cannot be traced in any true sense; and, further, that even if this were not so, the only remedy available to equity, viz., that of a declaration of charge would not produce an equitable result and is inapplicable accordingly.

In later cases this idea has been considered under the more generally known title of a change of position defence. The possibility of such a defence applying to tracing claims was recognized in *Lipkin Gorman v Karpnale* [1991] 2 AC 548.

··

● *Lipkin Gorman v Karpnale* [1991] 2 AC 548

Questions

KEY POINT
An innocent defendant might be able to resist a tracing claim on the grounds that it would be inequitable to make them restore the trust property.

Lord Goff at 579:

> The answer must be that, where an innocent defendant's position is so changed that he will suffer an injustice if called upon to repay or repay in full, the injustice of requiring him so to repay outweighs the injustice of denying the claimant restitution.

The court would have to weigh up the respective claims of the tracing claimant and the innocent volunteer, and decide whether it was right to make the volunteer repay. Lord Millett considered this defence in *Foskett v McKeown* [2001] 1 AC 102 at 129, but rejected it as inappropriate to a claim based on property rights, where the object was to return the claimant's property. The only defence available was the bona fide purchaser for value defence.

Conclusion

We have seen in this chapter that tracing is a powerful means of locating and then recovering trust property. That property may change hands, change into another form of property, be mixed with other property and even increase in value, and yet it can still be recovered. The person who has the property may be unaware of its true origin and guilty of no wrongdoing, but they may still be required to restore it to the beneficiaries of the trust. There is, though, an air of unreality about tracing. Common law tracing is based on the idea of locating and recovering a physical object, the classic example being a bag of gold. Then it was extended to the property changing its form into various kinds of financial instruments, which are just sets of rights with no physical existence, and even money in a bank account, which is just a debt that the bank owes to its customer. Equitable tracing took the process even further, as Lord Greene MR said in *Re Diplock* [1948] Ch 465, at 520: 'Equity adopted a more metaphysical approach', with its willingness to allow tracing into mixed funds. The idea was still that individual pieces of property could be identified, even though with modern bank transfers no money, no gold, nor even pieces of paper change hands. As Millett J said in *Agip (Africa) Ltd v Jackson* [1990] Ch 265 at 286, 'Nothing passed between Tunisia and London but a stream of electrons'. Yet the idea of the physical existence of the traced property remains in rules like the rule in *Clayton's Case* and the rule of the lowest intermediate balance. *Foskett v McKeown* [2001] 1 AC 102 called for a rethink of the differing rules that govern common law and equitable tracing, but it has yet to happen.

Questions

Self-test questions

1   Define tracing.

2   What is the difference between common law and equitable tracing?

3   Is it possible to trace money at common law?

4   Explain when a wrongdoer may make any claim to his or her own money.

5   Why is it not possible to trace into an overdrawn bank account?

6   Explain the first in, first out rule.

7   Can the person tracing claim the increased value of trust property?

Discussion questions

1   Do the differences between common law and equitable tracing make any sense nowadays?

2   Is the rule in *Clayton's Case* a rule of law or just a rule of convenience?

3   Should a tracing claimant be able to claim part of the increased value of a mixed fund?

4   Should innocent volunteers, who have done no wrong, be forced to hand back trust property?

Assessment question

Brian is the manager of a Premier League association football club, Bristol United. In 2004 Melchester United buy Bristol United's best player, Junior, for £5,000,000. As a condition of agreeing to the transfer, Brian insists that Melchester United secretly pay him £500,000. Bristol United knows nothing about this payment.

The money is paid by Melchester to Brian's solicitor, Heep. Heep has received similar payments in the past on behalf of Brian. He does not consider it to be part of his job to ask Brian where Brian's money comes from.

Brian uses £250,000 to buy a house for his wife, Mary. The house is registered in her name and Brian tells her that the money is his bonus for winning promotion for Bristol United last year. She believes him.

Brian opens a bank account at Floyds Bank and deposits the other £250,000 there. The Bank knows that Brian is a well-paid football manager and does not question where the money comes from. Brian spends the money on two expensive motor cars, a Mercedes and a BMW, gambling, visits to night clubs, and other amusements typically enjoyed by football managers.

A Football Association investigation uncovers the secret payment to Brian. Bristol United wants to claim the £500,000.

In 2006 Mary's house is worth £300,000, Brian's bank account is £50,000 overdrawn, but he still owns the Mercedes and the BMW. Heep still owns a firm of solicitors which is earning large profits.

Advise Bristol United whether equitable remedies such as constructive trusts and tracing could be used to recover the £500,000.

Key cases

- *Foskett v McKeown* [2001] 1 AC 102 **(at 17.1.1, 17.1.2, 17.3.7, and 17.4.1)**

- *Re Diplock* [1948] Ch 465 **(at 17.3.1, 17.4.2, and 17.4.3)**

- *Re Hallett's Estate* (1879–80) LR 13 ChD 696 **(at 17.3.1 and 17.3.3)**

- *Bishopsgate Investment Management Ltd v Homan* [1995] Ch 211 **(at 17.3.5)**

- *Barlow Clowes International Ltd v Vaughan* [1992] 4 All ER 22 **(at 17.3.6)**

 # Further reading

P Millett 'Tracing and the Proceeds of Fraud' (1991) 107 *LQR* 71
This article reviews the main features of common law and equitable tracing and how they relate to the remedies available such as constructive trusts.

M Pawlowski 'The Demise of the Rule in *Clayton's Case*' [2003] *Conv* 339
Pawlowski looks at *Barlow Clowes International Ltd v Vaughan* [1992] 4 All ER 22, which did not follow *Clayton's Case*, and considers to what extent the rule of first in, first out survives.

G Virgo 'Vindicating Vindication: *Foskett v McKeown* reviewed' in AS Hudson (ed) *New Perspectives in Property Law, Obligations and Restitution* (London: Cavendish, 2003)
This is one of a number of published papers from a conference that consider the controversial decision of *Foskett v McKeown* [2001] 1 AC 102.

18

Trusts of the family home

Learning objectives

This chapter will help you to:

- understand that cohabitation gives no special legal status
- understand that a trust of land must be in writing
- understand that resulting and constructive trusts are an exception to the writing requirement
- distinguish between the two categories of trust in *Lloyds Bank v Rosset*
- appreciate that the judgment in *Lloyds Bank v Rosset* does not solve all the problems in this area
- distinguish between the claim to an equitable interest in the property and the quantification of that interest.

Introduction

This is an area where traditional trust law has had to adapt to changing economic and social conditions. Before the 1950s only a minority of married couples owned their own homes and cohabitation by unmarried couples was not very common. Nowadays cohabitation is not unusual and the majority of cohabitants and married couples own their own homes. House prices have risen steeply, which they did not in the past, and these homes are now very valuable property indeed.

In the past, wealthier couples employed marriage settlements, where their property was held on trust by trustees. (See Chapter 5 'The formality requirements and incompletely constituted trusts'.) With other couples it was normal to put the legal estate in the home in the name of the man, who was likely to be the main wage earner. That would seem to indicate that the house belonged solely to the man and the woman had no claim.

There were doctrines available in equity which were seized on and developed in order to find a possible solution. How those developments have progressed is the theme of this chapter. The doctrine of resulting trust, which holds that a party gains an equitable interest in the property by making a financial contribution, has existed for hundreds of years. (See Chapter 8 'Resulting trusts'.) Constructive trusts enable a party to claim an equitable interest where it would be 'unconscionable' for the legal owner to deny his or her claim. (See Chapter 16 'Constructive trusts'.) Proprietary estoppel means that the legal owner of the land is 'estopped' from going back on his promise to another person that that person has a claim to the land. (See Chapter 6 'Proprietary estoppel'.) All of these doctrines could be used by a partner claiming a share in a house against the partner that held the legal estate. They have now been synthesized into one overarching concept, that of the common intention constructive trust.

18.1 The myth of common law marriage

Nowadays couples who live together often own their home. If the couple separate, then there may be a legal dispute as to who owns the house or, if they share the ownership, the size of their respective shares.

If the couple is married, then under the Matrimonial Causes Act 1973 the court has wide discretionary powers to order the distribution of the couple's property. The court is not bound by who owns the property legally or equitably. Same sex couples may also marry under the Marriage (Same Sex Couples) Act 2013. Under the Civil Partnership Act 2004, couples of the same sex may register their partnership. Again, if the couple separate, the court has discretion as to how to order the distribution of their property.

Unmarried couples who live together do not have these statutory protections. If they are of the opposite sex then they do not even have the option of registering a civil partnership. Cohabitation is becoming increasingly common and it seems that many couples are ignorant of their lack of statutory protection, believing that living together can have the same legal consequences as marriage. 'Common law marriage' was abolished by the Marriage Act of 1753!

● **Stack v Dowden** [2007] 2 AC 432

(This case also appears at 18.1, 18.2.2, 18.8.3, 18.9, and 18.10.2.)

Baroness Hale at 450:

> Inter vivos disputes between unmarried cohabiting couples are still governed by the ordinary law. These disputes have become increasingly visible in recent years as more and more couples live together without marrying. The full picture has recently been painted by the Law Commission in Cohabitation: The Financial Consequences of Relationship Breakdown—A Consultation Paper, [2006] Consultation Paper No 179, Part 2, and its overview paper, paras 2.3 to 2.11. For example, the 2001 Census recorded over 10 million married couples in England and Wales, with over 7.5 million dependent children; but it also recorded over 2 million cohabiting couples, with over 1.25 million children dependent upon them. This was a 67 per cent increase in cohabitation over the previous 10 years and a doubling of the numbers of such households with dependent children. The Government Actuaries Department predicts that the proportion of couples cohabiting will continue to grow, from the present one in six of all couples to one in four by 2031.
>
> Cohabitation is much more likely to end in separation than is marriage, and cohabitations which end in separation tend to last for a shorter time than marriages which end in divorce. But increasing numbers of couples cohabit for long periods without marrying and their reasons for doing so vary from conscious rejection of marriage as a legal institution to regarding themselves 'as good as married' anyway: Law Commission, Consultation Paper No 179, Part 2, para 2.45. There is evidence of a widespread myth of the 'common law marriage' in which unmarried couples acquire the same rights as married couples after a period of cohabitation.

KEY POINT
Increasing numbers of people live together without being married, without realizing that they do not have the same legal rights as divorcing couples.

18.2 Declarations of trust

18.2.1 Land requires a written declaration of trust

The solution for cohabiting couples would be to write down and legally agree how they intend to share the property. As it is land, this must be done in writing and would usually take the form of a declaration of trust.

Law of Property Act 1925, s. 53

(1) (b) A declaration of trust respecting any land or any interest therein must be manifested and proved by some writing signed by some person who is able to declare such trust...

(See 5.2.1 'Land', and 5.4 'When the writing requirements can be waived'.) But also note s. 53(2) of the Law of Property Act 1925;

A written declaration of trust is not required if a resulting or constructive trust is involved.

If the couple does make a written declaration of trust, the declaration will provide the solution to any legal or equitable dispute about the property.

....

● *Pettit v Pettit* [1970] AC 777

(This case can also be found at 18.2.1, 18.3.1, and 18.5.3.)

Lord Upjohn at 813E:

> If the property in question is land there must be some lease or conveyance which shows how it was acquired. If that document declares not merely in whom the legal title is to vest but in whom the beneficial title is to vest that necessarily concludes the question of title as between the spouses for all time, and in the absence of fraud or mistake at the time of the transaction the parties cannot go behind it at any time thereafter even on death or the break-up of the marriage.

Pettit concerned a married couple, but the principle is the same for cohabiting couples. When a house is bought the conveyance will say who holds the legal estate in the land. It can be one of the couple or both of them. What a cohabiting couple should do is to add a declaration of trust and state their beneficial interests or how they share the house in equity. They could state that they share it equally or in any proportions that they choose to declare. Despite changes in the law since *Pettit*, a written declaration of trust would still be regarded as conclusive: *Pankhania v Chandegra* [2012] EWCA Civ 1438.

....

● *Pankhania v Chandegra* [2012] EWCA Civ 1438

A family combined together to buy a house for Mr and Mrs Chandegra. The legal estate was held in the joint names of Mrs Chandegra and her nephew, Pankhania, as tenants in common in equal shares. This was done because the Chandegra's earnings were low, but Pankhania had a good salary, which enabled them to obtain a mortgage. Pankhania did not live in the house or help pay for it.

HELD: The Court of Appeal followed *Pettit v Pettit* [1970] AC 777.

Patten LJ at para 13:

> For whatever reason, the parties (both of them of full age) had executed an express declaration of trust over the property in favour of themselves as tenants in common in equal shares and had therefore set out their respective beneficial entitlement as part of the purchase itself. In these circumstances, there was no need for the imposition of a constructive or common intention trust of the kind discussed in *Stack v Dowden* nor any possibility of inferring one because, as Baroness Hale recognized in paragraph 4 of her speech in that case, such a declaration of trust is regarded as conclusive unless varied by subsequent agreement or affected by proprietary estoppel.

18.2.2 Joint tenants or tenants in common

Even if the couple has been to a solicitor when they buy the property, they may not have decided how the property is to be shared. The process is mainly concerned with who holds the legal estate and this is often all that is completed. The couple could put the legal estate in the name of one of them or in joint names, when they would be known as joint tenants. They should also consider, but rarely do, how they are to hold the equitable interests in the property. They could specify that they are joint tenants or that they are tenants in common of the equitable interests. If they go for joint tenants, they hold the property in equal shares and if one dies the other automatically inherits the share of the deceased, which is known as the right of survivorship. If they choose a tenancy in common, then the couple can specify the size of each of their shares: it does not have to be a 50:50 split.

● **Stack v Dowden** [2007] 2 AC 432

(This case also appears at 18.1, 18.8.3, 18.9, and 18.10.2.)

Barry Stack and Dehra Dowden lived together without being married and their house was registered in their joint names. The conveyance contained a standard clause which stated that: '[t]he transferees declare that the survivor of them can give a valid receipt for capital money arising on a disposition of the land'. Lawyers would know that this meant that they were declaring a joint tenancy, because one of the features of a joint tenancy is that all the property goes to the survivor, the one who lives the longest.

HELD: Lord Neuberger at 473:

> In the present case, for instance, there is a disagreement as to the effect of the declaration in the transfer of the house to the parties that the survivor 'can give a valid receipt for capital money arising on the disposition of the land'. At any rate in the absence of any evidence that the effect of this provision was explained to the parties, I would reject the contention that it has the effect of operating as a declaration of joint beneficial ownership ... *Huntingford v Hobbs* [1993] 1 FCR 45. Quite apart from that, it seems to me that, in the absence of any evidence of contemporaneous advice to the parties as to the effect of the declaration, the alleged inference would simply be too technical, sophisticated, and subtle to be sustainable, at least in the context of the purchase of a home by two lay people.

Baroness Hale at 947:

> The Land Registry form has since changed. Form TR1, in use from 1 April 1998, provides a box for the transferees to declare whether they are to hold the property on trust for themselves as joint tenants, or on trust for themselves as tenants in common in equal shares, or on some other trusts which are inserted on the form. If this is invariably complied with, the problem confronting us here will eventually disappear. Unfortunately, however, the transfer will be valid whether or not this part of the form is completed.

In an ideal world then, a couple will declare a trust in writing and settle the issue of who owns the house and what their respective shares are if they both own it. Unfortunately, in the real world, a couple will probably be confused by the legal jargon and will not want to seem unromantic by insisting on making the legal position clear. Because of this, equity has tried to come up with a solution to cases where the couple has not made a written declaration of trust.

KEY POINT A declaration of a trust of land must be in writing and needs to specify how the equitable interests are held. 'It concludes the question of title for all time.'

18.3 Solutions from equity (historical explanation)

Property disputes between couples began to become common in the 1950s and 1960s. Many of the early cases involved married couples, because this was before divorce law was reformed and before the courts were allowed to redistribute the married couple's property, irrespective of who 'owned' it. The courts found a number of ways of solving disputes where a person claimed a share in the property. An express declaration of a trust of land must be in writing, but this does not apply to resulting and constructive trusts. (See 18.2.1 'Land requires a written declaration of trust'.) Section 18.3 'Solutions from equity (historical explanation)' is designed to show how the law developed historically. As we shall see, from 18.4 'Sole name cases—acquiring a beneficial interest: the two categories in *Lloyds Bank v Rosset*' onwards, it was the constructive trust that proved to be the most suitable vehicle for determining family home disputes.

515

18.3.1 Resulting trust

● *Pettit v Pettit* [1970] AC ???

(This case can also be found at 18.2.1, 18.3.1, and 18.5.3.)

Hilda Pettit inherited a house, sold it, and purchased 'Tinkers Cottage' with the proceeds, where she lived with her husband Harold. The legal estate was in Hilda's name, but Harold claimed a share on the grounds that he had spent money and effort in redecorating the house.

HELD: The House of Lords rejected his claim, but discussed the different bases on which such claims were made.

Lord Upjohn at 815G:

One of these was resulting trust. His Lordship cited *Dyer v Dyer* 1788 2 Cox Eq Cases 92 (see 8.4.2).

> But where both spouses contribute to the acquisition of a property, then my own view (of course in the absence of evidence) is that they intended to be joint beneficial owners and this is so whether the purchase be in the joint names or in the name of one. This is the result of an application of the presumption of resulting trust.

A spouse or cohabitant could contribute financially by contributing towards a deposit or purchase price or by paying the mortgage instalments.

The principles of resulting trust could be used in property disputes between cohabitants. If that was the case, the person would gain an equitable interest in proportion to the size of his or her financial contribution. So if the contribution was for half the purchase price, then half the house would be his or hers. When we look at contributions, such as repaying the mortgage, it is harder to assess the size of an equitable interest. The doctrine of resulting trusts may not provide the ideal solution in the world of today.

Lord Diplock at 823–4:

> The consensus of judicial opinion which gave rise to the presumptions of 'advancement' and 'resulting trust' in transactions between husband and wife is to be found in cases relating to the propertied classes of the 19th century and the first quarter of the 20th century among whom marriage settlements were common, and it was unusual for the wife to contribute by her earnings to the family income. It was not until after World War II that the courts were required to consider the proprietary rights in family assets of a different social class. The advent of legal aid, the wider employment of married women in industry, commerce and the professions and the emergence of a property-owning, particularly a real-property-mortgaged-to-a-building-society-owning, democracy has compelled the courts to direct their attention to this during the last 20 years. It would, in my view, be an abuse of the legal technique for ascertaining or imputing intention to apply to transactions between the post-war generations of married couples 'presumptions' which are based on inferences of fact which an earlier generation of judges drew as to the most likely intentions of earlier generations of spouses belonging to the propertied classes of a different social era.

Lord Diplock's prophecy has proved true and nowadays, resulting trusts would not be used in a family home case. Instead, the resulting trust has been developed into the second type of constructive trust in *Lloyds v Rosset* [1991] 1 AC 107. (See 18.4.2 'Common intention constructive trust type 2—direct financial contributions'.)

KEY POINT Under a resulting trust, if a person contributes to the purchase of property, he or she will have an equitable interest in that property, proportionate to the size of that contribution.

18.3.2 Proprietary estoppel

(See Chapter 6 'Proprietary estoppel' for a fuller account.)

This is an old equitable principle, which can be useful in property disputes. There have been many attempts to define it, but nowadays, proprietary estoppel depends upon representation, reliance, and detriment.

In the cohabitation context one of the couple might believe that they have some sort of legal claim to the house. Because of this they might spend money to help buy the house or do work on the house thinking that they own at least part of it. This forms the reliance and the detriment. Their partner encourages them to do this, or at the very least does not tell them that they are wrong to believe that they have some sort of claim to the house. This is the representation.

● *Pascoe v Turner* [1979] 1 WLR 431

Mr Pascoe bought a house which was in his name alone and lived there with Ms Turner. He told her 'The house is yours and everything in it'. Mr Pascoe later left her and she spent £230 on repairs and improvements such as plumbing, new carpets, roof repairs, and redecoration. Mr Pascoe wanted her to leave the house.

HELD: Cumming-Bruce LJ: As this was land, writing of some kind would normally be needed to give Turner any claim to the house: s. 53 of the Law of Property Act 1925. Estoppel allowed an exception to this rule.

At 436:

> For this is a case of estoppel arising from the encouragement and acquiescence of the plaintiff between 1973 and 1976 when, in reliance upon his declaration that he was giving and, and later, that he had given the house to her, she spent a substantial part of her small capital upon repairs and improvements to the house.

At 438:

> …the court must decide what is the minimum equity to do justice to her having regard to the way in which she changed her position for the worse by reason of the acquiescence and encouragement of the legal owner.

At 439:

> Weighing such considerations this court concludes that the equity to which the facts in this case give rise can only be satisfied by compelling the plaintiff to give effect to his promise and her expectations.

The house was awarded to Ms Turner.

KEY POINT
Proprietary estoppel applies when the claimant acts to their detriment relying on the promise of another.

The thinking of the court was that Pascoe had promised Ms Turner the house and because she had believed him and acted to her detriment, he now had to make good his promise.

Proprietary estoppel has been absorbed into the first category of constructive trust in *Lloyds Bank v Rosset* [1991] 1 AC 107. (See 18.4.1 'Common intention constructive trust type 1—oral agreement and acting to one's detriment'.) Occasionally, estoppel is still used in family home cases, if no common intention can be found. See 6.8.2 'A proprietary estoppel can be based on a representation' for an example: *Southwell v Blackburn* [2014] EWCA Civ 1347.

18.3.3 Constructive trust

It is hard to define exactly what a constructive trust is. (See Chapter 16 'Constructive trusts' generally and 16.2 'General application of constructive trust' in particular.) The basic idea is that the holder of the legal estate has behaved unconscionably, by perhaps breaking a promise or deceiving the other party.

● *Paragon Finance plc v DB Thakerar & Co (a firm)* [1999] 1 All ER 401

Millett LJ at 409:

> The constructive trust arises by the operation of law whenever the facts are such that it would be unconscionable for an owner to deny that another person has acquired a beneficial interest in the property.

This principle can be applied to a situation of a cohabiting couple, where the legal owner is denying that their partner has any interest in the property. The difficulty that the courts have found is in defining what would be unconscionable.

● ***Eves v Eves*** [1975] 1 WLR 1338

(This case also appears at 18.5.1.)

Janet lived with Stuart Eves and changed her surname to Eves. They were both married to other people. Stuart bought a house and paid the mortgage. The legal estate was in his name alone, because he told Janet that her name could not go on the title deeds, as she was under 21. They had two children together and Janet did a lot of physical work on the house such as stripping wallpaper, painting, breaking up concrete with a 14lb sledgehammer, demolishing a shed, and gardening. Stuart left and married Gloria. They succeeded, by threats, in evicting Janet from the house, but she claimed a share in it.

HELD: Lord Denning MR at 1341:

> In strict law she has no claim on him whatever. She is not his wife. He is not bound to provide a roof over her head. He can turn her into the street. She is not entitled to any maintenance from him for herself. Such is the strict law. And a few years ago even equity would not have helped her. But things have altered now. Equity is not past the age of child bearing. One of her latest progeny is a constructive trust of a new model. Lord Diplock [in *Gissing v Gissing*] brought it into the world and we have nourished it.

At 1342:

> Although Janet did not make any financial contribution, it seems to me that this property was acquired and maintained by both by their joint efforts with the intention that it should be used for their joint benefit until they were married and thereafter as long as the marriage continued. At any rate, Stuart Eves cannot be heard to say the contrary. He told her that it was to be their home for them and their children. He gained her confidence by telling her that he intended to put it in their joint names (just as married couples often do) but that it was not possible until she was 21. The judge described this as a 'trick' and said that it 'did not do him much credit as a man of honour'. The man never intended to put it in joint names but always determined to have it in his own name. It seems to me that he should be judged by what he told her—by what he led her to believe—and not by his own intent which he kept to himself.

The other two members of the Court of Appeal did not wish to go as far as Lord Denning, but agreed with him that Janet should have a quarter share. They thought that there was an agreement or arrangement between Stuart and Janet upon which she had acted.

Brightman J at 1345:

> If, however, it was part of the bargain between the parties, expressed or to be implied, that the plaintiff should contribute her labour towards the reparation of a house in which she was to have some beneficial interest, then I think that the arrangement becomes one to which the law can give effect. This seems to be consistent with the reasoning of the speeches in *Gissing v Gissing*.

The House of Lords had tried to bring together the concepts of resulting trust, proprietary estoppel, and constructive trust in a very influential judgment.

KEY POINT
Constructive trusts allow the courts to enforce an oral agreement between a couple, if it would be unconscionable not to do so.

● ***Gissing v Gissing*** [1971] AC 886

(This case can also be found at 18.5.3, 18.6, 18.7, and 18.8.1.)

Lord Diplock at 905:

> A resulting, implied or constructive trust, and it is unnecessary for present purposes to distinguish between these three classes of trust, is created by a transaction between the trustee and the cestui que trust in connection with the acquisition by the trustee of a legal estate in land, whenever the trustee has so conducted himself that it would be inequitable to allow him to deny to the cestui que trust a beneficial interest in the land acquired. And he will be held so to have conducted himself if by his words or conduct he has induced the cestui que trust to act to his own detriment in the reasonable belief that by so acting he was acquiring a beneficial interest in the land.

The Court of Appeal in *Eves v Eves* [1975] 1 WLR 1338 claimed that they were following *Gissing*, but the individual judges came to different interpretations of the law. In the 1970s and 1980s there were many court decisions on the family home and judges had different approaches to the law: some based on resulting trust, some on estoppel, and some on constructive trust.

18.4 Sole name cases—acquiring a beneficial interest: the two categories in *Lloyds Bank v Rosset*

The House of Lords was forced to consider the issue again and restate the principles in *Gissing v Gissing* [1971] AC 886, but this time more clearly. They favoured the constructive trust approach as the most inclusive, but drew upon elements of resulting trust and proprietary estoppel to formulate their two types of common intention constructive trust. The party without the legal estate has to prove their entitlement to a beneficial interest against the holder of the legal estate, by establishing that one or both types of constructive trust exist.

18.4.1 Common intention constructive trust type 1—oral agreement and acting to one's detriment

● **Lloyds Bank plc v Rosset** [1991] 1 AC 107

Lord Bridge at 132–3:

> The first and fundamental question which must always be resolved is whether, independently of any inference to be drawn from the conduct of the parties in the course of sharing the house as their home and managing their joint affairs, there has at any time prior to acquisition, or exceptionally at some later date, been any agreement, arrangement or understanding reached between them that the property is to be shared beneficially. The finding of an agreement or arrangement to share in this sense can only, I think, be based on evidence of express discussions between the partners, however imperfectly remembered and however imprecise their terms may have been. Once a finding to this effect is made it will only be necessary for the partner asserting a claim to a beneficial interest against the partner entitled

to the legal estate to show that he or she has acted to his or her detriment or significantly altered his or her position in reliance on the agreement in order to give rise to a constructive trust or proprietary estoppel.

KEY POINT A claim to a beneficial interest in the family home can be based on an oral agreement between the couple, but the claimant must also act to their detriment in relying on the agreement.

18.4.2 Common intention constuctive trust type 2—direct financial contributions

● *Lloyds Bank plc v Rosset* [1991] 1 AC 107

Lord Bridge at 132–3:

> In sharp contrast with this situation is the very different one where there is no evidence to support a finding of an agreement or arrangement to share, however reasonable it might have been for the parties to reach such an arrangement if they had applied their minds to the question, and where the court must rely entirely on the conduct of the parties both as the basis from which to infer a common intention to share the property beneficially and as the conduct relied on to give rise to a constructive trust. In this situation direct contributions to the purchase price by the partner who is not the legal owner, whether initially or by payment of mortgage instalments, will readily justify the inference necessary to the creation of a constructive trust. But, as I read the authorities, it is at least extremely doubtful whether anything less will do.

(The facts of *Lloyds Bank v Rosset* can be found at 18.5.3 'Actions that do not qualify as detrimental reliance'.)

KEY POINT A claim to a beneficial interest in the family home can be based on a direct financial contribution to the purchase price or payment of mortgage instalments.

18.4.3 *Lloyds Bank v Rosset* and other cases

Lord Bridge was trying to summarize and make sense of the previous case law and he found it helpful to say that there were two distinct categories of case. The older cases had not made this clear-cut distinction and it is important to bear this in mind when studying the cases before 1991. He was also not very specific as to what type of trust this actually was, referring to constructive trust and proprietary estoppel in the first category and constructive trust in the second category. Previously, cases in the second category had usually been referred to as resulting trusts (see 18.3.1 'Resulting trust'). However, *Lloyds Bank v Rosset* [1991] 1 AC 107 is still regarded as the authoritative statement of the law and subsequent cases have followed it. Earlier cases are also now reinterpreted in the light of what Lord Bridge said. The House of Lords in *Stack v Dowden* [2007] 2 AC 432 and the Supreme Court in *Jones v Kernott* [2012] 1 AC 776 have confirmed that we are dealing with constructive trusts here, but have criticized the strictness of the *Rosset* approach. They recommend that the law should be further liberalized along the lines of the Law Commission reports summarized at 18.10 'Reform of the law'. For the moment though, *Lloyds Bank v Rosset* has not been overruled and it would take a Supreme Court case on that point to do so.

Oral agreement and detriment

18.5.1 The oral agreement

It is important to realize that the claimant must prove both requirements. There must be an oral agreement that the couple is to share the equitable interest in the house. The claimant must also prove that he or she did something to act to his or her detriment.

....

● **Eves v Eves** [1975] 1 WLR 1338

(This case also appears at 18.3.3.)

Brightman J at 1345:

> If, however, it was part of the bargain between the parties, expressed or to be implied, that the plaintiff should contribute her labour towards the reparation of a house in which she was to have some beneficial interest, then I think that the arrangement becomes one to which the law can give effect.

Janet Eves acted to her detriment by contributing considerable physical labour to repairing the house. She only did this because she thought that she had a share in the house.

Lloyds Bank v Rosset [1991] 1 AC 107 tightens the law in one respect. It is no longer acceptable to *imply* an agreement as Brightman J suggests. There must be evidence of the existence of an actual oral agreement, 'express discussions' as Lord Bridge calls them. The couple must have at some point, ideally when they acquired the house, sat down and agreed how they would share it. It is accepted, however, that their memories may now be faulty.

....

● **Grant v Edwards** [1986] Ch 638

Between 1967 and 1969 Grant, a married woman, had a casual relationship with Edwards. In 1969 Grant gave birth to a son, and the couple decided to buy a house and live together on a more permanent basis. Edwards paid the purchase price, the legal costs, and made the repayments on the mortgage and the house was put into the names of Edwards and his brother. Edwards told Grant that this was done in case her ownership of the house affected her divorce proceedings. This was just an excuse. From 1972 Grant was employed and she made a substantial contribution to the household budget, which made it easier for Edwards to pay the mortgage. In 1975 the house was damaged by fire and insurance money was paid out to Edwards. The money remaining after the house was repaired was paid into a joint building society account. The couple separated in 1980 and Grant claimed a share in the house.

HELD: Nourse LJ at 648–9:

> It would be possible to take the view that the mere moving into the house by the woman amounted to an acting upon the common intention. But that was evidently not the view of the majority in *Eves v Eves* [1975] 1 WLR 1338. And the reason for that may be that, in the absence of evidence, the law is not so cynical as to infer that a woman will only go to live with a man to whom she is not married if she understands that she is to have an interest in their home. So what sort of conduct is required? In my judgment it must be conduct on which the woman could not reasonably have been expected to embark unless she was to have

an interest in the house. If she was not to have such an interest, she could reasonably be expected to go and live with her lover, but not, for example to wield a 14lb sledge hammer in the front garden. In adopting the latter kind of conduct she is seen to act to her detriment on the faith of the common intention.

In order to see how the present case stands in the light of the views above expressed, I must summarise the crucial facts as found, expressly or impliedly, by the judge. They are the following. (1) The defendant told the plaintiff that her name was not going onto the title because it would cause some prejudice in the matrimonial proceedings between her and her husband. The defendant never had any real intention of replacing his brother with the plaintiff when those proceedings were at an end. Just as in *Eves v Eves*, these facts appear to me to raise a clear inference that there was an understanding between the plaintiff and the defendant, or a common intention, that the plaintiff was to have some sort of proprietary interest in the house; otherwise no excuse for not putting her name onto the title would have been needed.

Was the conduct of the plaintiff in making substantial indirect contributions to the instalments payable under both mortgages conduct upon which she could not reasonably have been expected to embark unless she was to have an interest in the house? I answer that question in the affirmative. I cannot see upon what other basis she could reasonably have been expected to give the defendant such substantial assistance in paying off mortgages on his house. I therefore conclude that the plaintiff did act to her detriment on the faith of the common intention between her and the defendant that she was to have some sort of proprietary interest in the house...

KEY POINT
An oral agreement *and* an indirect financial contribution that enables the other partner to pay the mortgage instalments secure an equitable interest in the property.

In *Grant v Edwards* it can be seen how the oral agreement and the detrimental reliance are entwined. Both are needed in order to claim a share in the house in equity. As in *Eves v Eves* [1975] 1 WLR 1338, there was an agreement between the couple that the woman should have an interest in the house. In both cases the man agreed that the woman had a share, but made excuses as to why it could not be put in writing. Relying on this agreement the woman acted to her detriment, physical work in *Eves*, a contribution to the household budget enabling the man to pay the mortgage in *Grant*.

It is possible for the couple to agree orally that one of them is *not* to have a share.

● ***Thomas v Fuller-Brown*** [1988] 1 FLR 237

Harry Fuller-Brown, a bricklayer, moved in with Pamela Thomas. Pamela bought a new house for them both to live in for £23,500. The legal estate was in her name and she paid £13,500 in cash, from the sale of her previous home, and took out a £10,000 mortgage for the rest. Harry, who was unemployed and claiming benefit, made no financial contribution and indeed Pamela allowed him some 'pocket money' each week. Later, Pamela received an improvement grant from the council and 'an agreement was reached that he (Harry) should carry out the work provided for by the council grant and organise it, in return for her keeping him'. Harry carried out £15,500 worth of work, which included a two-storey extension, a through-lounge, electrical and plumbing work, replastering and redecorating throughout, landscaping the garden, laying a driveway, repairing the chimney and the roof, repointing the gable end, building an entry hall, rebuilding the kitchen, and installing new stairs. Pamela moved out and wanted possession of the house, but Harry claimed that his work gave him a share in it, that Pamela had agreed to this, and indeed they had once planned to marry.

HELD: Slade LJ at 240:

It is perhaps understandable that the defendant, having devoted a substantial amount of labour to the house, though no money, and having seen it correspondingly increase in value, should consider that he should be entitled in law to claim some interest in it. However, it must be said that under English law the mere fact that A expends money or labour on B's property does not by itself entitle A to an interest in the property.

At 246:

…it is the *common intention* of the parties that is relevant. It takes two parties to make an agreement or form a common intention, not merely one. On the judge's findings of primary fact, which I think we cannot disturb, the plaintiff never did agree to marry him and never did lead him to suppose that by doing these improvements he would ever acquire an interest in the house.

18.5.2 Actions that qualify as detrimental reliance

Detriment can take many forms and the courts have never fully defined what is and is not acceptable as detriment. Physical work on the house was regarded as detrimental reliance in *Eves v Eves* [1975] 1 WLR 1338 and an indirect financial contribution was acceptable in *Grant v Edwards* [1986] Ch 638 at 18.5.1 'The oral agreement'.

● ***Ungurian v Lesnoff*** [1990] Ch 206

Anatole Ungurian, who was Lebanese, and Kamilla Lesnoff, who was Polish, formed a relationship and decided to live in London. He bought a house, 136 Muswell Hill Road, in 1970, in which they both lived together, until he left in 1974. Litigation began in 1980, when Ungurian claimed that it was his house and Lesnoff should leave. To be with Ungurian, Lesnoff had left her flat in Poland, which she could have lived in for the rest of her life, and her job at a university. She acquired the surname Lesnoff by entering into a marriage of convenience with a Frenchman. (It was easier for a French citizen to gain permission to stay in England than a Pole.) She had found the house in London and carried out extensive alteration work, for which Mr Ungurian had paid.

HELD: Vinelott J at 222:

I am satisfied that it was understood from Christmas 1968 onwards that, if Mrs Lesnoff threw in her lot with Mr Ungurian and made her home permanently abroad, he would provide her with the security of a home; something on which, amongst other things, she could rely if anything happened to him. Mrs Lesnoff was giving up a great deal, and moreover the two of them, with their experience of life behind the Iron Curtain, knew that the loss of her flat and the severance of her ties with Poland would be irrecoverable.

At 223:

In summary, therefore, I am not satisfied that the house was bought by Mr Ungurian with the intention that it would belong to Mrs Lesnoff, either immediately or when she gave up her flat in Poland and obtained permission to live permanently abroad; but I am satisfied that it was bought with the common intention that Mrs Lesnoff would be entitled to live there with her children, sharing it with Mr Ungurian when he was in England, and with any of his children who were here for the purpose of being educated.

At 224:

Mr Ungurian held the house on trust to permit Mrs Lesnoff to reside in it during her life unless and until Mr Ungurian, with her consent, sold the property and bought another residence for her in substitution for it.

Mrs Lesnoff succeeded in her claim, based on their oral agreement and her acting to her detriment. The judge does not make absolutely clear which of her actions were considered detrimental and which were not: it is rather the cumulative effect of them. The oral agreement is unusually specific for this type of case. Usually it is that a partner should have a share in the house, but the couple rarely discuss details such as the size of the share. Here the agreement was that she could stay in the house for her life, which is translated by the judge into legal terms as a life interest.

In the following case the 'detriment' is different again, rather than particularly related to the acquisition of the house.

● *Hammond v Mitchell* [1991] 1 WLR 1127

In the summer of 1977, Tom Hammond, a married man of 40 separated from his wife, was setting off for a ride in Epping Forest when he had a chance encounter with Miss Vicky Mitchell, a 21-year-old girl who had stopped her car to ask the way. Their conversation led to further meetings and within a very short time they were living together. He was a trader, dealing in those days principally in second-hand cars. She was a Bunny Girl employed at a high salary by the Playboy Club in Mayfair as one of their croupiers. They had two children together and participated together in various business enterprises. In 1979 Mr Hammond bought a bungalow in Essex, paying half in cash, from the sale of his flat, and the other half on mortgage. Later on their business activities shifted to Spain and again Mr Hammond bought a house, which they both used. He also bought Vicky a half share in a Spanish restaurant, which he put in her name. In 1988 Vicky left him and she claimed a share in his assets.

HELD: Waite J:

> Miss Mitchell had a half share in the bungalow, because that was what was agreed. There had never been any agreement that she should have a share in the Spanish properties.

At 1131:

Shortly after the purchase of the bungalow Hammond told Miss Mitchell:

> I'll have to put the house in my name because I have tax problems due to the fact that my wife burnt all my account books and my caravan was burnt down with all the records of my car sales in it. The tax man would be interested, and if I could prove my money had gone back into a property I'd be safeguarded. Later the same day he mentioned to her that he was going through a divorce and that it would be in his best interests if he was to put the property into his name. Soon after completion he said to her, 'Don't worry about the future because when we are married it will be half yours anyway and I'll always look after you and [the boy].'

At 1137:

Was there an oral agreement upon which Miss Mitchell had acted to her detriment?

> The answer to that question should, in my judgment, in both its parts be 'Yes'. In relation to the bungalow there was express discussion on the occasions I have already described which, although not directed with any precision as to proprietary interests, was sufficient to amount to an understanding at least that the bungalow was to be shared beneficially.
>
> Miss Mitchell, by her participation wholeheartedly in what may loosely be called the commercial activities based on the bungalow, not only acted consistently with that view of the situation but also acted to her detriment in that she gave her full support on two occasions to

speculative ventures which, had they turned out unfavourably, might have involved the entire bungalow property being sold up to repay the bank an indebtedness to which the house and land were all committed to the hilt.

At 1139:

The parties in such cases need to fully explain to the court what they claim to have agreed.

The primary emphasis accorded by the law in cases of this kind to express discussions between the parties ('however imperfectly remembered and however imprecise their terms') means that the tenderest exchanges of a common law courtship may assume an unforeseen significance many years later when they are brought under equity's microscope and subjected to an analysis under which many thousands of pounds of value may be liable to turn on fine questions as to whether the relevant words were spoken in earnest or in dalliance and with or without representational intent. This requires that the express discussions to which the court's initial inquiries will be addressed should be pleaded in the greatest detail, both as to language and as to circumstance.

Miss Mitchell and her partner agreed that she had an interest in the bungalow. When the bungalow was mortgaged to raise funds for their business enterprises she signed a form accepting that the bank's claims had priority over her claims to the property. She would not have done this unless she had thought that she had an equitable interest in the property. Both requirements were satisfied: there was an oral agreement and she acted to her detriment.

18.5.3 Actions that do not qualify as detrimental reliance

If we consider the facts of the key case, *Lloyds Bank v Rosset [1991] 1 AC 107* (at 18.4.1 'Common intention constructive trust type 1—oral agreement and acting to one's detriment' and 18.4.2 'Common intention constructive trust type 2—direct financial contributions'), we can see that Mrs Rosset failed on both the elements of an oral agreement and acting to her detriment.

· ·

● *Lloyds Bank plc v Rosset* [1991] 1 AC 107

Mr and Mrs Rosset had married in 1972 and had two children. In 1982 he inherited money from his grandmother in Switzerland. The Rossets decided to buy a dilapidated farmhouse. Mr Rosset used most of his inheritance to do this and borrowed money from his bank, Lloyds, secured on the farmhouse. The farmhouse was in Mr Rosset's sole name, because the trustee, his uncle, of the Swiss fund insisted that this should be so. The Rossets moved into the farmhouse and Mr Rosset paid for building work. Mrs Rosset coordinated and supervised the work of the builders, helped her husband plan the renovation, and decorated rooms. Mr Rosset could not pay the bank and the bank claimed possession of the farmhouse. Mrs Rosset and the two children remained living there and Mr Rosset moved out. Mrs Rosset resisted the bank, claiming that she had an equitable share in the house.

HELD: Lord Bridge at 127:

The case pleaded and carefully particularised by Mrs Rosset in support of her claim to an equitable interest in the property was that it had been expressly agreed between her and her husband in conversations before November 1982 that the property was to be jointly owned and that in reliance on this agreement she had made a significant contribution in kind to the acquisition of the property by the work she had personally undertaken in the course of the renovation of the property which was sufficient to give rise to a constructive trust in her favour.

Lord Bridge rejected this claim, as the judge in the original trial had concluded that there was no agreement:

At 128:

> It was settled that the property should be transferred into the name of the first defendant alone to achieve the provision of funds from Switzerland, but in the period from August 1982 to 23 November 1982 when the contracts were exchanged, the defendants did not decide whether the second defendant should have any interest in the property.

Mrs Rosset had not acted to her detriment.

At 131:

> It was common ground that Mrs Rosset was extremely anxious that the new matrimonial home should be ready for occupation before Christmas if possible. In these circumstances it would seem the most natural thing in the world for any wife, in the absence of her husband abroad, to spend all the time she could spare and to employ any skills she might have, such as the ability to decorate a room, in doing all she could to accelerate progress of the work quite irrespective of any expectation she might have of enjoying a beneficial interest in the property.

> On any view the monetary value of Mrs Rosset's work expressed as a contribution to a property acquired at a cost exceeding £70,000 must have been so trifling as to be almost **de minimis**. I should myself have had considerable doubt whether Mrs Rosset's contribution to the work of renovation was sufficient to support a claim to a constructive trust ...

De minimis— Latin—too small to matter.

KEY POINTS Two points can be observed from the facts of this case. First, the oral agreement should be made at the time the property was acquired and, secondly, the detriment has to be substantial to count. To make a comparison, Janet Eves in *Eves v Eves* [1975] WLR 1338 (see 18.3.3 'Constructive trust' and 18.5.1 'The oral agreement') did a lot more work on the house than Mrs Rosset and had an oral agreement with her partner.

Pettit v Pettit [1970] AC 777 is similar, as Mr Pettit claimed that he had spent £300 renovating the house, but this was not enough to secure an equitable interest.

● *Pettit v Pettit* [1970] AC 777

(This case can also be found at 18.2.1 and 18.3.1.)

HELD: Lord Morris at 805:

> I do not think that the mere circumstances taken by itself that one spouse does work of reno-vation to a house belonging to the other spouse has the result that some beneficial interest in the house is acquired by the former.

Child rearing and housekeeping alone are not regarded as detriment.

● *Burns v Burns* [1984] Ch 317

(This case can also be found at 18.7.)

Valerie Burns moved in with Patrick Burns in 1961 and they lived in rented accommodation. After their second child was born Patrick bought a house for them to live in, which he paid for and which was in his name. Valerie made no financial contribution, as she did not work, because she was looking after the house and children. After 1975 she did work, but her earnings were not needed to pay the household expenses. In 1980 Valerie left Patrick and she claimed a share in the house. Patrick sought possession of the house.

HELD: Fox LJ at 327–8:

> It seems to me that at the time of the acquisition of the house nothing occurred between the parties to raise an equity which would prevent the defendant denying the plaintiff's claim...there was no understanding or arrangement that the plaintiff would go out to work to assist with the family finances; the defendant did nothing to lead her to change her position in the belief that she would have an interest in the house. It is true that she contemplated living with the defendant in the house and, no doubt, that she would do housekeeping and look after the children. But those facts do not carry with them any implication of a common intention that the plaintiff should have an interest in the house. Taken by themselves they are simply not strong enough to bear such an implication.

At 331:

> But, one asks, can the fact that the plaintiff performed domestic duties in the house and looked after the children be taken into account? I think it is necessary to keep in mind the nature of the right which is being asserted. The court has no jurisdiction to make such order as it might think fair; the powers conferred by the *Matrimonial Causes Act 1973* in relation to the property of married persons do not apply to unmarried couples.
>
> But the mere fact that parties live together and do the ordinary domestic tasks is, in my view, no indication at all that they thereby intended to alter the existing property rights of either of them.

KEY POINT Valerie Burns lost because there was no evidence of an oral agreement, and even if there had been, being a housekeeper and mother did not qualify as detrimental reliance. People do not do these things because they think that they have an equitable interest in the house.

thinking points

Some actions count as detrimental reliance and some do not. Is this fair or logically justifiable? Heavy work on a garden and house is detrimental reliance, but bringing up children is not. The detriment must be something more than someone would normally do just while living in their home and indicate that they are doing this because they believe that they have some sort of claim to the home. The way that the evidence is portrayed in court can be crucial as to whether or not detriment is found and assumptions about what is 'normal' behaviour for men and women may enter into the process. See A Lawson 'The Things We Do For Love: Detrimental Reliance and the Family Home' (1996) Legal Studies 218.

18.6 Financial contributions

In this second category from *Lloyds Bank v Rosset [1991] 1 AC 107* (see 18.4.2 'Common intention constructive trust type 2—direct financial contributions') the claimant has to show that he or she contributed financially to the purchase of the house. The advantage for the claimant in this category is that he or she does not have to prove that there was ever any oral agreement about sharing the equitable interest in the home. The court will look at the conduct of the parties to 'infer a common intention'. The disadvantage for the claimant is that Lord Bridge only mentions two types of financial contribution: direct contribution to the original purchase price or paying the mortgage.

Some of the older cases show that lesser contributions do not secure an equitable interest.

● *Gissing v Gissing* [1971] AC 886

(This case can also be found at 18.3.3, 18.7, and 18.8.1.)

Violet and Raymond Gissing were a married couple and the family home was in Raymond's name. He took out a mortgage to pay for it and also had a loan from his employers. Violet's contributions were £220 from her savings to pay for a lawn and furniture. Later on she contributed from her earnings to the housekeeping and paid for her own and her son's clothes. In 1961 Raymond left Violet for a younger woman. Violet alleged that he told her 'Don't worry about the house: it's yours.' Later Raymond lost his job and wanted to sell the house, and Violet claimed that she owned a share of it.

HELD: Lord Diplock at 909:

> Where the wife has made no initial contribution to the cash deposit and legal charges and no direct contribution to the mortgage instalments nor *any adjustment to her contribution to other expenses of the household which it can be inferred was referable to the acquisition of the house*, there is in the absence of evidence of an express agreement between the parties no material to justify the court in inferring that it was the common intention of the parties that she should have any beneficial interest in a matrimonial home conveyed into the sole name of the husband, merely because she continued to contribute out of her own earnings or private income to other expenses of the household.

Yet again the claimant might have had a case under the first category in *Rosset* if there had been an oral agreement, but there was not. There would have had to have been a pre-existing agreement, probably when her husband acquired the house.

In *Gissing v Gissing*, Lord Diplock at 910:

KEY POINT
Minor contributions to household expenses do not secure an equitable interest in the house.

> The learned judge was prepared to accept that after the marriage had broken down the husband said to his wife: 'Don't worry about the house—it's yours'; but this had not been relied upon, at any rate in your Lordship's house, as an acknowledgement of a pre-existing agreement on which the wife had acted to her detriment so as to give rise to a resulting, implied or constructive trust...

Her limited, indirect, financial contributions were not enough to gain a share under the second *Rosset* category.

Indirect financial contributions

Generally couples who are living together pool their resources. Let us say that the man has agreed with the company providing the mortgage that he will be responsible for repaying it. It may be that he is only able to afford these payments because the woman (say) is contributing from her earnings to their shared household budget. We have already seen in 18.5.1 'The oral agreement', from *Grant v Edwards* [1986] Ch 638, that indirect financial contributions can count, if there is also an oral agreement that the claimant has a share in the house.

However, if there is *not* an oral agreement Lord Bridge in *Lloyds Bank v Rosset* [1991] 1 AC 107 seems to have excluded this kind of indirect financial contribution from his second category. He only mentions contributions to the purchase price and repaying the mortgage, and then says at 133: 'But as I read the authorities, it is at least extremely doubtful whether anything less will do.' (See 18.4.2 'Common intention constructive trust type 2—direct financial contributions' for the full wording.) However, on the same page Lord Bridge had confirmed that he was just attempting a brief survey of the existing law and he confirmed that *Gissing v Gissing* [1971] AC 886 was a leading case. That case seems to state that indirect financial contributions can secure an equitable interest in the house.

● *Gissing v Gissing* [1971] AC 886

(This case can also be found at 18.3.3, 18.6, and 18.8.1.)

Lord Diplock at 909:

> Where the wife has made no initial contribution to the cash deposit and legal charges and no direct contribution to the mortgage instalments nor any adjustment to her contribution to other expenses of the household which it can be inferred was referable to the acquisition of the house, there is in the absence of evidence of an express agreement between the parties no material to justify the court in inferring that it was the common intention of the parties that she should have any beneficial interest in a matrimonial home conveyed into the sole name of the husband, merely because she continued to contribute out of her own earnings or private income to other expenses of the household.

This is a repeat of the quotation given in 18.6 'Financial contributions', with the crucial words highlighted. It seems to suggest that indirect financial contributions can gain a party a share in the house. This is so even if there is no oral agreement between the partners.

A later case also supports the idea that substantial, indirect financial contributions can gain a claimant a share in the equitable interest of the house, without the need for an additional oral agreement.

● *Burns v Burns* [1984] Ch 317

The full facts are at 18.5.3 'Actions that do not qualify as detrimental reliance'. After 1975 Valerie Burns worked, but her earnings were not needed to pay the household expenses. In 1980 Patrick left and Valerie claimed a share in the house.

HELD: Fox LJ at 330–1:

> There remains the question of housekeeping and domestic duties. So far as housekeeping expenses are concerned, I do not doubt that (the house being bought in the man's name) if the woman goes out to work in order to provide money for the family expenses, as a result of which she spends her earnings on the housekeeping and the man is thus able to pay the mortgage instalments and other expenses out of his earnings, it can be inferred that there was a common intention that the woman should have an interest in the house—since she will have made an indirect financial contribution to the mortgage instalments. But that is not this case.
>
> I think it would be quite unreal to say that; overall, she made a substantial financial contribution towards the family expenses. That is not in any way a criticism of her; it is simply the factual position.
>
> What is asserted here is the creation of a trust arising by common intention of the parties. That common intention may be inferred where there has been a financial contribution, direct or indirect, to the acquisition of the house.

On the facts of both *Gissing v Gissing* [1971] AC 886 and *Burns v Burns* [1984] Ch 317, the female partner did not make a large enough financial contribution to the family budget to count as an indirect financial contribution towards the repayment of the mortgage instalments.

18.8 Quantifying the size of the equitable interests

18.8.1 This is the second stage of the process

Once the court has decided that a claimant has an equitable interest in the family home, it has to decide how large that share is. So there is a two-stage process:

1. Has the claimant any equitable interest at all?
2. If the answer is yes, then the court goes on to decide the size of the share.

In a single name case, the claimant first has to use *Lloyds v Rosset* [1991] 1 AC 107, to establish whether the claimant has any equitable interest at all. *Lloyds Bank v Rosset* [1991] 1 AC 107, has nothing to say about stage 2, as Mrs Rosset failed at stage 1. She did not have an equitable interest at all, so the court did not have to consider how they would decide its size. For House of Lords' guidance on how to decide the size of the share, we have to go back to *Gissing v Gissing* [1971] AC 886.

● ***Gissing v Gissing*** [1971] AC 886

(This case can also be found at 18.3.3, 18.6, and 18.7.)

Lord Diplock at 908 to 909 suggested a number of ways of calculating the size of the shares.

1. Look at the evidence to see whether they ever agreed the size of the shares.
2. If there is no evidence of a specific agreement, look closely at the facts to see whether there was any evidence of a common understanding.
3. Alternatively, look at the evidence over the couple's years together and add up the value of their contributions, direct and indirect, in order to decide fair shares.

As we shall see, the courts have tried to refine this approach in subsequent cases.

18.8.2 The whole course of dealing

The approach that has gained favour, derived from Lord Diplock in *Gissing v Gissing* [1971] AC 886, is to look at what the couple did in relation to the house during their life together. This would include direct and indirect financial contributions, but also other factors, as explained in this section. Looking at the whole course of dealing is supposed to shed light on the couple's common intention as to the respective size of shares.

. . . .

● **Midland Bank plc v Cooke** [1995] 4 All ER 562

Mr and Mrs Cooke married in 1971 and moved into a house which was put into Mr Cooke's name alone. The house cost £8,500 of which £6,450 was repayable by mortgage, £1,100 was a wedding gift to the couple from the husband's parents, and the remainder was from the husband's savings. The house had been remortgaged to the Midland Bank to support the husband's business, but they could not repay the loan, so the Bank sought possession of the house. The wife resisted this, claiming that half the house belonged to her. The county court agreed that she had a share, but said that it was 6.47 per cent, which was the proportion represented by the half share of the wedding present from her husband's parents (£550 out of £8,500 = 6.47 per cent).

HELD: The Court of Appeal disagreed and gave her a half share.

Waite LJ at 574:

> The general principle to be derived from *Gissing v Gissing* and *Grant v Edwards* can in my judgment be summarised in this way. When the court is proceeding, in cases like the present where the partner without legal title has successfully asserted an equitable interest through direct contribution, to determine (in the absence of express evidence of intention) what proportions the parties must be assumed to have intended for their beneficial ownership, the duty of the judge is to undertake a survey of the whole course of dealing between the parties relevant to their ownership and occupation of the property and their sharing of its burdens and advantages. That scrutiny will not confine itself to the limited range of acts of direct contribution of the sort that are needed to found a beneficial interest in the first place. It will take into consideration all conduct which throws light on the question what shares were intended. Only if that search proves inconclusive does the court fall back on the maxim that 'equality is equity'.

At 576:

> One could hardly have a clearer example of a couple who had agreed to share everything equally: the profits of his business while it prospered, and the risks of indebtedness suffered through its failure; the upbringing of the children; the rewards of her own career as a teacher; and, most relevantly, a home into which he had put his savings and to which she was to give over the years the benefit of the maintenance and improvement contribution. When to all that there is added the fact (still an important one) that this was a couple who had chosen to introduce into their relationship the additional commitment which marriage involves, the conclusion becomes inescapable that their presumed intention was to share the beneficial interest in the property in equal shares.

The courts must look at the whole course of dealing between the couple in order to decide the size of their respective shares. They do not just look at the limited range of factors mentioned in *Lloyds Bank v Rosset* [1991] 1 AC 107 in order to decide whether the claimant has any share at all.

KEY POINT Mrs Cooke had a share because of her direct financial contribution to the purchase price, which is *Rosset* category 2. Once that is decided, the court looks at a much wider range of factors in order to decide the size of the share.

The test put forward in *Midland Bank plc v Cooke* [1995] 4 All ER 562 is now generally accepted as the correct test, although the conclusion reached in *Cooke* has been criticized as over-generous to Mrs Cooke.

● *Oxley v Hiscock* [2005] Fam 211

Mrs Oxley and Mr Hiscock had bought a house for £127,000 that was put into Mr Hiscock's name. Mrs Oxley contributed £36,300 and Mr Hiscock contributed £60,700, and they also took out a £30,000 mortgage, which they repaid equally. When they separated, Mrs Oxley claimed half the house, but Mr Hiscock argued that, on resulting trust principles, his share should be proportionate to his contribution, giving him 60 per cent.

HELD: The court disliked the result in *Midland Bank plc v Cooke* [1995] 4 All ER 562 because, although there was clear evidence that the couple had *not* explicitly agreed the size of their respective shares, the court said that their *presumed* intention was a 50:50 split. The court is not allowed to 'invent' agreements that the parties did not actually make.

Chadwick LJ at 246–7:

> In those circumstances the first question is whether there is evidence from which to infer a common intention, communicated by each to the other, that each shall have a beneficial share in the property.

(Chadwick LJ then discusses Lord Bridge's two categories in *Lloyds Bank v Rosset* [1991] 1 AC 107.)

First, it has to be decided that each party actually has a beneficial interest.

> In those circumstances, the second question to be answered in cases of this nature is: 'what is the extent of the parties' respective beneficial interests in the property?' Again, in many such cases, the answer will be provided by evidence of what they said and did at the time of the acquisition. But, in a case where there is no evidence of any discussion between them as to the amount of the share which each was to have—and even in a case where the evidence is that there was no discussion on that point—the question still requires an answer. It must now be accepted that (at least in this court and below) the answer is that each is entitled to that share which the court considers fair having regard to the whole course of dealing between them in relation to the property. And, in that context, 'the whole course of dealing between them in relation to the property' includes the arrangements which they make from time to time in order to meet the outgoings (for example, mortgage contributions, council tax and utilities, repairs, insurance and housekeeping) which have to be met if they are to live in the property as their home.

At 248–9:

> The right question, in the circumstances of this case, was: 'what would be a fair share for each party having regard to the whole course of dealing between them in relation to the property?'
>
> I think that that is a question to which this court can, and should, give an answer. I do not think it necessary to remit the matter to the county court. In my view to declare that the parties were entitled in equal shares would be unfair to Mr Hiscock. It would give insufficient weight to the fact that his direct contribution to the purchase price (£60,700) was substantially greater than that of Mrs Oxley (£36,300). On the basis of the judge's finding that there was in this case 'a classic pooling of resources' and conduct consistent with an intention to share the burden of the property (by which she must, I think, have meant the outgoings referable to ownership and cohabitation), it would be fair to treat them as having made

approximately equal contributions to the balance of the purchase price (£30,000). Taking that into account with their direct contributions at the time of the purchase, I would hold that a fair division of the proceeds of sale of the property would be 60 per cent to Mr Hiscock and 40 per cent to Mrs Oxley.

This case confirms the two-stage approach. First, decide whether the claimant has a share at all. Secondly, decide the size of the share. To do this the court must decide 'what would be a fair share for each party having regard to the whole course of dealing between them in relation to the property?' In this particular case, to ignore the different size of their respective financial contributions would not have been fair.

The Court of Appeal took a similar approach in *Galarotti v Sebastianelli* [2012] EWCA Civ 685, which was a case involving two flat sharers, who were in a platonic relationship rather than cohabiting. There, the common intention changed.

KEY POINT: The common intention may change. Look at the whole course of dealing to ascertain this.

● *Galarotti v Sebastianelli* [2012] EWCA Civ 1865

The flat was in Mr Sebastianelli's sole name and he paid £86,500. Mr Gallarotti paid £26,896.20. The cost of the flat was £188,287.44, with the remainder being borrowed on a mortgage taken out by Mr Sebastianelli. They orally agreed that they would hold the flat in equal shares, with Mr Galarotti paying most of the mortgage repayments. As it turned out, Mr Galarotti was unable to do this.

HELD: Arden LJ at para 16:

> The recorder had found as a fact 'that the express agreement between the parties was that they would each have a 50% interest in the Flat, despite the unequal amounts contributed by each of them'. The conclusion was that they held in equal shares.

The Court of Appeal disagreed; circumstances had changed.

Arden LJ at para 21:

> In any event, the parties could not possibly have intended that the agreement should apply in those circumstances.

At para 26:

> . . . Mr Galarotti left the Flat. By that point in time, the only inference that could be drawn was that the parties intended the beneficial ownership should, in substance, reflect their financial contributions. It was wholly implausible that Mr Sebastianelli should make a substantial gift to Mr Galarotti. Here were two flat sharers who were not in a family unit.

The financial contributions indicated 75 per cent for Mr Sebastianelli and 25 per cent for Mr Gallarotti.

It is possible for the whole course of dealing to indicate that the legal owner holds the house 100% for the claimant, which would mean that the legal owner must transfer the legal estate to the claimant.

Sunil wanted to buy a house to run a bed and breakfast business, but he could not obtain a mortgage, because of his poor credit rating. So he agreed that his sister-in-law, Jaci, would take the legal title and mortgage in her name. Sunil claimed that he ran the business alone and provided all the money for her to pay the mortgage.

HELD: Sullivan LJ at para 13:

> In these circumstances, if Sunil was able to establish, on the balance of probabilities, that the agreement was that he should be the sole beneficial owner, then provided he could also show that he has acted to his detriment in reliance on that agreement, he would be able to discharge the onus of showing that the beneficial ownership differed from the legal ownership.

He could show that he had acted to his detriment by running the business, so the conclusion was that Jaci held on trust for him.

KEY POINT In order to decide the size of the parties' beneficial interests, the court must look at the whole course of dealing between them in relation to the property to decide their shares.

18.8.3 Joint tenants and the whole course of dealing

Midland Bank plc v Cooke [1995] 4 All ER 562 and *Oxley v Hiscock* [2005] Fam 211 were both sole name cases, the legal estate of the house was held by only one of the parties, in both cases the man. In joint names cases there is really only one issue, quantification, the size of their respective shares. It is presumed that the joint names give both of them an equitable interest. In contrast to a single name case, it does not have to be proved. It is becoming much more common for the house to be held in joint names. The House of Lords, in *Stack v Dowden* [2007] 2 AC 432 and the Supreme Court, in *Jones v Kernott* [2012] 1 AC 776, started from the presumption that if the house was legally held in joint names, then it would also be held that way in equity, giving the couple equal shares. If one of the couple disputed that, they would have to prove that the common intention was different. Then the court would consider 'the whole course of dealing'.

KEY POINT In joint name cases there is only one issue, quantification, the size of the shares, which is ascertained by looking at the whole course of dealing: *Stack v Dowden*.

In single name cases, there are two distinct stages.

1. The claimant must prove that they have a beneficial interest: *Lloyd v Rosset*.
2. If they pass stage 1, the court will then decide the size of the claimant's beneficial interest: *Stack v Dowden*.

Stack v Dowden and *Jones v Kernott* approved of *Oxley v Hiscock* (see 18.8.2 'The whole course of dealing') and the use of the whole course of dealing to decide the size of shares. Joint name cases had previously used resulting trusts to decide the size of shares, based only on financial contributions, in cases like *Springette v Defoe* [1992] 2 FLR 388, but this was decisively rejected. Now both single name and joint name cases use the whole course of dealing approach to decide the relative sizes of the beneficial interests.

● *Stack v Dowden* [2007] 2 AC 432

(This case also appears at 18.1, 18.2.2, 18.9, and 18.10.2.)

A relationship between Dehra Dowden and Barry Stack began in 1975, when Ms Dowden was 17 and Mr Stack was 19. Ms Dowden was an electrical engineer and Mr Stack was a builder. In 1983 Ms Dowden, who was the bigger earner of the two, bought a house, which she paid for and was legally in her name. Mr Stack lived with her and they had four children together. He made some improvements to the house, but the Court of Appeal held that he made no financial contribution and thus had no claim to this house. In 1993 Stack and Dowden bought another house, for £190,000, and this time put the legal estate in their joint names. Ms Dowden paid £128,813 in cash, which was £57,179 from her building society account and £65,025 from the sale of her previous house. The balance was paid by a mortgage of £65,025, which was in their joint names. Mr Stack paid off the mortgage interest and insurance policies, totalling £33,747. He also repaid £27,000 of the mortgage capital and she paid £38,435. The couple separated in 2002 and Stack claimed half the value of the house. Dowden was willing to give him 35 per cent, while she would take 65 per cent.

HELD: The House of Lords agreed with Dowden, that the split should be 65:35 per cent in her favour, but their Lordships stated that, usually if the couple put the property into joint names, it would be assumed that they intended a 50:50 share, unless there was evidence to the contrary.

Baroness Hale at 454:

> Just as the starting point where there is sole legal ownership is sole beneficial ownership, the starting point where there is joint legal ownership is joint beneficial ownership. The onus is upon the person seeking to show that the beneficial ownership is different from the legal ownership. So in sole ownership cases it is upon the non-owner to show that he has any interest at all. In joint ownership cases, it is upon the joint owner who claims to have other than a joint beneficial interest.

KEY POINT

Where there is joint legal ownership it is usual to assume that there is also joint equitable ownership, i.e. a 50:50 per cent split.

The court would need to look at many factors of the couple's relationship together, particularly financial ones, to decide the proportions in which the parties intended to share the house.

Baroness Hale endorsed *Oxley v Hiscock* [2005] Fam 211, but stressed that the court must look for what the parties *actually* intended, rather than what the court considered as fair.

At 456:

> First, it emphasises that the search is still for the result which reflects what the parties must, in the light of their conduct, be taken to have intended. Second, therefore, it does not enable the court to abandon that search in favour of the result which the court itself considers *fair*.

At 459 (paras 69 and 70):

> In law, 'context is everything' and the domestic context is very different from the commercial world. Each case will turn on its own facts. Many more factors than financial contributions may be relevant to divining the parties' true intentions. These include: any advice or discussions at the time of the transfer which cast light upon their intentions then; the reasons why the home was acquired in their joint names; the reasons why (if it be the

case) the survivor was authorised to give a receipt for the capital moneys; the purpose for which the home was acquired; the nature of the parties' relationship; whether they had children for whom they both had responsibility to provide a home; how the purchase was financed, both initially and subsequently; how the parties arranged their finances, whether separately or together or a bit of both; how they discharged the outgoings on the property and their other household expenses. When a couple are joint owners of the home and jointly liable for the mortgage, the inferences to be drawn from who pays for what may be very different from the inferences to be drawn when only one is owner of the home. The arithmetical calculation of how much was paid by each is also likely to be less important. It will be easier to draw the inference that they intended that each should contribute as much to the household as they reasonably could and that they would share the eventual benefit or burden equally. The parties' individual characters and personalities may also be a factor in deciding where their true intentions lay. In the cohabitation context, mercenary considerations may be more to the fore than they would be in marriage, but it should not be assumed that they always take pride of place over natural love and affection. At the end of the day, having taken all this into account, cases in which the joint legal owners are to be taken to have intended that their beneficial interests should be different from their legal interests will be very unusual.

This is not, of course, an exhaustive list. There may also be reason to conclude that, whatever the parties' intentions at the outset, these have now changed. An example might be where one party has financed (or constructed himself) an extension or substantial improvement to the property, so that what they have now is significantly different from what they had then.

KEY POINT In order to decide the size of the parties' beneficial interests, the court must look at the whole course of dealing between the parties in order to decide what the parties intended.

The evidence in this case showed that Stack and Dowden did not intend equal shares, particularly as the couple kept their finances separate.

Baroness Hale at 465:

> This is, therefore, a very unusual case. There cannot be many unmarried couples who have lived together for as long as this, who have had four children together, and whose affairs have been kept as rigidly separate as this couple's affairs were kept. This is all strongly indicative that they did not intend their shares, even in the property which was put into both their names, to be equal (still less that they intended a beneficial joint tenancy with the right of survivorship should one of them die before it was severed). Before the Court of Appeal, Ms Dowden contended for a 65 per cent share and in my view she has made good her case for that.

The ruling in *Stack v Dowden* caused some confusion, as shown by the case of *Jones v Kernott* [2012] 1 AC 776. There the unmarried couple held the house in joint names, but the man had left 14 years before. They both accepted at trial that their original intention and their intention at separation had been to hold the house in equal shares. Could the couple's common intention as to the size of their shares change? What did the couple have to do to change their common intention? The Court of Appeal thought that the couple would need to make a fresh oral agreement to indicate their changed common intention, but the Supreme Court disagreed. What the common intention was and whether it had changed could be ascertained by looking at the whole course of dealing between the couple, as indicated by Baroness Hale in *Stack v Dowden* [2007] 2 AC 459. (See earlier.)

The couple lived together from 1983 or 1984 and bought their house in 1985 for £30,000. Patricia paid £6,000, they took on a mortgage for the rest, and put the house in joint names. Leonard gave her £100 a week and built an extension that increased the value of the house by 50 per cent. From the £100, Patricia paid the mortgage and everything else. They had two children together and separated in 1993, which was the end of Leonard's financial contribution to the house. They both accepted that, at that point, they shared the house in equal shares. In 1995, they sold a joint insurance policy, so that Leonard could buy his own house.In 2007, he began proceedings to recover his 50 per cent share. Patricia argued that the course of dealing between them since 1993, and Leonard's non-existent contributions, indicated that their common intention had changed. The judge agreed and awarded her 90 per cent of the value of the house and 10 per cent to Leonard.

HELD:

Lady Walker and Lady Hale at 794:

(1) The starting point is that equity follows the law and they are joint tenants in law and equity.

(2) That presumption can be displaced by showing (a) that the parties had a different common intention at the time when they acquired the home, or (b) that they later formed the common intention that their respective shares would change.

(3) Their common intention is to be deduced objectively from their conduct: 'the relevant intention of each party is the intention which was reasonably understood by the other party to be manifested by that party's words and conduct notwithstanding that he did not consciously formulate that intention in his own mind or even acted with some different intention which he did not communicate to the other party' (Lord Diplock in *Gissing v Gissing* [1971] AC 886, 906). Examples of the sort of evidence which might be relevant to drawing such inferences are given in *Stack v Dowden* 2 AC 432 at 459. (See above).

(4) In those cases where it is clear either (a) that the parties did not intend joint tenancy at the outset, or (b) had changed their original intention, but it is not possible to ascertain by direct evidence or by inference what their actual intention was as to the shares in which they would own the property, 'the answer is that each is entitled to that share which the court considers fair having regard to the whole course of dealing between them in relation to the property'. Chadwick LJ in *Oxley v Hiscock* [2005] Fam 211, para 69. In our judgment, 'the whole course of dealing . . . in relation to the property' should be given a broad meaning, enabling a similar range of factors to be taken into account as may be relevant to ascertaining the parties' actual intentions.

(5) Each case will turn on its own facts. Financial contributions are relevant but there are many other factors which may enable the court to decide what shares were either intended (as in case (3)) or fair (4)). It is possible for the evidence to show that the original common intention has changed.

The evidence in this case showed a change of common intention, even though the couple had not expressly discussed their changed shares.What could be inferred from the evidence was this. When the couple separated, in 1993, the house was worth £60 to £70 thousand and they intended equal shares. That would give Leonard Kernott £30–35,000. The house was worth £245,000 in 2008, at the time of the original trial. £30–35,000 is between 12 per cent and 14 per cent of £245,000, so giving Leonard 10 per cent was close enough.

If it was clear that the parties did not intend equal shares, but there was no evidence, either direct or inferred, of what shares they actually did intend, then the court could impute an intention to the parties and award fair shares as described in (4). This was further explained by Lady Walker and Lady Hale at 792:

> But if it cannot deduce exactly what shares were intended, it may have no alternative but to ask what their intentions as reasonable and just people would have been had they thought about it at the time. This is a fallback position which some courts may not welcome, but the court has a duty to come to a conclusion on the dispute put before it.

The law stated here is very similar to that stated in *Stack v Dowden* [2007] 2 AC 432, with the possible exception that the Court admits that the evidence may not provide an answer to what was the common intention on the size of shares. In that situation the court has to impute or supply its own answer as to what would be fair shares.

KEY POINT The court can infer the common intention from the evidence. The common intention may change. If the evidence does not reveal the common intention, the court may impute one and award fair shares.

---

thinking points

The decision in Jones v Kernott *accepts that the common intention of the couple may change. The court must infer what they can from the evidence in order to decide this. If the evidence does not provide an answer, the court may impute their common intention and award fair shares. This approach may well lead to justice in the individual case, but it makes the outcome of any case hard to predict. All involved accept that the common intention constructive trust will continue to evolve and also affect cases that do not involve cohabitants, particularly as it seems unlikely that Parliament will legislate for a more precise solution to this type of dispute. See the* Conveyancer *[2012] for a variety of comment from pages 149–80. There are articles by Mark Pawlowski 'Imputing intent in joint ownership: a return to common sense:* Jones v Kernott' *149–158, Man Yip 'The rules applying to unmarried cohabitants' family homes:* Jones v Kernott', *159–67, and John Mee* 'Jones v Kernott: *inferring and imputing in Essex', 167–80.*

18.9 What sort of trust is this?

The older cases suggest that the trust of a family home is a resulting trust: *Pettit v Pettit* [1970] AC 777 (see 18.3.1 'Resulting trust'). *Gissing v Gissing* [1971] AC 886 (see 18.3.3 'Constructive trust') considers the question of type of trust unimportant, while *Lloyds Bank v Rosset* [1991] 1 AC 107 (see 18.4 'Sole name cases—acquiring a beneficial interest: the two categories in *Lloyds Bank v Rosset*') suggests that it is a constructive trust. The majority opinion now seems to be that this is a constructive trust, because this enables the court to look at a wider range of contributions, financial and otherwise. The court is also not bound to assess the size of the party's shares solely on a mathematical basis, proportionate to the size of their respective contributions, as they would have to do if it was a resulting trust. Baroness Hale refers to it as an '"ambulatory" constructive trust', quoting Lord Hoffmann, as 'the parties' intentions may change over the course of time': *Stack v Dowden* [2007] 2 All ER 929 at 950. She repeats this thought in *Lynn Anne Abbott v Dane Norman Lawrence Abbott* [2008] 1 FLR 1451, 2007 WL 2126565 at para 4:

> It is now clear that the constructive trust is generally the more appropriate tool of analysis in most matrimonial cases.

Yet, some still prefer the greater certainty and precision of the resulting trust: at least it is possible to calculate the size of the parties' shares accurately.

● ***Stack v Dowden*** [2007] 2 All ER 929

The majority preferred the constructive trust analysis, but Lord Neuberger dissented in favouring resulting trusts, although he agreed with the outcome of the case.

Lord Neuberger at 961:

> I note that the Court of Appeal's recent decisions in this case and in *Oxley v Hiscock* [2005] Fam 211 (both of which were rightly decided) produced an outcome which would be dictated by a resulting trust solution.
>
> He noted that the shares would be the same 65%–35%, if a resulting trust was used based on the respective size of the couple's financial contributions.

The Supreme Court returned to the issue in *Jones v Kernott* [2012] 1 AC 776 and again decisively rejected the use of the resulting trust in family home cases.

● ***Jones v Kernott*** [2012] 1 AC 776

Lady Hale and Lord Walker at 794:

> The assumptions as to human motivation, which led the courts to impute particular intentions by way of the resulting trust, are not appropriate to the ascertainment of beneficial interests in a family home. Whether they remain appropriate in other contexts is not the issue in this case.

The general view, therefore, is that a constructive trust based on the parties' common intention should be used. The 'other contexts' might be where, in what seems to be a family case, there was really a business motive for acquiring the property.

Just such a 'commercial' case occurred in *Laskar v Laskar* [2008] EWCA Civ 347 and Lord Neuberger was able to apply a resulting trust, so that the parties took the property in proportion to their financial contribution.

● ***Laskar v Laskar*** [2008] EWCA Civ 347

A mother and daughter bought the mother's council house and put it into their joint names. Neither party lived in the house and it was rented out.

HELD: The Court of Appeal decided not to apply the presumption in *Stack v Dowden* [2007] AC 432 that, as the house was in joint names, the beneficial ownership was shared equally. A division based on resulting trust principles, reflecting the relative size of their financial contributions, was more appropriate. This was a commercial case.

Neuberger LJ at para 17:

> In the latter sort of case, the reasoning in *Stack v Dowden* would not be appropriate and the resulting trust presumption still appears to apply. In this case, the primary purpose of the purchase of the property was as an investment, not as a home. In other words this was a purchase which, at least primarily, was not in 'the domestic consumer context' but in a commercial context.

KEY POINT
The trust of the family home is a constructive trust. Resulting trusts still apply in commercial cases.

And at para 33:

> ...involves a relatively strict mathematical approach, which, in the context of a property bought primarily as an investment, seems not unreasonable.

A resulting trust analysis was also used in a dispute concerning ownership of a hotel, between Mr Lee, a wealthy Hong Kong property magnate and his sexual companion, Ms Wu: *Favor Easy Management Ltd v Wu* [2012] EWCA Civ 1464.

18.10 Reform of the law

In recent years, the Law Commission has looked at this issue twice, but no legislation has been passed yet.

18.10.1 Law Commission: Sharing Homes

In 2002 the Law Commission published *Sharing Homes: A Discussion Paper* (Law Com No 278), which looked at all the different situations in which people might share homes without completing proper legal formalities. So it covered not just cohabitants, but relatives and friends sharing. Perhaps, not surprisingly, this proved such a complicated subject that the Commission decided that it could not recommend any specific legislation:

Law Commission. Sharing Homes (Law Com No 278), 7

> It is quite simply not possible to devise a statutory scheme for the ascertainment and quantification of beneficial interests in the shared home which can operate fairly and evenly across the diversity of domestic circumstances which are now to be encountered.

The Commission, however, did make some very relevant criticisms of the existing law, which are summarized at para 7 of the Executive Summary:

1. The court tries to identify the 'common intention' of the parties, but 'this can be a somewhat unrealistic exercise, as people do not tend to think about their home in such legalistic terms'.

2. 'Although certain contributions towards the acquisition of the home can give rise to an interest in it, it is not very clear where the line is drawn between contributions which count and contributions which do not'. Paying the mortgage instalments secures an interest in the home, but it is doubtful whether paying the household bills, in order that a partner may pay the mortgage, is enough by itself. The Commission suggested, in their Conclusions (para 15) that the courts could solve this themselves by 'taking a broader view of the kinds of contributions from which they might infer "common intention"'.

3. Looking after children and other domestic work does not grant a share.

4. Fixing the size of the share is difficult and court decisions are inconsistent. Again the Commission recommended in their Conclusions that the courts could take a broader approach.

5. The Law Commission also concluded that more couples should be encouraged to make their position clear, by executing a written declaration of trust. It also advocated the registration of civil partnerships, which is now permitted, for same-sex couples, by the Civil Partnership Act 2004.

18.10.2 Reform of the law by the courts

The House of Lords seemed to have accepted some of these suggestions in *Stack v Dowden* [2007] 2 AC 432, in particular taking a broader approach in quantifying the size of the shares. The House also criticized the need always to find an express oral agreement in category 1 of *Lloyds Bank v Rosset* [1991] 1 AC 107 and the rejection of indirect financial contributions in category 2.

. . . .

● *Stack v Dowden* [2007] 2 AC 432

Lord Walker commenting on whether indirect financial contributions were acceptable, at 445:

> Lord Bridge's extreme doubt 'whether anything less will do' was certainly consistent with many first-instance and Court of Appeal decisions, but I respectfully doubt whether it took full account of the views (conflicting though they were) expressed in *Gissing v Gissing* [1971] AC 886 (see especially Lord Reid at pp 896g–897b and Lord Diplock at 909d–h). It has attracted some trenchant criticism from scholars as potentially productive of injustice: see *Gray & Gray, Elements of Land Law*, 4th edn, paras 10.132 to 10.137, the last paragraph being headed 'A More Optimistic Future'. Whether or not Lord Bridge's observation was justified in 1990, in my opinion the law has moved on, and your Lordships should move it a little more in the same direction, while bearing in mind that the Law Commission may soon come forward with proposals which, if enacted by Parliament, may recast the law in this area.

This was only an obiter dicta comment and we do not yet know what the Supreme Court would do if presented with such a situation in a real case. Meanwhile, the Privy Council and lower courts seem to have already added a 'third category' of constructive trust in sole name cases, by looking at the 'whole course of dealing'.

. . . .

● *Lynn Anne Abbott v Dane Norman Lawrence Abbott* [2008] 1 FLR 1451

The house that the couple lived in was a gift from the husband's mother, but legally it was in the man's name alone.

HELD: Baroness Hale: The court had to search for the couple's shared intentions, by looking at their whole course of conduct in relation to the property.

At para 28:

> There should be a declaration that the husband holds the house in trust for them both in equal shares.

Some textbook writers have taken up the suggestion that even for the 'first stage' in sole name cases, to decide whether the claimant has any beneficial interest at all, the court need only look at the whole course of dealing.

. . . .

● *Hapeshi v Allnatt* [2010] EWHC 392 (Ch)

Mrs Hapeshi had bought her council house and put it into the joint names of herself and her son, Michael. His brother Kevin claimed that it had always been agreed that he would also have a share in the house, although his name had not been put on the title deeds. Kevin did not contribute financially to the purchase, but did contribute to electricity and gas bills, house insurance, and some household items. Later he paid about £1,800 to pay off mortgage arrears.

HELD: Judge Hodge QC quoted approvingly from Megarry and Wade 'The Law of Real Property' at para 17, to the effect that *Stack v Dowden* and *Abbott v Abbott* [2007] UKPC 53 added an additional category to the two types of constructive trust in *Lloyds Bank plc v Rosset* [1991] 1 AC 107:

> [I]n response to changing social and economic conditions, the common intention may be inferred (or perhaps imputed) from the parties' whole course of conduct in relation to the property.

The judge took a similar approach when deciding the size of the parties' shares at para 50:

> It seems to me that I should adopt what has been described as the 'holistic approach', undertaking a survey of the whole course of dealing between the parties, and taking account of all conduct which throws light on the question of what shares were intended.

Mrs Hapeshi was awarded 50 per cent and Michael and Kevin 25 per cent.

The same approach was taken in a 'sole name' case, *The Crown Prosecution Service v Graham Piper* [2011] EWHC 3570 (Admin).

● ***The Crown Prosecution Service v Graham Piper*** [2011] EWHC 3570 (Admin)

Mr Piper owned Heathfields Farm, in Essex, which was mortgage free and in his sole name. It was valued at £580,000 and it was wanted by the CPS under a criminal confiscation order, following his conviction for a serious drug offence. His wife, Janet, claimed that, in equity, 50 per cent of the farm belonged to her. She had contributed £30,000 and helped run an equestrian business from the farm.

HELD: Counsel for both sides and the judge, Holman J, agreed on the law.

At para 7:

> (3) Their common intention is to be deduced objectively from their conduct (Jones v Kernott)
>
> (6) The whole course of dealing in relation to that property is to be given a broad meaning (Jones v Kernott) and the law has moved on from what Lord Bridge of Harwich said in Lloyds Bank v Rosset [1991] 1 AC 107, (see Abbott v Abbott [2007] UKPC 53).

At para 69:

> . . . all satisfy me on a balance of probability that it was indeed the intention, attitude and understanding of the husband from in or before 1996 that his wife, who had contributed to it and with whom he was working closely in an equestrian business partnership, did have an interest which amounted to 'co-ownership' in Heathfields Farm. It was rarely discussed, but it was understood and did not need to be.

The judge declined to award Janet a share in proportion to the size of her financial contribution, which was uncertain anyway.

At para 73:

> I reject that approach, which appears to reflect the law more of a resulting trust than of deducing a common intention or deciding, in the court's discretion, what is fair. . . . I am in fact satisfied on a balance of probability that the common intention that she should have a share was indeed a common intention that she should have a half or equal share.

In a subsequent sole name case, *Apsden v Elvy* [2012] EWHC 1387, the judge again stated that 'the law had moved on' since *Lloyds Bank v Rosset* [1991] 1 AC 107 and preferred to use *Jones v Kernott* [2012] 1 AC 776 and *Stack v Dowden* [2007] 2 AC 432. The conclusion was as follows:

• *Apsden v Elvy* [2012] EWHC 1387

Behrens J:

> I think that the proper inference from the whole course of dealing is that there was a common intention that Mr Apsden should have some interest in Outlaithe Barn as a result of the very substantial contributions made to the conversion works.

Mr Apsden had in fact made a sizeable financial contribution to the building works.

The courts, however will still not award a beneficial interest just because the couple have been in a long relationship. There must have been some kind of contribution, preferably financial.

• *Geary v Rankine* [2012] EWCA Civ 555

Ms Geary and Mr Rankine had been together for 19 years. Mr Rankine had bought a business, in which she worked, but that did not mean that there was a common intention that they would share the business property.

In a similar case, the couple had lived together and run businesses together for over 30 years, but, by itself, that was not enough to give the woman a claim.

• *Curran v Collins* [2013] EWCA Civ 382

Toulson LJ at para 9:

> Sadly the appellant found herself in the classic position of a woman jilted in her early fifties, having very much made her life with the respondent for over thirty years. The law of property can be harsh on people, usually women, in that situation. That was the view of the Law Commission when it recommended reform of this area of the law, but its recommendations were rejected by the Government. Bluntly, the law remains potentially unfair to people in the appellant's position, but the judge was constrained to apply the law as it is.

18.10.3 Law Commission: cohabitation

The Law Commission returned to the issue with a paper issued in 2007, *Cohabitation: The Financial Consequences of Relationship Breakdown* (Law Com No 307), which sensibly confined itself to cohabitation and not the many other situations in which people might share a house. The recommendations were that the law should depart from the existing approach, based on property rights and give the courts similar powers, to redistribute property, to those that exist when a couple divorce.

> The Scheme might operate when a couple had been living together for two years. If couples wished they could make a written agreement that they did not want the statutory scheme to apply.

When the couple separated, a cohabitant could apply to the court for relief. The court would look at the economic benefits each party had brought to the relationship and also consider the economic disadvantages that each had suffered.

Benefits would not just include paying for the house, but contributing towards any other family savings and investments or even unpaid work in a family business. Child care and care of other family members would be included, as would providing financial support for the family.

Economic disadvantages would include giving up work or losing promotion opportunities, inability to pay for a pension and loss of the opportunity to save or invest.

When the couple separate the court would not just be restricted to ordering the sale of the house and deciding how the proceeds should be divided, but, as in divorce, they could order the transfer of the house or other property, division of pensions and payments by instalments. The court must have regard to the welfare of children, especially those under 18 and the financial needs and obligations of each of the parties.

KEY POINT Under the Law Commission's *Cohabitation* reform proposals, the courts would have to look at the whole life of the couple together and the life they would lead after separating, rather than just looking at what they did to acquire a house.

Although these proposals were favourably received by the government, it announced in 2008 that there were no immediate plans to legislate. First they wished to study the financial impact of similar reforms in Scotland. If they are enacted, most of the law in this chapter will no longer apply to cohabiting couples, although it would still apply to other situations of informal sharing of land and to couples who fell outside the statutory scheme.

An illustration of how the Scottish scheme works can be seen in *Whigham v Owen* [2013] Fam LR 30. It resembles a 'scaled down' version of divorce.

● ***Whigham v Owen*** [2013] Fam LR 30

Jacqueline Whigham and Steven Owen lived together between 1984 and 2011 and had three children. She did not pursue a career of her own, but looked after him and the children and supported him in his business. He built up a successful plumbing business, Dial a Rod.

HELD: Lord Drummond Young. At para 9:

> ...a cohabitation that has lasted many years, with many of the features of marriage, might be rated at 80 to 90 per cent of a marriage, and one that has not lasted long, or has been intermittent, might be rated at 10 to 20 per cent of a marriage.

At para 32;

> The pursuer [Whigham] made very substantial contributions, both financial and non-financial, to the family, and the defender [Owen] unquestionably benefitted from these.

Owen's wealth was £747,669 and Whigham was awarded £250,000.

[In a divorce she might have received half.]

The Scottish case *Gow v Grant* [2012] UKSC 29 was heard by the Supreme Court, which gave Lady Hale the opportunity to call for similar reform south of the border.

Lady Hale at paras 50 and 56:

> [50] Responding to the government's announcement (Law Commission, 6 September 2011), Professor Elizabeth Cooke, the Law Commissioner who leads the commission's work in family and property law, said this: 'We hope that implementation will not be delayed beyond the early days of the next Parliament, in view of the hardship and injustice caused by the current law. The prevalence of cohabitation, and the birth of children to couples who live together, means that the need for reform of the law can only become more pressing over time.'
>
> As Professor Cooke also pointed out, the 'existing law is uncertain and expensive to apply and, because it was not designed for cohabitants, often gives rise to results that are unjust'. The reality is that the 'sufficient basis for changing the law' had already been amply provided by the long-standing judicial calls for reform (dating back at least as far as Burns v Burns [1984] Ch, 332); by the Law Commission's analysis of the deficiencies in the present law and the injustices which can result; by the demographic trends towards cohabitation and births to cohabiting couples, which are even more marked south of the border than they are in the north; and by the widespread belief that cohabiting couples are already protected by something called 'common law marriage', which has never existed in the south. There was no need to wait for experience north of the border to make the case for reform.
>
> [56] The main lesson from this case, as also from the research so far, is that a remedy such as this is both practicable and fair. It does not impose upon unmarried couples the responsibilities of marriage but redresses the gains and losses flowing from their relationship. As the researchers comment, 'The Act has undoubtedly achieved a lot for Scottish cohabitants and their children'. English and Welsh cohabitants and their children deserve no less.

thinking points

The Law Commission published detailed proposals on how the law might be reformed for cohabitants. The report highlighted the problems caused by the existing law and examined whether cohabitants should be treated as though they were married. That approach was rejected, and reforms based on the economic advantage or disadvantage gained from the relationship and the general principle of fairness were proposed. The issue of whether couples should be able to 'opt-out' was also considered. These reforms have been implemented in Scotland as seen in Gow v Grant. *Would these reforms be a better solution than the existing law or would they cause a whole new set of problems? For example, many people, other than cohabiting couples, share a house informally, e.g.* Hapeshi v Allnatt, *and they would still be governed by the constructive trust regime. See Stuart Bridge, Law Commisioner's three part article 'Cohabitants: Why Law Reform is Necessary' [2007]* Family Law 911–15, *'Financial Relief for Cohabitants: How the Law Commission's Scheme Would Work' [2007]* Family Law 998–1003, *and 'Financial Relief for Cohabitants: Eligibility, Opt Out and Provision on Death' [2007]* Family Law 1076–81.

Conclusion

Cohabiting couples could save themselves considerable legal trouble and expense if they made a written declaration of trust when acquiring a home to live in, but most do not: *Pankhania v Chandegra* [2012] EWCA Civ 1438. Even if the couple fails to do this, it is likely nowadays that both of them will have a claim to an equitable interest in their home. If the house is in joint names, they will both have a claim according to *Stack v Dowden* [2007] 2 AC 432 and *Jones v Kernott* [2012] 1 AC 776. If the house is in the sole name of one of the parties, a financial contribution to the acquisition of their home would put them into the second category of *Lloyds Bank v Rosset* [1991] 1 AC 107.

The first category in *Lloyds Bank v Rosset*, oral agreement plus detriment, is the category that causes more difficulty. There may be no oral agreement and the detriment may not be considered sufficient to obtain a beneficial interest. The stay-at-home partner, either male or female, who never earns, but just stays at home looking after the house and children, may be rare today, but such 'housewives/househusbands' are in the weakest position in claiming an equitable interest. Current law says that they cannot, but the Law Commission's proposals would change that. Although the courts are increasingly using a 'whole course of dealing' approach, rather than the stricter *Rosset* approach, to decide whether the claimant has any equitable interest in the house, there have been no cases so far that lack any detrimental reliance or financial contribution.

If we move on to deciding the size of the respective beneficial interests, according to *Stack v Dowden* [2007] 2 AC 432 and *Jones v Kernott* [2012] 1 AC 776, in joint name cases it is presumed that equal shares are intended, unless a different common intention can be proved from the whole course of dealing. In single name cases, we also look at the whole course of dealing to decide what shares were intended by the parties.

? **Questions**

Self-test questions

1 Why has the family home become a legal battleground?

2 How is a trust of land declared and what are the exceptions to this rule?

3 What is the difference between a resulting trust and a constructive trust?

4 What are the basic principles of proprietary estoppel?

5 What are the two categories of trust in *Lloyds Bank v Rosset*?

6 What level of proof is required for an oral agreement?

7 What qualifies as detrimental reliance?

8 What sort of financial contributions secure an equitable interest?

9 How is the size of an equitable interest determined?

10 What proposals have been made for reform of the law?

Discussion questions

1 Is the *Lloyds Bank v Rosset* approach of dividing trusts of the family home into two distinct categories helpful?

2 Should the law insist upon the existence of an oral agreement?

3 Could detrimental reliance be better defined?

4 Should indirect financial contributions be acceptable?

5 Does the law provide an accurate means for deciding the size of an equitable interest?

6 How should the law be reformed?

Assessment question

Ali and Bianca are both stockbrokers and meet through work. They soon become a couple, going on holiday together, and Bianca (and her dog Tiger Lily) move into Ali's London penthouse flat. A month later the couple become engaged and Ali hands over a large diamond ring to Bianca with the words 'soon we will be man and wife. Then our lives together will really start. We will buy a house with a large garden and we shall live happily thereafter.' Bianca stops actively pursuing her career as a stockbroker.

Bianca spends considerable time searching for their dream home and finds a dilapidated house in Essex. Ali buys the house, paying £450,000 of the £480,000 asking price in cash and borrowing the rest upon a mortgage. The legal estate is registered in the name of Ali. He tells Bianca that this is a mere 'formality', because he has borrowed the money.

Bianca spends a year organizing the renovation of the house, which costs £150,000. Ali pays £130,000 of this and Bianca pays the other £20,000 from her own savings and a bank loan.

Soon after, Bianca and Ali separate. Bianca is living in Ali's London flat, but Ali is living elsewhere. She considers that she is entitled to at least a share of the flat and/or the house and seeks your advice.

Advise Bianca upon whether she has any claim to the flat or the house and how the court would decide the size of her share (if any).

# Key cases

Further reading

G Douglas, J Pearce, and H Woodward 'Dealing with Property Issues on Cohabitation Breakdown' [2007] *Family Law* 36
Couples are surprisingly ignorant of the true legal position.

See the *Conveyancer* [2012] for a variety of comment on *Jones v Kernott* from pp. 149–80
There are articles by Mark Pawlowski 'Imputing intent in joint ownership: a return to common sense: *Jones v Kernott*' 149–58, Man Yip 'The rules applying to unmarried cohabitants' family homes: *Jones v Kernott*' 159–67, and John Mee *'Jones v Kernott:* inferring and imputing in Essex' 167–80.

Jones v Kernott not only tried to restate the law on the quantification of beneficial interests, but also suggested that the first stage of the process, discovering whether any sharing of the beneficial interests was intended at all, should no longer be determined by the two types of constructive trust in *Lloyds v Rosset,* but by looking at the whole course of dealing.

A Lawson 'The Things We Do For Love: Detrimental Reliance and the Family Home' (1996) *Legal Studies* 218
What the court considers as detrimental reliance is crucially important, yet the average couple does not think in this legalistic way.

S Bridge, Law Commisioner's three-part article 'Cohabitants: Why Law Reform is Necessary' [2007] *Family Law* 911–15, 'Financial Relief for Cohabitants: How the Law Commission's Scheme Would Work' [2007] *Family Law* 998–1003, and 'Financial Relief for Cohabitants: Eligibility, Opt Out and Provision on Death' [2007] 1076–81.
Should there be reforming legislation in this area?

19

Equitable remedies

Learning objectives

This chapter will help you to:

- understand that the courts' powers to grant equitable remedies are discretionary

- understand that equitable remedies vary from case to case and there is no one size fits all

- distinguish the principles governing the grant of general and specific injunctions

- understand the principles governing the grant and refusal of specific performance

- understand that all equitable remedies are in personam and can be granted in respect of property outside the jurisdiction of the court.

Introduction

One of the abiding characteristics of equity is its ability to act in personam, that is, to bind the conscience of the wrongdoer. Unlike common law remedies—which are rigid and attach specifically to the property subject of dispute—equitable remedies are flexible and do not need to attach to the objects of litigation. In fact, equitable remedies can be granted in respect of items or defendants located outside the jurisdiction of the court making the order. However, extra-territorial injunctions would not normally be granted in respect of land outside the UK, and are subject to some limitations such as the feasibility of enforcing the order overseas, absence of any contrary local rules overseas, and that service of the judgment can be effected.

● **Carron Iron Co v Maclaran** (1855) 5 HL Cas 416

Cranworth LC said at 436–7:

> ...the court acts in personam, and will not suffer anyone within its reach to do what is contrary to its notion of equity, merely because the act to be done may be, in point of locality, beyond its jurisdiction.

KEY POINT
Equitable remedies can be granted where property is outside the court's jurisdiction.

There are several remedies available in equity to a party who has been wronged in law or against whom some legal or equitable wrong is threatened. This is because 'equity does not suffer a wrong without a remedy'. Equitable remedies range from orders made by the court of equity (now the High Court) exercising equitable jurisdiction mandating someone, usually the defendant, to do or refrain from doing some act (injunctions), to decrees made by the court compelling a party to perform a contract (specific performance) in whole or in part. Our focus in this chapter is to consider some very important remedies that are available to anybody who approaches the court of equity. In particular, we discuss two most important equitable remedies, namely injunctions and specific performance.

19.1 Injunctions

Injunction is one of the oldest remedies of equity and also one of the most popular and most flexible. Although injunction has existed almost for as long as equity itself and used to be granted by the Court of Chancery before such powers were conferred on common law courts later in the development of equity, the statutory authority to grant injunctive relief is now enshrined in the English Supreme Court Act 1981.

According to s. 37(1) of the Act:

> the High Court may by order (whether interlocutory or final) grant an injunction... in all cases in which it appears just and convenient to do so.

19.1.1 Injunctions are discretionary

As with most equitable remedies, injunctions are granted not as of right to applicants, but by the discretion of the court. But note that injunctions are not a remedy that the court may grant indiscriminately. The court must have reference to precedents, common sense, and justice.

● ***Pride of Derby and Derbyshire Angling Association Ltd v British Celanese Ltd*** [1953] 1 Ch 149

Evershed MR at 181, said of discretionary power of the court:

> It is, I think, well established that, if A proves that his proprietary rights are being wrongfully interfered with by B, and that B intends to continue his wrong, then A is prima facie entitled to an injunction, and he will be deprived of that remedy only if special circumstances exist, including the circumstance that damages are inadequate remedy for the wrong that he has suffered.

● ***Medow v Medow*** (1878) 9 ChD 89

Jessel MR at 93, states that injunctions are 'not by the caprice of the judge, but according to sufficient legal reasons or settled principles'.

● ***Sears, Roebuck & Co v Camp*** 124 NJ Eq 403 (E & A 1938)

Justice Heher aptly set out the broad extent of equity's power to remedy a wrong.

At 411–12:

> Equitable remedies are distinguished for their flexibility, their unlimited variety, their adaptability to circumstances, and the natural rules which govern their use. There is in fact no limit to their variety and application; the court of equity has the power of devising its remedy and shaping it so as to fit the changing circumstances of every case and the complex relations of all the parties.

19.1.2 Against whom can injunctive orders be made?

The classical rule was stated in *Iveson v Harris* (1802) 7 Ves 251, by Lord Eldon at 257: 'you cannot have an injunction except against a party to the suit'. This view has drastically changed in modern times due to developments in European Union legal systems and also due to the proactiveness of courts.

● ***Venables v News Group Newspaper Ltd*** [2001] All ER 908

Dame Elizabeth Butler-Sloss at 908:

> [I]n light of the implementation of the 1998 Act, we are entering a new era, and a requirement that the courts act in a way which is compatible with the convention, and have regard to European jurisprudence, adds a new dimension to those principles.

Injunctions are now regarded as capable of being granted *contra mundum*, that is, against the world.

• ***Bloomsbury Publishing Group plc v News Group Newspaper* [2003] EWHC 1087**

> . . . the person or persons who have offered the publishers of The Sun, The Daily Mail and The Daily Mirror newspapers a copy of the book Harry Potter and the Order of the Phoenix by JK Rowling or any part thereof and the person or persons who has or have physical possession of a copy of the said book or any part thereof without the consent of the claimants.

KEY POINT
Injunctions can be granted against the whole world.

19.2 Types of injunction

Broadly speaking, injunctions are of two types: interim (formerly known as interlocutory injunctions) and perpetual (alternatively called final injunctions, see later for detailed explanation). Interim injunctions are granted by the court to enable parties to a suit to maintain the status quo until the court has heard the merits of the case fully. A final injunction does what it says: it determines finally the rights and obligations of parties and hence can only be granted following the full hearing of the case by the court.

But before we consider the specific types of injunctions, let us first examine certain principles that apply to all types of injunctions.

19.2.1 Requirements for the grant of injunctions

To protect legal rights

As a general rule, the court will only grant injunctions to protect a legal or equitable right. Thus injunctions are not whimsically granted or granted simply to fill a vacuum left by law.

● ***Holmes v Millage*** [1893] 1 QB 551

Lindley LJ at 555:

> It is an old mistake to suppose that, because there is no effectual remedy at law, there must be one in equity.

Note that actual infringement on legal or equitable right is not necessary: a mere threat of infringement suffices.

● ***South Carolina Insurance v Assurance Maastchappij*** [1986] 3 All ER 487

Lord Brandon said:

> [T]he effect of these authorities, so far as is material to the present case, can be summarised by saying that the power of the High Court to grant an injunction is subject to two

exceptions...(1) is when one party to an action can show that the other party has either invaded, or *threatens to invade*, a legal or equitable right of the former for the enforcement of which the latter is amenable to the jurisdiction of the court.

Thus, where a claimant fails to establish a right or a threat to it, no injunction will be granted.

· ·

● *Day v Brownrigg* (1878) 10 ChD 294

The plaintiff brought an action in respect of their house which, according to them, had been called 'Ashford Lodge' for a period of 60 years and that the adjoining house had been called 'Ashford Villa' for some 40 years. Problems started when the defendant decided to change their house name to 'Ashford Lodge'. The plaintiff sought an injunction to restrain action on the ground that allowing the renaming of the house was inconvenient and could cause their own house to lose value.

HELD: Per James LJ at 305:

> ...this court can only interfere where there is an invasion of a legal or equitable right. No such legal or equitable right exists.

· ·

● *Paton v Trustees of British Pregnancy Advisory Service* [1979] QB 276

The claimant, a husband, sought an injunction to prevent his wife from committing an abortion. Did pregnancy constitute such a right that equitable remedy of injunction applied?

HELD: Sir George Baker P at 281:

> ...the husband had no legal right enforceable in law or in equity to stop his wife having this abortion or to stop the doctors from carrying out the abortion.

KEY POINTS

- An applicant for an injunctive relief must establish that he or she has a legal or equitable right in the issue concerned.

- However, such right could exist only in terms of potential or real threat to them.

19.2.2 Is there any limit to the court's jurisdiction to grant injunctions?

This is an important question because originally only the Court of Chancery could grant injunctions and in respect of *specific* issues as already seen in Chapter 1 'The birth of equity and trusts' dealing with the historical development of equity. However, following a series of legal developments, common law courts of old began to grant injunctions alongside the Chancery. As we know from Chapter 1, the 1873–5 Judicature Acts fused the jurisdictions of courts of equity and the common law, at least as far as the grant of injunctions is concerned. But this then raises the question what kind of injunctions can these courts grant thereafter? Are they confined to granting the same type of injunctions they could grant before the Judicature Acts was enacted, or can they now grant injunctions in respect of much wider issues?

There are two sides to the debate. One view is that s. 25(8) of the Judicature Act extended the scope of injunctions that the High Court might now grant by virtue of s. 37 of the 1981 Supreme Court Act. The other view denies such an interpretation. Let us now consider these views.

The narrow view

- *Cummins v Perkins* [1899] 1 Ch 16

Lindley and Chitty JJ argued that the High Court could not grant injunctions in respect of issues the old court of equity or common law court could not.

- *North London Rly Co v Great Northern Western Rly Co* (1883) 11 QB 30

Brett LJ at 36:

> If no court had the power of issuing an injunction before the Judicature Act, no part of the High Court has power to issue such an injunction.

The House of Lords approved this classical view in *Gouriet v Union of Post Office Workers* [1978] HL 541, where their Lordships held that the Judicature Act did no more than simply fuse the procedures of the two courts with no consequences whatsoever to their jurisdictions.

However, more recent case law tends to favour a more liberal interpretation of s. 37 of the 1981 Supreme Court Act powers conferred on courts to grant injunctions over the narrow more rigid common law practice.

The broad view

- *Chief Constable of Kent v V* [1983] QB 34

Lord Denning MR at 42:

> The section as it now stands plainly confers a new and extensive jurisdiction ... It is far wider than anything that had been known in our courts before.

- *Bayer AG v Winter* [1986] 1 WLR 497

Fox LJ at 502:

> ...Bearing in mind we are exercising a jurisdiction which is statutory and which is expressed in terms of considerable width, it seems to me that the court should not shrink, if it is of opinion that an injunction is necessary for the proper protection of a party to the action, from granting relief, notwithstanding it may, in its terms, be of a novel character.

● **North London Rly Co v Great Northern Western Rly Co** (1883) 11 QB 30

Cotton LJ at 40:

> where there is a legal right which was, independently of the [Judicature Act], capable of being enforced either at law or in equity, then whatever may have been the previous practice, the High Court may interfere by injunction in protection of that right.

● **Parker v Camden London Borough Council** [1985] 2 All ER 141

Lord Donaldson at 141:

> For my part I do not accept the pre-Judicature practices of the Court of Chancery or any other court should still rule us from their graves…As I see the matter the jurisdiction, as a jurisdiction, is quite general and, in terms, unlimited. Nevertheless it has to be exercised judicially and with due regard to authorities which are binding on the court.

Two years after *Parker*'s case, the House of Lords continued this liberal approach.

● **South Carolina Insurance v Assurantie Maatschappij** [1986] 3 All ER 487

Lord Goff at 487:

> I am reluctant to accept the proposition that the power to grant injunctions is restricted to certain exclusive categories.

For an interesting article on the impact of language on equitable remedies, see Dennis Kurzon 'A Whorfian View of Equitable Remedies: A Chapter in the Semiotics of English Legal Development' (1995) VIII(23) *International Journal of Semiotic Law* 155.

KEY POINT Lord Donaldson did not deny that the practice before the Judicature Act limited the courts to certain types of injunctions. His position was that there was no reason why such restrictive practice should still continue in the post Judicature Act era.

thinking points

- *In the light of recent case law, do you think that the South Carolina case should become the correct interpretation of the extent of courts' powers to grant injunction?*
- *Do you think that there is any real need to have one specific view of the effect of the Judicature Act with respect to the scope of the court's jurisdiction to grant injunctions, or should the issue be left to courts to determine depending on the circumstances of the individual cases before them?*
- *Injunctions are a powerful equitable remedy which the courts have used for centuries. They are used very cautiously and only after a careful consideration of the right of plaintiff and defendants. It is because injunctions have serious consequences for parties against whom they are granted that the courts are usually reluctant to widen the scope of their use. However, the fact that the social milieu of*

the modern world is different to the one that prevailed a century ago means that injunctions, like any other equitable remedies, must adapt to new situations. Several jurisdictions, including the UK, have recently extended the perimeters of such well-known injunctions such as Anton Piller orders to suit the modern exigencies. See Jeff Berryman 'Recent Developments in the Law of Equitable Remedies' (2002) 33 Victoria University of Wellington L Rev 51; Fionnghuala Cuncannon 'The Case for Specific Performance as the Primary Remedy for Breach of Contract in New Zealand' (2004) 35 Victoria University of Wellington L Rev 657.

19.3 Principles guiding the grant of injunctions

There are several principles applicable generally to the grant of injunctions, although some particular principles govern the grant of specific types of injunctions. For example, the principles governing the grant of interlocutory injunctions are different from those applicable to perpetual (final) injunctions, just as different principles apply to whether an injunctive relief is to be granted with notice or ex parte (without notice to the defendant). We first consider the general principles which apply to the grant of injunctions regardless of what type of injunction is sought.

19.3.1 Inappropriateness of legal remedies such as damages

● *London and Blackwell Rly Co v Cross* (1886) 31 ChD 354

Lindley LJ at 369:

> The very first principle of injunction law is that prima facie injunctions cannot be obtained to restrain actionable wrongs, for which damages are the proper remedy.

Thus, where legal remedies are not appropriate it is up to the court to intervene by ordering injunctive relief.

● *AG v Sheffield Gas Consumers Co* (1853) 3 De GM & G 304

Turner LJ at 321:

> Whether this is a case in which the law is so inadequate that the court ought to interfere, having regard to the legal remedy, the right and consequence of the court's interference.

This principle suggests that the court will first have to consider whether common law remedies are adequate before entertaining the application for an injunctive order. But the court does not have to award damages, even if these are adequate, where an injunction will be more appropriate: *Beswick v Beswick* [1968] AC 58. This may be in order to prevent the culprit from continuing the offending act after paying damages (see *Stevens v Chown* (1901) 1 Ch 894), or to prevent what is generally regarded as a situation in which the defendant is able to 'purchase' the right to commit a wrong through damages. We shall discuss the issue of award of injunctions in lieu of damages more fully later.

19.3.2 Past and future conduct of claimants

As we discussed in Chapter 2 'Maxims of equity', equity runs on a series of maxims. Two of these maxims which are very important are that 'he who comes to equity must come with clean hands' and 'he who seeks equity must do equity'. As explained in Chapter 2, the first deals with the past conduct of the claimant who seeks equity, while the second relates to the future conduct of the claimant. Thus a claimant whose previous conduct has been tarnished by an impropriety may be denied an injunctive relief by the court just as a claimant who refuses to do equity or undertake certain obligations (in respect of the future) to alleviate the plight of the defendant, were the application for injunction to succeed, may be declined by the court.

Past conduct

● *Cross v Cross* [1983] 4 FLR 235

Following a break-up of marriage between a couple and a divorce proceeding, issues arose as to payment of maintenance and mortgage on the matrimonial property. The husband, responsible for the mortgage payment, and the wife, responsible for paying rates, both defaulted. The husband eventually divested his interest in the house in full settlement of his obligation towards the mortgage in the mistaken belief that his ex-wife and son were still living in the matrimonial home. It turned out that the wife had moved out to live with her new husband as at the date the previous husband divested himself of his interest. The ex-husband reversed his decision. His ex-wife brought an application for specific performance of that agreement. The court looked at the conduct of both parties up to the proceedings and, on balance, refused the wife's application.

Wood J:

> He who comes to equity must come with clean hands and any conduct of the plaintiff, which would make a grant of specific performance inequitable, can prove a bar.

As we said in Chapter 2, it must be noted that the court is here concerned not with the general conduct of the claimant but with any such specific conduct that may affect his application.

● *Dering v Earl of Winchelsea* [1787] 1 Cox 318

Sir Edward Dering, the Earl of Winchelsea, was of a general bad character, which included encouraging his brother to gamble with government money.

Eyre LCB:

> …a man must come into a court of equity with clean hands; but when this is said, it does not mean a general depravity; it must have an immediate and necessary relation to the equity sued for, it must be a depravity in a legal as well as a moral sense.

Future conduct

● *Chappell v Times Newspapers* (1975) 2 All ER 233

(See full facts in Chapter 2.)

HELD:

> …in seeking an equitable remedy the plaintiffs had to be prepared to do equity, *and by refusing to give an undertaking not to disrupt newspaper production* they were in effect telling the employers that they must keep to their part of the contract even though the plaintiffs were not themselves ready or willing to keep to theirs. Accordingly, even though the plaintiffs might not have been in breach of their individual contracts of employment, they were not entitled to the equitable relief claimed in the interlocutory application and the appeal would fail. [Emphasis added.]

KEY POINT
The court is not concerned with the general conduct of the claimant but with his conduct that relates to his application.

● *Neesom v Clarkson* (1845) 4 Hare 97

Wigram VC at 101:

> … where a litigant requires the assistance of a court of equity to enforce his claim, he can be made to submit to conditions.

thinking points

Do you think it is always possible for the court to separate the specific from the general conduct of a claimant, and is there any persuasive reason why the court could not look into the general conduct of a claimant to determine his application? As we observed in Chapter 2, courts are more concerned with the specific conduct of a claimant for equitable remedy vis-à-vis the defendant in deciding whether or not to grant the order. This principle was laid down in the Highwayman (Everet v Williams, *Ex 1725 9 LQR 197), where the court dismissed with costs a case brought by a robber who filed a bill in equity to compel his partner to account for a sum of money, and cited the lawyers who brought the case for contempt of the court. See FP 'The Highwayman's Case (Everet v Williams)' (1893) 9(35) LQR 197.*

19.3.3 Futility of an order

Where it will be futile to grant an injunction or where, once granted, it will be impossible to execute an injunctive order, the court will not normally grant the application. This is in consonance with the maxim 'equity does not act in vain'. Thus, where, for instance, it will be impossible for the court to compel the defendant to undo what he has already done—which gave rise to the claimant's action—the court may refuse an injunctive order.

● *Evans v Manchester, Sheffield and Lincolnshire Rly Co* [1887] ChD 626

The court refused to grant an injunction to prevent the future subsidizing of a canal.

Kekewich J at 639:

> I think it would be wrong to enjoin a company or an individual from permitting that to be done which is really beyond his control…in the sense that he cannot by any precaution or by any works with reasonable certainty…comply with the order sought.

● **AG v Observer Ltd** [1990] 1 AC 109

In breach of his duty of confidentiality, a former member of the British security services published confidential information in his memoirs. The memoirs became the subject matter of litigation in Australia and were subsequently published in America. Two British newspapers published material derived from the memoirs, but not disclosed in open court in Australia. The Crown sought permanent injunctions to restrain the first two newspapers from commenting on and reporting the contents of the memoirs.

HELD: Inter alia, that the injunction sought by the Crown in respect of future information was too wide and too vague. The court saw no reason in maintaining an injunction restraining some newspapers from publishing Peter Wright's Memoirs—*Spycatcher*—which had been published worldwide.

When would the courts award damages instead of injunction?

As said earlier, injunctions will only be granted where, amongst other reasons, any remedy is either inadequate or inappropriate. This means that, under certain circumstances, the courts will refuse injunctions following consideration of the suitability of damages.

Some writers argue that the circumstances in which the court will award damages instead of injunctions include those situations where, prior to the Chancery Amendment Act 1858 (otherwise known as Lord Cairns's Act), they could easily award damages and no more. Others argue that the courts are now able to award damages regardless of whether they could have done so prior to Lord Cairns's Act. However, what should concern us here are the principles governing when the court could award damages in lieu of injunctions irrespective of whether the court is operating before or after Lord Cairns's Act, as no one has argued yet that different principles attach to the different generations of courts. (For more reading on this issue, see Philip Pettit *Equity and the Law of Trusts* (9th edn, London: Butterworths, 2001) 552–4.) Section 2 of the Chancery Amendment Act empowers the court to award damages 'in all cases in which the Court of Chancery has jurisdiction to entertain an application for an injunction'.

19.4.1 Principles applicable to the grant of damages in lieu of injunctions

The court has a discretion, following Lord Cairns's Act, on whether to award damages in lieu of injunction, just as it has a discretion, following the Judicature Act, to grant injunctions or award common law damages. However, to grant damages in lieu of injunctions, it is essential that the court determines the existence of certain principles. These principles were laid down by Smith LJ.

● **Shelfer v City of London Electric Co** [1895] 1 Ch 287

At 323:

> (1) where the injury to the claimant is not substantial
> (2) where the wrong suffered by the claimant can be quantified in monetary terms
> (3) where monetary compensation will be enough remedy
> (4) where it would be oppressive to the defendant to grant an injunction.

But this does not mean that once these conditions exist the courts have no choice but to award damages.

Lindley LJ at 316:

> Ever since Lord Cairns's Act was passed the Court of Chancery has repudiated the notion that it ought to allow a wrong to continue simply because the wrongdoer is able and willing to pay for the injury he may inflict.

Thus, the rationale for awarding damages in lieu of injunction is not to provide the affluent defendant with unlimited ammunition to purchase the right to wrong another.

● **Slack v Leeds Industrial Co-Operative Society Ltd** [1924] 2 Ch 475

Lord Summer at 872:

> For my part ... I doubt, as Sir George Jessel doubted, whether it is complete justice to allow the big man, with his big building and his enhanced rateable value and his improvement of the neighbourhood, to have his way, and to solace the little man for his darkened and stuffy little house by giving him a cheque he does not ask for.

The four rules established by Smith LJ were an expression of his own opinion and, as such, they are susceptible to change or different interpretations and assessments.

● **Fishenden v Higgs and Hill Ltd** (1935) 153 LT 128

Hanworth MR stated that the rules set 'the high water mark of what might be called definite rules'.

Maugham LJ at 144: Although Smith's rules might have been accepted as valid they are 'not universal or even sound rules in all cases of injury to light'.

● **Jaggard v Sawyer** [1995] 2 All ER 189

The plaintiff with her husband bought a house in 1980 in a development area, subject to a covenant not to be binding on successive owners, not to use any part of the unbuilt land other than as a private garden and to keep the relevant section of roadway in good repair. In 1987 the defendants purchased a house at the opposite end of the cul-de-sac from the plaintiff's property. They decided to build another property on a plot which would have infringed the covenant and inconvenienced the plaintiff's own property. The plaintiff brought an action for injunction to restrain the proposed use of the new plot, but only after construction had commenced and advanced despite her being aware of the defendant's plan to do so.

The judge found that although the proposed user of the land resulting from the construction of No 5A would involve breach of the covenant and a continuing trespass, the defendants had acted openly and in good faith, and through inexperience had not appreciated the problem of the covenant, that the plaintiff had failed to seek interlocutory relief, that the trespass itself would involve only light traffic over the plaintiff's section of the roadway, and that if an injunction were granted No 5A would have no access route. In those circumstances the judge refused to grant the injunction sought because it would be oppressive to the defendants, and instead held that the plaintiff should be awarded damages in lieu under s. 50 of the Supreme Court Act 1981.

On appeal the Court of Appeal confirmed the award of damages. Millett LJ applied Smith's rules without criticism or qualifications, commenting that 'Laid down just 100 years ago, AL Smith LJ's test has stood the test of time' (at 287). The Court of Appeal's decision was based on the fact that the outcome of a particular case usually depends on the application of the fourth of Smith's rules—that is, that damages would be granted in lieu of injunction where it would be oppressive to the defendant to grant an injunction.

However, in *Kennaway v Thompson* [1981] QB 88, although the Court of Appeal affirmed the approach in *Jaggard v Sawyer*, stating that '[t]he principles enunciated in Shelfer's case, which is binding on us, have been applied time and time again over the past 85 years', it granted an injunction, despite the fact that the court of first instance had awarded damages, to restrict a nuisance of noise generated by a motor boat race. The Court of Appeal's decision was on the basis that none of the first three rules set down by Smith LJ was fulfilled.

KEY POINT Even where a defendant is able to prove that the injury he has caused or, in some cases, intends to cause the claimant is not substantial, remediable financially, and that granting the injunction will be unfair to him, the court could still grant the injunction. This will be so if, for instance, on the balance of everything, the court is of the opinion that it serves the interest of justice and equity to do that.

As shown above, AL Smith LJ's rules are just guiding principles to aid the court in its discretion to know whether or not to award damages instead of injunction. So much depends on facts and circumstances of individual cases. But as Pettit correctly noted (*Equity and the Law of Trusts* at 557):

> …most of the cases in which an injunction has been refused and damages awarded are cases where the plaintiff has sought a mandatory injunction to pull down a building which infringes his right to light or which has been built in breach of a restrictive covenant. In such cases the court is faced with a fait accompli and to grant an injunction would subject the defendant to a loss out of all proportion to that which would be suffered by the plaintiff if it were refused.

It is thus clear that the socio-economic costs of granting an injunction—usually, in this scenario, one that would compel the defendant to destroy an already completed project such as a house—play a crucial role in the courts exercising their discretion.

· ·

● *Wrotham Park Estate Co v Parkside Homes Ltd* [1974] 2 All ER 321

The purchaser of some plots of land covenanted with the seller and his assigns the owner for the time being of Wrotham Park Estate that he and his successors in title would not develop the land for building purposes except in accordance with a plan approved by the seller. The defendants began, at some point, to start developing these lands in contravention of the covenant. The plaintiff, the successors in title to the original sellers, brought an action for a grant of an injunction to restrain further development of the land and to have the houses already built pulled down. The application was refused.

HELD: Brightman J at 337:

> The erection of the houses, whether one likes it or not, is a fait accompli, and the houses are now the homes of people. I accept that this fait accompli is reversible and could be undone. But I cannot close my eyes to the fact that the houses now exist. It would in my opinion, be an unpardonable waste of much needed houses to direct that they be pulled down and I have never had a moment's doubt during the hearing of this case that such an order ought to be refused.

This can be contrasted, however, with the next case.

● *Jaggard v Sawyer* [1995] 2 All ER 189

The defendant built a house in a manner that landlocked the claimant so that the latter's access to his own property would require the claimant to trespass on a private road. In an action for an injunction, the court followed *Wrotham Park* and awarded the claimant damages in lieu of the injunction sought.

HELD: The plaintiff was awarded damages to the tune of what the defendant would have paid for a right of way, had he constructed the house in accordance with proper processes.

Measure of damages

If the court will award damages in lieu of an injunction, what is the relevant date for calculating the measure of damages to be awarded? Is it damages as would have compensated the plaintiff at the time when the action is brought or when the judgment would have been rendered?

● *Johnson v Agnew* [1980] AC 367

Lord Wilberforce at 896:

> In cases where a breach of a contract of sale has occurred, and the innocent party reasonably continues to try to have the contract completed, it would appear to be more logical and just rather than tie him to the date of the original breach, to assess damages as at the date when (otherwise than by his default) the contract is lost.

In the *Wrotham Park* case, damages were awarded in accordance with the sum the plaintiff might have expected as reasonable for relaxing the covenant in favour of the defendant.

KEY POINT It does not automatically follow that because damages are appropriate the court will refuse injunctions. If damages will become a means of purchasing the power continuously to infringe a claimant's right, then an injunction will be ordered notwithstanding the adequacy or appropriateness of damages in that case.

Let us now move to consideration of interlocutory injunctions.

19.4.2 Principles guiding the grant of interim injunctions

As said earlier on, injunctions are of various types, even if generally they are either prohibitory (restraining the doing of an act) or mandatory (compelling the doing of an act). In specific terms, injunctions can be interim (granted for a short time) or *quia timet* (granted prospectively to prevent a breach from occurring). Even then, in the category of interim injunctions, some injunctions can be of specific use, such as to prevent the removal of assets from a jurisdiction where the defendant is being a subject of the dispute (freezing injunctions), and some injunctions could also be granted to prevent the removal of vital materials for evidence from the defendant's premises (search order).

But whatever the different varieties of interim injunctions, all of them are subject to the same principles which we now consider.

The old regime and the test of 'prima facie' case

Prior to 1975—the date that *American Cyanamid Co v Ethicon Ltd* [1975] 1 All ER 504 was decided—the golden principle was that an applicant for the grant of an interim injunction must show that he had a prima facie case in the court.

● ***American Cyanamid Co v Ethicon Ltd*** [1975] 1 All ER 504

Lord Diplock at 406:

> It was to mitigate the risk of injustice to the plaintiff during the period before that uncertainty could be resolved that the practice arose of granting him relief by way of interlocutory injunctions.

The new regime and the test of 'not frivolous or vexatious' case

This case related to an action brought by a company (Cyanamid) which registered a patent in the UK for the use as absorbable surgical sutures of filaments made of a particular kind of chain polymer known as 'a polyhydroxyacetic ester' (PHAE). At that date, the absorbable sutures commonly in use were made from catgut. A rival company (Ethicon) was the main supplier of catgut sutures in the UK. Cyanamid introduced its patented product in 1970 and by 1973 had captured some 15 per cent of the UK market for absorbable surgical sutures. In order to meet the competition from Cyanamid, Ethicon proposed to introduce its own artificial suture (XLG). The chemical substance of PHAE was a homopolymer, whereas the substance from which XLG was made was a copolymer. Cyanamid brought an action for a *quia timet* injunction to restrain the defendant from introducing its product onto the UK market.

Although the patent judge held that Cyanamid had proved a prima facie case and was so entitled, the Court of Appeal reversed the order. On appeal to the House of Lords, it was held as follows.

HELD:

> ...all that was necessary was that the court should be satisfied that the claim was not frivolous or vexatious, i.e. that there was a serious question to be tried.

According to the *American Cyanamid* case, in determining whether to grant an interim injunction the court should adopt the following approach:

1. That the claimant can show that there is a serious issue to be tried.

2. That the court considers where the balance of convenience lies. The important things to consider here are:

   (i) the court's ability to quantify likely damages;

   (ii) the sufficiency of the claimant's cross-undertaking in damages (if the defendant is successful at trial); and

   (iii) the sufficiency of the defendant's financial resources to compensate the claimant (if the claimant is successful at trial).

3. If there is no imbalance, then the status quo is preserved.

KEY POINT An applicant for an interim injunction no longer needs to show that he has a 'prima facie' case before he can bring an application. What he has to show now is that his case against the defendant is neither frivolous nor vexatious.

The rationale for the new principles governing the grant of interim injunctions was laid out.

Lord Diplock at 396:

> When an application for an interlocutory injunction to restrain a defendant from doing acts alleged to be in violation of the plaintiff's legal rights is made on contested facts, the decision whether or not to grant an interlocutory injunction has to be taken at a time when ex hypothesi the existence of the right or the violation of it, or both, is uncertain and will remain uncertain until final judgment is given in the action . . . the object of interlocutory injunction is to protect the plaintiff against injury by violations of his right for which he could not be adequately compensated in damages recoverable in the action if the uncertainty were resolved in his favour at the trial.

Lord Diplock went on to substitute the 'prima facie' test of the old order for a new 'frivolous or vexatious' test. Thus, an applicant for an interim injunction is no more required to prove that he has a prima facie case; all he has to show is that his substantive action is not frivolous or vexatious. Lord Diplock thought in *American Cyanamid* that in reality, there was no understanding amongst the law lords to insist on a prima facie test as a condition for granting interim injunctions.

19.4.3 What does 'frivolous or vexatious' mean in this context?

● *Mothercare Ltd v Robson Books Ltd* [1979] FSR 466

Megarry VC said these terms could lead to confusion. He ruled that the phrases simply mean that the plaintiff can show there is 'a real prospect of succeeding in his claim to a permanent injunction at the trial'.

One slight problem with *American Cyanamid* was that the House of Lords, in laying down the new test, did not refer to its decision in *JT Stratford & Sons v Lindley* [1965] AC 269, a case which was decided ten years before *American Cyanamid*. In *JT Stratford*, the House of Lords had ruled that a claimant could only be entitled to an interim injunction upon proof of a prima facie case in his favour.

Some attempts have been made to limit the effect of the *American Cyanamid* test. In *Hoffmann-La Roche & Co AG v Secretary of State and Industry* [1975] AC 295, Laddie J went back to the old test of a 'prima facie' case. However, Laddie J's approach was not regarded as rejecting the new test as laid down by Lord Diplock, but rather serving as a reminder for the background to the *Cyanamid* principle, which is that the test is not meant to be exclusive.

· ·

● *Series 5 Software Ltd v Philip Clarke and others* [1996] FSR 273

In this case involving confidential business information and trade secrets, Laddie J attempted to resuscitate the prima facie criterion by stating that the court should also consider the relative strength of parties' cases in deciding whether or not to grant an interim injunction. It must be noted, however, that later his decision has not been followed and cases have not, so far, referred to the judgment.

· ·

● *Barnsley Brewery Co Ltd v RBNB* [1997] FSR 462

Robert Walker J:

> ...that the application for interlocutory injunctions cannot be mini trials of disputed issues of facts and that the court has to do the best it can on a provisional basis, with the relatively modest aim of reducing so far as possible an unjust result.

But notwithstanding these bold attempts, most courts now adopt the 'frivolous or vexatious test'.

It must be stated that, although the 'frivolous or vexatious' test is the main test that determines whether an application for interlocutory injunctions can be made, there are other principles, according to Lord Diplock, that the court must consider in order to decide whether or not to grant the application. According to Lord Diplock, there are six such principles, which we now consider.

However, in recent cases dealing with pharmaceuticals, courts have attempted to clarify some of the test laid down in *American Cyanamid*. One such criterion is the question of damages.

In *SmithKline Beecham plc v Generics UK Ltd* (Patents Court) [2002] 25(1) IPD 25005 and *SmithKline Beecham plc v Apotex Europe Ltd* (Patents Court and Court of Appeal) [2003] WL 1202563, both relating to GB patent number 2 297 550, and both relating to a patent concerning specific salt of the selective serotonin re-uptake inhibitor paroxetine, the court had to determine the balance of convenience between the parties. In *SmithKline Beecham plc v Generics UK Ltd*, the plaintiff had become aware of the defendant's intention to launch their own generic paroxetine product, which they claimed infringed claim 3 of the '550 patent relating to paroxetine hydrochloride anhydrate'. In an application filed for interim injunction, Jacob J, in determining the question of where the balance of convenience lay, had to consider the adequacy/quantifiability of damages. In his judgment, Jacob J said that:

> ...as between the two, I will put it this way, the claimant's damage is more unquantifiable than that of the defendant's, but both are unquantifiable. There are degrees of unquantifiability, just as there are degrees of infinity.

Jacob J reaffirmed his view in *SmithKline Beecham plc v Apotex Europe Ltd*, of virtually similar facts. The judge stated:

> I remain of the same opinion as I was in the Generics case. Where litigation is bound to ensue if the defendant introduces his product, he can avoid all the problems of an interlocutory injunction if he clears the way first. That is what the procedures for revocation and declaration for non-infringement are for.

In July 2010 the Supreme Court of Papua New Guinea, in the *Ramu Nico* case, had to find a balance of convenience in a suit brought by some landowners against Ramu Nico's attempt to construct a deep sea tailings placement (DSTP) system which the applicants for an interim injunction claimed posed serious environmental hazards. In confirming the decision of the lower court to grant the order, the Supreme Court held that 'the potential environment harm far outweighs the lifting of the injunction'. (See Julia Daia Bore, 'Ramu fails to lift interim injunction on tailings disposal', available at: <http://www.minesandcommunities.org/article. php?a=10262>.)

19.4.4 *American Cyanamid's* six guiding principles for granting interim injunctions

1. The governing principle is that the court should first consider whether if the plaintiff were to succeed at the trial in establishing his right to a permanent injunction he would be adequately compensated by an award of damages for the loss he would have sustained as a result of the defendant's continuing to do what was sought to be enjoined between the time of the application and the time of the trial. If damages in the measure recoverable at common law would be an adequate remedy and the defendant would be in a financial position to pay them, no interlocutory injunction should normally be granted, however strong the plaintiff's claim appeared to be at that stage (see 511).

Pettit has rightly considered this principle to be a 'restatement of the established rule that a claimant should not be granted an interim injunction unless he is able to show that if it was not granted, he would suffer irreparable damage'. Consequently, the damage done or threatened must be substantial and unquantifiable in monetary terms.

· ·

● *Express Newspaper Ltd v Keys* [1980] IRLR 247

On the basis of an unlawful proposal by a trade union to induce the claimant's employees to break their contracts by participating in a political strike, the claimant was held entitled to an injunction on the basis that it would be difficult to calculate its loss.

2. If, on the other hand, damages would not provide an adequate remedy for the plaintiff in the event of his succeeding at the trial, the court should then consider whether, on the contrary hypothesis that the defendant were to succeed at the trial in establishing his right to do that which was sought to be enjoined, he would be adequately compensated under the plaintiff's undertaking as to damages for the loss he would have sustained by being prevented from doing so between the time of the application and the time of the trial. If damages in the measure recoverable under such an undertaking would be an adequate remedy and the plaintiff would be in a financial position to pay them, there would be no reason on this ground to refuse an interlocutory injunction.

This principle was applied in *Chancellor Masters and Scholars of Oxford University v Pergamon* (1977) 121 Sol Jo 758, where the court granted an interlocutory injunction to restrain the defendant from projecting Pergamon Press's *Dictionary of Perfect Spelling* as though it was one of the claimant's dictionaries by featuring the word 'Oxford' in the title. The court held that to deny an injunction in this case would amount to great but unascertainable damage to the claimant and that the defendants would be sufficiently covered by the claimant's financial undertaking towards them if the defendants were, on the final case, successful.

3. Where there is doubt as to the adequacy of the respective remedies in damages available to either party or to both, then the question of the balance of convenience arises. It would

be unwise even to attempt to list all the various matters which may need to be taken into consideration in deciding where the balance lies, let alone to suggest the relative weight to be attached to them. These will vary from case to case.

The principle of balance of convenience has proved to be controversial. In *Francome v Mirror Group Newspapers Ltd* [1984] 2 All ER 408 and in *AG v Barker* [1990] 3 All ER 257, Donaldson MR commented to the effect that the principle of balance of convenience is 'an unfortunate expression'. The judge also stated that the court should be concerned with justice, not balance of convenience.

The problem is that some judges do not think it is possible to achieve a real determination of 'balance of convenience' without somehow prejudging the substantive case.

....

● ***Fellowes & Son v Fisher*** [1976] QB 122

Browne LJ at 138:

> I cannot see how the 'balance of convenience' can be fairly or reasonably considered without taking some account as a factor of the relative strength of the parties' cases, but the House of Lords seems to have held that this is only the last resort.

....

● ***Cayne v Global Natural Resources plc*** [1984] 1 All ER 225

May LJ at 225:

> ...that the balance of convenience reads more like the 'balance of the risk of doing injustice'.

4. Where other factors appear to be evenly balanced it is a counsel of prudence to take such measures as are calculated to preserve the status quo. If the defendant is enjoined temporarily from doing something that he has not done before, the only effect of the interlocutory injunction in the event of his succeeding at the trial is to postpone the date at which he is able to embark on a course of action which he has not previously found it necessary to undertake; whereas to interrupt him in the conduct of an established enterprise would cause much greater inconvenience to him since he would have to start again to establish it in the event of his succeeding at the trial.

This principle seeks to ensure that all circumstances of the defendant are taken into consideration before deciding whether or not to grant an injunction against him. The rationale here is to determine whether he stands to suffer any harm by a mere postponement of the date he wishes to commence an act he normally does engage in.

In *European Dynamics SA v HM Treasury* [2009] EWHC 3419 (TCC), a tenderer who had not been successful for a bid for work with a contracting authority brought an action for an interim injunction against the authority on the basis that its tender had not been fairly treated.

In deciding whether or not to grant injunction, the court held that the balance of convenience favoured the discharge of the without notice injunction for the following reasons:

• There would be substantial prejudice to the contracting authority, as the existing frameworks were due to expire and customers were waiting for the new frameworks to be in place—customers would go elsewhere to get the services they required if they had to wait for new frameworks to be put in place.

- The earliest date for a full trial of the dispute between the parties was at least six months away. This delay could result in irreparable harm to the contracting authority's reputation.

- There was no obvious or clear evidence that the unsuccessful tenderer would lose market share or would not be able to seek other work to replace what it might have secured had it been successful.

- If the unsuccessful tenderer succeeded on liability, damages would be an adequate remedy.

- If an injunction was granted for as long as six months, there was a real risk that the whole tender process would have to be re-run and—given the knowledge acquired by the unsuccessful tenderer—it might be necessary to exclude the unsuccessful tenderer and indeed others who tendered on the basis that there would not and could not be equality of opportunity in the new tender process.

For a commentary on this case, see Christopher Hill, Steve Abraham, and Donald Warnock 'United Kingdom: Public Procurement, Interim Injunctions And Framework Agreements', 25 August 2010, available at: <http://www.mondaq.com/article.asp?articleid=106776>.

5. Save in the simplest cases, the decision to grant or to refuse an interlocutory injunction will cause to whichever party is unsuccessful on the application some disadvantages which his ultimate success at the trial may show he ought to have been spared, and the disadvantages may be such that the recovery of damages to which he would then be entitled, either in the action or under the plaintiff's undertaking, would not be sufficient to compensate him fully for all of them. The extent to which the disadvantages to each party would be incapable of being compensated in damages in the event of his succeeding at the trial is always a significant factor in assessing where the balance of convenience lies; and if the extent of the uncompensatable disadvantage to each party would not differ widely, it may not be improper to take into account in tipping the balance the relative strength of each party's case as revealed by the affidavit evidence adduced on the hearing of the application.

6. If the extent of the uncompensatable disadvantage to each party would not differ widely, it may not be improper to take into account in tipping the balance the relative strength of each party's case as revealed by the affidavit evidence adduced on the hearing of the application. This, however, should be done only where it is apparent on the facts disclosed by evidence as to which there is no credible dispute that the strength of one party's case is disproportionate to that of the other party. The court is not justified in embarking on anything resembling a trial of the action on conflicting affidavits in order to evaluate the strength of either party's case.

However, apart from the above, it has been held that other special factors also exist on the basis for deciding whether to grant interim injunctions.

● *American Cyanamid Co v Ethicon Ltd* [1975] 1 All ER 504

Lord Diplock:

> I would reiterate that, in addition to those to which I have referred, there may be many other special factors to be taken into consideration in the particular circumstances of individual cases. The instant appeal affords one example of this.

● *Bryanston Finance Ltd v de Vries (No 2)* [1976] Ch 63

The plaintiff brought an action for an injunctive order to restrain the defendant from bringing an application for a winding-up of a company. The facts do not fall under any of the six principles, so Buckley LJ held that this amounted to a special factor that the injunction sought by the claimant was to restrain the commencement of a proceeding limine.

There is ongoing academic debate about the exact impact of the special factor which is not relevant to us. (For a full discussion, see Pettit at 575ff.) See further *Cambridge Nutrition v BBC* [1990] 3 All ER 529.

19.4.5 Limits or exceptions to *American Cyanamid* principles

Not applicable to applications for mandatory orders

In general, the *Cyanamid* principles concern mainly the grant of prohibitory injunctions on an interim basis. Thus, it is extremely rare for the court to grant an application for a mandatory order for, as the court said in *Gale v Abbott* [1862] 10 WR 748: 'the court would not compel a man to do so serious a thing as to undo what he had done except at a hearing'.

Absence of difficult questions of law

American Cyanamid does not apply to all applications for interim injunctions. For instance, it will not apply where there is no difficult question of law or issue of evidence to decide.

● *Hubbard v Pitt* [1976] QB 142

The case concerned an action brought by the applicant to prevent the defendant from picketing its offices following an organized campaign by the defendant to compel the applicant to comply with the defendant's guidelines for conducting property transactions such as property development in the area. The application was granted.

Stamp LJ at 185:

> There are no circumstances in which the existence of special factors would take a case out of the general rule that it is not necessary for an interlocutory injunction to make out a prima facie case. The existence of special factors is only relevant in considering whether the balance of convenience justifies the grant of an injunction.

Restriction of the freedom of speech under the Human Rights Act 1998

The obligations created under the Human Rights Act 1998 with regard to freedom of expression in particular limit the application of the *Cyanamid* principles. Under s. 13 of the Act, 'No relief is to be granted so as to restrain publication before trial unless the court is satisfied that the applicant is likely to be able to establish that publication should not be allowed.' Although there is already a high test of 'serious question to be tried' imposed by the *Cyanamid* principles, the obligation laid down in the Human Rights Act 1998 raises the threshold much higher, especially in cases against the media as already noted by Lord Phillips in *Douglas v Hello!* [2005] ECWA Civ 595 at 258.

The full implication of this new threshold was confronted in *Cream Holding v Banerjee* [2004] 4 All ER 617. Here, following the termination of her appointment as an employee of a Liverpool nightclub, Ms Banerjee copied the files of the company and made them available to two

Merseyside newspapers. Cream Holdings, the company which ran the club, applied for a restraining order. The House of Lords, however, said that they had not shown that they were more likely than not to succeed at trial if the publication was to be prevented.

Despite the fact that the interpretation adopted in *Cream Holdings* by the House of Lords, in construing the word 'likely' in s. 12(3) of the Human Rights Act 1998, suggests that the court would require applicants for interim injunctions in media cases to prove a very high likelihood of success at trial, Lord Nicholls cautioned against the assumption that 'likely' in that section invariably means 'more likely than not'. His Lordship urged an avoidance of turning such a test into a universal standard and rather commended a case-by-case approach (see particularly at 624ff of that case).

Libel cases

Whereas s. 12(3) of the Human Rights Act 1998 has now affected the test laid down in *American Cyanamid* concerning a 'serious law question', the position of libel suits, however, remains as before. In other words, the higher threshold laid down in *Cream Holdings* does not apply to libel suits.

In *Martha Green v Associated Newspapers*, the claimant applied to restrain the publication of an allegedly defamatory article. Relying on the *Cream Holdings* principle, she claimed that she was more likely than not to succeed at the full trial. However, Brookes LJ rejected this. The judge distinguished between the instant case and *Cream Holdings* on the ground that while the latter concerned a question of confidential information, the article being restrained from publication in *Martha Greene* only related to defamation. According to the judge, the two do not weigh equally. As even Lord Nicholls stated in *Cream Holdings*, 'confidentiality once breached, is lost for ever' (at 624).

Specific interim injunctions

There are several types of interim injunctions in existence. There are some, however, that attract specific comments because they emerged more recently and constitute, in the words of Lord Denning, 'the greatest piece of judicial law reform in my time' or, according to Donaldson LJ, 'Law's two nuclear weapons'. These two injunctions are the freezing injunctions (formerly called Mareva injunctions) and search orders (previously known as Anton Piller orders).

19.5.1 Freezing injunctions: freezing the assets of the defendant

● *Mareva Compania Naviera SA v International Bulkcarriers SA* [1980] 1 All ER 213

The claimants brought an action for injunction ex parte (without notice to the defendant) to prevent the defendants from removing from their banks in London moneys which the claimants hoped would be used to satisfy a judgment against the defendants. The claim was in respect of unpaid hire and damages for repudiation of a charterparty.

The law before the *Mareva* case

Before the *Mareva* case was brought, the law prevailing in England with regard to how a defendant to a suit can deal with his money, was as stated in *Lister & Co v Stubbs* (1890) 45 ChD 1. The law was that nothing empowered a person to obtain an injunction which restrains another from dissipating his money or removing it out of jurisdiction of a court hearing a suit against him. So, if A sues B in England for payment of some sum to him (A), while the case is being heard A cannot take out an injunction to stop B who, fearing that he might lose the case and hence be made to pay A from his money in banks in London or other parts of England, decides to use his money quickly or remit it to foreign banks. Such a move is bad faith but not illegal under the *Lister v Stubbs* rule.

In *Mareva*, Donaldson LJ recognized this rule but nevertheless granted an injunction, although only lasting until a certain hour of that day. The defendants appealed.

The issue appealed revolved around how the court would reconcile the ancient rule in *Lister v Stubbs* entitling a defendant to deal with his money howsoever he pleased and the imperative-ness of ensuring that the judgment that the claimant might get against the defendant is not frustrated by lack of means to compensate him.

Mareva Compania Naviera SA v International Bulkcarriers SA at 215 (Lord Denning MR):

> In my opinion that principle applies to a creditor who has a right to be paid the debt owing to him, even before he has established his right by getting judgment for it. If it appears that the debt is due and owing, and there is a danger that the debtor may dispose of his assets so as to defeat it before judgment, the court has jurisdiction in a proper case to grant an interlocutory judgment so as to prevent him disposing of those assets. It seems to me that this is a proper case for the exercise of this jurisdiction.

In coming to this conclusion, Lord Denning did not throw away *Lister v Stubbs* lightly. Rather, he relied on the wide discretionary power granted to courts by s. 45 of the Supreme Court of Judicature (Consolidation) Act 1925, which repeats s. 25(8) of the Judicature Act 1873.

> A mandamus or an injunction may be granted or a receiver appointed by an interlocutory order of the court in all cases in which it shall appear to the court to be just or convenient ...

It must be noted that Lord Denning had already started this move before *Mareva* when, in *Nippon Yusen Kaisha v Karageorgis* [1975] 3 All ER 282, his Lordship held that a freezing order could be granted on the basis of s. 37(1) of the Supreme Court Act 1981, entitling the High Court to grant an injunction in all circumstances in which it appears it is just to do so.

19.5.2 Principles guiding the grant of freezing injunctions

Although freezing injunctions are a type of interlocutory injunction—and hence, subjected to the same principles applicable to all interlocutory injunctions—there are some specific principles that apply to the injunction.

In *Third Chandris Shipping Corpn v Unimarine SA*, Lord Denning set out the guidelines for granting freezing injunction as follows:

Lord Denning MR:

> Much as I am in favour of the *Mareva* injunction, it must not be stretched too far lest it be endangered. In endeavouring to set out some guidelines, I have had recourse to the practice of many other countries which have been put before us. They have been most helpful. These are the points which those who apply for it should bear in mind:
>
> (i) The plaintiff should make full and frank disclosure of all matters in his knowledge which are material for the judge to know: see *Negocios del Mar SA v Doric Shipping Corporation SA (The Assios)* [1979] 1 Lloyd's Rep 331.
>
> (ii) The plaintiff should give particulars of his claim against the defendant, stating the ground of his claim and the amount thereof, and fairly stating the points made against it by the defendant.
>
> (iii) The plaintiff should give some grounds for believing that the defendant has assets here … In most cases the plaintiff will not know the extent of the assets. He will only have indications of them. The existence of a bank account in England is enough, whether it is in overdraft or not.
>
> (iv) The plaintiff should give some grounds for believing that there is a risk of the assets being removed before the judgment or award is satisfied. The mere fact that the defendant is abroad is not by itself sufficient. No one would wish any reputable foreign company to be plagued with a *Mareva* injunction simply because it has agreed to London arbitration. But there are some foreign companies whose structure invites comment. We often see in this court a corporation which is registered in a country where the company law is so loose that nothing is known about it—where it does no work and has no officers and no assets. Nothing can be found out about the membership, or its control, or its assets, or the charges on them. Judgment cannot be enforced against it. There is no reciprocal enforcement of judgments. It is nothing more than a name grasped from the air, as elusive as the Cheshire Cat. *In such cases the very fact of incorporation there gives some ground for believing there is a risk that, if judgment or an award is obtained, it may go unsatisfied.* Such registration of such companies may carry many advantages to the individuals who control them, but they may suffer the disadvantage of having a *Mareva* injunction granted against them. The giving of security for a debt is a small price to pay for the convenience of such a registration. Security would certainly be required in New York. So also it may be in London. Other grounds may be shown for believing there is a risk. But some such should be shown.
>
> (v) The plaintiff must, of course, give an undertaking in damages—in case he fails in his claim or the injunction turns out to be unjustified. In a suitable case this should be supported by a bond or security: and the injunction only granted on it being given, or undertaken to be given.

Assets in foreign lands

In *Siskina (Cargo owners) v Distos Cia Naviera SA (The Siskina)* [1977] HL 542, it was held that whereas the court could generally grant a freezing injunction, it could not do so unless a substantive action existed in respect of which the court had jurisdiction. Consequently, where a claimant brought an action for injunction in a foreign court, in a country where the defendant had no assets, the court would not be able to grant such an order since there would be no way of satisfying the judgment.

However, s. 28 of the Civil Jurisdiction and Judgments Act 1982 has removed the bar and now courts are able to grant an interim order—including freezing injunctions—in any case in aid of substantive relief wherever the proceeding is taking place.

Latest developments in freezing injunctions: Mareva by letter and Mareva principles applied to arrest warrants of ships

From 2005, two important developments have occurred in relation to Mareva injunctions. These are (i) the emergence of a new method of granting Mareva injunctions in very complex fraud cases, and (ii) the application of the Mareva principles to arrest of ships.

Mareva by letter

As was explained recently by one commentator:

> In cases where the victim of fraud is dealing with a dishonest obligor with the propensity to transfer and conceal assets, the time taken to prepare and finalize a set of pleadings to ground a series of urgent *ex parte* asset-freezing applications to courts in what might be numerous foreign jurisdictions may well turn out to be time spent in vain. There is a risk that by the time a number of freezing orders are made, the subject property may no longer be in the location originally identified. The very fact that ill-gotten property is located within a foreign jurisdiction necessitates the retention of local counsel.

(See Martin S Kenney 'The Mareva by Letter: Destroying a Banker's Defence of Good Faith', International Law Office, available at: <http://www.internationallawoffice.com/Newsletters/detail.aspx?g=78cc0260-e7a7-4969-97d9-7e9671b1244f>.)

In order to prevent the kind of situation described, a new process has emerged, which is granting Mareva by letter. As Kenney explains:

> This involves placing a third-party guardian or holder of assets, such as a bank, on notice that those assets are imposed with a constructive trust in favour of someone other than the party who the guardian or holder has previously been led to believe is the true owner. In cases where a victim of fraud has information to the effect that targeted funds or assets are about to be transferred to another location where it might be impossible to gain access to them, an immediate and informal (or *de facto*) freeze of the assets may be effected by issuing a letter to the third-party asset holder in question, informing it of the true origin or beneficial ownership of the targeted funds or assets, and advising it of its potential accessory liability in the event of any transfer or disposal of the assets in question.

Quite clearly, this informal process involves a high-risk strategy and, as such, a claimant who wishes to pursue this route must show the following:

> [S]ufficient proof should be provided to the third-party holder of assets to provide comfort that the conclusion being urged upon it as to the origin or provenance of the assets is in fact a reasonable one to be drawn in the circumstances.

Applying Mareva principles to arrest warrants against ships.

. . . .

● *Hansen v Trinity, The* (2007) BCSC 225

The plaintiffs contracted with the defendants to build a steel-hulled sailboat in return for which they would pay $600,000. Upon delivery the plaintiffs had paid $316,000, but discovered that the hull weld plates were so inferior as to constitute a fundamental breach of the contract by the defendant. The plaintiff claimed for the return of the $316,000 paid under the contract on grounds of unjust enrichment, negligence, breach of contractual duty of good faith, and promissory estoppel. Previously, on 9 August 2005, the plaintiffs had made an application for a Mareva injunction on the same matter and for the same amount. That application was dismissed by Macaulay J on the basis that there was no evidence that the defendants were contractually bound to build to ABS standard or that there was any failure to meet that standard which rendered the vessels unseaworthy. Thus the plaintiffs had failed to establish a strong prima facie case of fundamental breach such as was required for the granting of a Mareva injunction.

Subsequently, the plaintiffs made the application for the arrest warrant. The defendants claim that there was a failure to make full and frank disclosure in the application because the plaintiffs did not disclose that there had been an application for a Mareva injunction which had been denied and the reasons for that denial. The defendants claimed that full disclosure was required because the arrest application was without notice to the defendants. The plaintiff denied this and argued that disclosure and without notice requirements did not apply to arrest warrants of ships.

The British Columbia Supreme Court held that:

> because the opposing party does not have the opportunity to respond or explain, there must be an obligation on the applicant to make full and frank disclosure. The plaintiffs in the present case had failed to meet this standard of disclosure and accordingly the warrant was set aside.

thinking points

Do you think that extending the scope of application of Mareva principles weakens the basis of the order? Freezing orders are a special class of orders which operate to deny parties to a suit their legal entitlement to their assets without any judgment being entered against them at the relevant time. To that extent, it is an order to be cautiously applied, and as Lord Denning MR stated in the Third Chandris Shipping Corpn v Unimarine SA *case, 'it must not be stretched too far lest it be endangered'. But this caution should not be regarded as authorizing a blanket ban on sensible extension of the Mareva scope as evolving circumstances and exigencies of the modern commercial world necessitate. What is important is for a court to ensure that in granting a freezing order by letter or in applying the Mareva principles to arrest of ships, it is satisfied by evidence of the need to so act and act expeditiously.*

19.6 Search order

19.6.1 The old law

The old law concerning searching a defendant's premises for incriminating or evidential materials was laid down in *Entick v Carrington* (1765) 2 Wils 275, that no court has any power to enter into a man's property to search, by means of a search warrant, in order to see if there are documents which might incriminate him in a proceeding on libel, copyright, or any other infringements.

19.6.2 The new law: the *Anton Piller* case

● ***Anton Piller KG v Manufacturing Processes Ltd*** [1976] Ch 55

The plaintiffs were foreign manufacturers who owned the copyright in the design of a high-frequency converter used to supply computers. They learnt that the defendants, their English agents, were planning to supply rival manufacturers with information belonging to the plaintiffs which would enable their rivals to produce a similar product. The plaintiffs wished to restrain the defendants from infringing the copyright, using confidential information, or making copies of their machines, but they were afraid that the defendants, if notified, would take steps to destroy the documents or would send them out of the jurisdiction so that there would be none in existence by the time the action reached the stage of discovery of documents. The plaintiffs accordingly made an ex parte application for an order requiring the defendants to permit the plaintiffs to enter the defendants' premises in order to inspect, remove, or make copies of documents belonging to the plaintiffs.

HELD: The court had an inherent jurisdiction to make such an order ex parte, but should exercise it only in an extreme case where there was grave danger of property being smuggled away or of vital evidence being destroyed. The plaintiff had to show that it was essential so that justice could be done between the parties and when it would do no real harm to the defendant or his case. The order was not, however, a search warrant authorizing a plaintiff to enter a defendant's premises against his will, but an order on the defendant in personam to permit the plaintiff's entry or be in peril of proceedings for contempt of court. In the instant case, there was sufficient justification for making the order on an undertaking by the plaintiffs in damages.

19.6.3 The rationale of search order distinguished from *Entick v Carrington*

Lord Denning MR explained the rationale of search order:

> Let me say at once that no court in this land has any power to issue a search warrant to enter a man's house so as to see if there are papers or documents there which are of an incriminating nature, whether libels or infringements of copyright or anything else of the kind. No constable or bailiff can knock at the door and demand entry so as to inspect papers or documents. The householder can shut the door in his face and say, 'Get out'. That was established in the leading case of *Entick v Carrington*. None of us would wish to whittle down that principle in the slightest. But the order sought in this case is not a search warrant. It does not authorise the plaintiffs' solicitors or anyone else to enter the defendants' premises against their will. It does not authorise the breaking down of any doors, nor the slipping in by a back door, nor getting in by an open door or window. It only authorises entry and inspection by the permission of the defendants.

Although the search order derived its name from the case that eventually popularized it, the new rule which it developed had been introduced a year earlier by *EMI Ltd v Pandit* [1975] 1 All ER 418.

....

● *EMI Ltd v Pandit* [1975] 1 All ER 418

The plaintiffs, who owned the copyright in certain sound recordings of Indian music, brought an action against the defendant for infringement of copyright and passing off. Accordingly it applied ex parte for an order under RSC Ord 29 r 2(1) and (2), that such persons as might be duly authorized by the plaintiffs be at liberty forthwith to enter the defendant's premises between specified hours for the following purposes: inspecting and photographing pre-recorded tapes and other infringing material, and invoices, bills, and other documents and correspondence which were relevant to the action; removing infringing articles, and inspecting, photographing, and testing typewriters, since the plaintiffs suspected that the typewriter which had been used to carry out the alleged forgery was one belonging to the defendant which might still be on the premises. The plaintiffs were apprehensive that if they served notice on the defendant of the application, as required by RSC Ord 29 r 2(5), he would destroy or remove from the premises all relevant documents and articles and that the plaintiff would be effectively debarred from obtaining further relief in the action.

HELD: (1) the court had jurisdiction to make an order giving the plaintiff substantially the relief which it claimed. Such an order would only be made on an ex parte application in exceptional circumstances where it plainly appeared that justice required the intervention of the court in that, in default of such an order, the plaintiffs might be substantially deprived of a remedy. The order would only be granted on terms which safeguarded the defendant, as far as possible, and which narrowed the relief so far as it might otherwise cause harm to the defendant; (2) in the circumstances an order giving substantially the relief claimed would be made on the ex parte application, since the plaintiffs had established that if notice of the application were given to the defendant it would almost certainly result in the immediate destruction of the articles and information to which it was entitled and which it sought. The order would, however, be in the form of a mandatory injunction requiring the defendant to allow the plaintiff to enter premises occupied or used by the defendant between reasonable hours to inspect, identify, and photograph infringing material and other articles to which it was entitled, to remove infringing copies, and to inspect and test all typewriters and photographic machines.

The law has now incorporated Anton Piller situations:

Civil Procedure Act, s. 7

(1) The court may make an order under this section for the purpose of securing, in the case of any existing or proposed proceedings in the court—

    (a) the preservation of evidence which is or may be relevant, or

    (b) the preservation of property which is or may be the subject-matter of the proceedings or as to which any question arises or may arise in the proceedings.

(2) A person who is, or appears to the court likely to be, a party to proceedings in the court may make an application for such an order.

(3) Such an order may direct any person to permit any person described in the order, or secure that any person so described is permitted—

    (a) to enter premises in England and Wales, and

    (b) while on the premises, to take in accordance with the terms of the order any of the following steps.

(4) Those steps are—

    (a) to carry out a search for or inspection of anything described in the order, and

    (b) to make or obtain a copy, photograph, sample or other record of anything so described.

(5) The order may also direct the person concerned—

    (a) to provide any person described in the order, or secure that any person so described is provided, with any information or article described in the order, and

    (b) to allow any person described in the order, or secure that any person so described is allowed, to retain for safe keeping anything described in the order.

(6) An order under this section is to have effect subject to such conditions as are specified in the order.

KEY POINT
A search order is not a search warrant and, therefore, does not violate the rule in *Entick v Carrington*.

This statutory provision not only describes the order, but also lays down the steps that the applicant must take to implement the order.

19.6.4 Guidelines for granting search order

Ormrod LJ in the *Anton Piller* case stated three conditions that must be established before granting Anton Piller orders:

> There are three essential pre-conditions for the making of such an order, in my judgment. First, there must be an extremely strong prima facie case. Secondly, the damage, potential or actual, must be very serious for the plaintiff. Thirdly, there must be clear evidence that the defendants have in their possession incriminating documents or things, and that there is a real possibility that they may destroy such material before any application inter partes can be made.

● ***Lock International v Beswick*** [1989] 1 WLR 1268

Hoffmann LJ:

> Not everyone who is misusing confidential information will destroy documents in the face of a court order requiring him to preserve them.

19.6.5 Safeguards to protect the defendants

Lord Denning laid down certain safeguards for protecting a defendant in a search order suit.

1. *'The plaintiffs must get the defendants' permission.* But it does do this: it brings pressure on the defendants to give permission. It does more. It actually orders them to give permission—with, I suppose, the result that if they do not give permission, they are guilty of contempt of court.'
2. *'The plaintiffs must act with due circumspection.* On the service of it, the plaintiffs should be attended by their solicitor, who is an officer of the court. They should give the defendants an opportunity of considering it and of consulting their own solicitor. If the defendants wish to apply to discharge the order as having been improperly obtained, they must be allowed to do so. If the defendants refused permission to enter or to inspect, the plaintiffs must not force their way in. They must accept that refusal, and bring it to the notice of the court afterwards, if need be on application to commit.'

Other guidelines include that:

1. the claimant must give an undertaking in damages, as applicable to all cases of injunctions;
2. the claimant must make full disclosure of facts concerning the case, otherwise an Anton Piller order will be refused and, if already granted, will be discharged accordingly as held in *Guess? Inc v Lee Seck Mon* [1987] FSR 125, where an Anton Piller order was discharged for lack of full disclosure; and
3. there can be no Anton Piller order if it would result in the defendants incriminating themselves, as was held by the House of Lords in *Rank Film Distribution Ltd v Video Information Centre* [1982] AC 380.

The principle that the defendant would not be compelled to disclose materials that will incriminate him has now been incorporated by s. 7(7) of the Civil Procedure Act. Although s. 7 generally gives the court powers to grant Anton Piller orders, subsection (7) states:

> This section does not affect any right of a person to refuse to do anything on the ground that to do so might tend to expose him or his spouse to proceedings for an offence or for the recovery of a penalty.

Due to what Scott LJ considered to be excessive use of Anton Piller orders in its first few years—mainly between 1974 and 1986—his Lordship decided to supply a raft of new guidelines for the grant of the order. This was in *Columbia Picture Industries Inc v Robinson* [1987] Ch 38.

1. It is essential that a detailed record of the material taken should be made by a solicitor who executes an Anton Piller order before the material is removed from the respondent's premises.

2. When an Anton Piller order is executed no material should be taken from the respondent's premises by the executing solicitor unless it is clearly covered by the terms of the order. In particular, it is unacceptable that the respondent be procured by the executing solicitor to give consent to additional material being removed.

3. It is inappropriate for seized material the ownership of which is in dispute, such as alleged pirate tapes, to be retained by the plaintiff's solicitor pending trial. Although the solicitor is an officer of the court, the main role of the solicitor for the plaintiff is to act for the plaintiff.

4. The nature of an Anton Piller order requires that an affidavit in support of the application for the order ought to err on the side of excessive disclosure because, in the case of material which falls into the area of possible relevance, the judge and not the plaintiff's solicitor should be the judge of relevance.

New development in Anton Piller orders: The 'rolling' order

In Canada, it is now possible to obtain a 'rolling' Anton Piller order to restrain not only a specific infringement, but a continuous one (hence 'rolling'). The aim of this type of Anton Piller order is to restrain not only known persons who might infringe legal rights of others (especially copyrights), but specifically applicable to unknown infringers such as itinerants who hawk CDs and other types of music albums on the street. It is because the defendants of the rolling Anton Piller orders are not identifiable at the time of the order that the common appellation 'John and Jane Doe' is attached to such orders by the court. As explained by a Canadian commentator:

> The genesis of the rolling order appears to have been a number of Anton Piller orders executed against known itinerant street and flea market vendors. These orders were brought by known trademark and copyright holders against defendants who had pirated video, CD and software, as well as jewellery, clothing and other apparel. The affidavit evidence offered in support provided specific details of infringement. After a number of site-specific Anton Piller orders were granted, these were then used as evidence to support new affidavit evidence from private investigators alleging widespread infringement occurring in many flea market locations across Canada. Because the plaintiff could not identify the defendants in advance, the appellation John and Jane Doe appeared on the style of cause. By the 1990s approximately 50 of these rolling orders were operating within the country at any one time, and each may have attracted several hundred defendants to the proceeding.

(See Jeff Berryman 'Thirty Years After: Anton Piller Orders and the Supreme and Federal Courts of Canada' (2007) 2(3) *J of International Commercial Law and Technology* 128.)

In addition to the usual criteria for granting the Anton Piller order, the Federal Court of Canada in *Netbored Inc v Avery Holdings Inc* 2005 FC 1405 added two new criteria:

1. that the execution of the order would not harm the defendant or its case;

2. the interests of justice would not be brought into disrepute.

● *Vinod Chopra Films Private Limited et al v John Doe* 2010 FC 387

Hughes J had to review a 'rolling' Anton Piller order granted by the Federal Court of Canada in a copyright infringement case to an Indian film production company and its Canadian licensee against various unnamed persons who (according to the claim) 'deal in counterfeit video recordings'. His Lordship set aside the order with costs to the defendant, on the basis that the evidence that the plaintiffs had relied upon in seeking the order was 'insufficient, careless and misleading'.

Hughes J's decision in this case is an affirmation of the Canadian Supreme Court's leading judgment on Anton Piller.

● *Celanese Canada Inc v Murray Demolition Corp* 2006 SCC 36 (CanLII), 2006 SCC 36, [2006] 2 SCR 189

Binnie J, delivering the unanimous decision for the court, stated at paras 1 and 28 to 32 that:

[a]n *Anton Piller* order bears an uncomfortable resemblance to a private search warrant. No notice is given to the party against whom it is issued. Indeed, defendants usually first learn of them when they are served and executed, without having had an opportunity to challenge them or the evidence on which they were granted. The defendant may have no idea a claim is even pending. The order is not placed in the hands of a public authority for execution, but authorizes a private party to insist on entrance to the premises of its opponent to conduct a surprise search, the purpose of which is to seize and preserve evidence to further its claim in a private dispute. *The only justification for such an extraordinary remedy is that the plaintiff has a strong prima facie case and can demonstrate that on the facts, absent such an order, there is a real possibility relevant evidence will be destroyed or otherwise made to disappear.* The protection of the party against whom an *Anton Piller* order is issued ought to be threefold: a carefully drawn order which identifies the material to be seized and sets out safeguards to deal, amongst other things, with privileged documents; a vigilant court-appointed supervising solicitor who is independent of the parties; and a sense of responsible self-restraint on the part of those executing the order. [Emphasis added.]

579

KEY POINTS

- It is important that the consent of the defendant is sought, although there is pressure to accept.

- The items to be removed must relate specifically to the suit before the court and not be of general nature.

- Defendants do not have to surrender materials that may incriminate them.

thinking points

To what extent can you distinguish between a search order and a search warrant? Consider Lord Denning's statement that a search order 'may seem to be a search warrant in disguise' when answering this question. There is a remarkable similarity between a search warrant and an Anton Piller order. Both of them involve searching someone's premises for evidence. However, we must always remember that whereas with search warrants there is no need to obtain the consent of the owner of the premises, an Anton Piller order requires this, although it is not expected that consent will be denied lest the party

Specific performance

Specific performance is another equitable remedy that is based on the discretion of the court. It is granted mainly due to the inadequacy of the common law remedy of damages to breach of contract, although the court must order 'specific performance... only when it can by that means do more perfect and complete justice', as Lord Selborne said in *Wilson v Northampton and Banbury Junctions Rly Co* (1874) 9 Ch App 279.

Specific performance is, like all equitable remedies, an action in personam and, as such, can be granted in respect of lands outside the UK.

. . . .

● ***Penn v Lord Baltimore*** (1750) 1 Ves Sen 444

The plaintiff and the defendant by an agreement reciting that controversies had arisen between them concerning the boundaries of their lands abroad, agreed that a particular line should be the boundary and that commissioners should delimit the boundary within a certain limited time which had expired before the suit was brought; the agreement provided for conveyances from the one party to the other accordingly. In a suit for specific performance of the agreement it was held as follows.

HELD: The agreement could be specifically performed even though the land was outside the court's jurisdiction.

The court may sometimes grant specific performance of a contract and then make a separate order for a freezing injunction restraining the defendant from dealing with all or part of the purchase money. However, the court could combine the two remedies in a single order.

. . . .

● ***Seven Seas Properties Ltd v Al Essa*** [1989] 1 All ER 164

The plaintiff agreed to purchase a leasehold property from the defendants for £1.435 million and on the same day contracted to sell the property to a sub-purchaser for £1.635 million. Both contracts provided for completion on the same day. The defendants failed to complete on time and the sub-purchaser rescinded its contract on the day notice to complete expired. The sub-purchaser later brought an action against the plaintiff claiming over £600,000 damages for breach of contract. The plaintiff brought an action against the defendants seeking specific performance and applied for an inquiry as to damages and an order that £650,000, representing the sub-purchaser's claim and the plaintiff's costs in defending that claim, be retained in an account in the joint names of the parties' solicitors and not paid out to the defendants when the specific performance order was enforced. The master made the order sought. The defendants appealed against that part of the order preventing the £650,000 from being paid out to them, contending that the court had no jurisdiction to include such a provision in an order for specific performance, and that in any event the amount to be retained was excessive.

HELD: Hoffmann J at 166:

> Since in an appropriate case the court could, when making an order for specific performance, make a separate Mareva injunction restraining the vendor from dealing with the purchase money, it was convenient to combine the two orders into one. The master had therefore had jurisdiction to include the retention order in the specific performance order.

KEY POINTS

- Specific performance is discretionary and normally awarded where damages will be inappropriate to remedy the breach of a contract.

- Specific performance can be awarded in respect of property outside the jurisdiction of the court.

On what grounds may the court refuse specific performance?

19.8.1 Contract relating to personalty

Unless a contract relates to a contract of land, as a general rule, specific performance will not be granted. Thus, where contracts relate to money per se, save in exceptional circumstances, specific performance will not be decreed. Even where land is involved, the breach of such contracts must not be remediable by damages alone for specific performance to apply.

● ***Fountain Forestry Ltd v Edwards*** [1975] Ch 1

Following the death of a man, his widow and son agreed to sell his property to the plaintiff. The son, pretending to sign on behalf of the two, signed the agreement which was declined by the widow. The plaintiffs brought proceedings for specific performance contending that the contract was binding on the deceased's estate since one of two or more personal representatives was entitled to enter into a contract for the sale of an asset so as to bind the estate without the consent of the other personal representative or representatives.

HELD: On the assumption that, by virtue of s. 2 of the Administration of Estates Act 1925, one of two executors had power to enter into a contract binding on the deceased's estate to sell freehold land, and that an administrator had the same power of disposition as an executor, nonetheless the plaintiffs were not entitled to specific performance, since the son had not bound himself to sell the property without the concurrence of the widow but had bound the estate on the assumption, which he warranted to be correct, that he had authority to sign as agent for her. That assumption having been falsified there was no contract to be enforced; all that could be sued on was the warranty of authority given by the son.

But where the items involved were of rarity, even if damages could have been enough, the court may grant specific performance.

....

● *Falcke v Gray* (1859) 4 Drew 651

The case involved a contract to sell two China jars of considerable value.

HELD: A court of equity will entertain a bill for specific performance of a contract for sale of a valuable chattel where adequate compensation cannot be obtained at law; but in a case where it was proved that the price was greatly inadequate, and the purchaser knew it to be so, the court, under the circumstances, refused to decree specific performance, and dismissed the bill, although it would not have given relief to a vendor seeking to set aside the contract.

The same will apply if there is a contract to sell a 'right' to someone exclusively.

....

● *Erskine MacDonald Ltd v Eyles* [1920] E 415

A writer entered into a written agreement with the plaintiff, a publisher, to publish over a stipulated period of time her works exclusively. They also agreed that the defendant would not allow any other publisher to publish any other variant of her work during the period. In breach of the agreement the writer entered into an agreement with another publisher, the defendant, to publish her work. In an action by the plaintiffs to restrain both defendants from publishing it was held as follows.

HELD: (1) The agreement was not a contract of personal service but was a contract by Mrs E to sell the products of her labour or industry, of which the court would grant specific performance by restraining her from disposing of the novel in breach of her agreement with the plaintiffs.

19.8.2 Contracts requiring constant supervision by the court

....

● *Ryan v Mutual Tontine Westminster Chambers Association* [1893] 1 Ch 116

The facts concern the lease of a residential flat subject to a covenant by which it was agreed and declared by and between the parties to the lease that the premises were let subject to the regulations made by the lessors with respect to the duties of the resident porter, which were set forth in a schedule thereto. The lessors appointed a resident porter who, due to another job, absented himself from the work. The lessee brought an action against the lessors for breach of the covenant.

HELD: The court could not grant specific performance in this case to prevent continuance of the breach of the covenant.

However, there has been an attempt to reconceptualize the whole issue of constant supervision by the court so that it seems no longer invariably true that once an order could require the court to supervise, the court will automatically decline to grant it.

● *Tito v Waddell (No 2)* [1977] Ch 106

The Banabans brought two actions arising from the mining of phosphate by the British Phosphate Commissioners on Ocean Island, known to the indigenous inhabitants as Banaba. The first claim was by Banaban landowners for specific performance of the contractual obligation to replant certain land with trees or shrubs or, alternatively, damages. They also claimed damages for the wrongful removal of sand and the destruction of the ground.

HELD: Megarry VC at 321:

> [T]he real question is whether there is sufficient definition of what has to be done to comply with the order of the court. That definition may be provided by the contract itself, or it may be supplied by the terms of the order, in which case there is sufficient support by implication or otherwise in the terms of the proposed order.

This more liberal approach was followed in *Posner v Scott-Lewis* [1987] Ch 25.

● *Posner v Scott-Lewis* [1987] Ch 25

The plaintiffs were tenants in a block of flats owned by the defendant landlords. Each plaintiff held his tenancy on the terms of a written lease which contained in cl 3(11) a covenant by the defendants to employ a resident porter to keep the communal areas clean, to be responsible for the central heating and boilers, and to collect rubbish from the flats. In 1985 the then resident porter left the defendants' employment but by arrangement with the defendants continued to carry out on a part-time basis the duties specified in cl 3(11). The plaintiffs sought specific performance of the covenant in cl 3(11) compelling the defendants to employ a porter who was resident, contending that the porter's duties were being carried out inadequately.

HELD: Mervyn Davies J at 36: In the circumstances it was open to the court to consider the making of an order for specific performance. The making of such an order depended on whether there was sufficient definition of what had to be done by way of compliance with the court's order, whether enforcing compliance would involve superintendence by the court to an unacceptable degree, and the amount of prejudice and hardship that would be suffered by the respective parties if the order was made.

19.8.3 Contracts to carry on a business or any comparable series of activities

● *Co-Operative Insurance Society Ltd v Argyll Stores (Holdings) Ltd* [1998] AC 1

The defendants were granted the lease of the largest unit in a shopping centre. At the time they were granted the lease, it was anticipated that they would operate at all times during the opening hours so that the unit would be an anchor unit, attracting trade to the smaller businesses in the shopping centre. Should the defendants ever close the unit, this would have serious consequences on all other units hence the agreement to ensure that the unit was open at all times. At a point in time, the defendants suffered financial loss and decided, in breach of contract, to close down the supermarket. The claimants brought an action for specific performance.

HELD: A covenant in a lease of retail premises to keep open for trade during the usual hours of business was not, other than in exceptional circumstances, specifically enforceable, since it was the settled practice of the court not to make an order requiring a person to carry on a business. That practice was based on sound sense, as such an order required constant supervision, was only enforceable by the quasi-criminal procedure of punishment for contempt, and might cause injustice by allowing the plaintiff to enrich himself at the defendant's expense if the defendant was forced to run a business at a loss.

The reasoning of Lord Hoffmann particularly in this case was that making a specific performance order in this instance might result in the defendant being oppressed by being made to do things under constant threat of the court's contempt for failure to perform. Also, his Lordship reasoned that a specific performance order here could lead to the claimants enriching themselves at the expense of the defendant.

However, in *Barrow v Chappell & Co Ltd* [1976] RPC 355, specific performance was granted in a case concerning a contract to publish music.

19.8.4 Contract for personal services

The general principle is that the court will not grant specific performance in a contract for personal services.

. . . .

● *Francesco v Barnum* (1890) 45 Ch 430

Fry LJ:

> ...the courts are bound to be jealous, lest they should turn contracts of service into contracts for slavery.

For Megarry J, there are other much more complex reasons for the courts' reluctance to grant specific performance in respect of contracts for services.

. . . .

● *CH Giles & Co Ltd v Morris* [1972] 1 All ER 960

Megarry J at 969: The plaintiffs sought specific performance to compel defendants who had refused to take the necessary steps to procure an appointment of someone as managing director in accordance with the consent order they agreed to. The order was refused.

> ...the reasons why the court is reluctant to decree specific performance of a contract for personal services [and I would regard it as a strong reluctance rather than a rule] are, I think, more complex and more firmly bottomed on human nature. If a singer contracts to sing, there could no doubt be proceedings for committal if, ordered to sing, the singer remained obstinately dumb. But if instead the singer sang flat, or sharp, or too fast, or too slowly, or too loudly, or too quietly, or resorted to a dozen of the manifestations of temperament traditionally associated with some singers, the threat of committal would reveal itself as a most unsatisfactory weapon; for who could say whether the imperfections of performance were natural or self-induced? To make an order with such possibilities of evasion would be vain.

19.8.5 Contract lacking in mutuality

A minor cannot bring an action for specific performance because such an order cannot be granted against him.

• *Flight v Bolland* [1824–34] All ER Rep 372

Sir John Leach MR:

> No case of a bill filed by an infant for the specific performance of a contract made by him has been found in the works. It is not disputed that it is a general principle of courts of equity to interpose only where the remedy is mutual.

However, the rule of mutuality does not apply to the sale and purchase of land. In such cases, the principle is that the seller is as much entitled to a decree of specific performance as the buyer, despite the fact that the latter's obligation is only to pay the purchase price.

• *Price v Strange* [1977] 3 All ER 371

The defendant agreed to a new lease to the claimant in a property in consideration of the latter undertaking some repairs. Although the claimant carried out repairs to the interior of the property, the defendant's repudiation of the agreement prevented him from carrying out exterior repairs.

In an action for specific performance, the court of first instance declined the claimant's application on the basis, inter alia, that damages were sufficient. This was, however, reversed by the Court of Appeal.

HELD: Buckley LJ:

> If one party were compelled to perform his obligations in accordance with the terms of the contract while the obligations of the other party under the contract, or some of them, remained unperformed, it might be unfair that the former party should be left to his remedy in damages if the latter party failed to perform any of his unperformed obligations.

19.8.6 Where specific performance will be futile

The court will not grant an order for specific performance if, in the court's opinion, to do so would be useless. Examples include a refusal to grant an order of specific performance for parties to enter into a partnership that will be dissolved almost immediately (*Hercy v Birch* (1804) 9 Ves 357).

Apart from these, the general bases for denying equitable interest such as delay and acquiescence and conduct of parties, as have been discussed under injunctions earlier in the chapter, all apply to specific performance as well.

Conclusion

Equity developed in order to meet the rigidity of the common law and to do justice as between parties where common law rules would have been either inadequate or too formalistic. It is in respect of equitable remedies that equity shows its great ability to adapt to different situations and to keep reinventing itself. Hence, whereas equity would not formally prevent a person from dealing with his assets located within a jurisdiction where a lawsuit is pending or being conducted against him, equity devised the freezing injunction to put an end to such sharp practices so that judgments would not be frustrated. The same principle also underpins equitable intervention with the Anton Piller order to prevent destruction of materials of serious evidential value. Where a person would have been poorly compensated, for instance with regard to his items of inestimable value, it is now possible to order specific performance to protect such items.

Therefore, equitable remedies are a very potent tool for equity to implement its flexible and adaptability agenda not against the common law, but in a complementary fashion that leaves even the rules and principles of common law better fulfilled.

Questions

Self-test questions

1   What are injunctions and how are they used?

2   What is specific performance and how do you distinguish between it and normal actions to remedy breaches of contract?

3   To what extent do you think that the new test of 'frivolity and vexatiousness' in awarding injunctions meets the shortcomings of the 'prima facie' test?

4   Can you distinguish between an Anton Piller order and a search warrant with respect to decided cases?

5   What principles would the court consider before ordering the grant of interlocutory injunctions?

Discussion questions

1   If a court would not have granted an injunction before the Judicature Act, it has no power to grant such today. To what extent does this statement reflect the current thinking and case law on the remedy of injunction?

2   The requirement of mutuality is indispensable in a consideration of specific performance. Do you agree?

3   The court would not normally grant an equitable remedy that will require its continuous supervision. Discuss.

4　Once a claimant can prove that damages are not enough to remedy a breach of wrong committed against him, the court will automatically grant an injunction. Evaluate this statement in light of case law and jurisprudence.

5　What do we mean when we speak of discretionary power of the courts to award equitable remedies?

Assessment question

James employs John, a building contractor, to construct blocks of flats on some acres of land James recently purchased. James paid an advance sum of £3 million to John's company, to commence the construction. John promptly started working, but after a few months, he abandoned the work. Up to that point he had undertaken construction worth up to £1.5 million, leaving a balance of £1.5 million in his bank account in London. James commenced an action in London against John, first, that the court should decree specific performance of the rest of the contract. While this action lasted, James also brought an action praying that the court should freeze James's account in London until the outcome of the case. Advise James.

Key cases

- *American Cyanamid Co v Ethicon Ltd* [1975] 1 All ER 504 **(at 19.4.2, 19.4.3, 19.4.4, and 19.4.5)**

- *Anton Piller KG v Manufacturing Processes Ltd* [1976] Ch 55 **(at 19.5, 19.6.2, 19.6.3, 19.6.4, and 19.6.5)**

- *Co-Operative Insurance Society Ltd v Argyll Stores (Holdings) Ltd* [1998] AC 1 **(at 19.8.3)**

- *Entick v Carrington* (1765) 2 Wils 275 **(at 19.6.1 and 19.6.3)**

- *Kennaway v Thompson* [1981] QB 88 **(at 19.4.1)**

- *Mareva Compania Naviera SA v International Bulk Carriers SA* [1980] 1 All ER 213 **(at 19.5, 19.5.1, and 19.5.2)**

- *Shelfer v City of London Electric Co* [1895] 1 Ch 287 **(at 19.4.1)**

- *Wilson v Northampton and Banbury Junctions Rly Co* (1874) 9 Ch App 279 **(at 19.7)**

Further reading

P Pettit *Equity and the Law of Trusts* (12th edn, Oxford: Oxford University Press, 2012)
Excellent analysis of equitable remedies.

FP 'The Highwayman's Case (Everet v Williams)' (1893) 9(35) *LQR* 197
On the maxims of equity.

J Berryman, 'Thirty Years After: Anton Piller Orders and the Supreme and Federal Courts of Canada' (2007) 2(3) *J of International Commercial Law and Technology* 128
For a comprehensive overview of Anton Piller orders.

Glossary

A priori—Latin—from the start

Administrator—the person appointed by the court to deal with the estate of a person who has died without making a will

Administratrix—feminine of the above

Ambulatory—literally movable or mobile, but here it means that the testator can always make a new will, which supersedes older wills

Anti-vivisectionists—those opposed to experiments upon live animals

Assignment—transferring a right or interest in property to another

Bailment—the person given the property, the bailee, has possession of the property. The bailor has a superior right and can retake possession. It is not intended that the bailee should keep the property

Beneficiary—the ultimate person who would enjoy the property. Beneficiaries could include a trustee

Bequest—personal property left in a will

Bona vacantia—Latin—literally means unoccupied property. More loosely translated it means ownerless goods. The government, or Crown, claims property that has no identifiable owner

Cestuis que trusts—beneficiaries

Charge—a loan secured on property, e.g. a mortgage. If the loan is not repaid, the loaner may claim the property

Choses in action—a type of property that has no physical existence. A valuable, personal right

Codicil—an amendment or addition to an earlier will. The codicil must also be signed and witnessed, just like the main will

Consideration—each party to a contract must promise something of value. The consideration need not be adequate, i.e. of equal value to the promise made by the other party, but it must be of some financial value

Conveyance—the formal legal document, a deed, required to transfer the legal estate in land

Covenant—a legally binding promise, made in a deed

Cy-près—French—near to or close to

Debenture—a loan secured on the assets of a company. If the loan is not repaid, the assets can be sold by the person who made the loan

Deed—a formal legal document, that has to be signed, witnessed, and delivered

Delivered—the person making the deed must hand it over to the person to whom it grants rights, with the intention that it is legally binding

De minimis—Latin—too small to matter

Denizens—inhabitants

Devise—land left in a will

Devisee—person to whom real property (land) is left in a will

Donee—person to whom a gift is made

Donor—person who makes a gift

Eo instanti—Latin—loosely translated it means 'there instantly'

Equitable—certain rights are regarded as equitable. The basis is historical. They were once rights recognized by the Court of Chancery

Estate—the period for which a person is entitled to hold property. Estate usually refers to land. Under s. 1 of the Law of Property Act 1925 only two legal estates are recognized in law: the fee simple and the term of years

Estate—the total of personal property available for distribution on bankruptcy or death

Estoppel—the principle that a person cannot deny what they have represented to another

Executor—the male person appointed in the will to carry out the deceased's instructions in the will, in particular to dispose of his/her property according to the will

Executrix—feminine of the above

Fiduciary—a person in a position of trust or confidence, who may act on behalf of their principal. The position of the fiduciary is similar to that of the trustee and the position of the principal is similar to that of the beneficiary

Gilt-edged stock—also known as gilts. These are fixed interest loan securities issued by the UK government. They are regarded as particularly safe investments

'Homer nodded'—even the best of us sometimes make mistakes. The 'Homer' referred to is the ancient Greek poet

Impotent—does not have its modern meaning of sexually incapable. It means disabled or ill

In loco parentis—Latin—in the place of the parent. It means the person who assumes parental responsibility for the child

In personam—Latin—literally means against the person. The Court of Chancery used to order parties to do something, such as to return property, and if they did not do it they were punished for contempt of court. This might involve fines, imprisonment, or seizure of assets

Innocent volunteer—volunteer means that the person has provided no consideration in return and therefore cannot enforce a promise made by another. Innocent means that they are unaware that they have received someone else's property

Inter vivos—Latin—literally, between the living. A gift made while someone is still alive

Interest—the period for which a person is entitled to hold property. Since the Law of Property Act 1925, all interests in land that are not regarded as Legal Estates are recognized only in Equity, as equitable interests, e.g. a life interest

Intestacy—statute lays down the near relatives to whom their property goes

Intestate—when a person dies without making a will

Joint will—the husband and wife make similar or identical wills. This could be in one document as in *Dufour* or, more usually, the husband and wife each make a separate will

Land—the statutory definition of land can be found in s. 205(1)(ix) of the Law of Property Act 1925 and includes not only land, but buildings, parts of buildings, rights over mines and minerals, and other rights, privileges, or benefits in, over, or derived from land

Legal—certain rights are regarded as legal. The basis is historical. They were once rights recognized by the Common Law courts

Legatee—a person left personal property in a will

Licence—permission to do some act which otherwise could not lawfully be done. A licence often refers to land and is permission to do what would otherwise be a trespass. A licence does not grant an estate or interest in the land

Lien—a right to keep possession of property belonging to another person until a debt owed by that person is discharged (Oxford English Dictionary)

Locus standi—Latin—the right to bring a case to court

Malus animus—Latin—an evil mind

Marriage settlement—a trust is established, on marriage, to provide for the husband and wife and the children that they hope to have. Commonly, the husband and wife would covenant, in a deed with the trustees, that they would transfer any property that they acquired in the future to the trust. The spouses and the children of the marriage may enforce the promise in the covenant despite the fact that the children do not provide any consideration, i.e. they do not promise anything in return

Mirror wills—the husband and wife make joint wills in separate documents

Mortgage—a loan secured on property, e.g. a mortgage. If the loan is not repaid, the loaner may claim the property

Negotiable instrument—a promise to pay money that itself can be transferred or sold, e.g. a cheque or bill of exchange

Old boys—ex pupils of the school

Option—a contractual right to acquire property on payment of consideration. A contractual right is a form of property that has economic value and can be bought and sold, just like any other kind of property

Overreaching—the purchaser only wants to buy the legal estate in the land and does not want to be concerned with who might be the beneficiaries of the trust and what interests they might hold in the property. So, if the purchaser buys from two trustees, the purchaser is not bound by any claims that the beneficiaries might have to the land. Instead, the beneficiaries may claim against the seller of the land for their share of the purchase price

Parens patriae—Latin—father of the country

Pari passu—Latin—literally means spread out equally. The depositors share out what is left in proportion to what was taken from them.

Pecuniary legacy—a sum of cash left in a will

Personal property—all property that is not land. This includes moveable and intangible property

Personal representatives—executors or administrators who deal with the property of the deceased

Power of appointment—a beneficiary, or sometimes a trustee, is given the power to choose who inherits the property next. They would name the persons appointed in their will or perhaps in a deed while they are still alive

Precatory words—'requesting words'

Pro tanto—Latin—literally 'for so much'. It means the same as 'completely' here

Probanda—Latin—things requiring to be proved

Probate—the executors of the will prove to the court that the document really is the will of the deceased. Unless the will is disputed, this is just a routine, administrative matter

Propositus—Latin—anyone who could come forward to claim

Proprietary—an interest or estate that gives the right to actual property, usually land

Proprietary estoppel—if party A represents to party B that party B has a right to some property held by party A, then if party B relies on this representation and acts to their detriment, party A cannot deny the right of party B

Protective trust—a trust where the main beneficiary holds the property for life, until he is declared bankrupt or gets into debt, etc. Then his life interest ends and the trustees hold the property on a discretionary trust for the former life interest, spouse and children. A protective trust is well named, because it protects a beneficiary from the consequences of getting into debt

Real property—rights over land, especially freehold rights over land

Receiver—a person appointed to collect debts that are owed

Residuary—what is left of the deceased's property when debts, taxes, and identified gifts have been paid

Residue—what is left of the deceased's estate after specific gifts are taken out

Settlement—this is another word for trust. It often refers to a trust established in order to provide for a family. A settlement is usually made in a deed

Settlor—living person who establishes a trust. One who intends to part with his or her property and leave it for the benefit of others by an instrument executed when he—the settlor—is still alive

Share capital—when a company is formed its promoters decide what value of shares the company will have and will be offered for sale. £250,000 indicates that the company will have a reasonable amount of money behind it. The paid up in cash requirement indicates that the shareholders have actually paid for their shares

Specific—the property is identified

Spes—Latin—hope

Sub modo—Latin—subject to a condition.

Sui juris—Latin—the persons referred to have full legal capacity, i.e. they are of full age and are not mentally disordered

Testator/Testatrix—dead person who establishes a trust in his/her will. One who intends to part with his or her property and leave it for the benefit of others by an instrument executed when he/she—the settlor—is dead

Trust—an arrangement created for the purpose of transferring property to the beneficiary via the trustee. It usually states the conditions of the trust with regard to the time of its maturity, termination, variation, and so on. A trust arrangement can either be made in writing through a legal instrument or orally

Trust corporation—a company that can act as a trustee. Most banks offer this service and there are many companies specifically formed to act as trustees

Trust instrument—this is the document that sets out the terms of the trust, identifies the trust property, specifies the beneficiaries and their beneficial interests, and names the trustees

Trustee—the middle person, the bridge between a settlor and the person whom the property is to benefit. It is the trustee that the property is 'vested' in, in trust for another

Value—something of financial worth. 'Value' is sometimes used as another word for consideration

Vest—the beneficiary becomes fully entitled, e.g. if the trust said 'to A for life, remainder to the children of A upon marriage', a child of A does not become fully entitled until he/she marries and A dies. When the child marries, his/her equitable interest vests in interest. When A dies, the interest vests in possession

Vesting—the transfer of the legal estate

Virtute officii—Latin—literally, by virtue of their office, meaning that the executor does not hold the property for their personal use, but for the benefit of the beneficiaries

Ward of court—the child is placed under the protection of the court

Will—the document that states to whom the property of the deceased should be distributed. A will must be signed by the testator or testatrix and the signature must be witnessed by two people

Index

Index

607

complete: law solution

Reading and making sense of original case extracts is a vital part of understanding how law works. But how do you know which sections of which cases to read?

Books in the **complete** series combine extracts from a wide range of primary materials with clear explanatory text to provide students with a complete introductory resource.

Each author carefully unfolds the complexities of the subject, exposing the reader to relevant case extracts and supporting them with illuminating commentary. Helpful learning features are clearly presented and effectively employed, ensuring each **complete** title provides students with a stimulating introduction to the subject.

complete
series

For further details about titles in the series, visit
www.oxfordtextbooks.co.uk/law/complete